CINEMATIC SOCIOLOGY

SECOND EDITION

To Savannah Sutherland Bindas;
from Bambi and The Lion King to Harry Potter and
anything Jim Carrey, watching movies with you (some of them
multiple times) continues to be one of life's greatest joys.
—jas

To my brother, David Feltey,
who never lost a round of our homemade movie trivia game;
since you left to sing karaoke with the angels, we've been missing you.
—kmf

CINEMATIC SOCIOLOGY

social life in film

SECOND EDITION

EDITORS

Jean-Anne Sutherland
University of North Carolina at Wilmington

Kathryn Feltey
The University of Akron

Los Angeles | London | New Delhi
Singapore | Washington DC

Los Angeles | London | New Delhi
Singapore | Washington DC

FOR INFORMATION:

SAGE Publications, Inc.
2455 Teller Road
Thousand Oaks, California 91320
E-mail: order@sagepub.com

SAGE Publications Ltd.
1 Oliver's Yard
55 City Road
London EC1Y 1SP
United Kingdom

SAGE Publications India Pvt. Ltd.
B 1/I 1 Mohan Cooperative Industrial Area
Mathura Road, New Delhi 110 044
India

SAGE Publications Asia-Pacific Pte. Ltd.
3 Church Street
#10-04 Samsung Hub
Singapore 049483

Printed in the United States of America

A catalog record of this book is available from the Library of Congress.

978-1-4129-9284-8

Acquisitions Editor: David Repetto
Associate Editor: Nathan Davidson
Editorial Assistant: Lydia Balian
Production Editor: Eric Garner
Copy Editor: Rachel Keith
Typesetter: C&M Digitals (P) Ltd.
Proofreader: Jennifer Gritt
Cover Designer: Anupama Krishnan
Marketing Manager: Erica DeLuca
Permissions Editor: Karen Ehrmann

This book is printed on acid-free paper.

12 13 14 15 16 10 9 8 7 6 5 4 3 2 1

Contents

Foreword

Elizabeth Higginbotham

The study of film provides an opportunity to connect history and technological changes with social ideologies. Film production has changed over time, in delivery as well as in content, and thus films capture and reflect shifts in ideologies and other thinking about social institutions and social positions. When I was growing up in New York City in the 1950s, going to the movies was a weekend ritual. My brothers and sisters would choose which movie theater on Second Avenue we would attend, often negotiating how much money we would have for popcorn and candy after paying admission, which was often between 15 and 25 cents. There was a matron who monitored the children's section, so going alone was safe. We might spend much of the afternoon watching two feature films. We didn't pay attention to start times but would come in during the middle of a movie, stay until it started over, and either stop when we reached the part where we had come in or watch the ending again, depending on when we had to be home. Those were the days when you had to go to a movie theater to see a movie and your choices were limited by geography. In New York City, we had a television station that played one old movie a week, so we became familiar with many of the classics. We hardly noticed the lack of people of color but celebrated when they appeared, even if they were villains. We were being entertained, but we were also viewing images of other parts of the country, seeing models of heroes and heroines, and gaining a healthy respect for heterosexual romance, without any sex—along with a skepticism for science, as most of the monster films were about mad scientists crossing boundaries.

When I describe to my students what those days were like, they are stunned. Their own film viewing practices began at home, and they take watching movies for granted. They have fond memories of watching features with their families on cable, VHS, or DVD, depending on their age. Going to see a new Disney release was a big family event. When they were older they would go to the multiplex and see one film while their parents saw another. As teenagers, they would go to the mall on the weekend to see well-publicized blockbusters with friends. Even as college students, they might relax at the end of the day by watching a segment of their favorite movie.

Our film viewing has changed because of new technologies that have made it easier for people not only to make and distribute films but also to view films in many different ways. DVDs, cable television, and streaming via the Internet now bring films from around the world to personal screens of many sizes. This technology means films penetrate our lives differently than they did in the past.

The study of film has also changed. Film studies was a small field in the 1950s and 1960s, often limited to cultural studies and to people on the east and west coasts who could access art theaters as well as screens controlled by Hollywood studios. This interdisciplinary field focused on the films as texts. Now, in addition to preparing collections on eras of film history, individual directors, genres, and film treatment of specific groups, sociologists write about fiction films to examine how their narratives and representations frame our world-views. This second edition of Jean-Anne Sutherland and Kathryn Feltey's *Cinematic Sociology: Social Life in Film* captures the development in the field as scholars decode films, consider how their themes reflect the social order, and discover how films play a powerful role in constructing our images of ourselves and others. The editors are still committed to helping readers examine how films explore social issues, including social ideologies, and providing them with tools to develop a critical analysis of how film production meets specific goals and how those constructs frame issues for audiences. This volume will help viewers evaluate what's on the screen and ask complicated questions about a film's narrative style, theoretical orientation, representation of groups, and presentation of institutions and their missions.

Sutherland and Feltey asked the authors to examine how films present or even critique social theories—our common understanding of social organizations and behaviors. Is social life presented as orderly where people accept prescribed roles and find them satisfying? Or do we watch films that depict alienation and despair as well as a range of ways that people confront these dehumanizing social conditions? As we are being entertained, we are also being introduced to the worldviews and social theories embedded in the films. If we have the necessary skills, we can unravel these presentations and think about them with greater clarity.

This edition of *Cinematic Sociology* expands its investigation of what films teach us about social class, race and ethnicity, gender and sexuality. Traditional Hollywood films have celebrated whiteness, certain manifestations of heterosexual masculinity and femininity, and narrow visions of middle class status. While sociologists study these constructs as dimensions of inequality, Hollywood films often present individual stories where people can readily overcome social barriers if they make the right choices. Such presentations can be reaffirming of the individualism germane to American culture, but they can obscure the ways that inequalities are embedded in social institutions and render invisible the efforts of individuals and groups to challenge restrictions. The authors use films as a lens for exploring the complexities of social class, race and ethnicity, gender and sexuality, and to propel our analysis of these inequalities in the past and in contemporary life.

Individuals operate within major social institutions, and films often teach us about these realms of social life. Films provide images of the families we would like to have, of appropriate expectations over the life course, and of the ways people move within educational and occupational settings. The visual power of images and strong narratives can shape expectations in ways we may be unaware of. The discussions of social institutions in this volume suggest the depth of those constructions and how we need to critique them and listen to the viewpoints of other viewers.

Sutherland and Feltey have edited a book that does much, but they remain cognizant of how each individual brings unique experiences to the viewing of any film. Because people decode films from their own social positions, many interpretations of the images and stories on the screen can be found within any audience. This volume is not about our seeing the same images, but about each of us gaining a more nuanced appreciation of the medium and learning to use a shared language to discuss what we do see. Because films from all over the world are now ready to be viewed, we can use the tools of sociologists to question the representations and stories directors use to give us a vision of a time and place. Those constructions may or may not reflect the social realities of people in those places at those times, but they do reflect a specific viewpoint worthy of discussion. In this era of globalization, images of others and their stories often come to us in films, and we need to be ready with a critical eye to view them, identify the ideologies encoded in them, and share what we see with others. The readings here provide resources for many lively conversations about films.

Preface

The first edition of *Cinematic Sociology: Social Life in Film* began with many conversations about how to teach a course called Sociology through Film. We both taught the course, and we knew what we wanted to assign our students to read, but we'd never found a complete textbook featuring the right combination of theory, method, and substantive material. Sharing our teaching strategies, film lists, and assignments, we developed a list of goals:

1. To create an accessible, engaging book of readings that addressed central issues in the discipline of sociology, such as class, race and ethnicity, gender and sexuality, social institutions, and social change.

2. To compile readings that creatively applied sociology, using film(s) as the subject matter.

3. To frame the readings with an overview of how to think about film as a cultural product that both reflects and shapes the social world in which we live.

4. To incorporate social constructionist and critical perspectives in order to uncover the multiple stories within film that might not be readily seen or understood.

5. To integrate the sociological imagination throughout to demonstrate how individual experiences occur in cultural and social contexts where structures constrain and enable individual action.

Once the book was in use, we heard from faculty and students about what they liked and what they wished had been included. This second edition fills those gaps:

1. The Introduction now includes more coverage of the sociological theories covered in most introductory sociology classes: functionalism, conflict, and symbolic interactionism.

2. New chapters have been added to cover the areas of theory; deviance, crime, and law; the life course; and social institutions.

3. New readings have been added to the Global Connections chapter and the Social Change chapter.

4. Two readings have been revised and updated.

5. "Outtakes" (text boxes) have been added to address a specific issue or question related to each chapter's topic.

The result, *Cinematic Sociology: Social Life in Film, Second Edition,* can be used on its own, as a supplement to a text, or in combination with other articles and monographs. It is designed for undergraduate students and can be used as a stand-alone text or reader for courses on sociology through film or as a supplement to a social problems, social inequality, or introductory sociology course.

Sociologists at the Movies

When we teach our Sociology through Film course, we find that a good starting point for exploring social life through film is to consider our personal relationship with film. We often ask the students in our respective classes to recall the movies they watched as children. What were their favorites? What were some of the major themes? Are there scenes that stand out? Can they recall the circumstances of their early film viewing? With whom did they watch movies? Inevitably we find that students not only fondly recall their childhood movies, but recall them in the context of family and friends.

Perhaps our earliest memories of film involved family and close friends. Perhaps they led us to games and fantasies that were integral to our young lives. They might have captured ideals we clung to in our childhood, such as princesses falling in love or action heroes saving the world. The first notes of a soundtrack might elicit memories that touch us deeply and personally, taking us back to a particular place and time or to memories of significant loved ones from our pasts.

The influence of movies (like all other forms of media) as agents of socialization cannot be underestimated. In asking our students to take a trip down movie memory lane, we are helping them to begin thinking like sociologists—to make the connection between their own lives and the social worlds to which they belong. Our own stories of growing up with movies serve as illustration.

Jean-Anne

When I was a kid, the small Central Florida town where I lived had one movie theater on Main Street that showed only one movie at a time. A few years later a second theater opened in town, this one with fancy red rocking chairs. It gave us a second option for Friday night movies, because that's what the kids did in our town—we went to movies on Friday night. I can recall my growing-up years by reflecting on the movies I saw and with whom I saw them. I remember when I was old enough to go to a movie without a parent: a friend and I saw *Young Frankenstein* and I still remember how hard we laughed. I remember seeing *Tommy* and looking down the aisle as several classmates hissed, "Jean-Anne, Jean-Anne, *move!*" because I didn't want to move down a seat. I loved Elton John and had gotten there early so I would be situated perfectly in the middle to see his Pinball Wizard. I *did* move down (albeit grudgingly), in part because Friday nights at the movies meant more than opportunities to see our heroes and idols on the big screen. We were also there to be together. We experienced our first dates, our first kisses, our many fights, our makeups. We experienced moments of popularity and social exclusion. When I reached high school age I got the best job in the world: at the movie theater. On Friday afternoons several of us would gather and preview the newly arrived films. The theater was ours until evening, when it would fill with the faces of those we'd known for years. One night I was alone in the small concession area when a man quickly left the theater in tears midway through a showing of *Apocalypse Now*. It moved me then, though I understand it more clearly now. I grew up watching movies—but the significance of those movies came from the community in which I experienced them.

Kathryn

My childhood memories of going to the movies include standing at attention, hand over heart, watching a screen-size American flag waving in the breeze as the national anthem played before the beginning of the feature film. My siblings and I were Air Force "brats" (Wertsch 2011), raised, for the most part, on military bases. But the first movie I remember seeing was off-base at the drive-in on a warm summer night when I was 10 years old. My parents and we four kids (soon to be five) packed into our 1963 Mercury station wagon with the fake wood paneling on the side. We parked backward, opened the back, and I lay side by side with my siblings as we entered a world where a nanny brought magic, wonder, and order into the lives of Jane and Michael Banks. I fell in love with the idea of Mary Poppins, a woman who flew in with the east wind, took charge, brought order, and left when her job was done. I most identified, of course, with Jane Banks, but I was keenly aware of her mother in the background, organizing and rallying for women's rights. For my birthday I asked for the book, and over the next couple of years I read all eight books in the series by P. L. Travers. To this day I remember all the words to the songs from the film, and when I'm with my siblings during holidays we sing those and other songs from childhood movies we saw together.

As we reflect back on our early movie memories, we look at the experiences through a sociological lens. While our stories appear to be very personal, they, like all stories, are best understood in social context. As sociologists, we experience what C. Wright Mills (1959) described as "the urge to know the social and historical meaning of the individual in the society" (p. 5). The way we view film and the meanings we derive are impacted by our locations and engagement with the social world.

For Jean-Anne, growing up in a small town, the theater was a pivotal site in building and sustaining social networks. In Goffman's (1959) terms, it was the setting for the front stage of adolescence in her community. Jean-Anne's memory of the man leaving *Apocalypse Now* in tears is part of her understanding of the ongoing legacy of Vietnam in the lives of those affected. For Kathryn, going to the movies, like all activities on a military base, was structured by patriotism and nationalism. She was an avid reader, and movies provided visual representation of the texts she read and directed her attention to social events outside of school curriculum and family life—such as the women's suffrage movement, which she had never heard about before seeing *Mary Poppins*.

Going through this exercise with our students, we learn how their lives have been affected by the films they've watched and invite them to think about films and film viewing differently than they have in the past. Many students tell us that their friends and family don't necessarily appreciate their sociological approach to watching movies; they complain, "You're not fun to go to the movies with anymore!" But overall, our students feel they have been enlightened and given a set of tools that will be useful throughout their lives. In any event, they say they will never again see movies in the same way!

References

Goffman, E. 1959. *The Presentation of Self in Everyday Life.* Garden City, NY: Doubleday Anchor Books.

Mills, C. W. 1959. *The Sociological Imagination.* New York: Oxford University Press.

Wertsch, M. W. 2011. *Military Brats: Legacies of Childhood inside the Fortress.* St. Louis: Brightwell.

Acknowledgments

We would like to thank the many students who have taken our Sociology through Film classes over the years. They have brought to this course ideas and insights (and film suggestions!) that have contributed to our approach to the course and informed the pedagogical framework we are developing.

We appreciate the support provided by our families and friends. Jean-Anne would like to thank Mark Cox for being the best of sounding boards. Thanks also to DeeAnna Merz Nagel for her flow of film-related e-mails, her constant encouragement, and her unconditional, lifelong friendship; and to Joy Skinner, who validates a long-standing assumption— the work-family juggling act can be tolerated only if a strong and hilarious friend is nearby. Kathryn would like to thank Diane Moran for being there always. Thanks also to Zach Feltey for sharing his stories and insights, and to Matt Lee for showing by example that shared laughter does help.

We thank the contributors to the book for their work using film to teach about the social world we share with one another. We appreciate SAGE Publications, our publisher, and David Repetto, our editor, as well as Nathan Davidson and Lydia Balian, sociology editorial assistants, all of whom guided us in shepherding the book through the publication process. We would also like to thank our fabulous copy editor, Rachel Keith, for her diligence and professionalism.

Many thanks to our friends and colleagues at the University of North Carolina Wilmington and the University of Akron for their support, including Kim Cook, Diane Levy, Dave Monahan, Becky Erickson, Bill Lyons, Mark Tausig, and John Zipp. We are especially grateful to our friend, colleague, and mentor Michael Kimmel, who encouraged, evaluated, advised, and ultimately empowered us to write from the heart. Michael, just as you encouraged us to work from our hearts, you daily modeled for us a colleague who worked unselfishly from his. Thank you for your relentless cheerleading and support.

CHAPTER 1

Introduction

Theo: Whatever you say, whatever you do, movies always got there first. Even that line you just said comes from a movie.

—Dot the I (2003)

American Society and Film

In U.S. society, "going to the movies" has been a favored pastime since the opening of the first movie theaters over 100 years ago. It is hard to imagine a small town, Anywhere, USA, without envisioning the movie theater on the town square, complete with marquee and ticket booth and moviegoers lined up to pay their admission fee. Not only was the movie theater an integral part of the creation of community on the movie set, but in-life, off-screen movie theaters were built in towns and cities across the United States. Indeed, the image of the town movie theater is a staple in movies and is often used, along with other institutions such as the pharmacy and barbershop, to convey a sense of community, a gemeinschaft haven in a changing world. For example, in the classic *It's a Wonderful Life* (1946), we see from the Bijou Theater marquee that *The Bells of Saint Mary's* is playing in Bedford Falls, a community protected from capitalist and political greed by the goodness of George Bailey (James Stewart). In a similar vein, when Marty (Michael J. Fox) in the first *Back to the Future* (1985) travels 30 years back in his hometown, Hill Valley, he orders a soda at the downtown drugstore and observes that the nearby Essex Theater is playing a Ronald Reagan film.

The antithesis of this communal setting is what towns could or would become if small-town values were sacrificed to modernization. When George Bailey is rescued from his Christmas Eve suicide attempt by his guardian angel, Clarence, he is shown the town that Bedford Falls would have been without his influence. Pottersville is a tawdry town with a main street dominated by pawn shops and sleazy bars. The theater marquee now boasts "Georgia's sensational striptease dance with Girls! Girls! Girls!" Community values have been replaced by individualism, cynicism, and distrust. In *Back to the Future's* alternate 1985 we see a run-down Essex Theater, now an adult movie house showing "Orgy,

Why is it inevitable
How can we see this in L. Immaterk legs york?

American Style." The deterioration of these theaters, along with the commodification of sexuality (in a place formerly reserved for family entertainment), symbolizes the alienation that accompanies modernization.

The process of modernization, however, included the rapid expansion of the motion picture industry in the first half of the twentieth century. Between 1914 and 1922, 4,000 new theaters were built in the United States (Starker 1989). Many of these were built in residential areas, signaling a new trend in the industry: the "neighborhood theater." During the 1920s, about 100 million people attended movie theaters each week, twice the number that attended church (Library of Congress N.d.). The popularity of the movies could, in part, be attributed to the low admission prices and unreserved "democratic" seating, making this leisure activity widely accessible to diverse audiences.

York

One of the functions of the theater in the early twentieth century was to aid in the assimilation of immigrants into the community, ensuring that a shared way of life was protected and passed on. For example, in some communities, theaters ran special features on Sundays (when theaters were not ordinarily open) "to educate and familiarize foreign speaking people with the customs, principles, and institutions of our American life" (Abel 2004:107). Many films during this period focused on the immigration story and life in the new country. Films such as *Making of an American* (1920) were sponsored by state level committees on Americanization with the goal of encouraging immigrants to assimilate by learning American customs and the English language (Roberts 1920).

Assimilation into the American mainstream was, of course, reserved for immigrants who most resembled the dominant group. Theaters, like other public institutions, reflected the racial, ethnic, and class-based divisions of the larger society in the content of the films shown and the treatment of the attending audiences. Until the latter part of the twentieth century, the policy of racial segregation was enforced at movie theaters by time (showing films for African American audiences late at night), by section (seating African American viewers in the balcony), by entrance (requiring African Americans to enter off a side alleyway), and by neighborhood, with black-only theaters serving patrons in African American neighborhoods, especially in northern cities (Hearne 2007). This history of racial segregation in theaters has been portrayed in recent movies. In *The Secret Life of Bees* (2008), set in 1964 South Carolina, Lily (Dakota Fanning) goes to the movies with Zach (Tristan Wilds), and she follows him to the balcony so they can sit together. Zach is dragged out of the theater and beaten by white men outraged at their transgression. In the film *Ray* (2004), Charles (Jamie Foxx) refuses to perform at a segregated concert after encountering young civil rights activists protesting outside the theater. In a less known movie, *Hope* (1997), a young African American boy dies in a theater fire when he is trapped in the balcony where there is no emergency exit.

In southwestern states, schools, public facilities, and movie theaters were segregated, with Asian and Mexican immigrants and citizens forced to sit in the balcony, even if seating was available downstairs (Ross 1998). In Kansas, Mexican Americans were restricted from some sections of city parks, churches, and other public facilities, and were routinely segregated in movie theaters through the mid twentieth century (Oppenheimer 1985). This institutional segregation, visible across communities, was based on an ideology of racism reflected in the official policies of organizations, businesses, and homeowners associations. Two of the most common settings of segregation, aside from schools, were movie theaters and swimming pools (Montoya 2001).

Moving through the decades of the twentieth century, changes in the film industry reflected societal and cultural changes. The location and structure of venues for movie viewing changed from the picture palaces of the early twentieth century, to the art deco architecture of the Depression era, to the drive-in movies of the mid twentieth century, to the multiplex and megaplex of the mid to late twentieth century. Just as the content of film celebrated the culture of consumerism and individualism, the way we watched movies became less public with the expansion of in-home movie viewing services and options. However, while 75 percent of Americans say they would rather watch a movie at home, between 1995 and 2006 there was only a 5 percent decline (from 31 percent to 26 percent) in those reporting they go out to see a movie at least once a month (Pew Research Center 2006). Among the group most coveted by the theater industry—younger, better educated, higher-income consumers—the decline was more pronounced (from 56 percent to 43 percent). However, 71 percent of Americans reported watching a movie once a week or more, while an additional 18 percent watched a movie at least once a month. As at-home and on-the-go movie technology become more widespread, our viewing practices may change, but regardless of where or how we watch, we are still "going to the movies" in our leisure time.

Sociology and Film[1]

All over the world, people go to the movies—to escape, to be enlightened, to be entertained. Indeed, movies are among the world's most popular social experiences. In 2007 there was a decline in movie attendance, but two years later, with a "teetering" economy, there was a "box-office surge" (Cieply and Barnes 2009). Amid complaints of rising box office prices, movie attendance dropped again in 2010 and 2011. At the same time, movie-on-demand rentals and online downloading numbers are increasing (Verna 2010). While rates of cinema attendance ebb and flow, the myriad forms of movie watching mean that even in times of economic crisis, we still watch movies.

> *Finn:* I'm not going to tell the story the way it happened. I'm going to tell it the way I remember it.
>
> —*Great Expectations* (1998)

everdlone weconnect

Going to the movies is a social event; we view movies with significant others and are affected by the experience in a social context. Consider the young dating couple who share a soda (or something stronger) after watching a movie together, talking earnestly, seriously, about their feelings for the characters. Or the child, seated between her parents, munching popcorn and watching *March of the Penguins* and deciding to become an oceanographer. Or families who share their anguish and deepen their understanding about social issues such as AIDS (*Philadelphia*), sexual harassment (*North Country*), race and ethnic relations (*Do the Right Thing*), personal heroism and sacrifice (*Saving Private Ryan*), or the cold cruelty of the Holocaust (*Schindler's List*). Or even the everyday people who, hit hard during troubled economic times, watch a musical or comedy and momentarily laugh their troubles away. As the lead character in *Sullivan's Travels* (1941) said in the final lines of the movie, "There's a lot to be said for making people laugh. Did you know that that's all some people have? It isn't much, but it's better than nothing in this cockeyed caravan."

Tagling
Knowing.

Frankly mydear, I Don't give a DAMN

Reading a Film Sociologically

Every field of study offers a slightly different way of seeing film. An Anthropology of Film class might integrate ethnographic films as a means of "seeing" culture. Older films might be considered historical artifacts, offering a window into the culture at particular points in time. Many documentaries are themselves products of anthropological interest in disclosing the practices and ceremonies of other peoples and cultures. A film course in the history department would take a look at historically significant films and question their authenticity, accuracy, and interpretation. For example, you might take a film like *Glory* and discuss the cinematic treatment of the Civil War; a film such as *Sense and Sensibility* might enhance discussions of class and gender relations during different historical periods.

In a Film Studies class, attention would be directed to film production, cinematography, mise-en-scène, film genres, film history, and film theory. In the mass media and cultural studies departments, perhaps the cousins of sociology in terms of film analysis, you might be asked to consider social and cultural "powers" at work in the film and in the film industry that remain largely unchallenged as social disseminators of cultural ideas. How does cinematic "form" work with (or against) the cinematic content?

Sociological perspectives draw from these traditions. In this text, we are less concerned with the technical aspects of film production and more concerned with the stories told through film, and how these stories are told. Is there something specific that a sociological perspective brings to the study of film? More important for our inquiry, sociology *through* film, how can film be used by sociologists to better understand the society in which we live?

The core of any sociological curriculum revolves around four interrelated themes: (1) identity, (2) interaction, (3) inequality, and (4) institutions. Sociologists can use films as social texts to explore these core themes.

Identity: Many films involve the development of individual characters as a central theme: how they come to know themselves, how they try out identities until they find one that fits, how they adapt their identities for strategic purposes. The sociological concept of the "looking glass self" and the dramaturgical metaphors made popular by Goffman and others are amply illustrated in films such as *In and Out*, in which a closeted gay teacher is outed in the national media and comes to accept his homosexuality, just as the small town in which he lives comes to accept him. In *Forrest Gump*, Forrest (Tom Hanks) and Jenny (Robin Wright) come to know who they are in very different ways. Forrest moves through his life, unconcerned about whether others see him as heroic, iconic, or mentally ill. In fact, we do not learn that Forrest is aware of his "difference" until late in the film when he asks Jenny about their son: " . . . is he smart or is he . . . ?" Jenny responds, "He's very smart. He is one of the smartest in his class." Jenny, on the other hand, is very aware of how others view her, and her sense of self develops in the context of unloving and abusive relationships beginning in her family of origin.

Interaction: All film involves social interaction, even when the story is one of isolation from others. For example, in *Cast Away*, Chuck (Tom Hanks) develops a friendship with Wilson the volleyball, who becomes his companion and confidant. As the viewing audience, we come to know Chuck through his interaction with Wilson. By watching film, we learn about social interaction in the context of relationships, everything from friendship (*Sisterhood of the Traveling Pants*) to romance and dating (*The Break-Up*) to family life (*The Joy Luck Club*) Indeed, many people probably first know what sex and intimacy look like from having seen it in the movies.

Inequality: A common theme in movies is inequality based on social class, race, gender, or nation. Many people who live in relative comfort encounter the stark reality of people oppressed in systems of inequality through the movies. A student spoke of her political apathy until she saw the film *Hotel Rwanda* at the university cinema. The film so moved her that she became involved in campus political organizations that confronted inequality and eventually changed her major to public sociology, making her newfound awareness of politics her future.[2] A friend told of his first memory of learning about the Holocaust while watching *Exodus* with his parents and grandparents as a young child, and for the first time his family began to talk about what had happened to the Jews of Europe. They had been silent; the film enabled them to give words to the unspeakable. How many films reveal the brutal injustices of the prison system (*Cool Hand Luke*; *The Green Mile*), or the Jim Crow South (*Driving Miss Daisy*; *To Kill a Mockingbird*), or slavery (*Amistad*; *Beloved*), or any other type of structured inequality? Films can engage us viscerally, making inequality palpable and real—and thus far less tolerable.

GME Sold — we are consumptionist

Institutions: Finally, film enables us to locate ourselves in the institutions that shape our lives. Films such as *Patton* and *A Few Good Men* illustrate more than the atrocities of war—they provide a lens into the military as organization and institutional force. In the same way, movies about work and the workplace (*Working Girl*; *Michael Clayton*) reveal the often invisible structural barriers encountered in institutions, whether it's the glass ceiling encountered by women or unethical business-as-usual practices. Institutions such as work, school, and religion shape our identities, and films, usually without our awareness, provide us with understandings of the social structure of these "spaces" where we live, work, learn, pray, and are entertained.

Sociologists explore these four themes in the film "content"—the stories presented in films. Sociologists also might look for patterns in viewership—the ways some movies target specific audiences by class, race, gender, or sexuality. Or they might examine the centrality of film in childhood socialization: many Americans might say that some of their most tender and powerful memories of childhood involve going to the movies. Sociologists may also consider the ways that films, like other media texts, elicit, structure, and facilitate the expression of different emotions to which we, as humans, need access. We consider the social dynamics of audiences, the effects of images on social life, the complex interaction of cinematic technique with the experiences of viewers. We consider the ways in which social problems and identities are represented in film—the manner in which films both reflect and create culture.

Key!

Reading films with a sociological eye makes us conscious of ourselves as we watch movies. In a sense we move from our seats in the theater to the projection booth. From there we can look at the audience as they "see" the film. Also, we can appreciate the film as *film*: a strip of material that produces images and ideas. From this angle we can recognize the social nature of the movie experience—people coming together for entertainment, for storytelling, for a view of our culture as well as the cultures of others. Movies are social experiences, and we often remember family events and experiences from our childhood through their associations with movies. Baby boomers (including the editors of this book) can probably still recall when small theaters sold pickles from a big jar at the concession stand, or biting through the outer layer of a Good & Plenty to get to the chewy licorice inside, or the sticky-sweet smell of black Jujubes that got stuck to the soles of your shoes in the theater. For many, a social life in high school meant meeting friends at the movies on a weekend night, where they would see dozens of classmates—friends and foes.

The dynamics of social interactions—homophobia, racial awareness, class interaction—are evident as we take our seats to watch the movies, just as much as they are in the movies themselves. For example, when two women go to the movies together, how many seats do they take? The answer is, invariably, "Two." But ask men how many seats they take. The typical answer is three; they leave the middle seat open, or put their coats there, because they don't want anyone to think they are "together."

The Film as a Text

But it is mostly what is on the screen that rightly preoccupies the sociologist of film. Like other forms of art—music, literature, paintings—films speak to us, exposing us to the ideas of writers, actors, and directors who use various techniques to explain, explore, or exploit our experiences. We can look at the history of cinema—the ways that a film will reference other "texts"—or the actual technology and technique, but only insofar as they enable the director, screenwriter, and actors to make a particular case to viewers. Applying the sociological imagination to film involves awareness of the economic, political, and social forces at the point in history when a particular film or set of films is produced. In fact, this is one of the strengths of film as a pedagogical tool: it can provide access to multiple sociohistorical contexts. However, it also reflects the (biased) view of the filmmaker(s) telling the story. Our interests are sociological—social—not aesthetic. We can appreciate the aesthetic beauty of, say, a Merchant Ivory production,[4] but our sociological imaginations are animated by the actual story and the moral lessons they present to us.

At the same time, reading films sociologically does not mean that we drain the fun out of the experience. While a sociological reading asks us to look beyond common sense thinking and long-held interpretations (in short, to be critical thinkers), we can still appreciate the entertainment value of movies. We can critique expressions of gender in film without dismissing Disney, a central piece of our childhood movie memories. Seeing films through a sociological lens does not make movie watching laborious. Rather, it should enhance our viewing experience, further developing our understanding of the society in which the film was produced and the people it portrays.

This book is about the ways in which films speak to us. It's about film as a text in the same way that a novel is a text—not only telling a story, but providing moral instruction, social observation, social context, and political judgment. In 1963, Lewis Coser's edited volume *Sociology through Literature: An Introductory Reader* sought to fuse social science and art, specifically literature. Coser made sociological thought within literary works visible and explored how classic works of literature express various classical preoccupations of sociologists. More current writing continues this tradition through analyses of literature and group identities, decoding systems, and the impact of life experiences on reader response (Griswold 1993). Works of literature are seen not only as products of the authors' imaginations and examples of shared meanings, but also as *social* texts that speak of culture, socialization, identity, inequalities, and social structures.

Literature is appreciated not only for the telling of a good story, but for the ways in which authors go about capturing social context, social and psychological struggles, and social problems. The great novels leave us with commentaries on social class (*The Great Gatsby*; *Pride and Prejudice*), race (*Huckleberry Finn*; *The Bluest Eye*), and gender (*The Awakening*; *The Scarlet Letter*). Narratives such as these provides frames through which we can understand a social class to which we do not belong, *feelings* associated with racial tensions, and social constraints associated with being male or female. Before motion pictures, these were the stories on which we relied.

In today's world, Americans attend movies far more often than they read fiction. In this sense, films have become a new kind of text through which we are provided stories, frames, and representations of social life. Films, of course, require a different kind of "read" than a novel. For instance, while the author of a novel might also be encouraged to consider production and sales, there are fewer investors to whom the author must answer. With film, there is the ever-present issue of currency—films cost an enormous amount of money to produce and, thus, must earn an even greater amount upon release. The issue of money has the potential to change the telling of the story so that it "satisfies" a much larger community. The novel can be as controversial as the author intends, since he or she has more autonomy. A film, on the other hand, must often play down controversy to reach a broader market. The novel is one voice—that of the author's. Film is the product of many voices—the screenwriters, the director, the actors, and so forth—thus potentially diluting the original voice (e.g., the author of the text on which the film is based). The interpretations of a novel lie mostly in the active imaginations of the reader. A film can use technology, utilizing visuals and sound to guide viewer response. Thus, while film is a modern text, we must read it conscious of the ways in which symbols, language, and author intentions are specific to this medium. Film studies' entrée into "film as text" attests to how we think of movies as "comprising visual language, verbal systems, dialogue, characterization, narrative and 'story'" (Shiel 2001: 3). Films reflect our culture while simultaneously serving as an element that constitutes it. We see our society through film and we see film through the prism of our social norms, values, and institutions.

Sociology *of* Film/Sociology *through* Film

Much earlier social scientific thought about popular culture was steeped in deterministic thinking. For example, the Frankfurt School warned that the "liberatory" power of jazz—antiauthoritarian, sensual, rebellious—actually served to further authoritarian domination because it temporarily "freed" individuals and thus muted or siphoned off anger at an unjust system. Any system that gives us such pleasure can't be all bad—thus the systemic domination is, ironically, legitimated by embracing its own resistance. Popular culture was an "opiate of the masses," to use Marx's famous phrase about religion, numbing us to the pain of inequality. "Keep you doped with religion and sex and TV/So you think you're so clever and classless and free," sang John Lennon in his devastatingly plaintive song "Working Class Hero."

Historically, too, sociology's interest in film had a deterministic bent. From the origin of the moving picture, social scientists worried that film would instruct people to passively

[handwritten margin note: Books take your mind, films takes your sunses & mind. Permission to. Collective consciousness]

People will passively

follow the normative instructions contained in the film. Somewhat like contemporary anxious parents, they worried that a film about crime would inspire a young person to commit crimes. Surely, pornography would cause rape, and cowboy movies would inspire violence. Ultimately sociologists renounced this image of the film audience as a passive sponge, soaking up messages and responding as Pavlovian dogs, with a more elitist conception of the audience as a gullible mass, somehow incapable of deciphering the descriptive from the normative.

In contrast, sociologists today have come to see the film audience more as decoder of symbols and meanings, actively engaged with the film itself, and as "contextualizer," constantly interpreting images within the contexts of social life. Film neither causes social problems nor simply reflects them.

This notion of the active audience lies at the foundation of current sociological interest in film—both in sociological studies of popular culture as they have gained broader acceptance and in the college courses on film and sociology that have become available to students. Some call the course "Sociology *of* Film." It is likely that classes will include topics such as filmmaking, film production, and film distribution as well as the content, form, and impact of films. Certainly when a course is "of" something, that something is the unit of analysis—gender, for example, in a Sociology of Gender class.

Others call the course "Sociology *through* Film." In these classes, *film* is not the unit of analysis per se. Rather, film is used as a concrete means of illustrating principals in the study of social life. The goal of the course involves learning to recognize sociological concepts in our life experiences (in movies, rather than relying solely on textbooks). Here we are concerned with the social construction of reality. (What do different films suggest about the meaning of gender or race or social status for people in society today? How does the "language" of film produce different meanings?) We are concerned with the repetition of images in our culture. (How is a group or a political system presented to us? Does this change over time?) We consider the socializing effects of film. (How and what do films teach us?) Our goal is to "see" movies differently.

We see this of/through distinction in studies of sociology and literature. Coser's text was called *Sociology through Literature,* not *Sociology of Literature.* Coser compiled an impressive (and abundant) collection of excerpted literature from Shakespeare to Norman Mailer, arguing that literature was yet another source from which we gain knowledge about society, and hence, ourselves. He said, ". . . if a novel, a play or a poem is a personal and direct impression of social life, the sociologist should respond to it with the same openness and willingness to learn that he [sic] displays when he interviews a respondent, observes a community, or classifies and analyzes data" (1963:xvi). This was a bold stance during a time when sociology tended toward more "serious" matters of scientific study (and typically relied on functionalist theory). What is important here is that Coser set out to explore literary works not for purposes of literary analysis, but as data to be analyzed regarding social experiences for sociological inquiry. He wrote:

> This book is not meant to be a contribution to the sociology of literature. Sociology of literature is a specialized area of study which focuses upon the relation between a work of art, its public, and the social in which it is produced and received . . . The attempt here is to use the work of literature for an understanding of society, rather

than to illuminate artistic production by reference to the society in which it arose . . . This collection, then, should help to teach modern sociology through illustrative material from literature. (P. xvii)

Coser went on to teach such substantive sociological topics as stratification (through George Orwell's "The Lower Classes Smell" from *The Road to Wigan Pier*); sex roles (through Virginia Woolf's *A Room of One's Own*); race relations (through Mark Twain's "Huck Breaks the White Code" from *Huckleberry Finn*); poverty (through Charles Dickens's "I Want Some More" from *Oliver Twist*); and family (through Lev Tolstoy's "The Perils and Dilemmas of Marital Choice" from *Anna Karenina*).

This book follows the model set forth by Coser. Thus, we consciously call it sociology *through* film. This book will teach you about the field of sociology, using film as the source. Thus far we have delineated the sociological perspective used in the analysis of film. But how exactly do sociologists do it? How do we decode a film as text? What tools do we have available to us?

The Sociological Toolkit

The sociological viewing, analysis, and interpretation of film require an understanding of the relationship among historical context, social structure, and individual experience (Shiel 2001). In Mills's (1959) terms, the sociological imagination enables us to grasp history and biography and the relations between the two. Engaging our sociological imaginations allows us to see how events that seem extraordinarily personal are in fact produced and shaped by social forces.

Take, for example, divorce. This life event seems to those involved to be the most private and personal decision two individuals can make. But as sociologists we note social factors contributing to the likelihood of divorce (e.g., marrying as a teenager, being poor, becoming unemployed, having a low level of education, perceiving that the division of household labor is unfair; see Amato 2010). Thus, divorces *are* personal and individual, occurring at the micro level, but they are also influenced by macro level societal structures. Divorces occur in societies with structured social orders, at a particular time in history, with different types of men and women inhabiting that place and time. Consequently, when we view *Kramer vs. Kramer,* a 1979 film about a couple who separate, leaving the dad to learn childcare and housework until the working mom returns and the custody battle begins, we must place it within context. Rather than viewing this as one couple's struggle with divorce—or even as *representing* divorce—our sociological imaginations allow us to read this film from the micro to the macro perspective. Consider the historical context of the 1970s: second-wave feminism was barely a decade old, so how might gender politics have impacted the telling of this story? We might also consider

> *Andrew:* Everyone is born with blinders on, knowing only that one station in life to which they are born. You, on the other hand, Madam, have had the rare privilege of removing your bonds for just a spell to see life from an entirely different perspective. How you choose to use that information is entirely up to you.
>
> —*Overboard* (1987)

social structure: how were "working moms" and "caregiving dads" represented in this film, considering "appropriate" gender roles at the time? And at the level of individual experience: what did the characters' emotional states and priorities reveal about divorce and child custody?

One of the benefits of studying sociology is the "toolkit" it provides for analyzing and understanding the social world. In this section we present theoretical perspectives and methodological approaches that can be used as a frame for reading films sociologically. As we have noted, film can be thought of as text in the sense that it provides material (data) subject to observation and analysis.

Theoretical Perspectives

In any Introduction to Sociology course, the student is introduced to theory. We need theory, after all, to guide both the questions we ask and our interpretations of the responses. More often than not, an introductory class will highlight the Big Three theories: structural functionalism, conflict theory, and symbolic interactionism. While the utilization of these theories is much more nuanced than a few bullet points can detail (as you will see from many of the readings within this book), it is also helpful to keep some of these points in mind, since the theoretical perspective you use depends on the types of questions you ask. If you want to consider macro level societal change, you might benefit from using *functionalism*. If you intend to explore power relations, including political power, patriarchy, or racial dominance, then a *conflict perspective* would be more appropriate. If your questions have to do with issues of representation ("meanings" in a film), socialization, or the social construction of reality, *symbolic interactionism* would provide the framing necessary.

Structural functionalism stems from the work of Émile Durkheim. Durkheim was concerned with social order—why does it exist and under what conditions will it fail? What holds society together? Thus, a classic functionalist perspective assumes the following:

- Society consists of "parts," all working together to maintain order (these parts include institutions such as law, family, economics, and religion).
- When a change or shift occurs in one part of society, changes and shifts occur in other parts as well.
- Cohesion is maintained via mutually agreed-upon norms and values.
- "Dysfunctions" occur when order and balance are upset.

Watching movies through a functionalist lens allows us to consider the interdependence of social institutions as well as how an event or behavior functions in society. Watching a movie about a family would lead us to consider how the family, as an institution, helps maintain an ordered society. A classic (and somewhat dated) functionalist view would argue that the family, especially the "traditional" family consisting of the breadwinner and the homemaker, helps maintain the equilibrium of society; each member has his or her roles. "Dysfunctions" occur when change occurs. For example, greater numbers of women from all social classes begin to enter the workforce. The "instrumental" and "expressive" roles of men and women become blurred as both men and women become responsible for economically supporting the family and taking care of the home and children. These changes in the family lead to changes in other institutions, such as education and religion. With more women working, fewer can volunteer at schools or in religious organizations. What, then, from a functionalist perspective, is the function of the homemaker? Her manifest (intended) function is to maintain societal equilibrium by raising children and creating a home to which the breadwinner can return. Her latent (unintended) functions include supporting the smooth running of other institutions and the community (through "free" labor or volunteerism).

At the core of conflict theory is the work of Karl Marx. Unlike functionalists, who focus on order and maintaining the status quo as society's goals, conflict theorists would claim that if stability lasts too long, then some group has too much power (and is enforcing it on others)! For instance, conflict theorists welcome shifts away from clear divisions of labor in the family, as men *and* women now have access to varied resources. Marx divided society into two classes (the owners and the workers). Because workers, during his time, had nothing to sell except their own labor, owners were able to exploit them, resulting in the workers' alienation, or separation, from themselves, others, and the products they made. Conflict theory holds the following assumptions:

- There is a scarcity of resources in society (e.g., money, education, jobs).
- Society consists of groups struggling for (scarce) resources.
- Conflict and change are good for a society, as they challenge the status quo.
- Power enables some groups to dominate others.

The conflict perspective reminds us that film is not a documented recording of social events or alternative worlds; film is carefully crafted and produced within industrial and economic relations of power (Giroux 2002). In contemporary sociology, many perspectives fall under the umbrella of conflict theory. For instance, a continuous critical approach (Lehman and Luhr 2002) allows for a view of film that shifts the center (Collins 2000) from dominant discourse to the matrix of domination along the axes of race, class, gender, sexuality, and geopolitical location. These interlocking systems operate from the individual to the social structural level. Critical theories provide the best vehicle for this approach. Feminist theory allows us to ask about prevailing attitudes and assumptions concerning gender as well as the structure of patriarchy. Critical race theory and critical white studies frame questions concerning racism, racial discrimination, and the acceptance of whiteness as the norm. Marxist theory can address power in the making of movies: who has the power to (re)produce ideologies? Pierre Bourdieu's theories allow an analysis of power via cultural capital: how do tastes and knowledge of culture "locate" people in social classes?

Symbolic Interactionism (SI) borrows from Max Weber's assertion that sociology should seek "to understand" society. The work of George Herbert Mead and Charles Cooley also form the basis of SI. In the SI (or constructionist) tradition, knowledge, truth, and reality are determined by "the context in which they are practiced" (O'Brien 2006:9). We engage in an interpretive process in which schemas and culturally specific common sense realities help us to arrive at meanings. Helping to shape those meanings are the values, norms, and ideologies of a culture that inform what is real. Thus, some assumptions of SI would be:

- Nothing has meaning until we give it meaning.
- Meanings are established through *interaction* with others.
- The exchange of symbols allows for the establishment of meanings.
- If we believe something to be real, it becomes real in its consequences (our interpretations guide our actions).

SI and social constructionism reminds us that race, ethnicity, gender, sexuality, and social class have no meaning until a society attaches meaning to a particular status or social location. Watching film and engaging with the content is part of the interpretive process where repetitive images take on meaning and become "real," often turning into "common sense knowledge." Through films we are told what it means to be man, woman, gay, lesbian, black, white, Asian, Latino, middle or working class. Whether the images and information are "objectively" real is irrelevant in terms of the consequences. Mediated images and information become part of the material that supports or contradicts our notions of what is real in the social world.

Methods

There are many methodological approaches to the study of film. We recommend the two processes outlined below.

The first approach is based on the process for conducting research, revised for film analysis.[4]

1. The Research Question
   a. What is the sociological question motivating the research?
   b. What is significant about your question?
   c. What is your argument?

2. Literature Review
   a. How have others approached this question? (Keep in mind that others may or may not have used film in addressing this question.)
   b. What were their contributions regarding the findings?
   c. What theories and methods have been used?
   d. What questions are left to be asked?
   e. Did reading this literature shape the way you are approaching your question?
   f. Is it important that you ask your question in another way?

3. Methods and Data
   a. How did you select your sample of films?
   b. How did you collect data?
      i. How did you watch the film(s)?
      ii. How did you take notes while watching?

   iii. Did you code the data, looking for patterns and trends?

   iv. What did you do with your notes when you were finished watching?

   v. Did these data help you to answer your question?

4. Data Analysis

   a. What are your findings?

   b. What do the data tell you regarding your research question?

   c. Use your data to make your argument (convince the reader).

   d. Relate your findings back to the literature review. Is this something new?

5. Conclusion

   a. Sum up your findings.

   b. What is the significance of this work?

   c. Are there implications for future research?

This model has several advantages. First, it does not deviate from traditional research models; thus, there may be some familiarity with the structure of the project. Second, it specifically guides not only the kinds of questions one might ask, but also the order in which to address them. While this model is familiar, the second recommended approach is representative of a different kind of qualitative methodology.

The second approach to analyzing film involves a five-step process drawn from the work of Norman Denzin (1989). The goal is to help students orient themselves to the content of film in the research role of nonparticipant observer (Tan and Ko 2004). In addition to honing skills of observation, this process incorporates an ethnographic tool called "thick description" (Geertz 1973). The key to thick, as opposed to thin, description is that even the simplest act can mean different things depending on the social and cultural context. Thus, it is the responsibility of the researcher to report not just actions, but the context of the practices and discourse within the society being observed. This means reading the text of the film at multiple levels and attending to implied as well as explicit content. The guiding question is how the film creates multiple meanings through language, action, and "what-goes-without-saying" (Barthes, as cited in Denzin 1989). This process should help you to "bracket" taken-for-granted assumptions about the social world to first observe and then analyze the content of the film.

1. Select the film and view it multiple times. While there are disadvantages to viewing a film outside the context for which it was made (e.g., large screen, particular sound system), one benefit to viewing a film at home is the ability to stop, rewind, and review throughout the process.

2. Outline the narrative themes of the film. Themes are patterns or constructs that, in qualitative research, are induced from texts in a process of open coding. Two strategies are worth mentioning here: the "social science query" and the "search for missing information" (Ryan and Russell Bernard 2003). In the first, the text is examined for topics important to social scientists, such as social conflict, cultural contradictions, methods of social control, and setting and context. In the second, attention is on what is not represented, including topics addressed in this text, such as class, culture, race and ethnicity, and sex and gender.

3. Conduct a realistic reading of the hegemonic interpretations of the text in terms of their dominant ideological meanings. This step involves a close reading of the film's characters, content, and dialogue. What universal features of the human condition are addressed? What stories are told that reproduce existing relations of power and inequity?

4. Develop a "subversive" or oppositional reading of the text such that the taken-for-granted hegemony is revealed by making the connections between particular lives and social organization visible and explicit (Ewick and Silbey 1995). Shifting away from characters, content, and dialogue, this analysis "focuses instead on how the film creates its meanings through the organization of signifying practices that organize the film's reality" (Denzin 1989:46). In this step, it is critical to attend to the individual-as-subject bias that structures much of film ideology—in other words, to apply the sociological imagination.

5. Compare the realistic/hegemonic and oppositional readings of the film. In this step the analysis is further developed as the results of the two previous steps are evaluated in relationship to one another. What is the story being told through the film, and how is it supported explicitly in how the characters are portrayed, what they say (and how they say it), and the events that construct a storyline? How does this compare to the "underlying ideological forces of the film" (Denzin 1989:46)?

In short, the way to apply sociology to film as data about social life is to answer the following questions when viewing the film (Brym 2008):

1. How does the movie reflect the social context?

2. How does the movie distort social reality?

3. To what degree does the movie shed light on common or universal social and human problems?

4. To what degree does the movie provide evidence for or against sociological theory and research?

5. To what degree does the movie connect biography, social structure, and history?

In This Book

> *Atticus Finch:* If you just learn a single trick, Scout, you'll get along a lot better with all kinds of folks. You never really understand a person until you consider things from his point

As Atticus Finch (Gregory Peck) explained to his daughter, the best way to understand others is to suspend what you think you know and see the world through their eyes. In sociology we call this the practice of *verstehen*, the term Weber used to refer to the social scientist's attempt to understand both the intention and the context of human action and interaction (Munch 1975). In this chapter, we have provided you with a toolkit (theory and method) and a data source (film) to put sociology into practice. Films can be effectively used in this way because they (1) give viewers access to social worlds beyond their own and (2) create the opportunity to understand the relationship between individual experience and "the broader social context which structures one's actions and choices" (Prendergast 1986:243).

Chapter 2 explores sociological theories and how they can be used to analyze and interpret film. In the Outtake, Rubinfeld applies the three theoretical perspectives to the Hollywood enterprise and the pictures it produces. Both readings in this chapter use the classical works of Marx and Weber and their critiques of modern society. Kimmel focuses on the transition of society from a traditional, feudal system to modern capitalism and the contrast between society as "an idyllic, pastoral culture, at peace with itself and deeply connected to nature, and a technocratic, bureaucratic modernist machine." The effects of rationalization as society becomes more bureaucratic are what Weber called the iron cage (or "a steel-hard casing," as Dahms points out in the second reading).

of view . . . Until you climb inside of his skin and walk around in it.

—*To Kill a Mockingbird* (1962)

Dahms distinguishes between two types of social theories: reflexive and reflective. Reflexive (critical) theories identify the conflicts and contradictions in modern society, while reflective theories explain that all of society (institutions, individuals, inventions) are reflections or manifestations of the values and beliefs of that society. Dahms explores these two theoretical orientations in *The Matrix*, noting that the trilogy "cuts to the heart of what *alienation* and *iron cage*, respectively, were meant to convey: that something rather insidious is at work in modern societies, that social theory is the means through which it can be illuminated—and what this means both for our lives and for the research orientation and self-understanding of sociology as a social science."

Chapter 3 addresses social class and inequality, Chapter 4 examines race and ethnicity, and Chapter 5 covers gender and sexuality. While the readings in these chapters focus on social class, race and ethnicity, and gender and sexuality, these are not separate dimensions in the lives of individuals or in larger social structures; they are intersecting systems of oppression (Collins 2000). Individuals have intersecting identities and locations; social organizations and institutions are structured in terms of intersecting inequalities. However, there are many methodological challenges to observing and analyzing intersectionality.

The readings in these three chapters use what Betsy Lucal (1996) called a "relational model" that includes both oppression and privilege: those who benefit (directly or indirectly) as well as those who are disadvantaged by inequality. In Chapter 3, Dowd introduces the concept of social mobility and cultural loyalty to the idea that upward mobility is not only possible but certain if individuals are motivated and industrious. Bulman directs our attention to the tension between middle class perspectives on education and upward mobility, and the realities of living and going to school in poor urban areas. In the Outtake, Feltey discusses two educational films about social class, one produced in the 1950s and the other at the turn of the twenty-first century, that address key sociological concepts regarding social inequality and opportunity.

Chapter 4 covers the topic of race and ethnicity in the movies. In the Outtake, Martinez applies the sociological imagination to her experience of watching *Pocahontas* and seeing a woman of color speak for her people and the ecosystem, both threatened by European conquest and colonization. In the third reading, Basler identifies stereotypes (in film and in life) that have been used by the dominant group to exclude or marginalize Latinos/as over time. She notes that "American film representations of Latinos/as help unveil persistent and pervasive stereotypes that 'other' Latinos/as, reinforcing their position as outsiders." This process operates in "trickle-down" fashion, as Guerrero illustrates in his discussion of the film *Rosewood* in the first reading. The film ends with the beating of a lower class white woman by her husband, offering resolution (payback?) for genocide by displacing the responsibility on what Guerrero calls "yet another Hollywood out-group, disenfranchised women." Both Basler and Guerrero claim that one hope for change lies in shifting the source of the story from the dominant group, who have historically controlled both access and resources, to tell the story of the "other." However, the knowledge produced from a privileged perspective cannot encompass the stories of those at the margins who have been excluded from film writing, filmmaking, and often even acting (as in films where people of color are played by white actors in "black face"). Basler notes a gradual change in film images, attributing it to the presence of Latino/a filmmakers in the industry. Guerrero describes the need for "wave after wave of new black filmmakers" with diverse experiences and standpoints. For example, gender differences in the filmmaking of black women and black men are apparent in the focus on character and drama versus action and violence.

In the second reading, Searls Giroux and Giroux go further than opening the field of film production to "others." They argue that the fight against racism on the screen and in the streets requires the commitment of all citizens to "critically engage and eliminate the conditions" that both produce structural racism and prevent true democracy. Further, the political arena is not the only site of action, since it is the responsibility of all citizens to create alliances across perceived racial differences in the community settings where they meet (and sometimes collide).

In Chapter 5, the readings on gender and sexuality provide new frameworks for thinking about power, patriarchy, and the social construction of gender and sexuality. In the Outtake, Sutherland spotlights the Geena Davis Institute on Gender in Media, an organization that uses social science research and the power of Hollywood to draw attention to the representations of girls and women in film and the paucity of women behind the cameras and the storytelling. In the third reading, Lucal and Miller call the sex/gender/sexuality binary, in which people are defined as male (masculine) or female (feminine), into question. They point out that the result of enforced categories (homosexual, woman) is the blinding erasure of identity where people's experiences, history, interactions, and emotions are collapsed into narrowly scripted roles. Bree, in *Transamerica*, is offered as a sign of hope in that she "queers the gender binary," not by going through sex reassignment surgery but by "comfortably mixing masculinity and femininity."

Bree's story is one of personal transformation: finding her place in a binary social world. She is persistent in reaching her goal of completing the transition from male to female, and in the process discovers the power she has to create change. In the second reading, Sutherland tells us that this would be the "power-to" model of social change for women. Like Bree, Ana in *Real Women Have Curves* and Celie in *The Color Purple* become increasingly aware of their objective conditions, and ways to get free. However, unless this form of empowerment is linked to collective action ("power-with"), gender as structure remains intact and unchanged. The real challenge to patriarchy and gender inequality is represented in films like *North Country*, where the oppressed come to see their circumstances as shared—or in Marx's terms, develop class consciousness.

As Josie (Charlize Theron) explained, sexual harassment is not a personal problem, and as a social issue it can be effectively challenged only by collective action. In a similar vein,

Messner in the first reading calls for collective action based on an ideal not of power-over, where might is the means to achieving desired ends, but rather of care and compassion. He challenges the masculine hegemonic, embodied in the film roles of Schwarzenegger (as the Terminator, for example) and Stallone (as Rambo).

In Chapter 6 we turn our attention to the public and private worlds of social life, work, and family. The division between public and private has been criticized for concealing "the underlying gender structures of the society" (Acker 2005:328), obscuring, for example, the ways that women are engaged in productive economic activities in the home. The readings in this chapter address the intricate links between public and private. In the Outtake, Rebecca Erickson introduces another dimension that crosses the public and private realms: the emotional labor involved in work performance and taking care of home and family.

In the first reading, Karla Erickson applies sociological questions usually reserved for research on family life to the workplace. She uses the films *As Good as It Gets* and *Office Space* to explore the public interactions that connect us to one another at the same time that these interactions become more controlled by corporate versions of self and community. Erickson encourages us to ask how film versions of work compare to our own experiences as workers and consumers in the modern marketplace.

In the second reading Cosbey suggests that we can use films to examine how the challenges of balancing work and family are represented. Beginning with the gendered division of labor, Cosbey explores the organization of the family with a stay-at-home mother, breadwinner husband, and dependent children. Although this family form is a historical anomaly, it is standard fare in film. When roles are reversed, as in *Mr. Mom* or *Daddy Daycare*, with mothers as breadwinners and fathers keeping the house and minding the children, it is comedy, a play on the expected social arrangements. Even when traded, the roles are intact: the person who cares for the children also cleans the house and provides support to the wage-earning spouse. Cosbey explores this further with the film *The Children Are All Right*, where the parents are both women but replicate traditional roles within the family.

Films that draw attention to the juggling act required of women who work for pay outside the home (since the division of household labor is still not equitable), such as *I Don't Know How She Does It*, present women's dilemma as one of identity (between occupation and mother). As sociologist Phyllis Moen (2003) points out, "In contemporary society, family and work roles are at odds with one another" (p. 17). Focusing on married couple families, Moen and other sociologists argue that organizations in the public domain still operate on a breadwinner model of family life, with built-in expectations about full-time (40 or more hours per week) work and the priority of work success in relationship to family (with the assumed "wife" fulfilling necessary duties). Change in this case cannot be crafted through individual adaptation, although couples do accommodate their relationships and lives to manage their public and private worlds. However, larger-scale structural changes are called for to address the realities of work and family today.

Chapter 7 explores the areas of deviance, crime, and law. In sociology these are three different, but related, subfields. Deviance encompasses behaviors, attitudes, or conditions that violate social norms in some way. Crime is behavior that violates norms codified in law. Whether or not an action, attitude, or condition will be defined as deviant or criminal depends on the time, place, and social order. In the first reading, Wonser and Boyns provide an overview of the sociology of deviance and crime, explaining the primary theoretical perspectives that have been developed and used by sociologists. Using the Batman films, the authors apply these theories to the world of Gotham City and the behaviors, identities, and statuses held by its inhabitants. They point out that which side of the law one stands on is shaped by "a rich interplay of sociological forces."

In the second reading, Rafter suggests that movies about crime are a form of "popular criminology" where many people learn about crime and criminals. The academic study of these films can give insight into the ideas people have about the nature of crime. Using films about sex crimes, Rafter demonstrates that some of these ideas overlap with academic criminology (e.g., the great frequency of sexual offenses and the threat of victimization from trusted members of the community, rather than the threat of "stranger danger"). These films also raise what Rafter identifies as "ethical, philosophical and psychological" issues outside the domain of academic criminology.

In the third reading, Callanan uses a constructionist approach to explore the sociology of law through film. The three films chosen, *Music Within*, *A Civil Action*, and *Erin Brockovich* all involve individuals who are willing (eventually) to take on a battle of David-Goliath proportions, fighting against all odds for justice. In the process, they are changed into better people, and the legitimacy of the legal system is upheld. As Callanan points out, viewers enjoy seeing the underdog prevail, but the individualist focus (on the protagonists and their clients) keeps the inherent class bias of the system safely out of the public eye and mind. The Outtake for this chapter also takes up the issue of corporate crime, in this case the largest criminal antitrust case in history and the subject of the film *The Informant!* The main character in this film, while providing evidence to the FBI for prosecution of his company, is also embezzling millions of dollars. The lightheartedness of the film is revealing in terms of societal views of "serious" crime, and Maume points out that white collar offenders often escape the label of criminal because of their respectability and social status.

Chapter 8 considers different stages in the life course as represented in film. The life course approach provides a framework for studying people in the context of statuses, roles, social groups, communities, and social institutions over time. While we generally think of the life course as unidirectional, from birth through childhood, adolescence, adulthood, and old age, Orange, in her Outtake, questions whether this still applies in society today, when nonlinear life stories are becoming more normative. In this chapter the readings focus on different age-graded trajectories in the life course: childhood, becoming a parent, and old age.

In the first reading, Lugo-Lugo and Bloodsworth-Lugo look at four animated films for children (*The Road to El Dorado*, *Shark Tale*, *Dinosaur*, and *Toy Story*) as examples of influential agents of socialization. Analyzing the themes in these films, the authors conclude that the content and delivery of the stories teach and reinforce stereotyped representations of race, ethnicity, gender, and sexuality. Children learn from these films stereotypical depictions of colonialism (good Europeans save childlike indigenous people), race and ethnicity (Mrs. García in *Shark Tale* is presented as an overweight, middle-aged, single, Mexican-accented female fish—with permanent rollers in her hair—who lives in the ghetto), and sexuality (in *Dinosaur*, boys and girls receive separate lessons on attracting the "opposite" sex, with girls being told to "keep the boys guessing"). Early research on the effect of movies on children and adolescents found that movies teach children about life, including attitudes, appearance norms, and sexual intimacy (e.g., how to kiss), and that 90 percent of children remember what they see in a movie long after the movie is over (Charters 1933).

The second reading moves from childhood to a transition point in adulthood: choosing to become a parent. In this reading, Holcomb explores alternative paths to motherhood using the films *Baby Mama*, *The Switch*, *Juno*, and *Knocked Up*. Rather than following the traditional route to motherhood (courtship and marriage), the main characters in these films are unmarried and off-age (a teen in one case, women over 35 in three others) as they grapple with the choice to become mothers. While the films provide models of nonnormative paths to motherhood, the effects of social class, race, and heteronormativity are assumed and audiences are given the standard happy ending of love and family, albeit out of order in terms of timing and context in the life course.

In the third reading, King uses three films—*About Schmidt*, *Gran Torino*, and (the animated) *Up*—to explore old age as a life stage, focusing on white men who have exited long-term social statuses that provided a source of identity and meaning in their lives (marriage, employment). Now widowed and retired, the story becomes one of isolation and, in sociological terms, alienation. However, in true Hollywood fashion, the main characters are rescued through a mentoring relationship with young male characters who are themselves at a transitional point in the life course. While the resolution is unrealistic (and even fatal in one case), King points out the ways in which aging masculinity is socially constructed and the high cost paid by men for their gendered power and privilege at earlier stages in the life course.

In Chapter 9, social institutions become the focus with four readings on different institutional domains: religion, sports, medicine, and the military. Social institutions, as defined by sociologists, are "a complex of positions, roles, norms and values lodged in particular types of social structures and organising relatively stable patterns of human activity with respect to fundamental problems in producing life-sustaining resources, in reproducing individuals, and in sustaining viable societal structures within a given environment" (Turner 1997:6). Further, institutions are interrelated through social practices, processes, and structures, as can be seen in the four institutions covered in Chapter 9.

In the first reading, Monahan explores the institution of religion in terms of structure and function. Religion, like all institutions, has a hierarchical set of social relations based on statuses and roles, as well as norms and beliefs separating the sacred and the profane. An inherent tension in institutions is the impetus toward or resistance to social change. Religion has served as a source of tradition, stability, and order at the same time that it has been a vehicle for radical social change extending beyond the realm of religious practice and into politics, economics, family life, and so on.

In the next reading, Montez de Oca examines sport as a social institution by focusing on football films. Central to the stories of football told through film are the themes of race, redemption, and social mobility. Sport intersects with the economic institution both to support competition and structured inequality and to reproduce inequality through the myth that playing hard and winning can contribute to upward class mobility. Boys are made into men through football and, as Montez de Oca points out, minority boys are given the opportunity to choose a normative life over deviance and crime.

The medical institution is the topic of Pescosolido and Oberlin's article. Using two central concepts from the subfield of medical sociology, the illness career and health disparities, the authors consider both the micro and macro level processes of health, illness, and disease. Institutional settings are central to the stories of the first two films considered,

Frances and *It's Kind of a Funny Story*. The main characters in each film spend time in a mental hospital, having been labeled by others or self-labeling as mentally ill. The relationship between politics and medicine is explored in the story of Frances, who is hospitalized in response to her unorthodox beliefs and behaviors.

The role of politics in health and illness is further developed as the authors focus on public health threats (e.g., industrial contamination of local water sources) and the legal battle to protect the public from disease and death. The reading ends with a discussion of the problems of health disparities and the probability of living (healthfully) or dying based on social class and access to resources. The Outtake in this chapter also addresses issues of health and illness with the zombie movie *28 Days Later*. Hund points out that preservation of human health is central to the story, as is the practice of "othering" those who are ill or infected.

The last reading of the chapter examines war as a social institution, complete with a social hierarchy based on status and power. Those who make the decisions are far removed from the soldiers engaged in the practice of war on the ground (or in the air or at sea). Martinez uses two films about the 1991 invasion of Iraq, *Three Kings* and *Jarhead*, to address the politics of war from the vantage point of soldiers. With their carefully delineated role expectations for soldiers (obeying orders, loyalty to the group and to the mission), these films tell different stories about structure and agency in the context of war.

In Chapter 10 the readings address economic globalization in the twenty-first century in terms of its effects on workers, whether they immigrate to global cities in search of employment or look for opportunities in their home countries in the midst of economic transformation. The concept of neoliberalism is central to understanding this economic transformation, since neoliberal globalization is "a process characterized by intensified economic exchange of goods, services, capital, labor, and new technologies across national borders" (Bandelj, Shorette, and Sowers 2011). In the Outtake for this chapter, Shaheen considers the question of global politics and what happens when governments and corporations "mix together greed, oil and terrorism in order to maintain their monopoly on Arab oil." He identifies two films that break the pattern of demonizing Arabs and Muslims, *Syriana* and *Munich*, pointing out that peace is not possible when force and violence are the mechanisms used to gain economic control.

In the first reading, Gonzales focuses on the role of low-wage migrant workers in the global economy with the film *Dirty Pretty Things*. Gonzales argues that the new economies of the global market have created a new "serving class" to meet the needs of a time-strapped professional class. Immigrant workers fill this need as a flexible, low-wage source of labor. From a functionalist perspective, immigrant labor keeps "society and economy running smoothly"; conflict theorists would argue that they are exploited labor. In *Dirty Pretty Things*, the effect of complex global economic systems on the individual lives of immigrant workers is made apparent. The intersection of the social institutions of economy (labor needs) and politics (regulatory power of the law) in the lives of individuals is seen in the ways that immigrant workers (barely) survive day to day. The costs for this survival are high as the immigrants are exploited not only for their labor, but for their very being—symbolized in the body parts that become marketable products in this new world economic order.

In the second reading, Moss and Hendricks use the film *Slumdog Millionaire* to explore the intersecting social processes of globalization and neoliberalism underlying the expansion of

Western capitalism. The authors point out that Mumbai can be seen as a *character* in the film as the different parts of the city "are shown to demonstrate social extremes; depressed economic conditions or booming capitalist industry, the wealth of crime bosses in mansions or the shacks of the slums, the bright lights and modern highway infrastructure or the dusty, grimy garbage dump with a makeshift tent where Jamal, Salim, and Latika sleep." While this film is largely celebrated as a "feel-good" movie, turning a sociological eye to the global economic and political processes at play reveals the ways that transporting a market economy fails when the history and culture of the receiving state are ignored.

The topic of Chapter 11 is social change, the environment, and social movements. The three readings in this section are concerned with the sources of social change, the nature of social relations (among social actors), and the relationships among social structure, the environment, tradition, and the anticipated future (Sztompka 1994). The readings consider questions related to the quality of life in human communities and how we envision and act toward a future that is more peaceful, egalitarian, and just.

In the first reading, Podeschi begins with the most basic of survival relationships: between humans and their environments. This focus has long interested sociologists; in the early twentieth century, the Chicago School conducted research on the city with the explicit goal of studying people, taking into account relations with the material environment and processes of adaptation (Gross 2004). Podeschi brings this concern into the twenty-first century using science fiction films to explore potential future scenarios for humankind and nature. The central theme is that of resistance (to the exploitative relationship between society and nature) versus reproduction (where nature is a resource to be exploited).

In the next reading, Feltey explores film stories involving nonviolence, both as an organizing principle in social movement activism (India's campaign for home rule; the civil rights movement in the southern U.S.) and in a gemeinschaft subculture (the Amish). Pointing out that violence is the dominant model of social relations from the micro to the macro level, Feltey suggests looking for models of nonviolent social order and change. Rather than power-over, dominance, and exploitation, what would society look like if the social order were based on cooperation, nonkilling, and peaceful coexistence?

In the third reading, Langstraat uses the films *The Long Walk Home*, *Norma Rae*, and *Milk* to explore the sociology of social movements. These three films focus on historical social movements in the U.S. that transformed social relations on the basis of race (the civil rights movement of the 1950s and 1960s), class or worker status (the labor and unionization movements of the twentieth century), and sexuality and gender (the LGBT movement of the late twentieth century). This reading, along with the Outtake for this chapter, offers hope that social change is possible and is rooted in the beliefs and actions of individuals working together toward envisioned change.

In the Outtake, Farr identifies what he calls "great activist movies" that "portray the ongoing struggle between the welfare of working people and larger societal forces." He encourages us to view these movies to understand the importance of taking a stand and fighting with the most vulnerable of society's members for the right to a decent life. The readings in the last chapter are ultimately concerned with questions of power—and leave us with important questions to consider about the future: will we create a social world where domination and exploitation of people and nature are the status quo, or will we engage in "progressive self-transformation" (Sztompka 1994) of ourselves, communities, and societies? In sum, *Cinematic Sociology: Social Life in Film* provides a way to explore our social world and the lives of those who share it with us. It is our belief that sociology offers the tools to interrogate and change the conditions that produce discord in relationships— individual, communal, national, and global. It is our hope that by turning the sociological lens on the movies we watch, we will be better equipped to contribute to these changes, together "dream better futures" (Feagin 2001:17), and create a world in which happy endings are not only found in the movies.

References

Abel, R. 2004. "History Can Work for You, If You Know How to Use It." *Cinema Journal* 44:107–12.

Acker, J. 2005. "Comments on Burawoy on Public Sociology." *Critical Sociology* 31:327–31.

Amato, P. 2010. "Research on Divorce: Continuing Trends and New Developments." *Journal of Marriage and Family* 72:650–66.

Bandelj, N., K. Shorette, and E. Sowers. 2011. "Work and Neoliberal Globalization: A Polanyian Synthesis." *Sociology Compass* 5:807–23. doi: 10.1111/j.1751–9020.2011.00408.x

Brym, R. 2008. "How to Write a Sociological Movie Review." Retrieved October 8, 2011 (http://projects.chass.utoronto.ca/soc101y/brym/MoviesREV.htm).

Charters, W. W. 1933. *Motion Pictures and Youth: A Summary.* New York: Macmillan. Retrieved December 29, 2011 (http://www.archive.org/stream/motionpicturesyo00charrich/motionpictures yo00charrich_djvu.txt).

Cieply, M. and B. Barnes. 2009. "In Downturn, Americans Flock to the Movies." *The New York Times,* February 28. Retrieved March 8, 2009 (http://www.nytimes.com/2009/03/01/movies/01films .html).

Collins, P. H. 2000. *Black Feminist Thought: Knowledge, Consciousness, and the Politics of Empowerment.* 2nd ed. New York: Routledge.

Coser, L. 1963. *Sociology through Literature.* Upper Saddle River, NJ: Prentice Hall.

Denzin, N. K. 1989. "Tender Mercies: Two Interpretations." *The Sociological Quarterly* 30:37–57.

Ewick, P. and S. Silbey. 1995. "Subversive Stories and Hegemonic Tales: Toward a Sociology of Narrative." *Law & Society* 29:197–226.

Feagin, J. 2001. "Social Justice and Sociology: Agendas for the Twenty-First Century." *American Sociological Review* 66:1–20.

Geertz, C. C. 1973. *The Interpretation of Cultures: Selected Essays.* New York: Basic Books.

Giroux, H. 2002. *Breaking in to the Movies: Film and the Culture of Politics.* Malden, MA: Blackwell.

Griswold, W. 1993. "Recent Moves in the Sociology of Literature." *Annual Review of Sociology* 19:455–67.

Gross, M. 2004. "Human Geography and Ecological Sociology: The Unfolding of Human Ecology, 1890 to 1930—and Beyond." *Social Science History* 24(4):575–605.

Hearne, J. 2007. "Race and Ethnicity." In *Schirmer Encyclopedia of Film,* edited by B. K. Grant, J. Staiger, J. Hillier, and D. Desser. Farmington Hills, MI: Thompson Gale.

Library of Congress. N.d. "Historical Comprehension: Picture Palaces." Retrieved February 19, 2012 (http://www.loc.gov/teachers/classroommaterials/connections/historic-buildings/thinking2.html)

Montoya, M. 2001. "A Brief History of Chicana/o School Segregation: One Rationale for Affirmative Action." *La Raza Law Journal* 12:159–72.

Munch, P. A. 1975. "'Sense' and 'Intention' in Max Weber's Theory of Social Action." *Sociological Inquiry* 45:59–65.

Lehman, P. and W. Luhr. 2003. *Thinking about Movies: Watching, Questioning, Enjoying.* 2nd ed. Malden, MA: Blackwell.

Lucal, B. 1996. "Oppression and Privilege: Toward a Relational Conceptualization of Race." *Teaching Sociology* 24:245–55.

Mills, C. W. 1959. *The Sociological Imagination.* New York: Oxford University Press.

Moen, P. 2003. "It's about Time: Couples and Careers." New York: Cornell University Press.

O'Brien, J. 2006. *The Production of Reality.* 4th ed. Thousand Oaks, CA: Sage.

Oppenheimer, R. 1985. "Acculturation or Assimilation: Mexican Immigrants in Kansas, 1900 to World War II." *The Western Historical Quarterly* 16:429–48.

Pew Research Center. 2006. "Increasingly, Americans Prefer Going to the Movies at Home. A Social Trends Report." Retrieved December 22, 2011 (http://pewresearch.org/assets/social/pdf/Movies .pdf).

Prendergast, C. 1986. "Cinema Sociology: Cultivating the Sociological Imagination through Popular Film." *Teaching Sociology* 14(3):243–48.

Roberts, P. 1920. *The Problem of Americanization.* New York: Macmillan.

Ross, S. 1998. "Working-Class Hollywood: Silent Film and the Shaping of Class in America." Princeton, NJ: Princeton University Press.

Ryan, G. W. and H. Russell Bernard. (2003). "Techniques to Identify Themes." *Field Methods* 15:85–109.

Shiel, M. 2001. "Cinema and the City in History and Theory." Pp. 1–18 in *Cinema and the City: Film and Urban Societies in a Global Context*, edited by M. Shiel and T. Fitzmaurice. Oxford, UK: Blackwell.

Starker, S. 1989. "Evil Influences: Crusades against the Mass Media." New Brunswick, NJ: Transaction.

Sztompka, P. 1994. *The Sociology of Social Change.* Cambridge, MA: Blackwell.

Tan, J. and Y. Ko. 2004. "Using Feature Films to Teach Observation in Undergraduate Research Methods." *Teaching Sociology* 32:109–18.

Turner, J. 1997. *The Institutional Order.* New York: Longman.

Verna, P. 2010. "Movie Industry Slouches toward Digital Future." Retrieved December 22, 2011 (http://www.emarketer.tv/Article.aspx?R=1007897).

Notes

1. This section was developed largely through conversations with Michael Kimmel. His contributions have made it possible to write about "sociology and film."
2. Jess MacDonald, presentation in Introduction to Sociology class, University of North Carolina Wilmington, 2008.
3. "Merchant Ivory Productions (MIP) has a special essence and meaning in the minds of viewers all over the world. Cultural interchanges, period pieces, lush photography, and an idyllic and charming world...." Retrieved December 28, 2011 (http://www.planetbollywood.com/Features/s021303-175631.php).
4. Bulman, R. 2007. Handout presented in Teaching Sociology through Film session, American Sociological Association, New York.

CHAPTER 2

Sociological Theory

Soap Opera Woman: Hey. Could we do that again? I know we haven't met, but I don't want to be an ant. You know? I mean, it's like we go through life with our antennas bouncing off one another, continuously on ant autopilot, with nothing really human required of us. Stop. Go. Walk here. Drive there. All action basically for survival. All communication simply to keep this ant colony buzzing along in an efficient, polite manner. "Here's your change." "Paper or plastic?" "Credit or debit?" "You want ketchup with that?" I don't want a straw. I want real human moments. I want to see you. I want you to see me. I don't want to give that up. I don't want to be ant, you know?

—*Waking Life* (2001)

Carol Van Sant: I'll just die if I don't get this recipe. I'll just die if I don't get this recipe. I'll just die if I don't get this recipe.

—*The Stepford Wives* (1975)

I n Introduction to Sociology courses we learn that sociology is the *systematic* study of social life and human behavior. Auguste Comte, the "father of sociology" (there's been no agreement on the "mother," to our knowledge) asserted that sociology, like the natural sciences, *could* apply rational, scientific methods to the study of society. How is this scientific approach achieved? Sociology is systematic in that we utilize specific theories and methodologies in our exploration of social life. We would not turn to several of our friends, ask them a few questions, and call that a "finding," nor would we dive into a research project without some sense of how we will interpret the questions we ask. Theory provides us with a lens through which we can view a social problem or concern; it "holds assorted observations and facts together" (Appelrouth and Edles 2012:2).

While sociology is indeed a social *science*, sociological theories differ from theories used in other sciences. Appelrouth and Edles argue that two main distinctions set sociological theories apart. First, while theories in the natural sciences are free from value judgments, some sociological theories have at their core a set of moral assumptions or assertions. However unbiased Comte claimed sociology could be (and many sociologists adhere to this approach), others are interested in "realizing a more just or equitable order" (p. 3). Thus, when we take a Marxist, or conflict, theoretical stance, certain moral beliefs about social life are contained in that lens (in this case, that the economic and social power one group holds over another is not "good").

Second, sociological theories differ from other natural science theories in that they, like society, are always in a state of change. Unlike other "things" in the social world, humans can't be held to universal laws. Human behavior is driven by multiple factors. Thus, sociological theories are as fluid as social life, reflecting the historical time and cultural landscape in which they were crafted. Marx argued that the social world was made up of two classes, the proletariats and the bourgeoisie, and that assertion may feel dated today—completely wedged into its historical place and time. Sociologist Erik Olin Wright, however, has managed to breathe contemporary life into Marx's work through his analysis of more complex class structures and more advanced capitalist societies.

Most of you know the story of *The Stepford Wives* (1975), even if you haven't seen the movie. Women move to the seemingly perfect community of Stepford with their husbands, who are active in a mysterious men's association. Soon after moving, Joanna (Katharine Ross) notices the bizarre behavior, dress, and speech of the women in Stepford. Their clothing is overly discreet and feminine, their breasts are unusually large and firm, their sex drives are mysteriously ravenous, their homes are spotlessly clean, and, as Carol Van Sant (Nannette Newman) repeats in bizarre repetition, finding the right recipe can be an obsession. Where would one begin analysis of this film? By starting from the foundations of a particular theory, we have a lens through which to interpret not only our questions, but also the data we acquire. For instance, a feminist perceptive would direct attention to the patriarchal structure of society (especially in the mid-1970s, when this film was released). A feminist analysis might read this film as a dark comedy/horror movie that sheds light on the backlash against women's struggles for equality in the 1970s. The Stepford men want to harness and control any autonomy or sense of individual power their wives exhibit. More and more women in the 1970s, no longer fulfilled as stay-at-home mothers and silent, supportive wives, began to demand equality, and the cultural reaction to this second-wave feminist movement was not quiet and accepting. Thus, while the notion of men turning women into robots to meet their every social, domestic, and sexual need is an extreme one, the metaphor can be made clear using a feminist perspective of the film.

The readings in this chapter not only illuminate how we can use a theory to better understand a movie, but they also show us how we can better understand a theory by watching certain movies. In the first reading, Michael Kimmel begins with the rise of the market and the social contract, using the film *Burn* to illustrate what capitalism creates and what it destroys in the process. This is followed by a consideration of the works of Karl Marx and Max Weber, which has provided the foundation for much of sociological theoretical thinking to the present day. Kimmel uses the epic *1900* to illustrate a Marxist perspective on the changing relationship between the ruling and working classes in the transition from feudalism to capitalism.

Kimmel then uses *Dances with Wolves* and *Avatar* to explicate a Rousseauian critique of modernity. Rousseau argued that as societies develop and humankind is increasingly separated from nature, inequalities are inevitable as we "run headlong into chains." The more we embrace science and technology, the more wicked and morally corrupt we become. These two films, Kimmel argues, "attempt to tap into that progressive critique of modern society," though in one-dimensional ways.

To explore Weber and the meaning of the Protestant ethic and cultures of self-denial as foundational to economic and social conditions under capitalism, Kimmel uses *Babette's Feast.* He then turns to the process of rationalization which, as stated earlier, was to Weber the most important characteristic of the development of Western society and capitalism. Drawing on the movies *The Godfather* and *The Godfather: Part II,* Kimmel follows the Corleone family and the transition from traditional authority to the rationalized "iron cage" in which power is concentrated at the top, but not without the loss of meaning, connection, and family.

In the second reading, Harry Dahms uses the *Matrix* trilogy to highlight the importance of Marx and Weber. Both of these classical theorists offered a critique of modern society, specifically questioning how the transition of society from a traditional, feudal system to a modern, capitalistic one has impacted the human spirit. To Marx, the result was alienation— the separation of individuals from themselves, their work, the product, and, indeed, others. Weber asserted that as we made the transition to modernity, society became increasingly rationalized. The cost of rationalization, according to Weber, meant that as we became a more bureaucratic society, we slowly locked ourselves into an iron cage (or "a steel-hard casing," as Dahms points out) of our own making. To Soap Opera Woman in *Waking Life,* alienation and the iron cage make her feel like an ant, running on ant autopilot.

According to Dahms, ". . . *The Matrix* cuts to the heart of what *alienation* and *iron cage* . . . were meant to convey." Dahms has us think further about sociological theory by distinguishing between reflexive and reflective theories. Reflexive (or critical) theories take a position. They illuminate the first distinction Appelrouth and Edles made when contrasting sociological theories with natural sciences theories. In the case of *The Matrix,* reflexive theories ask that we not take alienation as a given. Rather, we are to explore its causes, effects, and the ways in which alienation shapes our lives. Reflective theories, on the other hand, "recreate (rather than illuminate) the feedback loop running on alienation, which in turn influences norms and values, which in turn reinforce and amplify alienation." These theories might examine societies' norms and values without considering the ways in which the condition of alienation actually informs norms and values.

Both of these readings show us how we can recognize sociological theory in the movies. In movies, sociological theory can come alive and appear as more than a collection of abstract thoughts on a page. At the same time, we can use our knowledge of sociology to help us "read" movies. Rather than decreasing our enjoyment of the movies, it can make us more thoughtful about the world in which we live.

Reference

Appelrouth, S. and L. D. Edles. 2012. *Classical and Contemporary Sociological Theory.* 2nd ed. Thousand Oaks, CA: Pine Forge Press.

READING 2.1

SITTING IN THE DARK WITH MAX:
CLASSICAL SOCIOLOGICAL THEORY THROUGH FILM

Michael Kimmel

There's an old British joke that goes something like this:

Two Oxford professors, a physicist and a sociologist, were walking across a leafy college green. "I say, old chap," said the physicist, "what exactly do you teach in that sociology course of yours?"

"Well," replied the sociologist, "this week we're discussing the persistence of the class structure in America."

"I didn't even know they *had* a class structure in America," said the physicist.

The sociologist smiled. "How do you think it persists?"

While class—identity, structure, and inequality—is a core concept in sociology, few concepts prove more elusive. Ours is a doggedly psychological culture, in which structural problems are perceived as aggregated individual problems to be solved at the level of psychological motivation and individual good deeds. Thus poverty is not a social problem requiring structural solutions but a bunch of poor people who could get out of poverty if only they worked harder.

The entertainment industry typically isn't much help in this matter. In fact, it's sort of the problem. The classic Hollywood movie, after all, proposes an individual heroic solution to virtually any problem. Under attack by aliens? Call Bruce Willis or Tom Cruise. Bad guys bent on destroying the world? Call Harrison Ford or Bruce Willis. Mean outlaws riding into town? Call Clint Eastwood (and probably Bruce Willis). Social problems, we learn, are caused by bad people; eliminate them and the problems go away, the hero gets the girl, and they ride into the sunset. (Except John Wayne; he is so mythic a hero that he often eschews romantic entanglement with his "reward" and rides off alone, the last real man in America.) We live in a culture founded not on the recognition of "the power of the social," in Durkheim's famous phrase, but rather on its denial.

But social scientists also have, for decades, drawn on cultural expression—art, music, literature, film—to illustrate the sociological. For example, in his pathbreaking look at art, *Ways of Seeing*, John Berger (1972) uses the well-known painting *Mr. and Mrs. Andrews* by Thomas Gainsborough to illustrate the transformation of class relations in Europe in the eighteenth century and to chart the rise of the bourgeoisie. First, he shows us a painting of a sixteenth-century landscape—bucolic, rustic, pastoral. Rolling meadows, a cow grazing placidly, perhaps a church in the background. It's the "before" image. By the eighteenth century, though, that landscape painting has changed: Gainsborough puts an English squire on a bench, his wife next to him, and a hunting rifle across his lap. "They are not a couple in Nature as Rousseau imagined nature," Berger writes (1972:107). "They are landowners and their proprietary attitude towards what surrounds them is visible in their stance and their expressions." Berger exposes the transformation of the bucolic countryside when it turns into "property." "You see this land behind me," the squire seems to be saying, "I own it. It's mine." (And, given the gender politics of eighteenth-century England, he's also saying that about his "trophy wife.") Our view of the countryside changes as the countryside itself changes.

There is a long tradition of using other sorts of cultural texts—literature and music, as well as art—to illustrate these classical sociological themes. Examining the patronage system in the eighteenth-century Habsburg Empire sheds light not only on what subjects Mozart could, and could not, compose about, but also the sorts of musical techniques and instruments he could us. And Ian Watt (1959) argued that the rise of the novel was coincident with the rise of capitalism. The novel is the literary form of the rising bourgeoisie: with its disconnected individual hero seeking to make his fortune in a competitive and cynical world, the novel captures that decontextualized individual's struggle against the constraints of traditional society. For example, the early novels of Richardson, Defoe, and Fielding describe how upwardly mobile individuals like Tom Jones and Barry Lyndon calculate their next move up—only, nearly inevitably, to fall back where they came from, where they morally belong.

In the nineteenth century, the novel also became a weapon of the working class, as in Dickens's *Hard Times*, which imagined the noble long-suffering workers graining under the (Grad)grinding weight of bourgeois regimentation and exploitation. Reading that work next to Engels's contemporaneous *Conditions of the Working Class in England* gives one a palpable sense of the concreteness of class relations in a way that theoretical texts alone cannot often convey.

Film can also convey the themes of classical sociological theory. In this essay, I examine four films that suggest different core themes addressed by classical theorists:

1. The rise of the market, the historical emergence of the individual, and consent of the governed as the contractual basis of the state (presociological contract theorists)

2. The centrality of class and class conflict as the dynamic motor that drives historical development (Marx)

3. The importance of culture and especially religion in shaping the social and personal experience of class dynamics (Weber)

4. The influence of ethnicity and gender on class relations, and the effects of rationalization into the iron cage (Weber)

Burn and the Rise of Capitalism

One of the precursors to classical sociological theory was seventeenth-century British empiricism and contract theory. (The other was continental romanticism, as in Rousseau or Goethe.) Hobbes and Locke reasoned that society is not a social fact, as Durkheim said, *sui generis*, but rather it is formed through individuals coming together by rational contract to protect life (Hobbes) or property (Locke).

In his major work, *Leviathan* (1659), Hobbes provides a vigorous defense of absolute monarchy. In the state of nature, Hobbes argued, everyone is free and equal, which he saw as a terrifying prospect. Each of us is interested in furthering our own interests against everyone else's. If we're all free and equal, and we all want what everyone else has, then life will be very unstable and insecure. Hobbes believed that in our natural state, life is a "war of each against all" and our lives will be "solitary, poore, nasty, brutish, and short" (as cited in Kimmel 2006:7).

Fortunately, Hobbes believed, human beings also possess reason, which enables them to create society. Since the natural state of nature is that of war, the first move in building society must be to keep us safe and secure. The sole purpose of society is to ensure that war does not doom us all. No one can be trusted to refrain from harming others when it might benefit her or him to do so. We are thus happy to give up our individual power to a higher authority, the state (or "Leviathan," a ferocious and insatiable sea monster in the biblical story of Job). As long as we all give up our individual freedom, we can be safe and secure. This is the social contract—each individual agrees to give up her or his individual power. Only when the state has all the legal and military power can individuals feel safe. Anything less makes government unstable and social life impossible.

Locke's theory of the state of nature and the social contract was similar to that of Hobbes, but he came to rather different conclusions. Like Hobbes, Locke believed human beings first existed in a state of nature. But his view was that nature is relatively harmless, not a war of each against all. Nature is abundant, but nothing can be guaranteed from generation to generation. Locke believed that we enter a social contract to secure property. In his version of the social contract, people remain free, and surrender only the right to enforce laws. Government is limited; it exists only to resolve disagreements among individuals. Locke believed that if the government goes too far and becomes the sort of omnipotent state that Hobbes advocated, the people have a right to revolt and institute a new government. Locke's *Two Treatises on Government* served as the guiding document for Thomas Jefferson as he drafted the Declaration of Independence, which announced the American Revolution in 1776.

Adam Smith also deserves mention as a founding figure of the presociological enlightenment era. *The Wealth of Nations* ([1776] 1811) is the most influential economics book ever written, but its importance for sociology is profound. Smith set forth the doctrines of liberal capitalism and the ideology of laissez-faire (French for "leave alone"), or minimal, government. (Laissez-faire meant that the government should not interfere with the marketplace.) For Smith, competition in the marketplace of each industry against others is the source of prosperity. Smith's most original idea is that society as much as the individual is a system, or machine, whose workings are not the product of human intentions but of the unconscious "invisible hand." Contrary to the views of those who consider him an advocate of unrestrained capitalist greed, in actuality Smith saw individual appetites as naturally limited: why would people want more than they could possibly use? He also saw government as the active provider of public works, and suggested, "It is not very unreasonable that the rich should contribute to the public expense, not only in proportion to their revenue, but something more than in that proportion" (Smith [1776] 1811:286).

For all British presociological contract theorists, the move from the state of nature to society is a rational move. It is a morally positive move as well, preserving individual freedom and property. Rousseau's contract theory is quite a departure. In a state of nature, he argued in *Discourse on the Origin of Inequality* (1754), people are naturally good and innocent, distinguished from other animals only by their capacity for self-improvement and for compassion or sympathy. But private property causes inequality, and with that unhappiness and immorality. "Man was born free and everywhere he is in chains," he wrote in *The Social Contract* (1762:14). Our goal, then, is to try to recover the freedom and happiness of the state of nature. Through what Rousseau called the "general will," a kind of moral ethic that lives inside each person as well as in society as a whole, people become a community.

These two themes—the British emphasis on individual liberty and the French idea that society enhances freedom—collide in the 1970 film *Burn* (Gillo Pontecorvo). Pontecorvo takes up these themes as they are emerging in the eighteenth century—that is, at the time that Locke's and Rousseau's ideas are gaining sway throughout Europe—although the obscurity of the film today is based largely on its transparency as an allegory critical of American involvement in Vietnam.

The film follows the successful journey of a professional mercenary, Sir William Walker (Marlon Brando), who is dispatched by English merchants to the Caribbean island of Queimada, a Portuguese colony. The Portuguese control the island and its lucrative sugar plantations, in a traditionally colonial way, treating indigenous laborers as slaves and extracting all profits for repatriation to Portugal. The lives of local workers are, to use Hobbes's memorable phrase, "nasty, brutish, and short."

Walker is sent to the island by British capitalists to see if he can foment a slave rebellion and drive the Portuguese from the island, thus opening it up for a more rational sugar trade—namely, theirs. And in this he is quickly successful. True to the historical record of British trade, Walker enlists the help of a charismatic slave laborer, José Dolores (Evaristo Márquez), to lead the rebellion, and the Portuguese are quickly driven out.

A decade passes. We next see Walker, now a disillusioned alcoholic, suffering from bouts of conscience about what he has created. He is again approached by the same merchants, now firmly ensconced in Parliament, because the rebellion Walker helped ignite has never really died. Now that the slaves have tasted freedom from direct colonial oppression, they are finding capitalist wage slavery less to their liking than the sugar magnates had hoped. The rebellion has continued, with José Dolores now the leader of a popular nationalist and anti-capitalist insurrection. Walker is now dispatched to quell the very insurrection he helped begin because it now threatens those trade interests with ideas of national liberation and independence. Dissolute and cynical, Walker is dispassionately ruthless in its suppression, ultimately worse than the Portuguese.

Burn both explores and critiques the theories of presociological British philosophical ideas, especially Locke's contract theory and Smith's optimistic notions that the marketplace will tend toward morality. In both theories, disaggregated individuals pursue rationally calculated self-interest, and the result is a society that is more efficient and more moral. Both proclaim freedom and autonomy as the goal, rational calculation as the means to achieve it.

Pontecorvo doesn't believe it for a moment. Both Locke and Smith believed that the acquisitive appetite would be sated by "enough," and so neither could have predicted the avaricious amassing of stupendous fortunes by these rationally calculating individuals. The relentless rational pursuit of profit is, in their minds, a mental illness—that is, rationality in all matters is, itself, irrational.

In their stead, Pontecorvo begins to outline a Rousseauian critique of capitalism that centers on the simple morality of the traditional community that has been upset, first by the direct oppression of the Portuguese and later by the capitalist economic program. Whether you are a slave or a "wage-slave" makes little difference, Pontecorvo suggests: market relations poison interpersonal relations. British contract theorists celebrated what capitalism could create; Rousseau (and Pontecorvo) also mourn what capitalism destroys in the process.

The film is also a thinly disguised allegory of American involvement in Vietnam. In this allegory, the United States seduced the Vietnamese into throwing off the French colonialists, only to return a few years after Điện Biên Phủ to quell the nationalist insurrection our corporate interests had begun. The film's allegorical argument is that American efforts to suppress the human desire for freedom ended up far more brutal than French colonialism. And the process of substituting one immoral system for another in Vietnam is suggested as being as utterly corrosive to the American soul as it was to Walker in the film. (This Rousseauian argument explains why Marlon Brando, famous for his romanticized support of Native Americans, was so keen to take the part. And perhaps it also helps explain why a film starring Brando, at the height of his popularity—two years before *The Godfather*—was never released commercially in the United States. Perhaps the distributors thought American audiences wouldn't be able to relate to the bluntness of the allegory.)

To a sociologist, contract theory is incomplete; understanding society requires more than seeing it as the aggregation of autonomous individuals pursuing their self-interests in a marketplace, unfettered by government control. *Burn* makes a convincing case for the birth of sociological theory in the decades immediately following the years the film depicts. In a sense, William Walker's dispirited disillusionment with the rational marketplace is the emotional foundation of sociology.

1900 and the Transition from Feudalism to Capitalism

Burn helps us to understand the development of the capitalist world economy at the moment of its birth—through unequal trade relations in the eighteenth century. It amply illustrates Wallerstein's notions (1974, 1975) that capitalist class relations flow from this transformation of local economies as they are incorporated into capitalist trade relations. But we also have to understand how the events of the Industrial Revolution transformed everything about social life.

For example, between 1789 and 1848, the following words were first used with the meaning they have today: *industry, factory, middle class, democracy, class, intellectual, masses, commercialism, bureaucracy, capitalism, socialism, liberal, conservative, nationality, engineer, scientist, journalism, ideology*—and, of course, *sociology* (see Hobsbawm 1962:17). Think for a moment about how different our world would be without those words! As language is a window into the ideas of the time, you can easily get a sense, as a sociologist, that regardless of whether you think this was for the better or for the worse, it is undeniable that the new world was dramatically different from the old. How can we *see* this transition? How can we understand the consequences on our social and emotional lives?

I can think of few films that better illustrate this than *1900*, Bernardo Bertolucci's epic masterpiece. Running more than five hours, the film is panoramic in its sweep, tracing the transformation of Italian society from 1900 to the postwar era. At its center is the story of two boys, both born on New Year's Day, 1900, and their lives over the course of the first six decades of the century. Alfredo Berlinghieri (Robert De Niro) is the effete grandson of a wealthy landowner (Burt Lancaster), who has only family money to shield him from the consequences of his coddled fecklessness. His "other," his mirrored class foil, is Olmo Dalco (Gerard Depardieu), the grandson of the central peasant family that works on the Berlinghieri estate.

The relationship between the two is a microcosm of the changing relationship between ruling class and working class in the transition from feudalism to capitalism. As children, they play together, competitively, but in a relationship both take to be as natural as the land itself. Olmo is stronger and more sensuous. Alfredo is reserved, barely daring to imagine himself having fun, wide eyed at his playmate's playful abandon.

With a Marxist perspective, Bertolucci examines the human costs of capitalism's incursion on rural class relations. Marx had argued that capitalism was initially a revolutionary system itself, destroying all the older, more traditional forms of social life and replacing them with what he called "the cash nexus," in which one's position depends only on wealth, property, and class. But eventually, capitalism suppresses all humanity. We are not born greedy or materialistic; we become so under capitalism. In a memorable passage from *The Communist Manifesto*, Marx describes this process:

> The bourgeoisie, wherever it has got the upper hand, has put an end to all feudal, patriarchal idyllic relations. It has pitilessly torn asunder the motley feudal ties that bound man to his "natural superiors," and has left remaining no other nexus between man and man than naked self-interest, than callous "cash payment." It has drowned the most heavenly ecstasies of religious fervor, of chivalrous enthusiasm, of philistine sentimentalism, in the icy water of egotistical calculation. (As cited in Kimmel 2006:175)

This passage describes the film's many turning points. In the first decades of the century, the conditions of the peasants become worse after several economic crises. (These economic shock waves were felt all across Europe and propelled the continent toward the First World War.) The peasants on the manor begin to agitate for better wages and working conditions, and ask the padrone to meet with them. Traditionally, he would have listened; he would have seen the peasants as "his" peasants and recognized his obligations to them, as well as theirs to him. But capitalism has hardened his heart. Now he sees only potential profits. He turns his back, and one peasant makes a symbolic sacrifice that exposes that newfound indifference: he cuts his own ear off and hands it to the padrone.

And so, on the eve of the First World War, the peasants embrace communism as the alternative to rural feudalism. Both Olmo and Alfredo go off to fight in the war: Alfredo sees no action but returns in full uniform bedecked with ribbons and bows; Olmo is, naturally, a war hero. But the estate to which they return in the 1920s is vastly different from the one they left. Machines with gas engines have replaced peasant labor and the new enterprise is run by a young man from the city, up and coming and on the make. Neither a landowner nor a peasant, he represents something new in agrarian class relations: the urban lower middle class. Neither owner nor worker, he is a middleman, a manager. Attila Mellanchini (Donald Sutherland) is a cruel sadist, and he, of course, becomes a fascist Blackshirt. (Note that he is named after the famous marauding Hun; Bertolucci is never subtle.)

One of the film's greatest achievements, in my view, is that it so accurately portrays the historical origins of Italian fascism within a displaced urban lower middle class, a wedge between aristocratic frippery and an increasingly mobilized red peasantry. And the process is set in motion by the constant need for profits as the old agrarian system becomes increasingly commercialized. This alliance between the old aristocracy and the rising fascists thrust Italy into that earlier axis of evil in the Second World War—an insertion from which the nation has yet to fully recover.

Although its vista is panoramic, the tone of the film is heavy and didactic, and its characterization often follows political ideology rather than developmental psychology. Historical accuracy often slows the narrative to a crawl. Characters act because their class as a whole acted that way; form dictates content. And yet the three characters and their class experience express in miniature the interlocking fates of landlords, peasants, and urban classes in the twentieth century. And, at the film's end, one realizes that the dynamic tension, the camaraderie and the conflict both, between these two men—and the classes they represent—remains the animating social force in contemporary Italian society.

Dancing with Avatars: Rousseauian Nostalgia for the World We Have Lost

The early sociologists celebrated the transition from feudalism to capitalism, displacement of theology by science, the birth of modern society. As progressives, they were not blind to the new problems that industrial capitalism might bring with it, but they were all convinced that the new world was far superior to the old. This argument is evident at the birth of sociology itself. Auguste Comte, who coined the term *sociology*, was determined to develop a taxonomy of societies ranging from the most primitive and backward through the gradual replacement of theological explanations with rational scientific ones. In *The Course of Positive Philosophy* (1830–1842), Comte analyzed the evolution of intellectual thought over the course of human history and argued that it developed according to the Law of Three Stages. In the theological stage, supernatural forces are assumed to control the world; in the metaphysical stage, abstract forces and "personified abstractions" are thought to be the prime movers of history; and finally in the positive stage, events are explained through observation, experimentation, and analytical comparison. Just as humankind follows a set path in its development, Comte believed, so do the sciences, each of which he saw as progressing at a different rate depending on its relative complexity, generality, and independence from other subjects. Thus, Comte averred that astronomy was the first science to evolve, followed by physics, chemistry, biology, and eventually sociology. As the final science, sociology would shed light on the earlier sciences, synthesize all previous knowledge, and reveal the principles and laws affecting the functioning of societies.

Comte invented sociology as a riposte to another major strain of French intellectual thought, that offered by Jean-Jacques Rousseau. In the mid eighteenth century, Rousseau was, himself, responding to the work of Locke and Hobbes and other liberal thinkers who had argued that the historical progress of society was uniformly good, both economically and morally.

In 1749, while trudging to the prison of Vincennes to visit his friend, Diderot, Rousseau experienced the bolt of inspiration that set him on his path. Leafing through the newspaper, he fell upon the subject of a prize essay, announced by the Academy of Dijon: "Has the advancement of civilization tended to corrupt or improve morals?" While classical liberals like Locke would have argued that morals improved, Rousseau argued that mounting corruption went hand in hand with the progress of the arts and sciences. While primitive man had been naturally good and free, the present social order made men increasingly immoral and unhappy. Human beings must strive to recover the "rights of nature" and basic equality they once enjoyed. The sciences, industry, and the arts—here Rousseau pointed to his own friends, the proponents of Enlightenment—link men by bonds of self-interest instead of benevolence and mutual respect.

Published in 1754, his prizewinning essay, *Discourse on the Origin of Inequality*, was his greatest work. In the state of nature, he argued, man is innocent, distinguished from the other animals only by capacities for self-improvement and for compassion or sympathy. In the early stages, as human beings collaborate, they develop their feelings of sympathy, but other things also ensue. Cultivation of the earth gives rise to the idea of property, which causes the inequality of people's skills to lead to inequality in their fortunes. The wealthy enslave the poor, conflict erupts, and there arise demands for a system of law to impose order. With the establishment of law, which institutionalizes and increases inequality, human beings "run headlong into chains." As the first sentence of *The Social Contract* argues, "Man was born free and everywhere he is in chains."

This nostalgic argument—that the more "progress" we make in science and technology, the deeper we sink into a kind of moral depravity—inspired the work of two Oscar-winning epic films, *Dances with Wolves* (Kevin Costner, 1990) and *Avatar* (James Cameron, 2009). Though separated by two decades in reality and hundreds of years in cinematic time, these two films carry on a Rousseauian critique of modernity by contrasting an idyllic, pastoral culture, at peace with itself and deeply connected to nature, with a technocratic, bureaucratic modernist machine, a world by what Weber would call "the iron cage" of bureaucratic rationality.

There's a long strain of such antimodernism in American culture—from Grant Wood's paintings of plain folk, to Grandma Moses's even simpler paintings of even simpler folk, to literary and cinematic nostalgia for the world we have lost. Futuristic science fiction often represents a conservative critique of modernity by illustrating how unchecked technological and scientific developments will erode or corrupt our basic morality. Sometimes, however, this antimodernist impulse can be harnessed to a critique of unfettered capitalist greed, as in *It's a Wonderful Life*, which both celebrates small-town verities and critiques unbridled material acquisition.

Avatar and *Dances with Wolves* attempt to tap into that progressive critique of modern society, linking preindustrial cultures with community, emotional connectedness, and spiritual connection to eternal cosmic truths. Simplistic and naive, they tap into a general malaise among the middle class that modern society does not deliver on its promise, which make them both compelling and cartoonish. And along the way, they reiterate some very conservative ideas about race and gender.

In *Dances with Wolves*, Lieutenant Dunbar (Kevin Costner) is a dissolute, ne'er-do-well Civil War veteran who decides on a whim to see the West "before it's gone." Disillusioned with the Union Army's bureaucratic regime, he heads west, where he encounters the Oglala Sioux nation, defensive and hunted by marauding bands of demobilized military units making the big push west leading up to Custer's Battle of the Little Bighorn. Among the

(a)

(b)

Photo 2.1   Rousseauian nostalgia in *Dances with Wolves* and *Avatar*. Similar images in both films as the protagonist searches to find himself through a connection with the "native."

Sioux he finds a people living harmoniously with the land, who kill buffalo only when needed and use every single part of the animal (contrasted with the senseless slaughter of hundreds of buffalo by white hunters who want only their hides). He finds a people with little individualism and a lot of collective spirit, who respect their elders, tradition, and the old ways. And he finds love, in the form of Stands with a Fist (Mary McDonnell), a white woman who has been raised as Sioux after her family was wiped out. (How convenient that his love interest does not require miscegenation.) Forced, ultimately, to choose between the simple values of a people who live in harmony with nature and a modernizing technological society that seeks to conquer nature, he abandons his previous identity and catches up with the Sioux people just as they begin their retreat into historical oblivion. In one of cinematic history's most dishonest lines, Dunbar narrates that it was only when he heard his name, Dances with Wolves, spoken in Oglala, that he "knew who he really was."

The Rousseauian clash of cultures is reproduced in *Avatar*, which is the largest-grossing movie in history. (Evidently, Rousseauian nostalgia strikes a popular chord.) Here, a wounded (disabled) warrior, Jake Sully (Sam Worthington), encounters a primitive people of color (the color happens to be blue), the Na'vi, who inhabit the bucolic planet Pandora, a lush, verdant forest teeming with life. He encounters them as an avatar, mentally invading their world to find out about them for the Haliburton-like extractive mining company that wants to ravage the land to gain better access to a rare mineral called "unobtanium." (No one's ever accused Cameron of being a subtle director.) Indeed, the mining company flack, Parker Selfridge—get it?—(Giovanni Ribisi), calls Pandora "the most hostile environment known to man." Sully is mentored by Neytiri (Zoë Saldana), a Na'vi princess, and learns virtues such as patience, community, and love that are so obviously missing from the world of the technocrats. In his effort to make sure that no viewer could miss the symbolism, Cameron films the science and industry scenes with gray filters, so the scenes look nearly black and white, to better contrast with the verdant Garden of Eden that is Pandora. Eventually, Jake, like Lt. Dunbar, goes native, fighting off the mechanical robotic machines deployed by the military-industrial complex to ensure that the Na'vi can live in peace and harmony forever.

In both cases, it is not coincidental that the noble savages are people of color and the robotic technocrats are white. The contrast between primitive and modern is often played out as a racial drama. Here, as in many classic American novels, the young white man—naive, young, and wounded (both Sully and Dunbar have leg injuries at the start of the film)—are guided into the harmonious world of the primitive by a Native American spirit guide. As Leslie Fiedler pointed out decades ago, this pairing of the older man of color and the young white initiate is the traditional "couple" of the American novel: on the run, away from the feminizing clutches of civilization, off to the woods or to sea, the couple is Natty Bumppo and Chingachgook, Huck and Jim, Ishmael and Queequeg, the Lone Ranger and Tonto, Kirk and Spock—and now Dunbar and Kicking Bird, Sully and Neytiri. In these cases, the people of color are red and blue, not black or brown. But the effect is the same.

Combining the love interest with the Native American spirit guide into one character may make *Avatar* appear to be more progressive in its gender politics than *Dances with Wolves*. But Neytiri also is no feminist heroine; she will retreat to be a traditional Na'vi wife, connecting the next generation to all things pure and good. Contrast her with the actual feminist character in *Avatar*, the hard-drinking, chain-smoking, cussing, masculinized scientist Grace (Sigourney Weaver) who is ultimately sacrificed (as all strong feminist characters who seek genuine autonomy in a man's world must be) so that the Na'vi can remain a simple and harmonious people at peace.

Rousseauian nostalgia is almost always socially conservative even while attempting to offer a progressive critique of technological meaninglessness and the distortion of human values attendant upon materialism. By suggesting that the Na'vi or the Oglala are really more "advanced" than the advanced soulless technological machines that are set upon destroying them, they implicitly endorse the most conservative social relationships—relationships of "natural" and often hereditary hierarchies, of oppressive gender relations that restrict women's autonomy, and of racist assumptions that racial minorities somehow have a privileged access to natural rhythms.

Babette and the Culture of Guilt

If Marx provided the broad outlines of the transition to modern class society, Weber described how it felt—what motivated social action. Capitalism requires so much self-sacrifice, so much rational calculation, it's a wonder it could succeed at all. Weber argued that capitalist economics wasn't enough; there had to be a social psychology of capitalism, a mindset that established it, sustained it, animated it. After all, there had been forms of capitalism other than the one Marx described emerging in Western Europe in the sixteenth and seventeenth centuries. Ancient Jews, ancient China, and ancient India all had forms of capitalism, yet none became the self-sustained force that European capitalism did.

Weber's essay, *The Protestant Ethic and the Sprit of Capitalism*, explores that social psychology of capitalism. Weber begins with the observation that what distinguishes European capitalism from other forms is its rationality (as Marx observed in the above quote). But in Europe, capitalism did not appear first in the most "advanced" countries—France, Spain, and Italy—which were also Catholic, but rather in Protestant Britain, the Protestant parts of Germany, and the Netherlands. Much of the book explores the way Protestantism created a different mental landscape than Catholicism, one far more conducive to self-perpetuating capitalism. In that sense, the book charts *how* this religious ethic becomes the secular driving force of an entire economic system—how the Protestant ethic *became* the spirit of capitalism—and then how it ends up eroding the very sensibility it was intended to create.

What was that spirit of capitalism? Rational calculation. To succeed, any capitalist enterprise must reinvest profits. If you are a baker, you can't eat all your bread, or eventually you will go hungry. You have to deny yourself. You need to take what you earn and plow it back into the enterprise. You can't get ahead if you take all the money you earn during the day, go out partying with it all night, and spend it all. You need to save for the future. But why would you do that? What could possibly lead someone to deny immediate pleasures for the sake of a rational enterprise? Why would people deny themselves?

One can actually feel this contrast in the film *Babette's Feast* (1988). It is, in one sense, a movie about the most sumptuous meal ever created—a movie about appetite. Directed by Gabriel Axel, based on a novel by Karen Blixen (Isak Dinesen), the film is a gastronomical companion to Weber's masterpiece.

In the early nineteenth century, two sisters live in an isolated seaside village with their father, the pastor of a small Protestant church. The community of parishioners is an ascetic sect, plainly clothed, plain speaking, and utterly abstemious and self-denying. One day, a Frenchwoman, a refugee of the Revolution and the Terror, arrives at their door, penniless, desperate, and pitiful, and begs them to take her in. She agrees to work for them as a maid, housekeeper, and cook. They pay her a paltry wage, which she saves dutifully (especially since there is nothing at all in the village to spend it on).

Babette works for them for 14 years. Her sole connection to her past is a lottery ticket that a friend renews for her every year. One day, she receives news that she has won the lottery, and a sizable fortune has come her way. Does she put it in the bank, buy stocks and shares, invest it in a restaurant? No! She begs the sisters to allow her to use all of it to prepare a dinner party to commemorate the centennial of their father's birth. It is to be a celebration of Babette's gratitude for her station, an act of epic sacrifice.

The sisters hedge: Babette is a Catholic, French, a foreigner. But they allow her to proceed. Massive amounts of food are delivered, including a live sea turtle, cases of wine, and quails. The meal's preparation takes months. Indeed, Babette prepares what may be the most delicious meal in history. The sisters, meanwhile, come to believe that Babette is a witch and the meal is a trick to see if sensuous pleasure can break their iron-willed ascetic commitment. They determine to make no mention of the food during the dinner, and convince themselves that each sumptuous bite is really the blandest-tasting gruel—the equivalent, I should think, of eating a cardboard box.

So they sit, chewing each bite with hardly a hint of pleasure. They talk of everything *except* the food. Until, that is, another guest arrives. A lieutenant at the Swedish court, whose aunt has invited him to the dinner, sits down at the table, takes one bite, and realizes that the chef is Babette (whom he also loved as a young soldier), perhaps the most famous chef in prerevolutionary aristocratic France. (She had escaped the guillotine by coming to the Danish village.) His pleasure provides the catalyst for everyone's enjoyment of the meal.[1]

I cannot recall ever seeing a starker comparison between the two cultures—aristocratic and bourgeois, Catholic and Protestant, shame and guilt. Aristocratic abundance and sensuousness is seen by this Lutheran sect not with envy but with morally indignant horror. Shame-based cultures enable sensuous pleasures because they also promise some form of forgiveness. By contrast, guilt is relentless, unstoppable, and one can simply never do enough to unlock its grip. Thus Weber focuses initially on those countries in which rational, ascetic capitalism first thrived (Protestant Europe in the sixteenth and seventeenth centuries). Only there, with guilt as its implacable taskmaster, could people deny themselves enough pleasures to reinvest profits sufficiently to enable capitalism to take off.

Having established this, Weber shifts to the place where capitalism reached its apex: the United States. First, he finds in the aphorisms of Benjamin Franklin the full secularization of the Protestant ethic. Franklin's abstemiousness ("A penny saved is a penny earned") was matched only by his industrious inventiveness. A century later, though, Weber's mood turns sour as he considers what happens to people in this relentless pursuit of profit. The book ends with a haunting image of the "iron cage" of rationality, Weber's indictment of the dehumanizing effects of the modern world's overly controlled social order. Like Marx, Weber believed that the modern capitalist order brought out the worst in us. "In the field of its highest development, in the United States, the pursuit of wealth, stripped of its religious and ethical meaning, tends to become associated with purely mundane passions, which often actually give it the character of sport," he wrote (Weber [1905] 1967:184).

The bourgeois critique of aristocratic luxury is also a critique of the culture of shame: it lets people off the hook too easily. It promises forgiveness—which enables them to return to their sinning ways. I remember my first encounter with this. "When I go to confession, and I do my penance," a Catholic friend explained to me when I was 10. "God forgives and forgets." The bourgeoisie can afford neither succor and is driven into a frenzy of self-denying accumulation. When my neighbor told me that, I immediately went home and announced my intention to convert to Catholicism. I knew that "my" God, the Jewish God, forgot nothing, and would likely hold all sins against you until the next Day of Atonement. I wanted some of that forgiveness! (Of course, this was preteen cosmology, and bears little relation to actual Catholic or Jewish teachings. It does, however, expose the contrasting cultures.)

The film, like Weber, bases the contrast between those two cultures on nationality, religion, and temperament. Sensuous aristocratic culture may need discipline; ascetic Protestantism needs to loosen up. Marx, by contrast, saw the conflict as one between cultures based distinctly on class, the bourgeoisie being propelled more by anxiety than by guilt:

> The bourgeoisie cannot exist without constantly revolutionizing the instruments of production . . . Constant revolutionizing of production, uninterrupted disturbance of all social conditions, everlasting uncertainty and agitation distinguish the bourgeois epoch from all earlier ones. All fixed, fast-frozen relations . . . are swept away, all new-formed ones become antiquated before they can ossify. All that is solid melts into air, all that is holy is profaned, and man is at last compelled to face with sober senses, his real conditions of life, and his relation with his kind. (As cited in Kimmel 2006:175)

Both Marx and Weber foresaw the disenchantment and emptiness of such a culture, though they foresaw different political trajectories. *Babette's Feast* poses the question: can the bourgeoisie ever have any fun?[1]

Capitalist Rationalization as Intergenerational Succession in *The Godfather*

All these films illustrate the transition from feudalism to capitalism and the birth of modern society. Francis Ford Coppola's masterpieces, *The Godfather* (1972) and *The Godfather: Part II* (1974), illuminate these structural themes: the birth of capitalism and the rational capitalist enterprise as well as the social psychological themes of rationalization, disillusionment, and loss of meaning—all the while intertwining them in a discussion of ethnicity, immigration, and family dynamics. The canvas could not be grander: the two films together encompass the grand sweep of the American experience.

The Godfather illustrates many of the central themes of classical theory. For example, there is ethnicity (the contrast between Kay as an aloof WASP and the Corleones' boisterous ethnicity); the experience of different groups of immigrants in the early years of the twentieth century in America (especially as they gain an economic foothold in an ethnic enclave); gender development and the masculinities (in the contrast among passionate and violent Sonny; cold, calculating Michael; and happy-go-lucky and ultimately venal Fredo). It's a meditation on the intersections of ethnicity and gender relationships, on interracial dynamics and interethnic conflict in the mid twentieth century. It's a story of ethnicity and family, and the "proper" roles for women as the men go about their legitimate and illegitimate business. (Many doors are closed in women's faces in these films; there are some things that are simply for men.) And, of course, it's a saga about law enforcement's efforts to stop organized crime in New York—a gripping crime drama in which the police are more corrupt than the criminals.

The first film begins at the 1945 wedding of the daughter of Vito Corleone (Marlon Brando), the head of a New York Mafia "family." The sequel flashes back to his childhood in Sicily and his beginnings as a young Italian immigrant on the make in turn-of-the-century New York (where he is played by Robert De Niro). As the head of the family, Vito is traditional, patriarchal, and benevolent to those in his circle, steadfastly loyal and visibly loving to his old friends and family, but ruthless and merciless to those outside. Vito has three sons: the tempestuous hothead, Sonny (James Caan), sexually predatory and emotionally volatile; Fredo (James Casale), a ne'er-do-well, slightly retarded from an infant malady; and Michael (Al Pacino), a war hero who is the youngest, the smartest, and the son Vito has shielded from the family business.

Approached by another family to provide protection for the drug trade, Vito refuses, because although he knows there are great profits to be made, he considers drugs an ugly business, not dignified enough for his family operations. (His traditional authority joins effortlessly with his racism to suggest that the drug business be left to the black community.) This refusal sets the plot in motion: an assassination attempt on Vito, Sonny's murder, and Michael's eventual ascension to the role of Godfather.

Michael is both untroubled by traditional constraints and driven by a vision of taking the family business entirely legitimate in Las Vegas gambling. He is both more rational and calculating than his father, and also more ruthless and murderous. He leaves all old loyalties at the door; he sacrifices everything for the family business. He is the ultimate expression of the rational, calculating capitalist of which Weber warned.

Perhaps the central leitmotif of the film is the contrast between traditional and rational authority as discussed by Weber. The film's core theoretical insight is expressed in just three words spoken simply (and often) by Michael Corleone: "It's just business." In that phrase, he captures the transition from family-based benevolent patriarchy to a rational business enterprise, from traditional to legal rational authority.

Vito's way is the old way, eventually supplanted as Michael takes over. Michael takes those reins reluctantly; he doesn't want power, his approach is simply rational. Michael is cold, calculating, bureaucratic, and successful; he drowns all "heavenly ecstasies in the icy water of egotistical calculation." "Just business" is "only business" to Michael; he has all of the means but knows not the ends. He avenges every betrayal with cold-blooded murder, taking out his own brother, his brother-in-law (immediately after Michael stands in as his baby's godfather), and his father's best friend Tessio. Deliberate and decisive, he doesn't peacefully coexist with the other crime families in New York, as did his father; he methodically eliminates them and consolidates power entirely at the top.

Even though it is abstract, formal, and bureaucratic—indeed, as Weber reminds us, precisely *because* it manifests those qualities—legal rational authority is far more pervasive and far more powerful than traditional authority ever could be. By embedding its power in the formal rules, power is massively enhanced, and can be far more ruthless as it is accountable to no one but itself. What Michael calls "just business" can be very unjust.

In the end, Michael has more power than his father could have ever imagined—and more than he ever would have felt he needed. And for what? The film ends with an elegiac Weberian tone. Michael, desperate to take the rational business model legitimate, has rationally calculated himself into the iron cage. He sits alone, having abandoned all he loved, recalling the happy moments of that earlier family life—a man of enormous power, but empty inside, trapped by the machine of his own making.

Classical Theory and Pleasure

In one sense, the core of classical sociology has been to chart the transition from feudalism to capitalism, the birth of modern class society, the triumph of bureaucratic rationality over traditional authority relations based on kinship or religion. The grand narrative of capitalism is usually a triumphalist celebration of progress. And indeed, capitalism unleashed creativity and innovation beyond the wildest imaginations of those luxury-infected aristocrats.

But sociology's task has always been to peek underneath that triumphalist narrative, to tear back the curtain on the fraudulent wizard, to see the human costs of capitalist rationality, the deadening of the soul that invariably accompanies the accumulation of wealth and power. Sociology's unique contribution has always been to chart that grand irony: the way that efficiency becomes dull routine; that rational organization leads to a loss of meaning.

Each of the films I have discussed charts the passing of one historical era and the birth of the new, modern, era. And one main character in each film I have discussed—Olmo, Babette, José Dolores, and even Vito Corleone—represents the road not taken in that move toward modernity: the communitarian collectivism of Olmo's communist peasantry; the sensuousness embodied in Babette's feast; José Dolores's dream of national self-determination for all colonized peoples; the warm solidarity of familial ethics in Vito Corleone's world. They remind us that what is lost in the drive for profit may be the capacity for pleasure.

References

Berger, J. 1972. *Ways of Seeing*. New York: Penguin.

Fiedler, L. 1970. *Love and Death in the American Novel*. New York: Stein and Day.

Hobsbawm, E. J. 1962. *The Age of Capital*. New York: Scribner.

Kimmel, M., ed. 2006. *Classical Sociological Theory*. New York: Oxford University Press.

Rousseau, J.-J. 1762. *The Social Contract*. Translated by G. D. H. Cole.

Smith, A. [1776] 1811. *An Inquiry into the Nature and Causes of the Wealth of Nations*, Vol. 3. Printed for S. Doig and A. Stirling, Lackington, Allen and Co., Cradock and Joy, and T. Hamilton, London, and Wilson and Son, York.

Wallerstein, I. 1974. "The Rise and Future Demise of the World Capitalist System: Concepts for Comparative Analysis." *Comparative Studies in Society and History* 16(4):387–415.

Wallerstein, I. 1975. *The Modern World System*, Vol. 1. New York: Academic Press.

Watt, I. 1959. *The Rise of the Novel*. Berkeley: University of California Press.

Weber, M. [1905] 1967. *The Protestant Ethic and the Spirit of Capitalism*. New York: Scribner.

Note

1. A gastronomical note: In the early 1990s, Jakob de Neergaard, the chef who actually created the dishes in the film, reproduced the meal at Søllerød Kro, his restaurant outside Copenhagen. Having loved the film, I ate at the restaurant. I found it disappointing, the emphasis more on splendor of presentation than the food itself. But as an apposite coda you can't beat this: the restaurant, still billed as one of Denmark's best, is now owned by Michael Jordan.

*T*he *Matrix* (1999) was one of the most financially successful movies of the late twentieth century. More important, the movie almost instantly began to exert an unusually high degree of influence on popular culture, and the term *matrix*, despite its established usage in various areas of inquiry and research, quickly came to be associated with the film. Indeed, *The Matrix* represents such an effective formula linking action sequences, stunning visuals, and an intellectually compelling storyline that subsequent films belonging to the "tech-noir" genre (a combination of film noir and science fiction; see Meehan 2008) have been measured in terms of their ability to achieve a comparable combination. Arguably, despite numerous attempts, none to date has succeeded at outdoing (or equaling) the cult status and success of *The Matrix*.

Though the *Matrix* trilogy is far from flawless and has its share of detractors, the movies can be appreciated as both an expression of and a contribution to contemporary culture if they are understood as being centered on a message about the present age as well as the condition of modern societies in the late twentieth and early twenty-first century. In fact, there is a high degree of affinity between the underlying message of the *Matrix* trilogy on the one hand and sociology and modern social theory on the other. Yet, judging from the growing list of books and articles that have been published about the trilogy during the last decade, that similarity appears to have been lost on most of the films' critics and interpreters. As this literature has focused overwhelmingly on philosophy, religion, and postmodernism, the trilogy's social-theoretical message and its relevance to us today have remained neglected (see Constable 2009; Couch 2003; Grau 2005; Horsley 2003; Irwin 2002, 2005; Kapell and Doty 2004; Lawrence 2004; Seay and Garrett 2003; Worthing 2004; Yeffeth 2003; for a partial exception, see Diocaretz and Herbrechter 2006, especially the first three chapters).

The widespread neglect of the affinity between the *Matrix* trilogy and contemporary social theory is symptomatic of a growing lack of awareness ("reflexivity") with regard to the defining features of modern societies and their impact on how we live our lives. These features and related contradictions have been the theme and subject matter of social theory for almost two centuries, although particular theorists have been concerned with them in different ways and to differing degrees. In this reading, I distinguish between two types of social theories: reflexive and reflective. *Reflexive theories* are conceived to illuminate modern society as a social system fraught with a variety of contradictions and conflicts. Some of the conflicts are between surface appearances, ideologies, social and political groups, interpretive frames, and underlying economic, political, and social forces that shape empirical reality in many different ways. By contrast, *reflective theories* are less (if at all) concerned with how the contradictions and conflicts inherent in modern societies may influence, taint, or thwart the project of analyzing those societies. The *Matrix* trilogy provides an excellent illustration of these two types of social theories.

The *Matrix* Trilogy and the Social Theory of Jean Baudrillard

A few minutes into *The Matrix*, the hollowed-out version of a well-known book by post-modernist social philosopher Jean Baudrillard, *Simulacra and Simulation* ([1981] 1994), functions as a place to hide diskettes containing illegal computer programs. Baudrillard was one of the best known postmodern philosophers and the most prominent sociologist among the postmodernists. Since the 1980s, he has come to be regarded as one of the most important social theorists of the second half of the twentieth century. As Douglas Kellner put it:

> Baudrillard, a "strong simulacrist," claims that in the media and consumer society, people are caught in the play of images, spectacles, and simulacra, which have less and less relationship to an outside, to an external "reality," to such an extent that the very concepts of the social, political, or even "reality," no longer seem to have any meaning. And the narcoticized and mesmerized . . . media-saturated consciousness is in such a state of fascination with the image and spectacle that the concept of meaning itself (which depends on stable boundaries, fixed structures, shared consensus) dissolves. In this alarming and novel postmodernist situation, the referent, the behind, and the outside, along with depth, essence, and reality, all disappear, and with their disappearance, the possibility of all potential opposition vanishes as well. As simulations proliferate, they come to refer only to themselves: a carnival of mirrors reflecting images projected from other mirrors onto the omnipresent television screen and the screen of consciousness, which in turn refers the image to its previous storehouse of images, also produced by simulatory mirrors. Caught up in the universe of simulations, the "masses" are bathed in a media massage without messages or meaning, a mass age where classes disappear, and politics is dead, as are the grand dreams of disalienation, liberation, and revolution (Kellner 2011:321–22; see also Hazelrigg 1995:25–6).

As will become apparent, this apt characterization of Baudrillard's perspective describes the condition of those who are hooked into the Matrix, and their experience of "reality." Indeed, Baudrillard's perspective applies to the experiences of those who know only the Matrix (without knowing that there is a matrix, or anything outside of it). His theory does not apply to the totality of the *Matrix* universe,[1] however, and those who inhabit Zion. It is interesting that aside from the training programs, we do not see any forms of entertainment, such as televisions, radios, magazines, or videogames, in the Zion reality—the most ubiquitous entertainment venues that many of us today use to distract ourselves, and each other, from facing the "desert of the real"—e.g., unpleasant feelings caused by the fact that there are many forms of social injustice, that life is not necessarily great even if we own a lot of commodities, and so forth. As the reflexive critical theorist Kellner put it in the above quote: to those who exist outside the Matrix, there is a "referent, [a] behind, and [an] outside, along with depth, essence, and reality . . . and . . . the possibility of . . . potential opposition." Consequently, efforts to interpret the *Matrix* trilogy as a kind of "postmodernist manifesto" are misleading, inasmuch as the actions and concerns of the people living in the "real world" of Zion are characteristically modern, oriented toward and inspired by such ideas and ideals as *freedom*, *peace*, and *solidarity*.

Marx, Weber, and Modern Society as the Realm of Alienation

Although there are several scenes in *The Matrix* in which its social-theoretical thrust is readily apparent, the "pill scene" is the most obvious. Neo must choose between discovering the real world, symbolized by a red pill, and returning to the false reality of the Matrix, represented by a blue pill. When Neo meets Morpheus for the first time, the latter asks Neo whether he is willing to find out "how far the rabbit hole goes" (an obvious allusion to *Alice in Wonderland*). Neo indicates that he is ready to find out.

Morpheus: Let me tell you why you're here. You're here because you know something. What you know you can't explain. But you feel it. You've felt it your entire life. That there's something wrong with the world. You don't know what it is but it's there, like a splinter in your mind driving you mad. It is this feeling that has brought you to me. Do you know what I'm talking about?

Neo: The Matrix?

Morpheus: Do you want to know what it is? The Matrix is everywhere. It is all around us, even now in this very room. You can see it when you look out your window or when you turn on your television. You can feel it when you go to work, when you go to church, when you pay your taxes. It is the world that has been pulled over your eyes to blind you from the truth.

Neo: What truth?

Morpheus: That you are a slave, Neo. Like everyone else you were born into bondage, born into a prison that you cannot smell or taste or touch. A prison for your mind ... Unfortunately, no one can be told what the Matrix is. You have to see it for yourself. This is your last chance. After this there is no turning back. You take the blue pill, the story ends, you wake up in your bed and believe whatever you want to believe. You take the red pill, you stay in Wonderland, and I show you how deep the rabbit hole goes ... Remember, all I'm offering is the truth, nothing more ...

In this exchange, Morpheus communicates rather eloquently the gist of the theories of Marx and Weber, two significant founders of sociology, with Marx as the critic of alienation and Weber as the critic of the "iron cage."[2] In both regards, the language appears to be carefully chosen, and the message underlying *The Matrix* cuts to the heart of what *alienation* and *iron cage*, respectively, were meant to convey: that something rather insidious is at work in modern societies, that social theory is the means through which it can be illuminated—and what this means both for our lives, and for the research orientation and self-understanding of sociology as a social science.

Marx and Alienation

Marx's critique of alienation was directed at the linkages that sustain modern society—between the capitalist mode of production, the bourgeois social structure, the role of labor in individuals' lives, and the character of social relations—all of which translate into a rather peculiar relationship between the individual and reality. Marx identified alienation as occurring on four levels: (1) "man's alienation from the product of his labor, (2) from his life-activity, (3) from his species being," the consequence being (4) "the alienation of man from man"—in short: "the alienation of man from nature and from himself."[3] In *The Matrix*, there are four modes of alienation as well: (1) the simulation of the Matrix as "reality"; (2) human beings thinking that they live "normal lives," while in fact they vegetate in transparent pods and provide the machines with energy—the human "labor power"; (3) the "real world" of Morpheus and his comrades inside a hovercraft, with is presented as a world of war and work—of industrial labor; and (4) the specific reality of the Matrix: the world "as it was at the end of the twentieth century"—our world.

Viewed from the vantage point of the critique of alienation, modern society appears as a self-sustaining feedback loop (or force-field) among several dimensions of societal reality that become more and more aggravated with every generation. Over time, to maintain the stability and functioning of the system, mechanisms were established to buffer or alleviate both the destructive consequences resulting from the spread and inescapability of alienation that might threaten the survival of the system *and* the social and technological advances that accompany the spread of capitalism, and which could engender qualitative social transformations. In fact, every new generation experiences and internalizes as normal the preceding generation's experience of alienation, as well as the corresponding technological advances, so that the specifically modern condition of alienation that accompanied industrialization has been compounded over and over again since the beginning of the nineteenth century. As a consequence, as Morpheus puts it, "no one can be told what the Matrix is" (i.e., how modern society is the realm of alienation), since that would require a way of looking at reality that is not itself a function of specific societal conditions.

Thus, we generally perceive reality in ways that are directly an extension of how modern society functions, how modern society is a self-reinforcing feedback loop propelled ahead by the continuous deepening and proliferation of alienation. We not only perceive reality through alienation; even objectivity itself is the product of layers of alienation, and could not be imagined independent of it. Therefore, to tell another person that the world is governed by alienation is an utterly meaningless statement, unless the person is able (and willing, since willful ignorance—as it appears to be on the rise today—is an insurmountable obstacle to attaining the necessary understanding) to undergo the labor of seeing for herself or himself. As a result, "you can feel" how modern society is the realm of alienation, *especially* "when you go to work, when you go to church, when you pay your taxes," as Morpheus intones. Indeed, these are areas of social existence in which the paradoxes of modern life are

Photo 2.2 Alienation in *The Matrix*. Morpheus (Laurence Fishburne) walks among those who remain unaware that their reality is not real at all.

particularly pronounced, but *knowing* about it is a different story entirely, as it requires an effort to change *one's own self* to the degree that our specific identities replicate and extend concrete social conditions.

Weber and the "Iron Cage"

With regard to Weber's "iron cage," it is important to note that until recently, the related discussion in English-speaking sociology referred back to an incorrect translation, since Weber did not use the German version of that phrase. In his 1930 translation of Weber's *The Protestant Ethic and the Spirit of Capitalism*, Talcott Parsons, the later "pope" of post–World War II theory in sociology, turned Weber's term *stahlhartes Gehäuse* into "iron cage" (Weber [1904/5] 1958:181). Yet the expression Weber used should have been translated "steel-hard casing" (Weber [1904/5] 2002a:123), or "shell as hard as steel" (Weber [1904/5] 2002b:121). A *shell* or *casing as hard as steel* is an image rather distinct from a cage made of iron, in several regards. An iron cage is preindustrial, before the invention and proliferation of the Bessemer method that facilitated the conversion of iron into steel. While iron is vulnerable to the elements, steel does not rust and lasts much longer. Furthermore, *cage* and *casing* denote different surroundings: a person that is held in a cage usually is aware of that fact, while a person contained in a casing–encased, as it were–is much less likely to know of her or his condition. This, to be sure, is exactly what Weber tried to relay—that modern society, as a function of the Protestant ethic, is a prison that is not only difficult (or, indeed, impossible) to discern, but a prison that is part of ourselves, of our constructed identities: *The prison is part of us, and we are part of the prison.* Here, too, "no one can be told what the Matrix is" (i.e., what the implications of the casing as hard as steel are for how we exist; picture Neo and all the others in their pods, hooked into both the power plant and the Matrix), since appreciating this insight and its far-reaching implications is dependent entirely on the willingness of the individual to make the effort to understand, and to recognize that her or his world operates according to forces and imperatives that are quite different from what she or he had thought.

"There Is No Spoon"

Because of the sway of alienation and the steel-hard casing in modern society, the ability of individuals to contemplate the difference between the presumed as well as the imagined forces shaping social and individual life requires no less than the effort to "bend oneself"—or, to be more precise, to "bend one's self." In a sense, it is necessary to undo the bending that results from alienation and our existence inside the casing as hard as steel; as it were, we need to "straighten out." The seemingly cryptic exchange between Neo and the "Spoon Boy" in the Oracle's (Gloria Foster) living room pertains to the necessary precondition for Neo's ability to "change the Matrix":

Spoon Boy:　　Do not try to bend the spoon. That's impossible. Instead, only try to realize the truth.

Neo:　　What truth?

Spoon Boy: There is no spoon.

Neo: There is no spoon?

Spoon Boy: Then you'll see that it is not the spoon that bends, it is only yourself.

The challenge for the rebels, when they are inside the Matrix, is to realize and act on the fact that the Matrix is a system of power that works mostly because the ability of individuals to object to it—to recognize it as a system of power—is impaired. As a result, those who are aware of the existence of the Matrix, within the Matrix, still are not able to "think" that fact while acting in the Matrix, and as a consequence are de facto submitting to the power of the simulation. Put differently, the challenge is to recognize that we are alienated, and that we have to be aware that we are alienated in order to act in ways that are not an extension and function of the system of power we inhabit—even though this awareness alone is neither "disalienating" nor empowering. *Yet related reflexivity is a necessary precondition for efforts at disalienation and self-empowerment.* Even though initially, Neo does not know of his ability to "fight" the Matrix, what distinguishes him from the other rebels is that over the course of events, with their help, he acquires the capacity to realize that even though the Matrix appears to be real, it is not—and to act on this realization. Thus, inside the Matrix, although there may appear to be a spoon or any other material object or force, these cannot be bent by will alone, but by appreciating fully that they merely are the simulations of spoons, objects, or forces, and dependent on the rebels' willingness to submit to the logic they represent.

As becomes evident very quickly, the many choices Neo is compelled to make (and which he genuinely and "honestly" must make himself), as well as the training he is put through, are designed to enable him to become aware of the simulated nature of the Matrix while inside the Matrix, to act on this knowledge, and thus to attain a certain degree of control. Put simply, in *The Matrix*, we follow Neo's training as a transformative learning process induced by the rebels, especially Morpheus, under the sage guidance of the Oracle, *to hold two thoughts at once*: that the Matrix is real and unreal at the same time. To translate this insight into the language of social theory: because of our positions in society, we inevitably suffer from alienation, but our existence as alienated beings is not an essential feature of our nature. Instead, it is the result of clearly identifiable, interlinked, and historically grounded social, political, cultural, and economic processes. Presumably, it is not accidental that an African American male—Morpheus—and an African American woman—the Oracle—know more about Neo and his abilities than he does about himself—the white middle class guy who would not consider the possibility that he is alienated, on the one side, and two characters who are amply familiar with a multiplicity of forms of alienation (including especially the history of slavery), on the other. This is the meaning of *Temet nosce*—"Know thyself"—above the Oracle's kitchen door: without the help of others who have different social backgrounds and experiences that are the result of different locations according to race, class, and gender (as social manifestations of alienation), it is not possible to know our (alienated) selves fully, or even sufficiently, and the limitations (as well as capabilities) our positions in society impose on our ability to read, relate to, and act within the world.

The Matrix as a Critique of Everyday Life

The Matrix is alienation not primarily as a subjective experience, but as *a simultaneous social process and structural condition that manifests itself at the level of subjective experience.* It is not simply a general process resulting from industrialization and the spread of the capitalist mode of production, but sociologically something much more specific, as it pertains to a particular kind of relationship to nature—individually, socially, and environmentally/globally—that emerged alongside the formation of modern society.

In the above exchange between Morpheus and Neo, references to everyday life abound, hinting at the fact that what those hooked into the Matrix experience as the normalcy of everyday life is everything but normal and everyday, since in reality they are energy suppliers in a vast power plant, each placed in an adult-size pod filled with a gelatinous liquid. Morpheus elaborates in one of the later training programs, as he and Neo walk down a city street:

Morpheus: The Matrix is a system, Neo. That system is our enemy. But when you're inside, you look around. What do you see? Businesspeople, teachers, lawyers, carpenters. The very minds of the people we are trying to save. But until we do, these people are still a part of that system, and that makes them our enemy. You have to understand, most of these people are not ready to be unplugged. And many of them are so inert, so hopelessly dependent on the system, that they will fight to protect it.

The problem of overcoming the Matrix is also the problem of how to get across to those who are hooked into it that their experience of seemingly straightforward everyday life is a more or less total state of exception. (Shutting down the Matrix, even if the rebels could do that, would not be an option, given that millions of people would wake up in the power plant in a state of utter shock and horror from which most would likely not recover.) Thus, the central theme of *The Matrix* is the all-pervasive yet increasingly invisible prevalence of *alienation* in the world today, sustained and mediated by the media, including and especially in everyday life as the stage upon which the program of alienation is being played out, with corresponding difficulties in overcoming it.[4] When Morpheus first explains the Matrix to Neo, he describes it as a computer-generated, "neural-interactive simulation . . . a dream world built to keep us under control." The Matrix was engineered to conceal the omnipresence of alienation from human beings in order to extract the human life force. Yet how exactly does alienation continue to be an issue in this purportedly modern, if not postmodern, day and age, after two centuries of purported enlightenment in what feels like every conceivable direction?

Social Theory through *The Matrix*:
The *Matrix* Trilogy as Social Theory

Classical social theory, as it developed in Europe, started out from the experience of alienation, and its development accompanied successive transpositions of alienation to higher levels of mediation shaping cultural, social, political, economic, legal, and educational processes and institutions.[5] Everyday life is the arena where these transpositions occur and play out.

Concordantly, at the heart of *The Matrix* is the notion that everyday life in modern societies is highly problematic.[6] The basic premise is that we do not "naturally" grasp the true character of social life; the Matrix is a literal illustration of the fact that we tend to "live our lives, oblivious," as Agent Smith puts it, that modern society entices us to *think* that we understand the world in which we live while also relying on and perpetuating many strategies designed to provide disincentives for individuals to attain that understanding. Thus, we remain embedded in many layers of ideology, and even if social coexistence would be possible on the basis of the ability of members of society to relate to reality in undistorted ways (which is unlikely), *modern society in general, and its current transnational incarnation in particular, add specific layers of illusion and ideation that on their own would make it virtually and practically impossible to see political, social, cultural, and economic realities realistically.*

Indeed, it would never occur to most of us that modern society could function according to patterns and principles that have less to do with our notions about life, liberty, and the pursuit of happiness than with systemic imperatives and dynamics that contradict commonly held assumptions basic to the construction of meaningful life histories. Partly, these imperatives and dynamics are tied to the tension between human beings as biological life forms that are more or less "out of control" (i.e., not fully in control of themselves, their own lives, and their relations with others, especially the Other) and the world we have created: the world of industrialization and postindustrialization, of high technology and digitalization. Yet we inhabit a social world that requires us humans to be "in control" of both our collective affairs and our own selves. Still, for the most part, *we are not in control*. Thus, the issue is less that we do not know what is real, but that we are not in a good position to discern that the real as it appears on the surface of social life may itself be problematic, and to confront accurately the reality of modern society as the primary challenge.

The problem is that inevitably we rely on the cultural, political, and social representations of how modern society maintains order and functions as the basis from which we try to explain the totality of modern society, and our place within it. Yet these representations themselves are products of that which we try to understand and explain. In this sense, the effort to conceive of what drives modern society is similar to trying to understand the plots of many science fiction stories, novels, and movies in which early assumptions about reality turn out to be wrong (Gunn 2003)—and whose appeal may be related to the sense that prevailing perceptions of modern society may be problematic.

Beyond the Mirrors: Reflective and Reflexive Social Theories

Several authors have noted that in *The Matrix*, there are an abundance of mirrors (e.g., Clover 2005; also Brannigan 2002; Motter 2003). The mirrors provides a visual representation of the reflection-reflexivity divide. Interestingly, the history of social theory can be divided into two primary types: those that *reflect* how modern society is a realm of alienation, and those that adopt a *reflexive* stance with regard to the link between modern society and alienation, and critically reflect on it.

Social theories that *reflect* how modern society is the realm of alienation treat alienation as a given that is inevitable in industrialized societies, and thus not in need of special attention. Social theories of this type result from efforts to interpret conditions in existing modern societies in terms of widely accepted norms and cherished values. Yet, to a certain degree, those norms and values are bound to be manifestations of alienated conditions, rather than the basis for illuminating alienation. Such social theories recreate (rather than illuminate) the feedback loop running on alienation, which in turn influences norms and values, which in turn reinforce and amplify alienation. Theories that either reject or downplay the notion that alienation did and continues to play a key role in modern societies reduce their ability to consider and explicate the theoretical and practical issues and concerns that should be at the heart of social theory: how both the pursuit of prosperity *and* alienation have been shaping the evolution of modern societies to the present time. To the extent that particular social-theoretical agendas deny or neglect the fact that alienation is a process that constitutes a key dimension of modern societies, those agendas are in danger of concealing rather than revealing the matrix quality of present social, political, cultural, and economic conditions. This problem is especially virulent given that there are no theories that enable us to better confront the kinds of theoretical and practical challenges that Marx's theory was designed to address. If we reject Marx's critique of alienation as a legitimate and necessary endeavor, we run the risk of theorizing today's societies in ways that undercut novel ideas, visions, and perspectives relating to the future and the possibility of transformative social action. In *The Matrix*, reflective theories correspond to the blue pill: "You take the blue pill, the story ends, you wake up in your bed and believe whatever you want to believe," as Morpheus states. In social-theoretical terminology, taking the blue pill would be synonymous with choosing to interpret social reality according to principles that are themselves manifestations of the alienated social world. Paradoxically, we are socialized to read modern society in ways that are compatible with and reflect the realm of alienation, without reflecting on the processes and structures that sustain modern society as both the cause and consequence of the proliferation and compounding of alienation, in all areas of social life and all types of social identity. The culture—and cult—of consumerist individualism would be a prime example.

By contrast, *reflexive theories* endeavor to jolt our minds out of the peculiar combination of complacency and spectacle that sustains modern societies. Theories of this type encourage us to confront cognitive dissonance and its social-structural causes. We are encouraged to struggle against alienation (if only against the *effects* of alienation, to notice its sway), to recognize the causes of alienation, and to recognize how our own identities are shaped at least in part by existing alienated conditions. The impetus of reflexive theories—especially critical social theories—is revolutionary in terms of how we *see and conceive of the world*, though not necessarily in terms of how we act in and upon the "real world." Reflexive theories, thus, correspond with the red pill—a visualization of the willingness to find out what reality really looks like.

On the one hand, modern societies are not simply what they seem to be. On the other hand, our selves at least partly are the product of modern social reality and social structure. As a consequence, understanding modern society requires that we recognize that our selves are constituted by modern social reality, to whatever degree. While as inhabitants (both pillars and cogs) of the machinery of modern society, we are supposed to assume that we have the capacity to understand the machinery (inasmuch as we think we know the social world we live in), but without making the necessary effort we may be as deluded as those hooked into the Matrix. It should be the purpose of all social theories to contribute to our ability to recognize this fact.

The *Matrix* trilogy represents three stages in relation to alienation. *The Matrix* is about the (thrilling and/or disturbing) discovery that modern society is the realm of alienation (theory). *The Matrix Reloaded* is about what to do with that discovery (how to mediate theory and praxis: "I wish I knew what I'm supposed to do" is Neo's first statement of substance in *Reloaded*). *The Matrix Revolutions*, finally, is the effort to overcome alienation (praxis). The initial largely negative audience reactions to the second and third movies may be explained by the fact that discovering alienation is far more exciting than the rather tedious question of what to do with that discovery. Inevitably, the feel of *Reloaded* and *Revolutions* is different from that of *The Matrix*, since they do not culminate in unqualified liberation, but—more realistically and consistently—in a truce between the humans and the machines.

The *Matrix* Trilogy: A Critique of Work Society?

How might social theory help illuminate the thrust of the *Matrix* trilogy? In concrete terms, *The Matrix* is about how work continues to burden the majority of human beings, even though technological developments were supposed to bring liberation from toil. Paradoxically, alongside vast increases in productivity and technological advances, especially in the industrialized world, humans do not work less and do not have greater control over their lives. In fact, work continues to become more important for individuals' sense of self-worth, especially in the United States (and to a slightly lesser extent in Western Europe). How to explain this phenomenon? Rather than being ancillary to modern societies, a specific mode of labor constitutes their core. Labor is not something that happens and is organized in society, but society exists by being organized around the labor process: there is a direct link between how the majority of people "make a living" and how society is organized. This was the message Marx worked to formulate and tried to communicate (see Postone 1993).

Despite all the changes that appear to be taking place in existing modern capitalist societies, many of which are perceived to be far reaching indeed, the paradox is that the "fundamental structural features of capitalism" (Postone 1993:386) are stable by continuously being reconstituted. The social, political, and cultural structures remain stable while, under the impression of "globalization," the economic circumstances that surround their lives are changing rapidly. As the structural features of modern capitalist societies (especially race, class, and gender) have become ever more refined, a social structure has taken hold that seems to be so firmly ingrained that the possibility of a "beyond the Matrix" has become inconceivable to most human beings alive today.

There is no point in fighting the Matrix, or fighting to overcome the Matrix (i.e., alienation), if related efforts do not involve the qualitative transformation of relations between men and women, and between whites and members of other races and ethnicities (and, by implication, considering the state of Earth in the *Matrix* trilogy, also between humans and nature). In reverse, efforts to move beyond alienation can take the form of changing the nature of social relations in such a manner that at the very least *obvious, visible, conspicuous* forms of alienation, such as racism and sexism, lose their foundation in society—or, put differently, of asking what kind of social change would be needed to undercut the regeneration of forms of alienation so obvious as racism and sexism.

From the beginning, the Wachowskis conceived of *The Matrix* as an "intellectual action movie." It is not likely that the movie will lose its status as the most successful of such efforts for some time to come, the reason being the degree to which *The Matrix* is hooked into, reflects, and is critically reflexive of the increasingly problematic state of modern societies since the late twentieth century. In the absence of profound changes in politics, culture, economics, and society, with far-reaching implications for individuals' lives and identities—beyond modern society as *work society*—a similarly (or more) effective approach to designing a Hollywood movie to communicate a story of liberation from the specific kinds of repression, power, and built-in limitations characteristic of the present time and age, is difficult to imagine.

References

Baudrillard, J. [1981] 1994. *Simulacra and Simulation*. Translated by S. F. Glaser. Ann Arbor: University of Michigan Press.

Brannigan, M. 2002. "There is No Spoon: A Buddhist Mirror." Pp. 101–10 in The Matrix *and Philosophy: Welcome to the Desert of the Real*, edited by W. Irwin. Chicago: Open Court.

Clover, J. 2004. *The Matrix*. London: British Film Institute.

Constable, C. 2009. *Adapting Philosophy: Jean Baudrillard and the* Matrix *Trilogy*. Manchester, UK: Manchester University Press.

Couch, S., ed. 2003. *Matrix Revelations. A Thinking Fan's Guide to the* Matrix *Trilogy*. Southhampton, UK: Damaris.

Dahms, H. F. 2011. *The Vitality of Critical Theory*. Bingsley, UK: Emerald.

de Certeau, M. 1984. *The Practice of Everyday Life*. Translated by S. Rendall. Berkeley: University of California Press.

Diocaretz, M. and S. Herbrechter, eds. 2006. In *Critical Studies*. Vol. 29, *The* Matrix *in Theory*. Amsterdam, NY: Rodopi.

Geyer, F. and W. R. Heinz, eds. 1992. "Alienation, Society, and the Individual: Continuity and Change in Theory and Research." New Brunswick, NJ: Transaction.

Goonewardena, K. (2011). "Henri Lefebvre." Pp. 44–64 in *The Wiley-Blackwell Companion to Major Social Theorists*, Vol. 1, *Classical Social Theorists*, edited by G. Ritzer and J. Stepnisky. Malden, MA: Wiley-Blackwell.

Grau, C., ed. 2005. *Philosophers Explore* The Matrix. Oxford: Oxford University Press.

Gunn, J. 2003. "The Reality Paradox in *The Matrix*." Pp. 59–69 in *Taking the Red Pill: Science, Philosophy and Religion in* The Matrix, edited by G. Yeffeth. Dallas, TX: Benbella.

Hazelrigg, L. 1995. "Cultures of Nature. An Essay on the Production of Nature." In *Social Science and the Challenge of Relativism*, Vol. 3. Gainesville: University of Florida Press.

Horsley, J. 2003. *Matrix Warrior: Being the One*. New York: Thomas Dunne Books/St. Martin's Press.

Irwin, W., ed. 2002. The Matrix *and Philosophy: Welcome to the Desert of the Real*. Chicago: Open Court.

Irwin, W., ed. 2005. *More* Matrix *and Philosophy: Revolutions and Reloaded Decoded*. Chicago: Open Court.

Kapell, M., and W. G. Doty, eds. 2004. *Jacking in to the* Matrix *Franchise: Cultural Reception and Interpretation*. New York: Continuum.

Kellner, D. 2011. "Jean Baudrillard." Pp. 311–38 in *The Wiley-Blackwell Companion to Major Social Theorists*. Vol. 2, *Contemporary Social Theorists*, edited by G. Ritzer and J. Stepnisky. Malden, MA: Wiley-Blackwell.

Lawrence, M. 2004. *Like a Splinter in Your Mind. The Philosophy behind the* Matrix *Trilogy*. Malden, MA: Blackwell.

Lefebvre, H. [1947] 2002a. *Critique of Everyday Life,* Vol. 1. Translated by J. Moore. London: Verso.

Lefebvre, H. [1961] 2002b. *Critique of Everyday Life.* Vol. 2, *Foundations for a Sociology of the Everyday.* Translated by J. Moore. London: Verso.

Lefebvre, H. [1981] 2005. *Critique of Everyday Life.* Vol. 3, *From Modernity to Modernism.* Translated by G. Elliott. London: Verso

Marx, K. [1844] 1983. "From the First Manuscript: 'Alienated Labor.'" Pp. 66–125 in *The Portable Karl Marx,* edited by E. Kamenka. New York: Penguin Press.

Meehan, P. 2008. *Tech-Noir: The Fusion of Science-Fiction and Film Noir.* Jefferson, NC: McFarland.

Motter, D. 2003. "Alice in Metropolis, or It's All Done with Mirrors." Pp. 139–47 in *Exploring* The Matrix*: Visions of the Cyber Present,* edited by K. Haber. New York: St. Martin's Press.

Ollman, B. 1976. *Alienation: Marx's Concept of Man in Capitalist Society.* 2nd ed. Cambridge: Cambridge University Press.

Postone, M. 1993. *Time, Labor, and Social Domination. A Reinterpretation of Marx's Critical Theory.* Cambridge: Cambridge University Press.

Roberts, J. 2006. *Philosophizing the Everyday: Revolutionary Praxis and the Fate of Cultural Theory.* London: Pluto Press.

Seay, C. and G. Garrett. 2003. *The Gospel Reloaded: Exploring Spirituality and Faith in* The Matrix. Colorado Springs: Pinon Press.

Sheringham, M. 2006. *Everyday Life. Theories and Practices from Surrealism to the Present.* New York: Oxford University Press.

Smith, D. 1987. *The Everyday World as Problematic: A Feminist Sociology.* Boston: Northeastern University Press.

Weber, M. [1904/5] 1958. *The Protestant Ethic and the Spirit of Capitalism.* Translated by T. Parsons. New York: Scribner.

Weber, M. [1904/5] 2002a. *The Protestant Ethic and the "Spirit" of Capitalism and Other Writings.* Translated by P. Baehr and G. C. Wells. New York: Penguin.

Weber, M. [1904/5] 2002b. *The Protestant Ethic and the Spirit of Capitalism.* 3rd ed. Translated by S. Kalberg. Los Angeles: Roxbury.

Worthing, M. W. 2004. The Matrix *Revealed. The Theology of the* Matrix *Trilogy.* Millswood, Australia: Pantaenus Press.

Yeffeth, G., ed. 2003. *Taking the Red Pill: Science, Philosophy and Religion in* The Matrix. Dallas, TX: Benbella.

Notes

1. Although I will refer mostly to the first part of the trilogy, *The Matrix* (1999), I will also presuppose familiarity with *The Matrix Reloaded* and *The Matrix Revolutions* (both released in 2003), as well as *The Animatrix* (2003)—the set of animated background stories—especially the two segments entitled "The Second Renaissance," which could hardly be more sociological, with references to such things as the "vanity and corruption . . . of humanity's so-called 'civil societies,'" the Holocaust-like treatment of formerly submissive intelligent working machines as the threatening Other, narrow-minded politics, and environmental destruction–and how humans "were" responsible for all of it.

2. Marx did not have a high opinion of sociology as it was emerging during his lifetime, nor did he regard himself as a sociologist. In fact, it was not until the late 1960s that Marx's works came to be viewed as founding texts for sociology.

3. Marx [1844] 1983:138, 140. Note that the German word Marx used is *mensch*, meaning "human being."

4. The writings of the French sociologist Henri Lefebvre may be the best reference point for illuminating this dilemma. See also Sheringham (2006:135–37) and Goonewardena (2011). Since alienation is the experience that precipitated the rise of sociology (see, e.g., Dahms 2011:157–248; Geyer and Heinz 1992; Ollman 1976), the related literature is vast.

5. These transpositions have amplified and transformed alienation. In the related literature they have been theorized in terms of commodity fetishism, reification, instrumental reason, and functionalist reason. See Dahms (2011:93–157).

6. The literature on everyday life in social theory and philosophy has continued to expand. (See especially Certeau 1984; Lefebvre [1947] 2002a, [1961] 2002b, [1981] 2005; Roberts 2006; Sheringham 2006; Smith 1987.)

Outtake

**Lights, Camera, Theory: Picturing Hollywood
through Multiple Sociological Lenses**

Mark Rubinfeld

It's easy enough to knock Hollywood. Sure enough, choose any one of the three major sociological perspectives—functionalism, conflict theory, or symbolic interactionism—and you can find plenty about Hollywood to criticize. From the functionalist perspective, for example, building on the premise that healthy societies depend on strong values, norms, and institutions to maintain social order and solidify social ties, Hollywood has its faults. Whether it is all those nasty depictions of sex and violence appealing to the most animalistic of human urges, or all that squishy Hollywood liberalism and relativism undermining centuries of American traditionalism and exceptionalism, or simply all those wasted hours that could've been better spent doing something more productive than mindlessly watching one stupid Hollywood movie after another, if you want to use the functionalist perspective to argue that Hollywood diminishes us, then you can make that argument.

From the conflict theory perspective as well, there is plenty to criticize about Hollywood, even if the criticisms are premised on a very different set of assumptions. Starting with the supposition that the prevailing economic system in America, capitalism, serves only to further the interests of capitalists, Hollywood is just another tool of capitalism. Created by, financed by, and owned by capitalists, it exists not as an art, not even as a form of entertainment, but as an apparatus by which, under the guise of entertainment, we are indoctrinated into the core cultural components of capitalism—individualism, materialism, consumerism, commercialism, and narcissism. To be sure, Hollywood has never been alone in promoting these "isms," but it was the first to project them back to us in images larger than life and, even today, no other American institution conveys these images so vividly or ties them so wondrously to the American Dream. From this sociological lens, Hollywood's picture couldn't be clearer. If you are fortunate enough to live in America you can have it all—all the happiness that money can buy—as long as you can afford it. And if you can't, thanks to Hollywood, you can always dream you can.

The third of the three major sociological perspectives, the symbolic interactionist perspective, provides us with yet another critical lens to peer through. Focusing on all of the ways we derive symbolic meanings from everyday interactions and occurrences, the concern here is on Hollywood's representations. What do we see when we go to the movies, and if seeing is believing, what do we come to believe from all that seeing? Do we come away with a picture that says, for example, that all happy homes are white and middle class? That all happy couples are heterosexual couples? That all happy endings end with marriage? Or do we come away, perhaps, with a somewhat different picture that can be equally problematic? That all gun-toting terrorists speak with foreign accents? That all drug-dealing thugs are people of color? That all "hypersexed" women are dimwitted sluts while all the men they sleep with are, of course, conquering studs? As distorted and incomplete as Hollywood representations may be, they still matter because for more than 100 years now, through pervasiveness and persistency, they have helped to define what is—and which of us are—normal or deviant, admirable or unworthy, significant or irrelevant.

(Continued)

(Continued)

So given all this, which of these three sociological perspectives, if any, is right? Is one of them more useful for analyzing Hollywood than the others? The answer depends, in part, on one's own theoretical inclinations. All of these sociological perspectives, after all, are simply frames of reference. They are starting points, not finishing lines, for sociological exploration. Like any social phenomenon, Hollywood isn't any one thing. Rather, it is made up of multiple, often contradictory components that can only be fully understood by seeing those components through multiple, sometimes contradictory lenses. And while the focus here has been on the negative aspects of Hollywood, any one of the three sociological perspectives could be just as easily employed to pick out more positive attributes. So if you are interested in learning more about the sociological significance of Hollywood, it's up to you to choose your sociological perspective or combination of perspectives, identify your area of analysis, develop your research design, conduct your study, and go wherever your findings take you.

CHAPTER 3

Social Class

Professor Higgins:	You mean, you'd sell your daughter . . . Have you no morals, man?
Alfred Doolittle (Eliza's father):	No, I can't afford 'em, Governor. Neither could you if you was as poor as me. Look at it my way. What am I? I ask ya, what am I? I'm one o' the undeserving poor, that's what I am. Think what that means to a man. It means he's up against middle-class morality for all the time.

—*My Fair Lady* (1964)

Paul Barringer (English teacher):	You brats think that I and Miss Barrett stand up there day after day, talking about books, and the writing of books, just for the hell of it? You think it's got nothing to do with *you*? A writer creates a book. An individual creates a life. For a writer to create a masterpiece, he's got to think beyond what he knows. For an individual to create a life, even a halfway decent one, he's gotta go beyond what he knows. Go beyond the poverty, the dope, the disease, the degeneracy . . . Stick with what you think, and that's what you're gonna be stuck with. You may as well get out . . . All of you dismissed for the rest of your crummy lives.

—*Up the Down Staircase* (1967)

In the classic film *My Fair Lady*, Professor Higgins (Rex Harrison) tests his hypothesis that behavioral indicators of social class, such as "proper" English and comportment, can be learned. To prove his point, he takes on the challenge of transforming Eliza Doolittle (Audrey Hepburn) into a lady. Eliza's father (Stanley Holloway) shows up, shocking Higgins by asking for compensation for the use of his daughter, explaining that poor people cannot afford morality, a luxury of the middle class (who use it as a standard for the lower class). Ultimately, Higgins is successful in his endeavor, and in the end Eliza speaks "perfect" English, dresses in style, and behaves like a "lady." She observes that beyond learning how to act like a member of the privileged elite, "the difference between a lady and a flower girl is not how she behaves, but how she is treated. I shall always be a common flower girl to Professor Higgins, because he always treats me like a common flower girl, and always will." Of course, Professor Higgins has fallen in love with her because of her unpolished honesty (attributed to her class position) and her status as the "outsider within" (Collins 1999).

The movie *Pretty Woman* is a modern version of this fairy tale. In this film, prostitute Vivian Ward (Julia Roberts) and wealthy businessman Edward Lewis (Richard Gere) fall in love and Vivian leaves the streets to become an upper class wife-of-a-businessman. Along the way, Vivian is transformed by a new wardrobe, a makeover, learning proper etiquette and dinner manners, and Edward's appreciation for her frank honesty and basic goodness—characteristics he has failed to find in his world of financial high rollers. Vivian's childhood fairy-story fantasy comes to life as Edward rescues her, demonstrating his commitment by overcoming his fear of heights to climb the fire escape to her low-rent apartment. In her version of the story, the princess "rescues him right back," which we know is true for Edward since he abandons his unscrupulous business practices where making money is the endgame and chooses love over alienation.

"Rags to riches" is a common movie plot for both men and women, although men usually ascend through a combination of hard work, luck, and ingenuity, while women marry upward (are rescued) to exit the lower class. Celebration of the American Dream, based on the values of individualism, success, and hard work, is a constant in American film, reflecting the cultural belief in an open class system and reinforcing the attitude that failure is possible only in the absence of effort or desire.

Understanding and explaining social inequality is central to the discipline of sociology. Social inequality refers to differential access to and distribution of resources and rewards in society based on statuses such as social class, race, sex, and age, and the intersection of these in people's lives. In this chapter, the focus is on *social class*. There is variation in how sociologists define the concept of social class, depending on the theoretical perspective and the questions asked, but the overarching concern is with systems of economic inequality and differential location within those systems.

In the first reading, James Dowd uses three films, *Maid in Manhattan*, *Lady and the Tramp*, and *Good Will Hunting*, to explore the American Dream of upward social mobility. The cultural belief that individual motivation and effort are the keys to economic success (and conversely, that economic failure is the absence of motivation and effort) in American society is widely held by white Americans and increasingly embraced by African and Hispanic Americans (Hunt 2007). This belief is reflected in and reinforced by the movies we watch as children (*Lady and the Tramp*) and adults (*Maid in Manhattan* and *Good Will Hunting*). Despite the continued popularity of this view of individual success and upward mobility in the movies, it may be waning in the general population: in a 2006 opinion poll, over half of the Americans surveyed said the American Dream is no longer attainable for the majority of their fellow citizens (Sawhill and Morton 2007). In a Pew Research Center (2008) survey, over two thirds (69 percent) of the Americans surveyed agreed that the rich just get richer while the poor just get poorer.

In the second reading, Robert Bulman explores social class and education, focusing on the experiences of poor students in urban schools in contrast to those of middle class students in private or public suburban schools. According to sociologist Adam Gamoran (2001), students from class-privileged backgrounds have more academic success in school and are able to translate their education into economic success in the marketplace. In this way, economic, cultural, and social differences combine to preserve the position of the privileged from one generation to the next. Americans think of education as the means for achieving upward mobility and public education as the mechanism for creating a level playing field. However, economic inequality, racial segregation, and inequalities created by inherited wealth result in public schools that are separate and unequal, a direct contradiction to the ideology of the American Dream (Johnson 2006). As Rouse and Barrow (2006) concluded, "rather than encouraging upward mobility, U.S. public schools tend to reinforce the transmission of low socioeconomic status from parents to children" (p. 116).

In his reading, Bulman argues that the Hollywood version of urban high schools reveals middle class values based on rationality and individual achievement. This is exemplified by the idea that poor students have choices, a point made by Louanne Johnson (Michelle Pfieffer) in *Dangerous Minds*—they just need to make the right ones to be successful. The formula for the central story in the films that Bulman analyzes is that of an urban school plagued by poverty, drugs, gangs, violence, and rejection of middle class values saved by a lone teacher or principal who single-handedly rescues the students from a life of crime and/or early death. This theme has been a mainstay of film for decades, as the opening quote from *Up the Down Staircase* illustrates. Exhorting the students to go beyond their social location to become more than where they came from, the English teacher (Patrick Bedford) reinforces the idea that change occurs at the individual, not the institutional, level. Ignoring the structural inequalities that have created the urban school, these films are a celebration of individualism, might (often expressed through violence) as right, and conformity.

Exploring social class, the readings in this section invite you to consider the ways that inequality is structured economically, socially, and politically. As sociologists, we examine social class in terms of historical trends, global politics, and ideologies. We are particularly interested in the effect of economic inequality on life chances, including educational attainment and material well-being. Going to the movies is one way to learn about the ways that opportunity, mobility, and outcomes have been woven into cultural stories of social class across the years.

References

Collins, P. H. 1999. "Reflections on the Outsider Within." *Journal of Career Development* 26(1): 85–89.

Gamoran, A. 2001. "American Schooling and Educational Inequality: A Forecast for the 21st Century." *Sociology of Education* (Extra issue):135–53.

Hunt, M. O. 2007. "African American, Hispanic, and White Beliefs about Black/White Inequality, 1977–2004." *American Sociological Review* 72(June):390–415.

Johnson, H. B. 2006. *The American Dream and the Power of Wealth: Choosing Schools and Inheriting Inequality in the Land of Opportunity.* New York: Routledge.

Pew Research Center. 2008. "Inside the Middle Class: Bad Times Hit the Good Life." Retrieved December 29, 2011 (http://pewresearch.org/pubs/793/inside-the-middle-class).

Rouse, C. E. and L. Barrow. 2006. "U.S. Elementary and Secondary Schools: Equalizing Opportunity or Replicating the Status Quo?" *The Future of Children* 16:99–123.

Sawhill, I. V., and J. E. Morten. 2007. *Economic Mobility: Is the American Dream Alive and Well?* Retrieved December 29, 2011 (http://www.economicmobility.org/assets/pdfs/EMP%20American%20Dream%20Report.pdf).

READING 3.1

UNDERSTANDING SOCIAL MOBILITY THROUGH THE MOVIES

James J. Dowd

Movies are a particularly important vehicle for the transmission of cultural norms and understandings. As audience members we view movies in a relaxed mode, not fully appreciative of the ways that film narrative is structured to be consistent with the ideals, norms, and expectations of the surrounding culture. In this way, movies may be said to support the dominant culture and to serve as a means for its reproduction over time. But one may ask why audiences would find such movies enjoyable if all they do is impart cultural directives and prescriptions for proper living. Most of us would likely grow tired of such didactic movies and would probably come to see them as propaganda, similar to the cultural artwork that was common in the Soviet Union and other autocratic societies.

The simple answer to this question is that movies do more than present two-hour civics lessons or editorials on responsible behavior. They also tell stories that, in the end, we find satisfying. The bad guys are usually punished; the romantic couple almost always find each other despite the obstacles and difficulties they encounter on the path to true love; and the way we wish the world to be is how, in the movies, it more often than not winds up being. No doubt it is this utopian aspect of movies that accounts for why we enjoy them so much. The movies provide us with the happy endings and the just solutions we cherish in our hearts, even as we understand in our heads that they are not always found in the real world (Jameson 1990). Movies, then, offer both the happy, utopian ending that we love *and* the more conservative support of the dominant culture that guides behavior in "the real world."

Cultural ideas are transmitted to audiences without our discursive awareness and contribute to the social reproduction of society.[1] Although we may conduct ourselves effectively in routine social interactions, we do so without having to explain why we are engaged in this particular line of behavior. While we know what we are doing, we may not be able to explain how it is that we came to know what is usually done in these types of situations. This is where the movies and television shows that we watch, the music that we listen to, and the novels and magazines that we read come into play. They are all vehicles that transmit cultural information from cultural producers to audiences.

A core belief in American culture is that of social mobility. Social mobility can be understood as "the movement of individuals and groups between different class positions as a result of changes in occupation, wealth, or income"(Giddens, Duneier, and Applebaum 2007:234). Changes in class position across the life of an individual are referred to as *intragenerational mobility*. Generally, individuals change class positions over the course of their lives as a result of marriage, inheritance, illness, acquisition of human capital (such as education), promotion at work, and/or becoming a business owner. The belief in the possibility of upward social mobility and the dream of upward mobility in one's own life are ideas continually reinforced both in Hollywood movies and in the wider American culture more generally. In the next section, we examine three Hollywood films in which upward social mobility is central to the plot and the outcome of the story.

The Social Mobility of Deserving Individuals

We all know that certain individuals are economically more successful than others, and we are also aware that economic success tends to favor certain social groups more so than others. Yet the reality of social inequality has only occasionally been the source of social conflict within American society. More often, we accept the existence of social classes and economic inequality, believing that in one way or another inequality is inevitable, normal, and perhaps even beneficial for society. Even if we recognize the ideological basis of the social Darwinist views of social theorists from previous eras, such as Herbert Spencer and William Graham Sumner, we may still consider social inequality to constitute an inevitable part of human existence. As long as the system remains at least somewhat fluid, with the possibility of upward mobility existing for at least some if not all of us, we generally turn our attention to other matters more within our capacity to affect. Generally, we accept the reality of social classes and social inequality as legitimate and normal, reflecting the underlying differences in ability and ambition among individuals. It is this last point that finds its way into the stories told by Hollywood movies.

Movies that in some way purport to depict society in a naturalistic, if not perfectly realistic, way will often present characters whose natural abilities or positive qualities allow them to achieve a level of success that characters in similar positions, but without the necessary abilities or qualities, are highly unlikely to experience. When we view such movies, we often find the story compelling, uplifting, and enjoyable. We want the protagonist to succeed and are pleased that the movie's conclusion will almost always allow this mobility to occur. Although we may not spend much time analyzing our reactions to the film, we know at some level that such stories are moving because they confirm our beliefs that hard work and meritorious efforts can, at least sometimes, be recognized and rewarded.

In one way or another, the films in this chapter deal with social mobility. They include the romantic comedy *Maid in Manhattan*, the animated children's film *Lady and the Tramp*, and the coming-of-age film *Good Will Hunting*.[2] In each of these films the central character, though possessing definite virtues and talents, lives a life deeply rooted within the working class. All of these films end with the central characters (although not others who associate with them) becoming socially mobile. The protagonists of these films demonstrate through their behavior, talents, and other qualities that they have earned their mobility. Using these films, we can explore cultural understandings about social mobility in American society, particularly the belief that the possibility of upward mobility is open to everyone.

Maid in Manhattan (Wayne Wang, 2002)

Maid in Manhattan is a romantic comedy about the unlikely relationship between Christopher "Chris" Marshall (Ralph Fiennes), a New York assemblyman running for a seat in the U.S. Senate, and Marisa Ventura (Jennifer Lopez), a maid in a fancy New York City hotel and a single mother of a gifted child, Ty (Tyler Posey). They meet when Chris takes a room at the hotel where Marisa works. Chris mistakes Marisa for a wealthy socialite when he sees her in an expensive dress that actually belonged to one of the hotel's rich guests. The two characters begin a romantic relationship, although Marisa's hidden identity as a maid constitutes the main plot device that moves the story along to its conclusion. When Chris discovers Marisa's deceit, he breaks off the relationship, only to realize his mistake later when Ty confronts him at a press conference about the importance of giving people second chances. Chris and Marisa are reunited and, in the final few scenes of the film, the audience learns that both of them are successfully pursuing their chosen career goals.

The main storyline, then, concerns the romance between Chris and Marisa. But the secondary storyline, without which this film would not succeed, concerns the class differences between the two characters and Marisa's efforts to move up in the world. Although Marisa works as a maid, the audience is quickly made to see that she is both capable and deserving of far more prestigious and lucrative employment. Marisa defies any stereotype that we might hold of working class single mothers. She is energetic, dependable, intelligent, and possesses a pleasant disposition and vibrant personality that draws others to her and would be difficult not to notice. But the most telling evidence that Marisa deserves a better place in the world is her son. Ty is a remarkable child, a true gem. He is a dedicated student, an obedient son, and—like his mother—a charming and sweetly genuine personality. His tastes in music run not to hip-hop or other genres popular among youth but to the poetic lyricism of early Simon & Garfunkel. Ty also knows more about Richard Nixon than most adults, who may actually have lived through his presidency, further testifying to his individuality and warrant for more education and middle class status. Such a child does not develop by accident but requires the loving guidance of a caring and dedicated parent.

To add one last element to Marisa's quest for upward mobility, the film interjects information concerning her difficult background. It is clear that Marisa could easily adopt a defeatist attitude about life, considering her low pay, her long hours, her demanding family responsibilities, and the few opportunities that exist for someone like her to move up. This "realistic" understanding of Marisa's life is given voice by her mother, another hardworking but somewhat embittered woman whose presence in the film serves as a model for the type of life Marisa could easily anticipate as her own future. When her mother learns of her daughter's relationship with the rich politician, and learns as well of the means by which her daughter began this relationship, she advises Marisa to get back to work and think seriously and realistically about rent payments and similar issues of adult life. Although Marisa recognizes that her mother is well meaning, she refuses to accept the inferior status her mother has settled for. When her mother offers to help her find employment as a private household domestic,[3] Marisa responds:

> You're right, Ma. I'm a good cleaning lady. I'll start over. But not with Mrs. Rodriguez. I'm gonna find a job as a maid in some hotel. After some time passes, I'm gonna apply for the management program. And when I get the chance to be a manager . . . And I will, Ma. I know I will. I'm going to take that chance without any fear. Without your voice in my head telling me that I can't.

Marisa's happy ending, then, demonstrates that mobility and success are possible even for a working class daughter of Hispanic immigrants. With Marisa's mobility, the American Dream of success is further embellished and reinforced in the minds of the audience. We know this is "only a story," but it is a story central to the larger cultural narrative of the American Dream. Generations of immigrants have come to this country, worked hard, and found success. Further, the gendered story of women's ability to "marry up" in social class is reinforced in this film. While cross-national research indicates that, in general, marriage improves women's chances of upward mobility (Li and Singelmann 1998), women tend to marry men in the same social class as their fathers (Kearney 2006). Marisa's story is one of victory on both fronts: she works hard, has ability and talent, and is able to attract a man from a higher social class. Her story is an instance of the proven formula that ability, merit, and attractiveness will eventually yield success.

Lady and the Tramp (Clyde Geronimi, Wilfred Jackson, and Hamilton Luske, 1955)

The classic Disney animated feature *Lady and the Tramp* tells a very different story (although one with similar elements) of a romance involving two mismatched lovers. One is a respected and protected member of the upper middle class; the other is an uncollared, disreputable, freewheeling rascal. This time it is the male who is the outcast. *Lady and the Tramp* follows Lady, a cocker spaniel who lives a cosseted, insular existence in the home of Jim Dear and Darling and who, following the birth of her owners' first child, feels somewhat ignored and unloved. Leaving the protected environs of her suburban home, she finds herself in the unfamiliar slums of the city. Lady is pursued by a pack of menacing city dogs and eventually cornered in a back alley. Coming to her rescue, however, is Tramp, who—like a true knight in shining armor, defeats the pack and triumphantly watches as they scamper away. In this act of chivalry and heroism lie the beginnings of the romance between Lady and Tramp. The movie reaches its climax when Tramp is taken away to the pound after being falsely blamed for knocking over the baby's bed, presumably attempting to injure the infant in some way. As every viewer of this film will remember, however, Tramp was actually trying to protect the baby from being bitten by a large and sinister rat.

Demonstrating their decency, perceptiveness, and sense of noblesse oblige, Jock and Trusty—two respected members of the neighborhood's canine community—jump into action to save Tramp. The attempt is successful and a happy ending ensues. Lady's human family adopts Tramp, who is awarded with the preeminent symbol of respectability: an official collar. Tramp also wins the most cherished prize of all as he and Lady become a couple. The movie concludes with a Christmas scene showing Lady and Tramp, along with Trusty and Jock, playing with Lady and Tramp's litter of four energetic puppies.

Much of the film's plot revolves around the obstacles to romance and general social acceptance posed by social class and associated understandings of status hierarchy. When placed in the context of its own era, these themes are particularly resonant. When the film was released in 1955, the McCarthy hearings were fresh on the minds of Americans. The fear of being labeled a communist prompted middle and upper middle class Americans to hew closely to conservative principles and disavow any deviation from convention and propriety. Tramp, in one sense, is the rebel who rejects the restrictions on his freedom demanded by the middle class way of life. Like Johnny Strabler, the character played by Marlon Brando in the 1953 film *The Wild One*, who when asked what he was rebelling against famously answered, "What'd ya got?"; or Sal Paradise, Jack Kerouac's alter ego from his beat novel *On the Road* ([1957] 2007), Tramp's life is not one of quiet desperation and neither does he seem a likely candidate "to go to the grave with the song still in . . . [him] (Thoreau 1995).

Tramp tells Lady to open her eyes to what a dog's life can really be. When looking down at the suburbs with Lady, Tramp points out that the middle class, picket fence livelihood is "the world with a leash." This statement might be seen as a critique of the American Dream and of the contentedness of America during the Eisenhower era. However, echoing the sentiments of conservative middle class America, Jock the Scottie warns Tramp that "we have no need for mongrels and their radical ideas." Not surprisingly, the voices of both Jock and Trusty sound like old men, while Tramp speaks with a youthful exuberance consistent with the age of those who later brought the so-called youth counterculture into public notice.

In the end, however, the ideological theme of the American Dream and the status quo is upheld rather than changed, or even slightly altered, by Tramp. Despite all of Tramp's philosophies against "life on a leash," he ends up living with a middle class human family and even becomes the typical middle class husband and father. Only after he has acquired his collar and license, the badge of a dog's respectability, is he totally accepted by Jock and Trusty. His collar and license parallel the suburban home and nice car that mark one's status as middle class in today's America. Tramp's contentedness with family and friends around the Christmas tree at the end of the movie suggests that even active members of the counterculture, if fortune smiles upon them, can become upwardly mobile and, with age and maturity, even accept middle class values. The outspoken, streetwise Tramp has little to say in the film's final scene as he merely observes his puppies at play.

Certainly this ending could be viewed from a utopian standpoint if one focuses on the romance between Lady and Tramp. However, this would be a mistake if it caused one to overlook the film's continual references to the ideal of American middle class family life. Although Lady and Tramp presumably live "happily ever after," one wonders whether Tramp has settled in his own mind whether his incorporation into the home of Jim Dear and Darling, however comfortable his new existence might be, is worth the loss of his freedom. The film seems to couch the story in terms of what in the 1950s might have been understood as the traditional tale of the rambunctious male who settles down following a youthful period of sowing wild oats. Yet this traditional view of gender roles is not the only lens through which the story of Tramp can be analyzed. There is also the mobility lens.

By viewing the movie as a children's story filled with images of social class and ideas about the possibility of moving among the various classes, we can see Tramp as a character who lends credence to our culture's cherished myths of upward mobility. Tramp—like Marisa Ventura and many other characters from well-known Hollywood films (Vivian Ward, the beautiful prostitute in *Pretty Woman*, is another)—may love his freedom, but he also has the mettle and true grit of a successful entrepreneur, the verbal dexterity of a high-priced trial attorney, and the heart and spirit of an officer and gentleman. That it is Tramp (and not Boris, Pedro, or one of the other dogs that Lady meets during her stay at the pound) who eventually moves up in the world and wins his own collar is hardly surprising, since it is Tramp whom the film shows to be truly meritorious. His place in the bosom of Lady's human family is not an anomaly or a happenstance but, rather, a rectification of an earlier misplacement. Tramp demonstrated his value to society and, in return, society welcomed Tramp to its upper echelons. Mobility is possible but requires a demonstration of merit, talent, and virtue.

Good Will Hunting (Gus Van Sant, 1997)

Good Will Hunting, written by its two costars, Ben Affleck and Matt Damon, was a very popular coming-of-age drama set in the working class areas of South Boston. At the center of the story is Will Hunting (Damon), a troubled but brilliant youth blessed with singular intelligence and a love of learning who works as a janitor at one of America's most prestigious engineering schools, MIT. Will hangs out with a regular group of guys, foremost among them Chuckie (Affleck), a construction worker, nonpareil raconteur, and contented regular at the L Street Bar & Grille in Southie. The film sets out, then, with this puzzle: why does someone so brilliant content himself with a dead-end job and a social life spent with a group of childhood friends who, however loyal and funny, show no apparent signs of sharing any of Will's intellectual interests, let alone his mathematical brilliance? As the story unfolds, Will's internal rage and self-loathing continually get him into trouble until a judge finally determines that this bright but difficult lad needs to see a psychiatrist.

This film deftly develops four entangled storylines: (1) Will's mathematical genius, which brings him to the attention of an MIT professor Gerald Lambeau (Stellan Skarsgård); (2) Will's relationship with Sean Maguire (Robin Williams), his widowed psychiatrist, who years ago was a classmate of Professor Lambeau; (3) Will's budding romantic relationship with Skylar (Minnie Driver), a Harvard student he meets one evening in a bar near the college; and (4) the relationship between Will and his pals, primarily Chuckie. The fourth thread in this tangle is of particular interest here, since it is the relationship between Will and Chuckie that most clearly reflects the movie's point of view concerning intragenerational social mobility.

It is important to note that *Good Will Hunting* gets much right about social class. Will, Chuckie, and the lads drawn into their orbit are basically decent human beings. They are witty, verbally agile, and enjoy a good laugh, albeit often at the expense of one or another of them, usually Morgan. They probably drink too much, however, and have little if any ambition other than to meet some girls, go to a ballgame, or just hang out. Their futures are not difficult to imagine. As they grow older, they will almost certainly continue a life of generalized and low-paying physically demanding labor, looking forward to little other than the possibility of early retirement so that their aching bodies can rest. We know little if anything about their relationships with women, other than that none of them is currently in what might be termed a steady relationship. They entered adulthood as working class youth and will likely eventually exit this vale of tears as working class older men. Their odds of intragenerational upward mobility are quite long.

In this context, Will emerges as the one who is different (as in night from day). Although he shares in the jokes and verbal banter with his friends, he seems more comfortable off to the side, so to speak, rather than enjoying—as Chuckie does—being the center of attention. Will is also the only one in his crew whose abilities would almost certainly secure him a steady place among the upper middle class, home to those Max Weber (1968) described as the "propertyless intelligentsia." He is also the one among the lads who demonstrates an interest in developing a romantic friendship with a woman. As it turns out, it is Skylar's move to California that finally spurs Will to leave the comfortable but hopeless surrounds of South Boston to take a chance on love. But what is this film saying about social mobility?

Good Will Hunting's theory of social mobility can be discerned through a juxtaposition of the lives of Chuckie and Will. Chuckie, as the sun around which his friends predictably move, is clearly a young man with charisma, ability, and intelligence. Although we in the audience can only know about Chuckie what the film allows us to know, there is a quality about him that suggests the possibility of upper mobility. Yet the trajectory of the story clearly indicates that Chuckie has resigned himself to a peripheral existence solidly entrenched among the working class friends he knows and trusts. Out of this environment—as when the lads visit the Bow & Arrow, a bar in the Harvard neighborhood frequented mostly by the gifted and affluent students who attend schools like MIT and Harvard—Chuckie's working class habitus is clearly a liability. Will, in contrast, possesses the cultural capital that allows him to navigate the social scene at the Bow & Arrow just as easily as he does at the L Street Bar & Grill back home. Will comes to Chuckie's rescue as he deflates the pretensions of the Harvard graduate student attempting to humiliate Chuckie in order to impress Skylar and her girlfriend. As indicated in the following dialogue between Chuckie and Will, Chuckie is not blind to the differences between him and his closest friend, Will. At the same time, Will feels great ambivalence about leaving his social class and community of origin. Research on working class individuals who experience upward mobility reveals that they often feel they are letting down their own group by selling out and becoming part of the dominant, privileged class (Granfield 1991).

Chuckie: Are they hookin' you up with a job?

Will: Yeah, sit in a room and do long division for the next fifty years.

Chuckie: Yah, but it's better than this shit. At least you'd make some nice bank.

Will: Yeah, be a fuckin' lab rat.

Chuckie: It's a way outta here.

Will: What do I want a way outta here for? I want to live here the rest of my life. I want to be your next door neighbor. I want to take our kids to little league together up Foley Field.

Chuckie: Look, you're my best friend, so don't take this the wrong way, but in twenty years, if you're livin' next door to me, comin' over watchin' the fuckin' Patriots games and still workin' construction, I'll fuckin' kill you. And that's not a threat, that's a fact. I'll fuckin' kill you.

Will: Chuckie, what are you talkin' . . .

Chuckie: Listen, you got somethin' that none of us have.

Will: Why is it always this? I owe it to myself? What if I don't want to?

Chuckie: Fuck you. You owe it to me. Tomorrow I'm gonna wake up and I'll be fifty and I'll still be doin' this. And that's all right 'cause I'm gonna make a run at it. But you, you're sittin' on a winning lottery ticket and you're too much of a pussy to cash it in. And that's bullshit 'cause I'd do anything to have what you got! And so would any of these guys. It'd be a fuckin' insult to us if you're still here in twenty years.

Will: You don't know that.

Chuckie: Let me tell you what I do know. Every day I come by to pick you up, and we go out drinkin' or whatever and we have a few laughs. But you know what the best part of my day is? The ten seconds before I knock on the door 'cause I let myself think I might get there, and you'd be gone. I'd knock on the door and you wouldn't be there. You just left. . . . Now, I don't know much. But I know that.

Finally, if additional proof was needed, Will's ability to solve the math problems Professor Lambeau posted on a hallway bulletin board demonstrates that Will Hunting was meant for better things than pushing a broom with the rest of the night cleanup crew at MIT. The fact that, once his talent becomes known to Lambeau and others, offers of employment from private corporations and secret government agencies come rushing in seems inevitable, right, and satisfying, thus attesting both to our human longing for distributive justice and happy endings *and* to our collective belief in the flexibility and porousness of the American class structure.

Like Tramp and Marisa Ventura, Will Hunting is granted the opportunity to move up in the class structure. The main characters in all three films, but not their friends and acquaintances, create the opportunity for upward mobility through their talents, merit, and good character traits. They succeed because they deserve to. Implicit in this understanding of social mobility is the belief that those who do not move up are those who lack the requisite talent and skill.

Conclusion

Pierre Bourdieu (1984), sociologist and leading French intellectual, once was asked how sociologists explain the constant flux experienced by individuals in the postmodern world. In his answer, Bourdieu acknowledged the reality of change as experienced by the individual but pointed out that we often overlook the extent to which social life remains much the same, reproducing itself from generation to generation. Inequality persists in part because we are socialized to different ways of thinking and perceiving that are connected to our class position. We grow up so immersed in a particular habitus that provides us with ways to understand our immediate social worlds that it eventually become a sort of habit. We develop a "feel for the game," so to speak, that pushes into the background of human consciousness all of the information and behaviors necessary for us to negotiate a particular piece of social interaction.

Culture operates in ways we can consciously consider and discuss but also in ways of which we are far less cognizant. When we have to offer an account of our actions, we consciously understand which excuses might prove acceptable, given the particular circumstances we find ourselves in. In such situations, we use cultural ideas as we would a particular tool. We select the cultural notion as we would a screwdriver: certain jobs call for a Phillips head while others require an Allen wrench. Whichever idea we insert into the conversation to justify our actions, the point is that our motives are discursively available to us. They are not hidden. In some cases, however, we are far less aware of why we believe a certain claim to be true, or how we are to explain why certain social realities exist. Ideas about the social world become part of our worldview without our necessarily being aware of the source of the particular idea or that we even hold the idea at all. Beliefs about social mobility, I would argue, are like this.

We may never consciously give the social class structure of our society much thought, but this is not to say that we do not have particular beliefs about the class structure, and the reasons why some people are successful while others are not. In American society, it is commonly believed that individual success (or failure) is an accomplishment for which the individual is responsible. Indeed, some of our most cherished cultural beliefs have to do with individuals who struggle against the conventions of the day and, despite obstacles of all kinds, persevere and succeed. Many are satisfied to achieve only a modicum of success, not willing to exert themselves to the extent necessary to reach the higher echelons. Others are simply incapable of a strong performance in a demanding situation because they lack the skills, talents, or aptitude required.

No one could argue persuasively that individual talent plays only a minor role in success; the more widely held view is that individual characteristics are the single most important explanation of why individuals succeed or fail. The class structure is the eventual outcome, it is believed, of countless instances in which individuals of varying levels of ability encounter situations requiring certain levels of skill. My intent in this chapter is to demonstrate how our beliefs about the class structure and social mobility more generally (1) serve to reinforce existing levels of social inequality as inevitable and normal and (2) are replicated and supported through the countless popular films we have enjoyed from early childhood well into adulthood.

Hollywood movies are often considered by theatergoers to be vehicles for entertainment, opportunities for mindless enjoyment and the pleasure of viewing our favorite actors engaged in romantic, heroic, or otherwise interesting behaviors. Film producers also like to tout the educational aspects of film, pointing particularly to ways in which movies will increase our understanding of particular historical events or the lives of people in other places. Films do this, but the educational function of film is not restricted to such manifest lessons. Films also serve as vehicles or arenas for cultural learning, much of which is the learning of the basic, presumably commonsensical ideas that are part of the dominant culture.

References

Bourdieu, P. 1984. *Distinctions: A Social Critique of the Judgment of Taste.* Cambridge, MA: Harvard University Press.

Giddens, A. 1979. *Central Problems in Social Theory: Action, Structure, and Contradiction in Social Analysis.* Berkeley, CA: U. of California Press.

Giddens, A., M. Duneier, and S. Applebaum. 2007. *Introduction to Sociology.* 6th ed. New York: W. W. Norton.

Granfield, R. 1991. "Making It by Faking It: Working Class Students in an Elite Academic Environment." *Journal of Contemporary Ethnography* 20(3), 331–51.

Hondagneu-Sotelo, P. 2007. *Doméstica: Immigrant Workers Cleaning and Caring in the Shadows of Affluence.* Berkeley: University of California Press.

Jameson, F. 1990. "Reification and Utopia in Mass Culture." Pp. 9–34 in *Signatures of the Visible.* New York: Routledge.

Kearney, M. S. 2006. "Intergenerational Mobility for Women and Minorities in the United States." *The Future of Children* 16(2):37–53.

Kerouac, J. [1957] 2007. *On the Road.* New York: Viking Adult.

Li , J. H. and J. Singlemann. 1998. "Gender Differences in Class Mobility: A Comparative Study of the United States, Sweden, and West Germany." *Acta Sociologica* 41(4):315–33.

Thoreau, H. D. [1854] 1995. *Walden.* New York: Houghton Mifflin.

Weber, M. (1968). *Economy and Society: An Outline of Interpretive Sociology.* New York: Bedminster Press.

Notes

1. For Anthony Giddens (1979), social actors possess three types of consciousness: discursive consciousness, referring to those motivations we are able to analyze, articulate, and put into words; practical consciousness, which lies behind our capacity to perform the routinized or habituated practices of everyday life and which we generally do not dwell on and which, therefore, are not available to the actor's discursive comprehension; and, thirdly, the unconscious.

2. It is fair to say that the three films discussed in this chapter have all been widely viewed by American audiences. They have also all been quite profitable. *Good Will Hunting* cost approximately $10 million to produce. During its first weekend of wide release in early 1998, it recouped the $10 million and then some. By mid-1998, this film had grossed over $138 million in the United States alone and turned out to be one of the top-grossing films released in 1997. *Maid in Manhattan*, which didn't do quite so well, still clearly turned a profit for its investors. The movie cost an estimated $55 million to make, but a few months after its initial release in late 2002, it had taken in almost $100 million in gross receipts in the United States alone. And the children's animated film *Lady and the Tramp*, which cost in the neighborhood of $4 million to make in 1955 (hand animation being an extraordinarily difficult and time-consuming process and, therefore, a very expensive one), also turned a tidy profit for the Disney company. This film grossed almost $100 million by 1987 and almost half that amount in VHS and DVD rentals.

3. In urban centers such as New York City, where the film takes place, women from Mexico, the Caribbean, and Central American now predominate as nannies/housekeepers and housecleaners. Unlike European immigrant women of the early twentieth century, these women find themselves, generation after generation, stuck in the occupational ghetto of domestic work (Hondagneu-Sotelo 2007:15).

READING 3.2

CLASS IN THE CLASSROOM

Hollywood's Distorted View of Inequality[1]

Robert C. Bulman

To the casual viewer, a film about high school may be nothing more than simple entertainment. When the films are viewed collectively, however, the high school film genre reveals patterns that transcend entertainment and teach deeper lessons about American culture. Motion pictures do not necessarily reflect the high school experience accurately. Hollywood routinely twists and shapes reality to maximize dramatic or comic effects. Films must also frame complicated social relationships within two hours and on a two-dimensional canvas. Nevertheless, even if they are not precise social documents of real high schools and real adolescents, these high school films are still culturally meaningful. That is, they have something to teach us about how Americans make sense of education, adolescence, and class inequality.

As I argue in *Hollywood Goes to High School: Cinema, Schools, and American Culture* (2005a), there are significant differences in how Hollywood represents poor students in urban schools, middle-class students in suburban schools, and wealthy students in private schools. This chapter focuses primarily on the urban school films and the way in which Hollywood depicts social class.

By analyzing the representation of schools in film we find that Hollywood has a double-standard in how students from different social classes are depicted. Specifically, poor students are rarely allowed to be the heroes in Hollywood films (adults always must "save" them) while middle-class students are nearly always the heroes of the films in which they are featured (they are always wiser than the adults in the film). This double-standard, I argue, reflects the middle-class bias of American culture. The middle-class perspective is always the predominant and heroic perspective in film. While it would be nice to simply blame Hollywood for this double-standard, the truth is that these distorted images of poor and middle-class teens are a reflection of the distorted image that Americans in general have of different social classes. These representations are a fantasy of the middle class (that poor students are troubled and middle-class students are wise), but it is fantasy that transcends the middle class because the middle-class perspective in American society is hegemonic.

The middle class occupies a special place in the American economy and in American culture. In very rough terms, the middle class can be defined as that class of people who have a college degree, are employed in professional white collar jobs, exercise autonomy on the job, work for a salary rather than a wage, and own their own homes. After World War II the American economy expanded and with it expanded a new middle class to manage the industries and bureaucracies of the growing society. With the shift from an industrial based economy to an economy based in the information and service sectors, the educated and professional middle class has become even more important to the American economy. The middle class is not necessarily the most powerful class politically or economically in the United States. However, it is the most powerful class culturally. The image of the middle class has become the image of America. The definition of what it means to be an American in the popular imagination is closely linked to the stereotypical cultural images of middle-class life—suburban home ownership, heterosexual marriage and family life, educational and occupational achievement, and financial security (but not opulence).

I do not disagree with analyses of film that argue male or white perspectives tend to be privileged in Hollywood films. Indeed, Hollywood films are often framed in such a way as to highlight the perspective of male or white characters. Hollywood films are also, by and large, told from the perspective of the middle class and tend to privilege middle-class characters, middle-class values, and middle-class assumptions about the social world. The middle-class perspective of films is even harder to recognize by film audiences than racial or gender perspectives because class itself as a social category is difficult for Americans to wrap their minds around. Americans do not like to think in terms of class because we like to think that anyone, regardless of their background, can achieve anything in life provided they work hard enough. We often fail to recognize that there can be significant class barriers preventing individuals from achieving upward social mobility.

The High School Film Genre

The theme that high school movies have in common is an ethic of individualism. Adolescents in these films are expected to transcend the limitations of their communities, the narrow-mindedness of their families, the expectations of their parents, the conformity of their peers, the ineffectiveness of their schools, their social class status, and the insidious effects of racism in order to express themselves as individuals apart from social constraints. The source of their academic success and/or personal fulfillment is to be found within the heart and mind of each individual regardless of social context. There are dramatic differences, however, in the ways the theme of individualism plays out in films based in urban, suburban, and elite private high schools.

In the urban high school film a classroom filled with socially troubled and low-achieving students is dramatically transformed by the singular efforts of a new teacher or principal. All of this is accomplished to the consternation of the inept administrative staff and other teachers, who never believed that these students had such potential. This lone "teacher-hero" is always an outsider, one who has a troubled and mysterious past, little teaching experience, a good heart, and an unorthodox approach to teaching (Considine, 1985; Heilman, 1991; Burbach and Figgins, 1993; Thomsen, 1993; Ayers, 1996). Invariably, the outsider succeeds where veteran professional teachers and administrators have repeatedly failed. The outsider is able to defeat the culture of poverty that had previously inhibited academic achievement. In these films the poor and mostly nonwhite students must change their behavior and accept middle-class values and cultural capital in order to achieve academic success.

In the films based in suburban high schools, however, academic success is not a central focus of the plot. The suburban school films depict schools less as actual places of learning and more as social spaces where middle-class teenagers search for their identities and struggle with each other for the rewards of social status and popularity. In these suburban school films, schoolwork is secondary to the real drama of teen angst. Students must reject the conformity of their peers, the culture of popularity, and the constraints of adults in order to express their true selves. The hero is almost never an adult as in the urban school films, but always a student who is able to overcome the conformity of teen society or the authoritarianism of adult society.

In the films based in elite private high schools, academics are once again featured as an element of the story. However, whereas in the urban school films academic achievement is valued as the answer to the culture of poverty plaguing inner-city students, in the elite private school films the narrow focus on academic achievement is portrayed as an oppressive burden on students. The students in these films must conform to the wishes of their parents and the school in order to protect their social class status. The hero of these films is usually an outsider who challenges the culture of privilege that pervades the upper-class institution. This working- or middle-class hero works to expand the horizons of the upper-class students away from narrow academic achievement.

The upper-class students are challenged to risk their taken-for-granted position in the class hierarchy by finding and expressing their true selves independent of the expectations that elite culture has of them.

It is important to note that these different representations do not arise because of the actual differences between real urban, suburban, and private high schools. To be sure, there are real differences between these types of schools. However, the subgenres differ in significant ways because American culture makes sense of poor, middle-class, and wealthy youth in very different ways. The differences depicted on screen reflect the fantasies that Americans have about social class and inequality more than they reflect the realities of social class and inequality in the United States.

Because these high school films are made by and largely consumed by members of the middle class, and because middle-class culture is the hegemonic culture in the United States, these high school films tend to reflect middle-class worldviews and assumptions. Suburban school films represent middle-class frustration with the conformity and status hierarchy of suburban middle-class life and express fantasies of self-expression and individual rebellion against such a system. The elite private school films reflect middle-class resentment of the rich and a fantasy that to be truly happy it is not necessary to be rich, but it is necessary to be true to oneself as an individual.

The urban high school film genre represents the fantasies that suburban middle-class Americans have about life in urban high schools and the ease with which the problems in urban high schools could be rectified—if only the right type of person (a middle-class outsider) would apply the right methods (an unconventional pedagogy with a curriculum of middle-class norms and values). This teacher-hero represents middle-class hopes that poor students in urban schools can be rescued from their troubled lives not through significant social change, but by the individual application of common sense, good behavior, a positive outlook, and better choices.[2]

A Cinematic Culture of Poverty

In most of the urban high school films the plot revolves almost exclusively around the activities of one particular classroom of rowdy students and their heroic teacher in a troubled and violent school. The students in this class are depicted homogeneously: They all have similar social class characteristics and similar problems. We are rarely offered a glimpse into the complexities of their individual characters, their histories, their identities, or their families, as is the case in many of the suburban high school films. The urban high school students, for the most part, are from lower- and working-class homes, are often nonwhite (but not exclusively so), come from broken families that do not understand or do not care much about their child's education, have low educational aspirations and expectations, behave poorly in the classroom, and express a great deal of frustration with the formal structure of the school.

The students in these films represent the working- and lower-class populations as they are stereotypically imagined by suburban middle-class Americans. These students represent what middle-class people fear most about the poor urban youth: They are out of control, loud, disobedient, violent, and addicted to drugs; have no family values; and reject the dominant social institutions. The rejection of the school is particularly offensive to members of the middle class since they depend on educational credentials and because schools have served them quite well (Eckert, 1989).

One argument is that such stereotypical notions are the result of psychological projections—that the suburban middle class projects these images onto the residents of inner cities to relieve the burden of carrying such negative characteristics themselves. In other words, the identity of the middle-class suburban resident is formed in opposition to that of the inner-city resident, who is imagined to be impoverished both economically and morally. The growing social distance between suburban and urban America is reflected in the exaggerated representations of inner-city residents in the popular media. In response to the anxiety the middle class feels about life as it imagines it in the inner city, the suburban middle class seeks to impose its particular values and strategies for success on the residents of the inner city (McCarthy et al., 2004). What prevents inner-city residents from achieving educational and occupational attainment is believed by many in the middle class not to be a political or economic problem, but a moral one. Hollywood reinforces these middle-class fantasies about how best to address the problems of the inner city.

Hollywood's depiction of urban life and urban schools generally reflects the culture-of-poverty thesis. This view holds that residents of poor inner-city neighborhoods are poor not because they face racial and/or class discrimination or because they lack access to stable employment opportunities. Rather, it is argued that the urban poor are impoverished because they have the wrong values and the wrong attitudes about school, work, and family. In contrast to what is considered the normative cultural values of the middle class (material goals, rational calculation, and a belief in the efficacy of individual effort), the culture-of-poverty thesis implies an impoverished culture—a culture that is lacking in the requisite values to achieve individual success. The urban poor remain poor due to their failure to adopt middle-class values and to fully integrate into the dominant culture of the United States (Banfield, 1968).

Much social science research, however, has discredited the idea that cultural values are responsible for either success or failure in life (see, for instance, Bourdieu, 1977; Swidler, 1986; Lareau, 1987; Willis, 1981; Gibson and Ogbu, 1991; MacLeod, 1995). This research has shown that while cultural values and attitudes vary, they do so primarily as they adapt to larger historical, social, political, and economic conditions. As sociologists have studied the inner city, they have found that many of the social problems found there are less the result of cultural values and more the result of low levels of public investment in infrastructure, poor public housing, inadequate health care, poor schools, and a disappearing employment base (Wilson, 1996).

Nevertheless, the culture-of-poverty framework has found its way into the popular imagination, and it is difficult to dislodge. Rather than focusing on the social, political, and economic sources of the problems in the inner city, Americans prefer to place the blame on the moral failings and bad decision making of the residents of the inner city. National surveys have found that a majority of white Americans believe that a lack of personal motivation is the primary reason African-Americans, on average, have lower socioeconomic status than white Americans (Schuman et al., 1998). It is generally assumed that a solution to the problems in the inner city must be applied individually rather than structurally. As President George W. Bush remarked early in his first term, "Much of today's poverty has more to do with troubled lives than a troubled economy. And often when a life is broken, it can only be restored by another caring, concerned human being" (Hutcheson, 2001). Explaining poverty as the result of individual failure helps to relieve the suburban middle class of its share of responsibility for having politically and economically neglected the inner city. The frame that Hollywood uses to make sense of problems in urban high schools vividly reinforces the culture-of-poverty thesis and assists the middle class in its displacement of responsibility from troubled social structures to troubled lives.

Welcome to the Jungle: The Urban School in Hollywood Films

Many of the urban school films do acknowledge that inner-city students face the challenges of poverty, racial discrimination, and poor schools. However, the films portray the individual attitudes of the students as the primary obstacle to their academic achievement. These students don't have the right manners, the right behavior, or the right values to succeed in school. They have low aspirations and a low self-image, and they believe the odds are stacked against them. The schools, therefore, are unable to effectively educate these students. The reproduction of their low social status seems inevitable.

In the classic *Blackboard Jungle* (Richard Brooks, 1955) a class of working-class New York boys is depicted at first as nothing but a street gang who spend their days causing havoc in their vocational high school: A female teacher is nearly raped, a baseball is heaved at a teacher's head, a teacher's wife is harassed, and a newspaper truck is stolen. The metaphor in the film's title is all too literal: These students are seen as working-class animals. These are "beasts" that even music won't soothe; in one scene the students destroy a teacher's priceless collection of jazz records. In *The Principal* (Christopher Cain, 1987), one teacher compares the students to animals only to have another claim she would rather teach animals because at least animals do not carry knives. In *Teachers* (Arthur Hiller, 1984), the song "In the Jungle" plays while police search student lockers for drugs. In *Lean on Me* (John G. Avildsen, 1989), the high school is depicted explicitly as an untamed jungle. In the opening moments, we see students selling drugs, assaulting teachers, harassing women, and generally running amok. All of this takes place as the movie soundtrack plays Guns and Roses' loud and angry "Welcome to the Jungle" in the background.[3]

The jungle metaphor conveniently summarizes the imagined difference between middle-class suburban Americans and the poor urban students portrayed in these films. These are not students as middle-class Americans expect students to act. Their depiction as "animals" suggests that the problems in these schools are rooted in student behavior and, furthermore, that their behavior is rooted in an inferior culture.

In the opening scenes of *Teachers*, a student is stabbed, a student bites a teacher, the school psychologist has a nervous breakdown, and we see a teacher pack a gun in her briefcase. The assistant principal of the school casually explains these events as typical problems for a Monday. In *The Principal*, Rick Latimer (James Belushi) single-handedly breaks up a gang fight on his first day on the job as the principal of an inner-city school. In *The Substitute* (Robert Mandel, 1996), gang members have such firm control over an urban public high school that they attack a teacher with impunity. In *Dangerous Minds* (John N. Smith, 1995), the white, middle-class, and somewhat naive Ms. Johnson (Michelle Pfeiffer) walks into her class for the first time only to walk right back out after encountering nothing but abusive and hostile students, who first ignore and then ridicule her. These are the same students who, by the end of the movie, Ms. Johnson (and we the audience) will embrace warmly.

Or is it that by the end of the movie "they" (the at-risk, poor, and inner-city students) will have learned to embrace "us" (the educated, middle-class, and suburban audience as represented by Michelle Pfeiffer's portrayal of Ms. Johnson)? This distinction is an important one. Will the audience learn that these students are not animals after all? Have the students simply been misunderstood? Will the audience be the ones who learn a lesson? Or will the students radically change their behavior as they come under the civilizing influence of the middle-class teacher who will socialize them in the culture of middle-class life? With few exceptions, it is the students who must learn and change, not the audience.

The School Staff: Inept Bureaucrats and Incompetent Teachers

If the students are portrayed in a negative light, the school administrators and teaching staff are not depicted much more generously. The teachers and staff are generally shown as uncaring, cynical, incompetent, and ineffective educators. In short, the administrative and teaching staffs in these movies represent the worst fears that suburban residents have of urban public schools. These characters represent what many Americans believe to be typical of the urban public school "crisis"—a selfish, inept, wasteful, and uncaring bureaucracy. These are schools with no soul—just troubled students, failed educational methods, burned-out personnel, too many arcane rules, and too much paperwork.

If the harshest critics of public education (such as Lieberman, 1993, and Chubb and Moe, 1990) were to make a movie about the public schools, their fictional schools would look much like the schools in these films.

In *Blackboard Jungle*, the stern principal is offended by the suggestion that there are discipline problems in his school. He seems unaware of the disobedience that surrounds him. In *Dangerous Minds*, the soft-spoken principal is so narrowly focused on teaching the students to follow the most minor of rules that he is blind to their real life-and-death problems. Similarly, the administrators in *Up the Down Staircase* (Robert Mulligan, 1967) are more concerned that teachers follow the strict rules, obey the proper procedures, and fill out the right forms than they are with the welfare and education of their students. The principal in *Teachers* is blissfully ignorant of all the chaotic events in his school. Most of the administrative energy in the school is spent fighting a lawsuit filed by the family of a student who graduated without knowing how to read. The school authorities in *Stand and Deliver* (Ramón Menéndez, 1988) have little faith in their students and do not believe that they could possibly do well in an advanced math class. In *Coach Carter* (Thomas Carter, 2005) the principal of the school is furious that the coach is focused more on helping the players academically than he is focused on winning basketball games. In *Freedom Writers* (Richard LaGravenese, 2007) the chair of the English Department doesn't believe the low-income students in her school have the capacity to learn. She refuses to allow a young idealistic teacher to distribute *Romeo and Juliet* or *The Diary of Anne Frank* to her students, books that are otherwise collecting dust in the warehouse. In *Lean on Me*, the dramatic deterioration of the high school over the years is blamed on the actions of the selfish teachers' union and the corrupt politicians in City Hall. In *The Principal*, the teachers complain bitterly when the principal insists that the "thugs" of the school actually attend their classes. In *The Substitute*, the principal is actually one of the thugs. He has established an alliance with the dominant gang in the school to distribute drugs throughout the school district.

The vast majority of the teachers in these films have cynical attitudes about their jobs, and they seem to believe that most of the students are beyond hope. As one teacher from *Up the Down Staircase* summarizes her pedagogical philosophy, "You keep them off the streets and you give them a bit of fun and you've earned your keep." These veteran teachers are burned out and have failed to do what was assumed to be their professional obligation—to reform these students into respectable, educated, and well-behaved citizens.

The Outsider as the Teacher-Hero

While all of the students, all of the administrators, and most of the teachers are depicted as impediments to education, there is one bright light of hope in these films: the teacher-hero (or, in the case of *Lean On Me* and *The Principal*, the principal-hero). This lone figure is able to ignore the cynicism of veteran teachers, escape the iron cage of the school bureaucracy, and speak directly to the hearts and minds of these troubled youth who are, by the end of the film, transformed from apathetic working-class and poor students into studious and sincere students with middle-class aspirations.

The heroes of these films do not need teacher training, smaller class sizes, a supportive staff, strong leadership, parental participation, technological tools, corporate partnership, school restructuring, a higher salary, a longer school day, vouchers, or more financial resources. All they need to bring to the classroom is discipline, tough love, high expectations, and a little good old-fashioned middle-class common sense about individual achievement and personal responsibility.

In each of these movies the hero is someone new to the school, and often new to teaching entirely. The teacher-hero is a mysterious figure who literally becomes the savior of these students (Ayers, 1996). All hope would be lost if not for the intervention of this unconventional new teacher who breaks from the failed methods of the school and effectively reaches the students with a unique approach. The teacher-hero represents a likely fantasy of the suburban middle-class audience: A character they can identify with goes into a troubled urban high school and single-handedly rectifies its problems. The teacher- or principal-hero can clearly see through the confusion that has bewildered many educators and policymakers for years. She or he can identify the faults in these students and the problems in these schools and knows just what it takes to correct them. The teacher-heroes teach the students to escape the depressing and limiting world of their parents, to appreciate art and poetry, to learn manners and cultural skills, to develop new study habits, to set high goals, to have an optimistic attitude, and to believe that hard work pays off. In short, the teachers show the students how to overcome their culture of poverty. It is through this figure of the heroic outsider that the audience feels some sense of control over an otherwise chaotic situation.

In *Blackboard Jungle*, Mr. Dadier (Glenn Ford), a white man with plenty of upper-middle-class cultural capital (he recites Shakespeare in his job interview with the principal), enters the "jungle" (the "garbage can of the educational system," as one teacher puts it) and attempts to reform unruly thugs who don't even seem to care about an education. Mr. Dadier's wife wishes he would retreat to a middle-class school with well-behaved students. Mr. Dadier, however, is determined to reach the students in his "jungle." He wants them to care about an education, to learn "to think for themselves," and to make something positive of their lives. He takes a special interest in Gregory Miller (Sidney Poitier), the charismatic black leader of the class, and tells him that he should not settle for being an auto mechanic, that in 1955 racial discrimination and poverty are no longer excuses for blacks not to make something of their lives in the United States. Through his persistence and dedication Mr. Dadier is able to convince Miller to stay in school. They create a pact: Mr. Dadier will not quit his job if Miller doesn't drop out of school. In addition to Miller, Mr. Dadier eventually wins the respect and admiration of most of the other inhabitants of his classroom "jungle."

In *Dangerous Minds*, Ms. Johnson finds herself teaching some of the most difficult students in the school ("rejects from hell"). Her primary message to these students is that they can achieve anything they want, provided they put their minds to it. With only a superficial nod to their community, their poverty, their race, or their families, Ms. Johnson declares that their lives are defined by their individual choices, nothing more. As she tells her students, "If you want to pass, all you have to do is try." In order to give them the confidence that they can achieve anything they choose, she breaks from the traditional curriculum and uses "college-level" poetry to teach her students. Her class engages in intellectual debate about the similarities between the poetry of Dylan Thomas and Bob Dylan. The upper-middle-class cultural capital she imparts to them is in stark contrast to the poor and working-class family lives they lead. The grandmother of two brothers in her class doesn't see the point of all this book learning and withdraws the boys from Ms. Johnson's class. Nevertheless, most of her students begin to care about schooling and begin to believe that education, including poetry, can make a difference in their lives. Ms. Johnson develops a particular interest in one student, Raul (Renoly Santiago), and develops a pact with him: She loans him $200 but will allow him to pay back the money only on the day he graduates from high school. Ms. Johnson's love (and the candy bars she uses as bribery) inspires her students to believe in themselves and in the power of an education in spite of the hardships they face in the world outside the school.[4]

In *Coach Carter*, Ken Carter (Samuel L. Jackson) is not an educator. He is not even a basketball coach. He is a successful owner of a sporting goods store. His only qualification to coach or to teach, it seems, is that he was a basketball star at his high school in the 1970s. During a visit to his old school he notices with disappointment the lack of discipline among the players and their constant bickering. He is shocked to see the impoverished

Photo 3.1 The teacher-hero in *Dangerous Minds*. Ms. Johnson (Michelle Pfeiffer) tries to teach her "difficult" class through alternative teaching strategies, such as adopting supposed "urban" language.

state of the school and the destructive attitude of the students. "That school was tough when I went there," he says, "now it's off the charts . . . Those boys—so angry and undisciplined." It's up to him to set things straight. He sacrifices most of his free time to coach (and to teach life lessons to) the boys on the basketball team.[5]

In *Freedom Writers,* Erin Gruwell (Hilary Swank) is a young, naïve, and idealistic teacher who has never taught before. She declined opportunities to study law in order to become a teacher, so that she can reach young people before they find themselves in the criminal justice system. At first she faces stiff resistance in the classroom by hostile students. Her students are embroiled in gang wars and distrust anyone not of their own race. Ms. Gruwell eventually "reaches" her students by telling them about the greatest gang there ever was— the Nazis. She takes her students on a fieldtrip to the Museum of Tolerance and invites Holocaust survivors to speak to her class. By teaching about the Jewish Holocaust she breaks down the irrational prejudice her students have of each other. The students begin to exercise compassion toward each other and begin to care about schooling. The film reduces the problems in urban schools to gang violence and reduces the problems of gang violence to individual prejudice. Once prejudice is overcome anything becomes possible. Nothing else seems to be a barrier to individual success.

In *Stand and Deliver,* Mr. Escalante (Edward James Olmos) leaves a lucrative engineering job in order to teach high school math to Latino students in an East Los Angeles high school. Mr. Escalante insists on teaching calculus to students who normally would take regular or remedial math. His unconventional methods and his high expectations succeed. He is able to get his students to believe in themselves in spite of the doubts that their parents and the school authorities continue to have. His students pass the advanced-placement exam in calculus, and he inspires many of them to aspire to college. They begin to believe, as he tells one student who is covered in grease from working on his car, that it is better to design automobiles than to fix them. The only thing preventing them from designing cars, apparently, is a belief in themselves and the application of their abilities.

This same message about the ethic of hard work is repeated in film after film. As Mr. Thackeray (Sidney Poitier) tells his students in *To Sir, with Love* (James Clavell, 1967), "You can do anything you want with hard work." Similarly, in *Cooley High* (Michael Schultz, 1975), Mr. Mason (Garrett Morris) tells a student whose future may be working on an assembly line, "What is it you want? With your brains you can have it. Knowledge will get it for you." The simple power of knowledge to open up opportunities and to transform troubled lives is echoed by Ms. Johnson in *Dangerous Minds* as well: "The mind is like a muscle. If you want it to be really powerful you have to work it out. Each new fact gives you another choice." Coach Carter tells his players, "Go home tonight and look at your lives. Look at your parents' lives and ask yourself, 'Do I want better?'" As I have written elsewhere (Bulman, 2005b), it is not entirely clear what these poor and mostly African-American adolescent boys in a depressed inner-city neighborhood and under-resourced school are supposed to do to get a better life. The coach advises his students to show up to class and to study. It is hard to argue that this is bad advice. But the underlying message of the film is that the path to a better life is *entirely* in the hands of these low-income boys. It is a message of rugged individualism that denies the structural obstacles that these boys face on a daily basis. The message of the film is captured well by a poster hung prominently in the coach's office: "Life is Full of Choices: Choose Carefully." Life *is* full of choices. The film, however, doesn't even begin to suggest that some lives are offered more choices than others and that it takes much more than individual determination to succeed in life.

Coach Carter and the other films about poor urban youth suggest to audiences that for those who dream big, live disciplined lives, and work hard enough, anything is possible. The assumption in these movies (and too often in actual schools) is that aspiring to fix cars, to work on an assembly line, or to live a life similar to that of your parents is a sign of personal failure. This attitude serves to condemn those students who, for whatever reason, do not have college in their future. Furthermore, it is disingenuous to assume that the only obstacle standing in the way of middle-class occupational attainment for these students is their individual attitudes and their failure to exercise their brains.

Hollywood's Politically Conservative Worldview

What messages do these urban high school movies send to audiences about urban education? Do these films implicitly endorse any particular political solution to the problems in urban schools? In each of these movies the answer to the students' problems is revealed to be primarily an individual one: to reform the individual student, not the educational system or the wider society. The teacher-hero in all of these films must teach students the right values and manners, to convince them they have the power to improve their lives, and to insist they make better choices and take responsibility for those choices. As Principal Joe Clark (Morgan Freeman) in *Lean on Me* tells the students in his high school, "If you fail I want you to blame yourself. The responsibility is yours."

While there is certainly nothing wrong with encouraging personal responsibility among students, these movies dramatize only a portion of the story when they portray a lack of individual effort as the only reason the future of poor students is often limited. The serious business of school reform or revitalization of the inner-city economy takes a distant back seat to the individual reformation of these poor and working-class students. Success is a choice that each individual student must make. In the absence of a portrayal of the social, political, or economic context in which these individual choices are made, there is an implicit (and sometimes explicit) conservative political message conveyed in each of these films.

Near the end of each movie the teacher- or principal-hero faces a crisis that almost causes her or him to give up the mission. In each case, however, the crisis is heroically dealt with, and the teacher or principal stays on the job, having found her or his true calling in life. The dilemma facing the hero in the climax of each of these movies tells a significant political story about urban policy choices in late-20th-century America. Should the state play an active role in the structural reform of urban schools and urban economies? Or should the state retreat and let market forces work the magic of the invisible hand? Or is there a "compassionately conservative" third way, in which public policy addresses inequality, but only at the level of the individual?

In *Stand and Deliver*, Mr. Escalante's students are accused by the testing authorities of having cheated on their advanced-placement calculus exams. Mr. Escalante begins to doubt himself and wonders if he placed excessively high expectations on his students. In the end, however, the students retake the test, and they all pass. The students are redeemed. Even more important, however, Mr. Escalante is redeemed. In the face of bureaucratic resistance, he, as a newcomer to the profession of teaching, is able to apply new pedagogical methods and his students are able to succeed beyond any level the school has experienced before.

Several crises face Ms. Johnson in *Dangerous Minds*. One of her students, the charismatic leader of the class, is shot and killed by a crack addict. Another of her students, Callie, gets pregnant and is pressured by the school administration to attend an alternative school. Still other students drop out of school altogether. Ms. Johnson begins to lose hope and announces she will not return to teach the following year. Her students, however, protest vigorously. They feel angry and, ironically, victimized by Ms. Johnson's apparent betrayal. Callie returns to school on Ms. Johnson's last day to ask her to stay. Callie refers to one of the poems they have studied in class to make her point:

> I thought you'd always be here for me. . . . I decided, we decided, we aren't going to let you leave like that . . . you have to rage against the dying of the light . . . we see you as being our light. You are our teacher. You got what we need.

Moved by her students' testimonies, Ms. Johnson decides to continue teaching at the school.

In *Up the Down Staircase,* Sylvia Barrett (Sandy Dennis), a new teacher in a rough New York City high school, decides to resign after less than one semester on the job. Frustrated and angry with the school bureaucracy, saddened by a student's attempted suicide, and disheartened because several of her students plan to drop out of school, Ms. Barrett decides she is not up to the challenge of teaching at a "problem-area school." "A teacher should be able to get through to her students, even here," she complains. Near the end of the term Jose (Jose Rodriguez), a quiet, shy, and apparently depressed student, comes out of his shell and presides as the judge in a mock trial Ms. Barrett has organized for her English class. "I'm sorry you are leaving us," says Jose. "English was the greatest course I ever took." Thrilled that she has "gotten through" to Jose, Ms. Barrett changes her mind about quitting.

In *Blackboard Jungle*, several of Mr. Dadier's students assault him and harass his wife. Mr. Dadier loses the hope he had for all of his students and nearly takes a teaching job at an elite high school. In a fit of frustration toward the end of the film, Mr. Dadier asks, "What's the point of teaching if kids don't care about an education? And make no mistake about it. They don't!" However, Mr. Dadier soon regains faith in his students when they team up to defeat the most incorrigible troublemakers in class after they threaten Mr. Dadier with a knife.

In *Lean on Me*, the corrupt fire chief and mayor arrest Principal Clark for putting chains on the high school doors (in order to keep the drug dealers out). The students, however, rally to his defense. They surround the jail and demand his release with testaments to how much he has helped them. The news that 75% of the students have received a passing grade on the state's minimum skills test redeems him. He is released from jail and returns to lead his flock.

In *Freedom Writers*, Erin Gruwell's freshman and sophomore students learn that school policy prevents Ms. Gruwell from being their teacher in their junior year. The students, having finally learned to care for each other, to respect Ms. Gruwell, and to apply themselves in school, are incredulous that the school would make them take an English class with another teacher. In an attempt to allow an exception to the school policy, Erin Gruwell goes over the heads of the school administrators. After her efforts fail the students contemplate engaging in civil disobedience to keep their teacher. At the end of the film the superintendent of schools unexpectedly intervenes and allows Gruwell to continue to teach her students in their junior and senior year. The students rejoice. Apparently, in spite of the progress they have made academically, the students still need Ms. Gruwell.

Coach Carter, angry that his students have not been performing well in school, locks the team out of the gym and forfeits several basketball games. The students, the parents, and the community at large are furious with the coach. The school board holds a meeting to discuss the lockout. Carter announces at the board meeting that he will quit if the school board votes to end the lockout. Nevertheless, the board votes to end the lockout. The basketball season resumes, apparently without Coach Carter. The dejected coach clears out his locker and walks into the gym one last time. There, on the basketball court, he finds his players. They are not playing basketball. They are studying. The student he earlier threw against a wall emotionally recites a poem for his coach. He has apparently been transformed from a gangster to a scholar during the week of the basketball lockout. He says emotionally to the coach, "Sir, I just want to say thank you. You saved my life." With such powerful testimony of the way in which his players *need* him, Carter has a change of heart—he will not quit.

In each of these moments of crisis, the teachers are at the end of their rope. They are disappointed that they have failed as teachers, angry that the students have not responded to their lessons, or frustrated that the administration has tied their hands. This moment epitomizes the anxiety and frustration with urban schools expressed by politicians and many middle-class suburbanites; it is a representation of the neoconservative impulse to retreat from state efforts to solve social problems. It is as if the teacher-hero says, "Well, I've done my best to help these people but it failed. Let's cut school funding, eliminate affirmative action, end welfare, and insist on personal accountability. Their failure is no longer my responsibility."

In Hollywood, the well-intentioned middle-class reformer ultimately succeeds just when failure seems imminent. Success, however, is measured not by any institutional or social changes, but by the adoration of the students for the teacher-hero. With such admiration from the students, the "compassionately conservative" teacher-hero continues to work with the students. This is the moment of truth in these movies—proof to the teacher-hero that the students have been successfully reformed. They have progressed from lower-class animals to respectable middle-class students who finally understand and appreciate the efforts of their middle-class hero. Their troubled lives have been compassionately transformed by a caring and concerned human being.

However, in spite of an emphasis on the value of individual transformation and self-reliance, the students in these films continue to express a need for a relationship with their teacher. This is a need that the teacher-hero, in all good conscience, cannot ignore. Who else will save these students? In *Blackboard Jungle*, Miller agrees to stay in school provided that Mr. Dadier does not quit. In *Dangerous Minds*, Raul agrees to graduate only if Ms. Johnson does not leave the school. In *Up the Down Staircase*, Jose's transformation as a student is due entirely to the efforts of Ms. Barrett (who decides not to quit because of Jose's transformation). In *Teachers*, one student's decision to care about school is implicitly predicated on Mr. Jerrel's (Nick Nolte) decision to care about teaching. In *Lean on Me*, the crowd of students who gather to demand that Principal Clark be released from jail proclaim, "We don't want a good principal. We want Mr. Clark!" In *Coach Carter* the coach stays on the job only after a student credits him with saving his life.

There is an implicit assumption in most of these movies that if the teacher- or principal-hero does not agree to remain at the school, the students would quickly jettison the lessons they have learned and return to their apathetic underperformance and violent behavior. There is no other teacher (and certainly no school reform) that can reach these students. There is a dependence on the middle-class teacher by these lower-class students which points to an inherent contradiction in these movies.

The teachers encourage their students to transcend their dysfunctional families, their rotten peers, their lousy schools, and their culture of poverty. The teachers encourage their students to use their power as individuals to compete successfully and to attain a higher social status. Yet, to reach this goal, the students are necessarily placed in a position of dependence on the teacher- or principal-hero. For all of the rhetoric about independence and individual achievement, we never see the students in these urban high school films fully express their autonomy. Rather, their individualism is firmly embedded in their relationship with the teacher-hero. The lessons that these urban school films teach about autonomy, competition, and individual achievement ironically require a relationship of interdependence, cooperation, and shared goals. However, the lesson about interdependence, cooperation, and shared goals is left implicit. Independence and achievement, on the other hand, are heralded explicitly. They are heralded, however, without an awareness of the social connections and social institutions required to sustain them. This reflects the American culture's unwillingness to acknowledge our reliance on community. It also contributes to the sense of emptiness and loneliness that some sociologists have argued are part of the dark side of middle-class American life (Bellah et al., 1985).

Conclusion: The Urban School Frontier

With few exceptions, these urban high school films are a celebration of the middle-class values of rational calculation and individual achievement. There is no suggestion that a longer-term solution to the problems in urban public high schools must address employment in the inner city, equitable school funding, sensitivity to racial and class differences, or the restructuring of urban schools. In true Hollywood fashion, these teachers and principals have saved the day as solitary heroes. These educators—mysterious, troubled, well-intentioned, alone, selfless, and heroic—are the cowboys of the dangerous and untamed urban high school frontier. They represent the essence of American individualism—they stand outside society in order to save it. The students, meanwhile, are explicitly grateful for their salvation. However, the salvation the teacher-heroes offer is inevitably tangled up with the contradictions of American individualism: The independence they demand of students requires a relationship of dependence to achieve.

Certainly, a high score on a test, an emotional tribute to a beloved teacher, and happy and optimistic students make for a good dramatic conclusion. But what do these endings imply for the public's image of urban schools? The audience is left feeling triumphant and optimistic about the potential for improvement in urban public schools. However, by simplifying the many problems of urban public education and turning inner-city students and public school teachers into caricatures of their respective social classes, Hollywood is reflecting middle-class anxiety about the problems of inner-city schools and the naive hope that such problems need not be a sustained political commitment from all members of society, but merely the individual moral conversion of poor students.

References

Ayers, W. (1996). A teacher ain't nothin' but a hero: Teachers and teaching in film. In W. Ayers and P. Ford (Eds.), *City kids, city teachers: Reports from the front row.* New York: New Press.

Banfield, E. (1968). *The unheavenly city.* Boston: Little, Brown.

Bellah, R. N., Madsen, R., Sullivan, W. M., Swidler, A., and Tipton, S. M. (1985). *Habits of the heart: Individualism and commitment in American life.* New York: Harper & Row.

Bourdieu, P. (1977). Cultural reproduction and social reproduction. In J. Karabel and A. H. Halsey (Eds.), *Power and ideology in education.* New York: Oxford University Press.

Bulman, R. (2005a). *Hollywood goes to high school: Cinema, schools, and American culture.* New York: Worth.

Bulman, R. (2005b). Coach Carter: The urban cowboy rides again. *Contexts: Understanding People in Their Social Worlds, 4,* 73–75.

Burbach, H. J., and Figgins, M. A. (1993, Spring). A thematic profile of the images of teachers in film. *Teacher Education Quarterly,* pp. 65–75.

Chubb, J. E., and Moe, T. M. (1990). *Politics, markets, and America's schools.* Washington, DC: Brookings Institution.

Considine, D. M. (1985). *The cinema of adolescence.* Jefferson, NC: McFarland.

Eckert, P. (1989). *Jocks and burnouts: Social categories and identity in high school.* New York: Teachers College Press.

Ehrenreich, B. (1989). *Fear of falling: The inner life of the middle class.* New York: Harper Press.

Gibson, M. A., and Ogbu, J. U. (Eds.). (1991). *Minority status and schooling: A comparative study of immigrants and involuntary minorities.* New York: Garland.

Giroux, H. (1996). Race, pedagogy and whiteness in *Dangerous Minds. Cineaste, 22*(4), 46–50.

Heilman, R. B. (1991). The great-teacher myth. *American Scholar, 60*(3), 417–423.

Hutcheson, R. (2001, May 21). Bush calls for faith-based "assault on poverty." *Sacramento Bee,* p. A15.

Lareau, A. (1987). Social class differences in family-school relationships: The importance of cultural capital. *Sociology of Education, 60,* 73–85.

Lieberman, M. (1993). *Public education: An autopsy.* Cambridge, MA: Harvard University Press.

MacLeod, J. (1995). *Ain't no makin' it: Aspirations and attainment in a low-income neighborhood.* Boulder, CO: Westview Press.

McCarthy, C., Rodriguez, A., Meecham, S., David, S., Wilson-Brown, C., Godina, H., Supryia, A. E., and Buendia, E. (2004). Race, suburban resentment, and the representation of the inner city in contemporary film and television. In M. Fine (Ed.), *Off white: Readings on power, privilege, and resistance* (pp. 163–174). New York: Routledge.

Schuman, H., Steeh, C., Bobo, L., and Krysan, M. (1998). *Racial attitudes in America: Trends and interpretations.* Cambridge, MA: Harvard University Press.

Swidler, A. (1986). Culture in action: Symbols and strategies. *American Sociological Review, 51,* 273–286.

Thomsen, S. R. (1993, April 15). *A worm in the apple: Hollywood's influence on the public's perception of teachers.* Paper presented at the Southern States Communication Association and Central States Communication Association joint annual meeting, Lexington, KY.

Willis, P. (1981). *Learning to labor.* New York: Columbia University Press.

Wilson, W. J. (1996). *When work disappears.* New York: Knopf.

Notes

1. Significant portions of this chapter were previously published as "Teachers in the 'Hood: Hollywood's Middle Class Fantasy." *The Urban Review, 34*(3), September 2002, pp. 251–276. Published with kind permission from Springer Science+Business Media.

2. While the students in these urban school films are very often African-American and Latino, the social class differences between the students and their teacher-heroes are more significant than the racial differences between them. The middle-class protagonists of *To Sir, with Love; Lean on Me; 187; Only the Strong;* and *Stand and Deliver* are all African-American or Latino. Also, there are white working-class students in need of salvation from a middle-class hero in *Blackboard Jungle; To Sir, with Love; Class of 1984; Teachers; Summer School;* and *Cheaters.*

3. In contrast to the songs that refer to the urban high school students as jungle animals, several of the suburban school film soundtracks feature Pink Floyd's anthem of adolescent resistance, "Another Brick in the Wall," with the lyrics "Teachers, leave those kids alone!"

4. In his critique of *Dangerous Minds,* Henry Giroux (1996, p. 46) argues that the movie represents "whiteness" as the "archetype of rationality, authority, and cultural standards." While I agree generally with Giroux's critique of *Dangerous Minds,* I believe that these urban school films as a whole represent middle-class values, not whiteness, as the archetype of rationality, authority, and cultural standards. Americans generally lack the cultural language to make sense of social class. To the extent that they recognize social class, they often name it in racial terms. Similarly, racial differences in these films are very often conflated with and often stand in for social class differences. I agree with Barbara Ehrenreich (1989, p. 94), when she notes in her review of *The Wild One, Rebel Without a Cause,* and *Blackboard Jungle,* that these films deliver "impeccable middle-class messages: Crime doesn't pay; authority figures are usually right; you can get ahead by studying."

5. Some of my analysis of *Coach Carter* was originally published as "Coach Carter: The Urban Cowboy Rides Again." *Contexts: Understanding People in Their Social Worlds,* Summer 2005, 73–75.

Outtake

Social Class in America and *People Like Us*

Kathryn Feltey

Social Class in America (1957), a film produced to accompany the textbook *Sociology* by Arnold W. Green, traced the lives of three U.S. males from birth through adulthood. Their stories were contextualized by the social class position of their families, defined primarily by the occupational status of their fathers. The focus on intergenerational mobility between white fathers and sons reflects the dominant approach in sociology for much of the twentieth century, beginning with the publication of *Social Mobility* by Sorokin in 1927. Unlike the upbeat "anyone can get ahead if they work hard enough" theme of Hollywood movies, this educational film gave a fairly bleak view of the chances of upward mobility for those not born into a privileged social class. The three main characters represent the three major class categories: upper (Gil), middle (Ted), and lower (Dave). After high school, the three follow their class-designated destinies, with Gil traveling east to an elite Ivy league university ("to be with others like himself") and taking over his father's business after graduation, Ted becoming a white collar bookkeeper on the advice of his father (despite his longing to become an artist), and Dave working in a gas station to support his wife and children. Ted does experience what sociologists call *vertical mobility* when he moves to New York City to work in an advertising firm. However, his wife has left him by this point to advance her class position by one of the few mechanisms available to women in the 1950s: marrying "up" the class ladder, in this case by marrying Gil.

Over 40 years later, another educational film about social class was produced, *People Like Us: Social Class in America* (2000). In this PBS film, social class is explored through the stories of people and communities across the United States, "whether they live in Park Avenue penthouses, Appalachian trailer parks, bayou houseboats or suburban gated communities" (see PBS website[1]). There are different methods for measuring social class status and mobility, and *People Like Us* explores the question of how people see themselves in relation to the class system. This question becomes particularly poignant when people exceed the class in which they were born and raised, or have the desire to do so. Ginie Sayles, for example, "grew up poor but ended up marrying a millionaire." Capitalizing on the limited access women have to upward mobility, she has made a name for herself as a consultant training women to *appear* as if they belong in upper class social circles. Passing as a member of the elite involves a "makeover" not just in terms of what one wears, but in what sociologists call *cultural capital*, the knowledge and attitudes that provide advantages to the upper class. This is a popular story of love and social class in Hollywood—from *Cinderella* in animated children's film to adolescent love stories such as *Pretty in Pink* to adult "happily ever after" fairy tales like *Pretty Woman*. The reality is closer to the story of Tammy Crabtree, a single mother who supports her children by walking 10 miles a day to scrub toilets at the closest Burger King. The neighbors in the trailer park where she lives call her "trash," creating a class hierarchy in a setting outsiders would categorize as poor.

Note

1. Retrieved December 29, 2011 (http://www.pbs.org/peoplelikeus).

CHAPTER 4

Race and Ethnicity

Victor Joseph:	You gotta look mean or people won't respect you. White people will run all over you if you don't look mean. You gotta look like a warrior! You gotta look like you just came back from killing a buffalo!
Thomas Builds-the-Fire:	But our tribe never hunted buffalo—we were fishermen.
Victor Joseph:	What! You want to look like you just came back from catching a fish? This ain't "Dances with Salmon" you know!

—Smoke Signals (1998)

Mrs. Kline:	Those Latin people that were skulking around here earlier . . .
Peter:	Oh, they were looking at that house down the street.
Mrs. Kline:	Casing it?
Peter:	No, no, they were looking to buy.
Mrs. Kline:	Oh, please. If those people are on this block and not holding a leaf blower . . .

—Bringing Down the House (2003)

The history of race and ethnicity in Hollywood films reflects the racial and ethnic inequality of American society. In the early twentieth century, movies were created and exhibited to Eastern European immigrants to encourage assimilation. Whiteness was a status to be achieved, a way of life to emulate, with homogeneity as the goal, at least for immigrants from Europe. However, the portrayal of most nondominant groups in American film was the story of the "other," created and controlled through practices of exclusion, expulsion, and violence.

In 1915, D. W. Griffith made history with the first blockbuster film *Birth of a Nation.* Historians have called the film a major landmark for American cinema, and a "sacrifice of black humanity to the cause of racism" (Cripps 1977). The release of the film, with its demonizing of African Americans (played by white actors in black face) and sympathetic portrayal of the Ku Klux Klan, led to a nationwide protest of movie theaters organized by the National Association for the Advancement of Colored People (NAACP). In an interview about *Birth of a Nation,* sociologist and social reformer Jane Addams called it "unjust and untrue," noting that "one of the most unfortunate things about this film is that it appeals to race prejudice" ("Jane Addams Condemns" 1915).

Movies throughout the twentieth century reflected not just racial prejudice, but the subjugation of people through their absence or—when they were included—their narrowly defined, stereotypical roles. As Victor Joseph tries to explain to his hapless friend in the movie *Smoke Signals,* there is a stereotype associated with being Indian that is important for him to learn and use to survive in the white man's world. While many would agree that there has been significant progress in addressing racial inequality over the past century, there have also been major roadblocks.

In recent years there has been a reversal of the achievements of the mid twentieth century movements for racial justice, as evidenced by "the dramatic increase in black prisoners, and the growth of the prison-industrial complex, crumbling city infrastructures, segregated housing, soaring black and Latino unemployment . . . and deepening inequalities of incomes and wealth between blacks and whites" (Giroux 2002:237). Additionally, the "new racism" (Collins 2004) operates in the guise of a colorblind society where the successes of the civil rights movement have been achieved and racial equality has been realized.

Racist portrayals of African Americans in contemporary films are plentiful, with persistent linking of violence with men and "sexual promiscuity to the nature and identity of African American women" (Littlefield 2008:677). Such negative portrayals are not limited to the African Americans, but are also seen in images of Latinos/as (as criminals), Native Americans (as cliché savages), and Asian Americans (as immigrant shopkeepers or martial arts experts). Often, a (white) hero in a film is established through the creation of a minority enemy, or a "second fiddle" such as Tonto to the Lone Ranger or Kato to the Green Hornet.

The readings in this section focus on race and ethnicity in film. In the first reading, Ed Guerrero examines contemporary black screen violence, tracing its origins from Hollywood's blaxploitation period, to the 'hood-homeboy films of the 1990s, to "historical agonies" in black/African history. A central theme is the possibility of collective social change in the tradition of the black liberation movement versus "the grim, violent struggle for individual survival." Even when the latter is presented as a heroic action-adventure story, any political significance is undercut by what Guerrero calls "popcorn violence." Ultimately, he asks, "How does one make a feel-good Hollywood movie, with big box office expectations, about some of history's most wicked crimes: racism, genocide, and slavery?"

In the next reading, Susan Searls Giroux and Henry Giroux analyze the popular, award-winning film *Crash,* pointing out that the film begins with a paradox about the loss of community in modern society and ends in an exchange of racist slurs. In keeping with the "new racism" noted above, Searls Giroux and Giroux claim that "most Americans believe that racism is an unfortunate and bygone episode in American history, part of a past that has been more than adequately redressed and is now best forgotten." They are critical of *Crash* for presenting racism as a function of private discrimination, rather than a "systemic political force with often dire material consequences." Perhaps most tragic of all is that the conditions that produce structural racism also destroy the possibility for an engaged democracy.

In the last reading, Carleen Basler addresses the portrayal of Latinos/as in film over time. Beginning with a historical overview of Latinos/as, Basler examines the stereotypes that have been cemented in the American mind, noting that throughout history, there has existed an "us" (white Americans) and "them" (Latinos/as) attitude that is evident in the stereotyping of Latinos/as in film. She concludes by exploring the ways Latinos/as have found to subvert and resist negative stereotypes, typecasting, and status quo ways of making films, and calling for systematic research on the content of films, the identities and agendas of filmmakers, and Latino/a activism for social change.

References

Collins, P. H. 2004. *Black Sexual Politics: African Americans, Gender, and the New Racism.* New York: Routledge.

Cripps, T. 1977. *Slow Fade to Black: The Negro in American Film.* New York: Oxford University Press.

Giroux, H. A. 2002. *Breaking in to the Movies: Film and the Culture of Politics.* Malden, MA: Blackwell.

"Jane Addams Condemns Race Prejudice Film." 1915. *New York Evening Post,* March 13. Retrieved December 30, 2011 (http://historymatters.gmu.edu/d/4994/).

Littlefield, M. B. 2008. "The Media as a System of Racialization: Exploring Images of African American Women and the New Racism." *American Behavioral Scientist* 51:675–85.

THE SPECTACLE OF BLACK VIOLENCE AS CINEMA[1]

Ed Guerrero

The raw synergy of comedy and history is a revealing place to start an exploration of black violence in American commercial cinema. African Americans living today, more than 40 years after the end of the civil rights movement, are confronted with many daunting ironies and unsettling paradigm shifts. As Chris Rock, one of the incisive, funky heirs to the politicized early comedic style of Richard Pryor, acidly implores in his stage monologue, wherever you find a boulevard named after this nation's great apostle of nonviolence, Dr. Martin Luther King, Jr., "run . . . because there's some violence going down." One must now read the post–civil rights era in the broader, less optimistic twilight of "postslavery."

With declining resources, and the hegemony of race and class privilege reasserted in the neoconservative language of a post-9/11, post-Katrina world, the complexities of American society are sharp, and often very obvious. The 2008 election of the first black U.S. president, Barack Obama, is cast into ironic relief by the fact that far too many black people (along with much of the nonindustrial world) are slipping deeper into poverty and (globalized) ghettoization. For the restless many at the bottom, the only social "progress," it now seems, is that the main boulevards and public schools of these urban zones of disenfranchisement are named after the last generation's martyrs. Worse still, the great collective aspirations of the black freedom struggle, across the political spectrum from nonviolent action to "by any means necessary" militancy, have eroded into an ambivalent, self-focused consumerism of brand-name jeans and sneakers and intracommunal annihilation through gun-drug-gang violence.

In neoconservative, "running on emptiness—post-everything" America, where prisons surpass public education as lines in state budgets, black people have little say over their structurally determined condition at the bottom of the economic and social heap.[2] Despite the gains of a thinning, black middle class and the ornamental rhetoric of "black progress," for too many African Americans, stunted horizons and mean ghetto streets are the lived reality, now refracted in the 'hood-homeboy action flicks that have become such an influential, though fading, staple of what critics have dubbed the "new black film wave." While 'hood-homeboy violence is big box office, it's only one of the varied expressions of black violence on contemporary screens.

In this essay I would like to interrogate, historicize, and critically comment on some of the varied social, political, and psychic conditions factoring into black violence on the commercial cinema screen. In this process, perhaps I can address a few salient questions raised about black violence in the movies. For instance, what is the general framework within which dominant cinema violence, black and white, expresses itself? What are the origins of black violence in contemporary commercial cinema, and are there variations on the theme? And is black violence held to prefigured historical codes and a double standard by the dominant movie industry and its mainstream audience?

Violence in American Film

First and importantly, one must note that most black-focused films and black characters in mainstream films are not unique in portraying violence, and that blacks were latecomers to the screen violence game. With few exceptions, the stylistic range of black violence follows the overall configuration of mainstream white cinematic violence, which escalated in 1966 with the collapse of the Production Code and the advent of such technology-driven, stunningly violent box office successes as *Bonnie and Clyde* (1967), *Bullitt* (1968), and *The Wild Bunch* (1969; Amis, 1996).

Since then, we as a nation have become increasingly entertained by, and addicted to,[3] ever more graphic representations of violence expressed across a broad field of commercial movies with two loosely defined categories at either end of the violence continuum. At the most popular end is action-adventure or "popcorn" violence, with an emphasis on shoot-outs, car chases, pyrotechnics, quadraphonic noise, and ever increasing body counts. Except for shouted threats, curses, and screams, these films are light on dialogue, character development, and intellectual or psychological complexity. In industry terms, they are "sensation driven" and made for Hollywood's biggest and most influential demographic, the young (Gabler, 1997). Consequently, the violent action-adventure blockbuster delivers a jolting cinematic experience that's more akin to the thrill of a hyperkinetic amusement park ride or the action-packed computer games that, in terms of profit, outperform the average movie.

At the less profitable end are the social, psychological, or political dramas and historical epics made for older, baby boomer audiences seeking an aesthetic or intellectual experience at the movies. These films are considered by the industry to be "plot and character driven." When violence is depicted, it is aesthetically, socially, or morally edifying, erupting in such contexts as dramatic, character-focused conflicts or the broader sweep of history as in genocidal cataclysms, mass movements, political struggles, and social upheavals.

Responding to Hollywood's biggest audience (adolescent males 16–24), violence-driven, crime cinema, horror, and action-adventure flicks like the *Terminator* films (1984–2009), the *Die Hard* films (1988–2007), *True Romance* (1993), *Independence Day* (1996), *The Replacement Killers* (1998), *Kill Bill: Vol. 1 and Vol. 2* (2003–2004), *Saw I–V* (2004–2008), and *No Country for Old Men* (2008) abound. As a result, popcorn hyperviolence is one of Hollywood's biggest moneymaking ingredients. At the other end of the spectrum, films that explore the consequences of violence, like *The Pawnbroker* (1964), *Dr. Zhivago* (1965), *Gandhi* (1982), *Schindler's List* (1993), *Michael Collins* (1996), *The Passion of Christ* (2004), and *Apocalypto* (2006), are less common in the industry.

However, since some sort of violence is a necessary plot ingredient for box office success these days, these polarities are not discrete, and we find a great many feature films alloyed with violent moments regardless of the overall theme. Moreover, in the great mix of the middle reside films that sample graphic violence in an action-adventure style yet still strive to make an aesthetic, ideological, or psychological point, such as *Falling Down* (1993), *Boogie Nights* (1997), and *The Game* (1997). Even the industry's biggest blockbuster ever (at this writing), *Titanic* (1997), which is a romantic adventure staged in a historical context, cannot escape deploying liberal doses of the popcorn disaster violence first seen in its action-adventure-disaster ancestor *The Poseidon Adventure* (1972). There are also films that are graphically violent but claim to take an ironic view of violence, or to be statements against it, such as *Natural Born Killers* (1994) or classic Vietnam War films like symbolic *The Wild Bunch* (1969) and the literal *Platoon* (1986).

Violence in Black-Focused Commercial Films

In black-focused commercial films, we find a similar spectrum between the polar ends of cheap thrills and historical agonies. Features like *New Jack City* (1991), *Juice* (1992), *Trespass* (1992), *Menace II Society* (1993), *Posse* (1993), *Bad Boys I* and *II* (1995, 2003), and *Set It Off* (1996) and are all centered on violence as action-adventure entertainment and make up the popular end of the field. Then there's the hyperviolent romanticization of "the life" in *Belly* (1998), with its poster-bright colors and slick music video surface. At the other end, examples of black-focused films that attempt to depict violence in a historic, philosophical, or epic context include *Malcolm X* (1992), *Amistad* (1997), *Rosewood* (1997), and *Beloved* (1998). Films that are a mix of action-adventure violence and politicized or historicized theme include *Boyz n the Hood* (1991), *Dead Presidents* (1995), and *Panther* (1995), along with a more sanguine and cautionary tale of "the game," *noir* 'hood tour de force *Paid in Full* (2002). Moreover, perhaps ironically, both *Boyz n the Hood* and *Menace II Society*, and more successfully *Clockers* (1995), all make varied claims that their violent tales are meant to help stem black urban violence.

However we map this tangled field, one can convincingly argue that the origins of contemporary black screen violence are located in Hollywood's blaxploitation period, which consists of about 60 cheaply made black-focused action-adventure flicks released between 1969 and 1974. A scene in *The Dirty Dozen* (1967) marked a shift in Hollywood; star athlete turned actor Jim Brown sprinted down a line of ventilators, dropping grenades into them and blowing up a gathering of the elite Nazi German command (to the cheers of blacks and the approval of the mainstream white audience). The industry's long unspoken but strictly observed rules regarding the expression of black violence toward whites, and the sanctity of the white body, were beginning to erode under the political pressures of the civil rights movement and the surging "black power" aspirations of urban blacks.

Before this defining cinematic moment, with rare exceptions, like Paul Robeson killing a white prison guard (a scene cut by censor boards in the United States after the film's release) in *The Emperor Jones* (1933), or the obligatory threat of savage (Hollywood) tribesmen in the Tarzan flicks, or of the Mau Maus in *Something of Value* (1957), or the great siege battle in *Zulu* (1964), black lives were expendable and, in many instances, spectacularly devalued. Except for the functional purposes of staging threats and challenges to European supremacy to which whites could heroically respond, nonwhites were prohibited from inflicting violence upon whites, for compared to black life, white life was sacrosanct on the cinema screen (Shohat & Stam, 1994).

Blaxploitation Film

It was not too long after Jim Brown's grenade attack that a black superhero outlaw with revolutionary pretensions emerged in *Sweet Sweetback's Baadasssss Song* (1971) to maim or kill several white policemen, enjoy various dubious sexual escapades, and then escape a citywide dragnet to brag about it all. Thus the blaxploitation formula, which generally consisted of a black hero out of the ghetto underworld violently challenging "the Man" and triumphing over a corrupt, racist system, was born. What followed was a succession of detectives, gangsters, ex-cons, cowboys, dope dealers, pimps, insurgent slaves, and women vigilantes in flicks like *Shaft* (1971), *Across 110th Street* (1972), *Super Fly* (1972), *Black Caesar* (1973), *Black Mama, White Mama* (1973), *Boss Nigger* (1975), and *Drum* (1976), in which the protagonists shoot, punch, stab, and karate chop their way through a series of low-budget features that garnered megaprofits for Hollywood (Guerrero, 1993).

A couple of things are notable about the construction of violence in most blaxploitation period pieces. For one, because the technological advances of today's cinematic apparatus allow the industry to ever more convincingly represent or simulate anything that can be written or imagined, blaxploitation violence in many instances now appears crudely rendered and visually "camp" or naive in comparison to graphic blood- and brain-splashing shootouts in contemporary 'hood-homeboy action flicks. Also, the blaxploitation genre had a place for macho women in its pantheon of fierce action stars, women who echoed and upheld the cultural moment's call for reclamation of black manhood in the most violent, masculinist terms. Pam Grier in *Coffy* (1973) and *Foxy Brown* (1974) and Tamara Dobson in *Cleopatra Jones* (1973) play sexy black women adventurers configured to the social message of the times and black male adolescent fantasies that largely determined the success of blaxploitation films at the box office.

Blaxploitation films are full of fantastic moments of popcorn violence, like Foxy Brown (Pam Grier) triumphantly displaying the genitals of her archenemy in a jar, or vampire Blacula (William Marshall; *Blacula*, 1972) gleefully dispatching several white L.A. cops. However, in most cases, these films referenced black social reality, or transcoded,[4] however fancifully, black political struggles and aspirations of the times. The historical context in the urban north during this time involved increasing disenchantment with the limited gains of the civil rights movement among African Americans and a rise in black militancy with insurrections in hundreds of U.S. cities; these social energies found barely containable expression on the blaxploitation screen.

Super Fly (Gordon Parks, Jr., 1972)

The box office hit *Super Fly* exemplifies the social grounding of blaxploitation violence in a variety of expressions, even though the film was considered regressive by many black critics because of its blatant celebration of cocaine use and the hero's self-indulgent, drug pushing, hustling lifestyle. In the film's opening the protagonist dope dealer, Super Fly (Ron O'Neal), chases down and then brutally stomps a junkie mugger. However, the *mise-en-scène*[5] is insistently socially contextualized as the foot chase winds its way through the grimy alleys and dilapidated tenements of Harlem and culminates with the hapless derelict's getting the vomit kicked out of him in front of his impoverished wife and children; and all this to the overdub refrain of Curtis Mayfield singing the hit "Little Child Runnin' Wild." No matter what we think of Super Fly, or his nameless junkie victim, the social setting of this vignette forces us into a disturbing awareness of urban poverty, drugs, and the wicked symbiotic power relation between the junkie and the pusherman.

In contrast to the gritty realism of the black underworld informing *Super Fly*, where, interestingly, no guns are ever fired and most of the violence wears the cool mask of macho gesture, threat, and intimidation, the movie concludes with a rather fantastic athletic explosion of fisticuffs. In a cartoonish allusion to Popeye's love of spinach, Super Fly toots up on cocaine and then single-handedly whips three police detectives (in slow motion, no less), all while the corrupt police commissioner, literally known as "the Man," holds him at gunpoint. The social issues of this violent denouement emerge when Super Fly informs "the Man" that he's quitting the dope business, with a million dollars in drug profits. However, this retirement speech is also meant to recuperate the film's reactionary attitude and align it more closely with the political energies of the times. For Super Fly dramatically tells "the Man" off in the collective voice and terms of the black social insurgence of the late 1960s, thus framing what would be a totally implausible scene in the social yearnings of the historical moment. This type of politically conscious speech is fairly standard throughout the genre, from Ji-Tu Cumbuka's rousing gallows speech after an aborted slave revolt in *Mandingo* (1972) to Pam Grier's call to black unity and arms, against the backdrop of a wall-size George Jackson poster, in *Foxy Brown*.

Hood-Homeboy Film

One can argue that society's racial power relation hasn't changed all that significantly in the past 20 years (Bell, 1995), but it's clear that the psychic and social influences impelling the construction of black cinematic violence most certainly have changed. In comparison to the blaxploitation era, the 'hood-homeboy films of the 1990s are less obviously politically focused, and in their violent nihilism (and sometimes self-contempt) they hardly suggest the possibility of social change. Violence in the blaxploitation genre, no matter how crude or formulaic, captures the black liberation impulse of the 1960s. By contrast, the depiction of violence in the new black film wave, and especially the homeboy-action flick, rather than mediating black social and political yearnings, is concerned more with depicting the grim, violent struggle for individual survival left in the wake of the faded collective dreams of the 1960s. *The Toy* (1982) and *Trading Places* (1983) certainly signal this shift for black-focused mainstream cinema as surely as the rise of their respective stars, Richard Pryor and Eddie Murphy, followed the end of blaxploitation. The concentration of Hollywood's attention and production budgets on the rise of Pryor and Murphy coincides with the political and cultural shift from the "we" to "me" generation in mainstream culture and in representations of African Americans in commercial cinema. For no matter how imperfectly rendered its narratives, violence in much of blaxploitation either depicted or implied shaking off the "the Man's" oppression, and most important, moving toward the dream of a liberated future.

By contrast, violence in the new black film wave for the most part transcodes the collapse of those very hopes under the assaults of the Reagan and Bush years and their rollback policies on affirmative action, black social progress, multiculturalism, and the social progress of the welfare state in general. This is the ghettocentric 'hood-homeboy flick's most salient political point. With black inner-city neighborhoods ringed and contained by police departments, totally deindustrialized, chemically controlled with abundant drugs, fortified with malt liquor, and flooded with cheap guns, ghettos have become free-fire zones where the most self-destructive impulses are encouraged by every social and economic condition in the environment. As a cynical white cop in Spike Lee's *Clockers* (1995) coldly analogizes the situation, the urban ghetto has become "a self-cleaning oven." At best, then, turn-of-the-century cinematic 'hood-homeboy violence is socially diagnostic, an aesthetic attempt to raise consciousness by depicting the symptoms of a failed social and racial caste system. These depictions amount to endless variations on a theme: grotesque scenes of black and other nonwhite people trapped in ghettos and killing each other. Note Doughboy's (Ice Cube) "either they don't know, or they don't care" appeal for an awakening of conscience (and consciousness) at the end of *Boyz n the Hood*. The Hughes brothers, the directors of *Menace II Society*, rather disingenuously say it another way, declaring that they are not here to give people hope but rather to depict the realities of those trapped in the urban 'hood (Giles, 1993). Thus, one can discern the great distance between the political consciousness underpinning even the cheapest of blaxploitation, ghetto thrillers, and the "keepin' it real" nihilism of contemporary 'hood-homeboy flicks.

Yet, as with blaxploitation, the success of any commercial black film today is still eminently configured by the tastes of its (and Hollywood's) biggest aggregate, the youth audience, which mainly consumes action-adventure violence and generalized comedy, to the avoidance of drama and character focused films (Fabrikant, 1996). Consequently, the popular end of the black-focused film spectrum is crowded with productions deploying violence, very much in the style of dominant cinema, as a necessary action-adventure ingredient for box office success. Moreover, one can perceive a definite escalation or acceleration of violence from film to film. John Singleton's *Boyz n the Hood*, while punctuated with explicitly violent scenes, structured its narrative and ideology around the fates of good and bad brothers, Tre (Cuba Gooding) and Doughboy (Ice Cube). In this way the film at least holds out the possibility of escape from the 'hood through the time-honored, black race–building route of education. Conversely, the fates of Caine (Tyrin Turner) and O-Dog (Larenz Tate) are sealed when O-Dog brutally murders two Korean grocers in the opening moments of *Menace II Society*. From this gruesome beginning, the trajectory is straight down. And compared to *Boyz*, the body count increases exponentially; the action in *Menace* is best described as a sort of gruesome hyperviolence or autogenocide.

Correspondingly, many of the issues and debates regarding the depiction of extreme graphic violence as entertainment or realism were brought into focus with the release and box office success of *Menace II Society*. The Hughes brothers have claimed that their depiction of violence in *Menace* was a means to promote antiviolence efforts in the urban 'hood, telling the *New York Times*, "We wanted to show the realities of violence, we wanted to make a movie with a strong anti-violent theme and not like one of those Hollywood movies where hundreds of people die and everybody laughs and cheers" (Weintraub, 1993).

However, the film's violence and its impact on its audience would seem to annul this claim. As the brothers say, throughout most of *Menace*, violence is handled in an ugly, brutal fashion. The narrative is saturated with so many intensely violent scenes that violent action becomes the main structuring, captivating—and thus cumulatively entertaining—device in the film. What is more, in *Menace*'s final moments, when Caine is cut down in a hail of bullets, the scene is filmed in close-frame slow motion, thus fetishizing violence and evoking a style in the grammar of cinematic violence paying homage to Hollywood's foundational *Bonnie and Clyde* (1967; Massood, 1993). But perhaps more disturbing was *Menace*'s social impact, with film and media critics noting that youth audiences cheered the violent scenes, particularly the one in which the Korean grocers were killed. Because film is an intensely visual medium, audiences, whether impressionable or sophisticated, will always look past what a director says about a film's lofty intent to the visible evidence of what a film actually depicts on the big screen.

It is also important to note that ghettocentric violence is not always revealed through the lens of the 'hood-homeboy action formula and that in various ways some black artists have tried to counter its exploitation on the screen. When he stands up to the neighborhood bully, Ice Cube's character, Craig Jones, comes to a critical moment of extreme provocation in Ice Cube's popular 'hood-homeboy comedy *Friday* (1995). Flush with anger, Craig Jones pulls a gun, but instead of following the protocols of homeboy realism and "bustin' a cap" on the neighborhood bully, he pauses and reflects on the dire outcomes of such an act. Spike Lee's psychologically complex, character-focused drama *Clockers*, about a low-level drug dealer, covers the same issues, and on the same deadly turf. Like Ice Cube, Lee turns his eye more to the destructive consequences and grief that violence brings to the community, people's lives, and families. The violence in *Clockers* is minimal, awkward, low-key though realistic, and decidedly not of the action-entertainment variety. Marking the contrast between antiviolence strategies in *Clockers* and *Menace*, critic Leonard Quart (1996) comments that "Lee truly wants to turn his adolescent audience away from violence, rather than ostensibly moralize against it like *Menace*, which simultaneously makes the gory spectacle of people being slaughtered so exciting that the audience could howl with joy while watching."

Perhaps one of the most artful, sanguine tales about "the life" or "game," and its violent, nihilistic consequences, is *Paid in Full* (2002). Set in '80s Harlem, at the dawn of hip-hop, pagers, and the rise of sophisticated gang-drug organizations, violence here is a business matter. Nothing personal, violence is disciplinary. Show up late on the corner, or short on the count, or talk too much, and "you subject to get popped." Or in *Paid*'s narrative, as Rico (the rapper Cam'ron) rather unsympathetically tells Ace (Wood Harris), who has just survived a violent stickup, "Niggas get shot every day, B." This cautionary tale, articulated in the 'hood-homeboy film *noir* flashback, opens with Ace, a gaping head wound, soaked in blood, being asked by first-aid attendants who did this to him. In full, gory close-up, understanding where his actions have led him, Ace whispers, "I did." Violence here is socially and psychically mimetic. We traverse Ace's flashback year through the black world, and "the game" without benefit of guide or interpretation, to come full circle to the tale's reckoning and bloody conclusion.

Nowhere are the contrasts between sensation-driven and character/plot-driven films more evident than between the filmmaking practices of black men and black women, and how these gender differences are perceived by the dominant film industry and played out on the screen. Since Julie Dash's film *Daughters of the Dust* (1991), which had a reflective, dreamlike surface and no action-adventure violence, Hollywood has released into mainstream distribution a meager handful of features directed or written by black women—films like *Just Another Girl on the I.R.T.* (1993), directed by Leslie Harris; *I Like It Like That* (1994), directed by Darnell Martin; and *Eve's Bayou* (1997), *The Caveman's Valentine* (2001), and *Talk to Me* (2007), all directed by Kasi Lemmons. When it occurs, violence in these films is understated. It causes the protagonists a great deal of anguish and is used to dramatize the complexities of broader social or psychological situations.

Like other realms of cultural production, exclusion from positions of influence in the film industry intensifies with the number of minority statuses an individual holds. Hollywood's executive offices tend to view women's narratives as "soft," centered on drama and character and outside their most reliable moneymaking formulas, which, of course, mean liberal doses of action and violence. Black women experience "multiple jeopardy" based on sex and race (Collins, 2000), such that black male filmmakers have greater opportunities and are able to reach a wider (male) audience.

Differences in industry perception and audience consumption of black men's and women's products, especially concerning the uses of graphic violence, in part explain the box office success of *Menace II Society* and the comparative flop of *Just Another Girl on the I.R.T.*, which were both modest-budget black films released at the same box office moment.

It is also interesting to note that the gender hybrid originating in blaxploitation, the woman-focused action-adventure flick, has risen again in a series of variations and specific moments in films. *Set It Off* (1996), featuring Queen Latifah, Jada Pinkett, and Vivica A. Fox, is about an all-girl gang that tries to escape the ghetto by pulling a series of increasingly violent bank jobs. In Quentin Tarantino's blaxploitation reprise *Jackie Brown* (1997), the undisputed queen of black, campy violence, Pam Grier, returns to play a somewhat more subdued, middle-aged airline stewardess who rooks the streetwise gunrunner Ordell (Samuel L. Jackson) out of $500,000. One of Grier's big Freudian moments of reversal and castrating violence comes when she presses a gun to Ordell's dick and talks bad to him. Recalling blaxploitation's sexual ideology, in Ice Cube's *The Player's Club* (1998), homosexuality, the great threat to cultural nationalism, is punished as the beautiful stripper protagonist brutally defeats the "wicked" lesbian antiheroine in the film's culminating woman-on-woman fistfight.

Historical Agony: Racism and Violence

If violence is the principal and profitable cheap, popcorn thrill in the 'hood- homeboy action flick, it also finds expression at the other end of the black cinema spectrum as historical agony in such films as *Amistad, Beloved, Malcolm X, Rosewood,* and to a lesser degree in *Panther* (1995). As one of Spike Lee's most ambitious and publicized projects to date, *Malcolm X* grapples with a routine industry contradiction: it is a Hollywood biopic with blockbuster, crossover moneymaking pretensions, but at the same time, it aims to portray the life of a black revolutionary hero with some historical veracity. In pursuit of that broad audience in the middle, Lee mixes his renderings of violence by first entertaining us with the adventures of Malcolm as a hoodlum with his sidekick Shorty as they pursue the transgressive adventures of the hustling life. Lee even throws in a dance-musical number in zoot suits. But in the latter half of *Malcolm X*, the mood shifts and culminates with the brutally drawn out and explicit assassination of Malcolm X before a public assembly; the moment is both stunning and ambivalent in its effects. This scene has complex crosscurrents of political meaning, first working as historiographic realism to psychically shock us into fully recognizing the sacrifice that Malcolm X (and his family) made for black freedom and social progress. Yet the graphically violent surplus of the scene also turns it, in the Foucaldian sense, into spectacle, a public execution by firing squad rendered in brutal detail, thus punishing Malcolm for his beliefs. Accordingly, his last speech can also be viewed as a gallows speech (Foucault, 1979).

Like Lee's *Malcolm X*, and in contrast to his own "Panther" film, *The Huey P. Newton Story* (2001), Mario and Melvin Van Peebles's *Panther* aspires to historical distinction, this time by sympathetically depicting the rise of the Black Panther Party and the grievances of the black community that brought the party into being: police brutality, ghettoization, economic marginalization, and political disenfranchisement. However, while grappling with the same recurring contradictions between commerce and politics that appeared in *Malcolm X, Panther,* in pursuit of profits at the box office, relies mostly on the action-adventure violence of Hollywood's heroic individual. Thus, beyond the political insights about its historical moment that the film articulates, like in the shootout in which Bobby Hutton is killed, the film's deployment of popcorn violence in other scenes tends to undermine *Panther*'s claims to a historically realist style. Moreover, this tangle of issues involving varied styles of violence is certainly relevant to John Singleton's *Rosewood* and Steven Spielberg's *Amistad.* And perhaps these issues can be best explored by considering a question salient to both films: how does one make a feel-good Hollywood movie, with big box office expectations, about some of history's most wicked crimes: racism, genocide, and slavery?

Rosewood (John Singleton, 1997)

In *Rosewood*, John Singleton formulates the story about the real-life 1923 destruction of the all-black Florida town of Rosewood by a white mob as a revisionist Western, complete with an opening scene of the loner hero Mann (Ving Rhames) riding into town on his black "hoss," packing two .45 automatics and "lookin' for a nice place to settle down." As Lee did in *Malcolm X*, Singleton opts for a mix of action-adventure moments of popcorn violence, enveloped in a more shocking overall rendering of historicized violence. In one scene depicting the former, Mann hurries out of town to escape a deputized lynch mob, but he is set upon by a gang of whites and chased deep into the woods. Finally, Mann turns, stands his ground, and opens up with both of his .45s. Cut to the whites hauling ass out of the woods, with the punch line coming when they later excitedly exclaim that they were ambushed by a gang of "ten or fifteen niggers." The audience explodes with laughter. Singleton's timing and editorial touch with this classic scene from the archives of the cinematic Old West proves just right.

Overall, however, what happens to Rosewood on that gruesome night, as rendered by Singleton, is not at all funny or entertaining. At the height of the film's action, the disturbing sight of black men and women hanging from trees and telephone poles illuminated by the flames of their burning community seamlessly merges with those old *Life, Jet,* and archival photographs of real lynchings in America's gallery of historic horrors. Consequently, *Rosewood*'s panorama of violence is decidedly not escapist entertainment in the Hollywood sense. Violence here provokes the return of barely repressed collective nightmares and guilty complicities, as well as a painful examination of the national conscience which we as a national audience do not like to address, especially as entertainment, even in the darkness and anonymity of the movie theater. The historic agony of genocidal violence is brought into sharp focus in one of *Rosewood*'s culminating scenes, when one of the mob's prime instigators, proud of his crimes, forces his young son to look at a pile of black bodies awaiting disposal. Here, all of humanity's body counts are evoked, from Auschwitz to Wounded Knee to My Lai, Rwanda and beyond. Singleton's obvious point is that hope resides in the next generation, as the child rejects his father and runs away from home.

Rosewood is a mainstream commercial vehicle, and as such, its approach to violence is necessarily a mixed bag. If the film aspires to social conscience by shocking us with the historically repressed and oppressed, the lynch mob and its victims, it unfortunately lapses into the delusion of Hollywood formula in its portrayal of violence against women, black and white. Here we confront Hollywood's trickle-down theory of punishment, with the most powerless individuals in any hierarchy taking the rap for privileged elites hidden from critical interrogation. So, one must ask, why is it that the darkest black woman in the cast (Akosua Busia as Jewel), who opens the film with her legs spread, squealing from the pain of rape, is then in the film's closure gruesomely displayed as a murdered corpse, face up, eyes open in close-up? The argument here is that the narrative chain of significations, and the visual framing of her corpse, links the spectacle of Jewel's punishment to miscegenation, but also, implicitly, to her color. The whole issue of a devaluing, color-caste hierarchy, in this instance focused on those whom Alice Walker (1983) has referred to as *"black, black"* women, continues to be a troubling reality in mainstream commercial cinema.

Rosewood ends with the camera looking down in a long shot of a shack as we hear the screams of the white woman Fannie (Catherine Kellner), who initially yelled "nigger" to set things off, being brutally beaten by her husband, mixed with an overdub of lush, poignant cinematic music of the type used to signal narrative and ideological resolution. In Singleton's defense, one can speculate that a society that could burn an entire black town on drunken impulse would have no trouble thrashing one defenseless, lower-class white woman of loose reputation, especially one who has been set up by the narrative. Fannie does bear the historical burden of the oft-deployed false rape charge against black men. Yet with this beating the film reverts to a final cheap thrill, amounting to another act of symbolic punishment that displays the sacrificial offender/victim as spectacle while hiding the intrigues of the much more guilty and powerful. Coming in the film's closing moment, then, this beating concentrates blame for the genocide of a racial minority on yet another Hollywood out-group, disenfranchised white women (Girard, 1972).

In dominant cinema, moreover, the representation of black violence in the service of white narratives still circulates powerfully, animating some of Hollywood's most popular feature films. This is in part because the sign of blackness has become indispensable as the implicit, negative standard in neoconservative political rhetoric and moral panics about family, education, welfare, and crime. Simultaneously, the stylistic inventions and expressions of black culture powerfully influence every aspect of mainstream culture, especially urban youth styles, language, music, and dance. In many ways the films of writer-directors David Lynch and Quentin Tarantino epitomize the utility and profitability of black violence, as well as the deeply rooted psychological fantasies about the sign of blackness in the white popular imaginary.

David Lynch's crime-action-romance *Wild at Heart* (1990) opens with the gratuitous and brutally graphic murder of a black man who gets his brains publicly stomped out for the entertainment, and perhaps wish fulfillment, of the action-adventure audience. In this scene, in fact, David Lynch treats us to a "lynching," which also happens to be a play on his name and his style as invoked by the popular press (Willis, 1997). More broadly, Quentin Tarantino, in films like *Reservoir Dogs* (1992), *True Romance* (1993), *Pulp Fiction* (1994), *Get Shorty* (1995), and *Jackie Brown* (1997), appears to be deeply disturbed by barely repressed, ambivalent feelings about race in general, black masculinity in particular, as well as the issues of violence, miscegenation, and sex. Black male delinquents, while hip and alluring in Tarantino screenplays, wind up eliminated, raped, or murdered, with black male–white female miscegenation always punished. Conversely, black women are the exotic trophies of white male desire.

Perhaps the most troubling and historically predictable of Tarantino's constructions of black violence occurs in *True Romance* with the figure of the vicious pimp, drug-dealer Drexl (Gary Oldman). With this character, Tarantino's construction of the violent black male criminal becomes so grotesque and caricatured that it serves as an updated version of its explicitly racist historical referent, the "renegade Negro" Gus of *The Birth of a Nation* (1915). The similarities between the two are instructive. Gus, like Tarantino's drug-dealing pimp in dreadlocks, is a blackface caricature portrayed by a white man. Most significant, both Gus and Drexl represent sexual threats to white women and are ultimately punished with violent deaths. Gus's pursuit of white women becomes Griffith's rationalization for the organization and glorification of the Ku Klux Klan, which lynches Gus. Asserting the same basic threat, Tarantino evokes the rape-rescue paradigm in the actions of Clarence (Christian Slater), who, in a spectacularly violent scene, kills the black criminal Drexl to redeem his white girlfriend from sexual slavery. Considering this scene, and Tarantino's obsession with (for pleasure and profit, no less) the word *nigger*, which he says he wants to shout from the rooftops (Groth, 1997), one can speculate as to how little power relations and systems of representation have changed in the dominant film industry.

Amistad (Steven Spielberg, 1997)

The mid-to-big-budget, mainstream feature at the end of the scale of black violence as historical agony and realism is Steven Spielberg's *Amistad,* weighing in with production costs totaling $75 million. *Amistad* caps a trajectory well established by a number of films made during the blaxploitation period addressing the issue of slavery, like the action-sex-ploitation-driven *Mandingo* and *Drum*, and sustained in the 1990s with *Sankofa* (1993) and *Beloved*, all of which sharply reverse or debunk Hollywood's genteel sentimental depiction of slavery over the 80-year span of its "plantation genre" (Guerrero, 1993). Because *Amistad* recounts the actual events of a historic slave revolt on the high seas, and the successful repatriation of the rebellious Africans after an extensive court case, the film's narrative struggles with two issues pertaining to black violence that are not given much exposure in dominant commercial cinema. The first concerns the right, the necessity even, of the slave to rebel against the tyranny of his or her oppressors. The second issue has to do with the graphic revelation of the violence and oppression routinely inflicted on blacks by the daily operations of the slave system, and how that revelation recasts the perception of slavery in the American psyche, white and black.

Of course it's a long way from historical actuality to the big-budget Hollywood canvas, with its ultimate imperative that everybody's story be measured by its box office potential— that is, reduced to the compromises and revisions of its commodity status. Given the pressures on any blockbuster to return a profit at the ratio of three to one on an already hefty investment, it seems that in search of the broadest audience (read: white patronage), Spielberg approaches the issue of black revolt against European systems of tyranny, or even the frank depiction of those systems, with narrative restraint, to say the least. Yet, due to the inherent violent and irrepressible surplus of the subject matter, *Amistad*, unavoidably perhaps, unmasks the extreme cruelty of the slave system in historical realist terms.

Consequently, as in Spielberg's *Schindler's List* (1993), as well as the work of Lee and Singleton, here again we see the containing power of delimiting form and formula aimed at ensuring the biggest audience in direct conflict with the insurgent emancipation theme of *Amistad.*

Amistad opens with a spirited, furiously successful shipboard rebellion that soon goes adrift, with the black rebels being recaptured, imprisoned, and put on trial in New England. From here on the Africans are enslaved by the representational chains of Hollywood neo-liberalism as they are portrayed as confused, exotic creatures, denied all agency, voice, and centrality in what one would expect to be their story. The narrative drags, turning into a two-hour civics lesson about noble, well-intentioned whites defining and securing black freedom (Sale, 1998).[6]

When it comes to Hollywood's standard depiction of black freedom struggles, black characters tend to have no agency in the production of their own history and are reduced to passive victims emancipated by courageous whites (like the FBI in *Mississippi Burning* [1988] or the white lawyers in *Ghosts of Mississippi* [1996]). In fact, this stratagem is so cliché that Matthew McConaughey was recruited from *A Time to Kill* (1996) to play yet another dedicated white lawyer in defense of black liberation in *Amistad.* This convention is also present in *Schindler's List*, in which the narrative focus is on factory owner Oskar Schindler and concentration camp commander Amon Göth, with the Jews mostly reduced to the passivity of victims, a grim historical backdrop. What ever happened to the Warsaw Ghetto's resistance and rebellion?

However, any commercial film as visual commodity bears complex, contradictory forces and meanings that are not entirely containable, and are contested by many, often opposing, social perspectives. Regarding the depiction of violence in *Amistad*, this is no less the case. The slave revolt in *Amistad*'s opening, a revolt of oppressed against oppressor, has considerable action-adventure impact and historical appeal. Yet its placement is a subtle form of co-optation. Staging the insurrection in the opening moments of the narrative denies it any conclusive, cathartic force, thus displacing the insight that resistance against oppression in defense of one's freedom is a form of social justice, one afforded every white hero from John Wayne, Gary Cooper, and Henry Fonda onward. As we come to see, *Amistad*'s version of justice is a weary court case that essentially defines and celebrates constitutional definitions of *white* freedom. It is important to note that while the *Amistad* court case freed 38 Africans, it did nothing to alter the fate of millions of black people enslaved in the United States, or the efficient workings of the slave system itself. If anything, the slave system was further legally entrenched and refined by such sanctions as the Fugitive Slave Act of 1850 and the Dred Scott decision of 1857. In contrast, note who has agency, and the narrative positioning of the violent slave insurrection, in Haile Gerima's *Sankofa* (1993). Coming at the film's conclusion, this slave rebellion works as a resolution, underlining the brutality inflicted upon *Sankofa*'s blacks, broadcasting that they have agency, history, and justice in their own hands. What's at issue here is how the big-budget mainstream blockbuster, regardless of what its producers claim its subject is, almost always winds up talking about whiteness, guided by the persistent refrain of Eurocentrism that subtends its narrative (Dyer, 1997).

However, *Amistad* is punctuated with scenes that cannot be entirely repressed, scenes that are quite disturbing and challenging to comfortable, dominant notions of slavery, cinematic, psychic, or otherwise. As noted, Hollywood's depiction of slavery has experienced a sharp reversal of meaning since the resistant blaxploitation flicks of the 1970s. By now, the plantation more closely resembles the blood-soaked ground of the concentration camp than it does the majestic site of aristocratic Southern culture and gentility. So the irrepressible horror of the slave trade comes into disturbing focus with *Amistad's* depictions of the infamous Middle Passage, and with one particularly stunning scene when commerce and mass murder converge with brutal clarity. This happens when the Spanish slavers discover that they don't have enough rations to keep their entire human cargo alive for the Atlantic crossing. Echoing the death camp scene in *Schindler's List,* in which the weak are culled from the strong, in *Amistad* the cargo's weak and sickly are stripped naked, chained together, and very efficiently thrown overboard. Besides the naked, chained bodies, what is more disturbing about the scene's violence is the banal utility seen in the practices of maintaining human beings as slaves for profit. This insight is reinforced by other scenes of maintenance and discipline, in which slaves are fed, flogged, and washed in order to enhance their commodity value on the auction block in the New World. Very much like *Schindler's List, Amistad's* true force resides in its visual shock value, and in those resistant images, currents, and arguments that escape the policing of Hollywood's neoliberal, paternalist discourse. Relevant to the fundamental problem with both *Amistad* and *Schindler's List,* one critic puts it succinctly when he asks why *Schindler's List* "is so complicit with the Hollywood convention of showing catastrophe primarily from the point of view of the perpetrators" (Bernstein, 1994, p. 429).

No discussion of black violence as cinema would be complete without the mention of dominant cinema's depiction of contemporary, black Africa on the big screen. As Africa resides in the Western imaginary, *at best,* as a vast zone of war, poverty, disease and underdevelopment (without really understanding how it got, or is persistently kept, that way), Hollywood's recent mid-budget productions have depicted "the dark continent" mostly through the lens of violence as an assortment of historical agonies. Certainly recent examples, *Hotel Rwanda* (2004), *Blood Diamond* (2006), and *The Last King of Scotland* (2006), depicting genocide, dictatorship, and neoslavery, confirm this trope. Don Cheadle and Sophie Okonedo of *Hotel Rwanda* do an excellent job of dramatizing the Hollywood formula of presenting historical violence through the lens of the heroic individual, which flattens out and backgrounds the historical and social circumstances of this genocide.[7]

Besides their depiction of contemporary violence in the service of historical epic, *The Last King of Scotland* and *Blood Diamond* share variations on "the black/white buddy" theme. In *The Last King,* the paranoiac tyrant, Idi Amin (Forest Whitaker), is coupled with his Scotsman, physician confidant (James McAvoy); in *Blood Diamond,* work slave (Djimon Hounsou) is coupled with white redeemer (Leonardo DiCaprio). Considering the historical process of producing diamonds in Africa, from colonial conquest to apartheid to bush wars, there resides a nagging, ironic question implicit in the title *Blood Diamond:* is there only one? But also, if there are more, how can you tell which ones are drenched, or not, in blood?

Conclusion

I have no doubt that the cinematic depiction of black violence expressed in a variety of mixtures between entertainment and edification will continue to evolve as an inseparable part of Hollywood's accelerating commitment to all forms of cinematic violence as a technology-enabled, profit-driven industry strategy. Predictably, even though the 'hood-homeboy genre has been played out (Guerrero, 1998), the film industry will continue to produce a certain number of popcorn violence–saturated, empty entertainments like *Belly* or *State Property* (2002), or the more restrained, complex and socially grounded *Slam* (1998). Hope resides in the more innovative ways in which black filmmakers deploy violence in the service of their takes on realism, or the revision of social or historical issues from a black point of view. One can see suggestions of new directions in several recent black-inspired, black-cast commercial productions, including the Spike Lee–produced *Tales from the Hood* (1995) and the Oprah Winfrey–inspired and –produced *Beloved*.

A horror flick, *Tales from the Hood* makes it clear that for blacks, the horrific repressed fears returning in the form of the monstrous are markedly political and have to do with the great violent horrors of African American life: police brutality, lynching, racism, domestic abuse, and the catastrophic effects of overall social inequality. In its mix of popcorn and historical violence, the monsters that arise in *Tales* are more literal than metaphorical: corrupt, brutal cops framing black citizens, criminally violent 'hood-homeboys bent on autogenocide, and spouses who turn into violent monsters in front of their wives and children.

Similarly, *Beloved* struggles to innovate and frankly depict the reality and consequences of slavery's violence through the metaphor of scarring, both physical and psychic. The violent horror of slavery is revealed in "rememory" in a series of flame-lit, nightmarish flashbacks of hangings, whippings, and bizarre mutilations that continue to haunt and scar the psyches, the narrative present, and the bodies of the film's black cast. Ultimately, then, what will continue to subtly influence the trajectory of black screen violence and suggest new creative directions for its expression and critical understanding will be the persistent and conscientious visions of wave after wave of new black filmmakers, in all of their racial and heterogeneous incarnations as gays, women, men, subalterns, artists, intellectuals, and rebels, and their ability to bring fresh narrative, social, and representational possibilities to the big screen.

References

Amis, M. (1996). Blown away. In K. French (Ed.), *Screen violence* (pp. 12–15). London: Bloomsbury.

Bell, D. (1995). Racial realism—After we're gone: Prudent speculations on America in a post-racial epoch. In R. Delgado (Ed.), *Critical race theory: The cutting edge* (pp. 2–8). Philadelphia: Temple University Press.

Bernstein, M. A. (1994). The *Schindler's List* effect. *The American Scholar, 13*, 429–432.

Collins, P. H. (2000). *Black feminist thought: Knowledge, consciousness, and the politics of empowerment*. New York: Routledge.

Dyer, R. (1997). *White*. London: Routledge.

Fabrikant, G. (1996, November 11). Harder struggle to make and market black films. *The New York Times*, p. D1.

Foucault, M. (1979). *Discipline and punish: The birth of the prison*. New York: Vintage Books.

Gabler, N. (1997, November 16). The end of the middle. *New York Times Magazine*, pp. 76–78.

Giles, J. (1993, July 19). A "Menace" has Hollywood seeing double. *Newsweek*, p. 52.

Girard, R. (1972). *Violence and the sacred*. Baltimore: Johns Hopkins University Press.

Groth, G. (1997). A dream of perfect reception: The movies of Quentin Tarantino. In T. Frank & M. Weiland (Eds.), *Commodify your dissent* (p. 186). New York: W. W. Norton.

Guerrero, E. (1993). *Framing blackness: The African American image in film.* Philadelphia: Temple University Press.

Guerrero, E. (1998). A circus of dreams and lies: The black film wave reaches middle age. In J. Lewis (Ed.), *The New American Cinema* (pp. 328–352). Durham, NC: Duke University Press.

Hacker, A. (1997). *Money: Who has how much and why.* New York: Scribner.

Kolker, R. (2001). *Film form and culture.* McGraw-Hill.

Massood, P. (1993). *Menace II Society. Cineaste, 20*(2), 44–45.

Monk-Turner, E., Ciba, P., Cunningham, M., McIntire, P. G., Pollard, M., & Turner, R. (2004). A content analysis of violence in American war movies. *Analyses of Social Issues and Public Policy, 4,* 1–11.

Quart, L. (1996). Spike Lee's *Clockers:* A lament for the urban ghetto. *Cineaste, 22*(1), 9–11.

Sale, M. M. (1998). *The slumbering volcano: American slave ship revolts and the production of rebellious masculinity.* Durham, NC: Duke University Press.

Shohat, E., & Stam, R. (1994). *Unthinking Eurocentrism.* New York: Routledge.

Study finds white families' wealth advantage has grown. (2004, October 18). *The New York Times,* p. A13.

Walker, A. (1983). *In search of our mothers' gardens.* New York: Harcourt.

Weintraub, B. (1993, June 10). Twins' movie-making vision: Fighting violence with violence. *The New York Times,* p. C13.

Willis, S. (1997). *High contrast: Race and gender in contemporary Hollywood film.* Durham, NC: Duke University Press.

Notes

1. An earlier version of this chapter appeared as "Black Violence as Cinema: From Cheap Thrills to Historical Agonies" in *Violence and American Cinema,* edited by J. David Slocum (New York: Routledge, 2001).

2. The racial income gap reveals the relative position of black and white earners. In 1975, blacks made $605 for every $1,000 that whites earned; by 1995 that figure had dropped to a black $577 for every white $1,000 (Hacker, 1997). The "wealth gap" is even more telling; white households have a median net worth 14 times that of black households ("Study finds," 2004).

3. According to Monk-Turner et al. (2004), "a taste for violence, like any addiction, needs more of a fix over time. We believe that it will take more violence, and more graphic violence, to capture the attention of modern audiences" (p. 3).

4. Transcoding can be understood as the way that the social world is represented in film.

5. *Mise-en-scène* is a French term and originates in the theater. It means, literally, "put in the scene." For film, it has a broader meaning, and refers to almost everything that goes into the composition of the shot, including the composition itself: framing, movement of the camera and characters, lighting, set design and general visual environment, even sound as it helps elaborate the composition (Kolker, 2001).

6. Besides an excellent historical survey *of* the *Amistad* affair, Sale here gives a good account of how the *Amistad* rebels were constructed as passive "happy-go-lucky children in need of protection" at the bottom of the abolitionist defense council's hierarchy of concerns.

7. The HBO feature *Sometimes in April* (2005) provides a politically complex counterpoint to *Hotel Rwanda.*

DON'T WORRY, WE ARE ALL RACISTS!

Crash and the Politics of Privatization

Susan Searls Giroux and Henry A. Giroux

P
ublic reaction to the summer 2005 blockbuster *Crash* is a study in paradox. Well before it received the Oscar for Best Picture of the Year in 2006, Paul Haggis's directorial debut generated a great deal of discussion and no small amount of controversy in the media. Reviewers of the film tended to fall into two camps, describing it as gritty realism or sentimental manipulative melodrama; characters as believable or utterly stock; the central theme as committed to unmasking racism or to explaining it away in pious nostrums about the tragically flawed propensity of all humans to fear and distrust "the other." The heated debates over *Crash* show little sign of abatement—especially given its new life on the college film circuit. Indeed, on that most combustible of public issues—race—some critics even went so far as to publicly challenge colleagues who penned unfavorable reviews of the film, reducing intellectual integrity to a political litmus test in which disparagement of the film translated into an unqualified endorsement of racist expression and exclusion.

Crash narrates the interconnected lives of some 15 characters—black, white, Latina, Asian—within a 36-hour time frame on a cold Christmas day in post-riot, post-9/11 Los Angeles. The film begins with a paradox that captures the dominant mood about the politics and representations of race in America. Rear-ended on their way to a murder scene, Detective Graham Waters (Don Cheadle) and his partner and girlfriend Ria (Jennifer Esposito) respond to the accident in ways that communicate beyond the literal collision of metal and glass parts on foggy Mulholland Drive in car-obsessed Los Angeles. The scene reveals what happens when strangers are forced to rub against and engage each other across the divisive fault lines of race, class, ethnicity, and fear. For Waters, the collision gives rise to a doleful rumination about the loss of contact, if not of humanity, in a city where people appear atomized and isolated in their cars, homes, neighborhoods, workplaces, and daily lives. Desperate for a sense of community, if not for feeling itself, melancholic police detective Waters ponders, "In any real city, you walk, you know? You brush past people, people bump into you. In L.A., nobody touches you. We're always behind this metal and glass. I think we miss that touch so much that we crash into each other, just so we can feel something." Ria is less philosophical about the collision and jumps out of the car to confront the Asian woman who hit them. Any pretense to tolerance and human decency soon disappears, as the crash becomes a literal excuse for both women to hurl racial epithets at one another.

A scene that begins with a rumination about the loss of community and meaningful contact ends in an exchange of racist slurs inaugurating the polarities and paradoxes that are central to the structural, ideological, and political organization of the remainder of the film. Like *Magnolia* (1999), *Amores perros* (2000), *21 Grams* (2003), *Syriana* (2005), and

SOURCE: *Third Text* (2007). Vol. 21:6, pp. 745–759. Taylor & Francis (UK) Journals.

Babel (2006), among other celebrated films, *Crash* maps a series of interlocking stories with random characters linked by the gravity of racism and the diverse ways in which they inhabit, mediate, reproduce, and modify its toxic values, practices, and effects. Episodic encounters reveal not just a wellspring of seething resentment and universal prejudice, but also a vision of humanity marked by internal contradictions as characters exhibit values and behaviors at odds with the vile racism that more often than not offers them an outlet for their pent-up fear and hatred. Put on full display, racism is complicated by and pitted against the possibility of a polity enriched by its diversity, a possibility that increasingly appears as a utopian fantasy as the film comes to a conclusion.

The unexpected confrontation, the nerve-racking shocks, and the random conflicts throughout the film often require us to take notice of others, sometimes forcing us to recognize what is often not so hidden beneath the psychic and material relations that envelop our lives. But not always. Crashing into each other in an unregulated Hobbesian world where fear replaces any vestige of solidarity can also force us to retreat further into a privatized world far removed from the space of either civic life or common good. *Crash*'s director and screenwriter, Paul Haggis, plays on this double trope as a structuring principle that makes people uneasy, yet also in a more profound and troubling sense, more comfortable, especially if they are white. When racist acts are exposed in a progressive context, it is assumed that they will be revealing, furthering our understanding of the history, conditions, and agents that produce such acts. Equally important is the need to undo the stereotyping that gives meaning and legitimacy to racist ideologies. Haggis moves beyond the opening scene of his film to explore in detailed fashion the power of racial stereotyping and how it complicates the lives of the perpetrators and the victims, but ultimately *Crash* does very little to explore the historical, political, and economic conditions that produce racist practices and exclusions and how they work outside of the visibility of serendipitous interpersonal collisions in ways that might reveal the continuous, structural dimensions of everyday racism. *Crash* foregrounds racism, mimicking the logic of colorblindness currently embraced by both conservatives and liberals, but Haggis takes the truth out of such criticism by an appeal to the liberal logic of "flawed humanity" in an attempt to complicate the individual characters who allow deeply felt prejudices to govern their lives. *Crash* unfolds another paradox in which social life becomes more racially inflected and more exclusionary just as dominant discourses and representations of racism become increasingly privatized. In short, for all its pyrotechnics, *Crash* gives off more heat than light. It renders overt racist expression visible, only to banish its more subtle articulations to invisibility, along with its deeply structural and institutional dimensions. Theorizing racism as a function of private discrimination—a matter of individual attitude or psychology—denies its role as a systemic political force with often dire material consequences.

Yet the public conversation about *Crash* in all its vivid contradiction has something to teach us, revealing the widespread confusion over the meaning and political significance of race in an allegedly colorblind society. That the same film can be read as a searing indictment of America's deep-seated racism and also as its very denial, in the form of grand and forgiving assessments of the all-too-human tendency toward misunderstanding and fear, reflects the kind of schizophrenia that marks the politics of race in the post–civil rights era. That such a film can win an Oscar at a time marked by rabid racial backlash only underscores this tension. With the formal dismantling of institutional, legal segregation, most Americans believe that racism is an unfortunate and bygone episode in American history, part of a past that has been more than adequately redressed and is now best forgotten, even as informal, market-based resegregation proliferates in the private sector. In spite of ample research on race and inequality in the United States, many white Americans believe that white equality, integration, and racial justice are not just established ideals, but accomplished realities.[1] A recent report by the Pew Research Center found that 68 percent of whites did not believe that the government's response to Hurricane Katrina "revealed the persistence of racial inequality" whereas 71 percent of blacks viewed the response as an expression of discrimination on the part of the racial state (Allen, 2005). If inequality persists today between blacks and whites, so mainstream opinion goes, it is a function not of structural disadvantage (i.e., dilapidated, dysfunctional schools; rampant unemployment or underemployment; unequal access to loans and mortgages; police harassment and profiling or mass incarceration; etc.), but rather of poor character. Reinforced by the neoliberal mantra that negotiating life's problems is a singularly individual challenge, forms of racist expression and exclusion are denied their social origin and reduced to matters of personal psychology—a function of individual discrimination (or discretion, as archconservatives like Dinesh D'Souza would insist [Goldberg, 2002]). Not only are racial logics personalized, they are also radically depoliticized. As a complex set of historical and contemporary injustices, racisms—the plural underscoring their multiple and shifting nature—are analytically banished from the realm of the political. The role of the state, political economy, segregation, colonialism, capital, class exploitation, and imperialism are excised from public memory and from accounts of political conflict. As Wendy Brown (2006) observes, when emotional and personal vocabularies are substituted for political ones, when historically conditioned suffering and humiliation are reduced to basic forms of a presumably universal "difference," calls for "tolerance" or "respect for others" are substituted for real political transformation. Social justice and action devolves into sensitivity training, and the possibilities for political redress dissolve into self-help therapy. The oddly despairing and redemptive ethos of *Crash* marks the transition from an earlier generation's commitment to civil rights to the compromised contemporary insistence on civility, for which Rodney King's plaintive inquiry "Can't we all just get along?" provides the dominant refrain.

The intersection of racism and what we call its "humanization" comes into full view in a number of scenes in *Crash* that weave a diverse tapestry of actions held together by the intersections of difference, fear, and violence. Haggis begins the task of making racism visible—while implicating its victims and perpetrators—by structuring one of the most important scenes in the film around a carjacking. Haggis and his wife were actual victims of a carjacking in Los Angeles, an experience that provided the backdrop for writing the script.

Circling back to the afternoon before the first depicted crash on Mulholland Drive, two young black men in their 20s emerge from a bistro in an upscale white neighborhood. Anthony (Chris "Ludacris" Bridges) complains to Peter (Larenz Tate) about the daily stereotyping and humiliations visited upon poor people of color from both blacks and whites. He launches into the beginning of what will be an ongoing treatise on anti-black racism in America, ranging from the bad service he received in the restaurant by a black waitress to corporate hip-hop as a way of perpetuating black-on-black violence. Given a city wracked by two major racial uprisings and infamous for the racist violence of its police force, Anthony's assessment of internalized white supremacist beliefs would appear on target. His tirade is interrupted when he spots a wealthy white woman react in fear upon seeing him with his friend. Anthony is outraged:

Man, look around you, man! You couldn't find a whiter, safer, or better-lit part of the city right now, but yet this white woman sees two black guys who look like UCLA students strolling down the sidewalk, and her reaction is blind fear? I mean, look at us, dog! Are we dressed like gang-bangers? Huh? No. Do we look threatening? No. Fact: If anybody should be scared around here, it's us. We're the only two black faces surrounded by a sea of over-caffeinated white people patrolled by the trigger-happy LAPD. So you tell me, why aren't we scared?

Anthony responds with irony to this classic Fanonian moment of being "caught in the gaze," making it clear that if anyone should be afraid of racial violence it should be he and Peter, not white people, and especially not rich whites. Rather than allowing his audience to ponder this insight, Haggis performs a cheap reversal. Peter responds to Anthony's rhetorical question in wry tones, "Because we got guns." In a startling turn of events, the two young men then force the wealthy couple out of their black Lincoln Navigator and speed away from the crime scene. An encounter that at first seems to underscore the indignity and injustice of the racist gaze is dramatically canceled out when the white woman's fear proves legitimate. The stereotype of the dangerous black man is suddenly made all too real, an empirically justified fact. In an effort to underscore the basic contradictions that mark us all as human, Haggis undercuts whatever insight the film offers about the contemporary racist imagination, which often equates the culture of blackness with the culture of criminality.

Haggis plays on and extends the dominant presumption of black criminality in the following sequence. Waters and his partner soon find themselves at the scene of another crime: a white undercover detective named Conklin (Martin Norseman) has shot and killed a black man driving in a Mercedes. Unfortunately for Conklin, the black man turns out to be a police officer in the Hollywood division. Conklin claims he shot in self-defense, but this does not ring true to Waters, who quickly discovers that this is the third black man Conklin has killed in the line of duty. Haggis toys with a liberal sensibility that would assume this to be another tragic example of the violence of racial profiling, and Conklin a pernicious profiler. But he soon shatters this liberal presumption as the detectives discover that the black cop is dirty, having cut himself into the L.A. drug trade. In a series of intertwined scenes, black people are characterized as complicit with racist practices or as flawed individuals whose sorry plight has less to do with racial subjection than with their own lack of character, individual fortitude, or personal responsibility. And the stereotypes cut across gender and class lines.

For all of the pious defense of Haggis's rigorous antiracism among film critics, it is curious to note that none reflect on the utterly offensive portrayal of black women in the film, of whom we are introduced to three. The most damaging portrayal is of Waters's mother (Beverly Todd), who is represented as cruel and dysfunctional, a crack addict whose lack of discrimination and judgment results in her doting on her wayward son, Peter, who is a carjacker, to the exclusion of the more responsible and hardworking Waters, the only functional member of the family. Waters's mother is a grown-up version of the infamous "welfare queen," a slander coined by the presidential campaign of Ronald Reagan and kept in circulation by conservative and liberal ideologues who pushed for dismantling the welfare state. Similarly, the portrayal of an African American women named Shaniqua (Loretta Devine) as the heartless, bureaucratic insurance supervisor who works for the L.A. public health service is equally vicious. In an instance of alleged "reverse racism," she denies an elderly and probable prostate cancer victim in severe pain a visit to a specialist because his son is a white, racist cop. And if Shaniqua's bigotry is not clear enough in this instance, we meet her again at the end of the film when she is rear-ended at a traffic light. Emerging from her car, she angrily shouts at the Asian driver who hit her car, "Don't talk to me unless you speak American." Shaniqua stands in as the bad affirmative action hire willing to punish poor whites because of her own racial hostility. Why bother with a critique of the social state or the crumbling and discriminatory practices of an ineffectual welfare system when heartless, hapless, and cruel black women like Shaniqua can be conjured up from the deepest fears of the white racist unconscious? The third portrayal is of wealthy, light-skinned Christine (Thandie Newton), first encountered when she performs oral sex on husband Cameron (Terrence Howard) while he drives home from an awards dinner. She quickly becomes the overly sexed and out of control black woman with a big mouth who has no idea how to negotiate racial boundaries. After being pulled over by a white racist cop to whom she mouths off, she is subsequently subjected to a humiliating body search. As humiliating as is the violence she experiences from the racist and sadistic cop, Christine appears irresponsible and unsympathetic, if not quite deserving of the racial and sexual violence she has to endure. Even Waters, who provides a sense of complexity and integrity that holds together the different tangents of the story, is eventually portrayed as a corrupt cop willing to corroborate in a lie about the shooting of a black officer; he will end up framing a not quite innocent white cop in order to keep his brother out of jail, get a promotion, and provide political advantage with the black community for the L.A. District Attorney (Brendan Fraser). Such scenes participate in a "colorblinding racism" that tends to focus on white victimization while denying blacks grounds for protestation by rendering them complicitous with their own degradation.

But Haggis tempers his own confusion about the constitutive elements of the new racism, who perpetuates it, and under what conditions by powerfully organizing *Crash* around the central motif that everyone indulges in some form of prejudice. As Haggis explains in an interview for *LA Weekly*:

> We are each such bundles of contradictions...You can conduct your life with decency most of your days, only to be amazed by what will come out of your mouth in the wrong situation. Are you a racist? No—but you sure were in that situation! ... Our contradictions define us. (Feeney, 2005)

In other words, some racists can be decent, caring human beings and some decent caring human beings can also be racists. In this equal-opportunity scenario, racism assumes the public face of a deeper rage, fear, and frustration that appears universally shared and enacted by all of L.A.'s urban residents. This free-floating rage and fear, in Haggis's worldview, is the driving force behind racist expression and exclusion. Thus racism is reduced to individual prejudice, a kind of psychological mechanism for negotiating interpersonal conflict and situational difficulties made manifest in emotional outbursts and irrational fears. Without denying its psychological dimensions, what such a definition of racism cannot account for is precisely racism's collusion with rationality, the very "logical" use to which racism has *historically* been put to legitimate the consolidation of economic and political power in favor of white interests.

Perhaps more important, once questions of history and power are excised from public consciousness, racial inequality can be "transformed from its historical manifestations and effects perpetuated for the most part by whites against those who are not white into 'reverse discrimination' against whites who now suffer allegedly from preferential treatment" (Goldberg, 2002, p. 230). We offer two elaborated examples, perhaps the two most remarked upon scenes in *Crash*—the first sequence involving two LAPD cops, the utterly venomous, racist veteran cop Ryan (Matt Dillon) and his sympathetically drawn rookie partner, Hanson (Ryan Phillippe), who pull over the upper-middle-class black couple to whom we have already alluded. The other scene portrays a domestic dispute between utterly opportunistic district attorney Rick Chabot (Brendan Fraser) and his spoiled, overtly racist wife Jean (Sandra Bullock).

The first sequence involves Officer Ryan on the phone with the aforementioned HMO representative, Shaniqua—a conversation that ends on a very sour note. This prelude is important because it is intended to provide a context for the even more disturbing event about to unfold. When Ryan returns to the squad car, he and his partner witness a black SUV glide by, and they decide to follow. It is not the car involved in the earlier carjacking, but Ryan spies something amiss. In the afterglow of a little sexual foreplay, the couple is amused, but things turn more serious when Ryan asks a very sober husband, Cameron, to step out of the vehicle to see if he has been drinking. Christine, who has been drinking, takes offence and proceeds to verbally lambaste the officer as, unbidden, she too steps out of the SUV. Ryan calls the rookie for backup and insists the two put their hands against the vehicle to be patted down, a request that further infuriates Christine, whose assault has turned utterly profane and inflammatory—against the protests of her husband, who demands that she stop talking. But it is too late, she has crossed the line, and Ryan feels the couple needs to be taught a lesson. He proceeds to sexually molest Christine in the guise of police procedure while demanding from her husband, who helplessly looks on, an apology for their illicit behavior on the road. The producer and his wife return to their vehicle silenced, humiliated, and broken.

While the scene renders Ryan entirely unsympathetic and hateful, our judgment is presumably to be tempered by taking account of the context in which the abuse has unfolded. It also sets us up for Ryan's later redemption when he happens upon a car wreck and saves Christine from a blaze that is about to consume her and her SUV. In keeping with Haggis's understanding of how racist outbursts occur, racism is repeatedly represented in a series of isolated incidents rather than as a systemic and institutional phenomenon that informs every aspect of daily life. From Ryan's perspective, he has endured the assaults of two black women one after the other: he is the white victim of an allegedly incompetent affirmative action hire, as he later reveals, and of "reverse racism," since Christine called him "cracker," among other names, in a litany of personal assaults. Apparently Ryan has regained some equilibrium when, in a rather incredible coincidence, he saves Christine's life, in spite of her aggressive efforts to resist his initial attempt. Having staged a profound disidentification between the audience and Ryan, Haggis now repositions us to admire the officer's bravery and selflessness. Curiously, critics have read this scene as indicative of Ryan's contriteness, even moral growth, his coming to terms with the consequences of his earlier actions and his efforts to transcend a racist attitude. But is this really what we witness? Does remorse drive his "heroic actions" in saving Christine, or is he simply doing his job, which is to serve

Photo 4.1   From racist to savior in *Crash*, Ryan (Matt Dillon) saves Christine (Thandie Newton) from a near-fatal car accident.

and protect the public—a commitment he utterly violated scenes ago? Is there anything truly productive or uplifting in the pendulum swing of his character from racial victim to racial savior (with rapid downward momentum generating a brief sadistic lapse quickly forgotten if not forgiven in the upward arc of his transcendence)—or are these precisely the subject positions open to whites who refuse to engage self-reflectively and self-critically on deeply historical and power-infused social relations?

We are similarly set up for a "surprise" reversal (though by the end of the film the gesture has become well-nigh predictable) in the sequence involving the carjacking. As we've already argued, Haggis has flipped the script on two young African American men, who initially transcend the "thug" stereotype and appear educated, even critically conscious of such racist positioning, only to morph back into mainstream America's worst fears—a pair of gun-toting nightmares materialized in the flesh. Not only does the scene insert a kind of empirical validity to the presumption of black criminality, it manages to pathologize critical thought in the translation, a double demonization entirely in keeping with the conservativism of the colorblind commitments of the post–civil rights era. But Haggis's intentions become more curious still. Shortly, we find the victimized DA and his wife at home. The district attorney consults his staff, preoccupied with how to spin the situation so as not to lose either the "law and order vote" or that of the black community—a tongue-in-cheek moment satirizing the pretense to governmental colorblindness while the language of race is invoked in private policy decisions to strategize favorable outcomes. His wife Jean (Sandra Bullock), meanwhile, bristles in the kitchen as she watches a young Latino male, who she quickly surmises is a threatening gangbanger, change the locks. As with Ryan, the stress of the evening has gotten the better of her and she explodes in an emotional fit before her husband. She demands to have the locks changed again, referring to the evening's earlier incident when she had a gun pointed at her face:

It was my fault because I knew it was going to happen! But if a white person sees two black men walking towards her and she turns and walks in the other direction, she is a racist, right. Well I got scared and I didn't say anything and ten seconds later I had a gun in my face. And now I'm telling you that your amigo in there is going to sell our key to one of his homeys, and this time it would be really fucking great if you acted like you actually gave a shit!

Jean's comments are of particular interest for a number of reasons. Like Ryan, Jean for the moment appears barred from the human race—but only for the moment. Like Ryan, she assumes the posture of being victimized by the social dictates and policy measures associated with antiracism. For her, discrimination dissolves into discretion: if avoidance of certain groups is enacted through rational application of generalizations backed by statistical evidence about the dangers associated with those populations, then it can't be racist (Goldberg, 2002). Jean's fear at the very sight of two young black men proves justified. Before they do anything, they are guilty of blackness; they "are" a crime. Now she is angry at being thought of as a racist, and as such exhibits what Jean-Paul Sartre called "bad faith."[2] Jean throws herself into an emotional fit in order to take on an identity that enables her to evade herself. She presents herself manifestly as what she is (i.e., a racist) in order ironically to evade what she is.

We have spent some time unpacking these scenes because, we argue, they reveal in synecdochal form the broader politics of the film. In similar ways, *Crash* ironically evades the question of racism in all its sociohistorical force and political consequence while at the same time seeming to face it. It simultaneously insists that we take account of our own prejudices and their hateful, material consequences and unburdens us of the task at the same time by rendering such dispositions as timeless, universal attributes of a flawed humanity. Complicating further the gesture toward responsibility is the relatively unthinking way in which characters engage in racist verbal assault or physical violence and the frequently unthinking way in which they act humanely toward others. By rendering such actions as reflexive, emotive, or generally prereflective, *Crash* calls upon us to become consciously reflective and responsible for how we negotiate a post-9/11 urban context rife with fearsome strangers—a positioning it simultaneously undermines.

The apparent answer to the problem of white victimization is tolerance—and for their later expressions of tolerance, both Jean (by the simple gesture of affirming her Latina maid) and Officer Ryan are cinematically redeemed. The effort to humanize stark racists has earned Haggis critical accolades. Critics like David Denby (2005) were quick to seize on this alleged insight on the part of the film:

Crash is the first movie I know of to acknowledge not only that the intolerant are also human but, further, that something like white fear of black street crime . . . *isn't always irrational.* [emphasis added] . . . In Haggis's Los Angeles, the tangle of mistrust, misunderstanding, and foul temper envelops everyone; no one is entirely innocent or entirely guilty. (p. 110)

Within this equal-opportunity view of racism, the primary "insight" of the film trades in the worst banalities: there is good and bad in everyone. In such a context, the question of responsibility for the violence that racism inevitably produces becomes free-floating. It is a logic sadly reminiscent of the "banality of evil" that Hannah Arendt discovered during the Adolf Eichmann trial in Jerusalem; everyone, she recalled, looked for "Eichmann the monster," only to find a man very much like themselves. That such attempts at "humanization" should now be equated with redemption is a tragic denial of that history. The racism both on display and normalized in *Crash* is banal in Arendt's terms precisely because it is so thoughtless, or, as she later put it, a "curious, quite authentic inability to think" (2003, p. 159). A willful forgetting of such banality cannot elude the question of responsibility or forget that justice "'makes sense' only as a protest against injustice" (Bauman & Tester, 2001, p. 63). Any notion of humanization based on such forgetting is apparently the very precondition for the noncruel to do cruel things.[3]

Crash's delineation of racial conflict and its alteration of the concept of racism from a power-laden mode of exclusion into a clash of individual prejudices both privatizes and depoliticizes race, drowning out those discourses that reveal how it is mobilized "around material resources regarding education, employment conditions, and political power" (Goldberg, 1994, p. 13). When the conditions that produce racist exclusions are rendered invisible, as they are in *Crash*, politics and social responsibility dissolve either into privatized guilt (one feels bad and helpless) or disdain (victims become perpetrators responsible for their own plight). In a universe in which we are all racist pawns, it becomes difficult to talk about responsibility—let alone the conditions that actually produce enduring racist representations, injustices, and violence, the effects of which are experienced in vastly different and iniquitous ways by distinct groups. The universalizing gesture implicit in Haggis's theory of racism cannot address the dramatic impact of racism on individuals and families marginalized by class and color, particularly the incarceration of extraordinary numbers of young black and brown male prisoners and the growth of the prison-industrial complex; a spiraling health crisis that excludes large numbers of minorities from health insurance or adequate medical care; crumbling city infrastructures; segregated housing; soaring unemployment among youth of color; exorbitant school dropout rates among black and Latino youth, coupled with the realities of failing schools more generally; and deepening inequalities of income and wealth between blacks and whites.[4] Nor can it grasp the enduring inequality that centuries of racist state policy has produced and is still, as Supreme Court Justice Ruth Bader Ginsburg observes, "evident in our workplaces, markets and neighborhoods" ("Race on screen," 1997). It is also evident in child poverty levels, which statistics show are "24.7 percent among African Americans, 21.9 percent among Hispanics, and 8.6 percent among non-Hispanic whites" (Chelala, 2006).

David Shipler (1998) argues powerfully that race and class are the two most powerful determinants shaping an allegedly postracist, post–civil rights society. After interviewing hundreds of people over a five-year period, Shipler wrote in *A Country of Strangers* that he bore witness to a racism that "is a bit subtler in expression, more cleverly coded in public, but essentially unchanged as one of the 'deep abiding currents' in everyday life, in both the simplest and the most complex interactions of whites and blacks." Positioned against civil rights reform and racial justice are reactionary and moderate positions ranging from the extremism of right-wing skinheads and Jesse Helms–like conservatism to the moderate "colorblind" positions of liberals such as Randall Kennedy, to tepid forms of multiculturalism that serve to vacuously celebrate diversity while undermining and containing any critical discourse of difference.[5] But beneath its changing veneers and expressions, racism is fundamentally about the relationship between politics and power—a historical past and a living present where racist exclusions appear "calculated, brutally rational, and profitable" (Goldberg, 1993, p. 105). It is precisely this analysis of politics, power, and history that *Crash* leaves largely unacknowledged and unexamined—with the single exception of a cheap dismissal by the assistant district attorney Flanagan (William Fichtner).

At the same time, we recognize that part of the popularity of *Crash* is due to its neorealistic efforts to make the new post-9/11 racial realities visible in American cities, especially in light of a pervasive ideology of race transcendence that refuses to acknowledge the profound influence that race continues to exert on how most people experience their everyday lives and their relationship with the rest of the world. *Crash* brings to the attention of the audience how racial identities are played out under the pressures of class, violence, and displacement. *Crash* also pluralizes the American racial landscape, making it clear that racism affects not only black populations. It is also refreshing to recognize that the Los Angeles that *Crash* portrays (in contrast to, say, the L.A. of *Short Cuts*) is not entirely white, and that the public sphere is a diverse one that reflects a cosmopolitan American audience. Mostly, *Crash* explodes the assumption that racism is a thing of the past in America, but then blunts the insight by denying both power and history. Instead, Haggis implies that racism may be a public toxin, but we are all touched by it because we are all flawed. But drawing attention to race is not enough, especially when racism is depicted in utterly depoliticized terms, sliding into an expression of individualized rage far removed from hierarchies and structures of power. *Crash* seduces its audiences with edgy emotive force, but renders the truth of racism comfortable because it is removed from the realm of responsibility or judgment. It enacts the evasion of collective responsibility in the face of a pervasive system of racism bounded by relations of power and structures of inequality that encourage such failures. This is not a film about how racism undermines the social fabric of democracy; it is a film about how racism gets expressed by a disparate group of often angry, alienated, and confused—but often decent—individuals.

Racism in America has an enduring, centuries-old history that has generated a set of economic conditions, structural problems, and exclusions that cannot be reduced to forms of individual prejudice prevalent across a racially and ethnically mixed polity in equal measure. While the expression of racism and its burdens cannot be reduced to specific groups, it is politically and ethically irresponsible to overlook how some groups bear the burden of racism much more than others. How does one theorize the concept of individual responsibility, character, or equal-opportunity intolerance within a social order in which the national jobless rate is about 6 percent, but unemployment rates for young men of color in places such as south central Los Angeles have topped 50 percent? How does one ignore the fact that it is widely recognized that a high school diploma is essential to getting a job when more than "half of all black men still do not finish high school" (Eckholm, 2006, p. A1)? Law professor David Cole (1999, p. 144) points out in *No Equal Justice* that while "76 percent of illicit drug users were white, 14 percent black, and 8 percent Hispanic—figures which roughly match each group's share of the general population," African Americans constitute "35 percent of all drug arrests, 55 percent of all drug convictions, and 74 percent of all sentences for drug offences." Within such a context, the possibilities for treating a generation of young people of color with respect, dignity, and support vanish, and with them the hope of overcoming a racial abyss that makes a mockery out of justice and a travesty of democracy.

In addition, it is crucial to point out that *Crash* apologizes for the growing violence and militarization of urban public space that are part of a "war on crime" largely waged against black and brown youth by what David Theo Goldberg (2002, p. 4) has called "the racial state." As the state is stripped of its welfare functions and negates any commitment to the social contract, Goldberg argues, its priorities shift from social investment to racial containment and its militarizing functions begin to function more visibly as a state apparatus through its control over the modes of rule and representation that it employs. Unfortunately, the film's commitment to privatized understandings of racism leaves intact the myth that collective problems can only be addressed as tales of individual plight that reduce structural inequality to individual pathologies—fear, alienation, selfishness, laziness, or violent predisposition. But the visibility of racism is not simply an outcome of people randomly crashing into each other. The harsh and relentless consequences of racism are not merely present when individuals collide. Racism structures everyday life and for most people is suffered often in silence, outside of the sparks of unintended crashes (Essed, 1991). Only white people have the privilege of becoming aware of racism as a result of serendipitous encounters with the Other. The fight against racism will not be successfully waged simply through the inane recognition that we are all racists.

The popularity of a film as deeply contradictory and often reactionary as *Crash* must be understood in the context of the growing backlash against people of color, immigration policy, the ongoing assault on the welfare state, the undermining of civil liberties, and the concerted attempts on the part of the U.S. government and others to undermine civil rights. *Crash* misrecognizes the politics of racism and refashions it as a new age bromide, a matter of inner angst and prejudices that simply need to be recognized and transcended, an outgrowth of rage waiting to be overcome through conquering our own anxieties and our fears of the Other. We need to do much more to challenge racism in its newest incarnation. We should therefore be very attentive not to fight ancillary battles, viewing racism as merely an individual pathology with terrible consequences. *Crash* is not about viewing the crisis of racism as part of the crisis of democracy, but the crisis of the alienated and isolated self in a hostile (because increasingly diverse) urban environment. Consequently, it offers no solutions for addressing the most important challenge confronting an inclusive democracy—to critically engage and eliminate the conditions that not only produce the deep structures of racism but also destroy the possibility for a truly democratic politics. The struggle against racism is not a struggle to be waged through guilt or a retreat into racially homogenous enclaves; it is a struggle for the best that democracy can offer, which, as Bill Moyers (2007) points out, means putting into place the material and symbolic resources that constitute the "the means of dignifying people so they become fully free to claim their moral and political agency." It is a struggle that should be waged in the media as part of a politics of cultural representation; it is a struggle that needs to be waged against the neoliberal and racializing state and its failure both to equitably distribute power, resources, and social provisions and to create the basic conditions of engaged citizenship. It is also a struggle to be waged in neighborhoods, schools, and all of those places where people meet, talk, interact, sometimes colliding but mostly trying to build a new sense of political community where racist exclusion rather than difference is viewed as the enemy of democracy.

References

Allen, J. (2005, October 31). The black and white of public opinion: Did the racial divide in attitudes about Katrina mislead us? [Press release]. Washington, DC: Pew Research Center. Retrieved February 19, 2012, from http://www.people-press.org/2005/10/31/the-black-and-white-of-public-opinion/.

Arendt, H. (2003). *Responsibility and judgment* (J. Kohn, Ed.). New York: Schocken Books.

Bauman, Z., & Tester, K. (2001). *Conversations with Zygmunt Bauman.* Cambridge, UK: Polity Press.

Brown, W. (2006). *Regulating aversion: Tolerance in the age of identity and empire.* Princeton, NJ: Princeton University Press.

Chelala, C. (2006). Rich man, poor man: Hungry children in America. *Seattle Times.* Retrieved February 19, 2012, from http://www.commondreams.org/views06/0104-24.htm

Cole, D. (1999). *No equal justice: Race and class in the American criminal justice system.* New York: New Press.

Denby, D. (2005, May 2). Angry People—*Crash. The New Yorker,* pp. 110–111.

Eckholm, E. (2006, March 20). Plight deepens for black men, studies warn. *The New York Times,* p. A1.

Essed, P. (1991). *Understanding everyday racism.* Newbury Park, CA: Sage.

Feeney, F. X. (2005, May 5). Million dollar boomer. *LA Weekly.* Retrieved April 23, 2009, from http://www.laweekly.com/2005-05-05/film-tv/million-dollar-boomer/

Goldberg, D. (1993). *Racist culture.* Cambridge, MA: Basil Blackwell.

Goldberg, D. (1994). Introduction. *Multiculturalism: A critical reader.* Cambridge, MA: Blackwell.

Goldberg, D. (2002). *The Racial state.* Oxford, UK: Blackwell.

Moyers, B. (2007). A time for anger, a call to action [Speech transcript]. Retrieved January 9, 2012, from www.commondreams.org/views07/0322–24.htm.

Race on screen and off. (1997, December 29). *The Nation,* p. 6.

Shipler, D. (1998). *A country of strangers: Blacks and Whites in America.* New York: Vintage.

Notes

1. Richard Morin, "Misperceptions Cloud Whites' View of Blacks," *Washington Post* (July 11, 2001), p. A1. See, for example, David R. Williams, "Race, Socioeconomic Status, and Health: The Added Effects of Racism and Discrimination," *Annals of the New York Academy of Sciences,* Vol. 896 (December 1999), pp. 173–188; Eduardo Bonilla-Silva, *Racism Without Racists: Color-Blind Racism and the Persistence of Racial Inequality in the United States* (Boulder, CO: Rowman & Littlefield, 2006).

2. For an elaborated discussion of this concept as an analytic for understanding racism, see Lewis Gordon, *Bad Faith and Antiblack Racism* (Atlantic Highlands, NJ: Humanities Press, 1995).

3. This theme is taken up brilliantly in Zygmunt Bauman, *Life in Fragments* (Malden, MA: Blackwell, 1995).

4. For a compilation of figures suggesting the ongoing presence of racism in American society, see Ronald Walters, "The Criticality of Racism," *Black Scholar, 26*(1) (Winter 1996), pp. 2–8; and Children's Defense Fund, *The State of Children in America's Union: A 2002 Action Guide to Leave No Child Behind* (Washington, DC: Children's Defense Fund Publication, 2002), p. xvii.

5. For a devastating critique of Randall Kennedy's move to the right, see Derrick Bell, "The Strange Career of Randall Kennedy," *New Politics,* 7(1) (Summer 1998), pp. 55–69.

Reading 4.3

Latinos/as Through the Lens

Carleen R. Basler

Motion pictures' unique power of attraction lies in the semblance of reality they convey. Through visual images, the medium of film is capable of creating a convincing version of reality to the viewer. The stories told through film resonate with audiences because they speak to some shared aspect of lived experience in the social world. But not all lived experiences are represented in film, and some are skewed by *racism* and *ethnocentrism*. The absence of minority ethnic and racial groups in film tells a Eurocentric story, while stereotypical representations of racial and ethnic groups have wide-reaching consequences in the attitudes and beliefs of both stigmatized and dominant group members (Roman 2000–2001).

What is the Latino/a story in film? Latinos/as are underrepresented in film, and when they do appear their images tend to be criminalized, sexualized, or victimized (Ramirez Berg 2002). These images have the potential to persuade audience members that those representations are "real," accurate, or valid, especially if the viewer has had limited interaction with Latinos/as. It is important to note that much of the literature about how certain ethnic groups have been depicted in film actually creates and often reinforces its own distortions, creating "stereotypes of movie stereotypes" (Cortés 1992: 75). The result for the dominant (white) group is reinforcement of individual and institutional racism (Roman 2000–2001). Members of the stereotyped group are also affected and at risk for internalizing the discredited and demeaning characteristics portrayed (Garcia Berumen 1995; Roman 2000–2001).

At this intersection of realities, one based on lived experience and one media created and projected, we can use the *sociological imagination* to explore the Latino/a American story. C. Wright Mills (1959) introduced the sociological imagination as a way of connecting individual experience and history, for understanding the relationship between the private (personal) and public (structural). Without the sociological imagination, "the difference between the individual people who participate in social life and the relationships that connect them to one another and to groups and societies" is too often ignored (Johnson 2008:12).

Using film as a medium for sociological analysis provides a method for exploring cultural stories told about groups not considered part of the "American mainstream." Viewing film from a sociological perspective enables us to observe which groups are used to represent the mainstream and how "others" are located in relation to the social order. American film representations of Latinos/as help unveil persistent and pervasive stereotypes that "other" Latinos/as, reinforcing their position as outsiders and "foreigners" (Roman 2000–2001). At the same time, we can look for ways that contemporary films are changing, becoming more inclusive, or telling different stories rooted in the lived experiences of the diverse population categorically defined as Latino/a.

Although the sociological examination of Latinos/as in film is relatively new, scholars already debate which film theories best explain the Latino/a experience in the film industry and the impact of projected Latino/a images through film. However, most agree a chronological examination of Latino/a images in film reflects larger sociopolitical processes in American history. This reading focuses on the history of Latinos/as in the United States in the context of the broader issues of race, ethnicity, social class, and gender, as conveyed through the medium of film.

Stereotypes in Film

Film stereotypes are formed by gathering certain group traits, sometimes even across groups, and assembling them into a particular image. The shaped image embodies stereotypical "looks," behaviors, and actions that are then reified as an accurate representation of members of that group (Rodriguez 1997). Positive stereotypes in film are more often associated with representations of "mainstream," or Anglo, Americans, and negative stereotypes tend to be linked to racial and ethnic "others." Stereotypical depictions of Latinos/as in film are often negative, placing them in the racial and ethnic "other" category.

The American movie industry's general indifference to making films with authentic Latino/a themes is a significant marker of Latinos/as' being "othered." The majority of mainstream movies reflect an ignorance of the multidimensional Latino/a experience in the United States, and many films continue to misrepresent the diversity of Latino/a ethnicities by reducing them to a monocultural cinematic stereotype. Such actions by the film industry and filmmakers adversely affect Latinos/as in their everyday lives, especially if cinematic stereotypes are accepted as real by general audiences. Additionally, Latinos/as who are continually exposed to only negative representations of their ethnic group suffer a form of *symbolic annihilation* (Valdivia 2010). According to Coleman and Yochim (2008), symbolic annihilation, "as it pertains specifically to race, . . . means that those racial groups who are not presented as fully developed in media, be it through absence, trivialization, or condemnation, may see their social status diminished" (p. 5). Thus, symbolic annihilation is more than the absence of a group or the negative stereotypes projected onto a group but extends to outcomes related to economic, political, and social inequality.

This reading begins with an overview of the history of the Latino/a image in the U.S. film industry, then outlines dominant stereotypes found in major motion pictures. The various ways in which Latinos/as have attempted to subvert and resist negative stereotypes, typecasting, and status quo filmmaking, thus challenging earlier film images and general attitudes regarding Latinos/as in the United States, are addressed next. Last, contemporary challenges to Latino/a representation in the film industry are explored.

Latinos/as and American Film

The Latino/a presence in American cinema is complicated by several factors, most notably the labeling of Latinos/as as "others," the changing cinematic representations of Latinos/as over time, and the production and maintenance of Latino/a film stereotypes for the viewing audience.

Labeling Latinos/as as the Other

The two most common terms used to describe people and cultures of Latin America in the United States are *Hispanic* and *Latino*. However, these two umbrella terms contain multiple meanings, including those connected to such identity markers as race, ethnicity, gender, sexuality, and politics (Noriega and Lopez 1996). Both *Hispanic* (a label created by the U.S. government that infers Spanish heritage) and *Latino* (a more encompassing term referring to individuals of Mexican, Cuban, Puerto Rican, or other Latin American descent) condense and oversimplify the diverse and wide range of histories, cultures, and people they are meant to represent. Some Latinos/as trace their ethnic origins to indigenous populations (such as the Incas, the Mayans, and the Aztecs) who occupied the lands before the arrival of the Europeans, while others maintain an African heritage, a vestige of the Caribbean and Central and South America's involvement in the African slave trade.

Although most Latinos/as recognize that part of their lineage is tied to European colonization, the *racialization* of the Latino/a image in American film functions to mark them as nonwhite (and potentially non-American) "others" in relation to Anglo characters. In American film (as well as in real life), socially constructed concepts of *race* intersect with dominant ideas about *national origin* and *ethnicity*, privileging an Anglo European historical narrative. Assumptions about the superiority of whiteness (or European heritage) still exist in American society and are reflected in American films. However, the racial and ethnic "hybridity" of Latino/a identity and the rising economic power of the Latino population are challenging the American film industry to be more inclusive and less racist in Latino/a film representations.

The Multiple Images of Latinos/as in Film History

From the very beginning of American cinema, Latinos/as have been portrayed in ways reflecting American foreign policy and attitudes toward Latin America. Early film representations reveal the burgeoning industry's view of Latinos/as and Latin Americans as racially and ethnically different from, and inferior to, Anglo Americans.

The realization of America's *Manifest Destiny*, the idea that Anglo Americans were "destined" by God to own, inhabit, and control all the lands between the Atlantic and Pacific oceans in North America, was facilitated by racializing the Native American and Mexican American populations as not "white." Early America's aggressive westward expansion wrested from Mexico control of the territories that became Texas, Arizona, Nevada, California, and New Mexico. Individuals whose families had occupied those lands for generations were quickly labeled nonwhites, subjected to removal and relocation, and treated as second-class citizens or noncitizens.

Cinematic representations of how "foreigners" looked (nonwhite), spoke (accented or "broken" English), and behaved (usually threatening or amoral) helped reinforce Anglo notions of Latinos/as as not "real" Americans. Conveying the national narrative of Anglo American virtue and Mexican vice, the silent film *Martyrs of the Alamo* (1915) visually confirmed for audiences the alleged threat Mexicans posed to Anglo Americans. The film was directed by William "Christy" Cabanne, D. W. Griffith's assistant, but Griffith (who directed *Birth of a Nation*) supervised the making of the film. In this rendition of the famed military conflict at the Alamo, white actors in "brown face" played the role of morally depraved Mexicans who were drunken, lecherous (toward white women), and without regard for basic human dignity (e.g., they shot their prisoners of war, while the Americans let their prisoners go free). Other Hollywood films from this period also reinforced the image of "despicable Mexicans who robbed, raped, and murdered their way through the Southwest" (Bender 2003:xiv). Films such as *The Greaser's Gauntlet* (D. W. Griffith, 1908) and *Broncho Billy and the Greaser* (1914), written and directed by and starring Gilbert M. "Broncho Billy" Anderson, confirmed "the Mexican as an evil and sinister villain" (Reyes and Rubie 1994:6).

From the silent films into the first "talkies," Latinos/as were almost always portrayed in negative stereotypical ways. However, cinematic representations of Latinos/as took a more benevolent turn after the 1930s. One pressure brought to bear was the ban by Mexico and Panama on Hollywood movies that cast Latinos/as in a negative light (Benshoff and Griffin 2004). In response, Hollywood began to tone down some of the most offensive symbols and images. During the government's propaganda campaign of the 1940s, known as the Good Neighbor Policy, a more benign yet romanticized depiction of Latin Americans and Latinos/as emerged. This campaign developed out of the economic interests and vision of the Rockefellers, who lobbied for the establishment of a government office on Inter-American Affairs, including a "Motion Picture Division that would concentrate its efforts on seeing that Hollywood films that heretofore had, by and large, presented negative stereotypical images of Latin Americans would now present Latin Americans in more favorable images" (Adams 2007:290). For its part, Hollywood embraced the opportunity to open the film market in Latin America, especially since World War II had severely curtailed film distribution in the European market.

Disney's family films *Saludos Amigos* (1943) and *The Three Caballeros* (1945) are examples of Hollywood's participation in the campaign to circulate positive images of the people and cultures of Latin America. The prominence of these films during that time have led some to describe Walt Disney as the "chief propagandist for the Good Neighbor Policy" (Richard 1993:273). Importantly, these films revealed, for the first time to U.S. audiences, the modernity of Latin American cities and peoples, challenging the negative Latino/a stereotypes dominating film up to that point (Adams 2007).

During this period there was also a rise in Latin American–themed musicals, including *Down Argentine Way* (1940), *Week-End in Havana* (1941), and *That Night in Rio* (1941), all created to inspire positive feelings among Americans and Latin Americans about U.S. foreign policy and relations in Latin America. In fact, these films were referred to as "Good Neighbor" musicals by the movie industry and reviewers. In these films, music, camaraderie, humor, and dance bring people from North and South American together in business ventures, romance, and friendship. However, even these more neighborly representations of Latin culture reflected Anglo conceptions of nonwhite otherness that would contribute to enduring stereotypes of Latinos/as and Latin Americans. One need only think of Carmen Miranda, the "lady in the tutti-frutti hat," to realize the staying power of these stereotypes. While some have argued that the Good Neighbor Policy films represented progress in Hollywood's portrayal of Latinos/as, others ask if exchanging "lazy greaseball" stereotypes for positive "happy children" stereotypes really is a less racist representation (Roberts 1993:33). While the Good Neighbor Policy films praised and idealized Latin Americans in other countries (Argentina, Cuba, Brazil), movies featuring American Latino/a characters were rarely positive.

In a modest response, the film industry produced *social problem films* to address the discrimination Latinos/as faced in America. As Herbert Gans (1964) defined the genre, the social problems film "deals explicitly with social, sexual, and political problems and their solution" (p. 327). For example, *A Medal for Benny* (1945) is the story of a Mexican-American War hero who is awarded the Congressional Medal of Honor posthumously. Although the film explores the social injustices faced by many Mexican Americans, it reflects the standard filmmaking of the period in its homogenized portrait of Latino/a people.

Other social problem films include *The Lawless* (1950), *Right Cross* (1950), and *My Man and I* (1952). These three films address racism, prejudice, and discrimination. In both *The Lawless* and *My Man and I*, Mexican immigrants provided the low-cost labor needed by the farmer (*My Man and I*) and the fruit industry (*The Lawless*) in California. Struggling to survive, the Mexican laborers are confronted with the racism of the white community (e.g., in *The Lawless*, the Mexicans are called "fruit tramps" by the whites who live in what is known as "the friendly town" of Santa Maria) and the police, who assume guilt at every turn. *Right Cross* challenges conventions of the time with a story of an interethnic relationship between Pat O'Malley (June Allyson) and Johnny Monterez (Ricardo Montalbán). A theme across the three films is that of immigrant assimilation and pride in American identity versus resentment and anger over mistreatment by whites.

Probably the best-known Latino/a social problem films was *Salt of the Earth* (1953), based on the true story of Mexican American miners and their wives who managed a successful strike against the mine owners for unsafe and exploitive work conditions. These early social problem films were certainly progressive for their time, but as the 1950s' obsession with Communism spread and the Red Scare infiltrated Hollywood, filmmakers afraid of being blacklisted for producing movies critical of the government quickly backed away from many racial and social justice film projects.

Between the 1950s and 1970s, Hollywood's representations of Latinos/as returned to the stereotypical patterns and practices employed in the decades before the Good Neighbor Policy. For example, the screen adaptation of the musical *West Side Story* (1961) racialized Puerto Ricans as nonwhite, non-American "others." In the opening scene of the film we see members of the Jets, children of white European immigrants, claiming "ownership" of the streets and basketball court in the face of racial incursion from the Sharks, Puerto Rican immigrants to New York City.

The film captures the tensions of an interethnic romance between the young Puerto Rican immigrant Maria (portrayed by Anglo American actress Natalie Wood) and Tony (Richard Beymer), her working class Polish American beau. While the film is considered a social critique of racial prejudice and ethnic competition in working class neighborhoods, the ideological articulation of the stereotype and identity of Puerto Rican immigrants suggested their need to assimilate to the "American way." At the same time, there were no openings for assimilation, as the divisions between the two communities were drawn and protected. The Jets "judge the Puerto Rican migration to the urban center as an invasion of cockroaches which reproduces without control and infects the territory" (Sandoval Sanchez 1994). Thus the racist rhetoric of rampant reproduction and spread of contagious, life-threatening disease effectively designates the immigrant group as not only outsiders, but less than human.

American films of this period often reflected the ambivalent relationship the United States has with its southern neighbors. Films such as *Touch of Evil* (1958) and *The Border*

(1982) portray the United States–Mexico borderland as frightening and dangerous. Other films that depict Mexico and the border as wild and lawless include *Young Guns* (1988), *La Bamba* (1987), and *Born in East L.A.* (1987). However, a few films, like the excellent *Lone Star* (1996), attempted to highlight the difficulties and tensions surrounding issues of nationality, race and ethnicity, and immigration. Exploring the complexity of interethnic relationships at the community and individual levels, *Lone Star* does not offer up easy solutions to complex social relations.

More recently, American films have given greater depth to Latino/a characters in films, especially when the film centers on Latino/a individuals. Nevertheless, the characters usually reflect dominant stereotypes of Latino/a lower social position and deviant behavior. For example, in *I Like It Like That* (Darnell Martin, 1994), as a young Puerto Rican couple struggle to survive in the South Bronx, the husband is arrested and jailed for looting during a blackout while the wife goes to work and ends up sleeping with her boss.

Lead Latino/a characters are also portrayed as members of a racially oppressed, impoverished ethnic group needing or wanting to assimilate into Anglo American society. For example, in *Real Women Have Curves* (2003), Ana (America Ferrera) leaves her family in East Los Angeles, without her mother's blessing, and ends up at Columbia University with a new, more urban (read: nonethnic) appearance, moving outside and beyond her Mexican culture. In *Maid in Manhattan* (2002), Marisa Ventura (Jennifer Lopez) is a single mother working as a maid in an upscale hotel with dreams of upward mobility in employment (she seeks promotion to management) and lifestyle. She rejects her mother's acceptance of their "place" in life as maids, telling her that she is going to take a chance for something more without her mother's voice "in her head."

The Complexity of Latino/a Stereotypes in American Film

Stereotyping is a psychological mechanism that creates categories, allowing people to manage the massive amounts of data they encounter every day (Ramirez Berg 2002). Even though stereotyping may be a natural human process, how people use that process can turn the "natural" into a manufactured reality, creating a superior social location of one group over another. It is important to account for the ways that dominant groups assign selective characteristics to people—social, cultural, political, sexual, racial, class, and ethnic—to create "others."

Films have great potential to transmit both negative and positive stereotypes to mass audiences, especially if the viewer has no real contact with any member of the group portrayed in the film. Movies are part of the *societal curriculum*—the continual, informal collective of families, peer groups, neighborhoods, churches, organizations, institutions, and other societal influences that "educate" all of us throughout our lives (Cortés 1981). Movies teach by disseminating information about myriad topics, including race, ethnicity, culture, and nationality. Intentionally or not, movies contribute to intercultural, interracial, and interethnic understandings and misconceptions (Wilkinson 2007).

Stereotypical depictions of various outcast races, ethnicities, and cultures, often excruciatingly derogatory by contemporary standards, were commonplace in American popular culture before the invention of motion pictures (Petit 1980; Robinson 1977). Early films' racial and ethnic topics stemmed from popular forms of entertainment that predated cinema, including comic strips, vaudeville shows, and novels. Film escalated these depictions to new levels because of its capacity to heighten emotions as well as its ability to communicate to mass audiences. One side effect of the power of American cinema was that its often crushingly brutal portrayals of other races and cultures spread to audiences larger than ever before possible.

Stereotypes, learned through the process of socialization, are preexisting categories in any society or culture. There are two important features of stereotyping. First, when learned stereotypes are expressed, they are reinforced, and thus validated and perpetuated. Second, validation solidifies attitudes that suggest how certain individuals and groups should be treated (Miller 1982). Stereotypes persist not only because they are category labels, but also because they are implied programs for action (Royce 1982). Different stereotyping scenarios can be delineated depending on the power relationships between groups; they may be stratified, oppositional, or cooperative. If the groups are stratified, the dominant group creates subdominant stereotypes endowed with two sets of characteristics: *harmless* (with out-group members portrayed as childlike, irrational, and emotional), when they do not pose a threat; or *dangerous* (treacherous, deceitful, cunning), when they do pose a threat. Viewing film as "curriculum," we can use an interactionist perspective to deconstruct stereotypes and ascertain the *social intention* of the film.

According to Charles Ramirez Berg (2002), there are few nonstereotypical portrayals of Latinos/as in Hollywood cinema. Before *Zoot Suit* (1981), *La Bamba* (1987), and *Stand and Deliver* (1988), Latinos/as, even key or central characters, were mostly one-dimensional projections who often lacked self-determination or any real agency not directly influenced by the Anglo characters in the film.[1] Ramirez Berg (2002) delineated six classic Latino/a stereotypes based on American racial, ethnic, class, and linguistic stratification: the Bandito or "Greaser," the Latin Lover, the Half-Breed Harlot (or the Seductress), the Dark Lady, the Male Buffoon, and the Female Clown.

Bad Latinos and Good Latinos: El Bandito/Greaser versus the Latin Lover

One of the earliest and most common stereotypical representations of Latinos in U.S. cinema is the Greaser or Bandit. This male stereotype, with its roots in the silent "greaser" films, became the standard villain in many Hollywood Westerns. The Greaser/Bandit character in Western genre films was fundamental to the development of simplistic good guy versus bad guy story formulas. Typically, this character is treacherous, shifty, and dishonest. His reactions are emotional, irrational, and unusually violent. His intelligence is limited, resulting in flawed strategies. He is dirty and unkempt, usually displaying an unshaven face, missing teeth, and disheveled oily hair. Use of the Latino villain stereotype did not diminish along with "spaghetti" Westerns; it was simply reincarnated as the gang member or drug dealer in urban-violence films. For example, in *Falling Down* (1993), two Latino gang members threaten the Anglo protagonist, William Foster (Michael Douglas), trying to force him to pay a "toll" for crossing their turf. They are heavily armed and take pleasure in attempting to terrorize a man they do not consider a physical threat. This modern reiteration of the racialized good guy versus bad guy narrative not only reinvigorates the Greaser/Bandit stereotype of Latino males, but also conveys the message that Anglo violence against Latinos is justified because of the Latinos' criminal nature. The modern Greaser/Bandit image shows superficial changes in the stereotype without altering the original character's essence. "He has traded his black hat for a white suit and his tired horse for a glitzy Porsche, yet he is still driven to satisfy base cravings for money, power, and sexual pleasure—and routinely employs vicious and illegal means to obtain them" (Ramirez Berg 1997:113).

The resiliency of the Bandit/Greaser stereotype is evident in contemporary versions such as Latino gang member, foreign drug runner, rebel, and dictator. The association between Latinos and violence in film has increased dramatically with the extremely violent images presented in contemporary films such as *American Me* (1992), the fictionalized story of the rise of the Mexican "Mafia" in the California prison system. In *Carlito's Way* (1993), the main character is a Puerto Rican criminal who uses violence to advance his interests as well as to survive. In one scene he single-handedly shoots and kills a gang of Italian mobsters. In a similar vein, the *El Mariachi* trilogy (1992, 1995, 2003) has themes of drugs, imprisonment, violent gun battles, high body counts, and danger. From the half-breed villain in *Broncho Billy and the Greaser* (1914) to the cocaine-addicted, bloodthirsty power monger Tony Montana in *Scarface* (1983), the Latino Bandit is a demented, despicable character that usually ends up dying in a hail of bullets as punishment for his brutal behavior.[2]

A new twist on the old stereotype is the *Moral Bandit*. The Moral Bandit, unlike the original Latino Bandit character, has a noble purpose and is set as the moral foil to "bad" Latinos or corrupt Anglo characters. For example, Robert Rodriguez's *Desperado* (1995), the sequel to his 1992 *El Mariachi*, features Antonio Banderas as a gentle but deadly former mariachi seeking revenge against the local drug lord for the death of his former lover. While Rodriguez received high praise for both films, both movies capitalize on the negative stereotypes that are common fare in movies, such as the heavily armed renegade bandit. Several well-known Latino actors are cast as the stereotypical Greaser/Bandit types in both films. Moreover, the Mexican towns portrayed in the movies are but another tired stereotype of dirt-paved streets, free-roaming dogs, and dilapidated buildings.

Another example of the Moral Bandit is found in *Machete* (2010). Machete (Danny Trejo) is an ex-Mexican Federale out for revenge against a corrupt U.S. senator who traffics undocumented immigrants. Although Machete stays on the side of right, the image of his character is that of the scary, dangerous (and dark) Bandit/Greaser. He has long hair flowing down his back, a scarred and pockmarked face, and elaborate tattooing across his chest. He opens his coat to reveal large machete weapons lining both sides. Although the Moral Bandit is cast as the hero in these movies, the old Bandit/Greaser stereotype is still present in his enemies and parts of the character himself. Notably, the Mexican American filmmaker Robert Rodriguez is the creator of *Machete*, and planning to make a sequel. This leads us to question whether the filmmaker is attempting to rearticulate the old Greaser/Bandit stereotypes in his own cinematic vision or whether the stereotype is such a profitable commodity in the movie industry that even the most talented Latino/a directors are unwilling to discard them.

The Latin Lover can be juxtaposed to the Bandit/Greaser stereotype. Introduced during the 1920s, this character represents the Latino "other" as attractive, seductive, and romantic. Ironically, the Latin Lover stereotype originated from the screen work of Italian immigrant Rudolph Valentino (*Son of the Sheik* [1926]). The Latin Lover character is depicted as more passionate and sexually aggressive than his Anglo American male counterparts. His suave demeanor and accented English are often portrayed as charming and his cultural differences are seen as exotic and mysterious. The Latin Lover's masculinity is alluring but also presented as potentially volatile and dangerous. The Latin Lover character continues to be a consistent screen figure, played by a number of first-rate Latino actors including Cesar Romero, Ricardo Montalbán, Gilbert Roland, Fernando Lamas, Jimmy Smits, and Antonio Banderas. Even in contemporary family-oriented or animated films, the Latin Lover stereotype is pervasive. Popular examples include the characters of Puss (Antonio Banderas) in the *Shrek* movies (2001, 2004, 2007, 2010) and Ramon (Robin Williams) in *Happy Feet* (2006). In previews for *Puss in Boots* (2011), Puss strides through the town with Latin background music, sweeps his cape off to fight a bull, dazzles the townswomen with his accented voice and seductive eyes, accurately throws his sword across great distances, and rides off into the sunset on his steed. Adopting the same language and mannerisms found in traditional films, these seemingly innocuous animated characters carry on the Latin Lover stereotype for younger generations.

The visual image of the Latin Lover is opposite that of the Greaser. Whereas the Greaser is an overtly racialized "other," the Latin Lover is more of an ethnic type, usually a lighter-skinned individual that could potentially be assimilated into whiteness. Amorous or sexual relationships between a white female and a Bandit/Greaser are rare in films, whereas Latin Lovers are romantic leading men who regularly succeed in winning the hearts (if not the hands) of their white female leads. It is important to note that actors cast as Latin Lovers have significantly fairer complexions than actors hired to play Greasers. When Anglo or light-skinned Latino actors were cast as Greasers, Hollywood makeup artists darkened their complexions, putting them in "brown face" to make them more frightening (e.g., Eli Wallach in *The Magnificent Seven* [1960] and *The Good, the Bad and the Ugly* [1966]) or more racially ethnic (e.g., Charlton Heston in *A Touch of Evil* [1958] or Paul Muni in *Bordertown* [1935]). American filmmakers remain committed to the "good Latino" stereotype of Latin Lovers, and now the Moral Bandit, because they offer an acceptable "otherness" that remains appealing to audiences. The Greaser/Bandit image preserves the "bad Latino" stereotype, fueling Anglo audiences' fear of miscegenation and immigration. Although current moviegoers may be increasingly more aware of racial and ethnic stereotypes, the durability of these images in film over time highlights the continuing profitability of the Greaser/Bandit and Latin Lover stereotypes for the American movie industry.

Bad Latinas and Good Latinas: The Half-Breed Harlot versus the Dark Lady

According to Ramirez Berg (2002), the *Half-Breed Harlot* is the cinematic stereotype of Latinas and the female version of the Bandit/Greaser. She is a familiar stock figure in American film, particularly in Westerns. Like the Bandit, she is usually a secondary character. The Half-Breed Harlot is lusty and hot tempered, and the main function of her character is to provide as much sexual titillation as possible within industry standards (Pettit 1980). Doc Holliday's woman Chihuahua (Linda Darnell) in *My Darling Clementine* (1946) is a classic example. The Half-Breed Harlot, also known as the "seductress" stereotype, is a slave to her passions; her character is based on the premise that she is sexually driven. She is a prostitute because she enjoys the work and male attention, not because social or economic forces have limited her life choices and opportunities. Usually portrayed as the immoral foil to either male or female Anglo lead characters, the Half-Breed Harlot stereotype is often used to punish Latina sexuality, especially when it crosses racial lines.

The Half-Breed Harlot character often suffers for her love or relations with a white man. Contemporary examples of the Half-Breed Harlot stereotype are Eva Mendes's role as the sexy adulteress in *The Women* (2008) and Sofia Vergara as the cocktail waitress in *Chasing Papi* (2003).

Opposite the Half-Breed Harlot stereotype is the Dark Lady. She is mysterious, virginal, and inscrutable, and her cool distance makes her fascinating to Anglo males. She is circumspect and aloof where her Anglo counterpart is direct and forthright. She is reserved where the Anglo is boisterous, opaque where the Anglo is transparent. Actress Dolores del Río portrayed several versions of this stereotype, arousing American leading men's appetites the way no other Anglo woman could in the films *Flying down to Rio* (1933) and *Caliente* (1935).

The stereotype of the (not too) Dark Lady had irresistible erotic appeal to Anglo men. Anglo women are left to wonder, as a North American blond in *Flying Down to Rio* put it, "what have these South Americans got below the equator that we ain't got?" In a more recent example, Louisa Gomez (Maria Conchita Alonso) in *Colors* (1988) plays the Dark Lady as the romantic tension between white rookie police office Danny McGavin (Sean Penn) and Gomez builds (Ramirez Berg 2002). By infusing the Latin Lover and the Dark Lady characters with hypersexual characteristics lacking in their Anglo counterparts, American cinema has stereotyped and marginalized Latinos/as through racial idealization and sexual fantasy.

Not So Funny: The Male Buffoons, Female Clowns, and Spitfires

The Male Buffoon is the second banana in comic relief (Ramirez Berg 2002). Examples include the characters of Pancho (Leo Carrillo) in *The Cisco Kid* and Sergeant Garcia (Henry Calvin) in Walt Disney's *Zorro*. Many of the same physical and mental characteristics found in the Bandit/Greaser stereotype are present in the Male Buffoon, but instead of being the villain he is the target of ridicule. Comedy is used to deal with the Latino's accentuated differences, a way of taming his fearful qualities. Humor is supposedly found in his simplemindedness (the bumbling antics of Sgt. Garcia), his failure to master Standard English ("Let's went, Cisco!"), and his childish regression into emotionality (Agador's frustrated verbal explosions in Spanish in *The Birdcage* [1996]). The Male Buffoon stereotype, especially in the character of Cisco (e.g., the *Cisco Kid* series [1931–1941] and the *Cisco Kid* television movie [1994] starring Jimmy Smits and Cheech Marin) has endured in film despite Latino progress in American society. Contemporary portrayals of the Latino Male Buffoon as a simpleton, extremely ignorant, or in need of an Anglo character's assistance are pervasive in Hollywood comedies (e.g., Efren Ramirez's character Pedro in *Napoleon Dynamite* [2004]).

The Female Clown character alleviates through humor the overt sexual threat posed by the Half-Breed Harlot. This stereotype attempts to mitigate the Latina's eroticism by making her an object of comic derision. Although very physically attractive, the Female Clown is often portrayed as a dizzy yet alluring dingbat, expressing childlike emotionality and irrationality. When paired with traits of the Half-Breed Harlot, the Female Clown character may also be stereotyped as a "spitfire." Spitfires are often depicted as hot tempered, explosive, overly emotional, and enslaved by their passions. Some Female Clown or Spitfire characters are portrayed as innocent, such as the beautiful Mexican actress Lupe Vélez, star of the 1930s *Mexican Spitfire* movies, and Carmen Miranda as the "Lady in the Tutti-Frutti Hat" in *The Gang's All Here* (1943). The flamboyant nature of the Female Clown/Spitfire is set as the comic foil to the more tempered and restrained white female lead. However, contemporary Female Clown/Spitfire images are significantly hypersexualized, portraying Latinas as extremely curvaceous and unwittingly sexy. Notable examples are Salma Hayek in *Fools Rush In* (1997) and Penelope Cruz in *Vicky Cristina Barcelona* (2008).

Unacknowledged Stereotypes: The Latinos/as We Don't See

The marginalization of Latinos/as in the film industry has created a subset of stereotypes that are just as common but less prominent in critiques of Latino/a representation in film. Through film, these less acknowledged stereotypes endorse the political and social status quo. Images of Latinos/as maids, nannies, gardeners, construction workers, mechanics, day laborers, and undocumented immigrants are so pervasive in film they often escape notice, much less criticism. For example, the 2004 drama *Crash* about the racial and social tensions in Los Angeles, a city where Latinos/as are the largest racial/ethnic group (roughly 47.7 percent), featured only two significant Latino/a characters, a locksmith and a maid. In a city where Latinos/as represent all facets of the economic and occupational structure, the film's writer/director/producer Paul Haggis chose to highlight Latino/a roles most familiar to the moviegoing public. The film won the Academy Award for Best Picture in 2006 but was criticized for its negative portrayal of Asians, for failing to develop the Asian characters, and for reinforcing negative Asian stereotypes. The lack of criticism for the film's stereotypical depiction of Latinos/as highlights the general acceptance of such characterizations by both the film industry and the audience.

The overwhelming amount of negative images found in films that stereotype Latinos/as has profound implications for all members of the viewing audience. The stereotypes, both the glaring and the less obvious, tacitly endorse a system of social stratification that relegates Latinos/as to positions of subordination. Moreover, stereotypical Latino/a characters in these films are rewarded for passive traits (like assimilation, cooperation, and loyalty) as opposed to aggressive ones (like ambition and competitiveness), sending the message to Latinos/as to not challenge the dominant order (Larson 2005). In addition, the film industry's continual use of these stereotypes reinforces for the audience that there are "good" Latinos/as, "bad" Latinos/as, and Latinos/as we do not even need to "see."

Resist or Relent? The Challenge for Latino/a Filmmakers

In the late 1960s, as part of the Chicano political movement, Chicano film culture (or Chicano cinema) attempted to produce alternatives to the Hollywood film images of Latinos/as. By using oppositional forms of knowledge about Latinos/as, Chicano filmmakers intended to produce films that represented "Chicano counter-visions of history, identity, social reality, and resistance politics" (Fregoso 1993:xiv–xv). Chicano cinema films celebrated a different cultural identity than the one produced by the Hollywood film industry. Although racial politics dominated early Chicano films (e.g., *I Am Joaquin* [1969]), critiques of classism, sexism, and the treatment of immigrants were also present in many of them. Films such as *The Ballad of Gregorio Cortez* (1982) and *My Family/Mi Familia* (1995) portray Mexican immigrants and Mexican Americans who possess strength, dignity, and pride with group identities that are culturally reaffirming.

Contemporary Latino/a filmmakers are addressing more mainstream audiences and creating more commercial films. Some of the more economically successful movies from Latino/a filmmakers have been criticized (when compared to Chicano cinema) for not expressly denouncing systemic racial and ethnic inequality, not celebrating Latino/a culture and identity, and reifying the negative Latino/a stereotypes by including them in commercial films. On the other hand, Latino/a filmmakers are also credited with increasing the diversity of Latino/a images in contemporary Hollywood films. But has the increased diversity of Latino/a images mitigated the stereotypes found in American films?

Moreover, research on Latinos/as' presence and representation in film shows that not only have these common Latino/a stereotypes endured, but they are perpetuated through the selective exclusion of Latinos/as in the film industry (Larson 2005). Latinos/as are excluded in four major ways. First, Latinos/as continue to be highlighted in specific film genres, such as urban-crime or immigration-related themes. Second, Latino/a national heritages are considered interchangeable (for example, Jennifer Lopez played the title role of Mexican American *Selena* [1997] despite being of Puerto Rican descent), and Latinos/as' differing histories, cultures, and experiences are often conflated in the stereotypical representation of Latino/a characters. Third, "white" actors continue to play Latino/a roles (e.g., Natalie Wood in *West Side Story* [1961], Marissa Tomei in *The Perez Family* [1995], Robin Williams in *Happy Feet* [2006], Al Pacino in *Scarface* [1983]), resulting in misrepresentation and limited opportunities for Latino/a actors. Last, Latino/a actors are employed to portray Anglo and "ethnic" characters, which some scholars argue reifies the dominant representational forms of Anglo American culture (Cortés 1997; Williams 1997).

Conclusion

Identifying stereotypes of Latinos/as is not a sufficient examination of the larger social problem in the film industry. A comprehensive sociological analysis of image and content must also include an analysis of *control* (*why* such films were made that utilize these stereotypes) and *impact* (*how* the films actually influence viewers). Such an interrogation raises several important questions: Why must Latinos/as play roles that overgeneralize minor or even fictionalized aspects of their cultural backgrounds? Why are they often confined to playing "ethnic" or racialized characters? How can films accurately represent Latino/a culture and curtail the misrepresentations perpetuated by negative stereotypes?

Film representation needs to be understood within a social and historical context. The images of Latinos/as in American film do not exist in a vacuum but are part of the larger discourse on "otherness" in the United States. Beyond their existence as mental constructs or film images, stereotypes are part of the social conversation that reveals mainstream attitudes about Latinos/as as stereotyped "others." Deconstructing these stereotypes required an examination of the accepted norms of "good" filmmaking (including the star system, casting, screenwriting, camera angles, shot selection, direction, production design, editing, acting conventions, lighting, framing, makeup, costuming, and mise-en-scène) as well as the cultural context within which these activities occur.

The larger question we are left with is, what would Latino/a representation in film look like in the absence of stereotypical images? We are beginning to see glimpses of this in films made by and about Latinos/as. The growing political and activist presence of Latino/a populations also bodes well for a more diverse representation of Latino/a life. A student-led grassroots movement provides a model in its efforts to put Hollywood on notice that "there is more to Latino Culture than gang-bangers, suffering mothers, maids and drug dealers" (StudentNow N.d.). As sociologists we would do well to study such movements in addition to going to the movies.

References

Adams, D. 2007. "*Saludos Amigos*: Hollywood and FDR's Good Neighbor Policy." *Quarterly Review of Film & Video* 24(3):289–95.

Bender, S. 2003. *Greasers and Gringos: Latinos, Law and the American Imagination.* New York: New York University Press.

Benshoff, H. M. and S. Griffin. 2004. *America on Film: Representing Race, Class, Gender, and Sexuality at the Movies.* Malden, MA: Wiley-Blackwell.

Coleman, R. M. and E. C. Yochim. 2008. "The Symbolic Annihilation of Race: A Review of the 'Blackness' Literature." *African American Research Perspectives* 12:1–10.

Cortés, C. E. 1981. "The Societal Curriculum: Implications for a Multiethnic Education." Pp. 24–32 in *Education in the 80's: Multiethnic Education*, edited by J. A. Banks. Washington, DC: National Education Association.

Cortés, C. E. 1992. "Who is Maria? What Is Juan? Dilemmas of Analyzing the Chicano Image in U.S. Feature Films." Pp. 74–93 in *Chicanos and film: Essays on Chicano Representation and Resistance*, edited by C. A. Noriega. New York: Garland.

Cortés, C. E. 1997. "Chicanos in Film: History of the Image." In *Latin Looks: Images of Latinas and Latinos in the U.S. Media*, edited by C. E. Rodriguez. Boulder, CO: Westview Press.

Fregoso, R. L. (1993). *The Bronze Screen: Chicano and Chicana Film Culture.* Minneapolis: University of Minnesota Press.

Gans, H. 1964. "The Rise of the Problem-Film: An Analysis of Changes in Hollywood Films and the American Audience." *Social Problems* 11:327–36.

Garcia Berumen, F. J. 1995. *The Chicano/Hispanic Image in American Film.* New York: Vantage Press.

Johnson, A. 2008. *The Forest and the Trees: Sociology as Life, Practice, and Promise.* Philadelphia: Temple University Press.

Larson, S. G. 2005. *Media and Minorities: The Politics of Race and News in Entertainment.* New York: Rowman & Littlefield.

Miller, A. G. 1982. "Historical and Contemporary Perspectives on Stereotyping." P. 27 in *In the Eye of the Beholder: Contemporary Issues in Stereotyping*, edited by A. G. Miller. New York: Praeger.

Mills, C. W. 1959. *The Sociological Imagination.* New York: Oxford University Press.

Noriega, C. A. and A. M. Lopez. 1996. *The Ethnic Eye: Latino Media Arts.* Minneapolis: University of Minnesota Press.

Pettit, A. G. 1980. *Images of the Mexican American in Fiction and Film.* College Station: Texas A and M University Press.

Ramirez Berg, C. 1997. "Stereotyping in Films in General and of the Hispanic in Particular." In *Latin Looks: Images of Latinas and Latinos in the U.S. Media*, edited by C. E. Rodriguez. Boulder, CO: Westview Press.

Ramirez Berg, C. 2002. *Latino Images in Film: Stereotypes, Subversion, Resistance.* Austin: University of Texas Press.

Reyes, L. and P. Rubie. 1994. *Hispanics in Hollywood.* New York: Garland.

Richard, A. C., Jr. 1993. *Censorship and Hollywood's Hispanic Image: An Interpretive Filmography, 1936–1955.* Westport, CN: Greenwood.

Roberts, S. 1993. "'The Lady in the Tutti-Frutti Hat': Carmen Miranda, a Spectacle of Ethnicity." *Cinema Journal* 32:3–23.

Robinson, C. 1977. *Mexico and the Hispanic Southwest in American Literature.* Tucson: University of Arizona Press.

Rodríguez, C. E., ed. 1997. *Latin Looks: Images of Latinas and Latinos in the U.S. Media.* Boulder, CO: Westview Press.

Roman, E. 2000–2001. "Who Exactly is Living La Vida Loca? The Legal and Political Consequences of Latino-Latina Ethnic and Racial Stereotypes in Film and Other Media." *Journal of Gender Race & Justice* 41. Retrieved January 2, 2012 (http://law-journals-books.vlex.com/vid/exactly-vida-loca-latino-latina-film-445622).

Royce, A. P. (1982). *Ethnic Identity: Strategies of Diversity.* Bloomington: Indiana University Press.

Sandoval Sanchez, A. 1994. *West Side Story:* A Puerto Rican Reading of "America." *Jump Cut* 39:59–66. Retrieved January 10, 2012 (http://www.ejumpcut.org/archive/onlinessays/JC39folder/westSideStory.html).

StudentNow. N.d. "Activism: Positive Latino Films & The Premiere Weekend Club." Retrieved January 10, 2012 (http://www.studentnow.com/features/premiereweekend.html).

Valdivia, A. N. 2010. *Latina/os and the Media.* Cambridge, UK: Polity Press.

Wilkinson, L. C. 2007. "A Developmental Approach to Uses of Moving Pictures in Intercultural Education." *International Journal of Intercultural Relations* 37:1–27.

Williams, L. 1997. "Chicanos in Film: History of the Image." In *Latin Looks: Images of Latinas and Latinos in the U.S. Media,* edited by C. E. Rodriguez. Boulder, CO: Westview Press.

Notes

1. Katy Jurado's role as a resourceful businesswoman in *High Noon* (1952), Ricardo Montalbán's Mexican government agent in *Border Incident* (1949), and Anthony Quinn's dignified, defiant vaquero in *The Ox-Bow Incident* (1943) are exceptions to the oversimplified Latino/a characters in U.S. films during this time.

2. The original *Scarface* movie (1932) was based on an Italian immigrant character. The fact that the current version employs a Cuban immigrant (more specifically a *Marielito* second-wave Cuban immigrant) reflects the sociopolitical change of fear from early-twentieth-century worries regarding Italian immigrants to contemporary anxieties surrounding Latin American immigration.

Outtake

Pocahontas and Intersectionality: A Sociologist Reflects

Theresa Martinez

I remember going to see the movie *Pocahontas* in 1995. I took a *cholito*, whom I was mentoring at the time, and his girlfriend. To the uninitiated, *cholo* is a term mainly applied to Mexican American/Chicano males who have a certain style and swagger in the neighborhood. Some folks equate them with gang activity, though this stereotypical thinking doesn't take into account the issues young males of color face daily in the urban landscape.

So, here I was with a *cholito* and his girlfriend at this new Disney film called *Pocahontas.* They wanted to see it and I—well, I was skeptical. I am a Chicana baby boomer from a family of 12 kids, every one of us having experienced racism and classism even at a young age, with gendered norms never far from the surface. We had watched a grotesque panoply of horrific American Indian, Black, Chicana/o, and Asian representations during our growing up years. Countering these racist images, our mom raised us with a deeply held value for social justice— we knew all about the struggles of the Reverend Martin Luther King Jr. and Cesar Chavez and we boycotted grapes and lettuce long after the call for such a boycott.

The truth is, I was in that movie theater on sufferance and I watched with some discomfort as Pocahontas appeared on the screen—a brown-skinned Barbie doll image— and I figured I was in for a long, poor ride. And then, at some point in the film, something changed. It was when Pocahontas contradicts John Smith, who is talking of dividing up the land and giving it away. She tells him, quite forcefully, that the land belongs to no one and that the vast tapestry of land, air, and water as well as animal and humankind—in effect, the ecosystem all around them—is interconnected and interdependent. (Interestingly, this scene is a segue into the song "Colors of the Wind"). Here is a woman of color from a time when conquest and patriarchy were the norm, standing up to the pinnacle of privilege—a White European male—to speak for the vast interconnectedness of all life. Yes, it was a Disney cartoon, and yes, it was unrealistic, but I can admit that I was bawling. This stunned my *cholito* and his girlfriend, who asked what was the matter. At Baskin-Robbins after the movie, I told them.

Even though it was a Disney film and disappointing in parts, it was also in some ways a complete departure from past characters of color in film who did not speak up for themselves, let alone the ecosystem. Moreover, it was a remarkable example of the interplay of intersectionality in film. European males—privileged by race, class, and gender—invade territory to be confronted by indigenous peoples, penalized at that time by race and class, but whose males still asserted patriarchal power within their communities. The stage is set for a world forever changed in the theater of conquest. But there is an added angle of vision in this setting—the voice of an indigenous woman whose racial/class heritage and gendered self together are denied and desirable (in this instance) to her conquerors. Yet she is empowered to stand up for the richly drawn cultural heritage of her people and, in her woman's voice, to breathe a paradigm shift about the value of all life into the plot of a Disney movie and into the collective consciousness of the late twentieth century. When I considered that little girls and little boys across the country were watching her speak from intense personal power, it is no wonder I wept.

As for my dear *cholito* and his girlfriend, they consoled me that times were indeed a-changing. Even as we knew that they were often profiled by police and stereotyped by teachers and principals as young *cholos* and *cholas*—undesirables—in high school. Even as I faced disparaging remarks about being a "stupid Mexican woman" when I conducted diversity trainings in the community and on campus. Race, class, and gender are always present—together—in our lives.

CHAPTER 5

Gender and Sexuality

Ariel: But without my voice, how can I . . .

Ursula: You'll have your looks . . . your pretty face . . . and don't underestimate the importance of "bo-dy lan-guage." Ha!

Ursula The men up there don't like a lot of blabber / They think a girl who gossips is a
[singing]: bore / Yes, on land it's much preferred / for ladies not to say a word / After all, dear, what is idle prattle for? / Come on, they're not all that impressed with conversation / True gentlemen avoid it when they can / But they dote and swoon and fawn / On a lady who's withdrawn / It's she who holds her tongue who gets her man.

—*The Little Mermaid* (1989)

David: You're gay for saying that.

Cal: I'm gay for saying that?

David: You know how I know you're gay?

Cal: How? How do you know I'm gay?

David: Because you macramed yourself a pair of jean shorts.

Cal: You know how I know *you're* gay? You just told me you're not sleeping with women anymore.

David: You know how I know that you're gay?

Cal: How? Cuz you're gay? And you can tell who other gay people are?

David: You know how I know you're gay?

Cal: How?

David: You like Coldplay.

—*The 40-Year-Old Virgin* (2005)

W e go to the movies and we see tales of men and women, sex and sexuality. In film after film we see men and women coming together against remarkable odds. She's hardheaded; he's a slob (*The Break-Up*, 2006). She's desperate; he's a cad (*Bridget Jones's Diary*, 2001). She's liberal, he's conservative (*He Said, She Said*, 1991). She's driven; he's demeaned (*Why Did I Get Married?*, 2007). Given these differences, it's a wonder men and women ever get together. After all, men are from Mars and women are from Venus. We are so profoundly different, we hail from opposing planets, right? Many Hollywood films suggest as much. Film representations of relationships often reinforce popular notions concerning gender; that is, men and women are more different than we are alike, and this fact of difference is a "natural" part of our genetic makeup. Of course, sociologists know that there is almost nothing more *social* than gender, and have clearly established that "differences" between men and women are both socially constructed and greatly exaggerated (Kimmel 2007).

Gender, according to sociologists, refers to the meanings a society gives to masculinity and femininity. In daily interactions we are called on to perform as either masculine or feminine. Gender, then, is not just an identity or a status; it is a continual process of negotiation. Gender is something we "do" (West and Zimmerman 1987). Men are expected to maintain a masculinity that includes toughness, bravado, strength, assurance, and confidence, all with little display of emotion. Women are expected to perform a femininity that exudes beauty, caring, nurturance, neediness, and compassion, complete with every range of possible emotion.

If we play our roles wrongly, we often face social sanctioning. Of course, the price is much steeper for the man who drifts toward femininity, as we are a culture where the traits of masculinity are more highly valued. We see these roles strictly enforced in children's films. In the scene from *The Little Mermaid*, Ariel bemoans her fate if she loses voice, but recognizes that a woman who "holds her tongue" is preferred by men when it comes to romance. In Disney classics we find variations on this theme with repetitive images of the hapless princess, lacking any autonomy while in great need (of rescuing and of finding a husband/prince). The prince arrives, fully confident and capable of saving her from whatever forces bind her. They marry.

Research concerning these "differences" has shown that men and women are more alike than we tend to believe. For instance, many studies have found that *men* are the ones who hold strong ideological beliefs about romantic love (e.g., believe in love at first sight, fall in love more quickly; see Kimmel 2007). The problem is that, when we assume men and women to be somehow *innately* different, we fall into denial of culpability. We don't really have to work at communication when we assume that men and women simply *can't* communicate. Thus, films that present gendered relationships in this Mars versus Venus manner both reflect commonsensical assumptions of gender and contribute to a culture of gendered understandings of interaction. As Lorber (1994) points out, gendered social arrangements are justified by social institutions (e.g., religion) and cultural productions (e.g., films).

The relationships featured in film are based on the characters doing gender appropriately— that is, in ways that are congruent with their assumed biological sex. Further, sexuality is linked to the sex/gender binary such that "the possession of erotic desire for the feminine object is constructed as masculine and being the object of masculine desire is feminine" (Schippers 2007:90). Accordingly, heterosexuality is based on the presumed differences between and the complementariness of masculine and feminine. The scene from *40-Year-Old Virgin* captures the banter of two straight guys playing a video game. We can see the lengths men will go to *not* to appear as anything other than masculine and, since sexuality is linked to gender, heterosexual. It is important to maintain the image of manhood—especially in the company of one's guy friends. As Kimmel (1994) notes, often the performance of masculinity (and heterosexuality) happens *among* men *for* men.

The readings in this chapter explore the social construction of gender and sexuality. Masculinity in film is the subject of the first reading, in which Michael Messner considers how cinematic representations of hegemonic masculinity have seeped into the "theatre" that is U.S. politics. Using the case of movie star turned California governor Arnold Schwarzenegger, Messner explores the versions of masculinity Schwarzenegger's film roles captured, linking these to his "performances" as state governor. He focuses on the ways that Schwarzenegger, and the media, presented his political persona as the "Terminator" divorced from human compassion and emotions, and the "Kindergarten Commando" who is still a tough guy, but one who is vulnerable, compassionate, and caring (especially toward children). Messner argues that film images take on lives of their own—that power is rooted in these symbolic images and that the symbolic often becomes "real" as they are played out not by actors on the screen, but by politicians on the stage of government.

In the second reading, Sutherland explores how women with power are portrayed in film. Unpacking the concept of power, she identifies three forms of power and explores the meanings of these for women and the goals of feminism using examples from film. Women are using the power-over model when they enact masculine values and behaviors, as we see in *She Hate Me* when the women objectify and humiliate Jack on the basis of sex. This theme is continued with the film *The Devil Wears Prada*, with a female boss who is "chillingly mean, emotionless, and incapable of maintaining relationships." Another version of power, power-to, is more positive and life affirming, and involves an awakening, or raised consciousness, as seen in *Real Women Have Curves*, *The Color Purple*, and *Waitress*. But the move to organized action to create social change is rooted in the power-with model, as seen in the historic discrimination case represented in the film *North Country*.

"Doing gender" is elaborated on in Betsy Lucal and Andrea Miller's reading, in which they use a feminist constructionist analysis to explore the binary world of gender. We assume that men and women are opposites (Mars and Venus), and we assume a gendered duality that forces people to be "one or the other": you are man or woman, and you are heterosexual or homosexual. What is missing in this dualistic formula is the reality of many lives—that gender and sexuality are not fixed identities or experiences. However, with only two choices on both dimensions, the boundaries are made clear, at the same time that lived experiences are covered up or erased. Lucal and Miller explore the meaning of sexual desire and sexual identity, and the "either/or" constraints placed on changing and fluid human experiences, in the film *Chasing Amy*. With *Transamerica*, they draw our attention to the fixed categories of male/female and masculine/feminine as the main character seeks to bring sex (through surgery) into alignment with gender.

Exploring women and power, masculinity, and bisexual and transgender identities, the readings in this section invite you to consider the ways that gender and sexuality are socially constructed in film and in life. As sociologists, we begin with the understanding that gender is learned and then performed in interaction with others. Film is one of the media that provide us with the "meanings" that make up our gendered realities.

References

Kimmel, M. 1994. "Masculinity as Homophobia: Fear, Shame and Silence in the Construction of Gender Identity." Pp. 119–41 in *Theorizing Masculinity*, edited by H. Brod. Thousand Oaks, CA: Sage.

Kimmel, M. 2007. *The Gendered Society*. 3rd ed. New York: Oxford University Press.

Lorber, J. 1994. *The Paradoxes of Gender*. New Haven, CT: Yale University Press.

Schippers, M. 2007. "Recovering the Feminine Other: Masculinity, Femininity, and Gender Hegemony." *Theory & Society* 36:85–102.

West, C. and D. Zimmerman. 1987. "Doing Gender." *Gender & Society* 1:125–51.

The big news story on November 7, 2006, was that voters had returned control of the U.S. Congress to the Democrats. This represented a dramatic turning of the electoral tide against the policies of Republican President George W. Bush—especially against his stubborn mantra to "stay the course" in the war on Iraq. But apparently swimming against this tide was another story. On that same day, Republican Arnold Schwarzenegger was reelected as California governor by a landslide, winning 56% of the vote over Democratic challenger Phil Angelides's mere 39%. During a year of resurgent Democratic strength nationally, in a solidly Democratic state, and only a year after his popularity had plummeted with voters, how do we explain Schwarzenegger's resounding victory? In this article, I will explore this question by examining Schwarzenegger's public masculine image.

A key aspect of Schwarzenegger's public image, of course, is his celebrity status, grounded first in his career as a world champion bodybuilder, and even more so in his fame as one of the most successful action film stars of his generation (Boyle, 2006). My aim here is not to analyze Arnold Schwarzenegger's biography. Nor do I intend to offer a critical analysis of his films—I confess, I have watched some of them and not others (and I enjoy the ones that I have seen). Instead, my aim is both practical and theoretical: I will outline the beginnings of a cultural analysis of how and why Schwarzenegger rose to political power, what his appeal was and is, and how some current debates in gender theory might be useful in informing these questions. I will consider what Schwarzenegger's deployment of a shifting configuration of masculine imagery tells us about the limits and possibilities in current U.S. electoral politics. And I will deploy the concept of "hegemonic masculinity" to suggest how Schwarzenegger's case illustrates connections between the cultural politics of gender with those of race, class, and nation. In particular I hope to show how, when symbolically deployed by an exemplar like Arnold Schwarzenegger, hegemonic masculinity is never an entirely stable, secure, finished product; rather, it is always shifting with changes in the social context. Hegemonic masculinity is "hegemonic" to the extent that it succeeds, at least temporarily, in serving as a symbolic nexus around which a significant level of public consent coalesces. But as with all moments of hegemony, this consent is situational, always potentially unstable, existing in a dynamic tension with opposition.

Masculinities and Politics

Since the late 1980s, sociologists have tended to agree that we need to think of masculinity not as a singular "male sex role," but as multiple, contextual, and historically shifting configurations. At any given moment, a dominant—or hegemonic—form of masculinity exists in relation to other subordinated or marginalized forms of masculinity, and in relation to various forms of femininity (Connell, 1987). Very few men fully conform to hegemonic masculinity. In fact, it is nearly impossible for an individual man consistently to achieve and display the dominant conception of masculinity, and this is an important part of the psychological instability at the center of individual men's sense of their own masculinity. Instead, a few men (real or imagined) are positioned as symbolic exemplars for a hegemonic masculinity that legitimizes the global subordination of women and ensures men's access to privilege. What makes this masculinity hegemonic is not simply powerful men's displays of power, but also, crucially, less powerful men's (and many women's) consent and complicity with the institutions, social practices, and symbols that ensure some men's privileges (Messner, 2004). To adapt a term that is now popular in market-driven bureaucracies, hegemonic masculinity requires a *buy-in* by subordinated and marginalized men, and by many women, if it is to succeed as a strategy of domination.

Thus, the concept of hegemonic masculinity is most usefully deployed when we think of it not as something that an individual "has"—like big muscles, a large bank account, or an expensive car. But then, what is it? Where does it reside? Can we define it or is it something about which we simply say, "I know it when I see it"? To ask these kinds of questions, we need to develop ways of thinking about gender that are *global*, both in the geographic and in the conceptual sense of the word. Here, I want to explore the ways that we can think about hegemonic masculinity as a symbolically displayed "exemplar" of manhood around which power coalesces—and importantly, *not* just men's power over women, but also power in terms of race, class, and nation (Connell & Messerschmidt, 2005). I will suggest that it is in the symbolic realm where an apparently coherent, seemingly stable hegemonic masculinity can be forged (Gómez-Barris & Gray, 2006). We can track this symbolic masculinity as it reverberates into institutions—in the case of Arnold Schwarzenegger, into the realm of electoral politics—and we can see how hegemonic masculinity works in relation to what Collins (1990) calls a "matrix of domination," structured by race, class, gender, and sexuality.

Terminating the Feminized American Man

Arnold Schwarzenegger began his public career as a world champion bodybuilder. Many people mark his starring role in the award-winning 1977 documentary on bodybuilders, *Pumping Iron*, as his film debut. However, Schwarzenegger actually appeared in a few other television and B film roles before that, including a typecast role in the 1969 film *Hercules in New York*. Schwarzenegger's celebrity star rose rapidly in the early 1980s with a series of films that featured his muscular body as the ultimate fighting machine: *Conan the Barbarian* (1982), *Conan the Destroyer* (1984), *Commando* (1985), *Red Sonja* (1985), and *Predator* (1987). Among these popular 1980s films, it is *The Terminator* (1984) that most firmly established Schwarzenegger as a major film star and as king of a particular genre.

Conan, John Matrix, and the Terminator appear in the 1980s at the same time that Rambo and other hard, men-as-weapon, men-as-machine images filled the nation's screens. Susan Jeffords (1989) calls this cultural moment a "remasculinization of America," when the idea of real men as decisive, strong, and courageous arose from the confusion and humiliation of the U.S. loss in the Vietnam War and against the challenges of feminism and gay liberation. Jeffords's analyses of popular Vietnam films are especially insightful. The major common theme in these films is the Vietnam veteran as victimized by his own government, the war, the Vietnamese, American protestors, and the women's movement—all of which are portrayed as feminizing forces that have shamed and humiliated American men.

Two factors were central to the symbolic remasculinization that followed: First, these film heroes of the 1980s were rugged individuals, who stoically and rigidly stood up against bureaucrats who were undermining American power and pride with their indecisiveness and softness. Second, the muscular male body, often with massive weapons added as appendages, was the major symbolic expression of remasculinization. These men wasted very few words; instead, they spoke through explosive and decisively violent bodily actions. Jeffords argues that the male body-as-weapon serves as the ultimate spectacle and locus of masculine regeneration in post–Vietnam era films of the 1980s. There is a common moment in many of these films: the male hero is seemingly destroyed in an explosion of flames, and as his enemies laugh, he miraculously rises (in slow motion) from under water, firing his weapon and destroying the enemy. Drawing from Klaus Theweleit's (1987) analysis of the "soldier-men" of Nazi Germany, Jeffords argues that this moment symbolizes a "purification through fire and rebirth through immersion in water" (Jeffords, 1989, p. 130).

During this historical moment of cultural remasculinization, Schwarzenegger was the right body at the right time. Muscular Arnold, as image, reaffirmed the idea of categorical sex difference, in an era where such difference had been challenged on multiple levels. In this historical moment, the Terminator's most famous sentence, "I'll be back," may have invoked an image of a remasculinized American man, "back" from the cultural feminization of the 1960s and 1970s, as well as a resurgence of American power in the world.

It's possible to look at this remasculinized male subject in 1980s films as a symbolic configuration of hegemonic masculinity that restabilizes the centrality of men's bodies, and thus men's (at least white U.S. men's) power and privilege. Indeed, Messerschmidt's (2000) statement that "Hegemonic masculinity . . . emphasizes practices toward authority, control, independence, competitive individualism, aggressiveness, and the capacity for violence" (p. 10) seems to describe precisely the masculinity displayed by Schwarzenegger and Stallone in these 1980s films. But we need to be cautious about coming up with such a fixed definition of hegemonic masculinity. Though it clearly provided symbolic support for the resurgent conservatism of the Reagan era, this simplistic reversion to an atavistic symbology of violent, stoic, and muscular masculinity probably fueled tensions in gender relations as much as it stabilized them. As Connell and Messerschmidt (2005) note:

Gender relations are always arenas of tension. A given pattern of hegemonic masculinity is hegemonic to the extent that it provides a solution to these tensions,

Photo 5.1   Man as machine in *The Terminator.* Arnold Schwarzenegger, as Terminator, became a defining image of the remasculinization era of the 1980s.

tending to stabilize patriarchal power or reconstitute it in new conditions. A pattern of practice (i.e., a version of masculinity) that provided such a solution in past conditions but not in new conditions is open to challenge—in fact is certain to be challenged. (p. 853)

There's plenty of evidence that by the end of the 1980s, the remasculinized muscular hero who wreaks havoc with his guns (biceps and bazookas), while keeping verbal expression down to a few grunts or occasional three-word sentences delivered in monotone, was not playing well in Peoria. The 1988 installment of the Rambo series (*Rambo III*) was listed by the 1990 *Guinness Book of World Records* as the most violent movie, with 221 acts of violence and over 108 deaths. Despite (or because of?) this carnage, the film did not do well. Its gross in the United States was $10 million lower than the film's overall budget, and Stallone's tired one-liners (Zaysen: "Who are you?" Rambo: "Your worst nightmare") reportedly left audiences laughing derisively. Other icons of heroic masculine invulnerability tumbled from their pedestals: one of the actors who played the Marlboro man in cigarette ads died from lung cancer. By the late 1980s and early 1990s, the idea of men as invulnerable, nonemotional, working and fighting machines was frequently caricatured in popular culture and made fun of in everyday life. Health advocates grabbed on to this caricature with "culture jamming" counteradvertisements aimed at improving men's health. For instance, a counter ad distributed by the California Department of Health Services referenced years of "Marlboro Country" ads by depicting two rugged cowboys riding side-by-side on their horses with a caption that read, "Bob, I've got emphysema." These sorts of ads invert the intended meanings of the Marlboro Man, illustrating how narrow cultural conceptions of masculinity are unhealthy—even deadly—for the men who try to live up to them. This new cultural sensibility is directly a legacy of the feminist critique of hypermasculinity. By the 1990s, these kinds of counter ads could rely on readers to make the ironic connections, drawing on their own familiarity with the "straight" tobacco ads that were referenced, in addition to their familiarity with the increasingly prevalent cultural caricatures of hypermasculinity as dangerous, self-destructive, and (often) ridiculously laughable.

The Birth of the Kindergarten Commando

Many professional-class white men in the 1980s and 1990s began to symbolically distance themselves from this discredited view of "traditional masculinity," and forged new, more "sensitive" forms of masculinity. But this is not to say that successful and powerful men have fully swung toward an embrace of femininity and vulnerability. Some men's brief flirtations with "soft" "new man" styles in the 1970s—the actor Alan Alda comes to mind—were thoroughly discredited and marginalized. Instead, we have seen the emergence of a symbology of masculinity that is hybrid: toughness, decisiveness, and hardness are still central to hegemonic masculinity, but they are now normally linked with situationally appropriate moments of compassion and, sometimes, vulnerability. The 1980s and 1990s saw the increasingly common image of powerful men crying—not sobbing, but shedding a tear or two—in public: President Ronald Reagan in speaking of soldiers' sacrifices after the 1983 U.S. invasion of Grenada; General Norman Schwarzkopf at a press conference noting U.S. troops killed during the 1990–91 Gulf War; basketball player Michael Jordan in the immediate aftermath of winning his first NBA championship in 1991. These emotional displays may have been fully genuine, but I emphasize that they were not delivered in the aftermath of a loss, in a moment of vulnerability, failure, or humiliation. Try to imagine, for a moment, superstar NBA player Dirk Nowitzki after the Dallas Mavericks' 2006 loss in the NBA Finals, dropping to his knees at center court, overcome with grief, weeping openly with his face buried in his hands. That's not likely to happen. Tears are appropriate as public masculinity displays in the immediate aftermath of *winning* an NBA championship, or of having just successfully overrun a small third-world country with virtually no military. Powerful men have found it most safe to display public grief or compassion *not* in relation to their own failures, or to the pain of other men—this might be perceived as weakness— and *not* in terms of women's struggles for respect and equality—this might be perceived as being "pussywhipped" (a recently revived epithet in pop culture). Rather, the public compassion of this emergent masculinity is most often displayed as protective care—often for children—which brings us back to the Governator.

Schwarzenegger's original Terminator character was an unambiguously violent male-body-as-weapon, severed from any capacity for human compassion. But in the late 1980s, this image began to be rounded out by—not *replaced* with—a more compassionate persona. We can actually watch this transformation occur in *Terminator 2: Judgment Day* (1991). In this film, Schwarzenegger, though still a killing machine, becomes the good guy, even showing occasional glimpses of human compassion. And significantly, it is his connection with a young boy that begins to humanize him. Taken together, Schwarzenegger's films of the 1990s display a masculinity that oscillates between his more recognizable hard-guy image and an image of self-mocking vulnerability, compassion, and care, especially care for kids (e.g., *Kindergarten Cop,* 1990; *Jingle All the Way,* 1996). I call this emergent hybrid masculinity "The Kindergarten Commando." Indeed, in Schwarzenegger's first major foray into California politics in 2002, he plugged his ballot initiative for after-school activities for kids by saying that he had been "an action hero for kids in the movies; now I want to be an action hero for kids in real life." In the 1994 comedy *Junior,* Schwarzenegger appropriates an ultimate bodily sign of femaleness: pregnancy and childbirth. But Schwarzenegger's gender hybridity could never be mistaken as an embrace of a 1970s styled "androgyny." Instead, in the Kindergarten Commando masculinity of Arnold Schwarzenegger, we see the appropriation and situational display of particular aspects of femininity, strategically relocated within a powerfully masculine male body.

In his initial 2003 run for California governor, Schwarzenegger positioned himself as a centrist unifier, and his film-based masculine imagery supported the forging of this political image. Hardness and violence, plus compassion and care, is a potent equation for hegemonic masculinity in public symbology today. And what tethers these two seemingly opposed principles is *protection*—protection of children and women from bad guys, from evil robots from the future, or from faceless, violently irrational terrorists from outside our borders.

The post-9/11 world has provided an increasingly fertile ground for the ascent of the Kindergarten Commando as compassionate masculine protector. Iris Marion Young (2003) has argued that the emergent U.S. security state is founded on a renewed "logic of masculine protection." And as Stephan Ducat (2004) has argued in his book *The Wimp Factor,* right-wing movements have seized this moment to activate a fear among men of "the mommy state"—a bureaucratic state that embodies weakness, softness, and feminist values. The desire for a revived "daddy state" is activated through a culture of fear: only the man who really cares about us and is also tough enough to stand up to evil can be fully trusted to lead us in these dangerous times. The ascendance of this form of hegemonic masculinity is both a response to feminist and other critiques of the limits of a 1950s, John Wayne–style masculinity, *and* it thrives symbiotically with pervasive fears of threats by outsiders.

This is not a symmetrical symbiosis, though. In a male political leader today, compassion and care seem always to be subordinated to toughness, strength, and a single-minded resolve that is too often called "decisiveness," but that might otherwise accurately be characterized as stubborn narrow-mindedness. This asymmetry is reflected in Schwarzenegger's recent films, in which the violent, tough-guy hero has never been eclipsed by the vulnerable kid-loving guy: in *End of Days* (1999), Schwarzenegger saves the world from no less a force of evil than Satan himself. The emergent Kindergarten Commando masculinity is forged within a post-9/11 context in Schwarzenegger's 2002 film *Collateral Damage.* Here, firefighter Gordon Brewer is plunged into the complex and dangerous world of international terrorism after he loses his wife and child in a terrorist bombing. Frustrated with the official investigation and haunted by the thought that the man responsible for murdering his family might never be brought to justice, Brewer takes matters into his own hands and tracks his quarry ultimately to Colombia. By the time *Terminator 3: Rise of the Machines* hit the theaters in 2003, Schwarzenegger was governor of California. In *T3*, it was clear that the hero, though still an admirably efficient killing machine, had mobilized his human compassion to fight for humanity against the evil machines.

Hegemonic Masculinity in a Matrix of Domination

My argument thus far is that the currently ascendant hegemonic masculinity constructed through a combination of the film images of Arnold Schwarzenegger is neither the stoic masculine postwar hero image of John Wayne, nor is it the 1980s remasculinized man-as-machine image of Rambo or the Terminator. These one-dimensional masculine images, by the 1990s, were laughable. Instead, the ascendant hegemonic masculinity combines the kick-ass muscular heroic male body with situationally expressive moments of empathy, grounded in care for kids and a capacity to make us all feel safe. Feminism, antiwar movements, health advocates, and even modern business human relations management have delegitimized pure hypermasculinity. But many people still view effeminacy as illegitimate in men, especially those who are leaders. So, neither hard nor soft is fully legitimate, unless they are mixed, albeit with a much larger dose of the former than of the latter. And commercial interests have fruitfully taken up this hybrid masculine image: Heterosexual men, as we saw in the TV show *Queer Eye for the Straight Guy*, are seen as more attractive to women when softened—provided they still have power, muscles, and the money to purchase the correct draperies, fine cuisine, clothing, cosmetics, and other body-management products. Arnold, of course, has all of this. His masculinity displays were effective in securing power. But toward what ends? What do we see in the play of "hard" and "soft," in "strength" and "compassion" in terms of what he *does* as governor? Three events are very revealing, and I will discuss them very briefly. First, the governor's playfully aggressive use of references to his film and bodybuilder careers in his ongoing budget battles with the Democrats. Second, his class politics—particularly in his dealings with business and labor interests in California. And third, the "woman problem" that emerged during his first election.

Girlie Men and Political Intertextuality

During his earliest days in office, Schwarzenegger famously mobilized the "girlie men" epithet and turned it on his Democratic opponents in the California legislature. In doing so, he deployed references to his own *Terminator* films (urging voters to "terminate" his Democratic opponents), and the "girlie men" comments referenced the *Saturday Night Live* skit that had originally spoofed him. This illustrates the often-noted fact that cultural symbols don't float free: they emerge from, and in turn enter into, social relations. Schwarzenegger strategically deployed the imagery of the Kindergarten Commando to get himself elected. But in the real life of governing, when push came to shove, he fell back on the Terminator, not the lovable Kindergarten Cop "Protector of Children," as a strategy for deploying power.

Schwarzenegger's "girlie man" taunt is not the first time that a politician has drawn from popular commercial culture to invoke an image aimed to undermine his opponents. Recall, for instance, Vice President Walter Mondale's 1984 attempt to attack his Republican presidential race opponent's lack of substantive ideas by humorously deploying a "Where's the beef?" chant that referenced the then-popular Wendy's hamburger commercial. However, by comparison, Schwarzenegger's "girlie men" insult is a rather unprecedented multilevel image: it is a veritable Möbius strip of meanings, with life imitating ironic schlock, imitating life, imitating more schlock.

Audiences get a sense of pleasure and power—a sense of authorship from being insiders as they participate in decoding familiar intertextual messages like "Where's the beef?" "girlie man," or "I'll be back!" And if we think of the electorate as an audience (and certainly political parties use all the advertising expertise that they can muster), an election can be seen as a sort of poll of the audience's preferences. The electorate is buying a particular candidate who has been sold to them. Schwarzenegger's references to girlie men and to *The Terminator* appealed to his supporters, but they also set off a firestorm of criticism from feminists, gay/lesbian organizations, and Democratic legislators. The governor's plea to voters to "terminate" his Democratic foes in November not only disrupted his thus far carefully crafted image of bipartisan get-it-done compromiser, it also indicated the reemergence of a gloves-off muscular masculinity behind which the kind and compassionate Kindergarten Cop receded into the background. And this spelled some trouble for the Governator.

The symbolic symmetry of the new man—the Kindergarten Commando—was broken, leaving Schwarzenegger once again vulnerable both to sarcastic media caricature and to open questioning about the misogyny and homophobia that might lie behind the warm smile. However, the fact that Schwarzenegger's power was anchored so much in the symbolic realm facilitated his ability to deploy his power in a form that allowed for humorous, ironic interpretation; the implied self-mocking in his girlie man comments gets him off the hook, perhaps, from otherwise coming across as a bully: Democrats who decry the sexism or homophobia embedded in the girlie man comment appear perhaps to have no sense of humor. In the vernacular of the shock radio so popular with many young white males today, people who object to Schwarzenegger's comments as sexist or homophobic are "feminazis"; they just don't get the joke (Benwell, 2004; Messner & Montez de Oca, 2005).

Hegemonic Masculinity and Class Politics

Meanwhile, though, it's clear that the joke was on some of the most vulnerable people of California. My second example concerns Schwarzenegger's class politics. In August 2004, he vetoed a minimum wage increase. Simultaneously, he supported Walmart's economic colonization of the California retail industry. Walmart's importation of notoriously low-waged jobs has been resisted by organized retail unions and by several California cities and towns, yet it was clear which side Schwarzenegger took in this struggle. This illustrates how hegemonic masculinity enters into class relations. If there was compassion here, it was compassion for big business; if there was muscle to be deployed, it was against the collective interests of working people, defined by the governor's business logic as "special interests."

Governor Schwarzenegger also attacked public employees unions in his effort to control state spending. A National Public Radio story on March 15, 2005, noted that members of the California Nurses Association were showing up and protesting in every public venue in which he appeared. As he was giving a speech to supporters, one could hear the voices of the nurses chanting something in the background. Schwarzenegger commented to a cheering crowd, "Pay no attention to them. They are the *Special Interests*. They don't like me in Sacramento, because I am always kicking their butts!" Indeed, earlier that year Schwarzenegger had vetoed the rule that mandated a lower nurse/doctor ratio, and also took $350,000 in campaign contributions from pharmaceutical companies while opposing a prescription drugs law that would have helped consumers.

The ideological basis of these class politics and their links to the politics of race and immigration were further demonstrated in Schwarzenegger's speech at the 2004 Republican National Convention. He told his own rugged individualist immigrant story, with clear pull-yourself-up-by-your-bootstraps Horatio Alger themes. While positioning himself on the surface as someone who cares about and understands immigrants, his story reiterated conservative themes that are grounded in the experience of white ethnics, rather than in that of the vast majority of California's current immigrant population who deal daily with poverty, institutionalized racism, and escalating xenophobia. Schwarzenegger's narrative thus helps to reconstruct a white male subject and demonstrates how hegemonic masculinity is never just about gender: it is also about race and nation (Montez de Oca, 2005).

Hegemonic Masculinity as Heterosexy

My third example concerns Schwarzenegger's "woman problem." During the final weeks of the 2004 election, the *Los Angeles Times* broke a series of stories indicating that several women had complained of Schwarzenegger's having sexually harassed and humiliated them in various ways over the years. The women's claims were quickly trivialized by being more benignly defined as "unwanted groping." Ironically, these accusations probably enhanced Schwarzenegger's status with many men, and may have helped to secure the complicity of many women, as evidenced by the "Arnold, Grope Me!" signs seen at some of his rallies in the final days of his run for governor. Here, we can see that the hegemonic masculinity created by Schwarzenegger's symbolic fusing of opposites also involves the construction of a particular form of masculine *heterosexuality*. We should not underestimate the extent to which the imagery of hegemonic masculinity is electrified with an erotic charge—a charge that serves as a powerful linking process in constructing dominant forms of femininity, and through that, the consent of many women. In fact, it is likely that while the "groping" charges solidified an already-existing opposition to Schwarzenegger, it also pulled some voters more solidly into his camp.

A comparison with former President Bill Clinton is useful in this regard. Stephen Ducat (2004) discusses how during his first term as president, Clinton was vulnerable to questions about his masculinity due to his lack of military service, his support for women's and gay issues, and especially to the perception that his wife Hillary "wore the pants" in his family. Clinton, according to Ducat, lacked symbolic ownership of the phallus, necessary for a man with power. Attempts by Clinton's handlers to symbolically masculinize Bill, and to feminize Hillary, did little to help either of their images.

However, in the aftermath of the scandals surrounding Bill Clinton's sexual relations with White House intern Monica Lewinsky, Clinton's poll numbers skyrocketed. A 1998 Gallup poll conducted after the scandal broke found that Americans saw him as the most admired man in the world. He had morphed, in Ducat's words, from "emasculated house-husband to stud muffin," from "pussy" to "walking erection" (p. 150). Hillary Clinton's "stand by your man" posture apparently enhanced her popularity, too.

Hegemonic Masculinity and Women in Politics

To summarize, Arnold Schwarzenegger's sexy, hybrid mix of hardness and compassion is currently a configuration of symbols that forge a masculinity that is useful for securing power among men who already have it. But for a woman striving for power—at least in the context of the United States' current gender order—these opposites don't mesh as easily. Strength and compassion, when embodied in a woman leader, still appear to clash in ways that set her up for public crucifixion. U.S. congresswoman Pat Schroeder's brief flirtation with a presidential run in 1988—derailed by a public tear—comes to mind. Though Schroeder's many successful years in Congress, and especially her position as head of the Congressional Armed Services Committee, might have made her seem a serious candidate for the presidency, one public tear made her seem perhaps too feminine to become president. By contrast, during her years as first lady, Hillary Clinton was pilloried for her supposed "ballbusting" of her husband, for having her own ambitions to gain political power—in short, for being too much like a man. Former British prime minister Margaret Thatcher is no exception; she proves the rule. Thatcher was notoriously conservative with respect to slashing the British welfare state, and she complemented U.S. President Ronald Reagan with her militaristic saber rattling. An individual woman *can* occasionally out-masculine the men and be a strong leader. But, as with Thatcher, she'd better leave compassion and caring for the poor, for the sick, and for the aged literally at home.

The Dangers of a Compassionate Masculinity

Arnold Schwarzenegger is not the first male politician to attempt to craft a postfeminist hybrid symbology of hegemonic masculinity. George Bush, Sr., battled his own reputation as a bureaucratic wimp with a masculinizing project of waging war against Saddam Hussein. He signaled his compassionate side with speeches encouraging others (instead of the government) to be "a thousand points of light" to help the poor and homeless. And the 2004 presidential election between Kerry and George W. Bush seemed to devolve into another old *Saturday Night Live* satire: *quien es mas macho?* This reveals something important about the ascendant hegemonic masculinity. It did not seem to matter to many voters that Bush had been a lousy student who partied his youth away, and only escaped the shame of a drunk driving conviction, Vietnam War service evasion, and possible desertion from his National Guard service through his born-with-a-silver-spoon family connections. Nor did it seem to matter to many voters that John Kerry had served willingly in Vietnam and had been honored for bravery and war wounds. Kerry was still—with enough success to neutralize this apparent war hero advantage—stained by his association with "elite liberalism."

This is nothing new. Adlai Stevenson's unsuccessful runs for the presidency in 1952 and 1956 offer a good case in point. The conservative attack on Stevenson can be seen as part of the postwar hysteria about "reds" and "homosexuals." Kimmel (1996, p. 237) notes not only was Stevenson labeled "soft" on communism, but he was the classic "egghead." The candidate whom the *New York Daily News* called "Adelaide" used "tea cup words," which he "trilled" with his "fruity" voice, and was supported by "Harvard lace cuff liberals" and "lace panty diplomats."

A month before the 1952 Democratic Convention, FBI head, J. Edgar Hoover, ordered a "blind memorandum" be prepared on Stevenson. The "investigation" concluded that Stevenson was "one of the best known homosexuals" in Illinois (Theoharis, 2002, p. 180). Though the FBI memorandum was not made public at the time, attacks on Stevenson's masculinity (linked with his liberalism and intellectualism) formed a core of the contrast that Republicans successfully drew between Stevenson and war hero General Dwight D. Eisenhower, who handily won the election—and reelection four years later. For the past half-century, conservatives have used a version of this same gender strategy to wage a successful symbolic campaign that links liberalism with softness: book-learning and intellectual curiosity are viewed as a lack of inner strength and determination. Seeing the complications and gray areas in any public debate is viewed as a sign of waffling and a lack of an inner values-based compass. And compassion for the pain of others is seen as weakness.

To be sure, as President George W. Bush's slogan about "compassionate conservatism" showed, conservatives have incorporated the language of care into their project. As I have argued, a leadership masculinity without compassion is now symbolically untenable. But the new hybrid hegemonic masculinity always leads with the muscle. Muscle must first and foremost be evident; compassion is displayed at appropriate symbolic moments, suggesting a human side to the man. Liberalism suffers from the fact that it seems too often to lead with compassion, not with muscle. So when liberals try to look muscular, they are much more easily subjected to ridicule, like they are in some sort of gender drag, as evidenced by the infamous moment when 1988 Democratic presidential candidate Michael Dukakis tried to dress up like a commander-in-chief but ended up looking more like a schoolboy taking a joyride in a tank while wearing a too-large military costume.

George W. Bush's love of military dress-up did not draw the same kind of ridicule. Or, at least it can be said that this kind of ridicule does not seem to stick in the way it does when aimed at a supposed liberal. And so, very sadly I think, in recent presidential campaigns we saw both candidates trying their hardest to appear tough, strong, decisive, athletic, and militaristic, while suggesting—parenthetically, almost as an afterthought—that they care about all of us, that seniors should get prescription drugs, that no child should be left behind. The asymmetries in the ways that these two candidates were able to deploy this hybrid masculinity were apparent. When Kerry said that smart leadership would lead to a "more sensitive" waging of the war in Iraq, it was the only opening that any manly hunter would need; Vice President Dick Cheney needed no shotgun to jump right on this opportunity to blast the war hero with the feminized symbolism of weakness and liberalism.

Gender, Politics, and Justice

The accomplishment of a stable hegemonic masculinity by an individual man in daily interactions is nearly impossible. But what helps to anchor an otherwise unstable hegemonic masculinity is the play of masculine imagery in the symbolic realm. Today, for the moment, the gender imagery seen in the combined films of Arnold Schwarzenegger creates a hybrid masculinity I am calling the Kindergarten Commando. This image, when deployed in the realm of electoral politics, secures power and privilege in a moment of destabilized gender and race relations, economic insecurity, and concerns about immigration, all permeated with a culture of fear.

The widespread consent that accumulates around this form of masculinity is, I suggest, an example of hegemony at work. And—importantly—the power and privilege that this hegemonic masculinity secures is not necessarily or simply "men's power over women." The erotically charged masculinity of the famously cigar-loving Governator was effective in securing power in terms of race and nation, and in class relations in California. What I am suggesting here is that the public symbolism of hegemonic masculinity is a means of consolidating power in a matrix of class, race, and international politics. For California in 2004, it was Arnold Schwarzenegger's combination of muscle, heterosexuality, and whiteness—particularly the way his story reiterated the white European melting pot story of individualism and upward mobility in a meritocratic America—that formed a successful symbolic package that enough voters liked. As governor, Schwarzenegger mobilized this package first and foremost to wage class war on California's public workers and poor. But as Connell and Messerschmidt (2005) point out, hegemonic masculinity is always contingent and contextual. As contexts change, challenges are possible, perhaps inevitable. And California over the past few years has certainly been a site of rapid shifts and conflicts.

Schwarzenegger's attack on the underprivileged left him open to criticism of his own privilege and the possible use of his office to further his own interests. Opposition to Schwarzenegger mounted in 2005, as organized California teachers, nurses, firefighters, and other public employees waged massive protests and media campaigns against the governor. His having flexed his Terminator muscles left him open to questioning about whether he really cared about the elderly. Health activists and advocates for the elderly railed at the large donations he had accepted from the insurance and pharmaceutical industries, and his decisions that reflected those links. Perhaps, at least in California, a less conservative state than most, many of the governor's constituents wanted to see care and compassion reflected in *actual policies* rather than simply in some of his movies.

And so, after the ballot initiatives that he had sponsored were soundly defeated in the 2005 special election that he had called for, Schwarzenegger immediately shifted his strategy, leaving his combative Terminator persona behind and returning to the Kindergarten Commando. He began to promote some liberal issues, including signing landmark legislation to control global warming. He finally agreed to sign legislation to authorize a modest raise in California's minimum wage. But he also advocated cutting thousands of poor off of the welfare rolls and continued his ties with corporate elites in the pharmaceutical industry. Perhaps the new model for Schwarzenegger might be closer to the masculinity of Bill Clinton—combining a moderate liberalism on social issues like women's and gay rights with a fiscal conservatism that continues to enlarge the gap between rich and poor. The success of this new man leadership style is at once a visible sign of the ways that liberal feminist critiques of "traditional masculinity" have been incorporated and embodied into many professional-class men's interactional styles and displays. What results is a rounding of the hard edges off of hypermasculinity and a visible softening of powerful men's public styles and displays. But this should not be seen necessarily as a major victory for feminism. Rather, if I am correct that this more "sensitive" new man style tends to facilitate and legitimize privileged men's wielding of power over others, this is probably better seen as an example of feminism being co-opted into new forms of domination—in this case, class and race domination.

Schwarzenegger's return to Kindergarten Commando masculinity appears to have worked. His shift to more centrist stands—undoubtedly influenced by his more liberal wife, Maria Shriver—has calmed the anti-Arnold storms of 2005. And clearly, the muscle still matters: one of the largest advantages he had over his Democratic opponent in 2006 was that voters saw Schwarzenegger as a much stronger leader. A preelection poll conducted by the *Los Angeles Times* found that 60% of likely voters saw Schwarzenegger as a "strong leader," while only 20% viewed Phil Angelides as strong.

In short, I speculate that Governor Schwarzenegger's 2004–2005 rejection of the hybrid "Kindergarten Commando" masculine imagery that had gotten him elected contributed to a dramatic decline in his popularity, and to his thrashing in the special election of 2005. When he dropped the oppositional tough-guy approach and redeployed the Kindergarten Commando, his popularity again soared in 2006, contributing to his landslide reelection.

Conclusion

If we are to work toward economic justice for working people, immigrants, and the aged, toward equality for women and racial and sexual minorities, and if we are to work toward the creation of a more just and peaceful world, we need to tackle head-on the ways that dominant forms of masculinity—while always contested and shifting—continue to serve as a nexus of power that secures the privileges of the few at the expense of the many. Governor Arnold Schwarzenegger's strategic shifting of his public persona from Kindergarten Commando to Terminator and then back to Kindergarten Commando illustrates how, in the realm of electoral politics, hegemonic masculinity is a malleable symbolic strategy for wielding power.

In electoral politics, men's militaristic muscular posturing in seeking office limits women's abilities to seek high office in much the same ways that narrow masculine displays of dress, demeanor, voice, and style narrow women's chances in corporate and professional occupations. Women's activism in public life challenges these limitations, but if meaningful change is to occur, male leaders must also stop conforming to a singular masculine style of dress, demeanor, or leadership style.

It is unlikely that new, expansive, and progressive imagery will emanate from top male politicians. It's more likely that some men who seek high office but have progressive (even feminist) values may try to be "stealth feminists"—while posturing in military garb (like Dukakis in 1988), downplaying a deep commitment to reversing the human destruction of the environment (Gore in 2000), or overemphasizing long past military accomplishments (Kerry in 2004) instead of focusing on issues and values that they cherish. This doesn't work, partly because it is bad theatre. Even if this strategy succeeds in getting someone elected, it's unlikely that stealth feminism will work; men who get to the top using masculine muscle will rightly assume that, once in office, their constituents expect them to flex those muscles (e.g., President Jimmy Carter's ill-fated use of military power in 1980 in his attempt to end the Iran hostage crisis).

What we need is a renewed movement of ordinary women and men working side-by-side to push assertively for an ideal of the public that is founded first and foremost on compassion and caring. The seeds of such a movement currently exist—in feminist organizations, the peace movement, religious-based immigrant rights organizations, and union-based organizing for the rights of workers. A coalition of these progressive organizations can succeed in infusing local and national politics with the values of public compassion. This won't happen easily, or without opposition. We need to expect that such a movement will have to be tough, will have to fight—against entrenched privilege and against the politics of fear—in order to place compassion and care at the top of the public agenda. Out of such a movement, we can generate and support women and men who will *lead* with love and compassion and *follow* with the muscle.

References

Benwell, B. (2004). Ironic discourse: Evasive masculinity in men's lifestyle magazines. *Men and Masculinities, 7,* 3–21.

Boyle, E. (2006, November). *Memorializing muscle in the auto/biography(ies) of Arnold Schwarzenegger.* Paper delivered at the annual meetings of the North American Society for the Sociology of Sport, Vancouver, BC.

Collins, P. H. (1990). *Black feminist thought: Knowledge, consciousness, and the politics of empowerment.* Boston: Unwin Hyman.

Connell, R. W. (1987). *Gender & power.* Stanford, CA: Stanford University Press.

Connell, R. W., & Messerschmidt, J. W. (2005). Hegemonic masculinity: Rethinking the concept. *Gender & Society, 19,* 829–859.

Ducat, S. J. (2004). *The wimp factor: Gender gaps, holy wars, and the politics of anxious masculinity.* Boston: Beacon Press.

Gómez-Barris, M., & Gray, H. (2006). Michael Jackson, television and post-op disasters. *Television and New Media, 7,* 40–51.

Jeffords, S. (1989). *The remasculinization of America: Gender and the Vietnam war.* Bloomington: Indiana University Press.

Kimmel, M. (1996). *Manhood in America: A cultural history.* New York: Free Press.

Messerschmidt, J. W. (2000). *Nine lives: Adolescent masculinities, the body, and violence.* Boulder, CO: Westview.

Messner, M. A. (2004). On patriarchs and losers: Rethinking men's interests. *Berkeley Journal of Sociology, 48,* 76–88.

Messner, M. A., & Montez de Oca, J. (2005). The male consumer as loser: Beer and liquor ads in mega sports media events. *Signs: Journal of Women in Culture and Society, 30,* 1879–1909.

Montez de Oca, J. (2005). As our muscles get softer, our missile race becomes harder: Cultural citizenship and the muscle gap. *Journal of Historical Sociology, 18,* 145–171.

Theoharis, A. (2002). *Chasing spies.* Chicago: Ivan R. Dee.

Theweleit, K. (1987). *Male fantasies, volume 1: Women, floods, bodies, history.* Minneapolis: University of Minnesota Press.

Young, I. M. (2003). The logic of masculinist protection: Reflections on the current security state. *Signs: Journal of Women in Culture and Society, 29,* 1–25.

Notes

1. The term *Governator* became a widely used way to refer to Arnold Schwarzenegger in the popular media and among Californians in the aftermath of his election as California governor. The term symbolically links his job as governor with his best-known film role as the Terminator, and speaks to his successful construction of a hybrid celebrity personality that I discuss in this paper.

2. This article first appeared in *Gender & Society,* 21 (2007), pp. 461–480. Reprinted with the author's permission.

CONSTRUCTING EMPOWERED WOMEN

Cinematic Images of Power and Powerful Women

Jean-Anne Sutherland

f you were asked to think of a powerful woman in film, who might come to mind? Perhaps Sigourney Weaver in *Alien* (1979)? Maybe *Thelma & Louise* (1991)? Or Jennifer Lopez after her karate classes in *Enough* (2002)? Perhaps Nurse Ratched in *One Flew Over the Cuckoo's Nest* (1975) struck you as powerful, or *Norma Rae* (1979) when she stands on the table in the factory, holding the "UNION" sign as the loud machines slowly click off in support of her and the union. How many women would we come up with, and what would they look like?

As a starting point, it is important to observe the complexity of the presentation of powerful women in film. It is not straightforward. For instance, oftentimes when we see a powerful woman in a film, her power is the problem to be explained, overcome, or destroyed. Power is not the solution, as it is for men in film, but rather a flaw that must be rectified. Think of the two women in *Fatal Attraction* (1987). We are given Alex (Glenn Close), the confident, aggressive woman. She uses her sexual powers to lure Dan (Michael Douglas) into an affair. Her power is "bad." In fact, it is "mad," as in insane. Thus, the dutiful wife (Anne Archer) kills the seductress, quite legitimately (Alex killed their daughter's bunny, after all). Similarly, Catherine Tramell (Sharon Stone) in *Basic Instinct* (1992) may have indeed been powerful and clever, but her power, also highly sexualized, was to be overcome lest she continue to slaughter men. Annette Bening's character in *American Beauty* (1999) had many characteristics of a powerful male: she was passionately driven to succeed in her career, she wanted to maintain the lifestyle of the financially successful, she even engaged in an extramarital affair as many "successful" male characters have done in countless films. Yet, she is thought of as "the bitch," the relentless nag who "caused" poor Lester's (Kevin Spacey) breakdown.

If we are asked to think of powerful men in film, the question is less complicated. We might begin with Douglas Fairbanks, Edward G. Robinson, and Humphrey Bogart, covering several decades of early film. Then we could move to John Wayne, Clint Eastwood, Al Pacino, Sylvester Stallone, Michael Douglas, Arnold Schwarzenegger, Bruce Willis, Dwayne Johnson (aka "The Rock"), or Vin Diesel.[1] To be asked about "powerful men in film" might even strike us as a somewhat redundant question (that is, most men in film tend to be powerful—there's nothing remarkable about that). We've seen men exert power in film for so long that it seems odd to draw attention to it. The representation of men and power is rather straightforward—their "power" is more often than not the solution to whatever crisis the film revolves around.

Thus, we should pause and consider our ideas about power and women in film. Does Thelma's power (the kind that provoked her to run away from her constrained life) register as the same power Jennifer Lopez's character managed to muster (the kind that motivated her to kill her abusive husband)? Does either of these look like the kind of power Norma Rae had to gather to stand up for nonunionized factory workers? What does it mean to say that a woman is "powerful" in a film?

From 1929, when sound entered movies, until July 1, 1934, it was not at all unusual to see a film where the central character was a sexualized, self-sufficient woman. This period is what film critics have dubbed the "pre-Code" era of Hollywood. According to Mick LaSalle (2000), this era was dominated by films depicting multifaceted women who held jobs, took lovers, committed crimes, struggled with loss and the complexity of emotion, and claimed their sexuality. These films presented powerful women. They worked, they had sex, and they crossed boundaries. They acted a bit like men. These were not "women's films." Rather, these were the "movies the general public flocked to see." Alas, all of that came to an end—not gradually, but in one signing on the line. The so-called Legion of Decency, an organization of Catholic clergy, made their demands to the heads of studios: stop the indecency or we'll tell Catholics to stop seeing movies! An agreement was struck. The "codes" were enforced. Films no longer looked the same and neither did the women.

After the establishment of the Production Code, women returned home from work, denied their sexuality, sought marriage and motherhood above all else, and in general became more "ladylike." While we can find exceptions, as LaSalle points out, the change in women in film was startling and abrupt. But, we might ask if these pre-Code women were really powerful or whether they reinforced stereotypes of women using their sexuality as "vixens." We could then look at the films of the 1960s and 1970s that began to chisel away at the mostly dichotomous presentations of women in film: the virgin (Doris Day) and the whore (Sophia Loren). Was the critique of patriarchy in *The Stepford Wives* (1975) a step forward? Did Katharine Ross's character have power or did her eventual demise into robot perfection of femininity symbolize the futility of fighting against male expectations of women?

In this reading, I first discuss the concept of power. In order to decide who and what is powerful, it is necessary to first consider power and the multiple ways in which the term might be defined. I then discuss what those kinds of power tend to look like in film. Feminist scholarship acknowledges that some kind of acquisition of power is a necessary step in terms of women overcoming myriad layers of oppression. Thus, I also consider the extent to which these images of powerful women suggest social change for women—some crack in the traditions of sexual oppression and inequality. I will consider (1) what is power, (2) what do these varieties of power look like in film, and (3) do any of these representations actually offer a challenge to patriarchy?

What Is Power?

When we refer to power, it may well be that we take for granted what power is, without further consideration of the word. *Power*, after all, is a word we toss around in our lives almost daily. If we are asked to define it, perhaps we assume it looks only one way. Across disciplines, scholars have defined and conceptualized power in multiple ways. I have chosen three definitions most prominent in the literature, beginning with the most commonly understood notion of power.

Power-Over

The definition of power with perhaps the longest history in sociology, philosophy, and psychology is *power-over* (Nash, 2000, p.1; Yoder & Kahn, 1992). Power-over is the manner in which Weber defined power: the ability of one actor to carry out his (*sic*) will against another. Weber described it this way: "The chance of man or a number of men to realize their own will in a communal action even against the resistance of others who are participating in the action" (Nash, 2000). Chances are, if a student took an introduction to sociology course, this is the definition that emerged from his or her text. In a 1981 study, Paap found that nearly two-thirds of introduction to sociology texts defined power in this Weberian fashion. Not only is it a definition that runs through sociology and across disciplines, it also registers as the most "commonsense" definition. If a group has power, group members can achieve their goals. A person who has power can achieve his or her goals, and perhaps punch someone in the process.

Amy Allen (2000) argues that this conceptualization takes the form of a dyadic, master-subject relation; one is powered (master) and one is not (subject). In Marxist terms, the bourgeoisie have power (masters) and the proletariats have none (subjects). In that sense, the fate of the subjects is fully determined by the power wielded by the masters. This is a kind of masculinized power. When placed within the context of masculinity, power is seen in terms of force, inequality, and the ability to impose not only physical strength over others, but meanings and ideas as well (Connell, 1987). As Kimmel (1994) notes, manhood itself is equated with power. Hegemonic masculinity (the dominant culture's construction of manhood) is an image of men *in, with,* and *of* power.

According to Allen (1998), on the continuum of feminist analyses of power, the two ends are represented by those who see power as *domination* or *empowerment*. Domination theorists have focused their critiques on the ways in which men dominate or oppress women. Their analyses of domination, inequality, and the subjugation of women work within this power-over conceptualization. Prominent feminists such as Andrea Dworkin and Catharine MacKinnon have, according to Allen, grounded their analysis of inequality in the notion that masculinity means domination and femininity means subjection. The domination view holds that "what it means to be a woman is powerless, and what it means to be a man is to be powerful" (p. 23). These theorists do acknowledge that different men have different levels of power—white men more than black men, for example. But this perspective represents only a portion of a complete conceptualization of power. With their focus on men's domination of women, these theorists do not account for the moments in which women *do* assert their power over men and other women.

Important to note as we consider the feminist scholarship on power is that feminists are not working toward power-over for women. The goal of feminism is not to transfer domination and oppression (and masculinity) into the hands of women. Rather, feminists have exposed this type of power in order to dismantle it.

Power-To

If you were to search for the word *power* in the dictionary, whether the analog version (*Oxford English Dictionary*) or, more conveniently, online (dictionary.com), you would see that the first definition concerns the idea of personal control: "the ability to do or act." This "ability" is itself gendered in that research reveals that men tend to report higher levels of mastery than do women (Ross & Mirowsky, 2002).[2] If the ability to act requires a sense of control (or high levels of mastery), it is no wonder that research finds this more so in men than women. After all, at an early age we socialize boys toward notions of ability and strength and girls with notions of passivity and neediness (through childhood toys as well as film). Boys are taught to do and act while girls are encouraged to nurture others. Boys are taught to compete, and their levels of self-esteem generally rise throughout childhood. Girls learn the importance of physical attractiveness, and their levels of self-esteem tend to drop off in early adolescence.[3]

In social psychological terms, we associate *power-to* with what Bandura calls "personal control" or "self-efficacy" (see Yoder & Kahn, 1992). Bandura (1997) described self-efficacy as the extent to which we believe we have the ability to achieve results from our actions. This kind of personal empowerment is often conceptualized as "mastery," or the sense of having control over the circumstances of your life. In borrowing from these social psychological concepts, I mean to suggest a kind of power whereby a woman recognizes her own abilities and sense of agency. That is, do women have the power to act? Under what circumstances do women grasp their sense of agency and realize the control they have over the consequences of their lives?

"Empowerment theorists," as Allen (1998) dubs them, focus on "women's power to transform themselves, others, and the world" (p. 26). Carol Gilligan, Sara Ruddick, and Virginia Held have focused on the ways in which women's skills (e.g., nurturing, care giving, relationship building) have been devalued. These works build on the notion that as a woman performs care duties, particularly the role of mother, she is not powerless, but in fact empowered. Allen notes that to have power in the mothering role, according to Ruddick (1989, p. 37), is "to have the individual strength or the collective resources to pursue one's pleasure and projects." Nancy Hartsock makes a similar argument. By taking the standpoint of women, it is possible to create notions of power distinct from male analysis of power-over (in Sprague, 2005).

The empowerment theorists are working with a picture of power as power-to, the ability of a woman to recognize the control she has over her life, see the results of her actions, and recognize the power of the self. Empowerment theorists, like the domination theorists, lack a complete analysis. In other words, while noting that women draw power from previously undervalued roles (such as mothering), they fail to note the ways in which these roles are themselves determined by a gendered society.

For our purposes, these two definitions of power are incomplete. The first, power-over, while social is also hierarchical. It embraces a masculinist typology that equates power with domination. Domination theorists who work within this framework critique the ways in which men dominate women in society, but fail to account for ways in which women dominate or assert power. The second definition is also incomplete as it offers a view of power as individual and experiential. Utilizing this conceptualization takes power out of the social context. Empowerment theorists acknowledge feminine practices, but do so without consideration of male dominance. Neither of these two types of power offers any real "threat" to the patriarchal structure. In the first, we have women adopting the very modes of masculinity that feminists oppose. In the second, we have a step forward from that—women individually recognizing the ways in which they have personal power, but without the goal of *social* change. There is a third definition we must consider.

Power-With

A third, more integrative approach to power is needed in our analysis of powerful women in film. Allen (1998) calls this third approach *power-with*. She argues, "We must be able to think about the kind of power that diverse women can exercise collectively when we work together to define, and to strive to achieve, feminist aims" (p. 32). This kind of analysis would allow us to account for masculinist domination, female empowerment, and also address the coalition building that is necessary to fully address oppression and structured inequality.

This approach depicts power as a kind of solidarity. Beyond the masculine variety of power-over, and the social psychological power-to, power-with is the kind of power whereby women come together as a group to challenge systems of oppression and bring about social change. The masculinized power-over is not the sort of power feminists have strived for. And, while personal empowerment can mean movement from oppression, it is still that—personal. However, social change is possible when solidarity is formed and women work as a collective. It is the kind of power that has produced significant change in the lives of both women and men.

What do these forms of power look like in film?

Power-Over: Masculinity

Recall power-over in the Weberian sense, which asserts that one actor (or group of actors) has the ability to control the actions of another. Thus, A can get B to do what A desires, even if said action is not in the best interest of B. We see men exerting this sort of power in films all the time. We always have. Westerns, war films, gangster films, hero-conquers-all films—all of these depict a man (or group of men) with the power to control the actions of others. They are powerful because they are masculine. In these films, we have grown accustomed to seeing women as the barmaids, the prostitutes, the tragic vixens, the adoring wives, or the hapless beauties in need of rescue.

But wait! There has been some change, hasn't there? Women are increasingly playing roles that demonstrate a kind of power-over. Yet we have to ask, what does it look like when women use power-over? I argue that three things happen when women have this sort of power in film: (1) women become "powerful" by their adoption of masculine characteristics; (2) as masculine women they often engage in the exploitation of others; and (3) when physically strong, they are often highly sexualized. We find evidence of this through an analysis of three films: *She Hate Me, The Devil Wears Prada,* and *Lara Croft: Tomb Raider.*

She Hate Me (Spike Lee, 2004)

Spike Lee's *She Hate Me* is the story of Jack (Anthony Mackie), who has fallen on hard times. A formerly successful biotech executive, he finds himself penniless when his attempts to expose corruption at his corporation cost him his job. All of his assets frozen, he finds himself financially ruined. Enter his ex-fiancé Fatima (Kerry Washington), a stunningly gorgeous woman, now in a relationship with another stunningly gorgeous woman, Simona (Monica Bellucci). Fatima and Simona approach him with a business venture. They want to get pregnant. They ask if he will impregnate them for a very handsome fee. He rants and protests, but eventually agrees. Soon, all of their wealthy lesbian friends find out and a real business venture is under way—he gets them pregnant, they pay him lots of money. (Interestingly, all of these lesbian women, with the exception of Simona, choose the "old-fashioned method," as subsequent scenes show each having varieties of fairly aggressive intercourse with Jack.)

They have the money; he has the sperm. They have the power, thus they can get Jack to do what they want Jack to do. At first glance we might cheer just a little when we see successful women with substantial incomes aggressively getting what they want, and with such confidence. We might be inclined to chuckle at the reversal of roles: a man "putting out" to a group of demanding women. But, looking closely, we might be a bit more critical of the power we see. In fact, we see *women becoming "powerful" by their adoption of masculine characteristics.*

In one scene, the first group of women comes to Jack's home as Fatima and Simona explain the "deal." The women begin to agree to the terms and costs. One woman stops the conversation, asking how she can be sure of what she is "getting." She sits with her arm resting on the back of the couch (a rather masculine pose), and says to Jack, "Strip, bitch." In the moments that follow, Jack slowly begins to remove his clothes, starting with his shirt, until he stands naked before them. He is quiet, his face reflecting humiliation and shame. One of the women comments, "Now you know how it feels."

Is this a moment of powerful women in film? Or a moment when women are using the same kind of masculine power-over that results in the oppression of others? Later in the film one of the women says to Jack, "We see you as nothing but dick, sperm, and balls." To objectify a man as women have long been objectified is a seriously impoverished view of power. The goal of feminism is not to place the power of humiliation and abuse into the hands of women. Rather, that is the kind of oppressive power that feminists have challenged and sought to change.

The Devil Wears Prada (David Frankel, 2006)

Meryl Streep's performance as Miranda Priestly, the cold and cynical fashion magazine editor, was highly praised for its dead-on ruthlessness. Miranda is not just any magazine editor; she is THE editor whose decisions determine the fashion world. Hers is a powerful position, and she dominates those around her. When Andy (Anne Hathaway) lands a job as her personal assistant, she is unaware of the inner workings of the industry and thus unprepared for the scorn and cruelty she encounters at her new job. Her days are spent running, anxiety-ridden, here and there, trying desperately to satisfy a boss who only places further demands, mixed with cold criticism. We laugh at Andy's foibles and Miranda's tight-lipped criticisms. And we perhaps enjoy a film that centers on a woman as head of a powerful industry (albeit the fashion industry).

The Devil Wears Prada offers audiences a commanding and powerful woman. Instead of Michael Douglas in charge (as in *Wall Street*, 1987), we have Meryl Streep. The most powerful executive in the room is a woman. But, again we must ask what this really looks like. Miranda is a boss not unlike other bosses we've seen before. Cold, chillingly mean, emotionless, and incapable of maintaining relationships, Miranda could be any male executive that has come before.

Again, we see a woman with power, but it looks like the masculinized version of power-over that we have grown accustomed to, perhaps the only kind of power we recognize as "power." We simply cheer when we see women given a chance to do it. Is it any sign of progress when women perform as the kind of oppressive executives that feminists have criticized? Miranda represents yet another version of masculinized power that offers no alternative or dialogue concerning workplace dynamics (in which women are far more often the power*less*). In *The Devil Wears Prada,* we are presented with a masculinized woman, at least in the norms of bureaucratic leadership. And, in film, *as masculine women they often engage in the exploitation of others.*

Of course, another key to this film is the contrasting types of power between the two women. Miranda is presented as a negative role model of power—it looks too much like male power and denies her emotional connections to family and friends. Andy is driven toward a career, but not if the cost is her boyfriend or her relationship with friends. There is a certain "feminist/antifeminist" feel to this contrast. If women are to attain the power that Miranda holds, it must look different. And, yes, Andy should have a career, but not if it means she loses her adoring boyfriend.

Lara Croft: Tomb Raider (Simon West, 2001)

In *Lara Croft: Tomb Raider,* Angelina Jolie plays Lara Croft, the product of a wealthy British family, who has been expertly trained in weapons and combat. She goes about her adventures, collecting artifacts from tombs, temples, and ruins around the world. She stares down danger; she flips, fights, handles big guns, wears dark shades, and delivers wry, cold lines that reinforce her coolness. And she does it all while looking extraordinarily sexy. While we might have found Harrison Ford ruggedly attractive as Indiana Jones, Jolie is the very image of sexy in these films. Ford wore worn, baggy pants and jacket. Jolie is seen in tight-fitting clothes that accentuate her long legs, her shapely hips and her seemingly perfect breasts. Lara Croft is powerful, perhaps. But, make no mistake, she is HOT.

As in the *Kill Bill* (2003, 2004) series, *Lara Croft* presents us with a woman who can "fight like a man." In *Kill Bill: Vol. I* and *Vol. II,* Quentin Tarantino gave us sexualized women who could not only fight (some in little school-girl outfits), but chop off limbs with utter disregard. Lara Croft fights with impressive strength, but she too is highly sexualized while doing it. In these films, we are given strong women, but *when physically strong, they are often highly sexualized.*

We are offered images of women who can fight, and we may be inclined to see that as progress—as women gaining power in the form of muscle and strength. Of course, this too is masculine power of the power-over variety. As with the previous films, this kind of power offers no real movement from the forms of power feminists have critiqued. We can go as far as saying that power in this form is no threat at all to patriarchy. It either *is* patriarchy, redubbed with women, or it is physical power so heavily sexualized as to border on the comical. We can cheer for Lara Croft. We can even nudge our daughters and say, "See how strong she is?" But we must also recognize the limitations of such representations of power. First, they are based solidly on the sexuality of the woman. Her power is unconditionally linked to her physical attractiveness. Thus, our daughters might be motivated to lift weights, but quite possibly equally motivated to have breast implants. And second, the kind of power demonstrated in all three of these films—the kind that mimics masculinity, the variety that continues to oppress, and the physically strong yet highly sexual—none of these offers, serious threat to the traditions of patriarchy. In fact, they are drawn within the very limits of patriarchy, by patriarchy. There will never be enough Lara Crofts to really scare anyone.

Power-To: Agency and Autonomy

The second definition of power we considered was power-to, a personal sense of control. With this power, a woman can recognize the extent to which her actions determine her fate. She can come to know her own sense of agency and recognize her autonomy.

What does power-to tend to look like for women in film? We find this form of power begins to surface in films that portray women who, recognizing the restrictions of the norms dictating their lives, begin a search for "more." Lacking any real knowledge of personal empowerment (power-to) at the film's beginning, as the story unfolds, she comes to know something core about herself. These films have three prominent features. The women in these films tend to (1) separate from their lives, their cultures, and traditions as they begin to experience them as restrictive; (2) "wake up" from years of unconscious living and find agency where there was little; and (3) discover themselves through a discovery of their sexual selves or through the recognition that their lives are no longer dependent on having a man present. We'll take a look at these three features as they appear in *Real Women Have Curves*, *The Color Purple*, and *Waitress*.

Real Women Have Curves (Patricia Cardoso, 2002)

In this film, set in East Los Angeles, Ana (America Ferrera), a first generation Mexican American, has just graduated from high school. Her exceptional performance in school resulted in a full scholarship to Columbia University in New York City. Her family, a traditional Mexican family, struggles to survive financially on the earnings of Ana's sister, Estela's (Ingrid Oliu) sewing factory. Having given up her hopes for Columbia, Ana spends the summer working in Estela's factory with her sister, her mother, and several women from the neighborhood. Ana's mother is firmly rooted in the traditions of her culture and wants the same for Ana. At 18 years old, it is time for Ana to learn to sew, raise kids, and take care of a husband. She tells Ana, "A mother knows the right man for her daughter." Her advice to Ana: work hard, lose weight, find a man. As hard as Ana tries, she just can't find this advice acceptable.

Throughout the film, Ana *begins to separate from her life, her culture, and traditions, and begins to experience them as restrictive*. With a deep love for her family and a newfound respect for her sister's work, she still longs for the opportunities college offers. Not only has her mother's adherence to traditional ways proven restrictive of her future goals, her mother's sense of what it means to be a woman (get married, raise kids) has placed tremendous emphasis on physical beauty. Ana rebels against the notion that she is the "fatty" her mother calls her, instead finding a way to love her body, just as it is. Eventually, Ana finds the courage to tell her father that she must leave Los Angeles and take advantage of the opportunities available to her at Columbia. Her mother never comes out of the bedroom to "give her blessing," a heartbreaking image of one generation's fear of letting go and another's inability to *not* go. The last scene of the film shows Ana emerging from the subway in New York City, a confident and empowered smile on her face.

The Color Purple (Steven Spielberg, 1985)

The Color Purple tells the story of Celie (Whoopi Goldberg), a young black girl living in rural Georgia in the early to mid 20th century. Celie's father (Leonard Jackson) sexually abuses her, resulting in the birth of two children, which her father "took away." Celie is eventually married to a local farmer called Mister (Danny Glover), who soon begins to abuse her. Celia lives with Mister, his son Harpo (Willard E. Pugh), and Harpo's defiant wife Sofia (Oprah Winfrey). Mister's lover, Shug (Margaret Avery), comes to live in the house as well, and at first she is as hateful to Celie as Mister is. Eventually Sofia leaves the abuse of Harpo, taking her children (however, her spirit is eventually broken when she is separated from her children and forced to work for the mayor's wife). Celie and Shug grow closer, with Celie finding herself attracted to Shug's tenacity and spirit. Together the women uncover secrets from the past: Celie's father is not in fact her biological father; her sister, whom she thought dead, is in fact alive; and the children she birthed are alive, well, and in her sister's care. In a powerful scene, Celie, finally *having found some agency where once there was none,* confronts Mister for his years of abuse. Celie eventually moves to Tennessee and builds her own successful business. In the end, she returns to Georgia, this time an empowered woman.

In the course of this film, Celie emerges from the lowest possible social position. Not only is she a woman, but she is a poor, uneducated African American woman living in the segregated southern United States in the early 20th century. It was rare for a woman such as Celie to question the powerlessness of her life. When women, such as Sofia, did stand up for themselves, they were beaten, imprisoned, and forced into subservience. But even this experience did not break Sofia's spirit, and she stands with Celie as she is transformed from a woman lacking power (autonomy, agency, sense of control) to a self-supporting woman in control of her own fate.

Waitress (Adrienne Shelly, 2007)

In *Waitress*, we again encounter a woman living in an abusive marriage. Jenna (Keri Russell) is married to Earl (Jeremy Sisto), but she is miserably unhappy and hides the earnings from her job at the diner in hopes of leaving him. Meanwhile, she discovers she is pregnant. As the months go by, she becomes involved with her kind, dashing, and married obstetrician-gynecologist (Nathan Fillion), which further complicates her already complicated life. Not wanting to be pregnant, feeling miserable and stuck with Earl, Jenna feels powerless and without options. She pours her emotions into ideas for pies, such as "I Don't Want Earl's Baby Pie," but she has little besides her talent for baking. While she feels loved and respected by Dr. Pomatter, his marriage prevents them from being together. She has very little money of her own. She lacks the physical strength to stand up to Earl. She pins her hopes on the chances of winning $25,000 in a pie-baking contest. With that she could leave Earl.

What makes this film remarkable sociologically is its ending. If given only the paragraph above, and knowing something about the genre of light-hearted American films, we might assume the ending. She has the baby and manages to leave abusive Earl. The gorgeous doctor whom she has grown to love finds his way to her. But, in this film, that is not quite the case.

This is a film depicting a seemingly powerless woman who comes to power through her questioning and search for empowerment. This movie ends with Jenna indeed having her baby, a daughter. Before leaving the hospital she tells Earl she has no intention of going home with him—their marriage is over. Gone is the abusive husband. Then the twist. She tells the gorgeous doctor, who appears shaken and a bit devastated, that they too are finished. Jenna inherits some money from a customer (Andy Griffith) who recognized her potential. The film ends with Jenna, her daughter by her side, in her own pie-baking business on the site where once the diner stood.

The kind of empowerment that Jenna found involved the slow awareness that she had agency. In the course of the film, Jenna found that she could control the outcome of her life and, unlike so many films with happy endings for women, *she found this in the recognition that her life no longer depended upon men.*[4] Empowerment theorists might argue that her power stemmed from the birth of her daughter—from the sense of strength and power that accompanies the mothering role. Whether due to motherhood or her months of reflection and struggle (the process of "waking up"), or some combination of both, Jenna emerges in the end a woman empowered.

All three of these films offer hope. All suggest a very important kind of power, the kind that moves women to question their taken-for-granted circumstances. When we see this form of power in film, we are moved by women who find a place of core strength and a sense of agency and autonomy. More so than with films projecting a masculinized sense of power, these films offer images of power that actually change lives and lead women to step out of the expectations of femininity and womanhood and choose their own paths. Certainly, as we hope for films that inspire or reflect (or both) social change, this is movement.

But how much does it actually challenge the structure of patriarchy? I believe that it suggests a crack in the surface, that there is at least a consciousness of women and personal empowerment. That is an important image to portray in film, as it offers women a picture of their gendered trappings (as in *Kate Chopin: A Re-awakening,* 1998). But do these films offer critiques of the social context? Is the change suggested in these films social, or does it suggest a kind of experiential, personal change? While an important and valuable "change" occurs, it has yet to resemble *social* change. I believe that we see evidence of true social change in films that take power a step further.

Power-With: Collective Power of Women

Power-with involves women working together to define and achieve feminist goals. Consider some of the significant changes that have impacted women's lives over the past 50 years: women's suffrage, women's access to contraceptives, the right of women to initiate a divorce, protections against rape, laws against sexual harassment, equal pay laws, and women entering previously male-dominated jobs such as the police force, law, and medicine. While developing personal consciousness of these issues played a vital role in the lives of the women involved, it was the collective actions of women (and the men involved in the women's movement) that forced this consciousness into public social institutions, such as law, medicine, education and the media.

Films depicting women working together for change are far more common in the documentary genre (see the Film Index) than in Hollywood feature films. When we see power-with demonstrated in Hollywood films, they are the stories of women (1) struggling within the constraints of an oppressive system, (2) coming to realize the extent of their oppression, and then (3) working together to confront the system that oppresses them. In these films, as in the film discussed below, an individual woman begins to awaken to the oppressiveness of the system in which women operate. Hard as she might try, her individual attempts at change fail until the community of women comes together as a group.

North Country (Niki Caro, 2005)

Based on the book by Clara Bingham and Laura Leedy Gansler, *Class Action: The Story of Lois Jensen and the Landmark Case That Changed Sexual Harassment Law*, *North Country* tells the story of women working in the male-dominated world of mining and their fight against the abuse and harassment they receive from their male coworkers and bosses. Josey (Charlize Theron), a single mother of two, has recently left her abusive husband. Seeking employment that will allow her to care for her children, she is thrilled to land a secure job that offers a steady income. In the days before sexual harassment laws, the women in the mines suffered myriad forms of abuse from male coworkers who resented their very presence in their masculinized world. One supervisor tells the women, "there are all sorts of things a woman shouldn't do," and working at the mine was certainly one of them. On Josey's first day, she tells this same supervisor that her paperwork is in order, including the results of a physical. The man sneers. "Doc says you look real good under those clothes." When the women are silent, he retorts, "Sense of humor, ladies! Rule numero uno."

The workplace harassment and abuse is extensive. It begins with the verbal, "Which one of these ladies will be my bitch?" "Cunts" is written on the door to their locker room. It is psychological warfare. One woman finds that a man has ejaculated in her locker, on her clothing. Another is taunted as she tries to use the outdoor port-o-pot. When the men eventually turn the toilet on its side, she climbs out, covered in urine and feces, clearly traumatized by the event. The abuse turns physical when Josey is attacked and nearly choked and raped as her attacker tells her, "You're gonna learn the goddamn rules if I have to beat them into you myself." Clearly these women are *struggling within the restraints of an oppressive system*. They have no recourse—they can "tough it out" or they can quit their jobs. Of course, living in an economically depressed region, the women often make the case that they "need this job."

The abuse these women sustain builds camaraderie. They *come to realize the extent of their oppression* as the abuse they endure increases in frequency and intensity. However, they also realize their powerlessness. When Josey takes her complaints to management she is told sternly, "I suggest you spend less time stirring up your female coworkers, less time in the beds of your married coworkers," and more time at her actual job. Their reaction to her attempt at presenting a legitimate set of complaints stuns Josey in its hostility, not to mention the blatant disregard for truth (she is not sleeping with the married coworker, the lone male who sympathizes with the women's experiences), and the denial of their reality (they can't possibly focus on their jobs when each workday is spent in constant self-defense). When Josey tries to induce change, the women at first turn against her. They fear the loss of their jobs and make it clear they will not support her in the legal actions for the rights of the women to work in harassment-free environments. She asks one woman,

"What about what happened to *you*?" Her coworker replies, "It's my business." Josey tells her and the others, "Actually it's all of our business."

In the course of her court proceedings, it appears as though Josey's case is hopeless. She is attacked for her sexual history and the paternity of her children. She only needs three plaintiffs to come forward with similar grievances in order to make her individual charges into a class-action case, but the others remain fearful and sit quietly in court. In a pivotal scene, her lawyer (Woody Harrelson) demands that those present in the courtroom "stand up and tell the truth." Slowly, the women rise in support of Josey. First her coworkers, then her mother, then her father, and slowly other men in the room until most of the room stands in support. Her case is won and laws against sexual harassment and discrimination in the workplace slowly begin to change the lives of women.

Initially working alone, Josey had no chance of winning. But by *working together to confront an oppressive system*, social change became possible. It was not until the women stood together that life for women in the workplace would begin the slow process of change. The courtroom scene begins with the women rising to their feet and ends with first a few brave men, then slowly more and more men rising in support. This scene captures the kind of solidarity in the women's movement that includes men. Feminists don't want to turn the tables and oppress men; rather, they count on men to rise to their feet, along with women, and support them in their call for social change. Real change is possible when the collective power of women (power-with) takes a stand.

Conclusion

We have considered cinematic images of power and powerful women. In the process we have come up with multiple definitions of power and multiple images of power across films. This discovery has various implications for women, conceptually and politically. Beginning with the first kind of power, power-over, we could come up with numerous films that display powerful women in this manner. Oftentimes, when women are seen as possessing power-over, it is seen as a problem, not a solution. She is too powerful, thus she is evil, a temptress, a black widow, or a bitch. If she mimics masculinized power, she is likely to be "the bitch," or we find that she is humbled (or killed!) in the end. Those physically strong women are so highly sexualized as to offer no real threat. In fact, that kind of individual power may actually reinforce patriarchy as a system. It reminds women that patriarchy itself is not so oppressive. It can't be if we keep seeing images of these powerful women. Thus, any lack of power a woman might "feel" is wrong—she has only herself to blame.

We could also come up with a fairly nice list of films that present power-to. When we contrast this image to power-over, we certainly find it more pleasing. We even consider it feminist. Women in these films are bristling under the weight of gendered expectations. They leave their abusive husbands or have adventures. They often reach out to another woman or group of women in the process. And this is good. Personal empowerment is to be cheered. Conceptually it is much preferred to the former. But what does it say about the politics of gender? Does the content or message of these films offer a threat to patriarchy? If we compared it to the films in the power-over category, we would say yes, somewhat. They present us with women who develop the power to seek and find change. However, this is not the kind of power necessary for social change.

Significantly fewer films portray the power-with model. Both conceptually and politically, these films offer an actual challenge to the definition of power and to its social foundations. We move beyond a power-over depiction of women that, in reality, is merely repeating the masculinist patterns of patriarchy. And we step beyond power-to, which depicts individual women coming to terms with their lives. Power-with films offer us images of women, coming together in solidarity, in numbers to do what one woman cannot do alone. As we move beyond masculine and individualized definitions of power, let's hope that more directors are brave \enough to offer us cinematic images of the collective power of women.

References

Allen, A. (1998). Rethinking power. *Hypatia, 13*, 21–40.

Allen, A. (2000). *The power of feminist theory: Domination, resistance, solidarity.* Boulder, CO: Westview.

Bandura, A. (1997). *Self-efficacy: The exercise of control.* New York: W. H. Freeman.

Connell, R. W. (1987). *Gender and power: Society, the person and sexual politics.* Stanford, CA: Stanford University Press.

Kimmel, M. (1994). Masculinity as homophobia: Fear, shame and silence in the construction of gender identity. In H. Brod (Ed.), *Theorizing masculinity* (pp. 119–141). Thousand Oaks, CA: Sage.

LaSalle, M. (2000). *Complicated women: Sex and power in pre-code Hollywood.* New York: Thomas Dunn Books, St. Martin's Press.

Nash, K. (2000). *Contemporary political sociology: Globalization, politics, and power.* Malden, MA: Blackwell.

Paap, W. R. (1981). The concept of power: Treatment in fifty introductory sociology textbooks. *Teaching Sociology, 9*(1), 57–68.

Ross, K. E., & Mirowsky, J. (2002). Age and the gender gap in the personal sense of control. *Social Psychological Quarterly, 65*, 125–145.

Ruddick, S. (1989). *Maternal thinking: Towards a politics of peace.* New York: Ballantine.

Sprague, J. (2005). *Feminist methodologies for critical researchers.* Lanham, MD: AltaMira Press.

Yoder, J. D., & Kahn, A. S. (1992). Toward a feminist understanding of women and power. *Psychology of Women Quarterly, 16*(4), 381–388.

Notes

1. Noting the whiteness of this list of powerful men, we can consider the successful black actors that come to mind: James Earl Jones, Denzel Washington, Will Smith, Forest Whitaker, Don Cheadle, to name a few. Racial differences in terms of the representations of men and power in film are beyond the scope of this chapter, but necessary to note.

2. As Ross and Mirowsky point out, the gender gap in sense of control is affected by education, physical functioning, household income, and work history (working for pay increases personal control). They also find that the gender gap widens with age: as women age, their sense of control drops.

3. This decline in adolescent girls' self-esteem is less true of African American girls than for other racial/ethnic groups. See Tamara R. Buckley and Robert T. Carter, "Black Adolescent Girls: Do Gender Role and Racial Identity Impact Their Self-Esteem?" *Sex Roles*, Vol. 53 (9/10, 2005), pp. 647–661.

4. Other films, such as *How Stella Got Her Groove Back* (1998), depict the power that comes when a woman discovers her forgotten sexual self.

Stop for a moment and think about your most recent encounter with a stranger. How did you know if that person was a man or a woman? While you may not have been aware of it at the time, you most likely quickly made an assessment to allow you to proceed with the encounter under the assumption that you knew the individual's sex or gender. It may have been something about that person's appearance: the clothes he or she wore, the cut and style of hair. It may have been something he or she did: the timbre of voice that greeted you or the way that person walked.

Here's another question: Did your assessment include an attempt to determine whether that person was heterosexual or homosexual? Maybe not. Much of the time, we take for granted that the people we meet are heterosexual. In other words, our presumption of heterosexuality is so strong that we assume that others are heterosexual until something leads us to question that assumption. And, interestingly enough, the things that lead us to question such an assumption also relate to appearance and behavior. Perhaps it was a man who moved his hips a little too much when he walked or a woman who dressed in "masculine" clothing and had very short hair.

In our society, we make such assessments and behave based on those assessments all of the time. We also make decisions about our own appearance and behavior based on the assumption that others are making similar assessments of us.

Key to the sociological perspective is the understanding of gender and sexuality as social constructions, as social products. Gender and sexuality are not biologically determined; they are human creations, developed over a lifetime of interaction in the context of one's culture and society. We make a variety of assumptions about gender and sexuality that are a product of the social context in which we live.

First, there is our assumption about the relationship between sex and gender. Males are boys who grow up to be men; they look and act in "masculine" ways. Females are girls who grow up to be women; they look and act in "feminine" ways. Even though none of us looks or acts in exclusively masculine or feminine ways, we still tend to believe that men and women are "opposites." Similarly, masculine and feminine traits are conceptualized as opposites: boys are aggressive and girls are passive; men are prone to violence while women are prone to caretaking.

We grow up in a society that works very hard to ensure the persistence of these differences, yet, at the same time, we insist that the differences are "natural." Through the wonders of ultrasound technology, we need not wait until a baby is born to ask the most fundamental of all questions: "Is it a boy or a girl?" As soon as that question is answered, a pervasive process of gendering begins. We give different names, distinctive clothing, and different toys based on the answer. Throughout our lives, we expect men and women to see the world differently, to pursue different careers, and to have different priorities.

We train men and women to see each other as opposites and then expect them to fall in love, get married, and live happily ever after! For a society that provides so much support to heterosexual couples (e.g., all of the legal benefits of marriage), we also set them up for failure. How will they understand each other? Surely they won't have similar interests or like the same things. And, yet, people who couple with their opposites are the ones we see as normal—because, after all, *opposites attract!*

In the context of these assumptions, there is little room for the existence of complex identities, such as bisexuality and transgender. Dualistic gender and sexual identities are firmly rooted in our social landscape. However, this landscape is fraught with tensions and contradictions as it both *forces* and *relies on* social actors to imagine and experience their sexual and gendered identities as dichotomous (i.e., as being either one or the other). Even though lived experience shows us that sexual and gendered lives are rarely consistent, but usually dynamic (changing across contexts and over the course of a lifetime), these irregularities and shifts are ignored. Instead, they are subsumed, even hidden, under binary, dichotomous, "either/or" categories.

These dualistic categorizations are not mere conceptualizations existing only in the theoretical realm; they have real-world consequences for individuals who personally and socially identify as bisexual and/or transgender. For them, the dualistic conceptualizations of heterosexual/homosexual and man/woman are not enough because such conceptualizations do not reflect the reality of their experiences or identities. Identities are indeed complex; yet this complexity is wholly absent from the sexual duality of hetero/homo and the two-and-only-two gender categories that have come to serve as cornerstones of our social world.

Using a feminist social constructionist framework, in this chapter we examine how bisexuality and transgender can challenge either/or categorizations of sexual and/or gender identity, specifically as seen in the films *Chasing Amy* (1997) and *Transamerica* (2005). Using these films, we consider how sexual and gender categories have clear boundaries at the same time that people's experiences overflow and escape these strict categories.

Bisexuals and transgender individuals are oftentimes denied access to power and privileges otherwise granted to those who maintain "heterogender" (Ingraham, 1994) or "heterosexualized" patterns of behavior and interaction. This reading considers the depiction of bisexual and transgendered lives on film and reexamines *both* sexuality and gender identification categories through our analysis of *Chasing Amy* and *Transamerica*.

We begin by exploring the (in)visibility of bisexual and transgender identities. In *Transmen and FTMs*, Jason Cromwell (1999) argues that transgendered persons become "erased" when they "blend in and become unnoticeable and unremarkable as either a man or a woman" (p. 39). Likewise, when bisexuals are identified by social others as lesbian, gay, or straight, their identity as bisexual is erased. Thus, bisexuals, too, can appear "unremarkable." These identities become co-opted under the rubric of "heterogender" and homosexuality because they deviate from normative gender and sexual expectations. Thus, "doing bisexuality" (Miller, 2006) and "doing transgender" requires others to call their heteronormative assumptions into question—to rethink their own gender and sexuality assumptions. Using these two films we show how "changing gender [and/or sexuality] may be less empowering than changing how others *perceive* [italics added] our gender [and/or sexuality]" (Cromwell, 1999, p. 5).

Doing Gender/Doing Sexuality

With the groundbreaking work of West and Zimmerman (1987) in their article "Doing Gender," gender was repositioned as something that one accomplishes through his or her daily interactions with other people. The assumption is that individuals are constantly doing gender, whether they intend to or not. The social constructionist approach to gender reveals the potential individuals possess both to maintain and to deviate from what Lorber (1994) has referred to as "gendered processes," or those learned patterns that are enacted in order to conform, deviate from, or test gender-appropriate behavior.

What is perhaps most important with regard to this conceptual framework is the understanding of gender as a product of social interaction. One does not have to consciously perform his or her gender, for others will "do gender" for him or her regardless of what gender the social actor intended to project (Lucal, 1999). For example, those who participate in androgynous presentations of self (Goffman, 1959, 1976) to break down strict gender polarizations tend to be placed by others into one of the two available gender categories rather than into the gender-neutral category the androgynous actor may have intended (Frye, 1983; Lorber, 1994). Lucal (1999) has written about her experiences of being mistaken for a man, showing how important appearance cues are to people's assessment of gender. While Lucal is not trying to self-present as "masculine," her size, very short hair, nonfeminine clothing, and other cues lead people to read her as a "man" even though she is female.

When people are doing gender, they are also doing sexuality. A female who is feminine in her appearance and behavior is assumed to be "doing heterosexuality." On the other hand, a male whose appearance and behavior are deemed too feminine is assumed to be "doing homosexuality." We are surprised, for example, to find that a feminine female is a lesbian or that a masculine male is gay.

It is essential also to recognize that sexuality is not accomplished in isolation from one's gender (or race or social class) (Miller, 2006). By using the "doing gender" and "doing sexuality" approach, we emphasize that neither gender nor sexuality is muted. Instead, individual actors "do sexuality" similar to the ways in which they do gender. Recall here Garfinkel's (1967) assertion that, at the end of the day, we see persons as either male or female, masculine or feminine, and, consequently, as heterosexual or homosexual.

In the context of this schema, there is no room, it turns out, for an individual to "do bisexuality" (Miller, 2006). If conforming to gender norms means doing heterosexuality and deviating from gender norms is assumed to mean that one is gay or lesbian, then there is no way for individuals to signal their bisexuality, nor is there a way for others to attribute bisexuality to them. Next, we analyze the film *Chasing Amy* as an example of doing sexuality in the context of doing gender and of the (in)visibility associated with bisexuality.

Chasing Amy (Kevin Smith, 1997)

Bisexuality calls into question the either/or dualism of sex, gender, and sexuality, especially for those self-identified bisexuals in primary other-gender relationships, such as the character Alyssa Jones (Joey Lauren Adams) in the film *Chasing Amy*. In an attempt to deconstruct the rubric that supports either/or categories, we examine them in the context of biological essentialism and social constructionism. Using the film *Chasing Amy* provides us with a lens for considering how these competing theories impact "sexual truths," allowing us to see the processes involved with the erasure and delegitimization of bisexual identity in U.S. society.

Essentialist theories regarding sexuality are informed by a rubric that emphasizes the "natural" and biological aspects of sexuality. According to this model, dichotomous and mutually exclusive sex/gender categories (male/masculine and female/feminine) are associated with dichotomous, mutually exclusive sexuality categories (heterosexual/homosexual). In this context, bisexual identities are erased because their sexual identity does not exist within the heterosexual/homosexual binary—the only two possibilities recognized by this model.

Such assumptions are woven throughout the opening scene of the movie when Holden (Ben Affleck) and Alyssa, both comic book producers, meet at a comic book convention. She is sitting at the "minority voices" table—but since she is the only woman on a panel, the audience is left to guess whether her minority status is as a "woman" or as a "lesbian." After a casual introduction, Holden immediately takes a liking to Alyssa, and heterosexual assumptions prevail as Holden agrees to meet Alyssa at a club called Meow Mix in New York City. Upon arriving, Holden's business partner and best friend, Banky (Jason Lee), points out that there are a lot of women in the club. Holden notices Alyssa dancing and starts to approach her when his friend Hooper (a black gay male played by Dwight Ewell) says, "There is something you ought to know." Holden responds, "What? Does she have a boyfriend?" Hooper replies, "No." Holden smugly says, "Then what's to know, my friend? What's to know?" The assumption is that Alyssa is straight and, as long as she doesn't have a boyfriend, and is therefore available, there is nothing more to know.

As Holden and Alyssa reminisce about their common acquaintances (they grew up in the same town, but went to different high schools), Alyssa is invited up on stage to sing. Alyssa agrees and begins to sing a throaty love song. Holden believes she is singing this throaty love song for him and never notices the woman who has made her way through the crowd to get closer to the stage. When Alyssa finishes singing, she points to this woman and beckons her closer. Holden, of course, believes this summons is for him. Only when Alyssa walks off stage and dodges past him to kiss the woman does he finally understand what his friend wanted him to know. As the women continue to kiss, Holden stares in astonishment as his heteronormative assumptions begin to crumble.

Alyssa realizes that Holden is "weirded out," so she begins to "prove" her gay identity. She shares "war stories" with Banky, who seems more troubled with the techniques she uses to "fuck girls" than with her "gay" identity. For example, Banky and Alyssa talk about the permanent injuries they have received from performing oral sex on women. Here Alyssa continues to legitimate her identity as "gay" by talking about her encounters with other women, to the dismay of Holden, who quietly sits and listens.

Turning our attention to Alyssa and Holden's developing relationship, we see that their experiences challenge the "two-and-only-two" gender and sexuality paradigm and call into question the assumption that sex, gender, and sexuality are not stable and static categories, but instead fluid and ever-changing.

This contradiction of essentialism is evident when Alyssa, who refers to herself as "gay," contemplates her attraction to Holden, a self-declared heterosexual.[1] In the following scene, we see Alyssa grapple with her "true" sexual identity once Holden reveals his love for her while driving home from what their friends have come to call their "pseudo-dates."

Holden continues to declare his love for Alyssa and asks her if she has any hesitation about loving him. Alyssa sits quietly through Holden's soliloquy, but when he stops the car, she jumps out into the pouring rain. Holden follows after her and says, "Aren't you at least going to comment?" Alyssa responds, "Here's my comment—Fuck you!" Angrily, Alyssa verbally assaults Holden, asking him, "Do you remember for one second who I am?" Holden replies, "So? People change." Alyssa counters, "Oh, so it's that simple? You fall in love with me and want a romantic relationship? Nothing changes for you. But what about me, Holden?" Alyssa is astonished by this trivialization of her gay identity and shouts, "There is no period of adjustment, Holden, I am fucking gay!" Alyssa and Holden walk away from each other, but once Holden reaches his car, Alyssa jumps on him and they desperately kiss one another.

Despite what she says, Holden seems to assume that, based on her behavior, Alyssa has decided that she can in fact merely "change," with little consequence to her identity. Because Holden is a self-declared heterosexual, he does not have to contemplate a change in his sexual identity; his love for Alyssa only reconfirms the reality of his heterosexuality. We never really see Holden question his heterosexual identity because his partner, Alyssa, meets the standard relationship form. For Holden, his relationship with Alyssa supports the assumption that one's sex, gender, and sexuality remain both congruent and unchanged throughout one's life (Lorber, 1994).

Holden entirely dismisses Alyssa's past relationships with women and expects her attraction to him ultimately to override her other experiences. It seems that, in Holden's eyes, Alyssa has simply failed to find her "true" sexual identity until now. Alyssa herself can manage little more than an angry "fuck you" because she, too, feels that her attraction to Holden is an example of how she has failed at "gayness."

We see Alyssa confront essentialist notions about her "gay" identity in a scene with her all-woman friendship group. When Alyssa and her (apparently) lesbian friends get her comic book ready for mailing, the obfuscation begins. As Alyssa elusively attempts to describe her new lover, one of her friends accuses her of "playing the pronoun game." Alyssa denies this accusation; but, when her friends continue to confront her, she says, "Holden. His name is Holden." Finally, one woman lifts her wine glass as if to toast and says, "Here's to the both of you. Another one [lesbian] bites the dust."

The assumption here is that Alyssa must "pick a side." She is either gay (read lesbian) or straight. We see here that biphobia does not just occur in heterosexual society; in happens with great regularity in the so-called safe confines of lesbian and gay space (Miller, 2006). As a result, bisexuals participating in similar-gender or other-gender relationships are often mistaken for or misidentified as gay or straight. For example, recall the scene at Meow Mix when Holden assumes Alyssa is straight. Because Alyssa projects appropriate femininity, she is able to conform to heterogendered attributes (Ingraham, 1994). Hence, Holden's obvious bewilderment when he realizes Alyssa is gay. The feminine gender cues Holden read were not just that "Alyssa is a feminine woman" but also that "Alyssa is a feminine and heterosexual woman."

Social constructionist theory argues that social actors possess the agency to construct and participate in their own meaning-making systems. This approach calls into question the essentialist thesis that absolute sexual truths are necessary, as illustrated in a lovemaking scene. Holden, lying in bed with Alyssa, asks, "Why me? Why now?" She responds:

I've given that a lot of thought, you know. . . . I'm not with you because of what family, society, life tried to instill in me from day one. The way the world is; how seldom it is to meet that one person who just gets you. It's so rare. . . . And to cut oneself off from finding that person, to immediately halve your options by eliminating the possibility of finding that one person within your own gender, that just seems stupid to me. So I didn't. But then you came along—you—the one least likely. I mean, you were a guy. And while I was falling for you, I put a ceiling on that because you were a guy, until I remembered why I opened the door to women in the first place—to not limit the likelihood of finding that one person that would complement me so completely. So, here we are. I was thorough when I looked for you and I feel justified lying in your arms, 'cause I got here on my own terms and I have no question there wasn't someplace I didn't look. And for me that makes all of the difference.

Here Alyssa is not necessarily searching for the essentialist "truth" about her sexual identity, as she allows herself to experience her sexual activity and identity as being in flux. She is ready to confront the assumed impermeability of sexual identity categories and challenges Holden to move beyond the categories of "hetero" and "homo" to question the idea that sexuality is "fixed" or "exclusive."

For both Alyssa and Holden, traditional sexual identity categories cannot explain their *lived* experience. Alyssa, the "gay" woman, is in love with Holden, the "straight" man. Is she still gay? Is she bisexual? What is her sexual truth? What about Holden? Who is he if he sleeps with a gay woman? What becomes of his identity status as a straight man? Is he still straight when he has sex with someone who openly identifies as gay? Essentialist thinking does not allow for such lived experience, which challenges binary sexual categories. Such categories are inadequate, and people whose experiences confound them must try to "fit" their identities and sexual activities within the confines of categories that cannot contain their lives.

While Alyssa allows room for a fluid sexual identity, we never see this epiphany with the character development of Holden. In fact, instead of contemplating how his sexual identity may be destabilized by his relationship with Alyssa, he trivializes Alyssa's own identity negotiations by asking, "But can I at least tell people that all you needed was some serious deep dicking?" The chance for social-sexual reflection is abruptly interrupted and Holden never has to problematize his own identity. His homophobic response that all Alyssa needed was heterosexual intercourse reifies Holden's heteronormativity.

Indeed, Holden's relationship with Alyssa has no consequences for his identity, as he maintains his heterosexual privilege by using essentialist assumptions to his advantage. In other words, because others know Holden to be masculine and straight, his sexuality does not come under scrutiny when he develops an intimate relationship with Alyssa. In fact, this relationship only works to reaffirm sexual binary categories, since Alyssa's involvement with Holden proves that she must *really* be straight.

In keeping with a definition of sexuality based on what one does (and with whom), Holden's friend, Banky, cannot fathom why Holden would continue this relationship with Alyssa, since the fact that she is a lesbian means that Holden has no chance of fucking her. Banky pointedly questions Alyssa about the number of times that she has been in their apartment, asking, "Isn't that grounds enough for the pink mafia [i.e., lesbians] to throw you out of their club?" The attempts made by both Holden and Alyssa to date and eventually become intimate may be real on the surface but, as Banky predicts, their relationship is bound to end badly because Alyssa's previous relationships with women are the ultimate indicator of her true (i.e., essential) sexual identity.

To disregard the notion of any single sexual identity seems impractical to Banky. Arguing that sexualities are fluid and dynamic may make sense theoretically, but provides little justification for Alyssa's sexual identity. In other words, her varying experiences and relationships with similar- and same-gendered persons do not necessarily place her sexual identity in flux. The viewer is still led to decide only whether Alyssa is straight or gay. For example, while Alyssa never invokes the term *bisexual* (or, for that matter, *lesbian*) to describe herself, the viewer can see Alyssa's identity-questioning as an opportunity to examine the usefulness of stable categories like "hetero" and "homo."

We are not suggesting that the viewer should conclude that Alyssa is really bisexual—another absolute truth. But we do think her questioning helps to make the point that many people's sexual identities are in flux at some point in time, whether that flexibility is about attractions, preferences, fantasies, or actual relationships. Thus, the point is not to claim Alyssa as a true bisexual. Yet her character emphasizes that gender and sexuality are never determined once and for all and never function as mutually exclusive. Thus the question for the audience can become, "Why doesn't Alyssa use the term *bisexual* to describe her sexual identity?"

We can see Alyssa's character as an exemplar for rethinking the assumption that sexuality is some static personal attribute, property, or essence. Instead, Alyssa helps the viewer imagine bisexuality as one of the several available cultural categories from which she might choose. Through Alyssa's character development, we see that conventional categories that attempt to describe an individual's sexuality are usually misleading, for one category (e.g., homosexual, heterosexual, bisexual, asexual) does not adequately describe the variability of one's sexuality (Stein & Plummer, 1996).

The way in which categories are misleading is at the crux of *Chasing Amy*. For example, in a pivotal scene, the audience sees Banky throwing Alyssa's high school yearbook to Holden and pointing out Alyssa's senior picture with the words *finger cuffs* printed below it. Banky goes on to recount several rumors about Alyssa that he has heard from her sexual exploits with high-school boyfriends. Holden dismisses these rumors and tells Banky that "she's never even been with a guy."

Instead of looking at her past and concluding that it is evidence of her bisexuality, Holden cannot look past masculinist and heterosexist assumptions that suggest Alyssa's relationships with women were an acceptable part of her past, something that can easily be forgotten and forgiven once she cements her relationship with Holden. However, her sexual activities with men cannot simply be explained away as meaningless youthful indiscretions or some sort of "bi curiosity." Here, bisexuality is not only dismissed, but is actually erased because it is not positioned as a legitimate sexual identification category. Again, Alyssa never names herself as "bisexual." The assumption is that her sexual identity remains intelligible within the binary—she is lesbian/gay when she is partnered with a woman and heterosexual when she is with Holden. By excluding *bisexual* from her language, Alyssa provides a type of binary normalcy—a guise under which heteronormativity is perpetuated. In other words, *normal* is defined as two-and-only-two gender categories, justifying a binary logic that includes us all (and always excludes bisexuals).

Even though Alyssa does not claim a bisexual identity, her lived experiences at least allow viewers to witness sexual identity categories in flux, as well as to arrive at their own conclusions with regard to why Alyssa erases herself as bisexual. For example, even though a bisexual identity remains unspoken, unclaimed, and unremarked upon in *Chasing Amy,* its presence can be felt throughout the film. In Alyssa Jones, we have a character who is doing bisexuality without anyone—including herself—naming it as such. While she is unapologetic about any of her relationships, it is the assumptions of heteronormativity to which she ultimately refuses to conform. Alyssa and Holden do not live happily ever after.

The final scene of the movie occurs "one year later." Alyssa and Holden have not seen each other in a while when they meet at a comic book convention. Holden approaches Alyssa, who is sitting with another woman, promoting her comic. It is unclear whether this woman is a friend or a lover. The woman excuses herself from the table as Holden begins to make small talk.

When Alyssa's woman friend/lover returns to her side and asks, "Who was that?" Alyssa responds, "Oh, just some guy I knew." Here, Alyssa's sexual identity seems to be confirmed as really lesbian, since she does not say that she and Holden had a sexual relationship. Ultimately, any attempt to pin down a bisexual reading of Alyssa's character is thwarted.

In *Transamerica,* on the other hand, the visibility of transgender and the instability of gender categories permeate the film from the opening scene. In spite of the story of gender transition that is at the center of the movie, by the end of the film, the partitioning of gender categories remains in flux.

Transamerica (Duncan Tucker, 2005)

While all of us deviate from strict gender categorizations in some way, consider the lives of people who experience their sex and gender as incongruent, as not matching up in the expected ways. This describes the experiences of many *transgender* individuals. But this umbrella term can be used to refer to a whole spectrum of people who are more different from each other than we might expect, given their placement in a single category. Some identify as *genderqueers,* for example, and do not wish to change their bodies, just to live (full or part time) in a gender somehow different from their assigned sex. Others, for various reasons, seek some medical and/or surgical intervention; most commonly, they take hormones to change their bodies. Some others desire a full regimen of sex reassignment surgery (SRS).

Like bisexual identities, transgender subjectivities call into question the "natural" sex/gender/sexuality binaries. From an essentialist perspective, there are males and females, whose masculine and feminine genders, respectively, follow naturally from their sex. Transgender identities, however, raise the possibility that the relationship between sex and gender is, instead, a social construction and need not take the form of a mutually exclusive dichotomy.[2]

Photo 5.2 Challenging categorizations of sexual and gender identities in *Transamerica*. Bree (Felicity Huffman) wants to live life as a "normal" woman and does so through outward displays of femininity.

The opening scene of *Transamerica* leaves the viewer with no doubt about its subject matter. The film begins with a clip from *Finding Your Female Voice,* with Bree (Felicity Huffman) practicing a female voice along with the coach by repeating the mantra, "This is the voice I want to use." As Bree prepares for the day, we watch her dress, putting on heavy, opaque panty hose; shaping garments (a padded girdle and fake breasts); and makeup. Bree leaves the house decked out in pink; there is no doubt that she is very good at doing femininity.

As Bree walks to the bus stop, we hear a voiceover of her meeting with a doctor who must sign the consent form that will allow her to have SRS. The doctor asks which procedures she's already had, immediately signaling to the viewer that SRS involves much more than a single surgical procedure. Bree recounts three years of hormone therapy, electrolysis, facial feminization surgery, a tracheal shave (to make her Adam's apple less prominent), jaw recontouring, and a brow lift. The doctor tells her that she looks "very authentic."

Though she may look authentic, as Bree waits at the bus stop, she crouches down when she notices that she is taller than the men waiting for the bus. It seems unusual that a transwoman just a week away from her final surgery would still be so self-conscious. But perhaps the director is simply reinforcing the point that Bree is concerned about fitting in and being normal. As she tells the doctor, "I believe the term is 'being stealth.'" (Like the B-1 Stealth Bomber, a trans person who is stealth cannot be detected [or "read" or "clocked"].)

When the doctor reminds Bree that "gender dysphoria" is classified as a "very serious mental disorder," Bree quips, "Don't you find it odd that plastic surgery can cure a mental disorder?" This plastic surgery will rid Bree of the penis she finds so disgusting and will, in her eyes—and the eyes of society—complete her transition to full womanhood and allow her to fit easily into the binary. The result of this surgery, as she tells the doctor, will be female genitals that appear normal even to a gynecologist. Before she goes to bed that night, Bree tucks her penis between her legs, allowing her to envision herself as completely female (and as completely feminine in her gauzy night gown/robe). Bree's disgust for her penis reinforces the belief that, even for trans people, sex and gender are either/or. In a society that insists individuals must be either men or women—never both, let alone neither—it is, of course, not surprising that some trans people internalize these same beliefs.

Later in the film, we see another example of Bree's desire to live life as a "normal" woman. As she travels cross-country with Toby (Kevin Zegers), the son she fathered as a result of a "tragically lesbian" affair in college, Margaret (Elizabeth Peña), her therapist, has arranged for her to spend the night at the home of another transwoman, Mary Ellen (Bianca Leigh). Toby does not yet know that Bree is trans, and Bree is horrified to find that the woman and her transgender friends, who are in varying stages of transition, are in the midst of a party. It is not surprising that she panics and tells her hostess that she and Toby must leave. Toby, however, wants to join the party, later reporting to Bree that the people there were "nice."

Among the guests at the party are well-known transgender people like Calpernia Addams and David Harrison (the only transman in the film). David tells Toby that trans people are "gender-gifted" rather than "gender-challenged." When Toby says to him, "Dude, I thought you were a real guy," David's response is, "We walk among you." In a memorable scene, Bree tells her hostess that one of the women there could not pass "on a dark night at two hundred yards"; but it turns out that this Mary Kay cosmetics representative is a "G.G.," or "genuine girl" (or "genetic girl," as this abbreviation is often defined). Mary Ellen says that Bree needs to "check her T-dar." (In other words, Bree is not as good at spotting other transgendered people as she might think.) Here, we get the sense that gender is more complicated than the sex-equals-gender, either/or dichotomy might suggest.

Bree's concerns about what Toby thinks of her as a result of her association with other trans people are soon overshadowed by his finding out that she is not a "real" woman. Toby is driving when they stop along the roadside late at night so Bree can urinate. When he looks in the rearview mirror, he sees Bree's penis. When she returns to the car, he says nothing but speeds off. Soon after they have a confrontation at Sammy's Wigwam, a roadside souvenir stand. When Sammy (Forrie Smith) mistakes Bree for Toby's mother (as several people in the film do), Toby tells Sammy, "She's not even a real woman; she's got a dick," and goes on to call her a "fucking lying freak."

Here we see another example of the assumption that, to be a "real" woman, Bree must get rid of her penis (which we know she wants to do, given the disgust she expressed about it to the doctor at the beginning of the film). Despite the fact that Bree has lived as a woman throughout the film to this point, her womanhood is immediately called into question upon Toby's sighting of her penis. In his eyes—*and* in hers—only by "cutting it" off can she become a complete woman.

This belief is reinforced when Bree enters her parents' home later in the film. Bree's mother's first question is whether Bree is still a "boy." To find out, she grabs Bree's crotch and announces that, indeed, she is still male. But Bree grabs her mother's hand and forces her to touch Bree's breast, showing her that she is female, too. While this scene can be taken to counter the taken-for-granted assumption that male and female, masculine and feminine, cannot exist in the same body, the viewer already knows that this situation is temporary. Bree hates her penis and wants to have it turned into female genitals. There is no acknowledgment of the reality that some transwomen (by choice or because of limited resources) keep their penises (and even continue to use them as sexual organs).

Bree's mother's refusal to see her as a woman continues. When Bree comes into the living room wearing a flowing, pink chiffon dress, her mother tells her that she looks "perfectly ridiculous." When the family goes out to dinner, Bree's mother forces her to act like a man and pull her chair out for her so she can sit down. This action takes on a whole different meaning, however, when Toby pulls Bree's chair out for her, too. Without saying anything, Toby shows that he has a renewed belief in Bree's womanhood.

Bree finally returns to Los Angeles and has her surgery. When we see her in the bathtub touching her new genitals, obviously pleased with them, it is clear that her transformation into a "real" woman is complete. Her penis is gone, fashioned into female genitals, and she can now begin her new life. But the final scenes, when Toby reappears in her life, both reinforce and call into question the sex/gender dichotomy of either/or and the naturalness of these distinctions.

Bree rises from the sofa and starts walking out of the room to get Toby the beer he has requested. As she walks into the kitchen to get it, she stops, turns around and tells Toby that he will not be allowed to put his feet up on her brand new coffee table. The fact that she has seen what he is doing despite not watching him can be viewed as an example of her motherly (feminine) attributes. We usually think of mothers, not fathers, as having "eyes in the back of their heads," seeing everything a child does. It is evident that Bree's role in Toby's life will be a maternal and feminine one.

But the final scene (viewed from outside the apartment, through appropriately feminine gauzy curtains) is this: when Bree hands Toby a beer, he cannot open the bottle, so he hands it to her. She exchanges it for the one she has already cracked open and proceeds to open the other bottle as well. As viewers, then, we are left with a reminder of Bree's former life as Stanley; men, not women, are usually the ones with the strength to open a stubborn lid.

However, the impression here is not that Bree is still really Stanley. Instead, it appears that, because her transition is now complete, Bree can be comfortable mixing genders, something she consciously avoided before her final surgery. Indeed, in this scene, she is still wearing pink—but now her pink sleeveless blouse is paired with loose-fitting, flowered pants. The new Bree can show more skin (with a sleeveless shirt) and can wear pants (for the first time in the film). Freed from her concerns about being read, Bree can now do both femininity and masculinity. If Toby needs help with a "masculine" task, she can now provide it. The old Bree would have asked Toby to open *her* bottle.

On one hand, finalizing her transition with surgery makes Bree invisible as a trans person—much like Alyssa erases herself as bisexual in *Chasing Amy*. On the other hand, however, the ending of the film makes her visible for the first time as someone "gender-gifted," as transman David Harrison characterized transgender people earlier in the film. She can do both femininity and masculinity, thus questioning the natural, mutually exclusive status of these categories.

Conclusion

Many people experience their sex, gender, and sexuality as existing in the realm of the taken for granted. They learn the gendered appearance and behavior expectations associated with their sex category and do gender in ways that mostly conform to those expectations. Their common, everyday deviations from such norms and expectations are considered to be temporary and mundane, and do not call their sex, gender, or sexuality into question (Garfinkel, 1967; Kessler & McKenna, 1978). Heterosexual men can wear pink shirts and take care of babies, while heterosexual women can enjoy watching football (but probably not playing it) and wear T-shirts and jeans without leading to any questioning of their identities.

Other people, however, cannot take for granted such fundamental components of their identities. Feminine lesbians risk getting misread as heterosexual and being invisible to other lesbians (Maltz, 2002), while transwomen may face the prejudice and discrimination that they experience because our society is patriarchal and denigrates femininity (Serano, 2007). Like openly gay men, they risk violent reactions to their deviations from gender and sexual norms. Some heterosexual women's sexuality is called into question by people who believe they "look like lesbians," while the "Effeminate Heterosexual Man" was the title of a *Saturday Night Live* skit in the 1990s.

And, as the films analyzed here show, there are the issues and dilemmas of a transgendered and/or bisexual existence. As Cromwell (1999, p. 122) notes, "Transgender people and people with nonheterosexual identities queer the Western binaries of body-equals-sex-equals-gender-equals-identity as well as the binary of heterosexual and homosexual." Along with such queering, however, often comes invisibility.

In *Chasing Amy*, Alyssa's experiences can easily be read as evidence that she is bisexual and that she is doing bisexuality; we see her kissing a woman (and know that she is known as someone who has sexual/romantic relationships with women) *and* we see her sexual/romantic relationship with a man. But Alyssa identifies as gay, does not continue her relationship with Holden, and, in the end, chooses not to go public with the fact that she had a relationship with him. The fact that Alyssa's prior sexual relationships with men, rather than those with women (the ones that were clearly most important to her identity to that point), are most troubling to Holden further queers her identity.

In *Transamerica*, on the other hand, the viewer is left with little doubt about Bree's transgender status. But it is also made clear that her transgender existence is temporary and will be resolved by the end of the film. Before her final surgery, Bree is depicted several times as a woman (given her feminine appearance—she always wears pastel colors—and behavior) with a penis. It is also clear that she does not want to continue to have a penis, supporting the notion that, ultimately, male and female/woman and man cannot exist simultaneously. Her reluctance to be in the company of other trans people (seen at the party in Mary Ellen's house) also supports the idea that her transgender status is temporary and uncomfortable for her. Unlike these transgender people, Bree's preference is, as she told the doctor at the beginning of the film, to "try to fit in" and to be "stealth."

Ultimately, however, even Bree queers the gender binary. While the viewer is left with no doubt that Bree is happier after her final surgery, it is also made clear that she is also more comfortable mixing masculinity and femininity. Presurgery, Bree always wore skirts and was always self-conscious about her appearance. Postsurgery, however, she wears pants for the first time in the film and opens Toby's beer bottle, something presurgery Bree never would have done.

In the final analysis of *Chasing Amy* and *Transamerica*, what remains problematic is not necessarily that the characters do not name themselves as "bisexual" or "trans," but the ease with which Alyssa and, to a lesser extent, Bree erase or at least make more difficult the possibility of such naming. Alyssa never legitimizes a bisexual identity; her validation comes from retaining her gay identity, such as when we see her dismissing Holden as simply "some guy she once knew." Bree does not claim a trans identity; she now considers herself authentically female and a woman. This erasure of identity is blinding—for both characters, previous lives, lovers, practices, and interactions are dismissed and instead replaced and validated by the static, binary categories of homosexual and woman.

In this respect, *Chasing Amy* is ultimately more conservative than *Transamerica*. The viewer is left with validation of the belief that static, dualistic categories are the best for everyone involved. The final images of *Transamerica,* on the other hand, leave the viewer more optimistic about the future prospects of gender fluidity and flux. Ironically, as a result of her final SRS, Bree appears to have been freed, at least a bit, from her rigidly gendered self, leaving the viewer to ponder the possibilities of "working the boundaries" between categories.

References

Cromwell, J. (1999). *Transmen and FTMs: Identities, bodies, genders, and sexualities.* Urbana: University of Illinois Press.

Frye, M. (1983). *The politics of reality: Essays in feminist theory.* New York: Crossing Press.

Garfinkel, H. (1967). *Studies in ethnomethodology.* Englewood Cliffs, NJ: Prentice Hall.

Goffman, E. (1959). *The presentation of self in everyday life.* Garden City, NY: Doubleday.

Goffman, E. (1976). Gender display. *Studies in the Anthropology of Visual Communication, 3,* 69–77.

Ingraham, C. (1994). The heterosexual imaginary: Feminist sociology and theories of gender. *Sociological Theory, 12*(2), 203–219.

Kessler, S. J., & McKenna, W. (1978). *Gender: An ethnomethodological approach.* Chicago: University of Chicago Press.

Lorber, J. (1994). *Paradoxes of gender.* New Haven, CT: Yale University Press.

Lucal, B. (1999). What it means to be gendered me: Life on the boundaries of a dichotomous gender system. *Gender & Society, 13,* 781–797.

Maltz, R. (2002). Fading to pink. In J. Nestle, C. Howell, & R. Wilchins (Eds.), *Genderqueer: Voices from beyond the sexual binary* (pp. 161–165). Los Angeles: Alyson Books.

Miller, A. (2006). *Voices on binary objections: Binary identity misappropriation and bisexual resistance.* Unpublished dissertation, American University, Washington, DC.

Serano, J. (2007). *Whipping girl: A transsexual woman on sexism and the scapegoating of femininity.* Emeryville, CA: Seal Press.

Stein, A., & Plummer, K. (1996). I can't even think straight: Queer theory and the missing sexual revolution in sociology. In S. Seidman (Ed.), *Queer theory/sociology* (pp. 129–144). Cambridge, MA: Blackwell.

West, C., & Zimmerman, D. (1987). Doing gender. *Gender & Society, 1,* 125–151.

Notes

1. It is interesting to note that throughout the movie, while other characters refer to Alyssa as a "dyke" or "lesbian," Alyssa only refers to herself as "gay."
2. It should be noted that some people consider transgender to be a biological phenomenon.

Outtake

The Geena Davis Institute on Gender in Media

Jean-Anne Sutherland

We often see celebrities taking part in various "causes" such as AIDS, health, hunger, abuse, or environmental concerns. Less often do we hear of celebrities whose mission concerns the need for gender equality in the media! Geena Davis is the exception. Her organization seeks to "engage, educate, and influence the need for gender balance, reducing stereotyping and creating a wide variety of female characters for entertainment targeting children 11 and older."

Watching television and movies with her daughter, Davis was astonished when she noticed the minimal role girls play in children's media. And she did more than just talk about it—she enlisted Dr. Stacy Smith of the USC Annenberg School for Communication & Journalism to conduct research on gender in film and television. Smith and colleagues have produced some stunning research:

- Among top-grossing G-rated family films, boy characters outnumber girl characters three to one.
- Girls in family films tend to be hypersexualized and serve mostly as "eye candy."
- Equality has not been achieved in the industry: women make up only 7 percent of directors, 13 percent of writers, and 20 percent of producers.
- Gender stereotyping remains rampant in the movies: in G-rated family films from 2006 to 2009, not a single female was shown working in medical science, as a business leader, or working in law or politics. (In fact, 80.5 percent of all working characters are male.)
- There has been scant change in terms of gender imbalance in movies over the last 60 years.

As Smith and Choueiti note, women make up roughly 50 percent of the population and the workforce. Thus, it is alarming how family films not only tend to exclude girls (as significant characters) but also continue to cast them in highly stereotypical ways. While the young women of today will no doubt play a major role in tomorrow's world of business, technology, and science, they surely will not find much inspiration in the movies! They will see that females are valuable when they are youthful and have exposed skin and small waists. As sociologists, we realize that repeated images in films are more than simply "entertainment." Rather, the repetition of images means that those images become so normalized that questioning the status quo of moviemaking is not likely.

Not only are girls underrepresented in G-rated family films; women are grossly underrepresented as directors and writers. Not surprisingly, the percentage of girls and women who appear on screen increases if a woman serves as director or writer of a film. Davis's institute realizes that crucial to leveling the playing field in regard to girls in media is increased participation of women behind the scenes. Women, after all, are more likely to tell a girl's story. And, with increased numbers of women in the industry, the stories of girls and women will feel less risky. That is, fears that no one will go to see a girl's story will hopefully lessen as more of these films are made—and people (girls *and* boys) go to see them! As Davis has pointed out, it has to get to the point where these images look and feel *normal*.

(Continued)

(Continued)

Davis continues to support academic research on gender and media and spends a great deal of time speaking out on talk shows, at conferences, and in universities. During a 2011 talk at Georgetown University, Davis pointed out the correlation between watching television and a girl's sense of her options in life. It's a negative relationship, of course. The more TV she watches, the fewer options she feels she has. For boys, the more TV he watches, the more sexist his views are. "There is clearly a very strong, negative message about girls coming through," Davis noted.

The Geena Davis Institute on Gender in Media combines the resources of academia and Hollywood power. Utilizing data-driven analysis, the Institute is able to put forth an argument grounded in research. Davis can then use her power in Hollywood (as an Academy Award–winning actor) to spread the concerns. The message is both micro and macro. In the micro perspective, Davis recommends we spend more time engaging with the media our kids consume. At the macro level, Davis suggests significant changes in the structure of Hollywood and filmmaking.

Check out the website and see what's new: www.thegeenadavisinstitute.org.

CHAPTER 6

Private and Public Social Worlds

Buddy:	What I am concerned with is detail. I asked you go get me a packet of Sweet'N Low. You bring me back Equal. That isn't what I asked for. That isn't what I wanted. That isn't what I needed and that shit isn't going to work around here.
Guy:	I . . . I just thought . . .
Buddy:	You thought. Do me a fucking favor. Shut up, listen, and learn. Look, I know that this is your first day and you don't really know how things work around here, so I will tell you. You have no brain. No judgment calls are necessary. What you think means nothing. What you feel means nothing. You are here for me. You are here to protect my interests and to serve my needs. So, while it may look like a little thing to you, when I ask for a packet of Sweet'N Low, that's what I want. And it's your responsibility to see that I get what I want.

—Swimming with Sharks (1994)

Eliza Welch:	Every day from the second I wake up till the second I pass out cold, my day, like the day of almost every other mother I know, is made up of a series of concrete, specific actions. And they're actions that kind of wear away at passion, if you know what I mean. The actions are petty and small like . . . like refilling coffee cups or folding underwear. But they accumulate in this really debilitating way that diminishes my ability to focus on almost anything else. Bigger things like, you know, ideas or . . . politics or dreams of a better life.

—Motherhood (2009)

Sociology as a discipline developed in the nineteenth century, a time of rapid social, political, and economic transformation. The processes of industrialization and urbanization were reflected in the growth of capitalism and the factory system as well as the separation of home from work and production from consumption and repro-duction. The separation of home and family into the private sphere, and the economic and political into the public sphere, became a dominant model of social life based on gender. Women's participation in the domestic realm became life defining, as did men's participation in the political economy. Regardless of women's waged productive labor, women's primary role became that of wife and mother, while, in Marxist terms, men's position was defined by their relationship to the means of production (e.g., as workers in a waged economy).

Historically, sociology treated the private realm of home and family as separate and apart from the public realms of work, politics, and the economy. Further, the spaces we inhabit as social actors were conceptualized not just as physically separate, but also as involving sepa-rate functions and processes in our lives. Nowhere does this become more obvious than in the very narrow construction of normative family life in mid-twentieth-century United States. "Bedroom communities" were built in enclaves on the periphery of urban centers, and workers commuted from the privatized life of home and family to the public domain of work. Home was a place where bodies were nourished and cared for, emotional well-being nurtured, and meaning found in what sociologists call primary group relationships. Leaving home, we entered the public domain of secondary group relationships, engaging in contract-based exchange relationships and the life of the larger community.

Although we now recognize that public and private are interwoven at the individual and structural levels of social life, the ideological division is often reflected in the movies. As film stories unfold, the viewing audience follows the characters from one realm to the other, making sense of the plot and narrative based on where (public or private) the action occurs. In this chapter, the readings examine the private and public domains of social life through a sociological lens. In the first reading, Karla Erickson turns to the public sphere of social life, specifically the world of work, and applies sociological questions usually reserved for research on family life to the workplace. Using classical sociology, Erickson frames the transformation of work in a service economy with the concepts of community (gemeinschaft) and society (gesellschaft). She points out that more of our human interac-tions are taking place within the marketplace at the same time that more of our physical and emotional needs are being met by services for pay.

Using the film *As Good as It Gets*, Erickson explores connection, intimacy, and identity in the public space of an urban restaurant as a site of dining and social relationships. The second film, *Office Space*, provides a view of a suburban restaurant as one setting where workers are pitted against not just management, but the dehumanizing effects of corporate control of the self. As Buddy, who represents the corporate position, so harshly explains to Guy in *Swimming with Sharks*, "What you think means nothing. What you feel means nothing. You are here for me. You are here to protect my interests and to serve my needs." Yet people do more than serve the corporation in the context of work—they establish relationships, construct communities, and develop a sense of identity.

In the second reading, Janet Cosbey explores the challenges of balancing work and fam-ily as portrayed in the movies. She begins with two films to investigate the gendered model of family life as separate from the world of economy and work. Using *Mona Lisa Smile*,

Cosbey examines the construct of the "ideal family," consisting of a homemaker wife, breadwinner husband, and their children, and the reproduction of this ideal in the historical anomaly of the 1950s era. Although this ideal never represented the way we were, it has influenced the development of public and economic policies as well as individual choices and experiences into the present day. Cosbey uses a gendered twist on the ideal family with the film *Mr. Mom*, demonstrating the gendered division of labor between home and work, as well as within the home, and the inequalities embedded in this social arrangement. She returns to this theme at the end of the reading with the film *The Children Are All Right*. The gendered division of responsibilities in the family reflects the stay-at-home mother/breadwinner father model, although both parents are women.

Cosbey considers the "choice" parents make to either work outside the home or stay home full time. Of course this is a choice only in economically advantaged families where one parent is able to earn enough to support the family. Cosbey points to *I Don't Know How She Does It* as a film about the juggling act mothers who work often perform. Although the combined income of the two-career family provides a comfortable standard of living, including a nanny for care of the children, the central story line is the distress caused by the conflicting demands of home and family for Kate. Kate is highly invested in her career and derives great satisfaction from her success. However, she experiences a great deal of stress about how to manage her ever-expanding to-do lists for home and work.

Eliza in *Motherhood*, on the other hand, expresses regret and resentment at her full-time mother status, which she feels is eroding her ability to focus on "bigger things." In one scene, she tells her daughter, "It's good when mommies work. It keeps mommies happy. It keeps them from being mean, nasty, yelling mommies." While researchers have found that multiple role obligations (e.g., work and motherhood) can enhance well-being, they also increase stress in the form of the "double day."

As fathers participate more in home and childcare, they are experiencing more stress related to work-family conflicts. Interestingly, it is not the work of home and family producing the stress, but rather "increasing job demands, the blurring of boundaries between work and home life, declining job security and flat earnings" which led 60 percent of married fathers to report work-family conflict in 2008 (compared to 35 percent in 1977; Aumann, Galinsky, and Matos 2011:2).

Exploring the private and public domains, the readings in this section invite you to consider the ways that we live in the gemeinschaft of our homes and families as well as survive in the gesellschaft of work and commerce. As sociologists, we are interested in the ways our identities and experiences are shaped by gendered arrangements intersecting with race, ethnicity, and social class at home and at work. Going to the movies is one way to learn about social life in private and in public, as well as the connections in between.

Reference

Aumann, K., E. Galinsky and K. Matos. 2011. "The New Male Mystique." Retrieved January 4, 2012 (http://www.familiesandwork.org/site/research/reports/newmalemystique.pdf).

READING 6.1

SERVICE, SMILES, AND SELVES

Film Representations of Labor and the Sociology of Work

Karla A. Erickson

Workplaces are sites in our society where people are rejected, promoted, discriminated against, sexually harassed, politically awakened, and intellectually challenged. What humans can do, they do at work: fall in love, cheat, laugh, cry, scream, bleed, build, plan, present, think, and talk. Despite the richness of activities that take place within work, workplaces have historically been studied through a set of questions that situate work as distinct from private life. When studying private life, scholars frequently pursue questions about emotion, connection, intimacy, and conflict. Yet when scholars turn their curiosity toward work, the tendency has often been to ask a distinct set of questions about control, constraint, resistance, organization, power, and efficiency. Like many contemporary sociologists of work, I am compelled to apply questions previously reserved for private life to public life. How does work shape our sense of self? How do our work and the places where we labor influence our ideas about emotion, friendship, and even intimacy? What do we give to our work emotionally, intellectually, socially, and spiritually, and what do we receive in return?

As scholars of labor, when we apply questions about trust, pleasure, intimacy, and care to work processes and workplaces, we begin to treat work as a location and an experience that can be transformative, for better and for worse. Work is a powerful site for sociological inquiry because work can lead individuals to feel cheapened; work can act as a socializing agent, encouraging individuals to treat others with trust or, alternatively, with suspicion; and finally, work can profoundly influence individual ideas about other people's capacities, intentions, wants, needs, and skills. These questions, then, are important for studying contemporary social life in general, and are particularly important for scholars who seek to study service work. In this chapter, to introduce some of the concerns and theories that are central to the study of work, occupations, and organizations, I focus on scenes from two popular films that depict a series of social interactions in restaurants. A close analysis of scenes from *As Good as It Gets* (James L. Brooks, 1997) and *Office Space* (Mike Judge, 1999) provides a starting point from which to consider a series of questions about workers and consumers in the service sector: What kinds of connections are available to workers and consumers in the global economy? How do workers negotiate the terms of their labor? What do customers want, and what do they get emotionally and socially through for-pay interactions with service workers? In what follows, I focus on scenes in *As Good as It Gets* and *Office Space* that use restaurant interactions as commentary on social life, paying particular attention to the social meanings that emerge around work and identity.

Restaurants as Scenes of Connection

In movies, the social interactions highlighted in a scene can make use of the partial privacy of a particular table nestled in the hustle and activity of the marketplace. The sound of people at other tables talking, the clink and crash of work in the kitchen, and the buzz and aura produced by many bodies, smells, and sounds in one place can provide a rich backdrop for plot development. In *As Good as It Gets*, the restaurant provides much more than mere backdrop: the restaurant becomes a site where workers and consumers navigate the boundaries between individuals working and living in a service society.

In *As Good as It Gets*, viewers get to know two of the three main characters through their points of contact within a restaurant where one dines and the other works. Melvin Udall (Jack Nicholson) is an obsessive-compulsive man who spends most of his time self-sequestered in his well-appointed apartment writing romance novels. He is a bigot, riddled with compulsions from hand washing to checking the locks, unable to step on cracks in the sidewalk or eat with silverware washed by someone else. Despite his rather noteworthy limitations as a social actor, Melvin Udall somehow manages to write romantic fiction that is widely read. His abrasiveness toward others is routine. For example, when his editor's assistant, who has appreciatively read all of his many books, decides one day to eagerly inquire, "Mr. Udall, I just *have* to ask, how do you write women so well?" Udall responds without skipping a beat, "I think of a man and I take away reason and accountability." Like this exchange, most of Melvin Udall's points of contact with other people are characterized by fear, hurled insults, and abrasive attempts at achieving distance from others. Melvin spends his days trying to get other people to leave him alone, and he is largely successful through a combination of ornery behavior, obsessive-compulsive habits, and forceful insults that combine the worst of misogyny, racism, homophobia, and anti-Semitism.

When we first meet the character of Melvin Udall, there is reason to believe that the film will be taken up with his battle against others in a world (specifically, New York City in the 1990s) that requires contact with other people, both wanted and unwanted. Yet as the film progresses, Udall's battle to remain alone is replaced by a growing need to be connected to others—first Carol Connelly (Helen Hunt), his waitress at the restaurant he frequents; next a dog, Verdell, that he takes care of while his neighbor recovers from a violent attack; and finally, the neighbor himself, Simon Bishop (Greg Kinnear), who is trying to regain a foothold in life after his body has been brutalized and his spirit destroyed as a result of the attack against him. The movie is categorized as a romantic comedy, but it has none of the lightness often associated with that genre. It *is* funny, but often at the expense of the pain and absurdity of daily life, including children who are very sick but cannot receive consistent medical care, and the diffuse costs of homophobia within families, in communities, and between neighbors. For example, the title of the movie, *As Good as It Gets*, comes from a scene in which Melvin has "courageously" burst into his therapist's office (his self-proclaimed courage comes from the fact that he had to step on lines in the floor to get to the therapist), only to be thrown out because he does not have an appointment. In one of the great comic lines of the movie, Melvin exasperatedly shouts, "How can you diagnose me with obsessive compulsion and then act like I had some kind of choice in the matter?" After his therapist kicks him out, an irritated and disappointed Melvin surveys the room of people waiting for the therapist and asks in a tone that betrays both complacency and horror, "What if this is as good as it gets?" Like him, his audience of fellow patients look horrified, but too beaten down to respond at all. Against this backdrop of a contemporary urban environment, taxing at best and frequently demoralizing, Melvin, beleaguered and exhausted, heads to the same restaurant each day to eat his meal with disposable silverware that he brings with him in a plastic sandwich bag.

Melvin's routine patronage at this particular restaurant is a striking contrast with the rest of his routines, which seek to isolate him and protect him from contact with others. As he enters the restaurant for the first time, there is nothing particularly noteworthy, charming, or extraordinary about the restaurant itself that might inspire such loyalty. Like many regular customers, Melvin has a favorite table, and he is outraged to discover other people sitting in "his" booth. His behavior reveals his willingness to verbally accost strangers in an attempt to get what he wants, and introduces viewers to "his" waitress, Carol Connelly.

Carol is portrayed as the last bastion of goodness in a world gone wrong. As viewers, we get to know Carol through Melvin's contact with her at the restaurant. From watching her move quickly and effectively among tables, chatting with customers and coworkers, we learn that Carol is the mother of a chronically ill son. She lives with her mother and focuses all her energy and attention on her son, forming her own sort of obsession. Carol knows the names of her customers, seems respected by her coworkers, and has considerable influence with her manager, which she uses in the first scene to save Melvin from getting kicked out of the restaurant.

Scene 1: Melvin's Table

During the first scene staged at the restaurant, Carol tries to calm Melvin when he finds that "his" table is occupied.

Melvin [following Carol into the service area]:	I'm starving.
Carol:	Go on, sit down. You know better than to be back here.
Melvin:	There are Jews at my table.
Carol:	It's not your table. It's the place's table. Wait your turn. Behave. Maybe you can sit in someone else's section. [All the other waitresses gasp.]
Melvin [to the customers at "his" table]:	How much more do you have to eat? Your appetites aren't as big as your noses, huh?
Manager [preparing to move toward Melvin]:	That is it! Forget it! I don't care how many people buy his books . . .
Carol [holding out her hand to stop her manager]:	I know, I know. Just give me one more chance; I'll talk to him. [Walks over to talk to Melvin.]
Melvin:	[Shrugs, self-satisfied.] They left.

Carol:	Yeah, what do you know? Brian says he doesn't care how long you've been coming; you ever act like this again, you're barred for life. I'm going to miss the excitement, but I'll handle it.
Melvin:	[Nods assent.] Three eggs over easy, two sausage, six strips of bacon with fries . . .
Carol:	Fries today!
Melvin:	. . . a short stack, coffee with cream and sweetener.
Carol:	You're going to die soon with that diet, you know that.
Melvin:	We're all going to die someday. I will, you will, and it sure sounds like your son will.
Carol:	[Face drops, becomes silent. After a pause . . .] If you ever mention my son again, you will never be able to eat here again, do you understand? Do you understand? Give me some sign you understand or leave now. Do you understand me, you crazy fuck? Do you?
Melvin [nervously moving his plastic silverware around]:	Yes. [Quietly] Yes.

This first interaction between Carol and Melvin is richly staged emotionally, from the irritation of the manager and offense of the other customers to Carol's tightly contained rage when Melvin insinuates that her son is dying. This scene quickly establishes Carol as a deft manager of her own and other people's feelings. We see Carol as a skilled worker who is valued enough by her boss to be able to step in and protect a regular customer against her manager's desire to throw him out.

This first exchange between Carol and Melvin also displays both the potential and danger of service exchanges as social interactions. Carol is portrayed as being in control of her work environment. She chooses to share aspects of her personal life with her coworkers and customers. Yet despite her ability to control some aspects of her work, Melvin is able to use the knowledge he has overheard about her personal life to hurt her. Melvin is able to receive recognition and tolerance of his atypical, politically incorrect, and offensive behavior by dining out. By contrast, Carol is vulnerable to the risks of opening her self up to the emotional aspects of her job.

Like most service workers, Carol must learn how to put on multiple emotional performances simultaneously. As servers' bodies move among locations and slip between tables, they must also adjust their faces and affect to react to a range of customers. Sociologist Arlie Russell Hochschild (1983) defines these adjustments of feeling as "emotional labor." Hochschild uses the term *emotional labor* to describe work that "requires one to induce or suppress feeling in order to sustain the outward countenance that produces the proper state of mind in others" (p. 7). Hochschild and researchers who have followed in her footsteps to develop a sociology of emotion have directed attention to how service work makes use of workers' emotions on the job, the costs to workers of altering their emotional production for a wage, and the broader implications of moving through a service economy in which consumers *know* that feeling is being strategically altered and managed. Just as physical labor can tire and wear out the body, emotional labor can estrange workers from the part of their selves they use at work—their emotions (Hochschild 1983:7).

In *As Good as It Gets*, Carol and Melvin's interactions provide a context for examining the emotional stakes in service exchanges. Despite Carol's far superior emotional skill and appeal, Carol remains structurally vulnerable to Melvin's poor social skills. The power dynamics inherent in their commercial relationship set up unequal rights to feeling. As Hochschild (1983) explains, servers are situated to absorb their customers' emotional displays, both appropriate and inappropriate, while customers are not obliged to return the favor (p. 171). In the emotional subtext of the film, Carol is a form of medicine for Melvin, inspiring him and soothing him, but as the one who is paid to serve rather than be served, Carol's emotional returns are constrained by the circumstances of her employment. By virtue of her position as service provider, Carol assumes a weaker right to feeling than does Melvin.

While previous studies of emotional labor have focused on worker strategies for protecting themselves from emotional demands (Paules 1991; Pierce 1995), I argue that part of what lubricates the "crucial steadying effect" of emotional labor in our culture is that the workers who provide a warm meal, a haircut, a smile, or a token of recognition in the marketplace often come to enjoy the emotional demands of their work. In my study of a restaurant called the Hungry Cowboy, both customers and coworkers described the restaurant as a scene of familiarity and connection (Erickson 2004, 2005; Erickson and Pierce 2005). Customers said the restaurant provides them with recognition. "Everyone knows me here," said one regular customer. A waitress named Alex went further, comparing Friday to a reunion:

> I look forward to working on Friday night. I like to come in on Friday nights because it's like family reunion time. All of these customers that I haven't seen for a while—I can give them a hug, I can say it's good to see you, oh my god, you're getting so grown up. I have always looked forward to Friday nights. A good night is a lot of familiar faces, not a lot of money. Just to have fun and enjoy the people I'm waiting on.

Similarly, in *As Good as It Gets*—as the film develops—viewers come to realize that Carol, as the single mom of a sick child who lives with her mother, gets the majority of her adult interaction at work. We see Carol telling sweet stories about her son to her coworkers and customers, exchanging resources with her coworkers, and being recognized for the quality of her service by her customers and boss. Carol is routinely connected to others, and she relies on the restaurant as a significant site of connection as well. Carol is intent, even insistent, on producing meaningful interactions through her labor. So much so that she does not even give up on Melvin. The allegorical aspects of Melvin and Carol's relationship as a venue for commentary on contemporary life expand midway through the film when their relationship moves outside the restaurant on a day when Carol cannot come to work because her son is ill.

Scene 2: Carol Misses Work

As Americans consume more services, and more Americans work in the service sector, many more of our points of contact with other people take place within the context of a service exchange. In *As Good as It Gets*, it is this point of connection between customer and server that proves transformative for both Carol and Melvin. Unlike most consumer-provider relationships, Carol and Melvin's relationship is extended beyond the restaurant stage when Carol's son, Spencer, becomes ill and she misses work to care for him.

Melvin's day is ruined when she is not there to wait on him. Melvin pays the busboy for Carol's last name, finds her address, and goes to her house. She opens the door.

Melvin:	I'm hungry. You have ruined my whole day. I haven't eaten.
Carol [shocked]:	What are you doing here?
Melvin:	This is not a sexist thing. If you were a waiter, I'd be doing the same . . .
Carol [interrupting, exasperated]:	What are you doing? Are you totally gone? This is my private home!
Melvin:	I'm trying to keep emotion out of this, even though it's an important issue to me and I have strong feelings on the subject.
Carol:	On what "subject"? That I wasn't there to take crap from you and bring you some eggs? Do you have any control over how creepy you allow yourself to get?
Melvin [hurt]:	Yes, I do, as a matter of fact, and to prove it I have not gotten personal and you have. Why aren't you at work? Are you sick? You don't look sick, just tired and bitter.
Carol [noticeably relaxing]:	My son is sick, OK?
Melvin:	What about your mother?
Carol:	How do you know about my mother?
Melvin:	I hear you talking while I wait.

This scene is important to the development of both characters precisely because they have moved from the ordinary stage for their contact—tableside—to Carol's doorway. In Carol's understandable surprise at finding Melvin at her door, she reveals a secondary surprise at discovering that Melvin has in fact been listening to her while she talks to other people at the restaurant. Having put a moratorium on references to her son, she seems to assume that Melvin does not know much (or care much) about her except for her utility to him—specifically, her usefulness as the one who knows how to serve him his "one warm meal" in a way he finds soothing. It is Melvin, then, who is reaching beyond the parameters of the service exchange in two ways: first, by showing up on her home territory rather than the middle ground of the restaurant where they ordinarily meet, and second, by revealing an interest in her life that extends beyond the predictability of the service she provides. This scene in the doorway of Carol's apartment also becomes the catalyst for the next stage of their connection. Seeing that Spencer's health prevents Carol from getting to work, Melvin uses his wealth to insure that she can be there when he needs her. He pays for Spencer's medical care, and in doing so, pushes far beyond the preliminary point of contact at the table in the restaurant, catapulting their relationship into uncharted waters.

Service Interactions and Social Connections

In *As Good as It Gets*, contemporary social life is portrayed as lonesome, dangerous, and potentially crippling. Carol is at once in need of healing herself while also the source of that healing for others. Carol, like many waitresses who have turned up on the silver screen before her, is also a master of emotional management. Carol's tenacity—her emotional resilience in regard to Melvin's frequent verbal assaults on her character and her importance—inspire him, in his words, "to want to be a better man." Her emotional resiliency operates as an antidote to the emotional defeat in which Melvin and his neighbor, Simon Bishop, are tempted to indulge.

Melvin, the unredeemable, is redeemed by a waitress. Not a high-paid therapist, a doctor, or a friend, but his favorite waitress. This outcome is not very surprising if we are at all familiar with the romantic comedy genre, in which unlikely lovers find each other in unusual locations. However, what is quite unusual are the ways in which Carol's work persona remains central to Melvin's understanding of her, even as his affection for and attraction to her deepen. For example, Melvin tells Carol how he marvels that all her customers cannot see what he sees:

> I might be the only person on the face of the earth that knows you're the greatest woman on earth. I might be the only one who appreciates how amazing you are in every single thing that you do, and how you are with Spencer, "Spence," and in every single thought that you have, and how you say what you mean, and how you almost always mean something that's all about being straight and good. I think most people miss that about you, and I watch them, wondering how they can watch you bring their food, and clear their tables, and never get that they just met the greatest woman alive. And the fact that I get it makes me feel good, about me.

The manner in which Carol does her work is central to what Melvin believes he knows about her. This attentiveness to what her work communicates and reveals is in tension with a more generalized attitude that waiting tables is not an important means of making a living. In fact, the view that waiting tables is a superfluous or inconsequential form of labor is the necessary context for a funny scene later in the film. When Melvin arranges for a top physician, Dr. Martin Bettes (Harold Ramis), to care for Carol's son at Melvin's expense, the doctor is surprised to discover what Carol's "indispensable" job entails.

Dr. Bettes: My wife is Melvin Udall's publisher. She said that I was to take excellent care of this little guy because you are urgently needed back at work. What kind of work do you do?

Carol: I'm a waitress.

What makes this exchange funny is that waiting tables is viewed as unessential and unimportant labor. Being a doctor is important; being a waitress is not. And yet, within the context of the film, Carol's work is what brings Melvin into contact with her.

Thinking beyond the film, in the move from an economy dominated by industrial production to an economy dominated by services, our service interactions with others have become much more central to daily life. The sheer frequency of our market-based interactions with others inspires sociologists of labor to return to long-running questions about the nature of connections between individuals. Similarly, Carol and Melvin's relationship raises questions about the nature of market-initiated relations: Can relationships that begin in market exchanges transform into relationships characterized by more familial or intimate ties? What does it require to move a relationship that originates in the unequal structure of a service exchange and is characterized by emotional scripts and restraint on intimacy into a relationship that is expansive and personal? Thinking through these and similar questions encourages a return to the distinctions made by German theorist Ferdinand Tönnies (1957), who differentiated between two distinct types of relationships between people: gemeinschaft, which roughly translated means community, and gesellschaft, which means society. Gemeinschaft is characterized by close, intimate, kin or kinlike relations, while gesellschaft is characterized by impersonal and sometimes instrumental relations between people.

Tönnies's (1957) ideas continue to be relevant today when we, as participants in social life, and as scholars, attempt to differentiate the moods, tones, or substance of interactions between two or more people. The concepts gemeinschaft and gesellschaft—community and society—provide us with a vocabulary to distinguish between voluntary connections between similar individuals who support one another, and means-to-an-end connections between heterogeneous social actors who have limited connections with or responsibilities for one another. During his lifetime (1855–1936), Tönnies attempted to make sense of the rapid cultural changes wrought by industrialization. Today, the rapid expansion of the service economy means that more and more of our human interactions take place within the marketplace, while more and more of our needs are fulfilled by services for pay.

As Good as It Gets is a movie about connections and emotions that uses neighbors in an upscale apartment complex and customers and food servers in a neighborhood restaurant as two aspects of social life that thrust us toward each other, for better and for worse. Ultimately, the movie puts Melvin, Carol, and Simon—three characters connected through unlikely means—on a road trip together to Baltimore. The message of that road trip is that they are all (and perhaps we, the viewers, are, too) hurt emotionally by the cumulative damage of their lives. Their emotional needs, which arise from different events and ailments, are ultimately treated as *shared* needs. The connections among their needs are made explicit in a conversation that takes place between Carol and Simon, which Melvin interrupts. Simon is explaining to Carol why he has not been in touch with his parents for many years. Carol replies, "OK, we all have these terrible stories to get over, and you—"

She is interrupted by Melvin, who spouts off from the back seat, "It's not true. Some have great stories, pretty stories that take place at lakes with boats and friends, and noodle salad. Just no one in this car. But, a lot of people, that's their story. Good times, noodle salad. What makes it so hard is not that you had it bad, but that you're pissed that so many others had it good." This outburst from Melvin is significant because it connects to the title of the film and the abiding fear Melvin revealed earlier, "What if this is as good as it gets?" Melvin's will never be a life of noodle salad and boat ride memories, and yet he delivers this speech from the backseat of a convertible driven by a woman he is attracted to and whom he respects, and shared by his neighbor, toward whom he has, despite his homophobic tendencies, grown increasingly fond. If as viewers we believe that connections with other people are generally good, then for Melvin, for Carol, and arguably even for Simon, their former lives were not as good as it gets.

In this film, the neighborhood and the restaurant give rise to new connections between people. And the connections among the three people in the car are situated as more real than the often accidental and unwanted ways in which we touch each other, talk to one another, and are forced to interact with people as we make our way through late capitalism. In fact, the relations among the three people in the convertible are situated as curative and healing, in contrast with many other social relations that are largely disinterested and disheartening. When Simon's "party friends" and even his family abandon him, when Carol cannot find men to date who can handle the complexity of her life, and when Melvin cannot even get the attention of the therapist he pays to treat his illness, these three become unexpectedly connected. Melvin's reference to "noodle salad" paints a picture of lives of ease, lives that do not require careful navigation to find and meaningfully connect with one another. In contrast, the connections among the three main characters in this film are anything but easy; they are forged through trial and error, but emerge quite strong. To viewers, it is clear that Melvin's speech about noodle salad is itself mythological and nostalgic; he refers to a world as pretend as the romantic fiction he writes. Melvin longingly imagines a life that no one in the car—but also no one watching the film—ever *really* experiences. In contrast to a fantasy about noodle salads and boat rides, the connections among Melvin, Carol, and Simon are situated as ultimately superior to connections to some family and some friends, many of whom cannot be counted on to stand by when disaster or illness strikes. Ending on this note, the film offers one vantage point from which to think about how to apply Tönnies's (1957) terms to contemporary social life. These three people forge gemeinschaft-like relations out of gesellschaft points of connection. They build community amid the rubble of kinship.

I turn next to *Office Space*, a movie that situates the restaurant as one of many sites in which workers must struggle against the dehumanizing effects of corporate control of the self at work.

The Ironies of Cubicle Culture

Office Space, as the title suggests, is a movie about work. The primary plotline involves Peter (Ron Livingston), a burned-out office worker who has reached the limits of his tolerance for his work at a technology corporation named Initech. The perilous and mind-numbing conditions of work at Initech, where workers are faced daily with the threat of downsizing, are juxtaposed with the work conditions of Peter's love interest, Joanna (Jennifer Aniston), who works at a T.G.I. Friday's–lookalike restaurant called Chotchkie's. Chotchkie's is located between Chili's and Flinger's, in a strip mall situated in the concrete landscape of the suburb where Initech is located. The viewer first encounters Chotchkie's when the bored-to-death cubicle workers, Peter and his friends Samir

(Ajay Naidu) and Michael (David Herman) go for a coffee break after just 30 minutes of work on a particularly irritating Monday morning.

Scene 1: Brian, the Super Server

Unfortunately for Peter, Chotchkie's does not provide the refuge from corporate culture he had hoped for. At the restaurant, Peter, Samir, and Michael are accosted by a male waiter named Brian, who epitomizes the ideal server Chotchkie's seeks to mold. Brian is aggressive, trying to sell dessert to the three men at nine o'clock in the morning, and portrays an enthusiasm that is both sickeningly sweet and utterly unrealistic given the confines of his role and the time of day.

Brian: So can I get you gentlemen something more to drink? Or maybe something to nibble on? Some Pizza Shooters, Shrimp Poppers, or Extreme Fajitas?

Peter: Just coffee.

Brian: OK. Sounds like a case of the Mondays.

Writer and director Mike Judge, who also created the animated series *Beavis and Butthead* and *King of the Hill*, has captured with painful accuracy the irrationalities of consumer experiences in chain restaurants. In Brian's performance, the corporate script trumps the context. If Shrimp Poppers are what he's been instructed to sell, he'll suggest them to customers, even at nine o'clock in the morning. Like Judge's previous work, *Office Space* is cynically focused on the minutiae of suburban life, and here, in his first full-length motion picture, he has mapped the continuities between cubicle culture and corporate chain restaurants.

Office Space is a modern day rant about the alienating affects of work: about the unacceptable costs to the self extracted by jobs that belittle us, leaving us dreaming of a different life, and cubicles that are too small to contain us. For example, in one of the culminating, most famous scenes of the film, Peter steals the copy machine that Samir and Michael have struggled with the whole time they have worked at Initech. The three men take the machine out into a deserted cornfield and proceed to brutalize it with baseball bats and fists, like a group of gangsters beating up an enemy. The scene is set to the tune of "Still" by the Geto Boys, so as they punch, kick and mutilate the machine, the Geto Boys chant, "Cause it's die muthafuckas, die muthafuckas" (Geto Boys 1996). The critique *Office Space* offers of the unacceptable costs and dehumanizing effects of work is not subtle.

Unlike films that tangentially comment on the effects of business practices in late capitalism, here the criticism is centered in the dark and biting humor that emerges out of circumstances that have become all too common in the new economy. Throughout the film, Peter's struggle to escape the constraints of his work amid the continuous threat of downsizing is compared with Joanna's struggle to retain her dignity in her job at Chotchkie's. Like Peter, Joanna is portrayed as resisting the character-shaping demands of her work. While Joanna's character and struggle are substantially underplayed compared to the screen time devoted to Peter's struggle, the parallel structure of the two narratives is noteworthy, if only for the way waiting tables is treated as work that is *similar* to other forms of work, notably white collar work. By contrast, back in 1974, in *Alice Doesn't Live Here Anymore*, Alice's job as a waitress is portrayed as the ultimate failure and insult to her self. In that film, waiting tables is presented as overtly shameful work that is the domain of lower class people who are destined to toil, or of "fallen" middle class women. Thirty years later, in *Office Space*, the central waitress figure is depicted as a smart working class heroine whose compassion and charm make her a sought-after love interest, in part because she possesses enough street smarts to assert her independence and resist degradation in her job. Much like the character of Carol in *As Good as It Gets*, Joanna in *Office Space* can be trusted as a solid, honest, truth-telling woman who provides a healthy alternative to a world riddled with people who have been beaten down and compromised by their work. In fact, unlike the vast majority of people at Initech who have lost all trace of resistance, and certainly unlike the super server, Brian, who has given himself entirely to a corporate-sponsored presentation of self, Joanna still has substantial fight left in her.

Joanna's specific struggle is with her officious manager, who seems eternally disappointed by her reluctance to enthusiastically display what he calls "flair." At Chotchkie's, flair refers to the corporate-required buttons displaying funny, ironic statements that are provided by the company to "individualize the workers." During Joanna and Peter's first lunch date, Peter accidentally stumbles on the delicate matter of the flair.

Peter:	We're not in Kansas anymore.
Joanna:	[Laughs.] I know, really.
Peter [indicating the buttons on her chest]:	It's on your . . .
Joanna [looking down at the buttons she is wearing on her suspenders and uniform shirt]:	Oh, right. That's one of my pieces of flair.
Peter:	What's a piece of flair?
Joanna:	Oh, it's . . . We're required to . . . You know, the suspenders and these buttons and stuff, we're actually required to wear fifteen pieces of flair. It's really stupid actually.
Peter:	Do you get to pick them out yourself?
Joanna:	Yes, we are, although I didn't actually choose these; I just sort of grabbed fifteen buttons. I don't even know what they say. [Uncomfortably] I don't really like talking about my flair. OK?

If we think of what occurs initially between Melvin and Carol as a form of commercialized intimacy, then what Joanna is struggling with is the corporate management of the self. In service work, the very character and emotions of service workers become the terrain of struggle in manager and worker debates.

Joanna's arguments with her boss and her refusal to conduct herself like Brian, the super server, reveal ambiguities and tensions central to training service workers. Brian, the super server, and Stan, the manager, both seem to believe in servers' ability to perform a script that does not sound rehearsed—to reproduce a smile, again and again, without ever losing the sparkle. Within this framework, getting to know customers is a purely instrumental activity in that a connection with customers might provide servers with insight into how to get more money out of customers. According to the corporate philosophy, then, more flair equals more fun for customers, which equals more money for the company. Joanna pushes back against this outlook, arguing against more flair. From her vantage point, being forced to go over the required minimum of flair would falsely convey support for and enthusiasm about corporate mandates that she thinks are "stupid."

In short, what Joanna's manager is attempting to convince her to do is "speed up" her performance of self within the job. Sociologist Robin Leidner (1993) describes some of the tensions that arise when companies attempt to speed up human interactions:

> Organizations that routinize service interactions are acting on contradictory impulses. They want to treat customers as interchangeable units, but they also want to make the customers feel that they are receiving personal service. The tension inherent in this project was apparent when I asked one of the trainers at Hamburger University about McDonald's goals for customer service. He told me quite sincerely, "We want to treat each customer as an individual, in sixty seconds or less." (P. 179)

Joanna's manager wants her to act as if she wants to go above and beyond the minimum. He wants her to want what the company wants, and masks this behind a request for her to "express herself" by giving in and displaying more than the minimum 15 pieces of flair on her body. While Joanna's character is really tangential to the Herculean struggle that Peter and his friends at Initech undertake, she, too, struggles to retain an inviolable sense of self at work.

Scene 2: Scripted Selves

To understand the significance of the "flair wars" that Joanna and her manager play out, it is important to note that Chotchkie's is likely a play on words referring to the Yiddish word *tchotchke*, which means "an inexpensive trinket" ("Tchotchke" N.d.). Writer and director Mike Judge cleverly names the restaurant a word that refers to something worth collecting, but not antique or particularly valuable. Combine this with the fact that Judge plays the unflinchingly corporate manager of Chotchkie's who relentlessly attempts to get Joanna to "express herself" with flair, and the significance of the restaurant scenes to the larger meaning of the film becomes clear. Later in the film, in a conversation with her manager, Joanna debates the necessity of "speeding up" the personality demands of her job.

Manager: We need to talk about your flair.

Joanna: I have fifteen pieces of flair.

Manager: Fifteen is minimum.

Joanna: It's up to you if you want to do the bare minimum, like Brian.

Manager: They come to Chotchkie's for the attitude and the atmosphere, and the flair is part of it.

Joanna: So you want me to wear more?

Manager: [Rolls his eyes.] Look, we want you to express yourself . . .

Her struggles demonstrate the central tension between individualizing and management control. The manager's task is to encourage individuals to be who the company needs them to be under the guise of "expressing themselves," but Joanna refuses to play the game.

Later in the film, Joanna triumphs over her sniveling boss, even though to do so requires quitting her job.

Joanna:	You know what, Stan, if you want me to wear thirty-seven pieces of flair, like your pretty boy over there, Brian, why don't you just make the minimum thirty-seven pieces of flair?
Stan, Chotchkie's Manager:	Well, I thought I remembered you saying that you wanted to express yourself.
Joanna:	Yeah. You know what, yeah, I do. I do want to express myself, OK. And I don't need thirty-seven pieces of flair to do it. [Holds up both middle fingers and walks out.]

Joanna's victory is satisfying, if fleeting. By the end of the film, she is working for another corporate restaurant in the same strip mall.

Popular Culture and the Sociology of Work

What can the movies teach us about work in the new economy? Films can be used as a common text through which to discuss and debate changes in the conditions of work and the implications of work on how we construct selves and relate to one another under conditions of late capitalism. Familiarity with sociological theories and research on the conditions of work lead to making connections between what we get paid to do and who we think we are, in our own lives and in the larger society.

Occasionally movies and other media circulate back and get incorporated somehow into work itself. Witness how many workers have *Dilbert* cartoons up in their cubicles, for example. When I worked as a waitress, I was subjected daily to the power of pop culture to inform our vantage point on work. Since my name is Karla, customers constantly reminded me of the character of Carla Tortelli from the incredibly popular 1980s television sitcom *Cheers*. *Cheers* depicted a Boston bar in which the same customers interacted with the same workers every night, forming a tight community of friends. In my research on neighborhood restaurants, customers also used references to the fictional *Cheers* to explain why they frequented a particular restaurant. On comment cards, they would write, "It's like Cheers here!" or, when I asked them to describe their favorite place to dine out, they would say, "A place where everybody knows your name, like Cheers."

Not only can film offer us a fresh vantage point on work, but film occasionally informs how we make sense of our roles in the new economy. In fact, at one of the restaurants I studied, the movie *As Good as It Gets* came up in multiple interviews with both customers and servers. For example, like the comfort Carol provides Melvin, one waitress named Jessica had been a routine, habitual, reliable person in her customers' social landscape. Jessica volunteered the following story as an example of her connection to customers:

There are many people who don't realize what it means to be a waitress, and they probably make as much money or less than I do, but they all feel superior to me. I have customers who say I can never leave. They have told me that if they come in and find out I quit, they are going to be like Melvin in *As Good as It Gets* and go to my house and get me to come back and wait on them! They're just trying to tell me how much they appreciate my service, and I realize that. It's like a little warm fuzzy.

Jessica's use of the film reveals that servers are drawn into emotional performances through multiple routes—not only managerial strategies, but also their own sense of craft and the collaborative construction of a sense of community. Jessica's customers made use of *As Good as It Gets* as a common text that could help them explain her significance to them. Jessica retells the story to counter the more prevalent attitude of "many people who don't realize what it means to be a waitress." Taken together, these instances demonstrate that popular culture depictions of service workers do occasionally supplement or help explain people's responses to one another within market exchanges.

Popular culture representations of work and social life allow us to hold up fictional interactions at a distance and scrutinize them together: How do popular representations compare to our own experiences in the marketplace, the neighborhood, or the office? What are the social conditions and organizational cultures of the places we work and consume? As a scholar of work, I find films to be one of the many avenues of access to analyzing working life and improving the theoretical insights we use as tools to do our own intellectual and scholarly work. Film is one of many tools we can use as a vehicle for thinking critically about how we perform our roles in the new economy, with particular attention to how our sense of self is affected through the service interactions and the social connections that emerge within the marketplace.

References

Erickson, K. 2004. "Bodies at Work: Performing Service in American Restaurants." *Space and Culture* 7(1):76–89.

Erickson, K. 2005. "To Invest or Detach? Coping Strategies and Workplace Culture in Service Work." *Symbolic Interaction* 4(1):76–89.

Erickson, K. and J. Pierce. 2005. "Farewell to the Organization Man: The Feminization of Loyalty in High-End and Low-End Service Jobs." *Ethnography* 6(3):283–313.

Hochschild, A. R. 1983. *The Managed Heart: Commercialization of Human Feeling*. Berkeley: University of California Press.

Geto Boys. 1996. "Still." Track 2 on *The Resurrection*. CD.

Leidner, R. 1993. *Fast Food, Fast Talk: Service Work and the Routinization of Everyday Life*. Berkeley: University of California Press.

"Tchotchke." N.d. *Oxford English Dictionary*. Retrieved December 1, 2007 (http://www.oed.com/).

Paules, G. F. 1991. *Dishing It Out: Power and Resistance among Waitresses in a New Jersey Restaurant*. Philadelphia: Temple University Press.

Pierce, J. 1995. *Gender Trials: Emotional Lives in Contemporary Law Firms*. Berkeley: University of California Press.

Tönnies, F. [1912] 1957. *Community and Society* (Gemeinschaft und Gesellschaft). Translated and edited by C. P. Loomis. East Lansing: Michigan State University Press.

REEL FAMILIES

The Delicate Balance of Family and Work in Film

Janet Cosbey

P opular films reveal our ideals and expectations about family life in myriad ways. We watch films searching, consciously or unconsciously, for clues about how we should act, what our families should be like, and how to solve problems and dilemmas that we face in our daily lives. As moviegoing audiences, do we see families presented as a reflection of real life—as the actual lived experiences of families at particular points in time and in particular locations? While belief persists that movies reflect reality (hooks 1996), "reel life" is not a mirror for "real life." Movies screen and frame social reality, and they reflect ideological images of interaction, relationship, and community (Denzin 1991). Cultural ideals about families—how they are constituted and expected to act—are deeply ingrained. When we see what looks familiar or normative, we often accept those representations without question. In recent years, films have begun to address problems families face in real life, such as the patriarchal nature of family violence and the damage it causes to familial relationships. A contemporary challenge in families that has not been realistically represented in film is how to meet the competing demands of work and family life.

Someone has to earn a living that can support the family and provide food, shelter, clothing, and all the resources that a family needs to function and survive. Historically, family households were divided along gender lines with the man having the relationship to the outside world, bringing in the resources necessary to provide for his family. He was the breadwinner, playing the instrumental role in charge of "resource attainment." His wife, on the other hand, did not enter the world of work, but instead spent her time in expressive tasks, caring for her family and both literally and figuratively being a "homemaker." It must be noted, however, that this construction of family is based on race, class, and sexual status; that is, a largely white, heterosexual middle class experience. Historically, women—immigrant women, women of color, and women in the lower socioeconomic classes—have always worked for wages to economically support their families. Realistically, in today's society, most two-partner households find that both need to work in order to support and make a home for themselves and their children and other family members who may depend on them. So, if both partners are playing the instrumental role in the family, who plays the expressive role? That is, who makes the home: who does the laundry, cleans the house, buys and prepares the food, organizes family appointments, pays the bills, and so forth? Ideally, these everyday minutiae are balanced with the demands of life in the workplace and community.

"Real life" families and "reel life" families meet this challenge in a variety of ways. The shift from male-breadwinner to dual-earner couples and single-parent households has created a stressful balancing act that is very different in reality from the fictional stories of families we see on television (Heintz-Knowles 2001; Jacobs and Gerson 2001) and in the movies. Additionally, we still cling to the romanticized notion that stay-at-home mothers are the "ideal" way for families to provide for young children and organize all the tasks necessary for household management. Suggestions that career women choose to "opt out" of the workforce to stay home and care for families rather than continue working at highly paid, demanding yet satisfying jobs contributes to the cultural mythology that stay-at-home moms are best (Stone 2007).

Are fictional characters in film reflective of contemporary American families? How can women excel in the workforce, maintain a working relationship with their partner, and raise their children successfully? Why do women feel they have to do it all? This reading uses gender as a lens into patterns of family life related to the delicate balancing act that is work and family. Gender structures the family at the same time that individuals create and re-create gender within family relationships. Sociologists note that gender relations and family life are so intertwined that it is impossible to understand one without the other (Coltrane 1998). To explore the gender-family-work relationship, this reading focuses on five films.

The first two films, *Mona Lisa Smile* (2003) and *Mr. Mom* (1983), address the breadwinner-homemaker model of family life, historically known as the "cult of domesticity." Both films are centered on the question of gender and work outside the home versus caring for family. The second set of films, *I Don't Know How She Does It* (2011) and *Daddy Day Care* (2003), provide examples of the so-called "opting out" phenomenon for women and men. The last film, *The Kids Are All Right* (2010), focuses on the social construction of family and how, regardless of the sex of the partners, family life is structured by gendered assumptions related to wage earning, career commitment, parenting, and homemaking.

Gender and Families

Mona Lisa Smile and *Mr. Mom* are both stories about the breadwinner-homemaker model of family life, albeit from different vantage points. *Mona Lisa Smile* takes place in the 1950s and demonstrates the stronghold of the ideological view of family prevalent during that period. Functionalist theorists such as Parsons and Bales (1955) described this family arrangement in terms of the expressive, caregiving role for women and the instrumental, breadwinner role for men described above. Mr. Mom provides a modern adaptation of family roles and responsibilities. The wife plays the instrumental role while the man plays the expressive role. Significantly, these gender roles remain unchallenged and unchanged, regardless of who performs them. Both movies offer an opportunity to critically examine the traditional gendered structure of the family, one in historical context, the other in more contemporary society. Although the films themselves may not offer an answer to the challenges this model of family life brings to American families today, they do provide us with a means of questioning the gender roles that have accompanied this model.

Mona Lisa Smile (Mike Newell, 2003)

In *Mona Lisa Smile*, Katherine Watson (Julia Roberts), a feminist, forward-thinking, idealistic new professor takes a job teaching art at conservative all-female Wellesley College in the 1950s hoping to inspire her students to see beyond their expected roles.[1] Katherine leaves her boyfriend behind in California and begins her new life in Massachusetts ready to change the world, or at least women's place in the world. Katherine approaches her teaching with the earnest belief that she can open the minds of the young female students she meets so that they can challenge the traditional societal expectations of the day and do something more with their lives than become "just a housewife."

As a professor, Katherine is confident that she can use the art that she loves to challenge her students to think critically and question their life choices. Katherine soon finds the situation at Wellesley at odds with her expectations, and she considers leaving. Though she is teaching the best and brightest students who are always prepared for class, eager to learn and to demonstrate their knowledge, she is disappointed to find their sole ambition in life remains finding a husband. These young women, daughters of the upper class, are being groomed to fill their place as wives and mothers within that social class. As Katherine wryly comments early in the film, it seems as though she is at a finishing school rather that a college: "I thought that I was headed to a place that was going to turn out tomorrow's leaders, not their wives."

The breadwinner-homemaker model of family life that Katherine finds her students so committed to was part of the historical anomaly of the 1950s. During World War II, women had been recruited into factory work to replace the men who had gone to war. With the changes wrought by industrialization, including the separation of work from home, all women except the most economically privileged were part of the waged economy. The difference in the World War II era was that for the first time in history, women were doing men's work for men's wages. Once the war was over, women lost their jobs or were moved to lower-paying positions to open the labor market for the returning male soldiers. At the same time, there was a cultural emphasis on gender-specific roles with the family—and women's place was at home, caring for their husbands and children. Movies during that period reversed the government-produced advertising, designed to entice women into factories during the war, with images of women happily caring for home and family. Post–World War II movies were a celebration of "Harriet the Happy Homemaker," replacing the World War II images of "Rosie the Riveter" (Edelman 2008). This version of family life was supported by a strong postwar economy and government policies such as low-interest mortgages to veterans, making the American Dream of marriage, family, and home available to many working class as well as middle class families (Cherlin 2008).

In the aftermath of World War II, and in the wake of U.S. economic, political, and social transformation, the decade of the 1950s was a "throwback to the Victorian cult of domesticity with its polarized sex roles and almost religious reverence for home and hearth" (Skolnick 1991:52). The fact that Katherine was not successful with the students at Wellesley is not surprising; the majority of women who attended college in the 1950s had no career plans and dropped out in large numbers to marry (Skolnick 1991). However, it is important to remember that this was a reflection of the time, rather than a demographic or social trend, and that only members of the upper middle and upper classes could send their daughters to college. Although this period was short lived, and that most women have engaged in some type of wage labor throughout history, this ideology has been fixed in cultural construction and memories of family structure. Gendered expressions about the family have shaped public policy, as well as individual choices and experiences, across the generations, although in reality it was "the way we never were." (Coontz 1992). Regardless, the myth has lived on, shaping our beliefs and expectations about family life into the present day.

The depiction of 1950s femininity, etiquette classes, and homemaking skills is so far removed from the college experience of women today that we might feel a sense of superiority that we are no longer subject to these outmoded views about women. The beginning of the second-wave women's movement is often identified as the critique of the homemaker role, including the isolation and desperation of educated middle class women who were relegated to keeping house in the suburbs, described by Betty Friedan in *The Feminine Mystique* (1963). Despite the changes wrought by the women's movement, there are still many remnants of traditional gender roles at work in families today. Gendered ideas about women's and men's work and family roles are evident even in families who espouse support for women's working outside the home and more equitable relationships in the home. There may be more flexibility today for both women and men, but the legacy of the homemaker-breadwinner ideal continues to structure our lives, choices, and potential. The belief that the natural role for women is to be homemakers and the natural role for men is to be labor force participants continues to permeate our ideas of what is appropriate feminine and masculine behavior in our society even today.

Mr. Mom (Stan Dragoti, 1983)

The gendered division of labor in the public and private realms is the central theme of the movie *Mr. Mom*. With the economic downturn in the automobile industry, Jack Butler (Michael Keaton) loses his executive job. After failed attempts to find employment, he stays home to care for the house and children as "househusband" while his wife Carolyn (Teri Garr) goes to work as an executive for an advertising agency. Being a stay-at-home dad is usually a temporary situation, as it turns out to be in the case of Jack Butler. Many men take on this role by default, either by finding themselves unexpectedly unemployed or because of illness or disability. Though this film is a comedic look at this particular family situation, it aptly illustrates the gendered division of labor at home and work and the legacy of the cult of domesticity.

The mishaps Jack "Mr. Mom" Butler experiences during his domestic reign illustrate the stark gendered divisions in the homemaker-breadwinner model. The exaggerated tribulations Jack endures capture the 1950s model of family life, in which the mom was left in charge of the home while the dad was absorbed in his work. He does not know, or need to know, what is involved in maintaining the home and caring for their children: after all, that is the work of the housewife/mother. Thus, when Jack takes over the home, he is a bumbling mess. *Mr. Mom* illustrates that it is the role itself and not the sex of the person performing the role that is responsible for the frustrations and discontent the homemaker role encompasses. Sociological insight enables us to see that regardless of who is making the home and minding the children, expectations about what is done and how it is done are rooted in the sex/gender binary system. Jack, representing "everyman," is portrayed as innately incapable of fulfilling the homemaker role.

The stay-at-home parent role has many challenges and limitations, including isolation and lack of control over one's work. Jack soon finds himself overwhelmed with laundry, cooking, cleaning, and other household chores. He is frustrated with the never-ending menial tasks. The majority of these chores require little thought or skill, and on top of that, they need to be done constantly. His only social contacts during the day are his children, and though he tries to engage them and seeks their help with housework, he is left feeling

Photo 6.1 The gendered division of labor in *Mr. Mom*. Jack Butler (Michael Keaton) makes a mess of the homemaker role when his breadwinner role is temporarily suspended.

frustrated and alone. His reactions, humorous in the role reversal, illustrate the frustration and discontent of the suburban housewife described by Betty Friedan so long ago. Jack shouts at his wife, "My brain is like oatmeal. I yelled at Kenny today for coloring outside the lines! Megan and I are starting to watch the same TV shows and I'm liking them! I'm losing it."

While Caroline is also initially uncomfortable with the role switch, she grows increasingly enamored with her new job as Jack becomes increasingly disappointed with his. Carolyn is sympathetic to Jack as she confesses that she once felt much the same way. Prior to Jack's job loss, Carolyn had strictly adhered to the 1950s model of homemaker, including the belief that she freely chose this way of life because it was best for her family. However, her success at work fosters a new sense of confidence that she did not have in her life as a wife and mother. Carolyn loves her new role, yet she gives up her job when Jack finds employment because in the end it is best for her to be at home embracing her "natural" feminine role. The traditional family is restored, with perhaps greater empathy between Jack and Caroline about their respective roles, but no deeper understanding of how to break free of their gendered destinies.

It is not surprising that the Butlers' role switching experience did not bring greater enlightenment to the couple. Americans still feel that paid work is more important than unpaid work (Cherlin 2008). Therefore, the work that women, and in this case Jack as *Mr. Mom*, do at home in caring for children, cooking and cleaning, and providing emotional support to the family is not as important as work that is paid. On the one hand, we espouse the belief that caring for children and homemaking skills are valued work, but noneconomic activity is devalued in modern capitalist society. What we value most in our society is work that is rewarded economically. Furthermore, working without pay puts one in the position of financial dependency, with costly emotional consequences. Research suggests that the characteristics associated with the traditional housewife role do not lead to self-confidence and positive mental health. Studies on the difficulties embodied in this model of family life have shown that traditional women married to traditional men experience the most symptoms of stress, including feelings of worthlessness, fatigue, and depression. Traditional wives also express the most dissatisfaction with life in general (Spence, Deaux, and Helmreich 1985). Our gendered notions of family life have implications well beyond the role division that occurs in families. Although *Mr. Mom* appears to suggest that this switch in gender roles may be a viable model of family life, there are two outstanding issues: (1) the labor- and time-intensive constellation of work assigned to the homemaker role is not altered by the sex of the person doing the work; and (2) the stay-at-home role is not always desirable or healthy for those doing the work involved. Moreover, women who divide their time between home and career are violating contemporary notions of the "good mother." Thus, just as many mothers find satisfaction in their careers, the full-commitment expectations of mother-hood often lead to feelings of guilt and shame (Sutherland 2010).

Work-Family Balance

The traditional gendered model of family life that is valued and sustained in *Mona Lisa Smile* and *Mr. Mom* is no longer a reality for the majority of U.S. families. In 2009, in two-parent families with children under age 18, 96 percent had at least one parent employed and 59 percent had both parents employed (U.S. Department of Labor, Bureau of Labor Statistics N.d.). The shift from the male-breadwinner model to the dual-earner or single-parent household has created a stressful balancing act for most families in today's society. This balancing act is very different in real life than it is in the fictional world. In the movies, work and family roles very rarely come into contact, and if they do, parents easily manage childcare and household activities (Heintz-Knowles 2001). Other than the film *I Don't Know How She Does It*, no major motion picture has captured the dilemma of this balancing act that the majority of families face daily. In this film, a working mother, enjoying and excelling at her dream job as an account executive, struggles to get ahead in her career while still keeping everything together on the home front with her loving, but less than helpful, husband and two young children.

Twenty years after *Mr. Mom*, another film focusing on the problems families face when dad is out of work and mom is still in the workforce was released. Jack Butler's situation in the 1980s resonates with the current economic recession and an increasing rate of unemployment with many men losing their jobs. In *Daddy Day Care*, Charlie Hinton is faced with the same dilemma as Jack Butler, yet he handles his situation differently. As in the first set of films, the gender roles are not questioned and change very little regardless of who performs them. Both *I Don't Know How She Does It* and *Daddy Day Care* offer an opportunity to critically examine the gendered choices men and women make in their efforts to balance the worlds of work and home.

I Don't Know How She Does It (Douglas McGrath, 2011)

I Don't Know How She Does It, the statement frequently made about working mothers, is the title of a 2002 Allison Pearson novel that inspired the film by the same name. It is the story of Kate Reddy (Sarah Jessica Parker), an account executive and the mother of two young children trying to do it all: "bring home the bacon and fry it up in the pan," as the 1970s commercial for Enjoli perfume phrased it. Kate struggles to balance the needs of her family with the needs of her career. Her stress is palpable as she describes her difficulties falling asleep at night. She ponders researchers' confusion about why women with young children don't sleep through the night. "Instead of sleeping," she muses, "I do the list." She mentally imagines all of the many things she has to do the next day as she attempts to go to sleep at night. Kate's problems with sleep are eerily similar to the real life stories of working women that Arlie Hochschild collected for *The Second Shift* (2003); the working women she interviewed who were juggling home and career talked about sleep the way a hungry person would talk about food.

In this film, it is possible to look beneath the flippant jokes and crazy antics of the characters, to see the pain and anxiety parents feel as they try to bring balance to their lives. Kate and her husband Richard (Greg Kinnear) have two children, a nanny to care for them, and a lovely, comfortable home. Richard is more laid-back and easygoing, with a job that is less demanding than his wife's. Richard is always advising Kate to slow down, but Kate knows that Richard has no idea of the work she has to do to keep everything together for their household. In the novel upon which the movie is based, Kate wryly notes, "Women carry the puzzle of family life in their heads, they just do" (Pearson 2002:183).

Throughout the film, Kate debates with herself about the pluses and minuses of working at a job she loves versus staying home to care for her children. She experiences constant guilt about not measuring up to some unattainable standard of what a perfect wife, mother, and worker should be. Although she loves the work she does, she frets about missing meaningful moments in her children's lives and has a romantic fantasy that everything would be perfect if she could stay home with her children and care for them full time. Kate feels conflicted about her life and the choices she has. The trailer for the film asks in a male voice-over: "How do you keep your life together without losing it?"

Kate Reddy represents the millennial version of true womanhood. Unlike the models of Victorian domesticity, Kate not only has to care for her children and home, or at least see that both are cared for; she has to excel in the workplace as well. The quandary Kate faces reflects changes that have occurred with the dramatic increase in labor force participation of married women with young children. In the mid-twentieth century, only 10 percent of mothers with children under the age of six and 30 percent of mothers with school age children worked outside the home, compared to 60 percent and 80 percent, respectively, in the twenty-first century (Wright and Rogers 2010).

The majority of mothers may be in the labor force, but this alteration in men's and women's roles has been a "stalled revolution," with little change occurring at home (Hochschild 2003). Women may spend the day working for wages, but their workday does not end once they leave the workplace; they come home and perform the "second shift" in attending to household chores. In her study, Hochschild identified three types of couples in terms of handling the division of domestic duties. In the first type, *traditional* couples, the wife may work outside the home for wages, but she is still expected to come home in the evening and complete her domestic duties. In these families, household tasks are divided along gender lines, with the wife handling the traditional homemaker chores of housecleaning, cooking, shopping, laundry, and so forth, whereas the husband handles the traditional male chores of car and lawn maintenance, fixing things, and so forth. In the couples Hochschild designated as *transitional*, the husbands "help" their wives with the household chores. The smallest group of couples is *egalitarian*, with husbands and wives sharing the domestic labor. Helping a spouse with designated duties still leaves the majority of work with the "wife," but more important, the responsibility for organizing the chores, seeing that the work is done, and even knowing what tasks need to be completed remains the responsibility of women, still supporting the traditional gendered division of labor. Kate Reddy's comment about women carrying "the puzzle of family life in their heads" reflects the frustrations inherent for women in couples of the transitional type, where household accountability is still women's work.

This work-family balancing act takes a toll. The stress faced by dual-earner families and single working mothers is well documented. There are a multitude of factors that contribute to stress in a marriage, but recent evidence has shown that the division of household labor can be a constant source of contention in even the best of relationships. The most common problem for dual-earner couples is role overload, particularly when children are young. Role overload can lead to problems both at home and in the workplace. Parents, particularly mothers, who juggle competing demands are at risk for serious health problems. In the workplace, overwhelmed parents contribute to low morale with frequent absences, absenteeism, and decreased productivity. Many working parents report that they feel torn between the needs of children and home and their need to be a productive worker (DeGenova, Stinnett, and Stinnett 2011).

Remnants of the breadwinner-homemaker model of family life are still evident in the way some couples handle the division of labor concerning household tasks. For many men, the home is a refuge from work, a place of relaxation as it has traditionally been. For women, on the other hand, the home is often not a refuge, but a place where more work must be done, resulting in what Jessie Bernard (1982) termed "his" and "her" marriage. Not only is marriage a different experience for men and women, but research shows that men benefit more from this arrangement than women do. A recent study of dual-earner couples found that when men come home from work they want to be alone. Women, however, tend to spend time after work with one or more children. Their alone time was usually spent doing housework. This study looked at stress levels of men and women, finding that wives' stress levels drop when their husbands are helping with chores. On the other hand, men's stress levels fall when their wives are busy while they're relaxing (Saxbe, Repetti, and Graesch 2011).

For more than 40 years, since the women's movement initiated changes in the world of work and home, researchers have been studying the changes in family dynamics. Conventional wisdom continues to maintain that even though women are working longer hours on the job and cutting back on housework, men have not been making up the difference. There is, however, a slight indicator of change revealed in the time men and women spend on such household chores as cooking, meal cleanup, laundry, outdoor chores, repairs, paying bills, and childcare duties. These chores have traditionally been gender defined, and research continues to show that married women spend about three times more hours on housework than married men (Coltrane 2008). Other studies using a variety of research methods have concluded that although men are doing more at home at the same time that women are decreasing the amount of time they spend on housework, an equitable balance has not yet been reached (Coltrane 2008; Davis and Greenstein 2004; Hook 2004; Lee and Waite 2005).

The differences still evident in how men and women share, or don't share, household responsibilities underlie the dilemma faced by Kate Reddy in *I Don't Know How She Does It* as well as that faced by Charlie Hinton in the film *Daddy Day Care*. In the latter, Charlie's ultimate decision that his family comes first can be made because of the support he receives from his wife. As we saw in *Mr. Mom*, it is the structure of these gendered positions in the family that is difficult, if not impossible, to change. Although Charlie Hinton makes a different choice about his family life than Jack Butler did 20 years earlier, his options were more open than those of Kate Reddy.

Daddy Day Care (2003)

Daddy Day Care takes on the question of what happens when ad executive Charlie Hinton (Eddie Murphy) loses his job in product development at a large food company. Like *Mr. Mom*, the man in the family finds himself out of work and plays the expressive role by staying at home and caring for the household and children while his wife plays the instrumental role by working outside the home to support the family.

After being out of work just a short time, Charlie and his former coworker, Phil (Jeff Garlin), discover that new jobs are not easy to find and day care is incredibly expensive. They decide to open a day care facility to rival the one their children had previously attended, the exclusive Chapman Academy run by a strict and severe headmistress, Miss Harridan (Anjelica Huston). Initially, there is some hesitation on the part of parents, particularly moms, about placing their children in a day care facility run by men, but eventually the need for day care outweighs their concerns. Although the daddies occasionally seem overwhelmed by the antics of the children and unsure of what to do with them, they apply management techniques from their working experience and soon find the day care a success.[2] When Charlie is offered his job again, he returns to work only to decide that he prefers spending time with his son and returns to the world of Daddy Day Care. "I'd say this wasn't a bad trade-off," Charlie comments to his son at the end of the film.

The storyline in *Daddy Day Care* captures the real consequences of the economic recession for many men. Between 2007 and 2011, 6.1 million jobs were lost by men; only 28 percent have been regained (Institute for Women's Policy Research 2011). What makes Charlie's situation unique is that, unlike *Mr. Mom*, when given the choice, he opts out of his profession to spend more time with his child. The tug-and-pull of work commitments and family is generally thought of as a dilemma for women rather than men, who have been designated as the earners in family.

Charlie's decision to make childcare his focus is consistent with the area of home and family where men contribute most. That is, when men participate in family/home work, they are most likely to take on childcare tasks rather than mundane household chores. This is not surprising, since taking care of children is more intrinsically and emotionally rewarding than doing routine domestic tasks (Hochschild 2003). In addition, time spent caring for children is more interesting and fun—perhaps not as much fun as the film *Daddy Day Care* suggests, but more enjoyable than housework nonetheless. Research continues to support this trend; the most dramatic increase in men's household contributions in the past 20 or 30 years has been doing more childcare. Between 1965 and 2003, men tripled the amount of time they spent caring for their children (Bianchi, Robinson, and Milkie 2006).

The number of men staying at home to care for their families may have increased in recent years, but it is not likely to become a majority experience. Men in married-couple families with children are still most likely to work outside the home. When one parent stays home, it is most likely to be the mother. Of all married-couple families in 2010, men were the only workers in 19 percent of the families while women were the only workers in 8.6 percent (U.S. Department of Labor, Bureau of Labor Statistics 2011). Many stay-at-home dads are only temporarily in this position because of the economic downturn, but when jobs return, they will most likely return to the workforce. So, like the movie *Mr. Mom*, the movie *Daddy Day Care* is not foreshadowing a role reversal of great magnitude.

Similarly, Kate Reddy's torment fostered by juggling the roles of worker and mother does not reflect that working women will ultimately choose full-time mothering. The slight dip in women's labor force participation in recent years led some observers, particularly in the media, to proclaim that mothers were opting out of the work force (Williams, Manville, and Bornstein 2006). The implication was that women could not handle both a career and motherhood and were choosing to return to their more traditional gender roles. However, recent labor force fluctuations notwithstanding, women's labor force participation is not likely to change significantly in the years ahead. The struggle for families to balance work and home continues. However, gender convergence suggests that changes in family relationships that result in a more equitable distribution of work are possible.

Gender Convergence

While there is a consensus that the division of household labor is far from equal, some research suggests that more couples are sharing than ever before, especially in full-time dual-earner households. Each generation of men has appeared to take on a greater share of the work involved in running a home. While men's family work has not changed nearly as much as women's labor force participation has changed, there is evidence that men are becoming more involved in the work of home and family. Notably, expectations about men's involvement have changed, as Sullivan and Coltrane (2008) point out: "Men and women may not be fully equal yet, but the rules of the game have been profoundly and irreversibly changed" (p. 204).

These trends in men's work at home and women's employment status suggest an ongoing shift toward "gender convergence," an ever-increasing similarity in how men and women live and what they want from their lives (Lang and Risman 2010:408). This gender convergence varies by race, ethnicity, and social class, however, with dual-earner, middle and upper class white families exhibiting the most evidence of change. Unemployment, economic stress, and job insecurity contribute to resistance to change.

Although men may appear to be reluctant to take up the slack in household chores left by women who are contributing more hours to paid employment than to domestic duties, there are benefits for both partners when sharing occurs. Most Americans now see sharing household chores as a more important factor in marital success than such traditional measures as having children. In addition, couples who share employment and housework are less likely to divorce than couples who follow the gendered pattern of male breadwinner and female homemaker (Cooke 2010). A 2009 study, part of the University of Michigan Panel Study on Income Dynamics, found that men who do more housework also have more sex with their wives—a definite benefit to sharing household chores. Another benefit is evident in a recent study reporting on stress levels in relation to domestic duties. The bad news was that men wanted to spend time alone and that they would rather relax than help their wives, but the good news was that when men did help their wives with chores, their wives' stress levels fell (Saxbe et al. 2011).

In an early study of the ways in which couples work out work and family obligations, Philip Blumstein and Pepper Schwartz (1983) compared married, cohabiting, and same-sex couples. Couples who agreed that both partners in a relationship should work outside the home were, not surprisingly, found to be happier than those who disagreed on this issue. More important, "because working women bring money into the household, their work helps equalize the balance of power in their marriages" (Blumstein and Schwartz 1983:139). Wives who work also garner more respect from their husbands. This study also found that cohabiting couples had more egalitarian standards for doing housework, although women still did the majority of the domestic chores. In gay and lesbian couples, as in heterosexual couples, those who were not fully employed did a greater share of the housework.

One effect of heterosexism is that gender is assumed to align with sex, which is reflected in the household division of labor. While not all couples adhere to these traditionally gender-defined roles, they serve as a reference point. For same-sex couples, on the other hand, each element involved in running a household becomes a point of debate. Same-sex couples may be a step ahead of heterosexual couples in building an egalitarian relationship. When asked how they came to organize their relationship, same-sex couples reported that it was basically trial and error. They did what worked best for them in terms of their skills, interests, and desires. In the Blumstein and Schwartz (1983) study of couples, they found that in some ways lesbians also find the female role demeaning and wish to change it. They do not want a partner to dominate them, and they want both partners to be satisfied with the work that they do. They want a relationship in which their home life is important, but they also want a strong, ambitious, and independent partner (Blumstein and Schwartz 1983). The film *The Kids Are All Right* provides a look at a modern two-mom family and the opportunity to critique gender when sex is held constant (i.e., when both adults in the relationship are the same sex).

The Kids Are All Right (Lisa Cholodenko, 2010)

This film is an engaging look at a modern family raising two kids the best way they know how. The relationship between Nic (Annette Bening), a doctor, who is the breadwinner of the family, and Jules (Julianne Moore), the stay-at-home mom who wants to be a landscape designer, is challenged when the sperm-donor father of their two children, Paul (Mark Ruffalo), comes into the picture. What threatens the bond between the couple, however, is not someone from outside the relationship; instead, their marriage is threatened by changes that have occurred in their relationship over time. As the children have gotten older and more independent, Jules and Nic find themselves questioning the roles they play in the family and with each other.

Jules had been happily caring for her family, seemingly content to have Nic support the family economically. The moms are parents to a daughter Joni (Mia Wasikowska) and a son Laser (Josh Hutcherson). As the children are growing up and Joni is going off to college, Jules is beginning to search for a way to find more meaning in her life. She had majored in architecture in college and is hoping to put her skills to use as a landscape designer. During one argument, she accuses Nic of sabotaging her desires to work outside the home. She argues that Nic always wanted her to be the "wife," the one who stayed home and took care of the family, even while she encouraged her to try various businesses that would allow her to work from home. As this "marriage" consists of two women, the "choice" for Jules to stay home with the children was not based on sex. Rather, we assume that Nic's higher income as a medical doctor was a determining factor, placing her in the instrumental role of providing for the family.

As the story unfolds, Laser expresses an interest in learning about his biological father, and he enlists his sister's help in contacting him and setting up a meeting. When the moms find out that the kids have been secretly seeing Paul, they decide they need to meet him as well and invite him over to dinner. During the dinner conversation, as they are introducing themselves and their lives to each other, Jules expresses her desire to start a landscape design firm. Nic is skeptical about this enterprise, but Paul eagerly suggests that Jules take him on as a client. In this scene, we see a seemingly "gendered" moment transpire. Nic, playing the instrumental role, expresses doubt at the likelihood of Jules's success (reminiscent of a scene in which the husband doubts the stay-at-home mom's ability to do "more.") However, Paul enlists Jules to landscape property for him. Jules and Paul see each other daily as she works on the landscaping, and eventually they develop an attraction that leads to a sexual affair.

It is important to note that the roles Jules and Nic play in the family are not based on sex (i.e., male or female). It is the *positions* they occupy, instrumental and expressive, that determine the power, or the perceived latitude of "choice," in the family. As Kimmel (2011) notes, "many of the differences between women and men that we observe in our everyday lives are actually not gender differences at all, but rather differences that are a result of being in different positions" (p. 11). Thus, *The Kids Are All Right* captures what gender scholars have long argued: many of the "differences" that we observe between men and women have less to do with biology and everything to do with the meanings we construct concerning masculinity and femininity. The separation of spheres told us that women are "supposed" to be the caretakers and that it is "natural" for men to work outside the home. Gender inequality is often explained as resulting from gender "differences." But, as we see in this film, the inequality (as "measured" by access to power and decision making) is not sex based, but rooted in the position each partner occupies within her or his relationship and family.

Conclusion

We learn many lessons about family life from watching films. Many of the movies produced in Hollywood are unrealistic escapist fare, capitalizing on dramatic situations to sell tickets. However, we still look to films for messages about how we should live our lives. What we learn from the movies often provides us with a template for family life that we then use to measure our own experiences. Sometimes the images and ideals we glean from film can lead to stereotypical and unrealistic expectations about family life. These expectations can also divert us from the real issues that families face in today's society, such as stresses imposed by an increasingly competitive job market; instability in terms of wages and benefits; the possibility—sometimes the reality—of losing one's job due to downsizing or other factors; and lack of adequate health care benefits and fear of the devastation a serious illness or medical condition could bring.

However, there are motion pictures that challenge conventional stereotypes and tell gripping stories about realistic, albeit fictional, families. Films can be a powerful and persuasive vehicle for making us look at the world in a new and different way. Movies such as those discussed in this reading can inspire us to critically examine the lives we lead and understand ourselves and our relationships within families more clearly. Applying our sociological imagination to these films also enables us to develop a keener sense of awareness and understanding about the lives of others in families not like our own.

References

Bernard, J. 1982. *The Future of Marriage*. New Haven, CT: Yale University Press.

Bianchi, S. M., J. P. Robinson, and M. A. Milkie. 2006. *Changing Rhythms of American Family Life* (Rose Series in Sociology). New York: Russell Sage.

Blumstein, P. and P. Schwartz. 1983. *American Couples: Money, Work, Sex*. New York: William Morrow.

Cherlin, A. J. 2008. *Public and Private Families*. New York: McGraw-Hill.

Coltrane, S. 1998. *Gender and Families*. Thousand Oaks, CA: Pine Forge Press.

Cooke, L. 2010. "Briefing Paper: 'Traditional' Marriage Now Less Stable Than Ones Where Couples Share Work and Household Chores." Pp. 431–34 in *Families as They Really Are*, edited by B. Risman. New York: Norton.

Coontz, S. 1992. *The Way We Never Were: American Families and the Nostalgia Trap*. New York: Basic Books.

Davis, S. and T. Greenstein. 2004. "Cross-National Variations in the Division of Household Labor." *Journal of Marriage and Family* 66:1260–71.

DeGenova, M. K., N. Stinnett, and N. Stinnett. 2011. *Intimate Relationships, Marriages and Families*. New York: McGraw-Hill.

Denzin, N. 1991. *Hollywood Shot by Shot: Alcoholism in American Cinema*. New York: Walter De Gruyter.

Ebert, R. 2003. "*Mona Lisa Smile*." *Chicago Sun-Times*, December 19. Retrieved February 19, 2012 (http://rogerebert.suntimes.com/apps/pbcs.dll/article?AID=/20031219/REVIEWS/312190304/1023).

Edelman, R. 2008. *From Rosie the Riveter to Harriet the Happy Homemaker: Women on Screen during and after World War II*. Unpublished lecture, New York Council for the Humanities, Pember Library, March, Granville, NY.

Friedan, B. 1963. *The Feminine Mystique*. New York: Dell.

Heintz-Knowles, K. 2001. "Balancing Acts: Work-Family Issues on Prime-Time TV." Pp. 177–206 in *Television and the American Family*, edited by J. Bryant and J. A. Bryant. Mahwah, NJ: Erlbaum.

Hochschild, A. 2003. *The Second Shift*. New York: Penguin.

Hook, J. 2004. "Reconsidering the Division of Household Labor: Incorporating Volunteer Work and Informal Support." *Journal of Marriage and the Family* 66:101–17.

hooks, b. 1996. *Reel to Real: Race, Sex, and Class at the Movies*. New York: Routledge.

Institute for Women's Policy Research. 2011. "Job Gap Between Men and Women Persists in August." Retrieved February 19, 2012 (http://www.iwpr.org/publications/pubs/job-gap-between-women-and-men-persists-in-august).

Jacobs, J. A. and K. Gerson. 2001. "Overworked Individuals or Overworked Families? Explaining Trends in Work, Leisure and Family Time." *Work and Occupations* 28(1):40–63.

Kimmel, M. S. 2011. *The Gendered Society*. 4th ed. New York: Oxford University Press.

Lang, M. and B. Risman. 2010. "Briefing Paper: A Stalled Revolution or a Still Unfolding One?" Pp. 408–12 in *Families as They Really Are*, edited by B. Risman. New York: Norton.

Lee, Y. and L. Waite. 2004. "Husbands' and Wives' Time Spent on Housework: A Comparison of Measures." *Journal of Marriage and the Family* 67:328–36.

Parsons, T. and R. F. Bales. 1955. *Family, Socialization, and Interaction Process*. New York: Free Press.

Pearson, A. 2002. *I Don't Know How She Does It*. New York: Knopf.

Saxbe, D., R. Repetti, and A. Graesch. 2011. "Time Spent in Housework and Leisure: Links with Parents' Physiological Recovery from Work." *Journal of Family Psychology* 25:271–81.

Skolnick, A. 1991. *Embattled Paradise: The American Family in an Age of Uncertainty*. New York: Basic Books.

Spence, J T., K. Deaux, and R. L. Helmreich. 1985. "Sex Roles in Contemporary Society." In *Handbook of Social Psychology: Special Fields and Applications*, edited by G. Lindzey and E. Aronson. New York: Random House.

Stone, P. 2007. *Opting Out? Why Women Really Quit Careers and Head Home.* Berkeley: University of California Press.

Sullivan, O. and S. Coltrane. 2008. *A Discussion Paper on Changing Family Roles.* Prepared for the 11th Annual Conference of the Council on Contemporary Families, University of Illinois, Chicago. Retrieved January 11, 2012 (https://netfiles.uiuc.edu/r-ferrer/VisitationSchedule/Family%20Trends/ Contemporary%20Families.pdf).

Sutherland, J.-A. 2010. "Mothering, Guilt and Shame." *Sociology Compass* 4(5):310–21.

United States Department of Labor, Bureau of Labor Statistics. N.d. "Table 4. Families with own children: Employment status of parents by age of youngest child and family type, 2009–10 annual averages." Economic News Release. Retrieved January 10, 2012 (http://www.bls.gov/news.release/ famee.t04.htm).

United States Department of Labor, Bureau of Labor Statistics. 2011. "Employment Characteristics of Families Summary." Economic News Release. Retrieved January 10, 2012 (http://www.bls .gov/news.release/famee.nr0.htm).

Williams, J. C., J. Manvell, and S. Bornstein. 2006. *"Opt Out" or Pushed Out? How the Press Covers Work/Family Conflict: The Untold Story of Why Women Leave the Workforce.* Retrieved January 6, 2012 (http://www.worklifelaw.org/pubs/OptOutPushedOut.pdf).

Wright, E. O. and J. Rogers. 2010. *American Society: How it Really Works.* New York: Norton.

Notes

1. According to Roger Ebert (2003), the screenwriters based their script on Hillary Clinton's experiences at Wellesley in the 1960s.
2. Andrea Doucet, in *Do Men Mother? Fatherhood, Care, and Domestic Responsibilities,* finds that the stay-at-home dads in her study bring elements of masculinity to their new roles as full-time caregivers.

Outtake

Seeing the Emotional Dimensions of Work and Family Life

Rebecca J. Erickson

When scholars analyze "work and family," they tend to focus on balancing the demands of paid employment with those of family life or on the performance of housework and childcare. Time constraints, gendered ideologies, and inequalities in pay can often lead to strain or conflict concerning the work that needs to be accomplished within the family. What tends to be overlooked is the *emotion work* required to perform work and family roles. "Emotion work" refers to activities that are concerned with the enhancement of others' emotional well-being and with the provision of emotional support. Given that feelings of "love" are at the heart of many depictions of contemporary family life and that today's service economy demands more of our emotional selves on the job, the continued invisibility of the *work* that it takes to be emotionally present in our interactions with others is somewhat surprising.

Films can provide unique insights into the ways that people perform emotion work and, in so doing, can help us trace the course of gendered expectations surrounding work, family, and emotion. At the same time, seeing emotional experience as *work* can be difficult because our assumptions about the connection between gender and emotion are portrayed as "natural." As with other types of sociological analysis, observing violations of cultural expectations may be the best way to recognize the normative guidelines underlying them. Because films about family life often trace the emotional arc or journey of one or more characters, they are particularly helpful for identifying the emotion work that keeps families, workplaces, and other institutionalized settings running smoothly and the chaos that results when rules about feeling are violated.

For example, films such as *Office Space* (1999) and *The Devil Wears Prada* (2006) illustrate the different ways that men and women are held accountable for emotion at work—particularly in regard to anger. In *Office Space*, Peter's expression of irritation with bureaucratic red tape leads to a promotion within his IT firm while Joanna's lack of "flair" in her restaurant service job leads to her loss of employment. In *The Devil Wears Prada*, this type of gender accountability seems to be reversed as Miranda Priestly (Meryl Streep) sits atop the publishing world despite her mean-spirited expressions of irritation with all who are beneath her on the corporate ladder. These reversals are more apparent than real, however, given that the audience recognizes that this comedic portrayal of Miranda's violation of female emotion norms—norms that are exemplified by the initially deferential sweetness of Andy Sachs (Anne Hathaway)—will undoubtedly have negative consequences. In this case, although Miranda holds on to her job, she is divorced by her husband. Although we often think of workplaces as bureaucracies characterized by emotional neutrality, workplace films help us to see their culturally grounded emotional foundations.

Although most family films featuring a cultural violation or gendered role reversal focus on who makes the money and who is taking care of the kids and housework (e.g., *Mr. Mom* [1983], *Mrs. Doubtfire* [1993], *Daddy Day Care* [2003]), they can also be seen as providing lessons in emotion work. Each of the preceding films illustrates the critical role emotional connections play in maintaining family life—particularly between fathers and their children. In a twist on this theme, *The Kids Are All Right* (2010) tells the story of a lesbian couple whose kids search for and find their biological father. Despite its progressive premise, the film presents a quite traditional portrayal of how one's emotional life can be influenced by paid employment and how the greatest threat to family stability is not behavioral violations but emotional ones. Nic, a successful physician and the family's stressed-out authoritarian breadwinner, is portrayed as indulging her partner Jules's forays into a series of failed business ventures both financially and emotionally. However, when Paul (the sperm donor) comes on the scene, his authentic support of Jules's occupational aspirations, along with the possibility that he will connect emotionally with the kids, threatens Nic's position in the family. As the film proceeds, the threat becomes realized and raises questions about Nic's emotional presence in her family. Nic's drinking also reveals the role that alcohol may play in enabling family members to interact with one another at the same time that it constrains their ability to be emotionally available to their families.

Finally, the essential role of emotion work in maintaining family life is often at its clearest when families are dissolving. In *Revolutionary Road* (2008), married couple Frank (Leonardo DiCaprio) and April (Kate Winslet) believe they can transcend the gendered work and family expectations of white suburban life in the 1950s. During an emotionally charged disagreement early in the film, Frank expresses his commitment to this belief, proclaiming, "I don't happen to fit the role of dumb, insensitive suburban husband! You've been trying to lay that crap on me ever since we moved out here!" These words are almost immediately undermined as each character rejects the emotion work being done by the other. April accuses Frank of putting her "in a trap" by moving to suburbia and violating their commitment to individual freedom and creativity. Revealing that he is in fact shaped by the feeling rules governing a 1950s "organization man," Frank draws back his fist to hit her but then storms away before he completes the act. This scene reveals how difficult it can be to perform the emotional work that sustains family life.

CHAPTER 7

Deviance, Crime, and Law

Teacher:	Your current event, Napoleon.
Napoleon Dynamite:	Last week, Japanese scientists explaced . . . placed explosive detonators at the bottom of Lake Loch Ness to blow Nessie out of the water. Sir Cort Godfrey of the Nessie Alliance summoned the help of Scotland's local wizards to cast a protective spell over the lake and its local residents and all those who seek for the peaceful existence of our underwater ally.

—*Napoleon Dynamite* (2004)

Fenster:	They treat me like a criminal. I'll end up a criminal.
Hockney:	You are a criminal.
Fenster:	Why you gotta go and do that? I'm trying to make a point.

—*The Usual Suspects* (1995)

Arthur Kirkland [pointing at his client]:	That man is guilty! That man, there, that man is a slime! He is a *slime!* If he's allowed to go free, then something really wrong is goin' on here!
Judge Rayford:	Mr. Kirkland, you are out of order!
Arthur Kirkland:	You're out of order! You're out of order! The whole trial is out of order! They're out of order! That man, that sick, crazy, depraved man, raped and beat that woman there, and he'd like to do it again! He *told* me so! It's just a show! It's a show! It's *Let's Make a Deal!* *Let's Make a Deal!* Hey Frank, you wanna make a deal? I got an insane judge who likes to beat the shit out of women! Whaddya wanna gimme, Frank, three weeks' probation?

—*. . . And Justice for All* (1979)

n *Napoleon Dynamite* we are presented with some of the most deviant of film characters. While neither Napoleon nor his companions commit a crime, they are nonetheless
deviant. Like most of us do, some or most of the time, the characters in the film break
from social norms. Unlike crime, which is the violation of a norm or a law that results in
a legal sanction, deviance, in the sociological/criminological sense, refers to the violation
of a norm resulting in negative reactions from others. Stealing might land you in jail, while
presenting your high school current event on the protective spells cast over Loch Ness for
the protection of Nessie (in all seriousness) just might land you as a social outcast from
school peers.

Ballantine and Roberts (2011:169–70) debunk four misconceptions about deviance
and crime—misconceptions that stem from the kind of commonsensical thinking that
sociology/criminology often dispels through empirical research. First, "some acts are
inherently deviant." Sociologically, deviance is socially constructed. An act has no inherent
meaning until a society gives it meaning. The labeling of acts as deviant varies across cultures, time, places, and social groups; and since labels carry tremendous social power, even
those who engage in criminal activity might bristle at the label, as Fenster makes clear
above. Second, "those who deviate are socially identified and recognized." In terms of
criminal deviance, approximately one third of crime reported to the police results in an
arrest. This means the majority are never labeled as deviant (at least via the criminal justice
system). Third, "deviants purposely and knowingly break the law." Actually, not all acts of
deviance are motivated by rational, calculated choice; many are driven by emotions or
incongruous understandings of what is actually deviant. Last, "deviance occurs because
there is a dishonest, selfish element to human nature." Actually, research has been unable
to establish a relationship between deviance and personality characteristics.

In the first reading, Robert Wonser and David Boyns explicate the sociology of deviance,
particularly the main sociological/criminological theoretical perspectives, through analysis
of the Batman films. Though these movies are in the genre of fantasy, a sociological reading
of Gotham City, Batman, and the various villains allows us to consider the social construction of deviance. The typically dichotomous cinematic images of "good guy/bad guy" are
actually blurred in these films. The "good guy," Batman, is a social outcast, as are most of
his enemies. Thus, we are offered multidimensional deviants: the "bad" demonstrating
weaknesses that may not justify their actions, but certainly help to explain them, while the
"good" are often viewed by Gotham City residents as equally "psychotic."

Beyond social constructionism, the authors utilize a variety of theoretical perspectives
in their analysis of the Batman films. Durkheim argued that deviance is an expected component of society and functions to remind us of social boundaries (members of society
learn and relearn these boundaries as they bump against them). Drawing from Durkheim,
other functionalist perspectives that seek to explain deviance and crime include anomie
theory, social disorganization theory, and differential opportunity structures—all of which
are highlighted by Wonser and Boyns. Other theoretical perspectives are illustrated using
the Batman films, from macro level analyses (conflict theory) to micro level analyses (differential association).

In the second reading, Nicole Rafter explores the extent to which crime films contribute
to our understanding of crime and seeks to specify "crime films' relationship to academic

criminology." While academic analyses of law films continue to flourish, Rafter argues that we lack a similarly robust literature concerning crime movies. Using a selection of five sex crime movies, Rafter seeks to "illustrate the relationship of film to criminology." Recognizing the criminological relevance of movies, Rafter argues that "popular criminology" and criminology are not at present connected in the theoretical manner in which she proposes. In this reading she suggests that we "conceive of crime films as an aspect of popular criminology, and of popular criminology as an aspect of criminology itself."

Valerie Callanan also utilizes a constructionist approach in her analysis of the sociology of law. According to Callanan, research has spotlighted three stances toward law: (1) before the law, (2) with the law, and (3) up against the law. Moreover, we can hold these views simultaneously and contradictorily. Callanan notes that many popular films present a reverence of the law, whether "before" or "with" the law. Al Pacino as Arthur Kirkland, in his iconic courtroom scene in . . . *And Justice for All*, exemplifies the many other films that point out the flaws in a system that places people "up against the law."

While the protagonists in each of the films Callanan considers risk and lose much in their pursuit of justice, the sacredness of the law prevails. Erin Brockovich temporarily sacrifices a relationship and strains those with her children. Jan in *A Civil Action* is a lawyer but, like Brockovich, out of his league as he fights for the victims of corporate pollution. In these films the fight and victory of the individual hero mask the myriad underlying structural constraints. It's good movie fun to see the underdog win. But, as Callanan points out, these narratives of justice and the sacredness of law also avoid real-life struggles such as those between the real "haves" and "have-nots."

Reference

Ballantine, J. H. and K. A. Roberts. 2011. *Our Social World: Introduction to Sociology*. 3rd ed. Thousand Oaks, CA: Sage/Pine Forge.

What Batman Films Tell Us about Crime and Deviance

Robert Wonser and David Boyns

C inema can reveal a lot about the sociology of deviance. From their explorations of subcultures, criminal syndicates, institutional corruption, underworld activity, and corporate malfeasance, films provide a unique opportunity to illuminate social worlds that often run against the grain of conventional society. Many films explore issues of deviance by creating realistic portrayals of social worlds that exist on the boundaries of social experience. In such films, we are invited into the backroom worlds of corporate crime as in *Wall Street,* witness the grit and grime of police corruption like that of *Training Day,* or enter the microcosmic universes of inner city street life like that found in *Boyz n the Hood.* While these films provide fictional accounts of deviance, they also invite viewers into sociological worlds that would not be surprising to encounter beyond the screen. Other films stretch the boundaries of the imagination in their exploration of deviance and ask viewers to engage in what Samuel Taylor Coleridge ([1817] 1965:169) called the "willing suspension of disbelief." These films take us into sociological universes that are beyond the realm of our conventional experience but, at the same time, provide a cinematic reality that illuminates sociological themes present in our own social world.

One of the more imaginative and spectacular windows into the sociology of deviance can be found in the Batman films that have now spanned over two decades—for example, *Batman* (Tim Burton, 1989), *Batman Returns* (Tim Burton, 1992), *Batman Forever* (Joel Schumacher, 1995), *Batman Begins* (Christopher Nolan, 2005), and *The Dark Knight* (Christopher Nolan, 2008). As a group, the Batman films provide a fertile context for a discussion of the sociology of deviance as it is examined in modern societies.

Through the Batman films, we inhabit the fantasy world of Gotham City, a bustling, urban environment similar to modern American cities. Gotham is rife with social problems and filled with the same deviant and criminal activity that commonly makes the news in our own cities. In Gotham, corporate crime is widespread, police corruption is rampant, and deviant subcultures rule the inner city streets. But Batman's world is unique in that it is filled with fantastic beings waging war between justice and order on the one side and crime and chaos on the other. While the Batman films ask us to suspend disbelief regarding Gotham's unusual superheroes and villains, they also give us a unique opportunity to examine the sociology of deviance in a potent and engaging way.

Using the Batman films as a window to explore deviance, this reading begins with a discussion of key concepts and perspectives related to the sociology of deviance. We then apply these concepts to the cinematic Batman and examine him as both a champion of order and justice and a deviant. We also investigate Batman's urban world, Gotham City, using the concepts of functionalist theory. Gotham City is a dysfunctional social environment and provides a case study of how social disorganization produces deviance. Gotham's conflict, crime, and deviance are primarily the products of the city's criminal masterminds,

Batman's foes. These villains help us to explore the ways in which deviance is, in many ways, in the "eye of the beholder" and subject to a process of social construction. In the final section, drawing on insights from sociological research and theory, we use the villains of Gotham City to illuminate the dynamics of deviance.

The Sociology of Deviance

The study of deviance is one of the most enduring concerns in the discipline of sociology. In sociological analysis, *deviance* is understood as behaviors that circumvent, flaunt, and even challenge the normative conventions of a given culture. As Emile Durkheim ([1895] 1982) suggested over a century ago, deviance can be thought of as an inherent aspect of society out of which we forge and shape our collective sentiments and identities. In Durkheim's analysis, deviance provides boundaries for social groups and helps outline the standards for both inclusive and exclusive membership. From this perspective, societies cannot function properly and coherently without group boundaries. According to Durkheim, a social order of balance and justice is important, but the deviance that challenges this order is vital and normal.

For Durkheim, deviance is a normal component of any society, as opposed to a patho-logical expression of those actions that stand outside the boundaries of social control. From this perspective, deviance has a twofold relationship to the normative social order: it is both common and even expected sociologically, and it represents a transgression of cultural stan-dards that constitute the norm. Sociologists understand *norms* as conventionalized modes of behavior, thought, and belief that outline the activities of a social group. Norms are the cultural rules, laws, and codes of etiquette that members of a group are expected to follow. For Durkheim ([1912] 1995), norms can be prescriptive, outlining forms of expected and preferred thought and action (i.e., what one *should* do), or they can be proscriptive, empha-sizing those behaviors and beliefs that are unacceptable, taboo, and forbidden (i.e., what one *should not* do). In Durkheim's ([1893] 1997) view, one of the most important challenges for a social group is how it handles deviance. Durkheim argues that groups typically vary in the degree to which they either repress deviance outright (usually through severe punishment or group expulsion) or work toward the restitution of order that is unsettled by deviance. It is important to note that, in Durkheim's analysis, cultural standards of normative thought and action are relative to sociological context and even to situational circumstance. Thus, what is considered to be normal behavior in one culture or setting may be regarded as devi-ant in another. As sociologists often note, and as will be examined below, norms and devi-ance both are *social constructions* (Berger and Luckmann 1966; Best 1995).

Batman: Winged Crusader or Criminal Menace?

Batman is an unusual and enigmatic character who amplifies issues related to sociological marginalization. From his unique appearance to his technological enhancements, Batman straddles the sociological worlds of normalcy and deviance. As a crime fighter, he is a vigi-lante superhero who is a guardian of good, championing the causes of justice over corrup-tion, order over chaos, stability over deviance. Following the script of most superheroes, Batman distinguishes himself as a defender of the good with his highly stylized mode of dress, mysterious and double life, and supernormal crime fighting abilities. Batman works closely with law enforcement in combating deviance, crime, and corruption. However, although Batman appears to be on the side of justice and order, it is not always clear on which side of the law he stands. Batman's dubiousness makes him unique as a superhero in that his activities are motivated by a prominent inner struggle that causes him, as well as others, to question the moral orientation of his motivations and loyalties. It is largely due to this tension that Batman has earned the title "The Dark Knight."

Batman's real-world identity is that of multimillionaire Bruce Wayne, the eccentric owner of the high-tech and multifaceted company Wayne Enterprises. After seeing his parents murdered at a young age, Bruce inherits the family fortune and vows vengeance against all who threaten the people of Gotham City. Bruce's wealth is apparent throughout the Batman films, as exemplified by his upper class lifestyle and ability to invent and commission complex crime fighting technologies. He is a person with extraordinary advantages, circumstances that are certainly instrumental for his double life as Batman. This privileged background stands in sharp contrast to that of many of Batman's enemies, the inheritors of significant social and economic disadvantage that are a product of what have been described as the limited opportunities of social strain (Agnew 1992; Cloward and Ohlin 1960; Merton 1968). Although Bruce Wayne is generally viewed as a philanthropic playboy, this persona primarily serves to distract the general public from his alter ego as the superhero Batman.

One of the most sociologically interesting aspects of the Batman films is that Batman is portrayed as a deviant who challenges deviance. The mystery surrounding Batman's image and abilities is frequently conflated with the rumors of his activities. For example, in *Batman*, Batman's escapades are exaggerated by news reporters and by street criminals who find uncertainty in the midst of legends of a new, mystifying, crime-fighting "winged vigilante." While Wayne's choice of bat-inspired attire has personal connotations and works to frighten criminals, his unnatural abilities and secret identity also make him a suspect in a number of Gotham's crimes.

At the beginning of *The Dark Knight*, the television news in the police station runs the caption "Batman: Crusader or Menace?" Because the crime-fighting, vigilante Batman is "more than just a man," it is unsurprising that he is identified as deviant. In a scene in *Batman Begins*, Bruce Wayne's new mentor Henri Ducard (Liam Neeson) tells him, "If you make yourself more than just a man, if you devote yourself to an ideal, then you become something else entirely." Bruce (Christian Bale) takes this literally and becomes a norm-violating "bat" that takes the law into his own hands and exacts justice as he sees fit without the legal authority to do so. David Matza (1964) argues that through *techniques of neutralization*, rationalizations that excuse questionable behavior, deviants are able to move back and forth along conformist paths most of the time and deviant paths other times. We see that through his alter ego Batman, Bruce Wayne, like many deviants, is allowed to "drift" between deviance and conformity to society's expectations.

Gotham City: Functional Harmony in Crisis

Batman's home, Gotham City, is as central to the storyline as Batman and his foes. In Batman lore, the city itself is modeled after downtown Manhattan in New York City and, in fact, Gotham was a nineteenth-century nickname for New York City (Burrows and

Wallace 1999). With its skyscraper-peaked skyline, high-rise townhouses, and generous urban density, Gotham City is a bustling metropolis that reflects the social organization of many prominent American urban centers. Throughout the films, Gotham's history is described as one of harmony and civility, where law and order prevail. However, recent economic trouble and social conflict in Gotham have caused considerable urban decay, political corruption, and social disorganization. Such processes have produced what sociologists describe as *social strain* (Merton 1968), which has led to widespread criminal activity and the emergence of a rogue underworld inhabited by Batman's foes. As described below, the story of Gotham City illustrates a set of sociological trends paralleling dynamics that have been the focus of sociological studies of crime and deviance for over a century.

The sociological ethos of Gotham City is seemingly founded on the *functionalist perspective* of society, based on the metaphor of human communities structured as organic beings (see Durkheim [1893] 1997). For functionalists, social order and balance are the goals of society and the degree to which a society functions can be illustrated by the harmonious interdependence of its major social institutions—such as law, government, and the economy. In his defense of society, Batman is a paragon of social order, weeding out deviance and crime in the service of order and justice. True to the functionalist perspective, Batman seeks to restore equilibrium to the social dysfunctions of unbridled crime. In *Batman Begins*, Bruce Wayne's love interest Rachel Dawes (Katie Holmes) echoes this perspective when she argues with Bruce that personal revenge is motivated by selfish and individualistic interest, whereas a socially organized and impartial legal system helps to create a society where "justice is harmony."

This functionalist focus on harmony is a common theme throughout many of the Batman films. For example, in *Batman Begins* we learn the story of Gotham City's origins. Once a prominent and thriving metropolis, Gotham has slowly fallen into massive urban decay and corruption. Such events have brought Gotham to the attention of the League of Shadows, a group focused on restoring order and balance to a world increasingly rife with conflict and disharmony. The League is willing to use extreme, even violent, measures to destroy the forces of disharmony in order to restore social equilibrium. As Gotham is one of the world's greatest cities, its sprawling crime and political corruption have pushed it into massive disharmony, and the League believes that destroying the city will help to move the world back into proper, harmonious focus. In the past, the League has attempted to exacerbate Gotham's disequilibrium by intentionally spinning it into economic turmoil, dire poverty, and social disorganization. The result is what we see in the Batman films, a shadowy and menacing urban environment where the fearful citizens of Gotham stay indoors after nightfall, dark and uninviting alleyways abound, and criminals roam and rule the streets.

Philanthropists in Gotham, like Bruce Wayne and his parents, have unsuccessfully interfered in the League's schemes by providing economic subsidies to rectify the city's poverty. Motivated by a unique and even distorted vision of harmony, the League seeks to further accelerate the demise of the slowly decaying Gotham. In *Batman Begins*, on the brink of the League's next attack on the city, Henri Ducard (as the villain Ra's al Ghul), Bruce Wayne's mentor from the League of Shadows, outlines the League's new plans for the destruction of Gotham:

Ra's al Ghul: Tomorrow the world will watch in horror as its greatest city destroys itself. The movement back to harmony will be unstoppable this time.

Bruce Wayne: You attacked Gotham before?

Ra's al Ghul: Of course. Over the ages, our weapons have grown more sophisticated. With Gotham, we tried a new one: economics. But we underestimated certain of Gotham's citizens . . . such as your parents. Gunned down by one of the very people they were trying to help. Create enough hunger and everyone becomes a criminal. Their deaths galvanized the city into saving itself . . . and Gotham has limped on ever since. We are back to finish the job. And this time no misguided idealists will get in the way. Like your father, you lack the courage to do all that is necessary. If someone stands in the way of true justice . . . you simply walk up behind them and stab them in the heart.

As the theory of functionalism asserts, the ideal society is like an organic entity, composed of institutions in a state of interdependent homeostasis. However, functionalists argue that societies frequently experience *anomie*, dysfunctional tendencies that pose threats to a community's balance and social order. In the Batman films, the League of Shadows along with Batman's other villains is a metaphoric embodiment of these anomic threats.

Drawing from Durkheim, sociologists have examined the ways that anomie (i.e., a breakdown of social norms) can produce deviance in human communities. *Social disorganization theory* was one of the first theories developed by criminologists to explain crime in urban areas (Shaw and McKay 1972). This theory posits that when a region's social fabric breaks down, its social institutions become weakened and the involvement of its community members is attenuated. Such communities suffer from a lack of traditional social control stemming from established institutions like the family, church, and school. These areas become transitional neighborhoods where unsettled and socioeconomically marginalized populations converge, creating regions where unemployment is high for populations vulnerable to anomie and residents are fearful. When social disorganization manifests itself, communities deteriorate and residents become frightened to leave their homes. This trepidation advances the cycle of crime as the "eyes on the street" (Jacobs 1961:44), so central to the informal social control present in urban areas, disappear and residents become reluctant to involve themselves in their communities for fear of victimization.

In Gotham City, social disorganization is widespread, and as sociologists have suggested, one of the outcomes of social disorganization is social strain. Robert Merton (1968) theorized that the social strain of anomie can create deviance when paths toward legitimate opportunities are blocked. When confronted with a lack of opportunity, some individuals will be forced to seek innovative and alternative means (e.g., crime) toward the pursuit of traditional goals (e.g., money). Others may be compelled to reject conventional pursuits altogether and become social outlaws, enemies of normal and predicable standards of conformity.

Robert Agnew (1992) extended these ideas, arguing that the social strain of blocked opportunities has important sociopsychological consequences, creating negative emotional experiences that result in antisocial orientations and behaviors. Looking at the consequences of social strain, sociologists have found that different socioeconomic contexts create "*differential opportunity structures*" (Cloward and Ohlin 1960). When legitimate opportunities are blocked among the members of a community, the shared disenfranchisement of these individuals will converge and they will look to create new opportunity structures. Such opportunity structures frequently materialize as deviant or criminal communities, such as street gangs, urban subcultures, and organized crime. These types of communities are exemplified in the Batman films through the various crime syndicates that emerge. While Batman's foes have prominent identities of their own, they rarely exist in isolation and find themselves either working in tandem with other villains (as the Penguin and Max Shreck do in *Batman Returns*) or operating with an alliance of street criminals (as the Joker does in *The Dark Knight*). As a result of the anomie that increasingly saturates Gotham City, many of the villains in the Batman films are drawn to an existence on the margins of society, pushed into a deviant way of life, and find membership and even security in the subcultures of Gotham's underworld.

In addition to exploring the causes of Gotham's general decline, the Batman films illustrate something else central to the functionalist perspective of deviance: while deviance may be dysfunctional for the moral order of Gotham City, it is also seemingly intrinsic and fundamental to the Gotham community. Echoing Durkheim's pronouncement of the normalcy of deviance, the Batman films depict a social environment where a certain amount of crime is anticipated and even expected. Batman's world is one of a functional interdependence of parts, where law enforcement and criminal activity are mutually interrelated, each serving as a system of checks and balances for the other. In *The Dark Knight,* the Joker (Heath Ledger) best expresses the interdependence of order and deviance when asked by Batman why he is set on exterminating the Caped Crusader. The Joker responds, "I don't want to kill you! What would I do without you? Go back to ripping off mob dealers? No, no, *no!* No. You . . . you . . . complete me." Such a response echoes a branch of functionalist theory that argues that dysfunctional aspects of society, such as deviance and conflict, can have important, subsidiary functions (Coser 1956; Merton 1968). Indeed, Batman would not be necessary were it not for the existence of deviance in Gotham.

The Joker's observations about the interdependence of law enforcement and criminal activity are sociologically astute and reflect the idea that some deviance is sociologically normal. Only when social dysfunctions become too severe do they threaten the workings of society. Again in *The Dark Knight*, the Joker elucidates this theme in a discussion with Gotham's former district attorney, Harvey Dent, now the crime boss Two-Face (Aaron Eckhart). The Joker says:

> You know what I've noticed? Nobody panics when things go "according to plan." Even if the plan is horrifying! If, tomorrow, I tell the press that . . . a gangbanger will get shot, or a truckload of soldiers will be blown up, nobody panics, because it's all "part of the plan." . . . Introduce a little anarchy. Upset the established order, and everything becomes chaos. I'm an agent of chaos.

The Joker's danger to Gotham is that his criminal activities are anarchic, so contrary to conventional norms that they stand outside the functional interdependence of deviance and order. The Joker's modus operandi is beyond that of what is expected from simple "cops and robbers." Instead, he challenges the basic rules of morality by compelling the ordinary citizens of Gotham to question their own moral beliefs, and ultimately exposes Gotham's codes of both deviance and order as social constructions.

Who's Afraid of the Big, Black Bat? Batman and the Social Construction of Deviance

While the functionalist and strain approaches to deviance resonate throughout the Batman films, there are other cinematic devices that challenge these perspectives and explore different approaches to the sociology of deviance. In watching any one of the Batman films, the "good guys" and the "bad guys" become apparent. The "good" are represented as the everyday citizens of Gotham, helpless victims of Batman's villains. Law enforcement and political officials work to serve the citizens in the name of the "good." On the side of the "bad" are Batman's villains, the street criminals they organize, and the politicians, business leaders, and police who have fallen into corruption and made alliances with the denizens of the underworld. Such bimodal definitions are typical cinematic plot devices that help us catalog the characters in a storyline into understandable divisions. But in the Batman films, these divisions are somewhat artificial, and at times depend on the perspective to which one is sympathetic. Many of Batman's enemies are social outcasts, defenselessly and unjustly rejected from the world of the good with little compassion or concern. In *Batman Returns*, the young Penguin (Danny DeVito) is discarded by his parents because of a childhood deformity. In *The Dark Knight*, we hear the Joker describe his physical abuse as a child. Thus, the Batman films play with, and often twist, definitions of cultural norms, and in doing so help to illustrate the socially constructed nature of deviance.

The *social construction of deviance* suggests that definitions of both normal and deviant behavior are contingent on social and cultural context (Berger and Luckmann 1966; Best 1995). What is considered deviant in one context may be seen as normal in a different setting. However, the fact that cultural norms are socially constructed does not mean they do not have a real impact on people and their social experience. Norms may be socially defined, but when they are reified, they are treated as if they have a concrete reality. Batman himself is an example of the socially constructed nature of deviance. As we have discussed, Batman walks a thin line between the good and the bad, often using tactics outside the law to defend the good. Because of this, Batman is frequently considered by the inhabitants of Gotham to be of questionable, or at least ambiguous, moral standing. As the Riddler (Jim Carrey) questions in *Batman Forever*, "Riddle me this, riddle me that; who's afraid of the big, black bat?" Of course, the Riddler uses this puzzle mockingly, but the question is an important one in understanding Batman. The sociological answer to the Riddler's puzzle is that because deviance is a social construction, everyone in some way fears Batman.

The uncertainty regarding Batman helps to illustrate the socially constructed and often arbitrary definitions of deviance that abound in Gotham. For example, in *Batman*, reporter

Vicki Vale (Kim Basinger) compares Batman's (Michael Keaton) behavior to that of the Joker, and she questions Batman's loyalty to the citizens of Gotham:

Vicki Vale: A lot of people think you're as dangerous as the Joker.

Batman: He's psychotic.

Vicki Vale: Some people say the same thing about you.

Batman: What people?

Vicki Vale: Well, I mean, let's face it. You're not exactly normal, are you?

Batman: It's not exactly a normal world, is it?

Photo 7.1   Batman (Christian Bale) and Joker (Heath Ledger). Both are deviant social outcasts in *The Dark Knight*.

Batman's responses to Vicki Vale are telling. When she reveals to Batman that people speculate that he is psychotic, he shrugs off the notion of himself as pathological. However, Batman's world is clearly inhabited by deviants and villains of broad eccentricities; and Batman seems to fit right in. His perception that corrupt Gotham is not a "normal world" is expected, given the peculiarities of the characters who live there, but it also stands as justification for his own activities as a crime fighter who operates outside the law.

Perhaps the most revealing illustration of the social construction of deviance occurs in *The Dark Knight*. In one of the pivotal moments in the film, the Joker has designed a "social experiment" to test the ethical standards and moral fortitude of the citizens of Gotham. He arranges for two ferries to be set afloat in the Gotham harbor: one filled with everyday citizens of Gotham and the other containing inmates from Gotham's prison. While each boat carries explosives, each also carries a remote detonator that will allow passengers to destroy the other boat. The Joker describes the "experiment" for the passengers over the ferries' public address systems:

Tonight you're all gonna be part of a social experiment. Through the magic of diesel fuel and ammonium nitrate, I'm ready right now to blow you all sky high. Anyone attempts to get off their boat, you all die. Each of you has a remote . . . to blow up the other boat. At midnight, I blow you all up. If, however, one of you presses the button, I'll let that boat live. So, who's it going to be: Harvey Dent's most wanted scumbag collection, or the sweet and innocent civilians? You choose . . . oh, and you might want to decide quickly, because the people on the other boat might not be so noble.

The Joker's experiment is designed to see which set of passengers will be the first to compromise their own ethical standards and destroy the people carried by the other ferry. Because the Joker is essentially amoral, his experiment is not designed to create a certain outcome but, instead, to expose what he perceives as the arbitrary nature of morality. As the Joker states, "The only sensible way to live in this world is without rules." The cinematic result is a film moment in which both the film's characters and the viewing audience are asked to question their own sense of morality and contemplate the socially constructed nature of cultural norms. In considering what to do, will the passengers be bound by the standards of the law? Which group of passengers will be first to detonate the other ferry? Which group of passengers is more deserving of life? Is it proper to take a life to save one's own? Which individual life is more important than another? Such questions are poignantly evoked by this scene, highlighting the socially constructed nature of deviance and examining how the arbitrariness of deviance can be exposed in situations of incredible uncertainty.

Who's Rules Are They, Anyway?
Conflict Theory of Deviance

In the Batman films, scenes like the Joker's "experiment" illustrate another important perspective within the sociology of deviance. This perspective asks us to consider whose interests are actually served by the cultural standards of normalcy and deviance. Are cultural norms neutral? Who creates the laws and other social norms? And who benefits from them? Such questions are addressed by the *conflict perspective* (Chambliss 1976; Quinney 1970), which contends that deviance and crime are socially organized to benefit the dominant and powerful interests of a society, often at the expense of the marginalized and disenfranchised. Conflict theories contend that, instead of deviance being a normal component of a social community, as argued by functionalists, definitions of deviance are inherently ideological.

From the conflict perspective, some individuals are able to escape legal scrutiny because of their positions of privilege and power. Batman himself is one such individual. Privilege and power provide others with the ability to determine the contours of the law; in fact, some are representatives of the law. These individuals flourish in Gotham's criminal underworld. Take, for example, the many instances of institutional corruption in the Batman films. Gotham business mogul Max Shreck (Christopher Walken), one of Batman's enemies from *Batman Returns*, is a powerful corporate criminal who intends to build a power plant that will steal electricity from Gotham's electrical grid, thus giving him a monopoly over Gotham's electric power. Millionaire scientist Edward Nigma (Jim Carrey) is a disgruntled employee of Wayne Enterprises who, in *Batman Forever*, adopts the persona of the Riddler after his inventions are rejected, and he seeks revenge by using his technologies of mind control to steal the brainpower of the citizens of Gotham. In *The Dark Knight*, it is only through corruption in Gotham's police force that the Joker is able to install his hired thugs as police officers and attempt to assassinate Gotham's district attorney, Harvey Dent. In the Batman films, deviance is not simply a product of "normal" social dysfunctions; following the conflict approaches to deviance, it resides among Gotham's elites, who use their social privileges to intentionally create chaos within the city. Many of these elites are corporate criminals who, until they meet Batman, are able to avoid scrutiny by the law and continue their deeds with impunity.

As stated previously, even Bruce Wayne (as Batman) is allowed to skirt the law as he and others see fit. Not only does Batman never get arrested (despite police opportunities to do so), but he is even called upon by Harvey Dent and Lieutenant Gordon (Gary Oldman) to apprehend the crooked mob accountant Lau from Hong Kong. In *The Dark Knight,* we witness a rooftop conversation that illustrates the way powerful men in Gotham's police force plan to use their position of privilege to evade the confines of the law:

Harvey Dent [turning to Batman]:	We need Lau back, but the Chinese won't extradite a national under any circumstances.
Batman:	If I get him to you, can you get him to talk?
Harvey Dent:	I'll get him to *sing.*
Lt. James Gordon:	We're going after the mob's life savings. Things *will* get ugly.
Harvey Dent:	I knew the risks when I took this job, Lieutenant. Same as you. [Turns back to Batman.] How will you get him back, anyway? [Turns to where Batman is, or rather, where he should be, as he's already vanished.]
Lt. James Gordon:	He does that.

Neither Dent nor Gordon knows how Batman will finagle this operation, but they both know that he won't necessarily use legal means. We are also left with the impression that Dent might use unscrupulous methods for getting Lau to "sing." In this instance and others, we see those with power and privilege, even Batman, use their advantages to skirt the law.

Batman's Villains: Whatever Doesn't Kill You Simply Makes You Stranger

The social order of Gotham City is frequently challenged by villains who endeavor to undermine the normative order of Batman's world. In their own way, each of these villains illustrates the dynamics of the sociology of deviance. But as a group, these villains highlight a long-standing principle within the sociology of deviance: we become like those with whom we associate. This notion is the fundamental premise of the *theory of differential association* (Sutherland 1939), which argues that individuals learn and practice deviance through interaction with others. Most of Batman's foes inhabit what sociologists call *deviance subcultures* (Cohen 1972) that provide important training grounds for deviant lifestyles and criminal activity.

Batman's foes in these films (e.g., Max Shreck, the Penguin, the Joker, Two-Face) commonly question Batman's sense of justice and attempt to expose a putative hypocrisy behind his morality. These villains continually call into question the legitimacy of Gotham's law—either by exposing police corruption (as in *Batman*) or by challenging the morality of Gotham's citizens by pitting them against one another (as in *The Dark Knight*). Each of the main villains in the Batman films exhibits his own style of deviance, often in trademark, comic-book fashion. Much like representatives of the conflict approach, these villains compel Batman to question exactly whose interests he is defending, and frequently suggest that the interests being upheld by society's legal institutions are really the interests of elites. In the following discussion we examine some of these villains and highlight the sociological principles of deviance that their exploits reveal.

Max Shreck: Elites and Corporate Crime

In *Batman Returns*, the deviance of Max Shreck (Christopher Walken) can be understood through the conflict perspective, as he is what sociologists describe as a *white collar criminal* (Sutherland 1949) who uses his position among Gotham's elites for personal profit. More specifically, he is an example of one who adopts a *rational choice approach* to crime (Gibbs 1975), using the logic of a cost/benefit analysis to guide his criminal activities. Under the guise of a well-respected businessman in Gotham, Shreck plans to siphon electricity from the city for personal gain. Shreck reveals his application of rational calculations in committing his crimes in a conversation with the Penguin. When the Penguin proposes that the two create a criminal alliance, Shreck initially balks at the opportunity: why share profits with a partner when there is more to be gained as a solo criminal? However, when the Penguin exposes Shreck's misdeeds—spewing toxic waste into Gotham's sewers, shredding revealing documents, and even murdering his former partner—Shreck agrees to an alliance. For Shreck, there is more to gain from sharing profits with a partner than by not sharing and having his deviant exploits exposed to the public. Shreck is a threat in the corporate suites and on the streets, using both white collar and street criminal methods.

The Penguin: Deviant Labeling and Stigma

In the case of the Penguin (Danny DeVito), Shreck's criminal partner in *Batman Returns*, we see the effects of what sociologists of deviance would describe as a lifelong "labeling process" (Becker 1963; Matsueda 1992). Deformed from birth, the young Penguin (named Oswald Cobblepot) suffered from what Erving Goffman (1963) describes as a *physical stigma* that set him apart from other children. Penguin is abandoned by his parents in childhood, and his pariah status is a primary motivation for his life of crime. He reflects on this situation to Max Shreck:

> I wasn't born in the sewer, you know. I come from . . . [Looks to the drainage pipes above.] Like you. And like you, I want some respect. A recognition of my basic humanity. But most of all . . . I wanna find out who I really am. By finding my parents, learning my human name. Simple stuff that the good people of Gotham take for granted!

Because people responded in horror to his visage, the Penguin was forced to live underground and develop a deviant existence. His ascribed label as a "deviant" creates a *self-fulfilling prophesy* for him as, motivated by this label, he finds little alternative but to turn to a life of crime. We see the Penguin's deviance manifested when he is in adult, just as expected by his parents. In *Batman Returns*, the Penguin's observation regarding the similarities between himself and Max Shreck is telling: "Odd as it may seem, Max, you and I have something in common: we're both perceived as monsters. But somehow, you're a well-respected monster, and *I am, to* date, not." Penguin's quote is astute because it high-lights the power of a deviant label in creating both a person's self-identity and his or her motivations for action; it also provides an important contrast with Shreck, who secures more respect because of his powerful position in society.

The Joker: Deviance as Social Learning

Much like the Penguin, the Joker is also a victim of a terrible physical stigma in the form of facial scars in the shape of a crooked smile that he hides with clown makeup. While the Joker (Heath Ledger) provides conflicting accounts of how he got the scars, one retelling in *The Dark Knight* reveals his horrific upbringing fraught with child abuse and domestic violence:

> Wanna know how I got these scars? My father was . . . a drinker. And a fiend. And one night he goes off crazier than usual. Mommy gets the kitchen knife to defend herself. He doesn't like that. Not one bit. So—me watching—he takes the knife to her, laugh-ing while he does it! Turns to me, and he says, "Why so serious, son?" Comes at me with the knife . . ."Why so serious?" He sticks the blade in my mouth . . . "Let's put a smile on that face!" And . . .

We see that the Joker's amorality and predilection toward crime are rooted in his early childhood experiences of abuse and the subsequent stigma of being, literally, scarred by that experience. The film's explanation for the Joker's deviant appearance and subsequent behav-ior illustrate the basics of *social learning theory* (Akers et al. 1979; Bandura 1977), which argues that socialization occurs through role modeling and the social reinforcement of behavior. If one has deviant or violent role models, as the young Joker did, one is more likely to have high exposure to deviance, have such behavior reinforced, and learn to reproduce it.

Because the Joker appears to have experienced long-term socialization from deviant role models, it is not surprising that in *The Dark Knight* he is shown associating with the deni-zens of Gotham's underworld. But the Joker's deviance is more extreme than that of Batman's other villains, as he appears to be motivated not by personal gain but by a desire to push the boundaries of morality—even to the point of self-destruction. The Joker is a moral terrorist who through his life experiences has been socialized into deviance. As a result, he prides himself on deriding society's norms and causing disruption to Gotham's normative order, as illustrated in this exchange with a bank manager:

Manager of   Oh, criminals in this town used to believe in things. Honor. Respect.
Gotham   Look at you! What do you believe in, huh? What do you believe in?
National Bank:

[The Joker sticks a grenade in the manager's mouth.]

The Joker: I believe whatever doesn't kill you simply makes you . . . stranger.

Here we see the Joker's flagrant disregard for the norms of society as well as the normative order of the criminal underworld.

Two-Face: Deviance within Systems of Social Control

Harvey Dent's decline into villainy provides an interesting counterpoint to the other villains and to Batman himself. As the district attorney of Gotham City, Dent is celebrated as the paragon of justice by the city's inhabitants. However, after an accident that scars the left half of his face, Dent becomes cynical of the justice system and transforms into Two-Face, fighting crime outside the law and orchestrating his actions by the chance flip of his two-headed coin. We learn in *The Dark Knight* that Dent (Aaron Eckhart) was once hailed as "The White Knight" because he convicted scores of the city's organized criminals. Like Bruce Wayne, Dent adopts an alter ego after experiencing a life-changing accident (Bruce witnesses the murder of his parents, while Dent experiences the murder of his fiancée, Rachel Dawes). By comparing Dent to Wayne, we see opposite sides of the same coin: Batman is a fallen man thrust into heroism; Dent is a fallen hero transformed into a corrupt man. In *The Dark Knight*, Dent as Two-Face expresses his doubts to Batman about the efficacy of Gotham's legal system: "You thought we could be decent men in an indecent time. But you were wrong. The world is cruel, and the only morality in a cruel world is chance... [As he holds up his coin]... Unbiased. Unprejudiced. Fair." Two-Face discounts the institutional procedures of the criminal justice system, because they are subject to human error and corruption, in favor of a moral system that seems to stand outside the distortions of human intervention: chance.

Dent's transformation is motivated by his disgust with the corruption he encountered within Gotham's legal system. In fact, it was police corruption that prompted his rise to the position of district attorney, and later facilitated his attempted assassination by the Joker, the death of his fiancée, and inevitably his disfiguring accident. Dent's story is representative of research into the sociology of deviance that examines corruption within systems of social control. For example, while police corruption does not appear to be a normative practice, it is a growing concern within metropolitan areas (Punch 2009). Like concerns about police corruption, deviance within systems of social control has been an enduring paradox of social theory that examines how to best preserve and maintain the integrity of collective morality. Such a concern is perhaps best expressed by the classic question, "Who will guard the guardians?" (Juvenal 1982) and illustrates one of the most complex issues related to the sociology of deviance: how can we ensure that the guardians of the normative order are not deviant themselves? Two-Face's story represents the potency of this question as an enduring concern. His resolution to this problem is fatalistic: as ultimate arbiters of morality, people cannot be trusted, and the only fair method of justice is chance. As the following conversation from *The Dark Knight* reveals, Two-Face's pessimism about the efficacy of systems of social control runs deep:

Batman: What happened to Rachel wasn't chance. We decided to act! We three!

Two-Face: Then why was it me who was the only one who lost everything?

Batman: It wasn't.

Two-Face: The Joker chose *me!*

Batman: Because you were the best of us! He wanted to prove that even someone as good as you could fall.

Two-Face: And he was right.

Like the story of Two-Face, the accounts of Batman's villains illustrate that the sociology of deviance is complex and multifaceted. And while many of us exhibit behaviors that in some way might be considered deviant, like those of Batman and his villains, there is a rich interplay of sociological forces that ultimately serve to shape our actions and even determine the side of the law on which we stand.

Conclusion

The key dynamics outlined by the early sociologists of deviance still resonate in today's social world and in fictional worlds like that of Gotham City. Dense urban ecology, large population density, and anomie all create criminological conditions where crime and deviance become predictable. The villains of Gotham emerge from these conditions and provide a *raison d'*être for Batman in his deviant evolution. In this way, the Batman films are modern day morality plays, examining the sociological forces that circumscribe crime. In the imaginary world of Gotham City, crime is a very real threat, and fictional depictions can help us understand the sociology of crime and deviance. Through the analyses in this chapter we can see the myriad ways in which crime and deviance are omnipresent forces operating in the fantastic world of Gotham despite the efforts of Batman to preserve the harmony of the city. As glimpses into our collective consciousness, the Batman films help to illuminate the story of ourselves, our social worlds, and specifically how we see deviance.

References

Agnew, R. 1992. "Foundation for a General Strain Theory." *Criminology* 30(1), 47–87.

Akers, R., M. D. Krohn, L. Lanza-Kaduce, and M. Radosevich. 1979. "Social Learning and Deviant Behavior: A Specific Test of a General Theory." *American Sociological Review* 44(4):636–55.

Bandura, A. 1977. *Social Learning Theory.* New York: General Learning Press.

Becker, H. 1963. *Outsiders.* New York: Free Press.

Berger, P. and T. Luckmann. 1966. *The Social Construction of Reality: A Treatise in the Sociology of Knowledge.* New York: Doubleday.

Best, J. 1995. *Images of Issues: Typifying Contemporary Social Problems.* New Brunswick, NJ: Transaction.

Burrows, E. G. and M. Wallace. 1999. *Gotham: A History of New York City to 1898.* Oxford, England: Oxford University Press.

Chambliss, W. 1976. *Who's Law? What Order?* New York: Wiley.

Cloward, R. and L. Ohlin. 1960. *Delinquency and Opportunity.* New York: Free Press.

Cohen, P. 1972. *Sub-cultural Conflict and Working Class Community.* Working Paper in Cultural Studies No. 2, University of Birmingham, Birmingham, England.

Coleridge, S. T. [1817] 1965. *Biographia literaria.* London: Oxford University Press.

Coser, L. 1956. *The Functions of Social Conflict.* New York: Simon & Schuster.

Durkheim, E. [1893] 1997. *Division of Labor in Society.* New York: Free Press.

Durkheim, E. [1895] 1982. *The Rules of Sociological Method.* New York: Free Press.

Durkheim, E. [1912] 1995. *The Elementary Forms of Religious Life.* New York: Free Press.

Gibbs, J. 1975. *Crime, Punishment and Deterrence.* New York: Elsevier.

Goffman, E. 1963. *Stigma: Notes on the Management of Spoiled Identity.* New York: Simon & Schuster.

Jacobs, J. 1961. *The Death and Life of Great American Cities.* New York: Random House.

Juvenal. 1982. *The Sixteen Satires*, translated by P. Green. London: Penguin Books.

Matsueda, R. 1992. "Reflected Appraisals, Parental Labeling, and Delinquency: Specifying a Symbolic Interactionist Theory." *American Journal of Sociology* 97(6): 1577–611.

Matza, D. 1964. *Delinquency and Drift.* New York: Wiley.

Merton, R. K. 1968. *Social Theory and Social Structure.* New York: Free Press.

Punch, M. 2009. *Police Corruption: Deviance, Accountability and Reform in Policing.* Cullompton, England: Willan.

Quinney, R. 1970. *The Social Reality of Crime.* Boston: Little, Brown.

Shaw, C. R. and H. D. McKay. 1972. *Juvenile Delinquency in Urban Areas.* Rev. ed. Chicago: University of Chicago Press.

Sutherland, E. H. 1939. *Principles of Criminology.* Chicago: University of Chicago Press.

Sutherland, E. H. 1949. *White Collar Crime.* New York: Dryden Press.

A new development is taking place within criminology: a growing awareness that film contributes to understandings of crime and, as a result, a steady accumulation of studies analyzing crime films. Some of these studies focus on specific films (O'Brien et al., 2005, on *Gangs of New York*), while others treat crime films more generally (Tzanelli et al., 2005; Rafter, 2006). Some look at a particular genre or subgenre of crime films (King, 1999, at cop action; Rafter, 2005, at psychopath movies); others examine crime films in the context of a broader criminological phenomenon, such as the U.S. prison crisis (Brown, 2003), the militia movement (Chermak, 2002) or the social construction of serial homicide (Jenkins, 1994). Still others emphasize constructions of gender (Sparks, 1996; Bailey et al., 1998; Cavender, 1999). Such analyses—and the list could go on for several pages—differ from works in the domain of film studies that use crime categories heuristically to isolate a subgroup such as gangster films (Munby, 1999) or prostitution films (Campbell, 2005) for cinematic analysis. Instead, the books and articles of interest here are concerned with the potential of films to make a substantive contribution to criminology through the perspectives they provide on cops, drug mules, heisters, prisoners, serial killers, victims and so on.

In this article I explore the criminological relevance of this growing literature on crime films; my aim is to validate and encourage such research by specifying crime films' relationship to academic criminology. I begin by comparing the crime-films literature with work conducted in the field of legal studies on "law films"—a literature that is far better developed, with a clearer sense of purpose and more momentum. I suggest reasons for the differences, asking what crime-film scholars can learn from the law-films movement. I go on to discuss a group of recent movies about sex crimes, using them to probe and illustrate the relationship of film to criminology. Arguing that crime films constitute a form of *popular criminology*, a discourse parallel to academic criminology and of equal social significance, I next suggest a model for understanding the process through which crime films shape our thinking about crime. I conclude that crime-film studies could acquire the strength and vigor of the law-films movement by focusing more sharply and consistently on the criminological significance of crime films.

Crime Films and Law Films

In its current, still-emerging form, the crime-films literature remains amorphous, lacking the coherence of the closely related literature on law films. Films about law became a topic within legal studies in the 1980s, starting with studies of courtroom films and lawyers (e.g. Chase, 1986; Post, 1987) but rapidly expanding to include, first, all movies that deal explicitly with civil or criminal law (e.g. Bergman and Asimow, 1996; Denvir, 1996), and, later, even films that deal inexplicitly or indirectly with law (Chase, 2002; Freeman, 2005). Thus the law-films category now includes (for example) *Dirty Harry* (1971), a movie that deals explicitly with the legal tension between due process goals on the one hand and crime control goals on the other, albeit in terms of a cop-action hero instead of a lawyer. It also includes movies that deal fundamentally, even if inexplicitly, with individuals' relationships to law or law-like processes—for instance the *Godfather*s (1972, 1974, 1990), *Do the Right Thing* (1989) and *Falling Down* (1993). Unlike crime-film studies, research on law films developed rapidly, generating a movement within legal studies to build a literature, institute law-film courses and, ultimately, come to terms with the implications of law films for definitions of "law" (Robson, 2005). Within legal studies, law films are now regarded as not only a valid source of information on popular attitudes toward law but also a form of legal discourse, a constituent of law itself (Greenfield et al., 2001; Chase, 2002). While a number of factors account for this success, two are especially important. First, although the definition of "law films" evolved over time, law-film scholars usually agreed on the general object of their inquiry, just as today, they usually agree on a definition of *law film* that includes any movie that deals centrally with legal issues (e.g. Greenfield et al., 2001). This ongoing consensus about the topic under analysis has helped unify the law-film movement and create a base on which scholars can build.

Second, the movement has been successful because, although its literature is diverse in topic and approach, at a very general level most of the studies ask the same basic question: How do law films relate to law and to the study of law (e.g. Freeman, 2005)? Moreover, the studies tend to respond with a common answer: law films are integral to law itself, comprising a popular discourse that must be understood if the nature of law is to be fully understood. This overall consensus on the kinds of questions to ask and ways to frame the answers has given law-film scholars a sense of common purpose—even of mission. It has also made their inquiries relevant to legal studies as a field. The fundamental question and its answers have legitimated the study of law films, easing the introduction of courses into law-school curricula. If crime-film scholars can likewise find common ground, their literature can mature along similar lines.

Law films and crime films overlap. The best way to define *crime films*, as I explain in more depth elsewhere (Rafter, 2006), is to define them as movies in which crime or its consequences are central. Their relationship to law films becomes clear if we think of film categories in terms of tiers of differently sized boxes. On the bottom tier, in CD-sized boxes, are specific films such as Clint Eastwood's first *Dirty Harry* and *The Verdict* (1982), the Paul Newman film about an alcoholic lawyer with a medical malpractice case. On the next level up, in somewhat larger boxes, are groups of related films: all movies in the *Dirty Harry* series, for example, or all films about lawyers who overcome personal challenges to triumph in court. On the next higher level, still larger boxes hold genres: civil-action law films, cop films, women lawyer films, death penalty films, psycho films and so on. On the top level, the largest boxes represent broad categories such as *crime films* and *law films*. This model gives us a way to think about classification but also enables us to conceptually shift movies from one box to another in order to study their interrelationships and, on occasion, to add a new box to one of the shelves. (Tiso [n.d.] has recently added a new box on surveillance films, and Varese [2006] one on Japanese yakuza movies.) Moreover, the model makes it clear that a specific film can occupy more than one place. For example, *Dirty Harry* might be placed in either the law-film or the crime-film category depending on one's analytic purpose.

And yet, although crime films themselves can be clearly defined and their relationship to law films specified, the literature on crime films remains sprawling and lacking in an overall sense of direction. It may derive a theoretical infrastructure and impetus from the new "cultural criminology" movement (Ferrell and Sanders, 1995; Ferrell, 1999; Ferrell and Websdale, 1999; Ferrell et al., 2004; Hayward and Young, 2004), but so far, with a few exceptions (Epstein, 1995; Cavender, 1999), that movement has yielded little in the way of film analysis. This article aims at giving crime-film research a stronger sense of purpose by asking: *How do crime films relate to criminology?* This question parallels the one that has given the law-film movement impetus: How do law films relate to law and to the study of law? Similarly, my answer parallels the one that has brought coherence to the study of law films: *movies constitute an aspect of criminology, a popular discourse that needs to be recognized and analyzed if criminology—the study of crime and criminals—itself is to be fully understood.* Note that I am not asking what crime films say about the causes of crime. This is an important question (and one that I address elsewhere [Rafter, 2006]), but not the main issue here. My central concern in this article is the relationship between crime movies and criminology.

Studying Crime Films: A Note on Methodology

To address this issue, I examine five[2] recent films about sex crimes: *L.I.E.* (Michael Cuesta, 2001), *In the Cut* (Jane Campion, 2003), *Monster* (Patty Jenkins, 2003), *Mystic River* (Clint Eastwood, 2003) and *The Woodsman* (Nicole Kassell, 2004). Let me say a few words about my selection principles, for anyone studying crime films almost immediately confronts a methodological problem: the wide range of available examples makes it easy to support almost any argument, if one selects unsystematically. This problem, so far as I know, has been considered neither by film-studies specialists nor by law-films scholars. It is one that criminologists, many of whom have a background in sociological methods, *can* address, thereby contributing to film studies more generally. Neal King's *Heroes in Hard Times* (1999) is one of the few crime-film studies to surmount the problem (also see Cavender, 1999). King copes with the selection issue by carefully defining the universe of films with which he will be dealing—U.S. cop-action movies—and then examining every example produced in a specified time period.

Following King's example, I limited my sample to all U.S.-made dramas focused on sex crime and released 2000–4. I chose the year 2000 as my start date to see what was happening in the new millennium and 2004 as my cutoff date because I started the research early in 2005. To identify films that fell within my parameters, I did a "power search" through the Internet Movie Database (www.imdb.com), using "sex crimes" as my search phrase and excluding comedies, made-for-TV movies, shorts and direct-to-video productions. The limitations meant that I had to exclude from the discussion several excellent recent examples such as *Happiness* (1998) and *La mala educación (Bad Education)* (2004). However, the systematic nature of my sample enabled me to speak definitively about how U.S. movies made in the period 2000–4 "framed" sex crimes (Gamson et al., 1992)—how they gave the offenses meanings.

The five films vary considerably among themselves, but all share a distaste for analyzing issues in simplistic, black-and-white terms. Eschewing easy divisions between victims and perpetrators, they examine the intertwining of guilt and innocence, showing that the offenders may have once been victimized by such crimes, or that the victims themselves behaved ambiguously. Most are concerned with gaps between appearance and reality. Those concerned with children in particular ask whether steps taken to protect young people can backfire, causing more harm than good. A few ask if we should try to live with sex offenders in our communities and whether such people are morally responsible or mentally ill. They tend to use dark palettes, partly due to the grimness of their subject matter, partly because they seek to express moral murk, confusion and the pervasiveness of risk.

In the next section, I begin by putting the five films in context, briefly outlining the history of sex-crime movies and recent shifts in understandings of sex crimes themselves. Then I discuss my examples in terms of three primary themes: the difficulty of determining guilt and assigning blame in sex-crime cases; the ordinariness and ubiquity of sex-crime offenders ("the guy next door"); and the risks one incurs in searching for sexual authenticity.

Contemporary Sex-Crime Films

Until recently, movies avoided taking sex crime as their text. The topic was long forbidden by Hollywood's Production Code, which outlawed depiction of anything that might offend "common decency" (Ellis, 1979). The topic was also socially taboo, and in any case no one (including criminologists) knew much about it. (In graduate school in the 1970s, I was taught that incest is something that occurs in Appalachia when teenage girls walk around in slips in front of their stepfathers.) In addition, the complexity of victim-offender dynamics and relationships in sex crimes did not lend itself to Hollywood's usual easy distinctions between good and evil. Sometimes a notorious offense would inspire a film, as happened when Fritz Lang based *M* (1931) on the depredations of Peter Kürten, the "Dusseldorf vampire." At other times scriptwriters sneaked sex crime in by a side door, as in the case of *Cape Fear* (1961), in which the psychopath intends to rape his antagonist's daughter. But for the most part, the distasteful nature of the subject combined with censorship and ignorance to keep sex crime off the cinematic agenda.

Change began in the early 1980s when a moral panic about child sexual abuse by day care workers spread across the USA. Today these cases are generally remembered as the result of mass hysteria, a national witch-hunt fueled by hurried investigations and the implantation of false memories in toddlers (Nathan and Snedeker, 1995; Loftus and Ketcham, 1994; de Young, 2004).[3] But at the time they got people talking about the possibility of sexual exploitation by trusted figures in everyday life, and they stimulated legal debates over issues such as whether children should be required to give evidence in open court. Discussions of sex crimes opened up still further as cases of clergy abuse surfaced, along with evidence of mass coverups of child sexual exploitation by Catholic priests. Infamous individual cases further eroded the wall of secrecy that had traditionally protected sex offenders; for example, in the U.S., the tragedy of seven-year-old Megan Kanka, lured into a neighbor's house with the promise of seeing a puppy, only to be raped and murdered, caused national outrage, especially when it was learned that the neighbor had been previously convicted of sex offenses. Similarly, the bizarre sexual predilections of serial killers like Jeffrey Dahmer prompted widespread debates over the legal responsibility of those with psychosexual illnesses. Recognition of date rape, sexual harassment and stalking brought sex crime even more into the open, again increasing people's sense of vulnerability. False memories, recovered memories, accusations against religious and scouting leaders, sex offender registries and the ubiquity of danger became favorite issues of the news media. It was in this context that more sexually explicit sex-crime movies began to appear. Not surprisingly, some of them dealt with difficulties in perception.

The Hazards of Assigning Blame

Mystic River takes place in a Boston neighborhood where the Mystic River flows into the harbor, close to downtown but a world apart, a small, apparently stable, working-class community, Catholic, tough and standoffish with outsiders. The film, based on a novel by Dennis Lehane, opens with a scene of three boys playing. One is kidnapped by two adult men who hold him for several days in a basement and rape him repeatedly. The rest of the movie shows how effects of the original crime ripple through the boys' adult lives and into the next generation.

The teenage daughter of one of these adults, Jimmy Markum (Sean Penn), is brutally killed. She was about to leave him in any case, he discovers, to elope with a neighborhood youth. Jimmy, whose mom-and-pop store is a front for criminal enterprises, suspects that Dave Boyle (Tim Robbins), the character who was raped as a boy, is his daughter's killer. With thuggish friends aptly named the Savage brothers, Jimmy kills Dave at night on the river's edge. The third member of the original trio, state trooper Sean Devine (Kevin Bacon), investigates the daughter's death, figuring out who really killed her and also discovering that Jimmy killed Dave. However, for the moment at least, he lacks the evidence to bring Jimmy to justice. Thus the three central characters fill the roles of criminal, victim and avenger, although the avenger is unable to function effectively. His impotence is underlined by the fact that his wife has left him and he is unable to communicate with her.

The central themes of *Mystic River*—misperception, abandonment, loss of fathers, loss of partners and children, loss of childhood, vengeance—play out against a background of nighttime scenes and constricted interiors. These themes cut across the film's central conflict: the clash in values between the small, closed community and the broader society—the type of clash criminologists describe as "culture conflict" (Sellin, 1938). Change does occur—a Starbucks coffee shop moves into the neighborhood, for instance; but the solidarity of Jimmy's criminal enterprise, the neighborhood's code of silence and generations of hardscrabble resentment toward the outer world all work to thwart the police investigation and throw the community back on its own resources. Like Sean's wife, it is unable to speak, incapable of communicating beyond itself. The community's resistance to the outer world is summed up in the final scene by the smile that Jimmy's wife (Laura Linney) bestows on Dave's widow, a chilling, triumphant nod that says, we will let you survive here if you ask no questions and play by our rules. Her hunger for power and the widow's hunger for justice have met head on, and power has won. The neighborhood defines its own values.

A consideration of the interlacing of guilt and innocence can be found in *Monster,* the biography of the prostitute Aileen Wuornos (Charlize Theron) ("America's first female serial killer," the news media called her), executed by Florida in 2002 for a series of highway murders. Wuornos does not at first glance seem promising material for an argument about the hazards of determining culpability. But Patty Jenkins, the film's author and director, manages to dig through the layers of media obfuscation to the bedrock of Wuornos's personality.

That *Monster* succeeds is due in large part to the dramatic skills of Charlize Theron, the actor who portrays Wuornos. Theron is able to express a wide range of emotions—often conflicting emotions—through her face and body. When Wuornos is hooking, for instance, we see a mixture of distaste, apprehension and hope play across her countenance. As she becomes more desperate, her grimaces simultaneously reflect nervous tension, hurt, defiance and determination. Theron, who gained 30 pounds for the role, came to closely resemble Wuornos herself, hardscrabble and belligerent except when her face lights up with love.

While Jenkins's script stays close to the facts of Wuornos's life, it shapes those facts in a way designed to forestall easy moral condemnation. It does so, for instance, by portraying Selby, Wuornos's lover, as a virtual child, casting a small woman, Christina Ricci, in the role. Wuornos's sense of responsibility emerges in contrast to Selby's infantile dependency; we see Wuornos making heroic attempts to cope, braving hopeless odds to provide Selby with "a house, cars, the whole fucking shebang" by becoming "a business person, something like that." She buries her own fears to protect Selby, only to be betrayed by Selby in the end.

Wuornos's rage toward and terror of men become understandable when we learn that she was raped at the age of eight and had her first baby when she was thirteen. She is hideously victimized by a customer before she commences her killing spree, and many of her clients are criminalistic themselves, brutish and repellent. The film does not whitewash Wuornos's crimes, nor does it show her as anything other than slow-witted, mentally ill, foul-mouthed, socially illiterate and self-deluded:

> I'm good with the Lord . . . Who the fuck knows what God wants? . . . People kill each other every day, and for what, huh? for politics . . . and religion . . . and they're heroes. I'm not a bad person, I'm a real good person.

But her history of victimization and her self-hatred complicate our judgment of her. At the end, as Wuornos is hurried into the death chamber, we see her not as a serial killer we can hate, but as a pathetic woman in whom good mixed with evil.

The Guy Next Door

The day care sexual abuse cases and scandals involving predatory scoutmasters and priests sowed widespread mistrust of the familiar figures to whom parents entrust children and on whom they rely for help. This mistrust fed into the emergence of a new movie bad guy: the neighborhood pervert, camouflaged by ordinariness, all the more dangerous because he lacks the stagy, unmistakable stigmata of traditional movie-star criminals.

This new type of villain turns up in *Mystic River* and *The Woodsman*, but nowhere with greater force than in *L.I.E.*, director Michael Cuesta's semi-autobiographical film about a 15-year-old boy stalked by a patriotic pillar of the community. Equally remarkable is *L.I.E.*'s depiction of the child victim as not helpless quarry but an agent of his own fate.

L.I.E. opens with 15-year-old Howie Blitzer (Paul Dano) balanced dangerously on a bridge railing above the Long Island Expressway. In a voice-over he tells us that the road has killed many people, including his own mother. "I hope it doesn't get me," he continues, although he is clearly toying with the possibility of suicide. In the ensuing scenes Howie loses his best friend, fights kids who accuse him of "salami swiping" (masturbating other boys), is assaulted and apparently abandoned by his father and is arrested for the burglaries he has been committing with friends. Moreover, he is stalked by a neighborhood ex-Marine, Big John or BJ (Brian Cox), a large, vulgar and cunning predator with a gun collection in his basement as well as a bedroom for the motherless boys he "saves" from time to time.

In the key scene, BJ rescues Howie from juvenile detention and brings him home, sending Scottie, his current teenage companion, to a motel for a few days. BJ, suddenly paternal, teaches Howie to shave—tenderly, repulsively, dangerously. They then hug, and Howie indicates he is sexually ready for what seems sure to come; indeed, he may even be a little bit curious. However, BJ—touched by Howie's scared "raccoon look" and realizing that the boy has just been devastated by news of his father's imprisonment—refrains for the nonce from molesting him, instead settling him for the night in a single bed. At breakfast the next morning, BJ again throws himself into the role of the good father, bustling about to cook breakfast and arranging for Howie to visit his dad in prison.

We know better than to trust BJ, who has heartlessly exiled Scottie to a motel and is drawing the net around his new prey. On the other hand, this revolting pederast has for a few hours given Howie the parenting he needs, suggesting that even BJ, who earlier admitted to shame about his sexual compulsions, has a remnant of decency. Moreover, this dose of parenting puts Howie back on his feet, giving him the courage to confront his father and face the future. Meanwhile, Scottie, displaced and abandoned, shoots BJ while the latter cruises for boys along the L.I.E., an act that frees Howie from the sexual threat. The final scene returns us to the bridge above the expressway, where Howie still broods about the road's murderous potential but now concludes, in another voice-over, "I'm not going to let it get me."

A comparison with *Sleepers* (1996), an earlier movie about pederasty, highlights *L.I.E.*'s incorporation of recent understandings of sexual victimization. In *Sleepers* (1996), four boys convicted of a minor prank are sent to a juvenile home where guards sodomize and torture them over a period of months. The sodomites are one-dimensional bad guys, sadists, Nazi-like officers excited by cruelty; their depiction draws on a now-outmoded stereotype of the pederast as overtly monstrous. BJ, in contrast, is depicted as someone familiar, hearty and trustworthy; driven by remorse as well as lust, he is a pedophile as well as a pederast, terrifying but not totally evil. In *Sleepers*, the main guard (Kevin Bacon) is easily recognizable as a bad guy: wiry, greasy-haired, pathological. BJ, on the other hand, looks like a favorite uncle—until you figure out what he is doing. In *Sleepers* the good guys win and the bad guys lose; in *L.I.E.* a complicated bad guy does something generous, and instead of an uplifting hero the film closes on a sad kid who survives sexual predation.

In its reflections of recent research on sex crimes against children, *L.I.E.* more closely resembles another recent film, *The Woodsman*, starring Kevin Bacon as Walter, a pedophile who has just been released after 12 years in prison for molesting little girls. Director Nicole Kassell's film, based on a play by Steven Fechter, is dedicated entirely to the development of Walter's character. (He is called a woodsman partly because he used to be a carpenter, but mainly in recollection of the Little Red Riding Hood character who cuts open the wicked wolf and releases the girl the wolf had swallowed, intact. In this context, the woodsman is an ambiguous hero, a savior who nonetheless gets control of a little girl, just as Walter himself later does in a wooded park.) Walter, who wants desperately to go straight, endures daily struggles with his compulsion and with the fellow factory hands who try to mob him out of their workplace. Although he is helped by a new girlfriend, Walter leads a bleak existence, rejected by his family and loathed by a contemptuous parole officer (Mos Def). The film does not ask us to pity Walter but dispassionately follows his story, not to resolution but to a small, precarious victory at the end when he hugs the little girl on a park bench and then sends her home.

Recent films use the ordinary-guy image of the sex criminal to emphasize children's vulnerability and the difficulty of perceiving such offenses when they occur. Aileen Wuornos, we learn in *Monster*, was initially raped by a neighbor, and she seems to have been molested by her father as well. One of the abductors in *Mystic River* wears a priest's ring. BJ, the hearty Vietnam vet of *L.I.E.*, is another respected community figure and pal of the juvenile police officers who, with painful irony, release Howie into his care. *The Woodsman* casts doubt on nearly everyone: when Walter sends the girl on the bench home to her father, it is to a father who jiggles her on his lap; and from his window he observes a man luring boys into his car. We cannot tell where corruption lies, these films warn; and today's sex criminal may be yesterday's victim.

The films underscore the inability of communities to protect their children. *Mystic River*'s tight-knit neighborhood is in fact one of lost children and failed fathers. The parole officer of *Woodsman* may keep close tabs on Walter, but another man is preying on children just across the street, and Walter does not dare report him. Even the wealthy neighborhood in which Howie Blitzer lives, with its vast lawns and showcase houses, its school guidance counselors and juvenile court specialists, is impotent in the face of BJ's duplicity.

The Risks of Sexual Authenticity

L.I.E. and *The Woodsman* point to the dangers inherent in a search for sexual authenticity, but no film investigates those risks as thoroughly as *In the Cut* (2003), Jane Campion's film about a not-so-young schoolteacher (Meg Ryan) searching for love and meaning. *In the Cut*, based on a novel by Susanna Moore, was panned by critics and viewers alike.[4] Audiences complained that it was nothing more than a "cheap erotic thriller," that Meg Ryan had shed her usual good-girl persona to become sluttish and that her character should not have taken so many risks in a high-crime environment. "Lackluster *Fatal Attraction*," one annoyed reviewer wrote, while another reported that "The only shock factor in this movie is getting the chance to see Meg Ryan naked, though I think most men still prefer Halle Berry." As these comments indicate, viewers looked for a traditional Hollywood category in which to slot *In the Cut*, and when they failed to find one they were disappointed. Campion took this risk in making a film about sexual and emotional authenticity with a story line that keeps foraying into traditional genres (the love story, the cop buddy action movie, pornography, the serial killer film) and then pulling back to find its own groove. But the risk is also one of the film's virtues, for the difficulty of identifying one's own path is part of Campion's story.

That story concerns Frannie Avery, a high school teacher living in a crime-ridden section of New York's East Village, determined not to be intimidated by the city's violence, hoping to have a genuine erotic experience and to be true to her own ways of relating to students and the city. Dreamy and independent, Frannie pays little attention to her appearance (Ryan's unkempt hair drove some viewers wild) or conventional rules of behavior, instead allowing herself to be tugged along by her own values and sexuality. When a woman is killed and dismembered in her neighborhood, Frannie gets sexually involved with the cop who questions her, Malloy (Mark Ruffalo). But it seems possible that he is the killer. Other women are killed and "disarticulated," including her sister. Viewers, along with Frannie, begin to suspect a range of men: a student, Malloy, a former lover, an unidentified mugger. Frannie seems to put herself in dangerous situations—dressing provocatively, hanging out in unsafe places. In the background flickers the courtship of Frannie's parents, a frightful dream sequence in which the woman slips while ice-skating and the man skates through her legs, severing them. Eventually the killer comes after Frannie, but she manages to overcome him and returns at the end to Malloy.

In the Cut, then, is a film about a woman living with the constant threat of violence against women. It is also a sexually charged movie with graphic (and—in a change from most movie sex—convincing) love scenes. At one point, Frannie's sister muses unhappily that she always thinks about sex in terms of what men like, instead of her own preferences. Campion has made a movie about sexual experience from a woman's point of view—unconcerned whether men might prefer Halle Berry to Meg Ryan. Her refusal to objectify Frannie's desires makes *In the Cut* a bold exploration of what sex would be like if women called the shots as well as of the dangers inherent in following one's own vision.

Like Frannie, viewers cannot be sure they perceive her world accurately. Who is dangerous, who a friend? Which settings are menacing, and which are merely part of the city scenery? Should one keep up one's guard, avoiding sleazy bars and unknown men, or pursue one's authenticity, sleeping with the window wide open and traversing deserted streets despite the risks? The characters of the two cops dramatize the problems of trust and perception. Malloy himself is an ambiguous figure, edgy, brutal, incoherent, oblivious to boundaries, unknowable. A scene in which he drives Frannie to a wooded reservoir makes not only Frannie but also viewers apprehensive. Equally disquieting is Malloy's buddy, with his endless sexist and racist profanity. Campion plays with the audience, thwarting our expectation that the buddy cop will merely echo the dominant officer, again forcing us into Frannie's viewpoint and the realization that we simply cannot tell where danger lies. In this context, the serial killer becomes a metaphor for living with risk.

Crime Films as Criminology

If we define criminology as efforts to understand crime and criminals, it becomes clear that even a small, narrowly focused sample of films like the one just analyzed can yield fertile criminological material. The themes of crime films overlap with those of academic criminology: for instance, in the examples discussed here, one sees the idea of crime as a product of culture clash with the stereotypical guy-next-door presentation of the child molester. But crime films also deal with matters beyond the range of academic criminology. Philosophically, they raise questions concerning the nature of good and evil. Psychologically, they encourage viewers to identify with victims and offenders—even serial killers—whose sexualities, vulnerabilities and moralities may be totally unfamiliar. Ethically, they take passionate moral positions that would be out of place in academic analyses. Crime films constitute a type of discourse different from academic criminology, one with its own types of truth and its own constraints.

This discourse needs a name. I suggest calling it *popular criminology* and defining it as a category composed of discourses about crime found not only in film but also on the Internet, on television and in newspapers, novels and rap music and myth. Popular criminology differs from academic criminology in that it does not pretend to empirical accuracy or theoretical validity. But in scope, it covers as much territory—possibly more—if we consider the kinds of ethical and philosophical issues raised even by this small sample of movies. Popular criminology's audience is bigger (even a cinematic flop will reach a larger audience than this article). And its social significance is greater, for academic criminology cannot offer so wide a range of criminological wares. It cannot see into the mind of a woman like Frannie, weighing the possibility of being loved against the possibility of being murdered, and it cannot dig so deeply into the minds of pederasts as *L.I.E.* or *The Woodsman.* The two types of criminology, popular and academic, complement one another, each contributing in its own way to understandings of crime.

I am proposing that we think of "criminology" as an umbrella category that encompasses both academic and popular criminology. The subdivisions should not be conceived as opposites, one concerned with reason and the other emotion; one coming from the head and the other from the heart; one "hard" and "one soft." Such misleading polarities reinforce the familiar false hierarchy in which scientific knowing is deemed superior. Rather, I am suggesting an egalitarian epistemology in which the two ways of knowing are conceived as partners in the task of defining and explaining crime. In fact, the categories of academic and popular criminology are already blurring, for the cultural criminology movement has for a decade been eroding their conceptual boundaries, demonstrating that they interpenetrate. This article, then, is an attempt to speed up and bring direction to a process already under way.

As popular criminology gains scholarly recognition, a key task will be analyzing the process through which crime films affect beliefs about crime. The question here concerns perception and impact, not reception. Film scholars have produced excellent reception studies, asking who watches which films and why. (The classic is Carol Clover's work on teen terror flicks, *Men, Women, and Chainsaws* [1992].) However, much less attention has been paid to the processes through which movies influence perceptions of crime. Although I cannot explore this issue in depth here, I can sketch an explanatory model that seems to me worth pursuing, one derived from recent work on the sociology of cognition and sociology of culture.

In the mid-1980s, sociologists began rejecting the traditional view of culture as a body of beliefs, customs, goals, values and institutions accepted fairly uniformly by all members of a group, instead adopting a view of culture as a repository or "tool kit" (Swidler, 1986), or what sociologist Paul DiMaggio terms "a grab-bag of odds and ends: a pastiche of mediated representations, a repertoire of techniques" (1997:267). This view anticipates that individuals and groups will perceive (Zerubavel, 1997), interpret and remember movies differently, that interpretations will vary over time and that viewers will carry away from films different bits of cultural information (see, more generally, Philo, 1997; Swidler, 2001). The view fits well with actual reactions to films. One viewer may conclude that *In the Cut* endorses sexual risk-taking, while another may take away the message that women should get out of New York City. Although the new sociology of culture does not discuss films directly, it implies that movies provide fragments of culture (frames or organizing principles as well as bits of information) and that culture is to be found both in the heads of individual viewers and in the larger collective consciousness. (For a related analysis from the cultural-criminology perspective, see Ferrell [1999], and for related work in film studies, see Turner [1999]; Mitry [2000].)

Sociologists and psychologists have studied how people perceive and then organize the bits of culture in their heads (DiMaggio, 1997; Zerubavel, 1997; also see Morgan and Schwalbe, 1990; Gamson et al., 1992; Swidler and Arditi, 1994). While much of this work is speculative, it seems that the fragments of cultural information in our minds form themselves first into frames and then into schemata or templates—bigger and more solid frames—that we draw on in the form of assumptions, social norms, principles and so on, using them as handy guides to behavior so we are not obliged to think through every action or reaction from the start. Schemata then aggregate into even larger mental structures: ideologies (including assumptions about the nature of heroes and villains), paradigms, logics and narratives of the self (perhaps including the self as a victim or perpetrator of a sex crime).

In this view, movies are a source of cultural information, most of which simply rattles around in our heads, waiting to be called upon, but some of which feeds into our ideologies and other mental schemata. The schemata in turn interact with the external world, where we encounter real-life crime and popular criminology (including perhaps new movies about sex crimes) that then feed back into our schemata, reinforcing or disconfirming them. For example, we might unequivocally despise child molesters until we view their compulsion through an offender's eyes, as in *The Woodsman*, or confront their ambiguous complexity even when loathsome, as in *L.I.E.* This model of film–external world interactions needs elaboration, but it offers a platform on which criminologists concerned with film analysis can build.

Conclusion: Crime Films and Academic Criminology

"Defending the disciplinary identity of criminology against incursions from 'elsewhere,'" write Garland and Sparks (2000:2–3),

is now as unfeasible as it is undesirable . . . Given the centrality, the emotiveness and the political salience of crime issues today, academic criminology can no longer aspire to monopolize "criminological" discourse or hope to claim exclusive rights over the representation and disposition of crime.

The gradual accumulation of a literature on crime films noted at the start of this article, and my argument for recognizing popular criminology as a criminological discourse in its own right, are signs of the disciplinary shifts that Garland and Sparks discuss. It is no longer possible to equate "criminology" with "academic criminology" (also see Braithwaite, 2000; Zedner, 2007).

But if academic criminology has been slow to make room for the study of popular criminology, part of the problem has rested with the crime-films literature, which has grown in size and richness while remaining diffuse in its aims. In this respect it contrasts with the law-films literature, which came to maturity more rapidly and from the start demonstrated its relevance to legal studies. Crime-films research, I have been arguing, needs to concentrate more clearly and consistently on movies' criminological relevance.

I have attempted to establish that relevance. Using the example of recent sex-crime movies, I have recommended that we conceive of crime films as an aspect of popular criminology, and of popular criminology as an aspect of criminology itself. If we define *criminology* as the study of crime and criminals, then it becomes clear that film is one of the primary sources (albeit an unscientific one) through which people get their ideas about the nature of crime. Some of those ideas echo academic criminology—the understanding of the great frequency of sexual offenses, for instance, and the realization that such crimes are frequently committed by trusted members of the community. But other ideas developed by popular criminology bring to bear ethical, philosophical and psychological perspectives that are beyond the reach of academic research, at least in its current state. Recognition that popular criminology is integral to criminology could invigorate the study of crime films—and criminology itself.

References

Bailey, Frankie Y., Joycelyn M. Pollock and Sherry Schroder (1998) "The Best Defense: Images of Female Attorneys in Popular Films," in Frankie Bailey and Donna Hale (eds) *Popular Culture, Crime, and Justice*, pp. 180–95. Belmont, CA: West/Wadsworth.

Bergman, Paul and Michael Asimow (1996) *Reel Justice: The Courtroom Goes to the Movies*. Kansas City, MO: Andrews & McMeel.

Braithwaite, John (2000) "The New Regulatory State and the Transformation of Criminology," in David Garland and Richard Sparks (eds) *Criminology and Social Theory*, pp. 47–70. Oxford: Oxford University Press.

Brown, Michelle (2003) "Penological Crisis in America: Finding Meaning in Imprisonment Post-Rehabilitation," PhD diss., Indiana University, Dept of Criminal Justice and American Studies Program.

Campbell, Russell (2005) *Marked Women: Prostitutes and Prostitution in the Cinema*. Madison, WI: University of Wisconsin Press.

Cavender, Gray (1999) "Detecting Masculinity," in Jeff Ferrell and Neil Websdale (eds) *Making Trouble: Cultural Constructions of Crime, Deviance, & Control*, pp. 157–75. New York: Aldine de Gruyter.

Chase, Anthony (1986) "Lawyers and Popular Culture: A Review of Mass Media Portrayals of American Attorneys," *American Bar Foundation Research Journal* 11(2): 281–300.

Chase, Anthony (2002) *Movies on Trial: The Legal System on the Silver Screen*. New York: The New Press.

Chermak, Steven (2002) *Searching for a Demon: The Media Construction of the Militia Movement*. Boston, MA: Northeastern University Press.

Clover, Carol J. (1992) *Men, Women, and Chainsaws*. Princeton, NJ: Princeton University Press.

Denvir, John (ed.) (1996) *Legal Reelism: Movies as Legal Texts*. Urbana, IL: University of Illinois Press.

de Young, M. (2004) *The Day Care Ritual Abuse Moral Panic*. Jefferson, NC: McFarland & Company.

DiMaggio, Paul (1997) "Culture and Cognition," *Annual Review of Sociology* 23: 263–87.

Ellis, Jack C. (1979) *A History of Film*. Englewood Cliffs, NJ: Prentice-Hall.

Epstein, Su (1995) "The New Mythic Monster," in Jeff Ferrell and C.R. Sanders (eds) *Cultural Criminology*, pp. 66–79. Boston, MA: Northeastern University Press.

Ferrell, Jeff (1999) "Cultural Criminology," *Annual Review of Sociology* 25: 395–418.

Ferrell, Jeff and C.R. Sanders (eds) (1995) *Cultural Criminology*. Boston, MA: Northeastern University Press.

Ferrell, Jeff and Neil Websdale (eds) (1999) *Making Trouble: Cultural Constructions of Crime, Deviance, & Control*. New York: Aldine de Gruyter.

Ferrell, Jeff, Keith Hayward, Wayne Morrison and Mike Presdee (eds) (2004) *Cultural Criminology Unleashed*. London: GlassHouse Press.

Freeman, Michael (ed.) (2005) *Law and Popular Culture*. Oxford: Oxford University Press.

Gamson, William A., David Croteau, William Hoynes and Theodore Sasson (1992) "Media Images and the Social Construction of Reality," *Annual Review of Sociology* 18: 373–93.

Garland, David and Richard Sparks (eds) (2000) *Criminology and Social Theory*. Oxford: Oxford University Press.

Greenfield, Steve, Guy Osborn and Peter Robson (2001) *Film and the Law*. London: Cavendish.

Hayward, Keith J. and Jock Young (2004) "Cultural Criminology: Some Notes on the Script," *Theoretical Criminology* 8(3): 259–73.

Jenkins, Philip (1994) *Using Murder: The Social Construction of Serial Homicide*. New York: Aldine de Gruyter.

King, Neal (1999) *Heroes in Hard Times: Cop Action Movies in the U.S.* Philadelphia, PA: Temple University Press.

Loftus, E. and K. Ketcham (1994) *The Myth of Repressed Memory: False Memories and Allegations of Sexual Abuse*. New York: St Martin's Press.

Mitry, Jean (2000) *Semiotics and the Analysis of Film*. London: The Athlone Press.

Morgan, David L. and Michael L. Schwalbe (1990) "Mind and Self in Society: Linking Social Structure and Social Cognition," *Social Psychology Quarterly* 53(2): 148–64.

Munby, Jonathan (1999) *Public Enemies, Public Heroes: Screening the Gangster from* Little Caesar *to* Touch of Evil. Chicago, IL: University of Chicago Press.

Nathan, Debbie and Michael R. Snedeker (1995) *Satan's Silence: Ritual Abuse and the Making of a Modern American Witch Hunt*. New York: Basic Books.

O'Brien, Martin, Rodanthi Tzanelli, Majid Yar and Sue Penna (2005) "'The Spectacle of Fearsome Acts': Crime in the Melting P(l)ot in *Gangs of New York*," *Critical Criminology* 13(1): 17–35.

Philo, Greg (ed.) (1997) *Media and Mental Distress*. Glascow Media Group. London: Longman.

Post, Robert C. (1987) "On the Popular Image of the Lawyer: Reflections in a Dark Glass," *California Law Review* 75: 379–89.

Press, Joy (2003) "Making the Cut: Jane Campion's Feminist Film Noir Stirs Up Pheromones and Occult Mystery in a Malevolent East Village." Retrieved February 19, 2012 (http://www.village voice.com/2003-10-21/news/making-the-cut/)

Rafter, Nicole (2005) "Badfellas," in Michael Freeman (ed.) *Law and Popular Culture*, pp. 339–57. Oxford: Oxford University Press.

Rafter, Nicole (2006) *Shots in the Mirror: Crime Films and Society* (2nd edn). New York: Oxford University Press.

Robson, Peter (2005) "Law and Film Studies: Autonomy and Theory," in Michael Freeman (ed.) *Law and Popular Culture*, pp. 21–46. Oxford: Oxford University Press.

Sellin, Thorsten (1938) *Culture Conflict and Crime*. Bulletin 41. New York: Social Science Research Council.

Sparks, Richard (1996) "Masculinity and Heroism in the Hollywood Blockbuster," *British Journal of Criminology* 36(3): 348–60.

Swidler, Ann (1986) "Culture in Action: Symbols and Strategies," *American Sociological Review* 51(2): 273–86.

Swidler, Ann (2001) *Talk of Love: How Culture Matters.* Chicago, IL: University of Chicago Press.

Swidler, Ann and Jorge Arditi (1994) "The New Sociology of Knowledge," *Annual Review of Sociology* 20: 305–29.

Tiso, Giovanni (n.d.) "The Spectacle of Surveillance: Images of the Panopticon in Science-Fiction Cinema." Available at www.homepages.paradise.net.nz/gtiso/filmessay (accessed 14 October 2004).

Turner, Graeme (1999) *Film as Social Practice* (3rd edn). New York: Routledge.

Tzanelli, Rodanthi, Majid Yar and Martin O'Brien (2005) "Exploring Crime in the American Cinematic Imagination," *Theoretical Criminology* 9(1): 97–117.

Varese, Federico (2006) "The Secret History of Japanese Cinema: The Yakuza Movies," *Global Crime* 7(1): 107–26.

Zedner, Lucia (2007) "Pre-Crime and Post-Criminology?," *Theoretical Criminology* 11(2): 261–81.

Zerubavel, Evitar (1997) *Social Mindscapes: An Invitation to Cognitive Sociology.* Cambridge, MA: Harvard University Press.

Notes

1. This article first appeared in *Theoretical Criminology,* Vol. 11 (2007), pp. 403–420. Reprinted with the author's permission.

2. The original publication included six films, but *Capturing the Friedmans*, a documentary, was excluded for this version, since only feature films are included in *Cinematic Sociology.*

3. Several others countries, including England and New Zealand, experienced a wave of day care sexual abuse cases about the same time. A related Australian case, though not one involving charges of sexual abuse, provoked the Meryl Streep film *Cry in the Dark* (1988).

4. But some critics raved about *In the Cut*—see Anderson (2003) and Press (2003). For the viewer comments cited here and later in this section, I relied on the Internet Movie Database.

THE HERO, THE LAW, AND THE PEOPLE IN BETWEEN

Models of the Legal System in Hollywood Films

Valerie J. Callanan

Introduction

As with every other social institution, law is socially constructed. How a legal system is seen by the public it serves comes from learning about the system through family, peers, educators, social networks, and institutions, including the media. The American public tends to believe that the United States has the best legal system in the world. Yet Americans also complain that the system is too lenient with criminals and favors the rich and powerful (Maguire 2003). Less than half the population express confidence in the Supreme Court, and even fewer people are confident in the local courts (Sherman 2002); moreover, trust and confidence in these institutions has steadily eroded since the 1980s. How is it possible that people can hold such contradictory beliefs simultaneously?

Silbey and Ewick (2000) argue that this contradiction is possible because law embodies both the sacred and profane. Based on Durkheim's concepts ([1912] 2001), law rests on the sacred principles of fairness, equality, humaneness, and responsibility, ideals upheld in American culture. The profane aspects of law are the messy day-to-day workings of legal systems, replete with institutional discrimination that disadvantages the powerless and other marginalized groups.

The institution of law in a democratic society is relatively transparent, which allows the populace to see both the majesty of the law and its weaknesses. Importantly, if the legal system were socially constructed as always being rational and principled (i.e., sacred), citizens would lose faith in the legitimacy of the system the moment they experienced or learned of evidence to the contrary. Conversely, if law were socially constructed as always being irrational and corrupt (i.e., profane), citizens would not view the system as legitimate to begin with. Silbey and Ewick (2000) posit that it is precisely because law is viewed as both majestic and messy that the system maintains its legitimacy. Law that is only about principles and rationality is too brittle; law that is corrupt and unpredictable is too pliable.

Perceptions of the Law

Silbey and Ewick (2000) found that individuals hold multiple and contradictory views of the law. From their in-depths interviews with 430 individuals, they found that people tend to have three main stances toward the law. The first, and most common, is what they term "before the law" (from Franz Kafka's [1937] parable with the same name). Individuals perceive the law as transcendent and omnipotent and—given its majesty—something they seldom use. Law is viewed as a set of legal principles "operating on known and fixed rules" (p. 50), which promotes impartiality and objectivity. Law exists because it is just, which allows for legal change when existing laws or lack of laws is deemed unjust in a changing social landscape. In this regard, law is sacred and not to be invoked lightly.

The second stance that individuals have toward the law is "with the law." This perspective sees law as a game, a "terrain for tactical encounters" (Silbey and Ewick 2000:52) among those who are well versed or at least comfortable using law to serve their purposes. Law is not viewed as abstract, but a "world of legitimate competition" (p. 52) in which individuals bring their resources to bear on the system to outmaneuver their legal opponents. In doing so, they may resort to deceit and manipulation, but justify these behaviors as necessary in a legal system that favors the "haves."

The third perspective Silbey and Ewick found is "up against the law." Law is viewed as an unwanted intrusion that individuals are not able to withstand because they do not have the resources to play by the rules. Thus, they "do what they can to get what they need" (p. 53), although these feints are seldom illegal. Individuals "up against the law" do not work so much to challenge the law as they do to avoid it. But these actions are motivated by a strong sense of justice and fairness. Individuals recognize themselves as "have-nots" by virtue of a social system in which they are relatively powerless. Cognizant of this imbalance, they believe they are within their rights to resist the law, often resorting to loud scenes or threatening violence—anything "to get attention that is being denied by those with greater power" (p. 54).

The importance of Silbey and Ewick's research is that it uncovers the multiple ways in which individuals view the law, and that people hold these multiple, and frequently contradictory, perspectives simultaneously. Thus, the American public believes the legal system is both just and impartial *and* intrusive and biased. How could this be?

Films about the Law

In modern societies, one of the most dominant purveyors of information about law and the legal system is the media, so studying its cultural products is important. In this reading I argue that films about the legal system convey messages that uphold the reverence of law but also reveal its imperfections. Because a large portion of popular culture films dramatize true cases that challenge existing law or injustice, I suggest that these media productions influence how consumers perceive the legal system. Films depict flaws in the legal system itself, but these are usually framed as minor, local, or specific problems, not general ones. Thus, systemic problems, such as class bias, are revealed, but they are not tied into the larger structural reasons for inequity that colors all aspects of society. Moreover, in most of these films justice is realized—also a common theme deployed in television crime dramas (Sparks, 1992). Consumers of these products, then, may be more likely to believe that while the system is imperfect, in most cases the truth wins out. Given that over 95 percent of Americans get their information about the justice system from mass media (Surette 2007), the potential influence of dramatic legal films may be especially strong on consumers' attitudes and beliefs about the American legal system. Consequently, it behooves media scholars to study the messages embedded in films about the American legal system, particularly blockbuster films that reach a large audience.

Films about the legal system employ a narrative common in other crime-related genres—that of the singular heroic figure who becomes so impassioned by the inequities in the system that he or she is willing to lose everything in the pursuit of justice. These heroes confront barrier after barrier but struggle mightily to overcome these obstacles. Their perseverance pays off, for in the end, justice is achieved. This emphasis on heroism manages to reveal inequalities and inefficiencies of the legal system yet obfuscate the structural reasons for these problems. Thus, these narratives do not harm the legitimacy of the American legal system but instead maintain it.

The focus on the heroic individual obscures structural inequalities in the legal system that have long been documented. Instead, it sends the message that justice is attainable for those that work hard. In doing so, the reality of systemic biases in the legal system is hidden. Moreover, legal films tend to focus on issues involving civil or human rights, so when the hero-protagonist triumphs, the majesty of democracy through law is revealed as it widens to protect more minority groups, such as the disabled or persons of color. Thus, the satisfactory conclusion in most films about the legal system may contribute to Americans' reverence for the law, in spite of their awareness of its many flaws.

The common man as hero has long been a popular narrative in cinema. This is especially true in films that deal with law and justice. In particular, American cinema has long been infatuated with courtroom dramas in which the hero-protagonist takes on the system to render justice. Earlier examples of this are Atticus Finch (Gregory Peck) in *To Kill a Mockingbird* (Robert Mulligan, 1962) and Henry Fonda as Juror 8 in *12 Angry Men* (Sidney Lumet, 1957). This narrative is so commonplace in legal films as to be cliché, yet it remains in vogue because it restores our faith in the world and the belief that right overcomes might. Moreover, since many of these films are loosely based on real cases, viewers might think that justice is achieved more frequently than it is in actuality. They may not realize how singular these cases are, which is *why* their stories are so compelling.

Film Portrayals of Those "Before the Law," "With the Law," and "Up Against the Law"

This chapter will describe and analyze three films that portray the hero narrative: *Music Within* (Steven Sawalich, 1997), *A Civil Action* (Steven Zaillian, 1998), and *Erin Brockovich* (Steven Soderbergh, 2000). Fighting an inefficient, biased, and unjust system, the protagonists in these films persevere against all odds and risk nearly everything in their pursuit of justice. Two of the three films (*A Civil Action* and *Erin Brockovich*) were extremely popular and also received several Academy Award nominations. Based on true stories, these films were also chosen because they represent the three different perspectives found by Silbey and Ewick (2000).

The first film, *Music Within*, is about Richard Pimentel (Ron Livingston), who fought to create laws that protect the disabled. Richard can be described as a man "before the law," which is established very early in the movie. In spite of a tragic childhood with a mentally ill mother, he craves attention and works hard in school to win his mother's affection. Early on in school, he excels in public speaking, but in spite of winning a local speech competition a few years after graduating from high school, he is denied a scholarship for college, without which he cannot afford to attend. So Richard enlists in the Army and is deployed to Vietnam, where he volunteers for difficult missions, one time stating, "I always wanted to be a hero." He sustains a serious hearing injury, causing tinnitus—constant loud ringing in the ears—which plagues him the rest of his life. Upon his release from service, the Veterans Administration (VA) denies his college benefits because he cannot hear people's speech (hearing aids did not help). Although he curses at the administrator that declines his education funding, he does not act violently—unlike another veteran, who throws a heavy metal trash can through the glass door of the VA's office. The contrast between Richard and this other veteran is further evidence that Richard is "before the law." As Silbey and Ewick (2000) state, those "before the law" are more apt to see their own problems as too mundane to seek legal remedies. For many, refusing to use the law is "an indication of moral strength and independence" (p. 51), as seems to be the case with Richard.

Instead of challenging the VA's decision to deny him college funding, he works his way through college, making friends with another student who has cerebral palsy, Art Honeyman (Michael Sheen). He also befriends a group of disabled Vietnam veterans, most of whom are still struggling to find employment four years later when Richard lands a well-paying job at an insurance corporation after graduating from college. Because he could read lips, he "passed" as hearing in the job interview. He never reveals his disability and becomes successful early on. And although he sympathizes with his friends who are unemployed veterans, he does not take action on their behalf.

His life takes a significant turn several months later, however, when he and Art, his friend with cerebral palsy, are denied service at a local diner one night. In a particularly poignant scene, the waitress snaps at Art, who has harmlessly flirted with her. "Don't you dare! You are the most disgusting, ugly thing I've ever seen! I thought people like you died at birth! How do you expect people to eat around you?" When they refuse to leave, they are arrested for violating an "ugly law" that made it illegal for any diseased, maimed, deformed, unsightly, or disgusting person to appear in public places.

As Richard narrates, "That horrible waitress made me embrace my past." He quits his corporate job and labors without pay to find jobs for his disabled friends. He is so successful that he obtains a position with a government agency that assists disabled veterans in finding employment. Richard works endlessly, straining the relationship with his girlfriend with whom he has been living for several years. Still, he continues to work at a feverish pace and, after a few years, gains the attention of the governor of Oregon, who appoints Richard to create a program to train employers to hire and work with disabled persons. The resultant book/manual *Tilting at Windmills* takes Richard a year to write and is so well received that it becomes a blueprint for every federal agency in the United States. He goes on to conduct training sessions with the CIA, the VA, NASA, and numerous other agencies and organizations. The whirlwind of constant travel and public speaking is too much for his girlfriend, who ends the relationship. But instead of slowing down, Richard becomes involved in campaigning for the Americans with Disabilities Act (ADA). Angry with the glacial speed at which the bill is progressing, he drinks too much and alienates his friends. His entire life becomes consumed with advancing the rights of the disabled.

After a series of misfortunes, Richard has an awakening about the meaning of life and reconnects with friends. The movie ends by informing viewers that the ADA was passed in 1990 and that *Windmills* became the blueprint for diversity training in hundreds of organizations in 23 countries.

Richard clearly personifies an individual whose perspective is "before the law." In spite of the discrimination he received by the VA, he does not use the legal system to remedy his problem. Instead, he combats the systemic discrimination he encounters by working assiduously on his own to overcome these barriers (e.g., working his way through college and learning how to read lips). It is only when he becomes outraged by the way his disabled friends are treated by society that he uses the law to change discriminatory practices against the disabled. As Silbey and Ewick (2000) found, individuals whose primary stance is "before the law" mobilize the law only to remedy situations that cause collective harm. For them, this is *the* legitimate use of law.

The second film, *A Civil Action*, displays an individual who could be categorized as "with the law"—someone who views law as a game and the legal system as the arena in which battles are waged. The protagonist, Jan Schlichtmann (John Travolta), is a private injury attorney who heads a small law firm with a reputation for settling cases before trial to secure the easy payout. This is immediately established in the opening scene. Jan wheels the bent and paralyzed body of a scrawny young male into a courtroom as his voice narrates:

It's like this. A dead plaintiff is rarely worth as much as a living, severely maimed plaintiff. However, if it's a long, agonizing death as opposed to a quick drowning or car wreck, the value can rise considerably. A dead adult in his twenties is worth less than one in his middle age; a dead woman is worth less than a dead man, a single man less than one who is married, blacks less than whites, poor less than rich. The perfect victim is a white male professional, 40 years old at the height of his earning power struck down in his prime. And the most imperfect—well, in the calculus of personal injury law . . . a dead child is worth the least of all.

(This statement prefaces the case that is to be Jan's undoing).

Jan loosens the collar of the mangled boy. One of the female jurors starts weeping, and another is fighting back tears. Opposing counsel scribbles "1.2 million" on a Post-it note and flashes it to Jan. He shakes his head almost imperceptibly. He offers a glass of water to the boy, who has great difficulty swallowing. The defense writes "1.5 million," but Jan again declines. Finally, just as the trial is to begin, the defense hastily scribbles "2 million," which he accepts.

This scene makes it clear that law is a game to Jan, in which costs and benefits are strictly assessed in terms of money. He is a graduate of Cornell Law, and his firm has made him and his colleagues rich. He wears Armani suits, drives a Porsche, and is listed in *Boston* magazine as one of the city's top 10 bachelors the year he drives to Woburn, a small industrial town 40 miles away, to turn down a case one of his colleagues foolishly agreed to take. The case is an "orphan"— one that has bounced from law firm to law firm. Several of Woburn's children have died from leukemia; the residents are certain that the water has been poisoned from toxic waste illegally dumped into the river. They only want the entities that have engaged in illegal dumping to acknowledge these actions and to clean up the areas they have polluted. As Jan cynically states to his partners when questioning why the case is an orphan, " . . . I can appreciate the theatrical value of several dead kids . . . I mean I like that, but that's not enough."

Driving back to Boston after turning down the Woburn families, he stops at the river and discovers that the probable polluters are owned by two large conglomerates—W. R. Grace and Beatrice. This immediately piques his interest, for the potential defendants have deep pockets (Beatrice owned several nationally recognizable food companies and had annual profits in the hundreds of millions of dollars). Little does he realize what the cost will be for going up against Beatrice, represented by one of the most prestigious law firms in Boston.

The differences in resources are not lost on Jan. As he walks into the law firm of Hale and Dorr (counsel for Beatrice), steeped in history with its Persian rugs, Harvard degrees on the wall, and an extensive law library, his voice narrates, "Lawsuits are war. It's as simple as that . . . don't be intimidated. It's what they want. Like all bullies—that's how they win." This statement, among others, reiterates that Jan is "with the law." He is preparing for battle and is not frightened by the larger size of his opponent.

As Galanter (1974) noted, the haves are individuals and organizations that can marshal a large array of resources for their legal cases, including access to legal teams with considerable expertise and skill. By virtue of their experience, size, and connections, these established legal firms—what Galanter calls "repeat players"—advantage the haves, who are able to afford the extraordinarily high cost of such representation. In contrast, the have-nots only have access to "one-shotters"—lawyers and small firms who seldom use the courts and are usually not as well educated or connected.

Moreover, differences between the haves and the have-nots are even larger when one considers the desired outcomes of a legal case. Repeat players are hired to ensure that the case in question does not result in changing existing laws, which might open the door for further lawsuits against a defendant in the future. Thus, they will work to offer a settlement before the case goes to court, where the odds of a plaintiff winning are two to one. In contrast, the have-nots have everything riding on the one case, so the particular outcome is extremely important. As Jan states in the movie, "The whole idea of lawsuits is to settle, and you do that by spending, spending, and spending until one side settles . . . Whoever comes to their senses first, loses." Clearly, the have-nots are disadvantaged, which is why fewer than 2 percent of lawsuits ever go to trial (Galanter, 2004). Their counsel settles before the costs become unmanageable.

From the very beginning of the court process, we see how much Jan is out of his league. Presiding over the case, Judge Walter J. Skinner (John Lithgow) greets the lead counsel for Beatrice, Jerome Facher (Robert Duvall), with a remark about the Boston Red Sox. It's apparent that the two have a social relationship. The judge also makes his disdain for Jan clear from the very beginning. At the first hearing, when Jan claims that the opposing counsel is trying to humiliate him, Judge Skinner replies derisively, "Mr. Schlichtmann— you are a personal injury lawyer, are you not? I think you can survive that! Sit down!"

Jan's firm hemorrhages money as the costs mount for soil and groundwater experts, excavation, and other expenses necessary to prove that the soil and groundwater around the plants are poisoned. With costs nearing $4 million, Jan and his partners have to mortgage their homes and sell their cars when their bank refuses to loan any more money. W. R. Grace offers $20 million and all parties agree to meet. Facher walks in very late to the meeting, apologizing: "Sorry I'm late. I was just given a chair at Harvard, of all things [chuckles] . . . from my students." Perturbed, Jan begins to explain that W. R. Grace and Beatrice had $634 million in profit the year prior and lays out his conditions for a settlement: $25 million for damages, $25 million for a research center, and $1.5 million for every family for 30 years—$320 million total. After a stunned silence, Facher stands up and, without a word, walks out, followed by the legal counsel for W. R. Grace. When Jan's baffled partners ask why he made such ridiculous demands, he explains that he wants justice for the families. It's no longer about the money.

Unfortunately for Jan, Judge Skinner appears to favor Facher, which is apparent in a scene that alludes to an ex parte meeting between the judge and the codefendants before Jan arrives. At this meeting, the judge sets a high bar for the jury to find that the codefendants were complicit in the poisoning of Hinkley's groundwater by presenting them with very convoluted and difficult questions. The film cuts to the hallway outside the courtroom where Jan and Facher are awaiting the verdict. Facher approaches Jan:

Facher: It's going to come down to people, as it always does.

Jan: They'll see the truth.

Facher: The truth? I thought we were talking about a court of law. Come on, you've been around long enough to know that the courtroom isn't the place to look for the truth . . . You disagree? Since when?

Jan: Eight kids are dead, Jerry.

Facher: Jan, Jan . . . Your suit fits you better than the sentimentality. That's not how you made all that money these years, is it? This stopped being about kids the moment you filed that complaint, the minute it entered the justice system.

Facher offers $20 million during a cynical soliloquy in which he warns Jan to take the offer because he is going to lose. He concludes, "Now if you're looking for the truth, Jan . . . look for it where it really is—at the bottom of a bottomless pit." Jan refuses the offer.

Beatrice is excused from the lawsuit, and in the end, W. R. Grace offers Jan $8 million to settle, but only after a humiliating encounter with the company's executive vice president and general counsel, Al Eustis (Sydney Pollack). Jan shows up late to the meeting at the Harvard Club in Boston, explaining that he has never been there before. Eustis replies, "I thought you went to Harvard!" When Jan explains that he graduated from Cornell Law School, Eustis exclaims condescendingly, "Cornell is a damn good school!" He asks Jan what he wants; Jan immediately begins talking about the case. Eustis interrupts—"There's an unspoken rule of the Harvard Club. Business is never transacted here. I meant, what do you want to drink?" He proceeds to discuss sailing—seemingly surprised that Jan doesn't sail—interminably. When they finally discuss the case back at the vice president's office, he challenges Jan:

Now let's be honest. It's not the money; it [a finding for the plaintiff] says we're guilty. And that says to every two-bit personal injury lawyer in Boston [a slight to Jan]—let's run up to Woburn to sign up every jerk with a head cold! It would be a shark effect!

He offers $8 million to settle. Jan replies, "I can't go to families with $8 million. I owe them more than that! I can't go to them empty-handed!"

Toward the end of the movie, Jan is shown sitting in an office bare of furniture and personnel; it is apparent he is living in his office. He calls Al Eustis and settles for the $8 million. When the firm presents the settlement to the Woburn families, it is revealed that the offer does not include cleanup of the toxic site or any admission of responsibility from W.R. Grace. The families are dismayed upon hearing the offer, and Anne Anderson, the original plaintiff who lost her nine-year-old son to leukemia, exclaims, "I wanted an apology from someone . . . and you said money is the apology. That's how they apologize—with their checkbooks. But you call this an apology? What kind of apology is that!" Jan remorsefully responds, "The only meaningful apology you're going to get is from me. [Sincerely] I'm sorry." Anderson retorts, "That's not good enough!" and walks out.

This scene demonstrates the differences between what the defendants—the haves—and the plaintiffs—the have-nots—want in terms of a settlement. As Galanter (1979) argues, the have-nots have everything riding on a particular case, and they want acknowledgment of wrongdoing from the defendants. In contrast, the primary concern of the haves is to deny responsibility, so they will offer monetary settlements small enough to avoid the appearance of culpability. Even if they have to frequently settle, it is still less costly than admitting guilt, which might lead to a change in laws that would hamper ongoing business practices and decrease profitability.

The film ends with a montage of Jan's subsequent life. In serious debt after losing his firm, his partners, and all of his assets, he winds up practicing law in a one-room, one-person operation located in a poor Hispanic neighborhood. He takes the bus to work and lives in a tiny apartment in another run-down area. Feeling guilty, he can't put the Woburn lawsuit behind him. He has an epiphany about the evidence and quickly discovers the "smoking gun." But rather than pursuing a lawsuit, Jan decides to turn over all the evidence to the Environmental Protection Agency (EPA), which ends up fining W.R. Grace and Beatrice $69.4 million to clean up the sites. At the end of the film, we learn that it took Jan several years to pay off the debts he accrued from pursuing the Woburn lawsuit. But even so, he went into environmental law. In the long run, although he pursues environmental justice, he is still someone "with the law," since he continues to use the legal arena, applying his hard-won knowledge to better the odds against larger opponents.

The third film, *Erin Brockovich*, portrays the story of a crass, brash, and beautiful woman in her late twenties with no legal training or college education who uses every trick to pursue justice for a desert community that had been exposed to poisonous chemicals. In this role, she could be described as an individual "up against the law." As noted by Silbey and Ewick (2000), individuals with this predominant orientation toward the law recognize they are have-nots and "use what they can to get what they need" (p. 53). They use a variety of ploys to "get attention that is being denied by those with greater power" (p. 54).

The movie quickly establishes that Erin (Julia Roberts) is a stressed-out single mother, angry with a world that has constantly disappointed her. The opening scene is of Erin, dressed in a low-cut top and tight skirt, in a job interview that is not going well. We learn that she has not attended college and has three young children from two failed marriages. Driving home after the disastrous interview, she is hit by a car that runs a red light. Sustaining a neck injury and $17,000 in medical bills, she hires an attorney to sue the other driver, an emergency room physician. Her counsel, Ed Masry (Albert Finney), heads a small firm in a working class suburb of Los Angeles. During the trial, it is clear that he has not given much time to the case. On the stand, wearing her characteristic revealing attire, Erin's character is impugned while her lawyer sits mum. Becoming increasingly agitated on cross-examination, she points at the defendant and shouts, "That asshole smashed in my fucking neck!"

Furious with Masry for losing the case, she yells at him as they leave the courtroom.

Erin:　　Open and fucking shut!

Masry:　　That's exactly the kind of language that lost the case.

Erin:　　Oh, please! It was over long before that! You told me I'd be set!

Masry:　　Okay, okay, let's try and settle down here!

Erin:　　Fuck settling down! I've got seventy-four dollars in the bank! I can't afford to settle down!

When Ed apologizes, she angrily asks before storming off, "Do they teach lawyers to apologize? Because you suck at it!"

Unable to find work after weeks of searching, Erin places dozens of phone calls to Masry's firm, none of which are returned. One day she shows up at his office and begins working, telling the other employees that Ed has hired her. When he confronts Erin to tell her he doesn't need another employee, she retorts, "Bullshit! If you had a full staff this office would return a client's damn phone call! I'm smart, I'm hardworking, I'll do anything and I'm not leaving here without a job!" With the whole staff watching, she leans over and murmurs to Ed, "Don't make be beg. If it doesn't work out, fire me. Please don't make me beg." Erin's behavior in this scene is typical of individuals "up against the law." When conventional means to gain attention do not work, as Silbey and Ewick (2000) note, they will often "masquerade" by "pretending to be someone they are not" (p. 54) or resort to making scenes, both of which Erin does.

Ed Masry puts her to work as a file clerk. One day, Ed asks her to open the file for a pro bono real estate case. The plaintiff, Donna Jensen (Marg Helgenberger), is claiming that Pacific Gas and Electric (PG&E), the major supplier of energy to Southern California at the time, is offering too little to buy her home in Hinkley, a small desert community in which a PG&E plant is located. Erin is intrigued that the file also contains medical records from the Jensens. She soon discovers that Donna and numerous other Hinkley residents are suffering abnormally high rates of lethal cancers, miscarriages, and other serious health problems. Investigating, she uses her sex appeal to obtain documentation that PG&E lied about the chemicals being leached into the groundwater. When an incredulous Ed asks how she accomplished this, Erin retorts, "They're called boobs, Ed." Again we see that Erin, as someone "up against the law," uses what she has to obtain what she needs.

Just as Richard Pimentel in *Music Within* and Jan Schlichtmann in *A Civil Action*, Erin works long hours investigating the case, which strains a fledgling relationship with a boyfriend as well as those with her children, for whom he "babysits." But she continues to work 12 to 16 hour days, trying to uncover more evidence against PG&E and to sign up plaintiffs. In one scene, we see Erin at the door of a Hinkley resident with all three children in tow. Her boyfriend, tired of her long absences, had finally moved out.

Erin's disdain of lawyers helps her win over potential plaintiffs, whom she has to obtain one by one, meeting with them in their homes or at work. When one woman asks Erin if she is a lawyer, she laughs. "Hell no! I hate lawyers! I just work for one." At another meeting in a family's living room, Ed and Erin are trying to sign up potential litigants. When Ed describes his fee, the room goes silent and heads shake. Erin quickly says, "Boy, do I know how you feel. The first time I heard that number, I said, you've got to be kidding me! Forty goddamned percent?"

"Erin—" Masry interjects.

She doesn't stop talking and her voice rises. "I'm the one that's injured and this joker [gesturing toward Ed] sits behind a desk all day and he wants to walk away with almost half of my reward?"

"Erin, can I—?"

She keeps talking over Masry. "But then, I ask him what he makes if I don't get anything." Ed continues, "And then I don't get anything, either."

"Plus," Erin states, "he's out all of the costs." The families then agree to the lawsuit.

She persuades Masry to sue PG&E, but they are quickly outmanned and outmaneuvered by the defendant's extensive in-house and contracted legal counsel. Ed quickly decides to partner with one of the best attorneys in environmental law, who suggests that the case be taken to binding arbitration. When Erin asks what that means, the attorney explains that it is a "test trial" with only a judge, whose decision is final and not subject to appeal. Erin objects, "They [the Hinkley plaintiffs] won't understand. They're expecting a trial!" The attorney condescendingly explains to her why binding arbitration is the best course of action.

This scene demonstrates how Erin is a person "up against the law." In spite of working for a law firm, she still is unfamiliar with the system. Motivated by a "strong sense of justice and right" (Silbey and Ewick 2000:54), she can identify with the clients' need to have their day in court and to be *heard* by those in power.

The court decides that 90 percent of Hinkley's residents have to be on the lawsuit against PG&E before it can proceed to arbitration. In a matter of weeks, Erin secures the agreement of over 600 families, moving her children to a Hinkley motel in order to work around the clock. She calls on her ex-boyfriend to help her with the kids while she is working, and they soon rekindle their romance. She also finds the "smoking gun" that topples the defense. PG&E settles for $333 million, making it, at the time, the largest direct action lawsuit that has ever occurred in the United States. Ed moves to a newer and much larger office suite in a downtown high-rise; Erin continues to work for him as an investigator. In the final scene, she is shown in her office calling a client. Into the phone she says, "Tell her that I'm not a lawyer. That may help!" This clearly establishes that Erin remains "up against the law" even as she continues to work within the system.

Common Themes

While each hero has a different orientation toward the law, they all risk and lose almost everything they value in their years-long dogged pursuit of justice. Richard Pimentel loses his girlfriend and, for a time, his closest friends. Jan Schlichtmann becomes bankrupt and loses his firm and partners. Erin Brockovich severely strains her relationship with her young children and loses her partner for several months. But their suffering pays off in the long run, for in all three films, justice—a sacred aspect of law—triumphs.

In the heroes' dramatic explanations of why they risked everything, the sacredness of law is also revealed. For example, in *Music Within*, Richard Pimentel asks Art, his friend with cerebral palsy, to read the complete draft of *Tilting at Windmills*. After reading the manuscript, Art asks, "Why did you want me to read this?" Richard starts apologizing, thinking it was mediocre. Art interrupts:

> You don't have a clue how good this is. You know what we cripples want besides getting laid? To be seen! When they look at me . . . do you know what they see? *Nothing!* I am ignored . . . How can you ignore this? [Gesturing to his deformed body] But, they ignore me . . . because I am *so* . . . disturbing . . . to their definition of human . . . that I make them feel! [Pounding his heart] I love that! What you've created will help them feel!

This is why Richard works so hard—simply, fairness for his friends and others, which means invoking legal rights to make it happen. As Richard tends to be "before the law," he does not use the legal system until there is an important enough reason to do so. The law is not being used to sue a dry cleaner; it is being used to make those who are different feel they have value. This humaneness also embodies a sacred aspect of law—that all people deserve to be treated fairly. *Music Within* reminds us of this basic principle and, in doing so, evokes hallowed aspects of law. Moreover, the dramatic emphasis on an individual's pain, such as Art's, draws viewers in emotionally, which makes us care that justice is realized.

The focus on individual suffering, however, masks the structural inequalities in American society that lead to unequal pain within the population to begin with. For example, disabled veterans are typically from lower and working class backgrounds. They are more likely to enlist in the armed services, since other opportunities such as higher education are not as accessible to them as they are to those from higher classes. And even in times of conscription, as during the Vietnam War, those with resources are often able to avoid armed conflict if they are drafted. Inequality also patterns numerous other forms of disability in the general population, such as cognitive impairment and mental illness, which are higher among those from the lower socioeconomic classes.

The ending scene in *A Civil Action* also references the scared aspects of law. A crew is shown moving dozens of boxes, composing the Woburn case file, out of storage. Then Jan is shown writing a letter to the EPA, to which he forwards the case, even though he has discovered the evidence to take down Beatrice. The film ends with Jan's voice-over of the letter's content:

> The appeals process takes longer, costs more, and its outcome is even less promising. Only five [appeals] in fifty will win. I have the evidence, but no longer the resources or the gambling spirit to appeal the decision. If you calculate success and failure, as I always have, in dollars and cents neatly divided into human suffering . . . the arithmetic says . . . I failed completely.

The background music swells while the impressive columns of a courthouse appear. Jan continues:

What it doesn't say is if I could somehow go back, knowing what I know now, knowing where I'd end up if I got involved with these people, knowing all the numbers, all
the odds, all the angles . . . I'd do it again.

Jan, someone "with the law," who cynically viewed law as a combative arena and had
little regard for anything other than the monetary value of his clients, is transformed
into a caring advocate. When his car breaks down on a bridge in the pouring rain, he
imagines what it must have been like for one of his clients, who had to stop on a bridge
to try to revive his leukemic son. His son died in his arms as cars went rushing past.

Just as Richard Pimentel is galvanized by the predicament of his disabled friends, Jan is
moved by the plight of the Woburn plaintiffs and the unfairness with which they have been
treated by much more powerful adversaries, which motivates his decision to level the playing field by turning the case over to the EPA. In his doing so, not only is the legitimacy of
law upheld, since he continues to trust in government (which delivers in the end), but so
is the legitimacy of the legal process. That is, viewers learn that the state provides alternative avenues to ensure that justice is served.

But just as in *Music Within,* a focus on the suffering of individuals conceals the structural inequalities that pattern environmental injustice. Businesses do not pollute the environments in which rich people live, which is largely explained by the fact that factories and
plants are not located in upper class communities. Those with fewer resources live closer,
then, to the entities that pollute the environment. But there are also numerous cases in
which companies deliberately dumped toxic chemicals in poor communities, knowing full
well that the residents lacked the power and financial resources to achieve legal redress. In
the case of *A Civil Action,* the individuals aware of the illegal dumping were too frightened to speak out because they or a family member worked for the companies owned by
W. R. Grace and Beatrice. Since there were few other employment opportunities in
Woburn, they did not want to lose their jobs. However, this focus on the individuals' plight
is never tied to the pervasive and growing economic inequality in the United States. The blue
collar workers in Woburn and across the country have fewer and fewer options as corporations move their manufacturing concerns to other countries. This puts increasing pressure
on workers to accept working conditions and practices that are unethical, if not illegal.

Just like *Music Within* and *A Civil Action, Erin Brockovich* is peppered with references to
the sacred aspects of law. It is clear from the beginning of the movie that Erin is "up against
the law." She does not trust lawyers or the legal system even after several months of working
for Masry. Erin's motivation from the beginning is to uncover the truth about the chemicals PG&E used in Hinkley. She simply wants justice for its families, a sentiment that only
grows as she learns of the extent of the harm caused by PG&E. As someone who has felt the
intrusive and inequitable aspects of law but was powerless to achieve fair outcomes, she
identifies with the working class families of Hinkley. Yet although Erin displays contempt
for lawyers and the legal system, her relentless drive on behalf of the Hinkley residents suggests she believes in fundamental and sacred principles of law, such as equality, fairness,
objectivity, and humaneness. As Silbey and Ewick (2000) argue, those "up against the law"
are not cynical about the law, but rather, recognizing their lack of power in a system that
favors those with more resources, they "undertake small deceits and other violations of
conventional and legal norms with a strong sense of justice and right" (p. 54).

Erin demonstrates her strong sense of right in one scene when she vehemently insists on proceeding to trial to achieve justice for the Hinkley families. Ed argues for settling.

Ed: This is serious!

Erin: And what, Ed? I'm not serious?

Ed: You're emotional! You're erratic! You say any goddamned thing that comes into your head. You make this personal, and it's not!

Erin: Not *personal!* That is my work, my sweat, my time away from my kids! If that's not personal, I don't know what is!

The profane aspects of law are highlighted in each of these three films, from the apathy of the federal government toward veterans wounded in the Vietnam War in *Music Within*, to the cynicism toward law displayed by the legal counsel on both sides of the case in *A Civil Action*, to the plaintiffs' deserved mistrust of both their own and the opposing counsel in *Erin Brockovich*. Yet the legitimacy of law is upheld because justice, however slow, is eventually realized.

We also see the heroes undergo significant changes that also ultimately uphold the legitimacy of the legal system. And each is humanized in the process. Richard Pimentel learns how to temper his anger and singular focus so that he no longer drives away those he loves. He also learns to work effectively with legal systems and other government agencies. Jan Schlichtmann loses his entrepreneurial focus on potential cases and becomes truly concerned and involved with the problems of his clients, wanting to achieve justice for them rather than just a large settlement. Erin Brockovich changes her manners and attire, becoming less brash and dressing more conservatively, but she never loses her drive to achieve justice for those who cannot afford to pursue it. All together, the heroes uphold the legitimacy of the legal system because they continue to use it, and they become better people along the way.

Conclusion

While viewers may find satisfaction that the underdogs in these films obtain justice, the focus on the individual obfuscates the social class bias inherent in the American legal system. For example, we see that many of Richard Pimentel's disabled friends were able to gain viable employment and eventually became somewhat protected from discrimination in the employment sector. The problem of disabled veterans, a national concern, however, is never linked to the disproportionate number of soldiers that come from the lower and working classes. The plaintiffs in both *A Civil Action* and *Erin Brockovich* are clearly working class, but it is never mentioned that when companies pollute, they do so in communities in which residents lack resources to resist these actions. Moreover, viewers do not learn anything about the extent of toxic dumping in the United States, or the number of lawsuits filed in this area or their outcomes. These kinds of omissions conceal the structural conditions in the United States that underlie inequities in the law and legal system.

In spite of the profane aspects of the legal system depicted in the films described, the restoration of justice achieved in each upholds the sacred nature of law. The resolution of justice is common to all genres of dramatic entertainment, as is the focus on heroism and individual suffering. While this makes for dramatic entertainment, it conceals both the singularity of successful outcomes by the have-nots against the haves as well as the larger structural inequalities underlying biases in the legal system.

References

Durkheim, E. [1912] 2001. *The Elementary Forms of Religious Life.* Oxford, England: Oxford University Press.

Galanter, M. 1974. "Why the 'Haves' Come Out Ahead: Speculation on the Limits of the Legal Change." *Law & Society Review 9*(1):95–160.

Galanter, M. 2004. "The Vanishing Trial: An Examination of Trials and Related Matters in Federal and State Courts." *Journal of Empirical Legal Studies* 1(3):459–570.

Kafka, F. 1937. *The Trial.* New York: A. A. Knopf.

Maguire, K., ed. 2003. *Sourcebook of Criminal Justice Statistics.* Retrieved August 13, 2011 (http://www.albany.edu/sourcebook).

Sherman, L. W. 2002. "Trust and Confidence in Criminal Justice." *National Institute of Justice Journal* 248:22–31.

Silbey, S. S. and P. Ewick. 2000. "The Rule of Law—Sacred and Profane." *Society,* September/October, pp. 49–56.

Sparks, R. 1992. *Television and the Drama of Crime.* Buckingham, England: Open University Press.

Surette, R. 2007. *Media, Crime and Criminal Justice.* 3rd ed. Belmont, CA: Thompson Wadsworth.

Outtake

Corporate Crime and *The Informant!*

Mike Maume

In one of the largest criminal antitrust cases in history, the Archer Daniels Midland (ADM) corporation was fined $100 million for its role in fixing prices on two of its agricultural products with industry competitors. The U.S. Department of Justice was able to successfully prosecute the case based on the role ADM vice president Mark Whitacre played in the investigation. The film *The Informant!* (2006), based on real events depicted in the book by *New York Times* reporter Kurt Eichenwald (2000), follows Whitacre's story as a corporate executive who turns whistle-blower and eventually is sent to prison for embezzling $9.5 million from his own company.

The first and second acts of the film portray Whitacre as an enthusiastic and quirky charac-ter who truly believes that his cooperation with the FBI as an informant against his fellow executives will lead to his eventual promotion to CEO. Whitacre identifies himself as an "orga-nization man" who fully expects to be employed at ADM for life, despite his actions to bring down the company's top brass (Whyte 1956). Ultimately, Whitacre's lies are revealed as the case is built against ADM and in turn against Whitacre himself. Unlike other recent portrayals of corporate crime (e.g., *The Insider, Erin Brockovich, Wall Street, Money Never Sleeps*), the film's central character turns out to be more of an antihero than a hero.

Originally coined by Edwin Sutherland, the phrase *white collar crime* involves criminal acts perpetrated in the course of legitimate business, typically by respectable persons in positions of trust (Friedrichs 2010). Outside this context, of course, it is rare to use the word "respectable" in describing individuals involved in criminal behavior, and in fact sociologists and criminolo-gists who study white collar crime have noted the success with which white collar criminals avoid the label *criminal*. Film viewers will note that the only characters to refer to the actions of ADM and Whitacre as crimes are the FBI agents and government lawyers assigned to the case. The lighthearted tone of the film reinforces the farcical, rather than sinister, nature of the cor-porate executives' actions, perhaps to underscore the idea that no one at ADM seemed to know or be concerned about the criminal culture that developed at the company or the extent of the frauds committed. In fact, by the end of the film, even Whitacre doesn't seem to recall the amount of money stolen while he was employed at ADM.

As a tool for understanding white collar crime, *The Informant!* has two major advantages. First, because of the often secretive nature of big business, one of the only ways that we have learned about the nature and extent of corporate misbehavior is through the cooperation and stories shared by whistleblowers and informants. For example, in the Enron–Arthur Andersen debacle, portrayed in the documentary *Enron: The Smartest Guys in the Room*, a combination of whistleblowing (company executive Sherron Watkins) and investigative reporting helped reveal the details of the fraud and conspiracy committed by the top executives of the company. In *All the President's Men,* an insider in the administration (using the moniker "Deep Throat") aids the investigation by Bob Woodward of the *Washington Post*. Both sociological case studies and investigative journalism share this approach to obtaining knowledge of corporate crime from an insider's perspective (Simpson and Piquero 2001). As Geis (2007:106) points out, there is an unfortunate "absence of significant field research on corporate crime that might shed light on important, but unresolved matters [in understanding corporate crime]."

Second, Whitacre himself is a far cry from the violent, predatory criminals portrayed in films depicting street crime or drug trafficking. While Whitacre has a Ph.D. in biochemistry, he shows very little savvy with regard to avoiding the authorities. In that sense, his story is similar to those of opportunistic thieves such as embezzlers and fraudsters who commit their criminal behavior based on a pressing financial situation rather than a desire to initiate a criminal career. However, given his position of trust within the company, Whitacre was able to embezzle and conceal much more than a low- or mid-level employee could.

Estimates of annual losses due to street crime (e.g., robbery, burglary) make up a small fraction of the losses attributed to corporate fraud, which vary between $60 and $300 billion per year. Estimates of corporate crime losses vary considerably because, unlike crimes such as homicide and robbery, there is no comprehensive nationwide reporting system for losses due to fraud, corporate criminal indictments, or fines.

References

Eichenwald, K. 2000. *The Informant.* New York: Broadway Books.

Friedrichs, D. O. 2010. *Trusted Criminals.* 4th ed. Belmont, CA: Wadsworth.

Geis, G. 2007. *White-Collar and Corporate Crime.* Upper Saddle River, NJ: Prentice Hall.

Simpson, S. S. and N. L. Piquero. 2001. "The Archer Daniels Midland Antitrust Case Study of 1996: A Case Study." Pp. 175–194 in *Contemporary Issues in Criminal Justice: Essays in Honor of Gilbert Geis,* edited by H.N. Pontell and D. Shichor. Upper Saddle River, NJ: Prentice Hall.

Whyte, William H. (1956). *The Organization Man.* New York: Simon & Schuster.

CHAPTER 8

Sociology and the Life Course

G: Seventy-five years. That's how much time you get if you're lucky. Seventy-five years. Seventy-five winters, seventy-five springtimes, seventy-five summers, and seventy-five autumns. When you look at it like that, it's not a lot of time, is it? Don't waste them. Get your head out of the rat race and forget about the superficial things that preoccupy your existence and get back to what's important now.

—*Holy Man* (1998)

Benjamin   It has no time limit. You can start whenever you want. You can change or stay
Button: the same; there are no rules to this thing. We can make the best of it or the worst of it. I hope you make the best of it. I hope you see things that startle you. I hope you feel things that you never felt before. I hope you meet people with a different point of view. I hope you live a life you're proud of. And if you find you're not, I hope you have the strength to start all over again.

—*The Curious Case of Benjamin Button* (2008)

Dean: Yet even in certain defeat, the courageous Jonathan Trager secretly clung to the belief that life is not merely a series of meaningless accidents or coincidences. Rather it's a tapestry of events that culminate in an exquisite, sublime plan.

—*Serendipity* (2001)

T he life course perspective is used by sociologists to study human lives over time; life course refers to the sequence of activities and events from birth to death (Mayer 2009:413). From a life course perspective, individual lives take place in the context of social institutions within which people hold particular statuses and roles. The life course includes short-term transitions, such as graduating from school or retiring at the end of employment. These transitions are embedded in age-graded trajectories, such as being a student or marrying and having children. Four factors or themes are central to the life course approach: "the interplay of human lives and historical times, the timing of lives, linked or interdependent lives, and human agency in choice making" (Elder 1994:5).

The readings in this chapter address three different stages in the life course and what can be learned about age-graded events and experiences through feature films. In the first reading, Carmen Lugo-Lugo and Mary Bloodsworth-Lugo look at four animated films for children: *The Road to El Dorado*, *Shark Tale*, *Dinosaur*, and *Toy Story*. According to the authors, films made and marketed for children are influential agents of socialization that, in addition to portraying the ideals of conquering fears, working hard, and contributing to team effort, "guide U.S. children through the complexities of highly racialized and sexualized scenarios, normalizing certain dynamics and rendering others invisible in the process."

Taken together, these films contain stereotyped representations of race, ethnicity, gender, and sexuality. These representations resonate with children "because they simultaneously reinforce both contemporary and historical notions of race, gender, and sexuality." For example, in *El Dorado* the Spanish conquest of the "Americas" is presented as a story not of colonization, but of rescue of indigenous people by "good" Europeans (in contrast with the "evil" Cortés and high priest). In *Shark Tale*, the characters are identified in terms of race and ethnicity with stereotypical markers, such as accent, accessories (e.g., "bling" for Oscar), and ability/talent (Oscar can't sing reggae; Sykes can't learn the complicated "fin shake" from Oscar). Across all four films, characters in the form of toys, fish, dinosaurs, and people enact norms of heterosexuality through dialogue, expression, and action.

In the second reading, Jeanne Holcomb explores a significant turning point in the life course: becoming a parent. In contemporary society the normative pathway to parenthood is courtship, love, and marriage in early adulthood. Holcomb focuses on alternative paths to motherhood using the films *Baby Mama*, *The Switch*, *Juno*, and *Knocked Up*. All of the movies feature unmarried motherhood, including a teenage mother in *Juno* and women of "advanced maternal age" (35 years or older) in the other three films. Despite the theme of nonnormative paths to motherhood in the films, Holcomb points out that social class, race, and heteronormativity are woven throughout the stories and that the films come to a close with traditional "happy endings."

In the third reading, Neal King uses three films, *About Schmidt*, *Gran Torino*, and (the animated) *Up*, to explore the later stage of life for white men who have exited long-term statuses (they are retired and have recently been widowed). As King explains, the three main characters "suffer the isolation created by men's typical approaches to their jobs and family lives." These typical approaches are the product of the social construction of masculinity that involves work as a primary source of identity and narrow networks of social support highly dependent on the emotional labor of wives. Loss of these two sources of identity and belonging, as found in the research literature and these three films, results in isolation, depression, and potential health problems.

In an interesting twist, these Hollywood stories of old age for men involve redemption from their separation and loneliness in the form of a mentoring relationship with a young male character. In *Up* and *Gran Torino*, these relationships become paramount to Carl and Walt, respectively. Both men risk life and limb on behalf of the young men, redeeming themselves at the same time that they pass on important lessons about manhood. Carl's life takes a turn for the better as he returns home and continues his friendship with Russell;

Walt sacrifices his life to put gang members who threaten his friend Thao and his family behind bars. In *About Schmidt*, Warren finds a young friend in the form of a foster child in Africa. He ends up alone, but feeling that he has been appreciated for his efforts when he receives a "thank you" drawing from his foster child.

The life course provides a way of studying human lives in the context of time and relationships, structure, and process. Movies provide the stories of people situated in time and place at the intersections of race, class, gender, sexuality, and age. Applying the life course to these stories allows us to understand how history, timing, social networks and relationships, and agency shape trajectories and transitions in lives over time.

References

Elder, G. H., Jr. 1994. "Time, Human Agency, and Social Change: Perspectives on the Life Course." *Social Psychology Quarterly* 57:4–15.

Mayer, K. U. 2009. "New Directions in Life Course Research." *Annual Review of Sociology* 35:413–33.

Children's Films as Agents of Socialization

The last decade or so has witnessed a proliferation of successful animated films, the majority of which have been made by Disney, Disney and Pixar, and DreamWorks.[2] Full of fantastic computer-generated images and special effects, the characters in these films depart from the simpler, two-dimensional designs in earlier (mostly Disney) films and provide viewers with more sophisticated, three-dimensional, emotion-displaying characters. Technological advances notwithstanding, these films, on a social level, offer viewers all-too-familiar and ordinary lessons wrapped in extraordinary and sometimes-magical plots. In a basic sense, the narratives embedded within these recent stories provide children (their primary target audience), and even adults, with audio-visual reinforcement of ideologies concerning gender roles, the importance of conquering one's fears, the rewards of hard work, or the benefits of team effort, making these stories powerful agents of socialization. Elizabeth Freeman (2005) actually describes these films as "'portable professors' of a sort, offering diagnoses of culture for adults even as they enculturate children" (p. 85).

These successful animated films also offer lessons about accepting ourselves for who we are, the wonders of pulling ourselves up by our own bootstraps, and the idea that love conquers all—even seemingly insurmountable class differences, ill-intentioned acts, and evil characters. Similarly, the narratives teach very specific messages regarding clear-cut dichotomies such as good and evil; namely, that good and evil are mutually exclusive, self-contained monoliths and that the good will always be good whereas the evil will always be evil. Henry Giroux (1999) explains this best when he claims that with these films, the corporations involved (e.g., Disney, Pixar, and DreamWorks) are "regulating culture," and thus, profoundly influencing "children's culture and their everyday lives" (p. 2). The messages embedded within these films resonate with children and are reiterated through other sources, while they also resound with parents who have received the same lessons since childhood. As Helaine Silverman (2002) conveys, "As a quintessential form of American public culture, animated movies may be examined as a site where collective social understandings are created and in which the politics of signification are engaged" (p. 299). According to Giroux (1999), these films are part of a popular culture that "is the primary way in which youth learn about themselves, their relationship to others, and the larger world" (p. 2). He goes on to argue that media culture has become a substantial, if not the primary educational force in regulating the meanings, values, and tastes that set the norms, that offer up and legitimate particular subject positions—what it means to claim an identity as male, female, white, black, citizen, noncitizen (pp. 2–3).

Giroux (1999) insists that "entertainment is always an educational force" (p. 28). Within this "edutainment," "animated films operate . . . as the new teaching machines" and "they possess at least as much cultural authority and legitimacy for teaching roles, values, and ideals as more traditional sites of learning" (p. 84).

In this article, we argue that, as suggested by Giroux, animated films offer children intricate teachings about race and sexuality. Thus, as socializing agents or "teaching machines," these films guide U.S. children through the complexities of highly racialized and sexualized scenarios, normalizing certain dynamics and rendering others invisible in the process. We fundamentally disagree with Bell, Haas, and Sells (1995), who argue that "Disney's trademarked innocence operates on a systematic sanitation of violence, sexuality, and political struggle concomitant with an erasure or repression of difference" (p. 7). To the contrary, these films precisely teach children how to maneuver within the general terrain of "race" and "sexuality," and they highlight quite specific differences. It is our contention that films, in their role as agents of socialization and "portable professors," provide children with the necessary tools to reinforce expectations about normalized racial and sexual dynamics. To illustrate our points, we will focus on four specific films: *The Road to El Dorado* (Bibo Bergeron, Will Finn, Don Paul, David Silverman and Jeffrey Katzenberg, 2000), *Shark Tale* (Bibo Bergeron, Vicky Jensen and Rob Letterman, 2004), *Dinosaur* (Eric Leighton and Ralph Zondag, 2000), and *Toy Story* (John Lasseter, 1995). We could discuss race and sexuality as intersecting markers within the context of each film, but in the interest of clarity, we will discuss each category separately here.

Con Men and Fish: Racialized Representations and Animated Films

In her book, *Understanding Disney*, Janet Wasko (2001) lists the various elements found in any "classic" Disney narrative: style, story, characters, and themes/values, along with the formulaic components of each. We would like to focus on her description of characters, for it is through the characters that "we" piece together the story, learn the themes/values, and get a feel for the film's style. According to Wasko, Disney anthropomorphizes animal characters, presents formulaic heroes, heroines, and villains, and provides stereotypical representations of gender and ethnicity. We can offer two points in relation to Wasko's basic claims. First, Wasko's description of Disney's animated characters can likewise be extended to the animated characters in films made by DreamWorks and Pixar (as we will discuss in this article);[3] and second, her claim regarding stereotypical representations can be expanded in the following way: Even though animals (and other nonhuman characters) are anthropomorphized in children's animated films, these films also, unfailingly, racialize nonhuman characters in the process. That is to say, these characters are not simply transformed into some generic "human" (for there are no generic humans); rather, they are inscribed, for example, as White "humans," Black "humans," Asian "humans," or Latino "humans." Thus, we maintain that animal and other nonhuman characters undergo a kind of racialized anthropomorphism within animated films. Our discussion of *Shark Tale*, below, will illustrate this point.

Similarly, although human characters in animated films still "play" formulaic and stereotypical roles and adhere to strict dichotomies, the scope of these roles and the shape of these dichotomies seem to be broadening in recent films, adapting to contemporary definitions. We will use *The Road to El Dorado* to illustrate this point. Consequently, we also argue that while many "classic" animated films (often featuring human characters) tend to adhere to strict dichotomies (good/evil, hero/villain, etc.), there are also recent notable examples (generally featuring anthropomorphized characters) that create more nuanced constructions of these binaries. That is to say, while we still see films that enact clear sets of binaries and simultaneously racialize characters in accord with these roles, we are also witnessing very recent films that complicate classic structures. The two films discussed in this section provide examples of each sort of film.

Stereotypes and Dichotomies in *The Road to El Dorado*

We begin our discussion with a film that conforms to classic structures and dichotomies: DreamWorks' *The Road to El Dorado*. Adding to Wasko's discussion of stereotypical representations of race and ethnicity in children's films, and—we add—sexuality, we argue that stereotypical representations must be placed within a broader, more complicated historical context within which gendered, racialized, and sexualized dynamics take place. In other words, stereotyped representations are only relevant because they simultaneously reinforce both contemporary and historical notions of race, gender, and sexuality.[4] Let us take, for instance, representations of race in *The Road to El Dorado*. Set during "the Conquest" of the Americas, *The Road to El Dorado* begins in Spain and moves to a mysterious location in what is now known as Mexico. The film begins with Hernán Cortés delivering a speech just prior to his departure for "the New World," in which he boasts, "We sail to conquer another world, for Spain, for glory." Thus, in a superficial way, the film subtly points to the greed-induced injustices of the Spanish Conquest; however, when examined more closely, *The Road to El Dorado* tells a highly racialized and dichotomized story involving Spaniards and indigenous peoples in the Americas. This story is accomplished by romanticizing the Indigenous as childlike and innocent beings (always smiling, rarely speaking, and mostly in awe) who are positioned as being in need of rescue. This "rescue" comes in the form of Tulio and Miguel—the "good" kind of Europeans (in contrast to Cortés, the "bad" kind).

In the case of *The Road to El Dorado*, the evil characters are hopelessly evil (i.e., Cortés and the High Priest) and the good characters are ultimately good (i.e., Tulio/Miguel and the Chief). While Tulio and Miguel (described by DreamWorks as "a pair of two-wit con men") may sometimes lack good judgment, they are—in the end—good, decent people (as they *must* be given their place within the binary structure). Hernán Cortés, in his evil incarnation, becomes the damnation of the natives, while Tulio and Miguel discover their role as saviors of the doomed indigenous society.

The most interesting feature of Tulio's and Miguel's characters is that, mistaken as gods, they are able to become heroes and save the indigenous society from its own heartless high priest. In fact, in his role as one of the gods, and responding to the high priest's request for a human sacrifice, Miguel gives the natives their first commandment: "There will be no sacrifices, not now, not ever." In the film, El Dorado (the place) becomes a site of racial dynamics where the indigenous population not only dances, drinks, and is happily festive but also partakes in "uncivilized" practices such as human sacrifice. It is also in El Dorado

Photo 8.1   Conmen turned savior in *Road to El Dorado*. The good-hearted
Miguel frolics with the child-like "natives" of El Dorado.

that Spaniards, Tulio and Miguel (with their puzzling British accents), manage to save the place, even after Miguel informs the Chief that the Indigenous will not be able to fight off Cortés and his men who are rapidly approaching the city. Despite this claim, Tulio is able to arrive at a solution to save the city which entails blocking its only entrance, thus preventing Cortés (or anyone else) from ever finding the city. In turn, its residents are isolated from other human contact forever, thus repositioning them as perpetually innocent and child-like peoples in need of protection. While carrying out the plan, both "con men" renounce the gold they had planned to take, signaling a change of heart concerning their own greed and revealing that in the end—and different from Cortés—they *do* possess kind hearts. Nonetheless, given that Tulio and Miguel were "con men" who arrived at and stayed in El Dorado through deceptive actions, their portrayal as ultimately kind-hearted heroes broadens any former (and pure) construction of "the hero." Moreover, dichotomies notwithstanding in *The Road to El Dorado,* Europeans become both the damnation and the salvation of the indigenous characters.

Racialized Anthropomorphism in *Shark Tale*

We find an excellent example of racialized anthropomorphism in the DreamWorks film *Shark Tale,* in which Oscar, described by DreamWorks (2005) as "a little hustler fish," speaks in a clearly "Black" American accent and lives in the ghetto part (South side) of the reef. His blackness is found not only in his accent and place of residence but also in his mannerisms, behavior, and jewelry (i.e., "bling"), which are highly racialized signifiers. For instance, in one scene, Oscar tries to "hustle his way" out of a situation with his boss Sykes, a puffer fish. Oscar tries to connect with Sykes by performing a complicated "fin shake," but Sykes is unable to follow the steps. After a few attempts, Oscar gives up and says, "Don't sweat it, a lot of white fish can't do it." For children who are learning the intricacies of race (as a social signifier) and race relations, labeling Sykes as a "White fish" (and therefore, Oscar as a "Black fish") validates other societal messages. Children learn that our culture is strictly raced and racialized, since even fish can be Black *or* White.

In fact, Oscar and Sykes are not the only fish racialized in *Shark Tale.* We can also find Ernie and Bernie (two Rastafarian jellyfish, complete with Jamaican accents) who work for Sykes, Lino (an Italian American–accented Mob shark and master of the reef), and Mrs. García (an overweight, middle-aged, single, Mexican-accented, female fish, with permanent rollers in her hair) who also lives in the ghetto. These are just a few examples. However, we can also locate nuances in the ways that these characters are racialized. For instance, not only can we see Oscar being racialized as Black, but we also can see an ethnicization of race whereby Oscar is constructed as a Black *American.* This ethnicization is accomplished through his juxtaposition to Ernie and Bernie, with whom he interacts. In one scene, for example, Oscar attempts to sing reggae, to which Ernie retorts, "Don't like the way you sing that song, man." In this way, Oscar is reinscribed as Black, but this reinscription is promoted through contrasting Oscar, as Black American, with Ernie and Bernie, as Black *Jamaican* (where to be Jamaican means to be accepted by Rastafarian jellyfish). In addition, Sykes is actually finally able to perform the fin shake, once Oscar becomes a celebrity and Sykes becomes his manager. With Oscar's celebrity and Sykes' newfound investment, we see Sykes now able to do the fin shake and to speak "Black lingo." We could argue that Sykes' "Black performance" parallels that of White rap producers and others who "learn the lingo" to have better rapport with their "investments." In *Shark Tale,* furthermore, we witness ethnicization in "White," for Lino is not only racialized as White but also ethnicized as Italian by way of very specific signifiers. For instance, Lenny (his son) tells Oscar that Lino is the Godfather, Lino speaks with an accent usually associated with New York Italians, and Frankie (Lino's other son) receives a Catholic burial, performed in Latin, after he dies. While almost silly, these stereotypes serve as important signifiers of a particular *kind* of whiteness within the United States—the whiteness of a group that, until recently, was *not* actually seen as White.

Dinosaurs and Toys: Straightness, Heterosexism, and Animated Films

A few years ago, Tinky Winky (of the children's television show *Teletubbies*) was rendered a "homosexual" by Jerry Falwell. Falwell—a professed straight man—claimed to know the status of Tinky Winky vis-à-vis "his" sexuality. Even though Tinky Winky never said "I am gay," Falwell thought that Tinky Winky's color (purple) and his accessories (his purse) said "I am gay" very clearly; Tinky Winky need not utter the words. It is worth noting, in this case, that Falwell's assessment of Tinky Winky also followed a curious path: He first assigned Tinky Winky a sex (male), then assessed that sex (by reading the color and the accessory as "inappropriate" gender attributions for a male), and then conflated gender and sexuality (by labeling Tinky Winky a "homosexual" on the basis of these "inappropriate" gendered characteristics). In addition, it could be that Tinky Winky's triangle headpiece clinched the "homosexual" assessment for Falwell.

At the time of the Falwell incident, some members of the gay and lesbian community argued that cartoon characters *do not have* sexualities; hence, in musing over children's television programming, Falwell had "simply gone too far." This was a case, some gay men and lesbians argued, of homophobia run rampant. However, it seems undeniable that cartoon characters—especially in Disney, Pixar, and DreamWorks productions—certainly do have sexualities, which is to say, they have *hetero*sexualities. Despite a tenuous relevance, or an outright irrelevance, to the storylines, "heterosexuality" (in the form of heterosexual relationships or heterosexually oriented banter) pervades most films for children. Indeed, if there is a purpose to these seemingly pointless scenes, the aim could be taken to be the "indoctrination" of children into "the heterosexual lifestyle."

In the films discussed above, *The Road to El Dorado* and *Shark Tale*, we can easily find examples of heterosexual relationships and banter. In *The Road to El Dorado,* Tulio, who has warned Miguel regarding the dangers that Chel (the "native") could bring, ends up falling for her himself. The fact that it is Tulio, and not Miguel, who cannot resist the indigenous woman only underscores her danger, for Tulio is represented as the more level-headed member of the con men pairing. On first seeing Chel, after all, it is Miguel who states, "Maybe we should call this place 'Chel Dorado,'" while uttering sounds of sexual excitement. The introduction of Chel into the narrative occurs after a series of scenes in which the sexuality of the two main characters could be construed as unclear; for example, after the two men have recited to each other that they have made each other's lives more adventurous and rich (on thinking that death was imminent) and after the two men have bathed naked together (on arriving in "the New World"). Chel clarifies for the audience that these two men are, indeed, sexually "normal." Of course, this "normalcy"—played out in the relationship between Chel and the two Spaniards—also tells the audience that the indigenous woman is available for the White man's choosing and that, like El Dorado itself, no "normal" man could resist her temptation (leading to her/its conquest and possession).

In *Shark Tale,* the role of "woman as temptation and trouble" is played by Lola, who is positioned as a danger to Oscar's potential wealth as he places a "sure bet" on Lucky Day to win the ensuing seahorse race. As Oscar turns around and sees Lola seductively entering the room, a song unleashes the lyrics, "Better watch out, she'll take your cash. She's a gold digger." Of course, in *The Road to El Dorado*, Chel's initial interest in Tulio and Miguel also centers on the "escape" that they might offer, and she makes a deal with them to gain a share of their gold. However, in *Shark Tale*, the "type of woman" represented by Lola is also contrasted with two other sorts of women—the kind of woman with whom a man should eventually settle down (Angie), and the kind of woman that no "normal" man could find alluring (Mrs. García). Angie, unlike Lola and unbeknownst to Oscar, loved Oscar before his newfound life of fame and fortune. Oscar initially overlooks her affection, referring to her simply as his "best friend." But it is precisely one's best friend (as long as that best friend is of the "opposite" sex) who offers a man long-term possibilities, unlike the seductress who will leave him on a whim. Or, perhaps worse still, it is the "Lola type of woman" who will seek revenge if he leaves her first. Lola herself states that the only thing she likes better than money is revenge.

However, it is not Oscar, the film's main character, who is in the opening scene of *Shark Tale*. Rather, it is Lenny—the son of Lino, the "Don" of the reef. As a worm struggles on a fishing hook, eyeing Lenny swimming closer and closer (with the theme to *Jaws* playing), the audience senses the danger. But Lenny does the unexpected. Instead of gobbling down the worm, he releases it from the hook and lets it swim free. As we learn, the thought of eating any of this "meaty" sea life makes Lenny sick. Lenny eventually confides in Oscar, in a discussion that evokes a narrative of self-outing, that he is a vegetarian. However, his family has known for some time that something is "odd" with Lenny—he is not a "normal" shark. As Lino says to Lenny, "You. I'm hearing things. When you look weak, I look weak," and "Son, you're going to learn to be a shark whether you like it or not." Thus, being a "normal" shark is equated with being a shark as such, and being a shark means being a vicious master of the reef (and not a compassionate consumer of kelp). Lenny's brother, Frankie, likewise tells Lenny, "If you want to make Dad happy, you've got to kill something. You've got to be a shark."

While the issue of Lenny's sexuality is left open in *Shark Tale*, parallels between stereotypical representations of gay men and characteristics displayed by Lenny are played on throughout the film. Not only does Lenny "come out" to Oscar (as vegetarian), but he also dresses both as a cowboy and as a dolphin at one point in the film ("Sebastian, the Whale-Washing Dolphin"). This "dress up" evokes both the fondness for uniformed men within gay male culture (the most famous example being the array of figures represented by Village People) as well as the more general relationship between gay men and drag. When Lino sees Lenny dressed in this get-up, he asks, "What are you wearing? What *is* that? Do you have any idea how this looks?" Of course, while Oscar makes a plea for Lino's acceptance of Lenny at the end of the film, asking, "Why can't you love him as he is?" it is precisely Oscar who has subtly rejected Lenny at an earlier point in the film, stating the number one rule for friendship as "none of that snuggly buggly stuff. Whatever that was." Oscar thereby distances himself from any "abnormal" closeness between the two male characters (or two men in general) and designates such closeness as "icky." In fact, such intimacy is to be so desperately avoided that this particular rule for friendship is cited before Rule 2—the rule directly related to Oscar's self-preservation: "If you ever have a change of heart [about being a vegetarian], please don't gobble me down." With his rules for friendship, Oscar reconstitutes himself as the heterosexual man—the man who may have other men as friends (as do Tulio and Miguel), but whose sexual desires are firmly positioned where they *should* be.

A point of connection between the overall representations of sexuality in both *The Road to El Dorado* and *Shark Tale* involves the incorporation of (hetero)sexuality into the narratives of the films when the basic messages could have been served without it. In this respect, children's films do not function very differently from adult-centered Hollywood films which find a way to work a (heterosexual) love story into almost any plot. But unlike adults, whose sexualities have already been soundly established (it would appear), children are still learning the societal lessons of (hetero)sexuality—that heterosexuality is the "normal" sexuality and the desired outcome for "any healthy child." Thus, the seemingly unnecessary incorporation of heterosexuality into the narratives of children's films can actually be seen to serve a function. That is, it reiterates lessons that children receive elsewhere—that boys like girls and girls like boys, and men like women and women like men, even when the boys/men and girls/women are, for example, fish . . . or dinosaurs or toys.

(Needless) Heterosexuality in *Dinosaur*

In the film *Dinosaur*, the main character, Aladar, becomes orphaned when a bird picks up his egg and drops it far from Aladar's home. Aladar (a dinosaur) is subsequently adopted and raised by a clan of lemurs. While this unusual situation could, and perhaps does, offer lessons about "alternative families" or "families of choice," this message is fundamentally undermined given its repositioning within a framework of normative heterosexuality. This framework renders procreation as the only legitimate reason for sexual activity and the nuclear family as sexuality's only "natural" outcome. For instance, near the beginning of the film, a scene with questionable relevance to the plot unfolds (the plot being dinosaurs making their way to the "nesting grounds" after meteors strike and destroy much of the Earth), when male-female pairs of lemurs are shown "doing the wild thing." While an argument could be made for the relevance of this scene (i.e., it suggests the means of survival for a species, thereby foreshadowing the meteor scene which renders extinction possible), any such significance to this scene—in our view—is undermined by a blatant depiction of lemurs "doing it."

To prepare for the mating ritual, we see Zini (Aladar's "brother") practicing his pickup lines and remarking, "Girl, I'm the professor of love. And school's in session," and "Hey, sweetie. If you'll be my bride, I'll groom ya." At the same time, we hear the girl and boy lemurs being taught their separate mating lessons. The girls are told to be subtle with their intentions and to "keep the boys guessing." Of the boy who has successfully mated in the past, we hear the praise, "He put the 'prime' in primate." And, as the boys arrive to "go at it" with the girls, we are privy to their introduction: "Here's your buffet table of love." All of the lemurs then embark on heterosexual pairings, and all are successful, except for Zini, who reassures himself by saying, "Before you know it, she'll be wanting a bigger tree" (that is to say, "Women are trouble"). Zini is appointed the only bachelor of the clan—except for Aladar, who has not yet found others "like himself" (i.e., other dinosaurs). Thus, Zini and Aladar can be seen to form a connection on the basis of their mutual bachelorhood, and while Zini is unsuccessful with the ladies himself, he does not fail to offer advice to Aladar later when he meets Neera on the way to the nesting grounds. Zini remarks, "Hey, hey, there's your girlfriend. What you need is a little help from the love monkey." Finally, Aladar is able to settle down with "the right girl," and the two dinosaurs have "a little Aladar" who "looks just like his father." In the film's final scene, we see Zini encircled by a "harem" of female lemurs, suggesting that he too might finally mate successfully. Zini asks, in a moment of sexual excitement, "Are you ladies up for a game of monkey in the middle tonight?" His inquiry is followed by a cheesy grin of sexual anticipation.

The Love of Toys in *Toy Story*

Another example of heterosexual incorporation into a children's film can be seen in the popular *Toy Story* movies, in which the voice of Tom Hanks animates the character of Woody. In the opening scene of *Toy Story*, Woody's "boy" (Andy) acts out a playtime scene in which Woody saves the life of Little Bo Peep's flock. When Andy leaves his bedroom, all the toys come to life. Little Bo Peep gently whispers to Woody, kisses him, and thanks him for saving her sheep. She follows this gesture with the line, "What if I get someone to watch the sheep tonight? Can you come over?" Woody blushes, revealing his sexual anticipation through the cheesiness of his smile (much like Zini). At the end of the film, Little Bo Peep tells Woody, "Merry Christmas, Sheriff," as she pulls him toward her with her shepherd's hook. To her holiday greeting, Woody replies, "Hey, isn't that mistletoe up there?" The two toys then disappear, out of the frame, as the film closes.

This final scene arrives after Woody, throughout the film, has found himself having to compete not only for the affections of Andy but also for those of Little Bo Peep. While Woody was previously the mainstay of both Andy and Little Bo Peep, their loyalties are tested as Andy's new toy, Buzz Lightyear—the new and flashy sort of toy (guy)—enters the scene. Given that Andy's family will be moving to a new home in just a week, Woody has instructed the toys to locate partners for the move. Woody wants no toy to be lost or left behind. With the arrival of Buzz Lightyear, on the occasion of Andy's birthday, Little Bo Peep thinks that she has found her solution. As she remarks on first noticing Buzz, "I've found my moving buddy." Little Bo Peep thereby displaces Woody from the role that he would have likely assumed. In the end, however, Little Bo Peep returns to Woody, much as Oscar returns to Angie (in *Shark Tale*). The message, here, is that the steady guy—rather than the flashy one—is a girl's best option. While flashiness might offer temporary excitement, steadiness provides long-term stability. The "tried-and-true" is ultimately better than the "toy-of-the-day." It is worth noting that in a sustained *Toy Story* subplot, Mr. Potato Head spends the entire film awaiting the arrival of Mrs. Potato Head. She finally appears at the end of the film, on the occasion of Andy's sister's birthday. The arrival of Mrs. Potato Head is followed by the regular appearance of the united and happy couple throughout the film's sequel, *Toy Story 2*.

Conclusion

Given such depictions of race and sexuality enmeshed within the storylines of films primarily intended for children, it seems reasonable to maintain that racialization—including racialized anthropomorphism—takes place on various levels within these animated films. On a basic level, such films provide children with important signifiers that chart racialized, and *racist*, dynamics. On a more profound level, these films serve as tools that help to teach children to maintain the racial (and racist) ideologies that maintain the status quo. For instance, even though Oscar is no generic fish, we are taught that he should nonetheless be happy to be a fish (a Black fish), to live in the ghetto, and to enjoy the lot assigned to him in life. As Oscar, at the end of *Shark Tale*, settles into his newfound life as co-owner of the Whale Wash (with Sykes), we note that while he has indeed moved from his father's lot as longtime tongue scrubber, he has not risen so far as to make a White audience uncomfortable with the success of a Black man/fish. After all, Oscar shares his bourgeois success with a White man, Sykes. Similarly, in *The Road to El Dorado,* we learn that the conquest of the Americas is over, and there is the possibility that multitudes of indigenous folks did not die after all. Rather, their civilizations may actually be hidden behind large rock formations impossible for us to find—thus, we need not feel guilty about the extermination of entire cultures. We need not worry about rape either, for we are told that indigenous women were actually more than willing to leave their families to live adventurous lives with European men (as demonstrated by the relationship between Chel and Tulio). And slavery, we are instructed, was an institution for evil people who fundamentally deserved it (as depicted by the enslavement of the High Priest by Cortés).

Moreover, there is an ethnicization of race in more recent animated films for children, suggesting that children are being taught not only "crude" racial categories but also more intricate ways of conceiving "race" in relation to ethnic markers. While it might be argued that there are positive aspects to such portrayals (for instance, they complicate race by not homogenizing racial categories such as "Black" or "White"), we would argue that the real purpose of the ethnicization of race—in a film like *Shark Tale*—is to differentiate characters in not-so-positive ways. For example, Lino (Italian White) is contrasted with Sykes (nondescript White) in ways that promote negative stereotypes of Italians in comparison to "other" Whites. While Sykes may wish to exploit Oscar and his newfound fame, Sykes is himself victimized by Lino's perpetual bullying, thereby rendering Sykes a "better" kind of White fish than Lino.

Heterosexism plays a similar role within these films, for a heterosexist lens implies *no* sexuality where a case can be made for glaring *hetero*sexuality. Owing to the fact that heterosexuality is normative, depictions of it often go unnoticed. This claim seems a more accurate reflection of the actual status of sexuality within children's animated films than the position that animated characters have no sexualities. All of the main characters discussed above not only have (hetero)sexualities but also convey more nuanced lessons from within the category "heterosexual." That is to say, Oscar's attention is depicted as properly directed at *women*, while ultimately he must end up with the right *kind* of woman; Woody must compete for the affections of Little Bo Peep, while she is distracted by the flashiness of the wrong *sort* of man. Even when a character is introduced, like Lenny, whose sexuality is unclear, this lack of certainty only affords the sort of mild put-down illustrated by Oscar's "None of that snuggly buggly" comment. With this distancing remark, heterosexuality is recentered and given its rightful place as the only "normal" sexuality. In the case of Tulio and Miguel, any lack of clarity regarding the nature of the male-male relationship is resolved through the introduction of Chel, the irresistible woman.

Likewise, rather than construing animated characters as generally unmarked by race, it is more likely that these characters are raced as White (which is why mainstream audiences do not notice many characters' races) as well as non-White (which is why other characters jump from their backgrounds). Concerning the second part of this point, we might consider Native Hawaiian Lilo in Disney's *Lilo & Stitch*, or Spanish-accented Puss in Boots in DreamWorks' *Shrek 2*, as two additional examples. An interesting question arises here regarding how knowledge of the social location of the actors motivating the characters' voices might inform the way we (especially adults) perceive the characters, as well as how they are drawn and narrated. Our suggestion would be that while the participation of Tom Hanks certainly contributes to the heterosexuality and the whiteness of Woody in *Toy Story* and the voice of Will Smith contributes to the heterosexuality and the blackness of Oscar in *Shark Tale*, this is not the only relevant (or even, most significant) factor in situating the characters. Rather, it would seem more important to consider how the characters (not the actors) operate within a specific frame of reference where socialization involving race and sexuality is the key. It is also significant to note that, in the end, the importance of these films resides in the fact that they are sold as mindless state-of-the-art entertainment and not as agents of socialization. This may be the most powerful aspect of animated films for children.

References

Bell, E., Haas, L., & Sells, L. (1995). *From mouse to mermaid: The politics of film, gender, and culture.* Bloomington and Indianapolis: Indiana University Press.

Bryman, A. (2004). *The disneyization of society.* Thousand Oaks, CA: Sage.

Freeman, E. (2005). *Monsters, Inc.*: Notes on the Neoliberal Arts Education. *New Literary History, 36,* 83–95.

Giroux, H. A. (1999). The Mouse That Roared: *Disney and the end of innocence.* Lanham, MD: Rowman & Littlefield.

Silverman, H. (2002). Groovin' to Ancient Peru: A critical analysis of Disney's *The Emperor's New Groove. Journal of Social Archaeology, 2,* 298–322.

Wasko, J. (2001). *Understanding Disney.* Malden, MA: Polity Press.

Notes

1. "Look Out New World, Here We Come"?: Race, Racialization, and Sexuality in Four Children's Animated Films by Disney, Pixar, and DreamWorks, by Carmen R. Lugo and Mary K. Bloodsworth-Lugo. This article first appeared in *Cultural Studies↔Critical Methodologies, 9* (2009), pp. 166–178. Reprinted with the authors' permission.

2. Disney has released *Aladdin* (1992), *Atlantis* (2001), *Dinosaur* (1993), *Lilo & Stitch* (2002), and *The Emperor's New Groove* (2000). Disney and Pixar have released *A Bug's Life* (1998), *Finding Nemo* (2003), *Monsters, Inc.* (2001), *Toy Story* (1995), and *Toy Story 2* (1999). DreamWorks has released *Antz* (1998), *Chicken Run* (2000), *Joseph: King of Dreams* (2000), *The Road to El Dorado* (2000), *Shark Tale* (2004), *Shrek* (2001), *Shrek 2* (2004), *Spirit* (2002), and *The Prince of Egypt* (1998).

3. As Alan Bryman (2004) discusses in his book, *The Disneyization of Society*, "disneyization" as a practice is so pervasive in our society that Disney's "style is frequently copied," and "as a result, audiences are sometimes unsure about what is and is not a Disney film . . ." (p. 6). For such reasons, we insist on including Pixar and DreamWorks animated films in our analysis.

4. A film such as *The Road to El Dorado* not only presents ideas that we have of race relationships in the 15th century but also reflects our own contemporary ideas of those very relationships.

FIRST COMES THE BABY CARRIAGE?

Nonnormative Transitions to Parenthood in Film

Jeanne Holcomb

What we crave most in this world is connection. For some people, it happens at first sight. It's when you know you know, it's fate working its magic, and that's great for them. They get to live in a pop song, ride the express train. But that's not the way it really works. For the rest of us, it's a bit less romantic. It's a bit more complicated. It's messy.

—*The Switch*, 2010

Have you thought about using a surrogate?

No, it's weird. It's for weirdos.

—*Baby Mama*, 2008

This is a disaster.

—*Knocked Up*, 2007

Is this for real, for real?

Unfortunately, yes.

—*Juno*, 2007

I f you were asked to define family, how would you respond? For many of us, the epitome of family is the traditional, nuclear family consisting of mom, dad, and biologically related children. Dorothy Smith (1993) named this ideological model the standard North American family (SNAF) and defined it this way:

> It is a conception of family as a legally married couple sharing a household. The adult male is in paid employment; his earnings provide the economic basis of the family-household. The adult female may also earn income, but her primary responsibility is to the care of the husband, household, and children. Adult male and female may be parents (in whatever legal sense) of children also resident in the household. (P. 52)

Although SNAF may still hold ideological power, demographic data clearly illustrate that family life is being experienced in a variety of forms. For example, in 2008 about one fifth of families with children under the age of 18 fit the SNAF model (Boushey and O'Leary 2010). Of all married-couple households in 2010, 48 percent were dual-earner households

(Bureau of Labor Statistics 2011). Given the number of unmarried and divorced parents, many children experience at least some time in a single-parent household. According to Kids Count, in 2009, 25 percent of children resided in mother-only households and another 7 percent lived in father-only households (Annie E. Casey Foundation, 2009).

If you plan on having children, do you assume that you will most likely be married first? While SNAF reflects and informs ideas regarding family structure, life course perspectives encourage a focus on life course transitions and the processes involved in forming family (although not all families include children). For instance, there have traditionally been five markers of adulthood: finishing school, beginning full-time work, establishing residence apart from parents, getting married, and having children. These transitions typically took place in an ordered series, but there have been significant shifts in the timing and sequencing of these transitions. In Western culture, the assumed sequence of young adult life transitions is that people fall in love, get married, and have children. As the childhood rhyme goes: "First comes love, then comes marriage, then comes baby in a baby carriage." However, the sequencing of the markers of the transition to adulthood is becoming more varied. With regard to timing, people are waiting longer to get married and to have children, and it is taking longer to complete schooling. In addition to shifts in when events occur, there are also shifts in the order of events. Traditionally, marriage preceded children, but these two events are becoming less connected (Shanahan 2000). According to data from the Centers for Disease Control and Prevention, four in 10 births in the United States in 2007 were to unmarried women, whereas only 11 percent of births were to unmarried women in 1970 (Ventura 2009).

This growing disconnect between marriage and childbearing is evident as more couples decide not to have children and more children are born "to single mothers, same-sex parents, [and] unmarried cohabiting partners" (Smock and Greenland 2010:576). Elder's work on the life course (1994) encourages us to recognize not just transitions and the timing of transitions, but to also examine the role of historical context and human agency in broader shifts in life course transitions. By focusing on historical context, we must also understand how factors such as the availability of contraception, women's participation in paid labor, women's college attendance rates, and reproductive technologies have impacted fertility patterns (Agrillo and Nelini 2008). Within structural opportunities and constraints, people have agency and make choices based on their unique circumstances. Thus, while nonmarital childbirth may be seen as a nonnormative transition, it may be a deliberate choice for a particular person given the situation. Thus, life course perspectives encourage us to recognize both micro and macro influences on life course transitions.

In recent work, Roseanna Hertz (2006) identified three pathways to unmarried motherhood: donor-assisted pregnancy with a known or unknown sperm donor, adoption, and accidental or unplanned pregnancy. The women in Hertz's study chose to become mothers as part of a process in which they came to realize that waiting for the "first comes love, then comes marriage" stages of family formation might result in never having children. Ultimately, the "broader mandates of American culture that tie motherhood to womanhood, parenthood to adulthood" led them to choose single parenthood, abandoning "the belief that marriage is an essential part of the family equation" (Hertz 2006:19).

It is clear that there is increasing diversity in family structure and life course transitions that leads to a variety of lived experiences beyond SNAF and the assumed sequence of love, marriage, and children. In this reading, variations from the normative path to parenthood are explored through four films released between 2007 and 2010: *Baby Mama* (Michael McCullers, 2008), *The Switch* (Josh Gordon and Will Speck, 2010), *Juno* (Jason Reitman, 2007), and *Knocked Up* (Judd Apatow, 2007). These films were chosen because they illustrate configurations of family and transitions to parenthood beyond the often assumed path of love, marriage, and children. Including such diversity is commendable, but it is also important to note the stereotypes that are often present. While it may be beneficial to have diverse family forms present in popular films, negative stereotypes do little to challenge ideological models and assumptions about life trajectories. The following section examines key themes related to variation in family formation in these movies. Second, the ways that social class, motherhood, reproductive choice, and heteronormativity are presented in these films are analyzed. Last, the ways in which these films reinforce (rather than present an alternative to) the standard of the traditional heterosexual nuclear family are examined.

Variations in Family Formation

The four films selected challenge the normative pattern of love, marriage, and childbearing. As mentioned above, there has been an increase in births to single women over time. Although having children is normatively linked with marriage (Hertz 2006; McQuillan et al. 2008), increasing numbers of women are having children outside of marriage. The four movies included in this reading concern unmarried women having children, and in three of the films, the stories involve an older, unmarried woman's quest for a child.

The separation of parenthood from marriage is a point made early in the film *Baby Mama* when Kate (Tina Fey) and Rob (Greg Kinnear) have the following conversation:

Rob: Do you have any kids?

Kate: I've never been married.

Rob: Well, Kate, you don't have to be married to have a kid.

Similarly, in *Knocked Up*, as Ben (Seth Rogen) and Alison (Katherine Heigl) are having breakfast with her sister and her family, Ben announces that he and Alison are going to have a baby. One of the young girls responds, "Well, you're not married. Aren't you supposed to be married to have a baby?" Her father responds, "You don't have to be," but her mother follows up with, "But they should be. Because they love each other and people who love each other get married and have babies." The unspoken "because that is what you are supposed to do" echoes between the reality of the couple's situation and the ideal of love followed by marriage followed by babies as the normative transition to family formation.

Overall, *Juno* challenges the marriage-childbearing transition by presenting teen pregnancy as an avenue for married couples who are infertile to obtain a child to expand their family. For instance, when Juno's stepmom, Brenda (Allison Janney), first finds out Juno (Ellen Page) is pregnant and that she intends to maintain the pregnancy, she says, "Somebody else is going to find a precious blessing from Jesus in this garbage dump of a situation." She obviously believes that teenage pregnancy is outside the realm of acceptability (there are clear images conjured by a garbage dump). Yet she also sees the hidden "blessing" that will occur for a couple who wants a child and who we assume is in an appropriate position to raise a child (i.e., married adults). Juno's pregnancy falls outside the normative pathway for her life, but it means that someone can have a family closer to the ideal (through the addition of a child) as a result.

Last, *The Switch* illustrates the increasing acceptance of unmarried women's active pursuit of motherhood outside of marriage. First, Wally (Jason Bateman) is not immediately supportive of Kassie (Jennifer Aniston), but they have the following conversation at her insemination party. Kassie says, "I thought having a party would make it fun, but it's just really depressing. You think I'm crazy, don't you?" Wally responds, "I think you want to have a child and I think that's natural. You're not nuts. You're okay." Later at the party, there is a toast to Kassie in which Debbie (Juliette Lewis) says, "To our Kassie: You're an inspiration to all of us. It's amazing. We're doing it for ourselves!" Last, when Kassie reunites with the sperm donor years later, he tells her, "I didn't get to say this to you back then, but I really respect you, your choice, doing this the way you did. It took a lot of guts. It was courageous." These comments illustrate a positive reaction to taking an alternative route to motherhood, at the same time that they reinforce the idea that desiring to become a mother is "natural" for women.

Thus, all four films present the acceptability of nonnormative transitions to parenthood. The level of acceptability varies by film, and, as will be discussed later, this acceptability is often rooted in heteronormativity and "happy endings" that include heterosexual coupling. It is also important to note that all of the women who will be raising the children are employed and portrayed as having at least a middle class status. Race is also a factor, as all of these mothers are white. These films suggest that nonnormative transitions may be acceptable, but only under certain circumstances when other privileged statuses are held. The idea that challenges to normative transitions are undermined by reinforcements of social stereotypes will be considered in depth later. First, key areas of the research on the transition to parenthood are illustrated using examples from the films.

Single Mothers by Choice

The Switch, *Baby Mama*, *Juno*, and *Knocked Up* all offer examples of women becoming single mothers by choice. These women intentionally enter motherhood while single, actively making the decision to become mothers outside of marriage. In fact, birth rates among unmarried, educated women with professional and managerial jobs have increased (Bock 2000). Single mothers by choice typically use their age, social class, and level of responsibility to legitimize their decision to become pregnant and raise a child without being married to the father. While single mothers are typically negatively stereotyped, these women try to legitimize their position and separate themselves from the negative stereotypes of other single mothers, particularly young, poor single mothers (see Hertz 2006).

The Switch and *Baby Mama* offer the clearest examples of women's efforts to become mothers outside of marriage. In *The Switch*, Kassie knows she wants to have a child, though she is not in a relationship. She explains a recent visit to the doctor's office in which the doctor began "giving me the lecture about my age and I really started to hear her about the timing . . . then I thought to myself, 'Why wait?' I can do this. I have a killer job at the network and I don't need to have a man to have a baby." Later, Kassie says, "I'm not going to wait around for some version of this that might never happen. This wasn't my plan either. I didn't grow up in Minnesota dreaming of the day I'd put an ad out for a sperm donor on Craigslist, but I'm here and it's happening." Kassie did not plan on having a child on her own, but now that she is older, she has come to the realization that this is something she wants to do. Like many single mothers by choice, she is not completely rejecting the notion of love and marriage; however, she is altering the timing and sequencing of marriage and childbearing.

In *Knocked Up*, Alison provides a somewhat different portrayal of single motherhood by choice. She is not intending to get pregnant and does not immediately welcome the pregnancy. Even more interesting in terms of societal definitions of "legitimacy" is that Alison rejects Ben's marriage proposal, stating that she wants to wait longer to see how their relationship develops. Ben responds, "I thought you felt weird that we're having a baby but we're not engaged or anything." Alison does not see the pregnancy as a reason to become engaged or get married. She does not consciously decide to become pregnant while single, but she consciously decides to enter motherhood as a single person (although the ending of the film does imply that Alison and Ben stay together).

Vanessa (Jennifer Garner) also had a unique transition to becoming a single mother, as she was married when she and Mark began the adoption process. She is portrayed as the victim when her husband leaves, but she carries on with the adoption they started together. Like Alison, Vanessa reaches a choice point where she has to decide whether to raise a child as a single mother. While most research on single mothers by choice focuses on older women who struggle with the decision over time, as Kassie and Kate do, other single mothers by choice may face more abrupt transition points, as Alison and Vanessa do.

It is important to note that the mothers depicted in these films are white, financially stable women who can use their class status to justify their choice to raise a child as unmarried women. Single mothers by choice often have to justify their choice because, despite increases in single-parent and cohabiting households, single parents are often stigmatized and seen as a less than desirable family form (Waldfogel et al. 2010).

One issue that arises with these depictions of single mothers by choice is that, with the exception of Vanessa in *Juno*, all the mothers are seen in relationships at the films' conclusions. Alison and Ben aren't married, but it is clear that they are in a relationship. Kate and Rob are in a relationship at the end of *Baby Mama*, as are Kassie and Wally in *The Switch*. Thus, while the films show women having children outside of wedlock, all three show the women in a relationship at the conclusion. While these women might have started the journey to parenthood more or less on their own, by the end of the films they were clearly partnered.

Procreative Consciousness

Motherhood by choice implies a process of decision making resulting in a life course transition from child-free to parent. However, there is variation in the degree of deliberateness in reproduction across family types and situations. The concept of *procreative consciousness* can be used to explore how aware people are that they might become pregnant, give birth, and parent a child. Procreative consciousness has been defined as "the cognitive and emotional awareness and expression of self as a person capable of creating and caring for life" (Berkowitz and Marsiglio 2007:368). The term has been applied primarily to men, since women are more likely to consider procreative issues such as conception and pregnancy because of the immediate physical risks associated with heterosexual intercourse for women (Marsiglio and Hutchinson 2004). Men, on the other hand, have a lower level of physical connection with pregnancy and thus think less about reproductive issues. However, the concept can also be applied to women; we can think about women's varying levels of awareness of how likely they are to become pregnant, what birth control methods they use, and how they react to finding out they are pregnant. For our purposes, procreative consciousness can be used to understand preparedness for life course transitions; if you have never really considered the possibility of procreation and you are surprised by a pregnancy, you might have a more difficult time with the transition to parenthood.

It could be argued that the films included here present notions of procreative consciousness. Vanessa in *Juno* and Kate in *Baby Mama* are acutely aware of procreative issues through their difficulty conceiving. However, *The Switch* and *Knocked Up* offer the clearest examples of procreative consciousness. In both films, there are relatively lengthy scenes in which one of the main characters goes through the process of realizing either that she is pregnant or that he has fathered a child. The pregnancy or child comes as a surprise, and the main character is abruptly forced to recognize her or his procreative ability.

In *Knocked Up*, Alison slowly realizes that she could be pregnant. After she throws up several times at work, she has the following conversation with a coworker:

Coworker: Are you sick?

Alison: I don't know.

Coworker: What'd you eat?

Alison: I haven't eaten today yet.

Coworker: You have the flu?

Alison: I don't know.

Coworker: I hope you're not pregnant.

Alison: That's impossible. You have to have sex to get pregnant.

Then, in the background, her coworker is talking on the phone to someone else and says, "She looks like she just realized that she's pregnant." In the following scene, Alison is talking with her sister (Leslie Mann) and the following dialogue occurs:

Alison: No, I can't be pregnant, right?

Sister: Did you miss your period?

Alison: No. Wait. I don't know. Shit. I can't remember. I've been really stressed.

It is apparent that Alison has not really given much thought to the idea that having sex once could lead to pregnancy. She is also under the assumption that Ben wore a condom, which he did not. Regardless, it is clear that she is rather shocked by the realization that she could be, and indeed is, pregnant.

The Switch offers an example of procreative consciousness through Wally's realization that he is Sebastian's (Thomas Robinson) father. Kassie became pregnant through donor insemination. After a mishap with the vial containing the donor's sperm, Wally actually replaced it with his own, unbeknownst to Kassie. Wally himself did not remember the drunken incident. He slowly remembers the events of that night and becomes aware that he fathered Kassie's child. Because of employment opportunities and to be closer to family, Kassie moves away after becoming pregnant. However, she moves back to New York City after seven years. Sebastian has mannerisms similar to Wally, including the way he eats, the way he stands, and his concern about hypochondria. As Wally and Sebastian ride the bus home from the zoo, a woman questions Wally's denial that he is not Sebastian's father because their physical appearances are so similar. Later in the movie, Wally is at his friend's house when he goes through the process of remembering that he switched the donor semen and realizes that Sebastian is indeed his child.

One thing that is noteworthy in these two examples is the time between conception and the heightened sense of procreative consciousness. For Alison, she is aware that she is pregnant about eight weeks after having sex, and she tells Ben right away. Wally, on the other hand, is not aware that he has a child until seven years later. Prior to being confronted with morning sickness or a child extremely similar to himself, neither Alison nor Wally had a strong sense of procreative consciousness. These two scenes illustrate how procreative consciousness can be developed rather quickly, depending on the circumstances.

Each of the films discussed provides insight to a nonnormative pathway to parenthood. Juno, a pregnant teen, gives her child up for adoption, providing Vanessa with access to motherhood. Kassie conceives a child through insemination, not knowing that she has a relationship with the donor. Kate planned to have a child through surrogacy, but finds herself pregnant the "old-fashioned" way, through sexual intercourse in the context of an intimate relationship. Last, Alison tells a cautionary tale of hooking up. Taken together, the four films illustrate diversions from the normative pathway of love, marriage, and children. In addition to portraying diverse transitions to parenthood, the films offer examples of single mothers by choice and procreative consciousness. While these inclusions of diversity could be beneficial in terms of lessening the stigma associated with such options, the four films also include problematic stereotypes.

Increasing Diversity or Problematic Stereotypes?

As discussed above, all four of these films incorporate variations from the love, marriage, and children pattern of family formation. On the one hand, it could be argued that these diverse representations are a positive reflection of the lived experiences of increasing numbers of women. On the other hand, the films also reinforce assumptions about social class, the motherhood mystique, and heteronormativity. Thus, while variations in life course transitions are presented, they are portrayed in a manner that makes it clear that these are nonnormative and largely undesired ways to experience the transition to parenthood.

Social Class

All four films include class-based dialogue and images of lifestyles that make it clear that alternative pathways are only available for people with class privilege. Surrogacy, donor insemination, and adoption can be prohibitively expensive. The ways these options are portrayed in the films leave economic disadvantage relatively unexplored and unchallenged. The advantage/access of one group is dependent on the disadvantage and limited life choices of another group. For example, *Baby Mama* is a case of commercial surrogacy in which the surrogate engages in surrogacy for the financial remuneration. In the beginning of the film, Kate is at the agency contemplating the process. The following conversation occurs between Kate and the agency representative:

Representative: I started this business because I saw a growth market. We don't do our own taxes anymore; we don't program our computers. We outsource. And what is surrogacy if not outsourcing?

Kate: Wait. You're not saying my baby would be carried by some poor, underpaid woman in the third world? . . . . But why do these women do it? Is it just for the money?

Representative: You do your job for the money, but I bet you love it and you're good at it. Let me ask you a question. Do you plan on hiring a nanny?

Kate: Of course. I have to go to work.

Representative: How is this any different? A nanny is someone you hire to take care of your baby after it's born. A surrogate mother is someone you trust to take care of your baby before it's born.

Later, the agency representative explains that she started the business to "remove the stigma from surrogacy." Yet, despite the conversation's hinting at reasonable concerns related to "renting wombs" and financial motivations for surrogacy (Warner 2007), the film's main premise highlights differences between the wealthy, organic food–eating Kate and the lower-income, Tastykake–eating Angie (Amy Poehler). When Angie and Kate interview each other, Carl (Dax Shepard), Angie's boyfriend, is also present. Kate asks what Carl does, and Angie replies that he is an "inventor/entrepreneur." Carl adds that they are tight on cash at that particular moment; the implication is that the primary reason for engaging in surrogacy is for the money. Throughout the film, Angie and Carl are portrayed as poorer than Kate, but they are also portrayed as eccentric "poor white trash" (Wray 2006): they drive an older car, their housing is not as nice or clean, Angie urinates in the sink, Carl won't leave the house to win a radio contest, Angie can't open the door on Kate's car, and Angie watches *America's Funniest Home Videos*. Toward the end of the movie, Kate even states, "She's not my sister. She's an ignorant white trash woman that I paid to carry my kid."

Thus, even while the movie portrays surrogacy as an option, it does so within a problematic framework related to social class differences between surrogates and intended mothers. Sociologists have expressed concern about fertility tourism, surrogacy, and the reproductive exploitation of disadvantaged women (Rothman 2008; Warner 2007). However, instead of fully dealing with these concerns, the film focuses on the stereotype of the immature, money-hungry surrogate. While regulations regarding surrogacy vary by state, surrogates in the United States can be rejected if they are not financially secure or are receiving government assistance. Potential surrogates go through lengthy psychological testing and are generally screened out if their stated motivation is financial (Teman 2010). Surrogacy can be an important route to parenthood for same-sex couples and for those experiencing infertility. However, there is a general cultural uneasiness related to the commodification of reproduction and the blurring of family boundaries that is reflected in the exchange between the agency representative and Kate, as well as the outcome of Angie's pregnancy.

In *Juno*, the pregnant woman also has a lower class status relative to the adopting mother. Juno's dad is an air conditioning repair person, her stepmom owns a nail salon, and they drive an older van, all status symbols of social class. Vanessa and Mark describe themselves as an "educated, successful couple" in the adoption ad, and they live in a nicer neighborhood with larger houses. When Juno first meets Mark and Vanessa at their house, they have their attorney present. At one point, Vanessa asks Juno if she seeks any other compensation, in addition to coverage of medical costs. Although she declines, the offer implies that Vanessa and Mark could afford to pay Juno for her "services."

Knocked Up also emphasizes social class differences, albeit between the biological mother and father. Early in the movie, Alison is promoted to an on-air position at E! Entertainment Television. She lives in the pool house at her sister and brother-in-law's house, which is obviously located in a high-income neighborhood, and drives an expensive, new-model car. Ben has been living off settlement money he was awarded because he was hit by a postal truck when he was younger, but he says that he has only "about nine hundred dollars left." He drives a much older car and shares a house with four other guys. He doesn't have a paying job, and he doesn't have a cell phone because of what he terms "payment complications."

While social class differences are less visible in *The Switch*, there is a scene in which Wally asks the sperm donor why he is doing it. The man replies that he is donating his sperm because "we could use the money." As in *Baby Mama*, the notion that bodies and reproduction can be commodified and serve to generate income for the economically disadvantaged is mentioned, but not fully developed. Thus, all four films include problematic notions of social class. Whether through simplistic portrayals of people engaging in reproductive options for financial remuneration or through depictions of class privilege in which wealthier people are represented as more prepared and able to be parents, these films are rife with class biases.

The Motherhood Mystique

The motherhood mystique proposes that the ultimate fulfillment of womanhood is found in motherhood (Hoffnung 1998). It is assumed that all women want to become mothers; nonmothers are seen as less than complete (Oakley 1974). However, it is misleading to assume that all women want to have children. Women in the United States are delaying childbearing; childbearing among women in their 20s has declined, while first-birth rates among women over 35 have been rising (Agrillo and Nelini 2008). In addition to delayed childbearing, there has been an increase in the number of child-free women. In 1970, only about one in 10 women between the ages of 40 and 44 had never had a child. In

2008, this figure was 18 percent, closer to one in five (Livingston and Cohn 2010). Research also indicates that the percentage of voluntarily child-free women is increasing (Park 2005). Despite these increases, not having children continues to be stigmatized. Given our pronatalist culture in which children are seen as contributing to well-being, people who intentionally choose to remain child free are often negatively stereotyped. People, especially women, who choose not to have children are often seen as maladjusted, selfish, less nurturant, immature, and individualistic (Agrillo and Nelini 2008; Park 2005). Having children is seen as an important part of becoming an adult, and those who do not go through this normative transition are often marginalized.

Three of these four films are based on the essentialist premise that career-driven women who have chosen to delay childbearing eventually reach a place where the desire for a child is paramount. While reproductive technologies and adoptions can certainly help those who could not otherwise have children, it is also disingenuous to portray people as desperately needing a child in order to feel fulfilled (see Speier 2004). In *Baby Mama*, Kate is a 37-year-old, career-oriented single woman. Here is Kate's monologue at the beginning of the film:

> Is it fair that to be the youngest VP in my company, I will be the oldest mom at preschool? Not really, but that's part of the deal. I made a choice. Some women got pregnant. I got promotions. And I still aspire to fall in love and get married, but that's a very high-risk scenario and I want a baby now. I'm thirty-seven.

She tries insemination with donor sperm first, but that doesn't work. Then she looks into adoption but finds out that she might have to wait years. Thus, surrogacy is portrayed as a last-resort effort to get a child more quickly. Kassie in *The Switch* is very similar to Kate in that she, too, feels the pressures of advancing age and wants to have a child. The motherhood mystique is also portrayed through Vanessa, who talks about how she has always wanted to be a mother. As Speier (2004) observed, in a pronatalist culture such as ours, women often internalize the notion that to be a mother brings true fulfillment. While this is certainly not true of all women, Vanessa feels she was born to be a mother.

To some extent, it is realistic to present the challenges that older, career-oriented women encounter when it comes to having children. However, is it also problematic to present these women as desperate to become mothers. The lack of a happy, older, child-free woman in popular culture precludes a more rounded understanding of women's choices about childbearing. Hoffnung's motherhood mystique is perpetuated through the collective representation of women needing to have children in order to be fulfilled.

Linked Lives and Nonnormative Transitions

Another key theme in life course perspectives concerns *linked lives*, which refers to the idea that people are connected to and influenced by others, especially friends, family, and coworkers. Relating this concept to the films, the supporting characters make it clear that nonnormative life choices are problematic, possibly even the wrong decisions. *Baby Mama* and *Knocked Up* most clearly illustrate the "bad decision" theme, but *The Switch* and *Juno* also contain narratives indicating that the decision to conceive children in the context presented is nonnormative and relatively unacceptable. Despite the films' happy endings, all of them include a subtle narrative stating that some pathways to parenthood are more acceptable than others.

In *Baby Mama*, Angie, the surrogate, is pregnant with her own child, not with the fertilized embryo created from the intended mother's egg and donor sperm. The surrogate and intended mother have a tenuous relationship throughout the film, but when the possibility arises that the surrogate is pregnant with a child unrelated to the intended mother, they end up in a debacle consisting of DNA testing and a court hearing. At the end of the film, the surrogate gives birth to her child, whom she keeps, and the intended mother is pregnant with her own biologically related, naturally conceived child (after being told that she had a one in a million chance of conceiving). Thus, the time, energy, and emotion she put into the surrogate arrangement really did not help her get anywhere, although she perhaps went through a period of personal growth and formed new friendships. The point is that the whole process of surrogacy, and the linking of lives in this manner, is presented as fraught with the potential for things to go wrong, and in the end, it does not help Kate have a child.

In *Knocked Up*, the bad decision theme is primarily illustrated through Ben's character. Alison is presented as a beautiful woman who has a solid career with room for promotion. Ben, on the other hand, is depicted as an immature and unemployed person who smokes marijuana, lives with four other young men, and is working on developing a website that details nude scenes in movies. The reactions of Alison and her sister make it clear that they initially see Alison's pregnancy with Ben's child as unacceptable. Even though Ben is portrayed as coming through at the end of the film in a very minimal way (he reads the baby books and shows up at the hospital), hooking up with Ben is presented as a bad decision throughout the film.

When Alison first wakes up the morning after they have sex, she pokes Ben with her toes from a distance to wake him up and her facial expressions indicate that she is somewhat repulsed by his presence in her bed. She seems unenthusiastic when Ben asks for her number, and he even tells his friends, "She was totally repulsed by me. She just didn't seem to like me." When the doctor confirms the pregnancy, Alison cries while Ben looks stunned. Neither is happy or excited about the pregnancy.

In the following scene, Alison flat out tells her sister, Debbie, that she drank too much and that having sex with Ben was a mistake. As the scene continues, Alison and her sister have the following conversation:

Debbie: Did I meet him?

Alison: Yeah. He was kind of medium height, chubby, blond curly hair.

Debbie: With the man boobs?

Alison: Yes. Here. I have this video of him on my phone.

Debbie   Oh. Oh God. How did this happen?
[watching
the video]:

Later in the movie, Alison and Ben are discussing the pregnancy with their parents. Ben's father is supportive of the pregnancy, but Ben says, "This is a disaster." Alison's mother is less supportive. Alison tells her, "It's important that you be supportive." Her mom responds, "I cannot be supportive of this. This is a big mistake. This is a big, big mistake." The overall message is that having sex with Ben was a mistake, and that getting pregnant with him was an even bigger mistake.

Negative reactions show up in *The Switch* when Wally considers Kassie's efforts to conceive through donor insemination. When she is first considering pregnancy and sperm donors, Wally makes the following comments to Kassie:

Instead of biting off the next step, deal with the one before.

What are you talking about? Are you out of your mind? You're going to let Captain Douche be the father of your child?

I don't think you should do the baby thing. It's not right. It's not natural. What if you meet someone six months from now?

Wally's comments illustrate the underlying assumption of a normative pattern that is perceived to be a better path to having children. Wally feels a relationship should come prior to conception and childbirth and that reversing the order of these events is problematic. Although he is later supportive of her decision, he is initially very clear in his disapproval. Just as Alison's mother's response to her pregnancy reinforces the normative pathway to parenthood, so, too, does Wally's initial disapproval of Kassie's decision to become pregnant "on her own."

Juno emphasizes the unacceptability of teenage pregnancy. Juno faces negative reactions from her peers at school, but the mistake theme is best portrayed in the beginning of the film. For instance, after Juno takes several pregnancy tests and realizes that she is probably pregnant, her body language is quite telling. She hangs her head and hunches her shoulders. She also buys some licorice rope from the store, and on her way home she hangs it from a tree and makes a noose with it. The mistake theme is also evident through conversations Juno has with Leah, Paulie, and her parents. When Juno first tells Leah that she is pregnant, Leah asks, "Is this for real?" and Juno replies, "Unfortunately, yes." Leah then says, "Oh my God. Oh shit. Are you going to go to Havenbrook or Women Now? Because you know you need a note from your parents for Havenbrook." When Juno tells Paulie, he does not smile and simply says, "Do whatever you think we should do." Juno tells him, "I'm sorry I had sex with you."

Despite the portrayal of variations in family formation, and despite the apparent acceptability of such variations, all four films ultimately place those decisions in a framework of bad decisions and mistakes. All the films have "happy" (traditional) endings, but it is clear throughout the films that the choices women make in these films violate societal norms and values about love, family, and childbearing. Many of those closest to the female main characters are initially unsupportive of their decision and contribute to the sentiment that their pregnancy violates social norms.

Heteronormativity

Heteronormativity refers to the processes through which institutions reinforce the idea that there are only two sexes and that only relationships between these "opposite" sexes are legitimate (Queen, Farrell, and Gupta 2004). All four films end with cliché scenes of heterosexual couples madly in love. Thus, though possibly out of order, heterosexual love enters these films in significant ways. In *Baby Mama*, Kate and Rob are in a relationship and become pregnant within a few months of their first date. At the end, when the film skips forward a year, they are still together and have both their biological child and an adopted child. In *The Switch*, the movie closes with Kassie and Wally kissing, followed by a scene of Sebastian's birthday party, where they are married. The ending of *Knocked Up* implies that Ben and Alison are in love and intend to raise their child together. In *Juno*, heteronormativity is significant in that the intended couple is a heterosexual, married couple; they just happened to separate before the birth. With the exception of *Juno*, the films end with the mother in a heterosexual relationship, and in *Juno*, the heterosexuality of Vanessa is not questioned. Thus, all four films, although they include themes of variation in family formation, rely heavily on heteronormative contexts. Although the child might have come first, love and heterosexual marriage still enter the picture and, in a sense, save the day. Adoption, surrogacy, and donor insemination are important pathways to parenthood for gay and lesbian individuals and couples; excluding gay and lesbian couples and presenting these pathways as nonnormative only further stigmatizes gay and lesbian families and others who choose to form families through these methods.

Conclusion

While including diversity in transitions to parenthood can be seen as a positive step in recognizing and respecting family diversity, films still have a long way to go to present accurate and accepting portrayals of variation in family formation. Life course perspectives help us to understand how unique historical times and places impact individual transitions, including the transition to parenthood. Parenthood is becoming more loosely connected to marriage, and reproductive technologies have fundamentally altered approaches to bearing children. Within this context, people are active agents who make decisions within the opportunities available to them. Demographic trends indicate that women are waiting longer to have children, more births are occurring outside of marriage, and more people are deciding not to have children. As the films discussed here illustrate, many of these nonnormative transitions continue to be stigmatized. Media is meant for entertainment, but it is also a significant agent of socialization. Thus, it is important that we critically examine blockbuster films and consider how this form of media supports and resists social change.

References

Agrillo, C. and C. Nelini. 2008. "Childfree by Choice: A Review." *Journal of Cultural Geography* 25(3), 347–63.

Annie E. Casey Foundation. 2009. "Child Population by Household Type 2009." Retrieved May 31, 2009 (http://datacenter.kidscount.org/data/acrossstates/Rankings.aspx?ind=105).

Berkowitz, D. and W. Marsiglio. 2007. "Gay Men: Negotiating Procreative, Father, and Family Identities." *Journal of Marriage and Family* 69:366–81.

Bock, J. 2000. "Doing the Right Thing? Single Mothers by Choice and the Struggle for Legitimacy." *Gender & Society* 14(1):62–86.

Boushey, H. and A. O'Leary. 2010. "Our Working Nation." Retrieved January 23, 2012 (http://www .americanprogress.org/issues/2010/03/pdf/our_working_nation.pdf).

Bureau of Labor Statistics. 2011. "Employment Characteristics of Families Summary." Retrieved January 23, 2012 (http://www.bls.gov/news.release/famee.nr0.htm).

Elder, G. 1994. "Time, Human Agency, and Social Change: Perspective on the Life Course." *Social Psychology Quarterly* 57(1):4–15.

Hertz, R. 2006. *Single by Chance, Mothers by Choice.* New York: Oxford University Press.

Hoffnung, M. 1998. "Motherhood: Contemporary Conflict for Women." Pp. 271–91 in *Shifting the Center: Understanding Contemporary Families*, edited by S. J. Ferguson. Mountain View, CA: Mayfield.

Livingston, G. and D. Cohn. 2010. "More Women without Children." Retrieved July 8, 2011 (http:// pewresearch.org/pubs/1642/more-women-without-children).

Marsiglio, W. and S. Hutchinson. 2004. *Sex, Men and Babies: Stories of Awareness and Responsibility.* New York: New York University Press.

McQuillan, J., A. Greil, K. Shreffler, and V. Tichenor. 2008. "The Importance of Motherhood among Women in the Contemporary United States." *Gender & Society* 22(4):477–96.

Oakley, A. 1974. *Woman's Work: The Housewife, Past, and Present.* New York: Pantheon Books.

Park, K. 2005. "Choosing Childlessness: Weber's Typology of Action and Motives of the Voluntary Childless." *Sociological Inquiry* 75(3):372–402.

Queen, M., K. Farrell, and N. Gupta. 2004. "Introduction: Interrupting Expectations." Pp. 1–8 In *Interrupting Heteronormativity.* Retrieved July 7, 2011 (http://www.syr.edu/gradschool/pdf/resource booksvideos/Heteronormativity.pdf).

Rothman, B. K. 2008. "Sociologist Response to 'Wombs for Rent.'" Retrieved January 18, 2012 (http:// mojomom.blogspot.com/search/label/Barbara%20Katz%20Rothman).

Shanahan, M. 2000. "Pathways to Adulthood in Changing Societies: Variability and Mechanisms in Life Course Perspective." *Annual Review of Sociology* 26:667–92.

Smith, D. 1993. "The Standard North American Family: SNAF as an Ideological Code." *Journal of Family Issues* 14:50–65.

Smock, P. and F. Greenland. 2010. "Diversity in Pathways to Parenthood: Patterns, Implications, and Emerging Research Directions." *Journal of Marriage and Family* 72:576–612.

Speier, D. S. 2004. "Becoming a Mother." Pp. 141–153 in *Mother Matters: Motherhood as Discourse and Practice*, edited by A. O'Reilly. Toronto, Ontario: Association for Research on Mothering.

Teman, E. 2010. *Birthing a Mother: The Surrogate Body and the Pregnant Self.* Los Angeles: University of California Press.

Ventura, S. 2009. *Changing Patterns of Nonmarital Childbearing in the United States.* NCHS Data Brief No. 18. Hyattsville, MD: National Center for Health Statistics.

Waldfogel, J., T. Craigie, and J. Brooks-Gunn. 2010. "Fragile Families and Child Wellbeing." *Fragile Families* 20(2). Retrieved January 23, 2012 (http://www.princeton.edu/futureofchildren/publications /journals/article/indcx.xml?journalid=73&articleid=532).

Warner, J. 2007. "Outsourced Wombs." *The New York Times.* Retrieved January 18, 2012 (http:// opinionator.blogs.nytimes.com/2008/01/03/outsourced-wombs/?ref=opinion).

Wray, M. 2006. *Not Quite White: White Trash and the Boundaries of Whiteness.* Durham: Duke University Press.

READING 8.3

BATTLES AND BALLOONS

Old Manhood in Film

Neal King

P ixar's animated film *Up* (Pete Docter and Bob Peterson 2009) was widely celebrated as a touching work of art, the unique story of an old man who solved his problems with a balloon adventure, a little boy, and a pack of verbose dogs. As entertaining as any such film might be, sociologists see something more. We see, depicted on screen, patterns that resemble those confirmed by our research, such that we can use movies to illustrate our theories. We also see a story told, more than once, by an industry with rules that shape its production. From that sociological perspective, I look at *Up* in the context of other recent films with similar themes, and use parts of it to illustrate the findings of social gerontology and masculinity research.

Such scholarship views relations of age, race, nation, class, and gender as intersecting dimensions of inequality between groups (old and young, female and male, etc.), and has shown how standards of masculinity intertwine with those of age to create problems for old men. We can rehearse these theories by considering links between three recent Hollywood feature films, which relate the adventures of old, white, U.S. retirees who struggle with social isolation. Three protagonists, of the Jack Nicholson parody *About Schmidt* (Alexander Payne, 2002), Clint Eastwood's urban western *Gran Torino* (2009), and the cartoon *Up*, live without or estranged from children, have recently lost their wives, and suffer the isolation created by men's typical approaches to their jobs and family lives. I begin with brief accounts of sociological theories of intersecting relations of age and gender, research on masculinity and work, and the consequences of those for men's health. I then recount the three Hollywood depictions of old men to see how they illustrate those theories and findings. I conclude with a few remarks about what these Hollywood films exaggerate and omit, and why.

Age and Gender Relations in Old Manhood

Age relations are long-standing patterns in group behavior that privilege younger adults at the expense of the old (Calasanti 2003).[1] They intersect with relations of gender, race, and class to structure regional labor markets and retirement policies that shape the lives of everyone. For instance, the exclusion of even middle-aged women from most dating and courtship tends to focus attention on younger adults and reduce the companionship and familial support available to old women. Likewise, the stigma attached to signs of aging allows younger workers in many occupations to belittle and exclude old people as too frail or obsolete to keep their jobs. These inequities advantage men and all younger adults, who claim disproportionate shares of nurturance, authority, and income. The twentieth-century Western institution of retirement has sidelined the growing old population from the workforce, segregating populations by age such that old people have become a distinct and marginal group.

As a result of both widespread resistance to social insurance and their exclusion from employment, many old people live on sharply limited incomes and find that their wealth dwindles. In the United States, for instance (prior to the recent recession, which made matters even worse for many old people by reducing the value of their wealth), median family net worth fell from $181,500 for families headed by those 55 to 64 years of age to $151,400 for families headed by those 75 years and older (U.S. Census Bureau 2004:457). Distributions of wealth tend to polarize over the life span of a cohort, such that inequalities of wealth are most extreme for the old. Without government transfer programs, 44 percent of U.S. citizens older than 65 would fall below the poverty line. Ideologies of physical frailty and dependence on people who work for a living can be used to justify inequities and deprivations; they bolster Western forms of *ageism*, the exclusion of old people based on beliefs about their incompetence.

Today, many old people find themselves dependent on government pensions and collective insurance, such as the Social Security program in the United States, which have come under political attack as drains on workers by the unproductive and undeserving (Minkler and Robertson 1991). These programs developed as Western economies generated extensive surplus wealth, clashes between industrial labor and management, and a middle class that wished to free itself of unpredictable family burdens. Growing central states responded by constructing a whole category of persons as too old to keep their jobs and dependent in retirement on government largesse (Myles 1984; Olson 1982; Phillipson 1998; Walker 2000). Though the equation of old age with dependence predates nationalized retirement in advanced capitalist nations, it is now strongly linked to these public pensions, codifying the informal status in terms of national law. Old age is now a matter not only of family rank but of global political economy, which has cemented its subordinate status.

Once such institutions as mandatory retirement, pension programs, retirement communities, and nursing facilities segregate generations and make people sensitive to markers of age as they encounter others daily, groups hold people accountable for showing that they know to which categories they belong. That is, people find their social competence and entitlements assessed in terms of their accomplishments of categorical status: white old men, middle-aged Latinas, young straight boys, and so forth (Fenstermaker and West 2002; King 2006). These daily "doings" of age, gender, and so on serve as markers that determine who deserves what, shaping distributions of privilege and responsibility. For instance, Connell (1995) notes that "middle-class men . . . are increasingly defined as the bearers of skill" (p. 55) in a labor market in which "men's domination of women is now legitimated by the technical organization of production" (p. 164). Professional men maintain claims to authority and high pay by emphasizing technical qualifications and the coordination of highly skilled work within complex organizations as they describe and do their jobs, whereas working class masculinities are rooted in the shop floors and craft houses in which they developed values of "work skills, social pride, and economic security of the craft tradition." For both groups of men, their gender means "independence, mutuality, and pride in craft" (Meyer 1999:118) as the basis for their pay. Because men's jobs have generally been accorded higher status and pay than women's, many aspire to ideals of such labor, whether they hold those jobs or not. By presenting demeanors linked to these jobs, men can bolster their claims on their gender/age privileges.

In such gendered contexts, men conduct themselves, on the job and at home, in ways that distinguish their work from that of women. They do that with skill-and-task orientations that pointedly exclude both open expressions of vulnerability and primary responsibility for empathetic concern—the duties of women. Kimmel (2006) recounts a history of midcentury fears of emasculation among middle class men in the United States: "The truly nurturing dad, emotionally expressive and available [was] regarded as effeminate" by at least some cultural critics (p. 162). Contemporary research shows that most men still reject "tears," "crying," and other expressions of vulnerabilities; "ache" and "hurting" as out of bounds in their dealings with other men (Bird 1996:125–26; Nayak and Mehily 1996:223). Rubin's research on women's and men's friendships (1985) showed that men restrict these expressions mostly to their relations with women, whom they treat as ultimate confidants and givers of care—the feminine roles of self-sacrificing subordinates who give more than they take. Finally, studies of caregiving by old people shows that men are relatively likely to block emotions and focus on tasks, whatever the effects on their relationships, and women more likely to attend to emotional aspects of nurturing (Calasanti and King 2007).[2] Contemporary ideals of manhood have been based on these constraints on expression and nurturance as well as the occupational focus on skilled tasks and physical risk.

Most ideals of manly work also rule out the physical slowdowns of retirement. To forestall exclusion and marginal status, people often resist identifying themselves as old (Minichiello, Browne, and Kendig 2000), and many men strive to attain ideals of youth by spending money on chances to play and stay hard (Calasanti and King 2005). That is, they buy equipment for and admission into high-end recreational activities and purchase medical means to maintain sexual performance, both of which allow them to continue to demonstrate the ability to complete physically challenging tasks. These and a host of other antiaging products, widely advertised by an industry worth at least tens of billions of dollars, are coming to define old manhood as a social and medical disease for a large population, a status against which men must appear to struggle if they are to maintain their claims on the benefits they have known (Calasanti 2007; Katz 2000; U.S. Senate Special Committee on Aging 2001).

The study of men's physical aggression and relative lack of self-care suggests that holding on to privilege can drive many to sacrifice health, both of their bodies and of the intimate networks on which they lean for support. Researchers have documented the harms that men do to themselves directly as they compete for status on their jobs and at home. Whether disenfranchised men of color in neighborhoods of concentrated poverty (Franklin 1987; Staples 1995), athletes desperate to perform as champions (Dworkin and Messner 1999), or ordinary men expressing rage through violence (Harris 2000) and refusing to consult physicians when ill (Courtenay 2000), all manner of men undercut themselves and endanger their lives in the pursuit of their ideals of task-oriented skill, indifference to pain, and physical risk.

Injury in manhood's pursuit extends to social networks, which men more often than women neglect, to the point of near isolation and desolation (Arber, Davidson, and Ginn 2003). Research has long shown that men benefit more from marriage than women do, largely because women do most of the nurturing work. By the time they reach old age, neglect of intimate ties can leave men isolated:

Women do have more extensive networks of intimate relationships than men. They are more involved than men in maintaining family contacts and make a greater emotional investment in family and friend relationships . . . As a consequence, men more often than women rely on their spouses as sole confidant (Connidis 2001:59).

Once divided from spouses, by divorce or by death, men receive less support from friends and kin than women do, in large part because they have invested less in those bonds, withholding the emotional expressions of nurture and need that can generate intimacy. They shortchange those relations in pursuit or enjoyment of the privileges of manhood, but often find meager payoff when they retire or lose their wives. For those not killed outright, the accumulated damage to bodies and bonds results in debilitating injury and chronic disease, leading to depression and fatal heart conditions (Sabo and Gordon 1995), and high rates of suicide born of despair (Stack 2000).

The point is that the society depicted in the films discussed below is one in which the activities by which men maintain their privileges over women, and adults maintain their dominance over the old, become difficult to sustain in old age, in part because they degrade their bodies and social networks. It is with these privileges and problems, at the intersections of age, gender, and other relations of inequality, that old men in movies struggle. I focus on three who begin by losing their wives, face desolation, and then find renewal through adventure and the company of boys. To illustrate these theories of gender and age, I begin with a look at two recent movies that tell roughly the same story.

Up and *Gran Torino*

The plots of the 2009 releases *Gran Torino* and *Up* run similar courses, suggesting a common view, among filmmakers at least, of old manhood as dependent on contact with youth. Per Hollywood convention, the plots divide their heroes' journeys into four dramatic acts. In both films, those plots turn on their developing relations with the boys they informally adopt. First acts take the old men from the funerals of their wives to the possibility of engagement with youth, which they initially refuse out of distrust of others. Second acts lead them to change their minds and assume responsibility for the boys. Third acts end on dark notes, when villains strike and make it seem as though heroes have failed their young friends. Fourth-act conflicts redeem the old men, who put their lives on the line in violent clashes on behalf of the boys who need them.

By plotting action-adventure stories in this way—by hinging plots on developments in relations with youth—Hollywood filmmakers focus attention on intergenerational mentoring as linchpins of these old men's lives. This is a grandfathering of sorts, the only mentoring left to do for old men retired from jobs and denied or estranged from children of their own. In some respects, this account of old manhood renewed amounts to Hollywood hokum: the absence of old women, the revival of manhood through contact with youth, and the role of bloodshed in that rebirth. Little of this has bearing in mundane experience and results instead from routines of generic storytelling in Hollywood (a point to which I return at the close of this essay). As fanciful as this view of old manhood may be, however, the depictions of task orientation, emotional distance, and social isolation that motivate these journeys allow us to illustrate the findings of social gerontology reviewed above, which support a view of old men as in need of some loving attention. In those first-act depictions, we find a truth in this storytelling.

Up begins with a quick summary of the shared lives of Carl and Ellie, who worked together at an amusement park and dreamed of childrearing and international travel but had to do without either. Ellie dies in old age, leaving retired Carl with a home and little to do but defend it, both from developers who would tear it down and from passersby who annoy him. A young scout offers services in pursuit of a merit badge, and Carl gruffly refuses. When Carl later wields a weapon in defense against the intrusive developers, they force Carl from his home. Booked into a retirement community, he resorts to a fantastical escape, up into the air via thousands of the balloons he had sold on his job. To Carl's dismay, he then discovers the young scout, Russell, inadvertently stowed on board. He wishes the boy away; but, high up in the air, he can do little about it.

The first act of *Gran Torino* proceeds in remarkably similar fashion: retiree Walt (Clint Eastwood) buries his wife, rejects condescension from his grown children and greedy grandkids (one of whom asks to take Walt's valuables so she can use them when she moves to college), and spurns his solicitous neighbors out of spite (he is white and racist, they Vietnamese immigrants). Where Carl of *Up* feared loss of his home to a corporation, Walt fears loss of his to immigration. Indeed, when a local Vietnamese American gang tries to steal his beloved Gran Torino from his garage, Vietnam veteran Walt raises his old military rifle in defense of all he has, and later rejects the neighbor boy's offer to make it up to him.

Photo 8.2   Masculine redemption in *Gran Torino*. Walt (Clint Eastwood) protects his Vietnamese neighbors from threatening gang members.

So go the first acts of these films, which establish protagonists as old men left without emotional support by the losses of their wives, now vulnerable to the incursions of the sorts of strangers whom middle class whites might find threatening (Asian immigrants in *Gran Torino*, wealthy developers in *Up*) as well as the marginalization of old people typical of retirement-oriented societies. These old men grow defensive in these conflicts and wish mainly to be left alone. Offered the company of boys but trusting no one, they first refuse their mentoring roles.

In the second act of *Up*, the unlikely companions must fly to South America together, a destination Ellie had dreamed of visiting her whole life. There, young Russell commits himself to the rescue of a female bird from a hunter and talks a reluctant Carl into looking after them both. The bird is a mother, attempting to return to her nest and nurture her young. Likewise, Walt finds himself stuck with solicitous neighbors in *Gran Torino*, gets to know their teenage boy Thao and his nurturing sister Sue, and refuses entreaties from his own kids to enter a retirement home. As in *Up*, the females whom heroes defend are members of groups whom whites would find foreign (one is a bird, after all). And, as in *Up*, only females among them engage in direct nurturance—through the provision of care and efforts to make others feel better. Walt's skills lie instead in demonstrating how to accomplish tasks and express contempt (in a running joke, he teaches earnest, polite Thao the sarcastic, profane banter that he maintains with working white men). Just as *Up*'s Carl assumes protection of the bird and guidance of the boy, Walt reluctantly decides to take on the protection of Sue and other female neighbors from the local gang as well as the education of Thao in manly work. At the midpoint of both films, then, protagonists begin to direct boys in the protection of threatened females and the skilled accomplishment of physical tasks.

In Hollywood storytelling, third acts pursue the consequences of decisions made at these midpoints but mostly end on cliffhanging notes of failure, and by doing so set up the satisfying climaxes in which justice can be done. In *Gran Torino*, third-act male bonding through shared tasks goes well, but the local gang grows more violent, strafing the neighbor home with guns and raping and beating Sue. In *Up*, the two companions enjoy adventures together until the hunter threatens them and steals the bird. At the end of the third acts of both films, old men and boys alike despair of their failure to protect the females around them.

Hollywood's fourth acts resolve heroes' problems, often with violent combat. In *Up*, Carl realizes that, with Ellie gone, his only purpose in life is to aid and rescue young Russell and his bird, now that the boy has put himself in danger to save her. In *Gran Torino*, Walt realizes that he too must put his life on the line to help and save Thao, who moves to confront the gang that has shot at his family and raped and beaten his sister. Both old men wade into violence, taking the places of the boys in the gunsights of their foes. Carl defeats the hunter and returns home with the boy to continue their friendship. Walt sacrifices his life to have the gang members sent to prison for his murder, but he has willed Thao his prized titular car. Both men are redeemed, all females safe, and both boys grateful.

In summary, heroes of these two films respond to attempts to sideline old men by growing hostile to neighbors, both take on youth when they see that they can teach valuable skills, both enjoy their joint efforts to rescue threatened females, and both put their lives on the line to stand up for youth when conflicts grow bloody. Both leave boys with important skills, making their lives meaningful. This is a manly approach to relationships in that shared tasks, especially dangerous, violent ones in the protection of females, suit the men best. They dwell not on personal revelation or nurturance through care, but on gruff conversation and joint physical effort in chivalrous struggle. Female characters are caregivers, onlookers, and victims, expressive and kind but unable to fight, never equals or peers.

Thus do we find vivid but strikingly sexist depictions of many of the patterns noted in the sociological literature: men root identities in roles as husbands and skilled workers on their jobs, and they leave nurturing expression and investment in supportive kinship to their wives. Once left to care for themselves, they can become isolated and may, after some gruff refusal, benefit from attention.

Note the rejection, in both of these films, of immediate family as any kind of aid to old manhood. Carl never has kids, and Walt spurns his own for their ageist disrespect. One might conclude from these depictions that such stories have little place for female kin, but another recent depiction of a man in old age does focus on his relations with his daughter once his wife has passed on. I turn to the links between that third film and *Up* in order to review gendered patterns in familial care.

Up and *About Schmidt*

Like *Up*, *About Schmidt* begins with the hero's retirement and his plans, with his wife, to pursue her dreams of adventures on the road (for which they have jointly contributed to purchase a recreational vehicle). Like Carl in *Up*, the hero, Warren Schmidt (Jack Nicholson), has no immediate family nearby. His grown daughter, Jeannie, lives in the next state, but he has left parental nurturance, and the intimacy that it forged, to his wife. When she dies during the film's first act, Warren finds himself alone in the house they shared.

By this time, the film has portrayed Warren as a man largely bereft of imagination, romance, and generosity. Like the title of the film, he is officious and dull. Also, like *Up*'s Carl, he claims in his recollections to have dreamed of adventure but to have given it up for his American Dream: a stable household and secure job. Both men have risked disappointing their adventurous spouses by staying so close to the safety of home. Indeed, the main difference between Warren and Carl is that Warren misses the nurturance women provide as much as he misses the status granted by his job. At the prospect of life without employment or spousal care, Schmidt seeks connection in the two ways that make sense to him. First, he asks his daughter to give up her (sweet-natured but dim) fiancé and move back in to care for her dad instead. Jeannie makes clear that she has never liked how Warren took advantage of her mother's care and returned so little of the support he was shown. ("She waited on you, hand and foot. Couldn't you have splurged on her just once?" she says of the cheap casket he has bought.) She is dutifully affectionate but angry with her father for doing so little to support her mother's bids for adventure. In an easy decision, she refuses his request to assume her mother's duties.

That connection largely closed, Schmidt pursues another. He has responded to an advertisement for a charitable adoption of sorts, in which a modest check and occasional letter make him sponsor of a child in an African village. He proceeds in the meager, officious fashion with which he tends all of his bonds. He sends a few dollars and writes, in formal style, what turn out to be lengthy accounts of his own concerns.

One letter to that foster child provides Warren's nearly scientific assessment of his plight: friends and family drove hundreds of miles to attend his wife's funeral in "a very moving tribute" to her status in a broad, sturdy social network. He, by contrast, has no one to call when his car breaks down and must take a cab back to the "big old house" his wife maintained. There, he uses his retired insurance-actuary logic to reckon his odds in the face of isolation.

Warren: If I'm given a man's race, age, profession, place of residence, marital status, and medical history, I can calculate, with great probability, how long that man will live. In my own case, now that my wife has died, there is a 73 percent chance that I will die within nine years, provided that I do not remarry.

Indeed, little more than two weeks of garbage-strewn dissolution at home pass before Schmidt admits that he feels "pretty broken up" and realizes "how lucky I was to have a wife like Helen." Despondently searching through her things, he makes matters worse when he runs across love letters fondly kept, evidence of an affair she once enjoyed with a family friend. Faced with his failures as a husband, Warren cannot bear to stay in the home, decides that his daughter is endangered by imminent marriage to an unsuitable man, and leaves that night in the RV purchased for the adventure of his wife's dreams.

As in *Up*, the hero has fled adversity by beginning a journey once planned by his wife and has assumed the role of protector of a female, while narrating all of this to a young boy. But where the heroes of *Up* and *Gran Torino* seem content to be alone and must relearn the joys of social relations and joint adventure, Warren Schmidt has a child he loves, understands how isolated he has become, and pursues family support more directly. As a result, the story is much more explicit about the role of family in the lives of old men.

Desperate for care, Warren returns his focus to his daughter and what he regards as the danger she is in. He drives the RV toward her home several hundred miles away, a few days early for the wedding. Rebuffed (over the phone, Jeannie firmly tells him not to show up until the day before the ceremony, as planned), Warren then meanders across country, revisiting places from his past. The next passages of the story, counterparts of Carl's balloon travel in *Up*, parody Warren's isolation and the social ineptitude that it has wrought. He narrates to the foster child his successes in life while actually boring fraternity brothers on his old campus, patronizing American Indians in shops along the road, making an unwanted pass at a woman who pays him attention, and buying gift shop curios that mean nothing to him. At night, stricken with loneliness, he looks to the sky and confesses his failures as a husband.

The rest of the movie features Warren's horror at the clan into which his daughter will marry. The groom's kin are caring, affectionate, and welcoming but also intemperate and prone to violate his standards of middle class propriety: one makes a pass at him, another pitches pyramid marketing schemes, and they yell in anger over trivia. Warren makes a final pitch to his daughter to drop her engagement, but she retorts with her dim view of his paltry fathering.

Jeannie: All of the sudden, you're taking an interest in what I do? You have an opinion about my life, *now*?

She implies that Warren angles more for his own care than for her happiness, and commands him to sit through the wedding that will both repulse him and cement his isolation. Where the heroes of *Gran Torino* and *Up* save female characters from predatory men, Warren can do nothing to change his daughter's course and must toast her marriage to a man who falls far short of his ideals of manhood.

Returning home in defeat, Warren confesses to the foster child, the only witness he has left.

Warren: What in the world is better because of me? When I was out in Denver I tried to do the right thing, tried to convince Jeannie she was making a big mistake, but I failed . . . Relatively soon, I will die; maybe in 20 years, maybe tomorrow. It doesn't matter. Once I am dead and everyone who knew me dies too, it will be as if I never existed. What difference has my life made to anyone? None that I can think of.

The story ends with a small redemption, when the African charity replies with a note of thanks. It includes a child's drawing, unrecognizable as anyone in particular, but ostensibly showing the foster child holding Warren's hand and smiling. This is enough for Schmidt, who weeps with joy at the hint of a bond. He knows little of the faraway child, and can barely speak to those nearby, but savors credit for his modest efforts. He labors at tasks where others wrestle with love, is drawn to the control he has over formal duties, and avoids the many compromises required by mundane care and intimacy. He remains manly in his approaches to the work required by family life. Constricting expression and care as men tend to do, he finds solace in thanks for jobs well done.

Only in *Up* do we see male bonding sustained when Carl takes the place of young Russell's distant dad, in a friendship focused on the playful competition (many men prefer sports talk, but these two count cars on the road) that sustains so much of the company of men. The friendship on display does not obviously include the self-revelations of pain and concern that men restrict mainly to talks with women they trust. But it can sustain a lesser solidarity, born of mutual expectation of routine interaction. Carl remains isolated from intimacy, but at least knows some loyal friendship. Heroes of the other two stories seem beyond social repair, one dead and the other left only to the most distant of ties.

These are snapshots of the risks that men, as a large group, run as they organize family and professional lives. They claim first-class citizenship in part by restricting expressions of fear, pain, and grief to intimacy with members of a subordinate class (women). For most of their lives, this works to their advantage, cementing their status as first-class protectors of others and their claims on women's nurturing work. But they risk severe isolation once those intimates are gone and suffer high rates of mortality and depression as a result.

Sociology *of* Film

Though it remains beyond the scope of this chapter to trace the sources of the many fictions in these three stories, I conclude by breaking from the sociology-through-film paradigm to provide just a little sociology *of* film, to see how the workings of Hollywood distort its views of social life. I do this to prevent readers and viewers from concluding that all aspects of these stories illustrate sociological theory and findings.

Produced several years apart, arising in different genres and maintaining widely varying tones, these films demonstrate remarkable consistencies in plotting and theme. The nearly identical storylines of *Up* and *Gran Torino*, in particular, suggest sources in a single network of storytelling professionals who work in an industry with age and gender relations of its own.

First, Hollywood storytellers have little use for old actresses, whose aging they hide with medical procedures and other tricks or whom they abandon in middle age, which is when most movie actresses' careers wind down (Addison 2006; Bazzini et al. 1997). Feature film-makers focus most cameras instead on women in their 20s, 30s, and 40s, model-gorgeous performers whose roles as objects can confirm the higher status of powerful men and whose performances of desire can make those men feel great. Note that, across the three movies discussed here, major female roles vary from daughter to bird (!) but share in common their status as threatened parties whom men must rescue. They are never peers, need not even be human; and those who come close to equality with male heroes are killed off right away. Avoiding old women, casting agents pair old men romantically with youthful lovers, often played by actresses decades younger than male stars (Gates 2010; King 2010). This has more to do with the preferences of the old men in charge of storytelling compa-nies than with any reality of social life, in which old women outnumber old men and marry spouses of comparable age. For this reason, to flatter men atop ladders of status in Hollywood, depictions of old age exclude most of the people who are old.

Indeed, this near banishment of old women from the screen requires casting of others as romantic or platonic buddies and foils. For this reason, these stories of old men come populated by youth, which leads to the second distortion. In fact, few old people find renewal through adventures with youth. Though contact with grandchildren is common, it tends to be once a week or once a month for those not providing primary care, and those who do look after grandchildren report higher rates of stress and depression as a result (Minkler 1999; Strawbridge et al. 1997). Old men tend to enjoy the company of other old people, and most youth remain segregated in youth-oriented institutions such as school and community activities that structure their daily lives. Depictions of old men in intensive contact with nonfamily youth owe mainly to the ability of old stars, such as Eastwood and Nicholson, to attract funding to stories centered on their characters. Such actors make mov-ies about old men because they have little choice. And scenarists surround them with more youthful performers because that is how Hollywood markets its wares: male stars and youth.

Third, the adventures that these heroes enjoy, from the RV road trip and sexual flirting of *About Schmidt* to the aerial dogfights of *Up*, resemble, to greater and lesser degrees, the "playing hard" touted by merchants of antiaging and "successful aging" (Calasanti and King 2005; Katz 2000) and attempts to keep action stars and children's films marketable to their fans. Though exploitation of and violence against women remain social problems, few old men answer calls to chivalrous combat in real life. The physical exertions of these heroes, celebrated in the action films and parodied in *About Schmidt*, more resemble the careers of action stars, the generic routines of children's cartoons, and the pictures of adventure that appear in ads for vacations, sports equipment, and drugs sold by the antiag-ing industry. These are stories of a strenuous manhood, defined by its gruff, physically trying domination of women.

The way masculinity is presented by such antiaging ads as those for Viagra, for instance, looks a lot like the stories told by these films: in either case, men cannot fight the corrosive effects of social aging without simultaneously reinforcing unequal gender relations, taking the lead, leaving unpaid nurturance to women where possible. Any movement away from a more dominant form of masculinity and toward, say, open expression of pain, fear, and need, or the regular provision of care, serves as a sign of aging and emasculation. These heroes will have none of it. In reality, by contrast, old men engage in little violent combat but mostly consume it by watching movie stars in action films. The increasing fragility of their bodies leads to relatively sedate lifestyles, whereas old men on screen stay robust. The recent antiaging boom in the advanced capitalist world sells the implicit notion that relaxation equals death or at least defeat and that, once he retires, only high-priced recreation keeps a man a man. In these respects, these movies look like antiaging ads, produced by an industry that overtly markets its wares to young audiences, celebrating the denial of old age through playing hard.

This thumbnail sketch of a storytelling industry merely suggests what pressures shape tales of old manhood on screen. Consumers of popular film should bear in mind not only the ways it illustrates what sociologists know about relations of gender and age, but also how it spins fantasies that have more to do with the production subculture and its business models than with the lives the rest of us lead.

In any case, these visions of old manhood combine truths about the ways in which men's attempts, in youth and middle age, to secure social privileges can restrict their options later on. Relations of gender and age combine to bolster many men's incomes and secure decades of unpaid support from women in their families, and then leave many men with little emotional support when they need it most. Where these fictions resolve the problems with chivalrous combat, one might instead suggest that men drop some of their rules against emotional intimacy, the giving of care, and tolerance of parity with women. We would see fewer battles and balloons, but more success instead.

References

Addison, H. 2006. "'Must the Players Keep Young?' Early Hollywood's Cult of Youth." *Cinema Journal* 45(4):3–25.

Arber, S., K. Davidson, and J. Ginn, eds. 2003. *Gender and Ageing: Changing Roles and Relationships.* Philadelphia: Open University Press.

Bazzini, D. G., W. D. McIntosh, S. M. Smith, S. Cook, and C. Harris. 1997. "The Aging Woman in Popular Film: Underrepresented, Unattractive, Unfriendly, and Unintelligent." *Sex Roles* 36(7–8), 531–43.

Bird, S. R. 1996. "Welcome to the Men's Club: Homosociality and the Maintenance of Hegemonic Masculinity." *Gender & Society* 10(2):120–32.

Calasanti, T. M. 2003. "Theorizing Age Relations." Pp. 199–218 in *The Need for Theory: Critical Approaches to Social Gerontology for the 21st Century*, edited by S. Biggs, A. Lowenstein, and J. Hendricks. Amityville, NY: Baywood.

Calasanti, T. 2007. "Bodacious Berry, Potency Wood and the Aging Monster: Gender and Age Relations in Anti-Aging Ads." *Social Forces* 86(1):335–55.

Calasanti, T. and N. King. 2005. "Firming the Floppy Penis: Age, Class, and Gender Relations in the Lives of Old Men." *Men and Masculinities* 8(1):3–23.

Calasanti, T. and N. King. 2007. "Taking 'Women's Work' 'Like a Man': Husbands' Experiences of Care Work." *The Gerontologist* 47(4):516–27.

Calasanti, T. M. and K. F. Slevin. 2001. *Gender, Social Inequalities, and Aging.* Walnut Creek, CA: AltaMira Press.

Connell, R. W. 1995. *Masculinities.* Berkeley: University of California Press.

Connidis, I. A. 2001. *Family Ties & Aging.* 1st ed. Thousand Oaks, CA: Sage.

Courtenay, W. H. 2000. "Social Work, Counseling, and Psychotherapeutic Interventions with Men and Boys: A Bibliography: 1980 to Present." *Men and Masculinities* 2(3):330–352.

Dworkin, S. L. and M. A. Messner. 1999. "'Just Do . . . What?' Sport, Bodies, Gender." Pp. 341–61 in *Revisioning Gender,* edited by M. Ferree, J. Lorber, and B. B. Hess. Thousand Oaks, CA: Sage.

Fenstermaker, S. and C. West. 2002. *Doing Gender, Doing Difference: Inequality, Power, and Institutional Change.* New York: Routledge.

Franklin, C. 1987. "Surviving the Institutional Decimation of Black Males: Causes, Consequences, and Intervention." Pp. 155–69 in *The Making of Masculinities: The New Men's Studies,* edited by H. Brod. Winchester, MA: Allen & Unwin.

Gates, P. 2010. "Acting His Age? The Resurrection of the 80s Action Heroes and Their Aging Stars." *Quarterly Review of Film and Video* 27(4), 276–89.

Harris, A. P. 2000. "Gender, Violence, Race, and Criminal Justice." *Stanford Law Review* 52(4):777–807.

Katz, S. 2000. "Busy Bodies: Activity, Aging, and the Management of Everyday Life." *Journal of Aging Studies* 14(2):135–52.

Kimmel, M. S. 2006. *Manhood in America: A Cultural History.* 2nd ed. New York: Oxford University Press.

King, N. 2006. "The Lengthening List: Age Relations and the Feminist Study of Inequality." Pp. 47–74 in *Age Matters: Realigning Feminist Thinking,* edited by T. M. Calasanti and K. F. Slevin. New York: Routledge.

King, N. 2010. "Old Cops: Occupational Aging in a Film Genre." In *Staging Age: The Performance of Age in Theatre, Dance, and Film,* edited by B. Lipscomb and L. Marshall. New York: Palgrave Macmillan.

Meyer, S. 1999. "Work, Play, and Power: Masculine Culture on the Automotive Shop Floor, 1930–1960." *Men and Masculinities* 2(2):115–34.

Minichiello, V., J. A. N. Browne, and H. A. L. Kendig. 2000. "Perceptions and Consequences of Ageism: Views of Older People." *Ageing and Society* 20(3):253–78.

Minkler, M. 1999. "Intergenerational Households Headed by Grandparents: Contexts, Realities, and Implications for Policy." *Journal of Aging Studies* 13(2):199–218.

Minkler, M., & Robertson, A. 1991. "The Ideology of 'Age/Race Wars': Deconstructing a Social Problem." *Ageing & Society* 11(1):1–22.

Myles, J. 1984. *Old Age in the Welfare State: The Political Economy of Public Pensions.* Boston: Little, Brown.

Nayak, A. and M. J. Kehily. 1996. "Playing It Straight: Masculinities, Homophobias and Schooling." *Journal of Gender Studies* 5(2):211–30.

Olson, L. K. 1982. *The Political Economy of Aging: The State, Private Powers, and Social Welfare.* New York: Columbia University Press.

Phillipson, C. 1998. *Reconstructing Old Age: New Agendas in Social Theory and Practice.* Thousand Oaks, CA: Sage.

Rubin, L. B. 1985. *Just Friends: The Role of Friendship in Our Lives.* New York: Harper & Row.

Sabo, D. F. and D. Gordon. 1995. *Men's Health and Illness: Gender, Power, and the Body.* Thousand Oaks, CA: Sage.

Stack, S. 2000. "Suicide: A 15-Year Review of the Sociological Literature." Part I, "Cultural and Economic Factors." *Suicide and Life-Threatening Behavior* 30(2):145–62.

Staples, R. 1995. "Health among Afro-American Males." Pp. 121–38 in *Men's Health and Illness: Gender, Power, and the Body,* edited by D. Sabo and D. F. Gordon. Thousand Oaks, CA: Sage.

Strawbridge, W. J., M. I. Wallhagen, S. J. Shema, and G. A. Kaplan. 1997. "New Burdens or More of the Same? Comparing Grandparent, Spouse, and Adult-Child Caregivers." *The Gerontologist* 37(4):505–10.

U.S. Census Bureau. 2004. "Statistical Abstracts of the United States: 2004–2005." Retrieved June 2005 (http://www.census.gov/prod/2004pubs/04statab/income.pdf).

U.S. Senate Special Committee on Aging. 2001. *Swindlers, Hucksters and Snake-Oil Salesman: Hype and Hope Marketing Anti-Aging Products to Seniors.* Serial No. 107–14. Washington, DC: U.S. Government Printing Office.

Walker, A. 2000. "Public Policy and the Construction of Old Age in Europe." *Gerontologist* 40(3):304–8.

Notes

1. For the purposes of this paper, I define old as retirement age and older. Calasanti and Slevin (2001) argue for this expansive view of the group as a gesture of political solidarity in that wide-spread public identification as old-and-proud may reduce the stigma that accompanies the term.

2. My point is not that women provide better care, which is a separate issue (men may, because of their task orientation, be able to care for demented spouses longer than women do, for instance), but rather that men invest less in intimacy than women tend to.

Outtake

Growth of the Nonlinear Life Trajectory

Erica Orange

Storytelling is as old as human history. Traditionally, we have thought of all stories as having a beginning, a middle and an end. But it appears that the non-linear approach is becoming more common in the world today. The popular filmmaker Christopher Nolan exemplifies this approach in his movies. Back in 2000, his film *Memento* told the story of a man whose memory does not exist. The film's events unfold in two separate, alternating narratives—one in color, and the other in black and white. The black and white sections are told in chronological order, and the color sequences are told in reverse chronological order. In Nolan's most recent film, *Inception*, non-linear storytelling forces the audience on a journey through a world where technology exists to enter the human mind through many levels of dream invasion.

But this trend is not only true in storytelling and movies. The idea that there are definitive beginning, middle and end stages to an individual's life is also shifting. People are now more likely to quit work and go back to school or retire and then take up a new career than ever before. As we have seen over and over again, life is less and less likely to follow a linear path. This will only become more common as the average life span grows longer. The move away from a linear life path for younger people is partially reflective of their expectation that you can invent your own story, choose your own ending, and not wait until the end for rewards.

It is possible that in the networked world in which we now live, and in which connections are now made in a web-like pattern as opposed to a straight line, we will continue to move away from linear narratives in many aspects of our lives. As children and youth, with their more malleable brains, develop in an increasingly networked world, it does not seem unreasonable to assume that they will be comfortable creating and functioning in a culture where non-linear narratives are the norm. If young brains start out processing information in a non-linear fashion, then it may be possible that growing up in a networked world will encourage the brain to stay with that sort of processing.

An increasingly non-linear path in the life cycle will add to the difficulty of raising a family, which is already increasing as a result of the incredibly dynamic culture in which we live. Individuals, lacking a norm or standard to compare themselves to at various times in their lives, will question if they are doing the right thing at the right time. In the workplace, boredom is likely to increase for those who can't stick with a linear narrative. The gamer generation will require the re-framing of tasks so as to inspire them and allay their boredom and disinterest. This will present a challenge to managers unable to adapt to the non-linear approach. Schools, too, must make changes—the old methods of teaching do not reach, or prepare, students living in an increasingly web-structured world.

And just as all of us may be increasingly confused in the world in which we now live, confusion reigns in the lives of the young. But what is also confusing is the way in which we define "youth" in the coming economy. Up through the last half of the 20th century, adolescence was

(Continued)

(Continued)

viewed as an important life stage that marked the transition years between childhood and adulthood. The modern life cycle came to contain multiple phases of youth: infancy, toddler, childhood, adolescence, late teens and early adulthood. What is emerging in the early years of the 21st century is a blending of these phases, and an extension of youth into what we might have considered full adulthood.

As the lines become increasingly blurred, absolute demarcations between populations and generations will no longer exist. Demographic variables will be increasingly hard to quantify—lines become more nebulous. Tangible definitions of household, income level, age, gender, race and ethnicity, employment status, religious affiliation, location, educational attainment, mobility, and marital status will all be inadequate for the nonlinear world into which we are moving.

SOURCE: Originally published on www.wfs.org. Used with permission from the World Future Society (www.wfs.org).

CHAPTER 9

Social Institutions

Bella Swan:	Hey Dad, I was wondering . . . why didn't you get remarried, after mom?
Charlie Swan:	Uh, I don't know . . . uh, I guess I haven't met the right gal. Why?
Bella Swan:	I don't know. I thought you just maybe gave up on the whole institution of it, of marriage . . . But do you think there's any value in it?
Charlie Swan:	Yep. Yeah, marriage has value . . . when you're older, much older. Like your mother, uh, seemed to work out fine for her the second time around, later in life.
Bella Swan:	Yeah I guess.

—The Twilight Saga: Eclipse (2010)

Rufus:	His only real beef with mankind is the shit that gets carried out in His name. Wars, bigotry, televangelism; the big one, though, is the fractioning of all of the religions. He said mankind got it all wrong by taking a good idea and building a belief structure on it.
Bethany:	You're saying having beliefs is a bad thing?
Rufus:	I just think it's better to have ideas. I mean, you can *change* an idea; changing a belief is trickier. People die for it, people kill for it. The whole of existence is in jeopardy right now . . .

—Dogma (1999)

Dave:	As all of you know, my former chief of staff has implicated me in a scandal involving Fidelity Savings and Loan . . . And once people start talking about scandal it's hard for them to talk about anything else. So fine. Let's talk about it. Bob Alexander has accused me of—[pulls some notes from his pocket] let me read this to make sure I get it right—"illegally influencing government regulators on behalf of major campaign contributors—interfering

with an ongoing Justice Department investigation and violating federal election laws in the area of campaign finance."

—*Dave* (1993)

I n common parlance, the term *institution* is used to describe an organization and/or physical place, such as a school or jail. In sociology, *social institutions* are defined as "patterns of behavior governed by rules that are maintained through repetition, tradition, and legal support" (Korgen and White 2011:161). Every society has social institutions that meet the basic needs of the population. As the quotes above indicate, marriage, religion, the state, and the economy are examples of social institutions. According to Patricia Yancey Martin (2004), institutions: are social and interactive, endure and persist; entail recurrent social practices; both constrain and enable social action; have interrelated social positions (e.g., gender, religion) with cultural norms; are (re)constituted by embodied agents; are internalized as identities and selves; have a legitimating ideology; are filled with inconsistency and conflict; are continuously changing; are organized by power relations; and are mutually constituted with individuals.

In this chapter the institutions of religion, sports, medicine, and the military are considered through the cinematic lens. In the first reading, Susanne Monahan explains that as an institution, religion is both structural and cultural, "serv[ing] as a rich social context for those embedded in it." Using the film *Doubt*, she identifies the interrelated social positions organized by power relations in the church based on gender, age, and occupation (parish priest and school principal nun). As a lay member of the church tells the school principal, "Sister, you ain't going against no *man* in a *robe* and win. He's got the position." Monahan also taps into one of the characteristics identified by Martin (above), noting that Sister Aloysius's resistance to the progressive change Father Flynn represents is not unusual, since institutional change is threatening to those who have been participants in creating and maintaining a particular social order.

Monahan also provides an overview of the social needs or functions that the institution of religion serves, pointing out the theoretical variation in sociology. Religion can be a source of community and belonging, as illustrated with the film *Chariots of Fire*, and provide social order, as illustrated with the film *A Serious Man*. At the same time, using Marx's explanation of religion as the "opium of the people," religion reinforces systems of inequality. But religion can also be a force for social change, as illustrated by the film *Romero*. Through this film, Monahan demonstrates the interrelatedness of social institutions (social, religious, political, economic) and how a religious leader can become an agent for revolutionary change across these institutional domains.

In the next reading, Jeff Montez de Oca examines sport as a social institution, focusing on football films and their relationship to the "American Dream." Sport, as a social institution, is interrelated with all other social institutions and "entwined with the state" (Martin 2004:1258). Montez de Oca points out that contemporary sport both reflects and creates the "competitive, goal-oriented culture and the social inequalities that characterize a capitalist society." Using "narratives of redemption" in football films, he explores the intersection of race, gender, and class with the theme of social mobility. While the view that sports can be a vehicle for changing one's social position is widespread, this is true for only a very small percentage of all who participate. This reality does not seem to weaken the myth of sports as a pathway to upward mobility. In keeping with the theme of redemption, religion is sometimes woven throughout the story, as seen in *Hometown Legend*.

Montez de Oca distinguishes between films featuring white male football players (from small towns) and those highlighting race relations. In the latter, the experience of racial redemption is key to the story, as the white characters in the film are "cleansed of the sin of racism" through their experience with "black angels" in the form of players and coaches. Racism, as told in these stories, is an individual level phenomenon rooted in ignorance and social distance. Once individuals change, the problem is solved. In a similar vein, using the "gangster-athlete binary and uncritical belief that sports teach moral discipline," Montez de Oca examines the promotion of sports as a pathway out of the gangster/deviant life for African American males in films such as *They Call Me Sirr*, *The Blind Side*, and *Gridiron Gang*. The reading ends with consideration of the intersection of race and gender and commodification of the body for men and women.

In the third reading, the medical institution is put through the lens as Bernice Pescosolido and Kathleen Oberlin explore "the connection between social context and determinants and individual experiences and choices in the realm of health and illness." Using two central concepts from the subfield of medical sociology, the illness career and health disparities, the authors consider both the micro and macro level processes of health, illness, and disease. The case of mental illness in two films, *Frances* and *It's Kind of a Funny Story*, illustrates the stages of illness from recognition (by self or others) through diagnosis, "treatment," and outcome. The juxtaposition of these two films reveals the power of labeling and the role of medicine in controlling deviant behavior that threatens the status quo on the one hand, and the opportunity for change (and growth) made possible in a treatment (versus punishment) model on the other. Both films involve the *total institution* of the mental hospital, but with very different stories and outcomes.

The sickness model also provides a framework for understanding a newly identified public health threat over time. The films *A Civil Action* and *Erin Brockovich* provide case studies of the interrelated social institutions of medicine, industry, and politics. Both involve "real-life" cases of environmental contamination by corporations, discovery of the damage through health crises experienced in local communities (statistically high cancer rates, especially among children), and the adversarial contest between the communities and corporations over risk and responsibility (fought out between two sets of lawyers in a court of law). Last, the structure of "health disparities along social fault lines" such as social class, race, and ethnicity is considered through the films *Titanic* and *John Q*. The most basic of health criteria, living over dying, is not a random outcome but rather depends on social status, which positions people differently in relationship to mechanisms of survival (life jackets and boats in the case of *Titanic*, surgical intervention and eligibility for a donor organ in *John Q*).

In the last reading, the politics of war in the social institution of the military is presented by Elizabeth Martinez. Martinez points out the contradictory social messages about the use and legitimacy of violence as a means to an end at the micro level versus the macro level. War is justified in the public domain through cooperative institutional processes by the state, civil society organizations, and the media. In fact, there has been such a close relationship between Hollywood and the Department of Defense that Jack Valenti, president of the

Motion Picture Association of America, has been credited as stating that "Washington and Hollywood spring from the same DNA."[1]

Martinez draws upon two films to explore the institution of war in the last decade of the twentieth century, specifically the 1991 Iraq invasion: *Jarhead* and *Three Kings*. The actions of higher-level officials of the state and military are the backdrop to the war, while the actual war is carried out at "the level of the soldier carrying out orders." The focus in this reading is on the soldiers and how the meaning of the war plays out in their position at the bottom of the hierarchy.

These four readings together provide insight to the model of institutions outlined by Martin (2004) above. Whether we are talking about religion, football, medicine, or war, people are inside institutional processes and the structure of institutions both facilitates and constrains their action. Further institutions reflect and produce structures of inequality in terms of gender, race/ethnicity, class, sexuality and "other axes of difference" (Martin 2004:1263). Importantly, all institutions are embodied, whether those bodies are prostrate in prayer, running the length of a football field, being medicated, or fighting for their nation (and their lives). Watching these films, we can examine and critique social institutions and develop a deeper understanding of the connection between personal experience and the structures we live within and help to create.

References

Korgen, K. O. and J. White. 2011. *The Engaged Sociologist: Connecting the Classroom to the Community.* Thousand Oaks, CA: Sage/Pine Forge Press.

Martin, P. Y. 2004. "Gender as a Social Institution." *Social Forces* 82:1249–73.

Note

1. The top leadership of the association has, from its beginnings, been culled from the realm of politics, exemplified by the recent appointment of Chris Dodd, former U.S. senator, as chairman and CEO.

| *Teresa Santangelo:* | God is everywhere . . . it's so clear to me that God is over there with those lovers by the car. Helping those women cross the street. And I can look at Leonard Villanova and know that God has sent him to me. |

—Household Saints (1993)

Household Saints (Nancy Savoca, 1993) recounts the story of three generations in an Italian-Catholic family between the end of World War II and the late 1960s. Catholicism pervades the lives of the films' characters. The elderly Mrs. Santangelo (Judith Malina) is deeply religious and experiences visions of her dead husband. Her son Joseph (Vincent D'Onofrio), though often cynical and skeptical, turns to his religion to understand his daughter's extreme religiosity, possible mental illness, and death at an early age. His wife Catherine (Tracey Ullman) follows the norms of gender and sexuality laid out for her by her faith as she marries and becomes a housewife and mother. Joseph and Catherine's daughter Teresa (Lili Taylor) is the most devout of all. Raised in a Catholic family and community, educated in parochial schools, and from a very young age seeking to serve God in ordinary ways, Teresa sees her whole world through the lens of her religion.

Teresa's claim that God is everywhere and intervenes in our lives is not unique. Many people, in a range of faith traditions, agree that a supernatural being or force shapes our lives. But the "God" of which Teresa speaks is not empirically verifiable. That is, Teresa's God cannot be observed using the five senses. And like other "supernatural" phenomena, Teresa's God is outside the natural world and therefore not available for observers to see and agree on what they see. For this reason, sociologists cannot assess the truth of Teresa's claim that God is everywhere.

That does not, however, prevent sociologists from studying *religion* as a social phenomenon built around a belief in the unobservable. We can empirically observe *belief* in God or other supernatural beings, as well as the social *institutions* that arise around such belief. Thus, although sociologists cannot say whether God is everywhere or whether he sent Leonard into Teresa's life, we can see *religion* all around us. According to a 2009 study by the Pew Forum on Religion & Public Life, 56 percent of Americans say religion is very important in their lives, 39 percent attend religious services at least once a week, 58 percent pray at least once a day, and 71 percent say they believe in God with absolute certainty. We see religion in personal attire: a veil, a yarmulke, a cross worn as a pendant. We see it in the moral foundations of communities: the Ten Commandments, Sharia law, the Torah. We see it in public displays: a crèche, a menorah, a statue of Buddha. We see it in gathering places: temples, churches, sacred circles. These symbols, or collective representations, of religion evoke a sense of sacredness, wonder, and awe among believers. Often, they are also recognizable to nonadherents, even though they may not have the same meaning or elicit the same response.

Not all of us hold religious beliefs, and even among adherents there is a remarkable range of beliefs and practices. The extent to which you "see" such symbols—that is, notice them and understand their meaning—depends in part on where you live, whom you know, and what media you consume. It also depends on how attuned you are to the presence and meaning of things that mean one thing to you and something quite different to others. Nonetheless, religious symbols, practice, and groups are everywhere, suggesting that religion itself is pervasive in human society.

Religion as a Social Institution

So, what is religion? You might take an inductive approach to answer: that is, gather what you know about religions and then identify commonalities. Your definition might look something like Melford Spiro's: religion is "an institution consisting of culturally patterned interaction with culturally patterned superhuman beings" (1996:98). Spiro's focus on interactions and superhuman beings that are *culturally patterned* aligns with how sociologists and anthropologists understand religion and captures important aspects of most major religions. Religion is a collective phenomenon created by human societies and practiced in *communities*. Religion is not invented and practiced by isolated individuals. Spiro also allows for multiple "superhuman beings" so that we do not exclude polytheistic faiths from our definition of religion.[1]

Spiro's definition captures the breadth of religion by invoking the term *institution*. Babbie (1993:28) notes that "the term *institution* is reserved for the system of institutional norms and values, roles and statuses that generally organize relations within some broad sector of social life." Social institutions comprise both structure and culture. Structurally, religion consists of organizations and groups that provide social locations for individuals, telling us what we are and how we are expected to behave. In turn, those organizations and groups are configured into a societal domain of religion. Suffused throughout an institution is culture—beliefs, norms, practices, knowledge—that shape how people think about their world. By identifying religion as an institution, Spiro encourages us to look beyond particular beliefs to the larger social system of which those beliefs are part.

The film *Doubt* (John Patrick Shanley, 2009) highlights how religion as an institution encompasses both structure and culture, and how it serves as a rich social context for those embedded in it. Set in the 1960s, *Doubt* is about a nun who suspects a priest of sexually abusing an altar boy. In the film, we see religion as social structure: patterned interactions among actors filling positions in a social system. In the Catholic Church, the positions include "parish priest," "school principal" (in this case also a "nun"), "teacher" (again a "nun"), "altar boy," and "parishioner." These positions are arranged into hierarchies and networks that structure interaction.

A key tension in *Doubt* is the struggle for power between characters whose social locations are defined by the Catholic Church: a younger priest and an older nun; a parish priest and a school principal; a man and woman in the gendered social structure of the Catholic Church. The existence of these structures and norms is revealed in this exchange between

Photo 9.1   Defying the social structure of religion in *Doubt*. Sister Aloysius
(Meryl Streep) ignores her position at the bottom of the church
hierarchy when she accuses Father Flynn (Philip Seymour
Hoffman) of sexually abusing a young boy.

Father Flynn (Philip Seymour Hoffman) and Sister Aloysius (Meryl Streep):

Sister Aloysius: This morning, before I spoke with Mrs. Miller [the victim's mother], I took
the precaution of calling your last parish.

Father Flynn: What'd he say?

Sister Aloysius: Who?

Father Flynn: The Pastor.

Sister Aloysius: I did not speak to the Pastor. I spoke to a nun.

Father Flynn: You should have spoken to the Pastor.

Sister Aloysius: I spoke to a nun.

Father Flynn: You know that's not the proper route for you to have taken, Sister! The
Church is very clear. You're supposed to go through the Pastor.

Father Flynn expects Sister Aloysius to contact the *priest* at his last parish. But Sister
Aloysius responds that she has contacted another nun, bypassing the church hierarchy and
instead drawing on an alternative network. Father Flynn's indignation suggests the reality
of the existing social structure. There are *routes*, and they are *clear.*

Sister Aloysius knows there are established ways to pursue her concerns. At two earlier
points in the film she speaks specifically of the chain of command above her. Her social
location near the bottom of the Catholic Church's hierarchy is not, however, conducive to
being heard or being told the truth. She is a nun, not a priest, in a system that weighs these

statuses differently. She is a woman, not a man, in a system that embodies male headship. She is older and more traditional, accusing someone younger and more progressive. The young boy's mother also recognizes the constraints. When Mrs. Miller (Viola Davis) learns of Sister Aloysius's plan to report Father Flynn, she responds, "Sister, you ain't going against no *man* in a *robe* and win. He's got the position."

Social institutions are characterized by stability, but they do change over time. Systems may become more or less hierarchical, roles may be redistributed, and values and norms may shift. Such change is destabilizing and confusing, and resistance to institutional change is not unusual. Father Flynn's unconventionality is an underlying source of Sister Aloysius's concern: his interactions with the children are warmer than was typical of that time, he embraces doubt and not certainty as a basis for community cohesion, he is open to importing secular elements into religious practice (e.g., considering performing "Frosty the Snowman" at the Christmas pageant), and—horrors—he uses ballpoint pens. These divergences, some major and others trivial, have accumulated into Sister Aloysius's deeply held suspicions about the younger, more progressive priest.

Although the major characters in *Doubt* are religious professionals, the film also reflects the central role of religion and religious organization in the lives of ordinary believers. Father Flynn stands accused of sexually abusing Donald (Joseph Foster), an African American altar boy who comes to the church from a troubled family and who has had difficulties in school. His mother wants to protect her son from harm, but she also believes that his prospects are intertwined with the church. For this misfit child, the church is a haven from an abusive father and cruel schoolmates. Donald has even said that he wants to become a priest and give sermons like Father Flynn's. Sister Aloysius does not understand why Donald Miller's mother is not more outraged by the accusations against Father Flynn. While Mrs. Miller understands the harm the priest might have done, she sees a bigger harm in removing him from the opportunities provided by the church, including an opportunity to be guided by Father Flynn:

Mrs. Miller [to Sister Aloysius]: My boy came to your school 'cause they were going to kill him in the public school. His father don't like him. He come to your school, kids don't like him. One man is good to him. This priest. Then does the man have his reasons? Yes. Everybody does. *You* have your reasons. But do I ask the man why he's good to my son? No. I don't care why. My son needs some man to care about him and to see him through the way he wants to go. I thank God, this educated man with some kindness in him wants to do just that.

For this mother, religion and her church are neither all good nor all bad. Like all social institutions, religion is populated with human beings who have complex motives and flaws. Her understanding is both horrifying and sociologically aware. She understands the significant structural disadvantages her son's race and emerging sexual identity may pose and sees the church as an imperfect way to manage them.

Religion, as understood by sociologists, is *social*. It is the institutionalization of belief and practice into a social structure occupied by people and a culture enacted by people. *Doubt* exemplifies this by focusing on the institutional structure of the Catholic Church and how adherents understand and negotiate it. *Doubt* does not, however, focus on the "culturally patterned superhuman beings" that Spiro includes in his definition of religion.

In the entire film, there are but 12 uses of "God." Most are exclamations ("God bless you!") or words of hymns sung in the background. Few are substantive references to a "culturally patterned superhuman being." In *Doubt*, religion really is the social institution.

While it is useful to think about what religion *is*, it is perhaps even more useful to think about what religion *does*. That is, what are the functions of religion in society? Sociologists have posited different answers to this question. Émile Durkheim understood religion as a kind of glue that holds society together into a cohesive community. Peter Berger argued that religion is "the audacious attempt to conceive of the entire universe as humanly significant" (1967:28). Karl Marx famously argued that "religion is the opium of the people," while contemporary sociologists have identified a range of situations where religion has been a source of social change.

Religion and Community

In Durkheim's view, the ultimate purpose of religion is to define and strengthen the boundaries around the social group. He defined religion as "a unified system of beliefs and practices relative to sacred things, that is to say, things set apart and forbidden—beliefs and practices which unite into one single moral community called a Church, all those who adhere to them" ([1912] 1995:44).

Inclusion in the community is defined and enacted by shared beliefs and communal practices around the sacred. These practices can include participation in publicly celebrated collective rituals (e.g., prayers, holy communion) and personal observances of shared rituals (e.g., ritual hand washing before a meal, genuflecting, praying five times a day). Both the private and the public remind believers of their *shared* beliefs about the sacred. It is the sharing of beliefs and the collective enactment of rituals around the sacred that remind believers of their membership in a community that also shares those beliefs. *Chariots of Fire* (Hugh Hudson, 1981), a film about two British track athletes who competed in the 1924 Olympics, provides a useful venue for unpacking Durkheim's ideas and their implications.

Belonging: Costs and Benefits

Chariots of Fire focuses on what it is to be a member of a "moral community called a Church." Sprinter Eric Liddell (Ian Charleson), born of missionaries and called to missionary work in China, trains to run in the 1924 Olympics while his sister Jennie (Cheryl Campbell) worries that his running will distract him from his missionary work, or worse, from his faith. A test of Liddell's adherence to his faith arises: a qualifying heat for the 100-meter race is scheduled for a Sunday, and running that race would violate Liddell's faith. The day is sacred and is not to be sullied with something so profane as the pursuit of human glory through sport.

You might wonder: "Why doesn't he just run? It's just one race and it's the Olympics!" That was the tack taken by the British Olympic Committee, who were frustrated with Liddell's refusal to put "king first and then God" and reluctant to ask the French to reschedule the race, as that would make England beholden to France. They prod Liddell to set aside his beliefs, for just one race.

Liddell:	I'm afraid there are no ways, sir. I won't run on a Sabbath, and that's final. I intended to confirm this with Lord Birkenhead tonight, even before you called me up in front of this inquisition.
Lord Cadogan, Chair of the British Olympic Committee (Patrick Magee):	Don't be impertinent, Liddell.
Liddell:	The impertinence lies, sir, with those who seek to influence a man to deny his beliefs.
Lord Birkenhead (Nigel Davenport):	On the contrary, Liddell, we're appealing to your beliefs, to your country, your king, your loyalties to them.
Lord Cadogan:	Hear, hear. In my day it was king first and then God.
Duke of Sutherland (Peter Egan):	Yes, and the war to end all wars bitterly proved your point.
Liddell:	God makes countries and God makes kings, and the rules by which they govern. And those rules say that the Sabbath is his. And I for one intend to keep it that way.
Prince of Wales (David Yelland):	Mr. Liddell, you're a child of our race as I am. We share a common heritage, a common bond, a common loyalty. There are times when we are asked to make sacrifices in the name of that loyalty. Without them, our allegiance is worthless. As I see it, for you, this is such a time.
Liddell:	Sir, God knows I love my country, but I can't make that sacrifice.

It is useful to think about what this sacrifice means for Liddell. In his study of world religions, Durkheim ([1912] 1995) identified only one universal quality of the sacred: that which is sacred is completely different and separate from the profane, the this-worldly. Heterogeneity, as Durkheim called it, requires that the sacred be treated with great care to buffer it from the profane. To run on Sunday, for Liddell, would improperly meld the sacred (i.e., the Sabbath) and the profane (i.e., running to win on behalf of a political entity). There are interpersonal consequences: he would disappoint his sister and likely his father, vital members of his moral community. He has internalized the moral code of his community, and even hears his sister's voice as he struggles with how to train and serve God as a missionary. In addition, Liddell would violate a central tenet of his faith. Adhering to his faith is costly, but it is entirely within his control. "Sacrificing," as the British Olympic Committee puts it, would place Liddell outside the boundaries of his moral community. Adhering to the Sabbath, especially when it is costly, reaffirms his beliefs and his membership in his "moral community called a Church."

Outsiders

Communities include but they also exclude. Boundaries place some inside the group while leaving others outside. If boundaries excluded no one, they would be meaningless;

the definition of insiders is often clarified through contrast with outsiders. That is, insiders understand themselves in terms of both who they are and what they share with others in the group, but also what they are not and how they differ from nonmembers. In *Chariots of Fire*, Eric Liddell struggles with a dilemma of belonging, how to balance the demands of his religious group with secular demands. Harold Abrahams (Ben Cross), a Jewish runner, struggles with being an outsider due to his religion. Abrahams personally experiences exclusion. As he describes to Aubrey Montague (Nicholas Farrell), a friend at Cambridge University:

Abrahams: It's an ache, a helplessness, and an anger. One feels humiliated. Sometimes I say to myself you're imagining this. Then I catch that look again, catch it on the end of a remark, see the cold reluctance in a handshake. [Indicates a photo.] That's my father. A Lithuanian Jew. He is an alien. He's as foreign as a frankfurter.

Montague: And a kosher one at that.

Abrahams: [Looks surprised and then laughs.] I love and admire him. He worships this country. From nothing, he built what he believed was enough to make true Englishmen of his sons. My brother's a doctor. A leader in his field . . . He wanted for nothing. And here am I setting up shop in the finest university in the land. But the old man forgot one thing. This England is Christian and Anglo-Saxon, and so are her corridors of power. And those who stalk them guard them with jealousy and venom.

Abrahams experiences being an outsider in his day-to-day interactions. And he feels the walls that block him from respect and belonging; social rewards are denied him because of his family's religion.

Abrahams is not imagining things, though the slurs in the film happen out of his presence. Upon his arrival at Cambridge, a porter notes his name and comments (out of Abrahams's earshot), "One thing's certain. Name like Abrahams, he won't be in the chapel choir." When Abrahams successfully completes a very difficult challenge, running the perimeter of the college courtyard in the time it takes the clock to toll 12 noon, the Master of Trinity (John Gielgud) quips, "Perhaps they really are God's chosen people after all." In so doing, he highlights Abraham's otherness by using the word *they* (they, which implies not us) and links it to his religious background. And when Abrahams hires a private coach, the Master of Trinity admonishes him for putting himself above the team:

[Our games] create character; they foster courage, honesty, and leadership, but most of all an unassailable spirit of loyalty, comradeship, and mutual responsibility . . . For the past year you have focused on perfecting your own technique in the headlong pursuit of, may I suggest, individual glory. Not a policy very conducive to the fostering of esprit de corps.

In other words, sport creates belonging and subsumes the individual within the group. By hiring a private coach, one who is half Italian and half Arab, Abrahams has betrayed values held sacred by his community and the community itself. After Abrahams departs the room, the Master of Trinity again attributes Abrahams's difference to his religion: "Well, there goes your Semite, Hugh. A different God, a different mountaintop." The social marginalization of Abrahams provides an opportunity for the community, in this case Cambridge University, to clarify its boundaries and expectations of its members.

In *Chariots of Fire*, Abrahams is seldom publicly observant of his faith. The only reference to a specific practice is an awkward moment where his date orders pork trotters for him before realizing he is Jewish. But Abrahams does not have to openly claim or practice his faith to be identified with it. That is another aspect of boundaries around moral communities: we are not always in control of how our case for belonging is evaluated. We do not have to agree with our exclusion for it to happen. Abrahams is well aware of this. As Abrahams observed about his father's oversight, the status of "true Englishman" is conferred, not claimed. And in response to the Master of Trinity's accusation of disloyalty, Abrahams defends himself: "I am a Cambridge man, first and last. I am an Englishman, first and last. What I have achieved, what I intend to achieve, is for my family, my university, and my country." But this does not satisfy his accusers. Abrahams is a cultural and religious outsider assumed to hold different things, and the wrong things, sacred.

Religion and Order

To Durkheim, the contrast between the sacred and the profane is key to religion. Sociologist Peter Berger (1967:26) also emphasized the importance of this difference, noting that "the dichotomization of reality into sacred and profane spheres . . . is intrinsic to the religious enterprise." But Berger argues that another contrast is even more basic to the function of religion: the distinction between order and chaos.

Berger views humans as meaning-seeking creatures. Because we lack inborn instincts to order our existence, humans create nomos: an order that is generated, maintained, and transmitted socially. That is, in the absence of a biological base to order our experience, we rely on systems of *meaning* to fill the gap. Nomos encompasses systems that we mostly take for granted—phenomena such as culture, science, law, and folklore. A stable nomos effectively orders social life by providing categories for our experiences as well as ideas about cause and effect. It allows us to take what might otherwise seem like random, disconnected events and place them into a larger, ordered context. It provides a way for us to make *sense* of things.

A nomos that is neither questioned nor doubted enhances social stability. Berger describes the most stable of social orders:

> Let the institutional order be so interpreted as to hide, as much as possible, its constructed character. Let that which has been stamped out of the ground *ex nihilo* appear as the manifestation of something that has been existent from the beginning of time, or at least from the beginning of this group. Let people forget that this order was established by men and continues to be dependent upon the consent of men. Let them believe that, in acting out the institutional programs that have been imposed upon them, they are but realizing the deepest aspirations of their own being and putting themselves in harmony with the fundamental order of the universe. (Berger 1967:33)

This brings us to religion. Berger calls religion *cosmos*, a special class of nomos that is understood as transcending human beings. That is, religion generally posits that there is a cosmic order that exists independent of human beings. Our experiences are seen as integrated into that larger system. Although religion is as much a human product as culture or law or science, we think of cosmos as an overarching order to the entire universe, an order that makes our experiences meaningful beyond the context of human society. This, according to Berger, allows us to fend off imminent chaos: the sense that nothing means anything. Religion gives us a way to believe that everything means something and that human experience plays out in an order linked to that of the broader universe.

In *A Serious Man* (Ethan Coen and Joel Coen, 2009), Larry (Michael Stuhlbarg) is a Jewish math professor living in the Midwest in the 1970s. His life is on a precipice. He had things we associate with success: a wife, children, a house in the suburbs, a stable job. Then in short order he learns his wife is in love with another man, an anonymous letter writer tries to derail his tenure application, a student offers him a bribe to change a grade, and his brother gets into legal trouble. When his wife's new love dies suddenly in a car crash and she expects him to pay for the funeral, Larry's displacement is complete. His sense of security in a taken-for-granted order is thoroughly upended. An old friend, Mimi Nudell (Katherine Borowitz), encourages him to seek answers in his religion.

Mimi: Sometimes these things just aren't meant to be, and it can take some time to see what was always there. For better or for worse.

Larry: I never felt it! It was like a bolt from the blue. What does that mean, that everything I thought was one way turns out to be another?

Mimi: Then it's an opportunity to learn how things really are. And I don't want to sound glib. It's not always easy to decipher what God is trying to tell you. It's not something you have to figure out all by yourself. We're Jews. We've got that well of tradition to draw on, to help us understand. When we're puzzled we have all the stories handed down from people who had the same problems. Have you talked to Rabbi Nachtner? Why not see him?

Note how Mimi refers to an underlying structure to our world. She speaks of "what was always there," "how things really are," and "what God is trying to tell you"—universal, transcendent truths. Where Larry presently experiences nothing but chaos, Mimi is convinced there is order, even if it is invisible to Larry. And she directs him to the institution of religion—Jewish beliefs, stories, and leaders—to seek new grounding.

Visiting the second of three rabbis, Larry asks some big questions:

Larry: I don't know where it all leaves me. Sy's death. Obviously it's not going to go back like it was.

Rabbi Nachtner (George Wyner)*:* Would you even want that, Larry?

Larry: No. Yeah. Sometimes. I don't know. I guess the honest answer is I don't know. What was my life before? What does it all mean? What is Hashem[2] trying to tell me, making me pay for Sy Ableman's funeral? And did I tell you I had a car accident the same time Sy had his? The same instant for all I know. Is Hashem trying to tell me that Sy Ableman is me? Or that we are all one or something?

His world destabilized by changes he cannot make sense of, Larry seeks assurance that there is order, not chaos, in the world. He seeks to again know for sure what his place is and what it means, like he thought he knew before all the changes.

Such searching is common. We see it when people refer to "God's plan," shorthand for an order that cannot be seen but is nonetheless presumed to be there. We see it when people seek meaning in the intolerable: a natural disaster, a sudden illness, the death of a child. We often seek evidence that our suffering is not isolated or random but instead fits in an *ordered* and *meaningful* world. We suffer in the moment from the disruptions, large and small, striking us. But we also suffer in a more general way, Berger argues, when we cannot make sense of those disruptions in a way that allows us to believe that human beings *matter* in the larger scheme of things. It is the difference between discrete suffering and more generalized anomie, where anomie is the feeling evoked by a lack of structure or meaning. The discrete disruptions in Larry's life have added up to a sense of anomie. It is to religion that Larry turns to rediscover meaning and order.

While we are most conscious of our search for meaning when disruptions have negative effects on our lives, Berger notes that unusually good things also require explanation. Have you ever watched a postchampionship game interview with a victorious athlete? Often, the athlete will specifically attribute his or her performance to a transcendent power (e.g., God, our Lord and Savior Jesus Christ). We place not just the bad but also the good within a framework of cosmos. Returning briefly to *Chariots of Fire*, we hear how Eric Liddell understands his remarkable ability to run fast:

I believe God made me for a purpose [to be a missionary in China]. But he also made me fast. And when I run, I feel his pleasure.

In a sermon he delivers after a race in Ireland, Eric Liddell connects his act of running with the everyday and the transcendent:

I have no formula for winning a race. Everyone runs in her own way or his own way. Where does the power come from to see the race to its end? From within. Jesus said, "Behold, the kingdom of God is within you. If with all your heart you truly seek me, you shall ever find me." If you commit yourself to the love of Christ, then that is how you run a straight race.

Liddell is part of a religious community, a community that provides him with a certainty that his life and his running are not just human pursuits of this world but imbued with cosmic meaning. Liddell does not suffer from the sort of anomie afflicting Larry in *A Serious Man.*

Religion and Social Stability

Religion helps people make sense of their own lives. As Peter Berger and Karl Marx argued, religion also works as a sense-making device on the collective level, providing answers to questions about why *social arrangements* look as they do. Why do we distribute political power as we do, be it democracy, monarchy, or authoritarianism? Why are economic resources distributed as they are, so that some have more than others? Why do some have better living conditions than others? Religion's answers to these questions enhance social stability by connecting human experience, including social arrangements that on their face may seem unfair or unjust, to a reality understood as transcending human beings. Karl Marx critiqued this function of religion:

> Religion is the general theory of that [manmade] world, its encyclopaedic compendium, its logic in popular form, its spiritualistic point d'honneur, its enthusiasm, its moral sanction, its solemn complement, its universal source of consolation . . . Religion is the sigh of the oppressed creature, the heart of a heartless world, just as it is the spirit of spiritless conditions. It is the opium of the people. (Marx 1978:53–54)

According to this view, by quelling dissatisfaction with existing social arrangements and anesthetizing the pain of human suffering, religion makes it less likely people will recognize the sources of their suffering and organize to do something about it.

People invoke "God's will" to explain suffering from both random sources and from systematic social arrangements. This is typified in an early scene in *Romero* (John Duigan, 1989), a film about Óscar Romero, who served as the Catholic Archbishop of El Salvador from 1977 through his assassination in 1980. The film follows Romero's transformation from other-worldly intellectual, hesitant to become involved in political or economic matters, to leader of a people's social movement against the intersecting groups of large landowners, government officials, and military leaders who closely guard political and economic power in El Salvador. At a small political gathering, participants dispute how God views their suffering:

Man: They came and said we had to go [leave the land]. We were only sharecroppers. We had no rights. When we wouldn't go, they burned our homes. Left us with nothing.

Old Man: It's God's will.

Young Woman: Who says it's God's will?

Young Woman: I think God looks at it and vomits.

"It's God's will" is both an explanation for suffering but also a logic for not more vigorously questioning the social arrangements that lead to suffering. If suffering is part of a transcendent truth, then who are we to question or challenge it? Thus, religion can serve as a buffer against pain as well as a barrier to change.

Romero also illustrates resistance to social change among religious leaders, especially those most closely tied to El Salvador's economic and political elites. After a series of violent clashes, Archbishop Romero (Raúl Juliá) asks Father Villez (Tony Perez) to draft a pastoral letter, but the letter leads to a dispute:

Villez:	This is not the way God wants his children to live. It cries out to heaven for redress. Therefore, even at the risk of being misunderstood, or persecuted, the Church must lift its voice in protest in a society so permeated with injustice.
Another Bishop:	It is inflammatory. The people will take to the streets.
Cordova (Eduardo López Rojas)*:*	But there is nothing but the truth in the statement and it must be said. I believe it should be read at all the Masses this Sunday.
Romero:	I'm not sure.
Villez:	You asked for the statement, Monsignor.
Romero:	I know.
Villez:	And now you want to give it up.
Romero:	No, just toned down. It mustn't be incendiary.

In their concern for order and the maintenance of existing social arrangements, some Church leaders argue for toning down the content of the letter. This is especially true of Bishop Estrada (Al Ruscio), who works with El Salvador's military. He argues repeatedly for restraint when he claims that "the Church's job is to preach the gospel . . . this is going to be interpreted as a political statement" and "the Church has always been a stabilizing influence. . . . if we abandon this role now, what will happen?" Thus, in *Romero*, some religious leaders argue that the Church should be a stabilizing influence, in effect aligning the Church with a status quo that embodies substantial economic and political inequalities. Early in the film, this is also Archbishop Romero's approach. It is not until later in the film that Romero embraces what Christian Smith (1996) terms "disruptive religion."

Religion and Social Change

The examples in *Romero* notwithstanding, Marx's claims do not consistently fit with the evidence on the role of religion in social change. Scholars note that religion provides valuable resources to social change movements and that there are circumstances where religious organizations and leaders play key roles in upending long-standing social arrangements. Leland Robinson (1987) identifies conditions under which religion can drive social change rather than support the status quo. First, "a preponderantly religious worldview among revolutionary classes" coalesces dissent and links it to truths that transcend human society (p. 53). Christian Smith (1996) concurs with Robinson, noting that religion provides powerful motivations for social change when dissenters are able to link proposed change to transcendent meaning systems or to core values such as justice or equity.

We see the power of religious worldviews in *Romero*. The poor in El Salvador are depicted as devoutly Catholic. Church structures are sacred spaces, Catholic priests are revered, and rituals such as Mass are central to their lives. Importantly, the poor come to understand their plight—poverty, oppression by the government and the large landowners, violence at the hands of the military—in light of a religious worldview of liberation theology. Henri Gooren (2002) explains the key tenets of liberation theology:

> Because liberation theology rejects the separation between spirituality and worldliness, the supposed apolitical character of the Church is strongly criticized as supporting the status quo and hence the wealthy. Social conflicts and class struggles, a term borrowed from Marxism, are an essential part of history and should not be ignored by the Church by appealing to a harmony model of Church unity. Most revolutionary was the idea of liberation theologians that the Kingdom of God could be established here on earth by trying to accomplish social justice and fighting poverty. To accomplish these goals, the social order should be analyzed, first of all by the poor themselves. (P. 29)

Liberation theology is explicitly "a theology at variance with the existing social order," Robinson's second necessary condition for religion to drive social change. The protesters focus on the *divergence* between the ideals set out by a Catholic theology focused on peace and justice and the reality of their lives. They acknowledge the absence of harmony and seek more just social arrangements in the here and now. Father Rutilio Grande (Richard Jordan) is a Catholic priest who ministers directly to the poor in the village of Aguilares. Early in the film, he explains to Romero why he is willing to be called "subversive" and an "agitator":

> Remember who else they called such names. Jesus is not somewhere up in the clouds sitting in a hammock. Jesus is down here with us building a kingdom. Oscar, what else can I do? I cannot love God, who I do not see, if I do not love my brothers and sisters whom I can see.

After dozens are killed by members of the National Guard while celebrating Mass in Aguilares's town square, Father Grande again explains himself to now Archbishop Romero.

Grande: Don't you see what's going on around here? Anyone who says what he thinks about land reform or wages or God or human rights, automatically he's labeled a communist. He lives in fear. They take him away. They torture him. They kill him. You don't believe me. Good-bye, Oscar.

Romero: Where are you going?

Grande: Back to Aguilares to serve them, to work with them, to strengthen them, while they're still alive.

Grande references religious ideals. He focuses on bringing those ideals to life in this world through organized social change rather than accepting this world as it is or hoping for something better in the next world. Religious narratives and metaphors can be powerful tools to communicate and strengthen the argument for social change.

Beyond ideological support, religion can also provide organizational resources to social change movements. Among the most valuable is ready-made leadership in the form of clergy who are respected and experienced at community organizing. Recognizing this, Robinson (1987) identifies a third condition for religion to drive social change: "clergy who [are] closely associated with the revolutionary classes" (p. 53). When such clergy lead people with a strong religious worldview at odds with existing social arrangements, Robinson argues that the pieces are in place for religion to drive social change. *Romero* features three priests, Fathers Grande, Osuna (Alejandro Bracho), and Morantes (Tony Plana), who live and work in the village of Aguilares. These priests live among the people, maintaining strong relationships with congregants through interactions that go beyond meeting in church on Sundays. The priests are involved in the community's political meetings and in working for economic justice and land reform.

In *The Religious Roots of Rebellion,* Phillip Berryman (1986) describes how priests deeply embedded in the social world of Aguilares engaged in intentional community building. Dividing Aguilares into 10 districts, the priests worked with these smaller communities, gathering data and meeting one on one and in larger groups with as many people as possible. The priests drew from religious scripture, linking it to the conditions of people's lives. Living and working among the people and drawing on their standing as Catholic priests, they used their skills in organizing religious congregations to pull together a social movement.

Religious organizations are also repositories for all sorts of organizational resources: meeting space, equipment, money and other materials, labor, and communication networks (Smith 1996). For example, when protesters in *Romero* are threatened by the military, they take refuge in the church sanctuary. Participants in the change movement are recruited from among existing congregations. Information is spread among protesters through religiously based social networks.

In *Romero,* we see both sides of religion and its relation to social change. There is resistance to broader societal change in the Catholic institutions of El Salvador. Most obviously, such resistance emanates from those leaders with close ties to the existing centers of power. But the resistance is more widespread, encompassing even Oscar Romero early in the film. As Marx argued, religion's focus on the otherworldly can blind the religious from seeing the conditions of their lives in this world, and perhaps more important, from seeing the causes of injustice. But we also see the necessary and sufficient conditions for religion to *support* social change in the shared religious worldview of the protestors, the divergence of religious ideals from the reality of their lives, and the close engagement of clergy leaders in the lives of the poor.

Conclusion

Recent film satires (e.g., *Easy A*, *Saved!*, *Religulous*) treat religion as a source of holier-than-thou hypocrisy. Other films (e.g., *A Walk to Remember*) suggest that religion produces moral behavior. The films analyzed here suggest something different: that religion is a mechanism for people to belong to a community and find meaning in their existence. Depending on other factors, religion can support social arrangements or challenge them.

From a sociological perspective, religion is not good or bad. Rather, it is an expression of human community, evidence of our very human impulse toward meaning making, and a mechanism for both social stability and social change.

References

Babbie, E. 1993. *What Is Society?* Newbury Park, CA: Pine Forge.

Berger, P. 1967. *The Sacred Canopy.* New York: Doubleday.

Berryman, P. 1986. *The Religious Roots of Rebellion.* Eugene, OR: Wipf and Stock.

Durkheim, É. [1912] 1995. *The Elementary Forms of Religious Life.* Translated by K. Fields. New York: Free Press.

Gooren, H. 2002. "Catholic and Non-Catholic Theologies of Liberation: Poverty, Self-Improvement, and Ethics among Small-Scale Entrepreneurs in Guatemala City." *Journal for the Scientific Study of Religion* 41(1):29–45.

Marx, K. 1978. In *The Marx-Engels Reader.* 2nd ed., edited by R. C. Tucker. New York: W. W. Norton.

Robinson, L. 1987. "When Will Revolutionary Movements Use Religion?" In *Church-State Relations,* edited by T. Robbins and R. Robertson. New Brunswick, NJ: Transaction.

Smith, C. 1996. *Disruptive Religion.* New York: Routledge.

Notes

1. But Spiro's definition still excludes some phenomena that are generally understood as "religion." Pantheistic faiths, ones that find nature suffused with the sacred, lack a superhuman being. And faiths like Buddhism are oriented around practices rather than belief in supernatural phenomena.
2. *Hashem* is a term for God used in nonsacred settings. It is used to avoid saying "God," which is considered sacred and thus dangerous to utter.

READING 9.2

SPORT AS SOCIAL INSTITUTION

Football Films and the American Dream

Jeff Montez de Oca

Sport sociology studies the operation of power and inequality in society through theoretical and empirical studies of sport as a social institution (Coakley 2009). Sport is often seen simply as a reflection or "microcosm" of society; however, contemporary sport sociologists see sport also as an active force in society through which people construct and negotiate identities as well as transform social arrangements (Carrington 2010). This understanding of sport emphasizes its constructed, dynamic nature rather than seeing sport as universal and timeless. In the United States, people typically understand sport as rule-bound physical competitions sanctioned and regulated by large formal institutions such as the American Youth Soccer Organization or the National Football League. This version of sport based on competition, written rules, governing bodies, disciplined training, and record keeping originated in the British public schools during the mid nineteenth century and was part of the interrelated processes of nation-state formation, imperialism, and industrialization (Dunning 1972, 1975; Eichberg 1986; Elias and Dunning 1986; Guttman 1978; Morford and McIntosh 1993; Stoddart 1988). So while contemporary sports may reflect the competitive relations of a capitalist culture, they also participated in creating the competitive, goal-oriented culture and the social inequalities that characterize a capitalist society.

Given the emergence of modern sport during the era of nation-state formation, imperialism, and industrialization as well as its displacement of earlier sporting traditions, we can see in modern sport social problems endemic to contemporary society such as class, race, and gender inequalities. Intersectionality, or the study of how different systems of domination intersect to form social relations, identities, and lived experiences, provides sociologists an important method for studying inequalities in social institutions, including modern sport (Knoppers and McDonald 2010). This reading uses an intersectional approach to look at how social mobility, race, and gender are socially constructed in 16 recent football films.[1] These films provide an uncritical celebration of the American Dream that promises that anyone, regardless of the circumstances of his or her birth, has the ability to achieve prosperity and success when he or she commits to determined, disciplined effort and plays by the rules. By telling recognizable stories through familiar narratives, these films draw on common stocks of knowledge rooted in a generalized "American experience." By drawing on the mundane and familiar in patterned ways, football films do not simply reflect a given social world; they help contour the ways in which viewers perceive the organization and workings of society. They help to define normality, the way the world works, and how people should act. In other words, football films are powerful ideological vehicles for telling stories and offering ways of understanding everyday life in the United States that simultaneously limit a person's understanding of his or her social world.

Different ideological narratives that relate to and represent social mobility, race, and gender run through these films. I refer to the primary narrative as "narratives of redemption." In these narratives, the protagonist experiences a life-altering transformation through his commitment to and sacrifice within football. Narratives of redemption mythologize sport as an avenue of social mobility regardless of contrary evidence. Narratives of redemption become "narratives of racial redemption" and "narratives of moral discipline" when race becomes a salient issue in the film. Both racial narratives open access to the American Dream for minority characters, while narratives of racial redemption wash white characters free of the sin of racism and narratives of moral discipline provide a path out of "the ghetto" for minority youth. Racial narratives in football films understand racism in purely individual terms and obscure the institutional or structural organization of race relations in the United States. "Narratives of gender" are also important in football films, since football is a masculinizing institution, a social institution where boys both learn and perform a masculine identity. Since manhood in America is predicated on its repudiation of femininity, female characters are generally marginalized in football films, and when present they serve to validate the manhood of a male character (Daniels 2005; Pearson 2001; Whannel 1993).[2]

The fact that football films are powerful ideological vehicles does not mean that they are "wrong," that they lack valuable lessons, or that they do not reflect many people's experiences. Instead, football films in their great consistency provide a narrow way of understanding the world that can obscure alternative truths and understandings of society. This is not to say that everyone interprets a film the same way. Our different social positions and mental frameworks allow for a range of interpretations. These different narratives are more like guides that encourage a particular understanding over others. However, the consistency of football films demonstrates core beliefs that viewers see and respond to because people operate within an existing set of social relations and make conscious choices based on what is and what appears to be available (Hall 1986). Narratives representing social mobility, race, and gender in football films provide powerful ideological frames through which people can understand and act on the world they live in without reflecting on it or recognizing contradictions. This reading studies football films to question how the institution of football, with its history, values, and norms, is used in recent popular films to construct common understandings of class, race, and gender.

Redemption as Narrative of Self-Transformation and Mobility

Sport sociologist Stanley Eitzen argues that while individual success stories perpetuate the belief that "sport is a path to social mobility," systematic research finds sport is much less effective in achieving mobility (1999:132). Eitzen identifies six common myths[3] that coalesce in the belief that sport operates as a vehicle of the American Dream. While each myth is based in truth, the myths are true for only a small minority of people (Eitzen 1999). Although very few people actually gain measurable, material benefits from sports participation, sport as a pathway to the American Dream is an axiom (a self-evident truth that organizes the narrative) in football films. This axiomatic belief is represented in football films through what I call narratives of redemption, or stories that highlight the transformation of a protagonist through his commitment to and sacrifice within football. The narrative of redemption is a flexible rhetorical device that does not only center on social mobility. For instance, Paul "Bear" Bryant is washed clean of the sin of pride and for putting a group of young men's lives in peril in *The Junction Boys* because his dangerous training regimen transformed a group of soft boys into hard men. In *We Are Marshall*, a single victory redeems Huntington, West Virginia, after a terrible plane crash in 1970 took the lives of almost the entire Marshall football team. Despite variation, the narrative of redemption generally operates around social mobility.

The representation of social mobility through football is clearly seen in the avowedly Christian film *Hometown Legend*, which tells the story of Athens, Alabama (a small town experiencing an economic crisis after the loss of the railroads), and a poor orphaned boy named Elvis Jackson (Nick Cornish). Jackson is a latter-day Huck Finn who squats in an unused barn on the edge of town, is deeply cynical and decidedly un-Christian. The film begins with the voice-over narration of Rachel Sawyer (Lacy Chabert), the middle class daughter of the assistant coach of the Athens High School Crusaders, as she prays for her town. In her prayer, she tells the viewer that Athens needs a miracle: it needs a successful football season to save both the town and the school.

The fusing of Athens's destiny with that of Elvis is illustrated when he becomes the starting quarterback and his success on the field leads to a revival within the community. However, just as the team heads into the championship game, Elvis learns that the scholarship he hoped to win has been defunded. Without the promise of a scholarship, he sees no reason to play and exaggerates an injury to sit out of the championship. While the Athens Crusaders face a slaughter in the big game, Elvis sits alone in his dark barn. Looking up into the night sky, he asks, "Alright, God, you've got something to say to me?" Turning away from the window with disappointment, he lights a lamp, and it illuminates a table covered with get-well pies and notes of encouragement from townsfolk thanking him for making the game fun and for reigniting the spirit of community. Elvis looks up from the table and is startled to see a strange black man's face in the lamplight. The man owns the barn, but Elvis sees God in his peculiar face. Filled with a righteous spirit that overcomes his earlier self-centered materialism, Elvis rushes to the stadium. The Crusaders lose the game, but they win a moral victory that allows Elvis and the town of Athens to attain redemption. The town achieves unity and pride despite its economic downturn. And in the last scene, Elvis sits casually in a boxcar with Rachel while wearing a University of Alabama sweatshirt that symbolizes his entrance into college and path to the good life. The film then ends as it began, with a voice-over prayer by Rachel in which she gives thanks to God "for showing up and showing off."

Rachel's prayer sets up a narrative focused on the efforts of individuals, but the narrative largely ignores the larger social forces that create economic deprivation in small towns across the country. The economy of Athens, Alabama, was rooted in Southern rural capitalism, particularly cotton and the railroads that collapsed in the mid twentieth century. Although a winning football team and renewed faith may make people feel better in the face of economic hardship, it does little to address the actual economic processes that have created widespread downward economic mobility for people in small towns. The emphasis on individualism shifts attention away from political and economic social institutions that create our conditions of opportunity and reduces macro economic processes into personal problems instead of fostering a critical understanding of the institutions that directly affect people's lives (Hilliard 1994).

Narratives of redemption give football films coherence, familiarity, and a sentimentality that allows for emotional connection to what is essentially a magical (and implausible) transformation in contemporary society. *Hometown Legend* is virtually identical to *Full Ride*, which came out only a year earlier, minus the overtly Christian symbolism. Both films are organized around the class transcendence of young white male characters that hearken to Huck Finn. However, without western territories to "light out for," these boys use football to integrate themselves into U.S. society—symbolized by winning a college education and an adoring girl. Even if sport's efficacy in achieving the American Dream is empirically questionable, the mythology is unquestioned in these films even at a time when people across the country are experiencing widespread downward mobility. What makes the narrative of redemption in football films so ideologically powerful is that it takes a highly conventional success narrative and infuses it with a spiritual quality that makes the unlikely seem achievable, natural, and permeated with moral imperative.

Football Films and the Dynamics of Race

Football films are an interesting subgenre to study in regard to race, given that African Americans dominate the game at its highest levels and Americans widely believe that sports are an avenue of social mobility. The films studied in this chapter consistently support dominant U.S. racial ideology. They embrace the idea that equality of treatment leads to individual advancement through disciplined and persistent effort, which is the foundation of the American Dream. Racial inequality is consistently represented in football films as either the result of individual racism (i.e., prejudicial attitudes and discriminatory behavior of individuals) or individuals' poor choices and lack of moral discipline. Moreover, racial inequality is represented as a problem primarily because it constrains a person's ability to achieve individual success and self-realization. Since football is represented as a vehicle of social mobility for boys who make the effort and sacrifice, those who fail to achieve mobility refused to either try or play the game by its rules. Therefore, socially imposed limits become self-imposed and the organization of society is inherently right and just. So, although all of the movies studied are either antiracist or racially neutral (racism is ignored), the individual understanding of racism reduces social issues to personal problems (Hilliard 1994) and reinforces a predominant racial ideology in the United States: because America has moved beyond legal and explicit racism, the problems of racial minorities are their own fault and policies of racial amelioration are unnecessary and discriminatory (Bobo, Kluegel, and Smith 1996).

Films like *Hometown Legend* and *Full Ride* represent one model for representing race. White protagonists are consistently poor small town boys who are troubled because of an emotionally unstable or absent parent, but with coaching from an older male they are able to go to college. This character is seen in *Varsity Blues*, *The Slaughter Rule*, *Full Ride*, *Hometown Legend*, *Friday Night Lights*, and *Gridiron Gang*. Black characters, on the other hand, never seem to come from small towns even if their white counterparts appear to.[4] In

Hometown Legend, *Full Ride*, and *Radio*, the teams have two or three African American players to represent diversity. However, any kid could substitute for them without affecting the story. Given football films' understanding of racism, these films present race as an issue only for people who are not white. Organizing the narrative around a white protagonist, these films proceed as if race and racial inequality do not exist and the transformation of the protagonist is purely in terms of individual class mobility. In this sense, football films construct a normative whiteness where working class, rural characters (often southern) stand in for "traditional" or "real" Americans and individual class mobility is achieved through hard work, discipline, and buying into the American system. We might even conjecture that the white characters are burdened by a moral obligation to achieve social mobility. It is in this sense that whiteness becomes synonymous with the American Dream and a white character who fails to achieve social mobility represents a lack of morality.

Football as Racial Redemption

Narratives of redemption also structure football films featuring African American protagonists. However, the historical period in which the film takes place profoundly affects the articulation of the narrative and the antagonistic force that creates the film's drama. If the story is set in the past, then white racism operates as the antagonistic force or obstacle that the black protagonist must overcome. *The Express*, for instance, explicitly frames the life of Ernie Davis (Rob Brown) within a narrative of racial war that Ernie's civil rights activism will transcend. Black characters in historical films like *The Express* achieve heroic status by stoically enduring the slings and arrows of white racism while they doggedly pursue football success. Contemporary films such as *The Blind Side*, *Gridiron Gang*, and *They Call Me Sirr* do not represent white racism as an antagonist force. Instead, it is the moral chaos and violence of inner city life that the black protagonist must overcome. If significant white characters are present in contemporary films, as in *The Blind Side*, they help the protagonist use football to escape the moral chaos and violence of the inner city (Chambers 2009).

The narrative of redemption in films that highlight race relations becomes a narrative of racial redemption for white characters who are cleansed of the sin of racism. This allows for a representation of normative whiteness as racially innocent through what literary scholars call "black magic," or the idea that the whiteness of white characters is dependent on the presence of blackness—a "black angel"—through which they produce themselves as virtuous and pure (Chambers 2009; Gabbard 2004). In other words, black angels serve the narrative function of making normative white characters appear virtuous and hence white. The farm owner in *Hometown Legend* who appears at the moment Elvis has his revelation typifies the black angel, since he exists only to mark Elvis's transformation. In *The Express*, Coach Schwartzwalder (Dennis Quaid) begins the film as a closet racist but becomes "a good man" through his relationship with Ernie Davis. In *Remember the Titans* and *Radio*, the cities of Alexandria, Virginia, and Anderson, South Carolina, are redeemed by the presence and honorable actions of black angels, Coach Herman Boone (Denzel Washington) and Radio (Cuba Gooding, Jr.), respectively. In *The Blind Side*, when one of Leigh Anne Tuohy's friends says to her over lunch, "I think that what you are doing is so great . . . Honey, you're changing that boy's life," Leigh Anne responds, "No, he's changing mine." In each case, the African American character becomes the object that white characters act upon to demonstrate their lack of individual racism. In this way, historical and contemporary films locate white racism in the past and as something that normative whiteness has overcome.

Change is one of the most important experiences for normative white characters. At a certain point in the film, a black angel will do something, generally related to a performance of manhood, and it changes a white character from being an antagonist to an ally of the black angel. In *Radio*, a racist football player named Johnny (Riley Smith) initially torments Radio, but he becomes an ally when Radio nobly refuses to reveal Johnny as one of his tormentors, which would place Johnny's scholarship in jeopardy. In *Remember the Titans*, the black player Julius (Wood Harris) lectures Gerry (Ryan Hurst) that racism is keeping him from acting as a true leader. Later, during a grueling training session, Gerry publicly supports Julius against his white teammates. Julius and Gerry then become best friends and a symbol of football's power to achieve racial reconciliation. In *The Express*, Ernie Davis faces two racist white foils, Coach Schwartzwalder and fellow player Bill Bell (Danny McCarthy). During the game at West Virginia University, Davis stands up for racial equality against the violent racism of the white WVU fans and Schwartzwalder's subtle racism. Davis's manly display of courage and integrity transforms Schwartzwalder and Bell into allies who help Davis to become the first African American player to win the Heisman Trophy.

Narratives of racial redemption rely on defining racism as individual racism. The logic of individual racism is that prejudice and discrimination are the products of ignorance and social distance; if we close social distance, people will get to know each other and realize that underneath the superficial difference of skin color, we are all really the same. The realization of an essential sameness in the human condition should lead to social integration and the dissipation of racial inequality. This is how the eminent sociologist Robert Park theorized race relations in 1914 and predicted a future end to racial inequality. The past hundred years have not borne out Park's prediction, but his optimistic beliefs reflect the bedrock of assumptions in football films that repeatedly show a white character getting to know a black angel as an individual, recognizing his humanity, and then acting on him as a *man* rather than an object. In *Remember the Titans*, the experience of an integrated training camp, removed from the racial conflict in Alexandria, allows the players to individualize and humanize each other. Coach Boone and Julius act as black angels, allowing the white characters to see their own individual racism, to transcend it, and to demonstrate their virtuousness. Individual racism in these films allows for easy narrative closure and racial redemption even if they demonstrate the exception rather than the rule. As early as 1963, Nathan Glazer and Daniel Moynihan recognized that larger social forces kept the races segregated and made ethnic identities salient long after social scientists had predicted (Glazer and Moynihan1970).

Racial Deviance and the Irredeemable

If football films represent white racism as something that existed in the past but was overcome through racial redemption, how can the persistence of racial inequality be explained? This may sound like an unfair question if one thinks of football films as "just entertainment." However, 10 of the 16 films discussed in this reading are "based on a true story" and therefore profess to represent a lived reality. Moreover, reviewers on film message boards consistently endorse these films as providing inspirational life lessons. Therefore, we can reasonably expect historical and sociological insight from these films.[5] In football films, it is individuals who work against social progress that maintain inequality in race relations. An inability or unwillingness to change, more than anything else, separates deviant whites from normative whiteness. As a result, deviant whites are unrepentant racists who are self-centered, prejudicial, and discriminatory.

Historical films cast deviant white characters as villains who prove the goodness of normative white characters. In *Radio*, the town's banker Frank (Chris Mulkey) plays a foil to Coach Jones (Ed Harris) by scheming to get Radio removed from the school.[6] In *The Express*, the states of West Virginia and Texas represent an anachronistic and deviant whiteness that the civil rights movement left behind.[7] In contemporary films, a defensive player, typically a linebacker, whom we see only through his face mask, is the primary representation of deviant whiteness. These players hop around on the field as they taunt the African American protagonist. They also shout after every successful play in what can be described as a "rebel yell." These minor characters play a major role in *The Blind Side* (the kid Michael Oher pushes over the fence) and *Gridiron Gang* (Willie Weathers's [Jade Yorker] nemesis). The image invoked by these characters is not a good-natured but a misdirected Huck Finn. They invoke the image of a backward, racist white man who deserves the ritual beating that he invariably receives. These nameless characters, like overseers in plantation literature, embody the violence of white supremacy and cleanse normative white characters of racist culpability (Costello 2007).

Although deviant whites in football films embody white racism, whether as an individual character or an entire state, they are also highly contained. Deviant whites in control of institutional power only appear in historical films; thus they are contained to the past, typically the South. The black angels in *Remember the Titans* and *Radio* change their southern towns, and Ernie Davis, who symbolizes the civil rights movement, changes the nation. At the end of *The Express*, a letter from President John F. Kennedy read at Davis's funeral is displayed on the screen: "He was an outstanding young man of great character who served—and, my hope is, will continue to serve—as an inspiration to the young people of this country." In contemporary films, deviant whites are the violent young men discussed above or older white women who make racist comments at meals, as in *The Blind Side* and *Friday Night Lights*. In fact, the lunch scene where Leigh Anne Tuohy's friends make racist comments gives her the opportunity to demonstrate that she is an enlightened southern woman by righteously saying, "Shame on you." In short, football films conform to the belief that the United States is on a linear historical trajectory away from a problematic racial past and into a happy postracial present. Unfortunately, this belief does not explain the persistent racial inequality that in fact permeates social institutions such as sport and structures contemporary society.

Football and Moral Discipline as Cure for Social Disorder

The primary ideological limitation of most football films is the narrow focus on individual racism that overlooks structural processes. This limits ways of imagining the causes of persistent racial inequality and ignores complex processes such as deindustrialization, which has led to staggering unemployment levels and intensified poverty in many inner city communities of color. The intensification of poverty in inner cities leads to a whole range of poverty-related problems such as increased crime and violence, drug and alcohol use, diet-related illnesses, and decreased life expectancy (Wilson 1987; Zenk et al. 2005). An analysis of inner city life is important, since it forms the location and antagonistic force confronting African American characters in contemporary football films. *They Call Me Sirr* narrates Sirr Parker's successful "escape" from the gangs, drugs, and desperation of South Central Los Angeles when he wins a football scholarship to Texas A&M. *The Blind Side* tells the rags-to-riches story of Michael Oher, who escaped the gangs, drugs, and desperation of Hurt Village to end up on the starting lineup of the Baltimore Ravens. Both Sirr Parker and Michael Oher also overcome dysfunctional, drug-addicted mothers who lack the ability to impart moral discipline to their sons. *They Call Me Sirr* attributes Sir Parker's success to an incredible individual drive and the racial class solidarity of an older gangster friend, while *The Blind Side* attributes Michael Oher's success to his preternatural physical gifts and the beneficence of the Tuohys.

In contemporary films featuring African American characters, football represents a prosocial alternative to gangs. "The gang life" is the obstacle that protagonists in contemporary films must overcome to achieve the American Dream, as opposed to the entrenched white racism of historical films. These films simultaneously construct the inner city as an authentic black space—the place where real black people live—and a space of moral disorder that a person needs to escape by making correct choices. Football films thus reproduce a binary opposition of athlete-citizen and gangster-deviant that animates a good deal of contemporary sport media (Cole 1996). The athlete-gangster binary is driven by the belief that sport provides moral discipline and serves as an antidote for the degenerative conditions of inner city life (Hartmann 2001).

The film *Gridiron Gang* uses the gangster-athlete binary to construct a redemptive narrative of moral discipline. Its representation of the gangster-athlete binary and uncritical belief that sports teach moral discipline produces dramatically engaging narratives of redemption but sidesteps and obscures a more complex racial reality of structural inequalities. *Gridiron Gang* tells the "true story" of how Sean Porter (Dwayne Johnson), a former football player and juvenile detention center guard, organized a football team made up of inmates at Camp Kilpatrick in Southern California. The film defines juvenile delinquency as a serious national epidemic through the rhetorical use of undocumented statistics. The film begins with white text on a black screen that states, "There are over 120,000 juveniles incarcerated in detention centers across the United States . . . Upon release, 75% will either return to prison or die on the street." This opening has the dual effect of connecting viewers to the plight of America's youth and establishing the "unquestionable truth" of the film through its somber presentation of statistics.[8] The rest of the movie details how Sean Porter uses football to inculcate moral discipline in Camp Kilpatrick's inmates so they can learn to make prosocial choices.

According to the film, Porter picked football because he was frustrated by his inability to keep the kids out of the gang life when they returned to the streets. In language akin to that of functionalist sociology, Porter argues to a coworker (Xzibit) that pulling kids out of a gang leaves a void in their lives. Without either a community or family, they experience isolation from society that produces a state of moral disorder and deviance. Porter theorizes that without membership in a group, the kids lack an identity and will inevitably be drawn back into the gang life. Like other members of the "social problems industry" (Hartmann 2001), Porter argues that the athletic gang will fill the void created by leaving the street gang and will inculcate the moral discipline in the kids that their families and communities did not. Football will transform the kids from "losers" (gangster-deviants) into "winners" (athlete-citizens). The athletic gang is valorized over the street gang for its ability to accommodate urban youth to conditions of deprivation rather than create their own underground economy. The apparent efficacy of football as a means of social control (i.e., reducing youth deviance by instilling civil norms) is heightened when the film tells us that most of the players have beaten the odds and turned their lives around. Ultimately, *Gridiron Gang* suggests that physical force, training, and pain on the football field forge a manly bond that transcends gang loyalties and overcomes the problems of a dysfunctional childhood.

The uplifting story in *Gridiron Gang* is predicated on accepting the sport-as-social-control hypothesis as unambiguously true. Unfortunately, the initial hypothesis did not draw on empirical research, and as a result the thesis is more ideological than factual (Hartmann 2001). Although individual success stories do exist, such as the one represented in *Gridiron Gang*, systematic research in the United States and the United Kingdom on youth athletics and deviance has *at best* found mixed results (Coakley 2011; Hartmann and Depro 2006; Hartmann and Massoglia 2007; Smith and Waddington 2004). In fact, youth sport participation can also encourage violent, antisocial behavior (Messner and Stevens 2002; Miller et al. 2007). A key limitation of the sport-as-social-control hypothesis is that it reduces patterns of behavior, like gang membership, to individual choices without recognizing the complex social conditions that lead a person to make one choice over another.

Gang members tend to experience a world structured by "multiple marginalities" in that they inhabit marginal neighborhoods, a marginal position in the economy, a marginal racial identity, and so forth. All of these positions come together to create "a web of ecological, socioeconomic, cultural, and psychological factors" in which gang life, despite its dangers, appears reasonable and desirable (Vigil 1988:9). Given that gang participation cannot be reduced to any one single causal factor, there can similarly be no singular remedy, such as sport participation. *Gridiron Gang*, like other football films, reduces the complexity of social life down to a singular explanation; deviance results from a lack of moral discipline. *Gridiron Gang* ultimately operates as a morality tale where football is presented as the singular remedy to a complex social problem without actually addressing the multiple marginalities that produce street gangs. By representing a lack of moral discipline as *the* obstacle minority youth must overcome to achieve the American Dream, football films mistake the symptoms of institutional racism for the cause of racial inequality. The film further obscures the fact that the racial privilege enjoyed by middle and upper class whites also produces the very conditions that foster street gangs.

Narratives of Gender and the Commodified Body

To this point, I have theorized football films in terms of class by arguing that narratives of redemption provide an individualistic frame for understanding social mobility and in terms of race by arguing that narratives of racial redemption and moral discipline provide a similar frame for understanding racial inequality. However, classed and raced actors are always also gendered actors (Ferber 2007). This is especially true in the masculinizing institution of football, where boys learn and perform a narrow model of manhood (Whannel 1993). The willingness and pleasure in delivering and enduring pain is central to performing an honorable manhood in football films, despite the fact that football rarely leads to social mobility but often leads to debilitating injury (Eitzen 1999). As a result, grueling training sessions that involve players vomiting and enduring injury to achieve glory are fixtures of football films. When a boy wills his body to rise above pain, suffering, and insecurity, football films suggest, he becomes a man and, in doing so, proves he is not a woman.

This means that although women are generally marginal in football, they play an important ideological role in football films by validating the man that the protagonist wants to become (Cheever 2006). This is the function of Rachel in *Hometown Legend*'s narrative of redemption. As an attractive young woman, she symbolizes goodness and middle class virtue. In fact, Rachel was the favorite wife of Jacob in the Bible, and today the name means purity and beauty. The daughter of the team's assistant coach, she is a leading community booster and an avid football fan assigned to act as Elvis's "prayer warrior." Rachel ultimately leads Elvis on his faith walk at the same time that she leads the fight to save both the high school and the town. In this sense, her body is the vessel through which Elvis and the town achieve redemption. Elvis's redemption is spiritual, material, and immediate: accepting Jesus Christ and forgoing the life of a self-centered egoist lead to an immediate movement into the middle class, symbolized by winning a college education and a beautiful middle class girl. Indeed, in *Hometown Legend*, *Full Ride*, *Jerry Maguire*, and *Gridiron Gang*, "getting the girl" and overcoming physical or mental anguish symbolizes the protagonist's achievement of manhood and transcendence.

Since escaping social fixity, or the idea that characters are trapped by their life circumstances, is central to narratives of redemption, it is revealing to see how football films represent men's and women's strategies to transcend fixity. Whether white or black, the young men in these films see their athletic abilities, their own human resources, as the ticket out of social fixity. So although the sources of fixity are racialized in the films, the use of the athletic male body to transcend social circumstances becomes a universal male behavior. White female characters also use their bodies to escape social fixity, but white female bodies are represented as sexual rather than athletic. In this sense, both young men and women create instrumental relationships to transcend fixity. White women use their bodies to attach themselves to a rising football star and move toward a better life; male characters need an older man, usually a coach, to achieve the same ends. Although Darcy Sears's (Ali Larter) whipped cream bikini in *Varsity Blues* is the most iconic image of the sexualized female body, Amy Lear (Meredith Monroe) articulates this gendered dynamic when she tells Matt Sabo (Riley Smith) in *Full Ride*, "We both put out to get out"—she for the players and he for the coaches. The bodies of men and white women in football films thus become commodities exchanged for social mobility.

None of the films under consideration represent African American women as commodifying their bodies.[9] Young African American women are consistently represented as college educated and smart. Most of the women are represented as proper ladies in that they are well spoken, heterosexually attractive, and deferential to their men. All of the young African American women exist in relation to an athletic male as either a wife or girlfriend, and their relationship to the male character is consistently based on romantic attachment, a legitimate normative motivation in bourgeois culture. The relationship therefore is presented as the choice of an educated, responsible young woman who does not need to rely on sexual commodification.

The representation of young African American women in these films may appear positive, given their generally negative image in U.S. popular culture. However, the domesticated image presented in these films does not challenge the pervasive "angry Black woman" stereotype (West 2008). Marcee Tidwell (Regina King) in *Jerry Maguire* provides an example of the merging of positive characteristics with this stereotype. Married to Rod Tidwell (Cuba Gooding, Jr.), Marcee is a strong, smart, proud, and college-educated black woman with a degree in marketing. However, she is also represented as angry, cynical, flamboyant, self-centered, fertile, and loud. When Rod Tidwell is offered an insultingly low contract and Jerry (Tom Cruise) calmly offers to follow up with the team, Marcee screams, "And say what? Would you please take your dick from my ass?" Dorothy (Renée Zellweger) responds by lecturing Marcee on decorum and humility. Once put in her place by a "proper lady," a contrite Marcee realizes that supporting Jerry and her husband is what matters most.

Although black women's bodies are not commodified in these films, they still fair worse than white women. White women's bodies are commodified in football films because men's possession of their sexuality symbolizes success and integration into U.S. society. Thus, characters like Rachel Sawyer and Amy Lear symbolize achievement of the American Dream. African American women are narrowly represented as either "good," in that they are domesticated and submissive to their men, or as "bad," drug-addicted mothers, as seen in *The Blind Side* and *They Call Me Sirr*. Unlike white women, African American women never come to symbolize success in the United States and therefore are unable to commodify their sexuality in football films. And when African American women are vocally upset about being denigrated relative to the valorization of white women, they are represented as problematic, as Marcee is in *Jerry Maguire*.

Conclusion

Football may be a team sport, but individualism looms very large in football films. Individualism is such a powerful ideology in the United States that it is an axiom of the Declaration of Independence: "We hold these truths to be self-evident, that all men are created equal, that they are endowed by their Creator with certain unalienable Rights, that among these are Life, Liberty and the pursuit of Happiness." Individualism provides a powerful mental framework that people in the United States use to clarify, understand, and represent the way in which society works, regardless of contradictions. Like any other ideology, individualism regularly faces contradictory evidence, and so it needs constant reinforcement from official society and popular culture. Narratives of redemption in their many permutations accept individualism as an unchallenged truth or axiom to organize compelling even if implausible stories of success and legitimate the organization of society. Even when football films point to flaws in society, especially racism, it is generally to suggest that these social problems result from the poor choices of individuals, not from the very organization of society itself.

Sport sociology tries to provide students with alternative mental frameworks, since individualism provides a narrow view of how society actually works. Football films' focus on individualism obscures the institutional forces that structures people's lives and contours the decisions they make. The individualism represented in football films like *Gridiron Gang* leads to what Lawrence Bobo calls laissez-faire racism, which "involves persistent negative stereotyping of African Americans, a tendency to blame blacks themselves for the black-white gap in socioeconomic standing, and resistance to meaningful policy efforts to ameliorate America's racist social conditions and institutions" (Bobo et al. 1996:16). Rather than recognizing the multiple marginalities that produce street gangs, a film like *Gridiron Gang* mistakes symptoms for causes by reducing street gangs to a lack of moral discipline.

By looking at sport as a historically based social institution through the perspective of intersectionality, we recognize that sport is neither a timeless reflection of society nor apolitical. Indeed, sport and its representation on film help to contour people's understandings of the world, themselves, and their place in the world. Moreover, sport has been integrated into educational curriculum since the early twentieth century as a means to produce desirable citizens (O'Hanlon 1980). Sport is a central institution of the modern world, and it has also been a site for transforming the world. The film *Not Just a Game* (Dave Zirin, 2010) profiles athletes such as Jack Johnson, Muhammad Ali, and Billie Jean King to demonstrate how sport serves as a powerful force in society, not just in creating the status quo but also in transforming how we understand racism and sexism. The goal of sport sociology is to understand how sport, whether in the stadium, on television, or on film, fits into the architecture of society, and how it can help us transform our social world.

References

Bobo, L., J. R. Kluegel, and R. A. Smith. 1996. "Laissez-Faire Racism: The Crystallization of a Kinder, Gentler, Antiblack Ideology." Pp. 15–42 in *Racial Attitudes in the 1990s: Continuity and Change*, edited by S. A. Tuch and J. Martin. Westport, CT: Praeger.

Carrington, B. 2010. *Race, Sport and Politics: The Sporting Black Diaspora*. Thousand Oaks, CA: Sage.

Chambers, C. 2009. "*The Blind Side* an Obvious Appeal to White Guilt." *The Grio*, November 20. Retrieved February 17, 2011 (http://www.thegrio.com/opinion/the-blind-side-an-obvious-appeal-to-white-guilt.php).

Cheever, A. 2006. "The Man He Almost Is": Jerry Maguire and Judith Butler. *Arizona Quarterly* 62(4):71–91.

Coakley, J. 2009. *Sport in Society: Issues and Controversies*. 10th ed. Boston: McGraw-Hill.

Coakley, J. 2011. "Youth Sports: What Counts as 'Positive Development'?" In *Introduction to Sport and Development*, edited by R. Schinke and S. Hanrahan. London: Routledge.

Cole, C. L. 1996. "American Jordan: P.L.A.Y., Consensus, and Punishment." *Sociology of Sport Journal* 13(4):366–97.

Costello, B. 2007. *Plantation Airs: Racial Paternalism and the Transformations of Class in Southern Fiction, 1945–1971*. Baton Rogue: Louisiana State University Press.

Daniels, D. B. 2005. "You Throw Like a Girl: Sport and Misogyny on the Silver Screen." *Film & History: An Interdisciplinary Journal of Film and Television* 35(1):29–38.

Dunning, E. 1972. "The Development of Modern Football." Pp. 133–51 in *Sport: Readings from a Sociological Perspective*, edited by E. Dunning. Toronto: University of Toronto Press.

Dunning, E. 1975. "Industrialization and the Incipient Modernization of Football: A Study in Historical Sociology." *Stadion: Journal of the History of Sport and Physical Education* 1(1):101–39.

Eichberg, H. 1986. "The Enclosure of the Body—On the Historical Relativity of 'Health,' 'Nature' and the Environment of Sport." *Journal of Contemporary History* 21(1):99–121.

Eitzen, D. S. 1999. *Fair and Foul: Beyond the Myths and Paradoxes of Sport.* Lanham, MD: Rowman & Littlefield.

Elias, N. and E. Dunning, eds. 1986. *Quest for Excitement: Sport and Leisure in the Civilizing Process.* Oxford, England: Basil Blackwell.

Ferber, A. L. 2007. "Whiteness Studies and the Erasure of Gender." *Sociology Compass* 1(1):265–82.

Gabbard, K. 2004. *Black Magic: White Hollywood and African American Culture.* New Brunswick, NJ: Rutgers University Press.

Glazer, N. and D. P. Moynihan, D. P. 1970. *Beyond the Melting Pot: The Negroes, Puerto Ricans, Jews, Italians, and Irish of New York City.* Cambridge, MA: MIT Press.

Guttman, A. 1978. *From Ritual to Record: The Nature of Modern Sports.* New York: Columbia University Press.

Hall, S. 1986. "The Problem of Ideology—Marxism without Guarantees." *Journal of Communication Inquiry* 10(2):28–44.

Hartmann, D. 2001. "Notes on Midnight Basketball and the Cultural Politics of Recreation, Race, and At-Risk Urban Youth." *Journal of Sport & Social Issues* 25(4):339–71.

Hartmann, D. and B. Depro. 2006. "Rethinking Sports-Based Community Crime Prevention: A Preliminary Analysis of the Relationship between Midnight Basketball and Urban Crime Rates." *Journal of Sport & Social Issues* 30(2):180–96.

Hartmann, D. and M. Massoglia. 2007. "Reassessing the Relationship between High School Sports Participation and Deviance: Evidence of Enduring, Bifurcated Effects." *The Sociological Quarterly* 48(3):485–505.

Hilliard, D. C. 1994. "Televised Sport and the (Anti) Sociological Imagination." *Journal of Sport and Social Issues* 18(1):88–99.

Knoppers, A. and M. McDonald. 2010. "Scholarship on Gender and Sport in Sex Roles and Beyond." *Sex Roles* 63(5–6):311–23.

Messner, M. A. and M. A. Stevens. 2002. "Scoring without Consent: Confronting Male Athletes' Violence against Women." In *Paradoxes of Youth and Sport*, edited by M. Gatz, M. A. Messner, and S. J. Ball-Rokeach. Albany: State University of New York Press.

Miller, K. E., M. J. Melnick, G. M. Barnes, D. Sabo, and M. P. Farrell. 2007. "Athletic Involvement and Adolescent Delinquency." *Journal of Youth Adolescence* 36:711–23.

Montez de Oca, J. In press. "White Domestic Goddess on a Postmodern Plantation: Charity and Commodity Racism in *The Blind Side. Sociology of Sport Journal* 29(2).

Morford, W. R. and M. J. McIntosh. 1993. "Sport and the Victorian Gentleman." Pp. 51–76 in *Sport in Social Development: Traditions, Transitions, and Transformations*, edited by A. G. Ingham and J. W. Loy. Champaign, IL: Human Kinetics.

O'Hanlon, T. 1980. "Interscholastic Athletics, 1900–1940: Shaping Citizens for Unequal Roles in the Modern Industrial State." *Educational Theory* 30(2):89–103.

Park, R. E. 1914. "Racial Assimilation in Secondary Groups with Particular Reference to the Negro." *The American Journal of Sociology* 19(5):606–23.

Pearson, D. W. 2001. "The Depictions and Characterization of Women in Sport Film." *Women in Sport & Physical Activity Journal* 10(1):103–24.

Persall, S. 2008. "Teammates Say *The Express* Changes History." *Tampa Bay Times*, October 5. Retrieved January 19, 2012 (http://www.tampabay.com/features/movies/article837721.ece).

Smith, A. and I. Waddington. 2004. "Using 'Sport in the Community Schemes' to Tackle Crime and Drug Use among Young People: Some Policy Issues and Problems." *European Physical Education Review* 10(3):279–98.

Stoddart, B. 1988. "Sport, Cultural Imperialism, and Colonial Response in the British Empire." *Comparative Studies in Society and History* 30(4):649–73.

Thompson, M. 2008. "New Movie 'Based on True Story' Shows WVU Fans in False, Ugly Light." *The Times West Virginia*, October 8. Retrieved January 19, 2012 (http://timeswv.com/wvu_sports/x681684807/New-movie-based-on-true-story-shows-WVU-fans-in-false-ugly-light).

U.S. Department of Justice. 2010. "Juveniles in Residential Placement, 1997–2008." Retrieved January 19, 2012 (https://www.ncjrs.gov/pdffiles1/ojjdp/229379.pdf).

Vigil, J. D. 1988. *Barrio Gangs: Street Life and Identity in Southern California*. Austin: University of Texas Press.

West, C. M. 2008. "Mammy, Jezebel, Saphire, and Their Homegirls: Developing an 'Oppositional Gaze' toward the Images of Black Women." Pp. 286–99 in *Lectures on the Psychology of Women*. 4th ed., edited by J. C. Chrisler, C. Golden, and P. D. Rozee. New York: McGraw-Hill.

Whannel, G. 1993. "No Room for Uncertainty: Gridiron Masculinity in *North Dallas Forty*." Pp. 200–211 in *You Tarzan: Masculinity, Movies, Men*, edited by P. Kirkham and J. Thumim. New York: St Martin's Press.

Wilson, W. J. 1987. *The Truly Disadvantaged: The Inner City, the Underclass, and Public Policy*. Chicago: University of Chicago Press.

Zenk, S. N., A. J. Schulz, B. A. Israel, S. A. James, S. Bao, and M. L. Wilson. 2005. "Neighborhood Racial Composition, Neighborhood Poverty, and the Spatial Accessibility of Supermarkets in Metropolitan Detroit." *American Journal of Public Health* 95(4):660–69.

Notes

1. The sample includes the following films released between 1996 and 2009: *The Blind Side* (John Lee Hancock, 2009), *Big Fan* (Robert D. Siegel, 2009), *The Express* (Gary Fleder, 2008), *Gridiron Gang* (Phil Joanou, 2006), *We Are Marshall* (McG, 2006), *Friday Night Lights* (Peter Berg, 2004), *Radio* (Mike Tollin, 2003), *Hometown Legend* (James Anderson, 2002), *The Slaughter Rule* (Alex Smith and Andrew J. Smith, 2002), *The Junction Boys* (Mike Robe, 2002), *Full Ride* (Mark Hoeger, 2002), *They Call Me Sirr* (Robert Munic, 2001), *Remember the Titans* (Boaz Yakin, 2000), *Any Given Sunday* (Oliver Stone, 1999), *Varsity Blues* (Brian Robbins, 1999), and *Jerry Maguire* (Cameron Crowe, 1996). Documentaries and comedies were excluded in favor of football dramas.

2. *The Blind Side* is in some ways an exception, since Leigh Anne Tuohy (Sandra Bullock) is the film's key protagonist (Chambers 2009; Montez de Oca In press).

3. They are: "(1) Sport provides free college education; (2) sport leads to a college degree; (3) a professional sports career is possible; (4) sport is a way out of poverty, especially for racial minorities; (5) Title IX has created many opportunities for upward mobility through sport for women; and (6) a professional sport career provides security for life" (Eitzen 1999:133).

4. The one exception is *Radio*, which centers on a developmentally challenged African American man.

5. Reviewers also consistently criticize the films for factual *inaccuracies* and artistic license in the representation of history.

6. Frank's son Johnny, mentioned above, turns against his own father, who is acting on his son's behalf when Johnny realizes that racism is wrong.

7. In fact, the film had to take tremendous artistic license to represent the South as especially racist (Persall 2008; Thompson 2008).

8. According to the U. S. Department of Justice (2010), the number of juveniles in public and private detention centers in the United States declined from a high of about 108,000 in 2000 to about 81,000 in 2008. There is no national data on recidivism rates, given state variations, but the highest rate of recidivism reported at the state level was 55 percent for rearrest only and ranged from 12 percent to 33 percent for reincarceration in 2008.

9. Terri (Jade Dixon) in *Full Ride* is *almost* an exception. Terri and Amy both pursue football players as a ticket out of fixity. However, Terri remains in the town even after Amy successfully escapes with Matt.

Introduction

In the most advanced, contemporary societies, issues of health, well-being, and even happiness take on greater value compared to societies with higher morbidity and mortality (Inglehart 1997). Ironically, the dominant discourse that surrounds these issues focuses on individual choices and lifestyles, even as the public embrace of deterministic genetic attributions for everything from mental illness to asthma has grown (Pescosolido et al. 2010). The modern *social institution* of medicine has at its disposal the most powerful technology ever known and the most generous public financial support ever provided, yet it is severely criticized for its failure to cure society's ills, unresponsiveness to patients and providers, and inaccessibility to much of the world's population. The United States devotes the greatest amount of gross domestic product (GDP) to health and health care, but infant mortality, life span, and other similar measures—all common indicators used to assess how well a country meets the health needs of its population—fall well below those of many other advanced Western and Asian countries.

At the heart of these ironies lies a curious focus on individual rights to choose, individual responsibilities to uphold, and individual consequences to bear—to purchase insurance or not, to exercise or not, to eat healthy foods or not, to get sick or not. The litany of individual choices extends to medical practitioners and the health care system in which they work—to accept insurance or not, to provide care or not, to specialize or not. Deeply engrained in the public mind, particularly in the United States, exists the target for understanding and improving life and avoiding premature death—the individual. Sociology, on the other hand, provides a different vantage point. From the beginning of the discipline, sociologists including Marx, Weber, and Durkheim, and later in the Chicago School, Park and Burgess, pointed to larger societal patterns such as mortality, morbidity, and access to health care as critical windows to understanding the power of structured inequalities in society on personal fates (Pescosolido 1996).

Thus, the "doggedly psychological culture" (to quote Michael Kimmel in Chapter 2) that characterizes American society finds similar expression in all medical areas. Issues dealing with health and medical care are ones with which we all have experience. How do sociologists deal with popular notions that health, illness, healing, and even disease are simply random biological phenomena or neutral scientific matters or the product of individual behaviors and choices, since we argue that they are also systematically, socially patterned? Yesteryear's debates about nature versus nurture are obsolete; we now know they operate together, sometimes reinforcing and other times canceling each other out. In sociology's early years, the sheer recognition and demonstration of social forces and social factors at work in health and medicine was a surprise to many. The already established sciences looked to individual rationality, the cell, elementary particles, and personality. Now, in the last several decades, the disciplinary boundaries and increasing specialization that characterized the last hundred years have been replaced by calls for connection across traditional intellectual boundaries and for more subtle and sophisticated explanations that avoid the "either/or" character of earlier debates (Pescosolido 2006).

The challenge becomes clear, but complex: How does the "power of the social" work in light of known disease-causing processes and vectors, scientific medical knowledge, and the demonstrated benefits of modern medicine? To show that the *sociological imagination* provides a key perspective to understanding life, death, and medicine now requires conveying *both* (1) that the lives of the physician, the patient, the health administrator, and the health policy maker are all shaped by the larger social context and (2) that even individual level health/medical behaviors (e.g., exercise, smoking, nursing school) and choices (e.g., going to a doctor, determining a diagnosis) intersect with social determinants (e.g., age, gender, race, socioeconomic status) to produce systematic social patterns of health, disease, and treatment. That is, the foundation of the sociological contribution lies in what sociologists have always known—life is regular and patterned, even if complicated and messy (Pescosolido 2011), and personal troubles are deeply embedded in public issues (Mills 1959). In sum, the point is not to reject our faith in science and medicine as social institutions, but rather to broaden our perspectives to see that these are inextricably tied to the social world, both shaping and being shaped by it.

Sociologists of culture have provided us with intellectual tools to use film to see the social world and social forces in operation. We know that popular films are not simply depictions of reality, but social constructions of it. Through Tilly's (1999) insights, we are aware that films, particularly American films, are in the category of "standard stories," leaning toward a rational accounting with ends neatly tied up. Self-motivated characters, and not social processes, tend to dominate. In addition, we know that audiences do not simply absorb what is depicted on film—they interpret, they read into, and they misread. However, as sociologists we can use the "standard stories" of popular film to wrestle with fundamental questions in active rather than passive mode, to take advantage of the greater visual orientation we have in contemporary times, and to go from concrete situations to general theories (Howe and Strauss 2000). As Sutherland and Feltey maintain in the Introduction to this volume, film provides a concrete means of illustrating principals on the study of social life. It allows a medium to demonstrate how macro levels of context "above" the individual (community, institutional, and support network systems) and the levels "below" (individual and molecular systems) shape the "typical" micro level experience of health, illness, and disease with which we are all familiar (Pescosolido 1990). In learning to think sociologically about the medical social institution and individual health and illness outcomes, films "serve as a bridge between the world of the classroom and the day-to-day world in which the student lives" (Demerath 1981:712).

To explore the connection between social context and determinants and individual experiences and choices in the realm of health and illness, two central ideas from medical sociology—the illness career and health disparities—are particularly helpful. We first consider the micro level, using films that provide a dramatic but reality-based look at the unfolding process for individuals or for a newly identified public health threat over time. The Illness Career Model provides a helpful tool for examining the stages of illness over the course of time as experienced at the individual level and understanding how a public health threat comes to be defined as such and its evolution through social and political dynamics. We will apply this model through the life of one person as showcased in film: on mental illness in *Frances* and *It's Kind of a Funny Story* and on environmental toxins in *A Civil Action* and *Erin Brockovich*. We then turn to the macro level processes of health disparities along social fault lines in the United States, such as socioeconomic status or class and race. Life chances, including the most basic of health outcomes, living or dying, depend in large part on social status rather than on simply being at the wrong place at the wrong time. Drawing on the Hollywood films *Titanic* and *John Q*, we explore the ways that class, race, and gender shape chances of survival.

The Illness Career for Individuals and Public Health

One recent attempt to synthesize the contributions of sociologists from different traditions (qualitative/quantitative, social constructivist/social epidemiologist/services research) has been rethinking health and medicine in light of the life course. The illness career has been conceptualized and studied in terms of individual response from the onset of symptoms with a focus on stages and signposts, role changes, and shifts in identity (Charmaz 1991; Davis 1963; Goffman 1959; Parsons 1951; Perrucci and Targ 1982; Suchman 1964). Early research established the trajectory of the illness career, while later research examined social factors associated with behaviors such as going to a doctor, filling prescriptions, and recovering. Unfortunately, the contingency-focused approaches usually lost the sense of context-based dynamics.

The Illness Career Model (see Figure 9.1) provides a conceptualization of health-related behaviors as embedded in the life course (see Chapter 8 in this volume). This approach emphasizes that any health-related behavior (e.g., dieting, taking pills) can be bracketed by "episodes" which are deeply rooted in "linked lives" (Elder 1978) and social context, usually accompanied by shifts in self-conceptualization, experiences in social institutions, and life chances. These are as relevant to the physician as they are to the individual in the community; as salient for understanding how a medical professional evaluates a symptom as they are to how a 13-year-old (i.e., the average age at which doctors report they made their decision) commits to going to medical school; and central to whether societies jail their midwives or train them. While the illness career follows an individual through the process, it opens up the possibility of looking at communities, health care systems, and historical periods. Most important, it involves a constant examination of the interface of community and treatment systems (Pescosolido 1996).

The illness career helps tie together the introduction of the "social" across different scientific topics in health and medicine (social epidemiology, medicalization, service utilization, and healing systems) or explanatory factors in health (gender, social class, race/ethnicity). By framing a sociological look at these issues under one overarching process, themes are not brought up and moved past but addressed and revisited. For example, the focus on Recognition (i.e., the decision that something is wrong) allows an examination of

Figure 9.1   The Illness Career Model

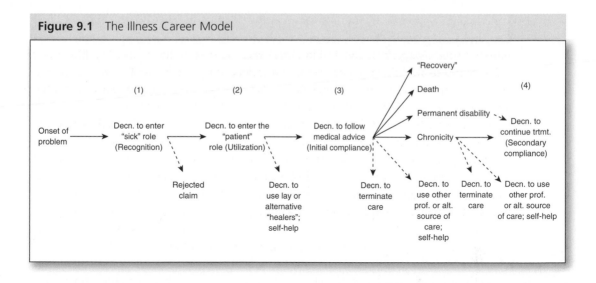

classic differences in how social class influences perceptions of illness (an individual's self-assessment). It simultaneously offers the opportunity to examine whether and how some claims for disease status (observable health indicators) at the medical or societal level are rejected, accepted, or transformed (e.g., see Figert 1996 on PMS). Looking at how people, organizations, and societies respond to new health challenges reveals the social construction of illness—how life's problems become medicalized (Clarke et al. 2003; Conrad 2005) and how health-based social movements bring individuals together (Brown et al. 2011).

Located squarely within the community, the social dynamics of the Recognition process most often begin outside the doctor's office and the health care system, since the decision to make a claim for the sick role, be forced into it, or be denied entry is one that is adjudicated in individuals' social networks (Pescosolido, Brooks-Gardner, and Lubell 1998). The illness career begins, according to Perrucci and Targ (1982), with the first occasion on which an individual displays behavior that is judged by others (or by the individual) as different. When the individual's mental or physical functioning lies outside a range considered by others as "normal" for that individual in that social context (Twaddle and Hessler 1987), entrance into the illness career becomes one potential response. Note that entry into the illness career occurs at the level of the individuals, the family, social control agents, and societies. Role "entrances" and "exits" are "punctuation points" in the social process of illness, setting up the importance of timing and spacing (when transitions occur), duration (the time it takes to complete a transition), and order (the sequencing of role changes; Pescosolido 1992).

Frances and *It's Kind of a Funny Story:* Illness Careers and the Myth of Mental Illness

The notion that "crazy" behavior is socially defined flies in the face of perceptions about the power of the biomedical model to diagnose and treat disease (Goffman 1963; Horwitz and Wakefield 2007; Scheff 1984). Often, we draw from the historical past or distant tribal societies where people with emotional problems were seen as possessed by demons or hailed as healers. *Frances* (Graeme Clifford, 1982) is the story of Frances Farmer (Jessica Lange), traced from her adolescence in Seattle to Hollywood actress fame and then to the end of her life (postlobotomy) as a local talk show host in Indianapolis. The film covers important historical periods in medicine and society (the 1930s to the 1970s) and portrays mental health as polemical regarding what individuals face when their behavior is defined as "strange" or out of the ordinary.

Labeling theory is particularly helpful in understanding how the film makes problematic the distinction between mental illness and "normal" behavior, particularly regarding gender and political roles. A variety of alternative labels are applied to Frances (atheist, Communist sympathizer, Hollywood troublemaker, alcoholic) depending on the audience and their political/economic/social motivations. The reactions of others to Frances's "deviant" behavior change as her social power increases and then decreases. Frances's rejection of social norms regarding women (she wears pants and asserts her opinions), Hollywood stars (she drives an old jalopy and appears without makeup), and patriotic citizenship (she is sympathetic to the plight of the unemployed masses and socialist politics) lead people in her social network to view her first as rebellious and ultimately as "crazy." Over time, Frances's behavior becomes more extreme, although given the context, it seems that many of her actions and reactions make sense given the abuse she endures from family, work, and the criminal justice and mental health institutions. Her unwillingness to conform to the expectations of her mother, studio executives, and psychiatrists leads to her institutionalization, shock therapy, and eventually a lobotomy.[1] Toward the end of the movie, Frances is interviewed on the television show *This Is Your Life* about her history and diagnosis:

Interviewer: . . . Dwayne Steele divorced you, and from this point on, your story takes a darker turn. Shunned by the Hollywood you criticized so harshly, alienated from your family and friends, you turn your back on professional commitments in New York, and alcohol and drugs enter your life. These are sad, desperate times for you . . . until finally your mother finds it necessary to commit you to a state mental institution. Were you mentally ill, Frances?

Frances: No, Ralph. I don't believe I ever was sick. But when you're treated like a patient long enough, you're apt to act like one.

Frances's response captures the essence of labeling theory—that once successfully labeled as mentally ill, especially in the context of a total institution, the patient experiences resocialization that involves acceptance of the definition/diagnosis of mentally ill (Goffman 1961). Mental illness is not often clear-cut, and social factors, from social networks to gender to political power (Rosenfield 1982), have been documented as critical to the process of "naming and framing" (Brown 1995) someone with a mental illness.

A more recent film, *It's Kind of a Funny Story* (Anna Boden and Ryan Fleck, 2010), tells a different story about hospitalization for mental illness. In the film, based on the book with the same title (Vizzini 2006), 15-year-old Craig (Keir Gilchrist) lives with his upper middle class family in Brooklyn, where he attends a prestigious, highly competitive private school geared toward professional occupations. He requests hospitalization for a series of problems, including academic stress, unrequited love, and suicidal ideation, only to find himself placed in an adult psychiatric unit (more than he bargained for), since the current fiscal strains of the mental health treatment system resulted in the closure of the adolescent unit. The film focuses on his relationships with others in the hospital and the reactions of family and friends, and even other patients (particularly Bobby, played by Zach Galifianakis), to his hospitalization. In the course of his hospitalization he discovers his artistic, rather than scientific or mathematical, abilities through a developing romantic relationship with another teenage patient, Noelle (Emma Roberts). Unlike Frances's inpatient experiences, Craig finds friendship, love, and the path to healing. There are fleeting references to societal expectations or standards as the source of individual problems (rather than flawed individuals who fail to accept and live up to those expectations), such as this exchange between Bobby and another patient:

Bobby: I don't get wrapped up in a bunch of stuff I can't have.

Johnny: Relax, it's just for fun, bro.

Bobby: That's not fun. That's propaganda, man. All those Madison Avenue types telling you how to live your life. Fast cars, hot chicks . . . Reese's Pieces . . . Gucci . . . Werther's Original. I don't buy into that bullshit!

However, the overarching story is one of individual effort and the power to choose a healthy (versus mentally ill) life. In fact, in one short week we witness Craig's transformation from boy on the verge of suicide to young man with hopes and dreams for his future, as he explains:

Okay, I know you're thinking: "What is this? Kid spends a few days in the hospital and all his problems are cured?" But I'm not. I know I'm not. I can tell this is just the beginning. I still need to face my homework, my school, my friends. My dad. But the difference between today and last Saturday is that for the first time in a while, I can look forward to the things I want to do in my life. Bike, eat, drink, talk. Ride the subway, read, read maps. Make maps, make art. Finish the Gates application. Tell my dad not to stress about it. Hug my mom. Kiss my little sister. Kiss my dad. Make out with Noelle. Make out with her more. Take her on a picnic. See a movie with her. See a movie with Aaron. Heck, see a movie with Nia. Have a party. Tell people my story. Volunteer at 3 North. Help people like Bobby. Like Muqtada. Like me. Draw more. Draw a person. Draw a naked person. Draw Noelle naked. Run, travel, swim, skip. Yeah, I know it's lame, but whatever. Skip anyway. Breathe . . . Live.

While both Frances and Craig were labeled as mentally ill, Frances ultimately rejected the label, concluding that her behavior was an adaptation to the context, a *self-fulfilling prophecy.* Craig, on the other hand, knows he is not "cured," that his hospitalization is "just the beginning." His illness and treatment are interwoven with other markers of adolescence—attraction, dating, and first kiss. For Craig, young love has transformative power, opening the artist within who has been stifled by pressures to follow in his father's footsteps. The ending is a happy one for Craig, his family, and the mental health system that changes peoples' lives for the better.

A Civil Action and *Erin Brockovich*:
The Illness Career in Context

As we've seen, films on mental illness are prime examples for application of the illness career allowing us to follow individuals through the interconnected process. However, we know that the illness career extends well beyond individual experiences, and that issues of health and illness are contextualized within broader societal concerns. Films that link disease and illness with situations beyond the control of individual life circumstances provide examples of the link between disease risk and outcomes and the larger social context. In this section we look at two such films, *A Civil Action* (Steven Zaillian, 1998) and *Erin Brockovich* (Steven Soderbergh, 2000). Both films are based on actual people, events, and communities.

In *A Civil Action*, unusually high cancer diagnosis and death are observed in a small Massachusetts community where the primary employer is a tannery production company. In fact, eight children have died of leukemia in a short period of time. The affected families seek legal recourse; their goal is to demand cleanup of the site where toxic dumping has contaminated the water supply as well as to obtain an apology to the community from the responsible party. Initially Jan Schlichtmann (John Travolta) meets with the affected families to inform them that his small law firm cannot pursue a case without a known defendant. However, during his drive back to Boston, and in a dramatic walk upstream of the local river, he sees shipments leaving the tannery that connect it to two large multinational corporations. That discovery makes the case more attractive (read: lucrative), despite the depressed "value" of the individuals who have been diagnosed with or died from cancer. Jan sums up the system of stratification in valuing human life when he explains:

> It's like this. A dead plaintiff is rarely worth more than a living, severely maimed plaintiff. However, if it's a long, slow, agonizing death as opposed to a quick drowning or car wreck, the value can rise considerably. A dead adult in his twenties is generally worth less than one who is middle aged. A dead woman less than a dead man. A single adult less than one who's married. Black less than white. Poor less than rich. The perfect victim is a white male professional, 40 years old, at the height of his earning power, struck down at his prime. And the most imperfect—well, in the calculus of personal injury law, a dead child is worth the least of all.

The film highlights the often strained relationship between a local employer, the community suffering from environmental toxins, and the willingness of outside stakeholders to allow (and even defend) public health violations to protect monetary interests.

Similarly, *Erin Brockovich* centers on a legal assistant who mobilizes a rural California community to speak out about the chromium contamination of the local water supply by Pacific Gas and Electric Company due to faulty (and illegal) handling of environmental toxins. The "David and Goliath" theme of the movie is a popular one in Hollywood. A lone individual, an outsider (indeed an outcast) to the dominant system, takes on a powerful corporation (albeit with help begrudgingly accepted from others) and wins against all odds. Where Jan outlined the value of victims in terms of payout, Erin demanded that the corporate lawyers use their own bodies and health as the standard for calculation. When the PG&E lawyer intones that "twenty million dollars is more money than these people have ever dreamed of," Erin responds:

Oh see, now, that pisses me off. First of all, since the demur we have more than 400 plaintiffs and . . . let's be honest, we all know there are more out there. They may not be the most sophisticated people but they do know how to divide, and twenty million isn't shit when you split it between them. Second of all, these people don't dream about being rich. They dream about being able to watch their kids swim in a pool without worrying that they'll have to have a hysterectomy at the age of twenty. Like Rosa Diaz, a client of ours. Or have their spine deteriorate, like Stan Blume, another client of ours. So before you come back here with another lame-ass offer, I want you to think real hard about what your spine is worth, Mr. Walker. Or what you might expect someone to pay you for your uterus, Ms. Sanchez. Then you take out your calculator and you multiply that number by a hundred. Anything less than that is a waste of our time.

In the happy ending to the movie, the families win the lawsuit, Erin and her boss move up in the legal world (symbolized by their brand new upscale offices), and Erin transcends her status as a poor single mother to champion the powerless against corporate wrongdoing. Ultimately, however, the links between corporate responsibility, environmental degradation, and public health are unchallenged and unchanged.

An older film that is also based on real-life events, *Silkwood* (Mike Nichols, 1983), dramatizes the growing concern and activism of Karen Gay Silkwood regarding safety standards at the nuclear fuel production plant where she worked. The actual case on which the film was based provoked a great deal of antinuclear controversy, including the allegation that the auto crash in which she died was "arranged" by the Kerr-McGee Corporation. The film portrays key issues, including exposure to radiation as a fact of life for employment in a small town in Oklahoma with minimal job opportunities, and internal local-national union tension that pits employees' concerns about their livelihood and national union concerns with the ability to negotiate contracts and legally pursue claims. Given the events at the Fukushima Nuclear Power Plant in Japan following the March 12, 2011, magnitude 9 earthquake and subsequent tsunami, this film is disturbingly relevant nearly three decades after its production.

All of these films call attention to multiple dimensions of social justice (environmental safety, financial reimbursement, and community empowerment), structural sources of power and control held outside of any individual, and tensions between different societal institutions. The reality of illness and death at the intersection of the political economy and environmental degradation remind us that individual choices about health and safety will not change these structural conditions.

Titanic and *John Q*: Social Inequalities and Life Chances/Health

There is little question that structured inequalities understood in social context represent the backbone of sociology's contribution to the health sciences. Documenting stratification plays itself out, in part, through morbidity and mortality statistics representing a principal theme of theory, empirical investigation, and the design of interventions. Yet these issues have taken on greater prominence in recent discussions across society and medicine, repackaged at least a bit as "health disparities" or "health care disparities"

(Agency for Healthcare Research and Quality 2003; Institute of Medicine 2002). From research to policy and even to the popular press, the unmasking of the disparities in health and health care for individuals based on social class, race, and ethnicity has become a dominant theme (van Ryn and Fu 2003). While attention to these matters is welcome by sociologists and other social scientists, the existence of inequality in health, illness, and healing is hardly a revelation (e.g., see Link and Phelan 1995; Lutfey and Freese 2005). Indeed, social status has long been recognized as influencing the most basic of life chances: whether one lives or dies.

A classic example of survival linked to inequality long used by sociologists is the *Titanic* disaster. This historical event is a vivid illustration of inequality and life chances by gender and social class (the latter marked, in this case, by passage categories; Atkins and Moy 2005). Of the 2,201 individuals on board (with a lifeboat capacity of 1,178 people), 711 survived. Thanks to Hollywood's preoccupation with this event, as opposed to other equally disastrous shipwreck cases (e.g., *RMS Empress of Ireland*, *RMS Tayleur*, *RMS Lusitania*, and *RMS Carpathia*, which, ironically, came to the rescue of *RMS Titanic* before its own demise six years later by German torpedo), there are a number of films about the *Titanic*.[2] The two most popular film efforts were 20th Century Fox's *Titanic* (Jean Negulesco, 1953), based on *A Night to Remember* (Lord 1955), and the more recent James Cameron film released in 1997. In the latter, told through the fictitious, ill-fated relationship that develops between Jack (Leonardo DiCaprio), a poor Irish immigrant traveling in steerage class, and Rose (Kate Winslet), a wealthy New Yorker betrothed in a class-match to a life restricted by gender norms of the time, *Titanic* graphically depicts the startling class- and gender-based survival rates. Over 60 percent of first-class passengers survived, while only 44 percent of those in second class and 25 percent of those in steerage lived. And, with each class, the odds of women surviving were much greater (97 percent of first-class women survived; 86 percent of second-class women survived; 46 percent of women in steerage survived; see http://www.anesi.com/titanic.htm).

The 1997 film has pivotal scenes that dramatize some of the key social class divisions and their effects, such as when Jack Dawson is locked in steerage along with other Irish and Italian immigrants to avoid crowding out the first-class passengers boarding the lifeboats. In *Titanic*, social structure found a vector of life and death—this time in social classes, as marked by the wealth and ethnic, as well as gender and age, differences among the passengers. We witnessed this play out in recent history with events surrounding Hurricane Katrina along the Gulf Coast, with the central dividing line being that of race and class (see Boisseau et al. 2008; Quinn 2006; Squires and Hartman 2006).

Turning from large-scale community disaster to individual calamity, in the film *John Q* (Nick Cassavetes, 2002) we see a desperate father take a hospital hostage in an effort to save his son, who needs a heart transplant to live. The hospital administration has refused to put his son's name on the list of eligible donor recipients since John's insurance will not cover the surgery and he and his wife do not have the $75,000 (30 percent of the cost of surgery) required to secure a place on the list. The film is rare in that it directly and forcefully addresses the issues of access and affordability in health care, as well as the role of insurance carriers in the private market where we purchase health care services, in a way that is usually found only in documentaries.

The situation is not simplified to insured versus uninsured, since John is in fact employed and does have health care coverage. However, he has recently been cut from full to part time and his benefits have been adjusted accordingly. Because of the economic downturn and his reduced employment status, he no longer has insurance that will cover the surgery his son needs to live. The overall message of the film is fairly straightforward: chances of survival and quality of life increase with income and wealth. In this sense, the son might as well be on the *Titanic* in steerage class, where only 34 percent of the children survived compared to 100 percent of the children in first class. The difference is that John Q resorts to violence to secure surgery for his child, a move that makes the hospital administrator nervous, as she explains to the police chief:

If you give in to this guy, there's gonna be guns in every hospital in the country. What, you think Mr. Archibald's the only one who has a sick child? Have you checked out the HIV ward? There's a whole floor full. People get sick, they die. That's the way it goes. I'm faced with decisions like this every single day. The fact is that there are 50 million people in this country without medical insurance. If you'd like to change it, you should call your congressman.

While her reaction seems callous in the context of the film, she is also pointing out the obvious: that without major health care reform, many more children will suffer the consequences of unequal access to the medical institution.

Bringing It All Together: Film as Space and Place Microscope

Health and health care, like mortality, reflect the inequalities that divide society (Klinenberg 2003). Devastating health and health care consequences are set in terms of difference, real or constructed, of ethnicity, race, social class, or any other factor that is used to cleave the underprivileged from the privileged. Depicting life and death on the screen takes an often formulaic, and often American, take on individual triumph, even when characters die. Rarely do we find a film (and more rarely still, a film to our liking) on doctors, medical schools, or hospitals that comes anywhere close to providing a contextual and realistic portrayal of the day-to-day forces that shape outcomes for patients and providers. Films on these topics tend to focus on the unusual case, the brilliant doctor, and the love lives of interns and residents, with health and medicine only providing a backdrop (e.g., *Flatliners*, *Doc Hollywood*, *Gross Anatomy*, and even *Patch Adams*). However, some films on life and death escape Tilly's charge of "standard stories" and allow us a visible look at inequality and its consequences in and for health, illness, and healing. The portrayal of C. W. Mills's sociological imagination may offer a particular challenge, since sociology is essentially a comparative discipline, with the power of social forces and processes best seen in looking over time, across cases, and beyond traditional boundaries. Films that do so themselves, or that allow us to create a pastiche, as we have described here, can bring a vivid and often resonant tool to the classroom. Perhaps it should be no surprise that the docudrama, which owes some semblance of truth to the actual case, provides the artistic vehicle that best matches what sociologists need to convey through celluloid stories. In relating a tale about a real time and place rather than a story of "everyman" and "any man," the complexities of human health and the response to it are, on occasion, vividly exposed.

References

Agency for Healthcare Research and Quality. 2003. "National Healthcare Disparities Report." Agency for Healthcare Research and Quality, Rockville, MD.

Atkins, D. and E. M. Moy. 2005. "Left Behind: The Legacy of Hurricane Katrina." *British Medical Journal* 331:916–18.

Boisseau, T. J., K. M. Feltey, K. Flynn, L. Gelfand, and M. Triece. 2008. "New Orleans: A Special Issue on the Gender Politics of Place and Displacement." *NWSA Journal* 20(3).

Braslow, J. 1997. *Mental Ills and Bodily Cures: Psychiatric Treatment in the First Half of the Twentieth Century.* Berkeley: University of California Press.

Brown, P. 1995. "Naming and Framing: The Social Construction of Diagnosis and Illness." *Journal of Health and Social Behavior* Extra Issue:34–52.

Brown, P., R. Morello-Frosch, S. Zavestoski, L. Senier, R. G. Altman, E. Hoover, S. McCormick, B. Mayer, and C. Adams. 2011. "Health Social Movements: Advancing Traditional Medical Sociology Concepts." Pp. 117–138 in *Handbook of the Sociology of Health, Illness, and Healing: A Blueprint for the 21st Century*, edited by B. A. Pescosolido, J. K. Martin, J. D. McLeod, and A. Rogers. New York: Springer.

Charmaz, K. 1991. *Good Days, Bad Days: The Self In Chronic Illness and Time.* New Brunswick, NJ: Rutgers University Press.

Clarke, A. E., L. Mamo, J. R. Fishman, J. K. Shim, and J. R. Fosket. 2003. "Biomedicalization: Technoscientific Transformations of Health, Illness, and U.S. Biomedicine." *American Sociological Review* 68:161–94.

Conrad, P. 2005. "The Shifting Engines of Medicalization." *Journal of Health & Social Behavior* 46:3–14.

Davis, F. 1963. *Passage through Crisis: Polio Victims and Their Families.* Indianapolis, IN: Bobbs-Merrill.

Demerath, N. J. 1981. "Through a Double-Crossed Eye: Sociology and the Movies." *Teaching Sociology* 9:69–82.

Elder, G. H., Jr. 1978. "Family and the Life Course." Pp. 16–61 in *Transitions: The Life Course in Historical Perspective*, edited by T. K. Hareven. New York: Academic Press.

Figert, A. E. 1996. *Women and the Ownership of PMS: The Structuring of a Psychiatric Disease.* Hawthorne, NY: Aldine de Gruyter.

Goffman, E. 1959. *The Presentation of Self in Everyday Life.* New York: Anchor.

Goffman, E. 1961. *Asylums: Essays on the Social Situation of Mental Patients and Other Inmates.* NY: Doubleday Anchor.

Goffman, E. 1963. *Stigma: Notes on the Management of Spoiled Identity.* Englewood Cliffs, NJ: Prentice Hall.

Horwitz, A. V. and J. C. Wakefield. 2007. *The Loss of Sadness: How Psychiatry Transformed Normal Sorrow into Depressive Disorder.* New York: Oxford University Press.

Howe, N. and W. Strauss. 2000. *Millennials Rising: The Next Great Generation.* New York: Vintage Books.

Inglehart, R. 1997. *Modernization and Postmodernization: Cultural, Economic and Political Change in 43 Societies.* Princeton, NJ: Princeton University Press.

Institute of Medicine. 2002. *Unequal Treatment: Confronting Racial and Ethnic Disparities in Health Care,* edited by B. D. Smedley, A. Y. Stith, and A. Nelson. Washington, DC: National Academies Press.

Klinenberg, E. 2003. *Heat Wave: A Social Autopsy of Disaster in Chicago.* Chicago: University of Chicago Press.

Link, B. G. and J. C. Phelan. 1995. "Social Conditions as Fundamental Causes of Disease." *Journal of Health and Social Behavior* Extra Issue:80–94.

Lord, Walter. 1955. *A Night to Remember.* New York: Holt Paperbacks.

Lutfey, K. E. and J. Freese. 2005. "Toward Some Fundamentals of Fundamental Causality: Socioeconomic Status and Health in the Routine Clinic Visit for Diabetes." *American Journal of Sociology* 110:1326–72.

Mills, C. W. 1959. *The Sociological Imagination.* New York: Oxford University Press.

Parsons, T. 1951. *The Social System: The Major Exposition of the Author's Conceptual Scheme for the Analysis of the Dynamics of the Social System.* New York: Free Press.

Perrucci, R. and D. B. Targ. 1982. "Network Structure and Reactions to Primary Deviance of Mental Patients." *Journal of Health and Social Behavior* 23:2–17.

Pescosolido, B. A. 1990. "Teaching Medical Sociology through Film: Theoretical Perspectives and Practical Tools." *Teaching Sociology* 18:337–48.

Pescosolido, B. A. 1992. "Beyond Rational Choice: The Social Dynamics of How People Seek Help." *American Journal of Sociology* 97:1096–138.

Pescosolido, B. A. 1996. "Bringing the 'Community' into Utilization Models: How Social Networks Link Individuals to Changing Systems of Care." Pp. 171–198 in *Research in the Sociology of Health Care.* Vol. 13, edited by J. Kronenfeld. Greenwich, CT: JAI Press.

Pescosolido, B. A. 2006. "Of Pride and Prejudice: The Role of Sociology and Social Networks In Integrating the Health Sciences." *Journal of Health and Social Behavior* 47:189–208.

Pescosolido, B. A. 2011. "Organizing the Sociological Landscape for the Next Decades of Health and Health Care Research: The Network Episode Model III-R as Cartographic Subfield Guide." Pp. 39–66 in *The Handbook of the Sociology of Health, Illness, and Healing: Blueprint for the 21st Century,* edited by B. A. Pescosolido, J. K. Martin, J. D. McLeod, and A. Rogers. New York: Springer.

Pescosolido, B. A., C. Brooks-Gardner, and K. M. Lubell. 1998. "How People Get into Mental Health Services: Stories of Choice, Coercion and 'Muddling Through' from 'First-Timers.'" *Social Science and Medicine* 46:275–86.

Pescosolido, B. A., J. K. Martin, J. S. Long, T. R. Medina, J. C. Phelan, and B. G. Link. 2010. "'A Disease Like Any Other?' A Decade of Change in Public Reactions to Schizophrenia, Depression and Alcohol Dependence." *American Journal of Psychiatry* 167:1321–30.

Quinn, S. C. 2006. "Hurricane Katrina: A Social And Public Health Disaster." *American Journal of Public Health* 96:204.

Rosenfield, S. 1982. "Sex Roles and Societal Reactions to Mental Illness: The Labeling of 'Deviant' Deviance." *Journal of Health and Social Behavior* 23:18–24.

Scheff, T. J. 1984. "The Taboo on Coarse Emotions." *Review of Personality and Social Psychology* 5:146–69.

Squires, G. and C. Hartman. 2006. *There is No Such Thing as a Natural Disaster: Race, Class and Katrina.* New York: Routledge.

Suchman, E. A. 1964. "Sociomedical Variations among Ethnic Groups." *American Journal of Sociology* 70:319–31.

Tilly, C. 1999. "The Trouble with Stories." Pp. 256–70 in *The Social Worlds of Higher Education: Handbook for Teaching in a New Century,* edited by B. A. Pescosolido and R. Aminzade. Thousand Oaks, CA: Pine Forge Press.

Twaddle, A. C. and R. M. Hessler. 1987. *A Sociology of Health.* Boston: Allyn & Bacon.

van Ryn, M. and S. Fu. 2003. "Paved with Good Intentions: Do Public Health and Human Service Providers Contribute to Racial/Ethnic Disparities in Health?" *American Journal of Public Health* 93:248–55.

Vizzini, N. 2006. *It's Kind of a Funny Story.* New York: Hyperion.

Notes

1. Psychiatrist and historian Joel Braslow (1997) notes in his study of lobotomies performed in the mid twentieth century at a California facility that the majority were performed on women considered to be "violent, disruptive, and uncooperative."
2. See http://www.media-awareness.ca/english/resources/educational/teachable_moments/deconstructing_titanic_4.cfm for a complete listing of both good and bad efforts.

READING 9.4

THE 1991 IRAQ INVASION IN CINEMATIC PERSPECTIVE

Jarhead and *Three Kings*

Elizabeth E. Martinez

Anthony Swofford: Every war is different, every war is the same.

—*Jarhead* (1999)

F ilms about war are a staple of the Hollywood machine, and war is a staple of the political machine. Indeed, collective violence appears to be a consistent part of the human experience. Yet there is also the commonsensical notion that violence is not the answer to conflict. Fighting does not resolve problems. Teachers and parents, as agents of our socialization, taught many of us to try consensus or compromise, instead of violence, to resolve disagreements. Most of us have heard, whether at home or school, the advice to "take a time out" or "use your words." These admonitions are supposed to teach us that problems should be resolved peaceably—not violently. As individuals, we are expected to find ways to avoid interpersonal violence and resolve disagreements peaceably.

A contradiction exists between what we are taught as individuals regarding the futility of violence and the persistence of collective violence in the form of war, ethnic conflicts, and revolution. Simply defined, *war* is collective violence. For many reasons, the collective violence of war has to be justified in the public sphere by institutional actors, such as states, civil society organizations, and media outlets. In the politics of war, states and other actors debate the question of what constitutes a just war, or a legitimate war effort, addressing such topics as the purpose of a specific military action and the acceptable conduct of war. *Just war theory* addresses the arguments for and against war.

In this reading, we will examine the problem of legitimating war as a form of collective violence. Rather than looking at the politics of war as discussed in the public sphere by states and the media, we will examine how moral explanations from just war theory relate to the social structure that separates public policy debates from the actions and experiences of ordinary soldiers. Warfare as experienced on the ground level is different from debates in the public sphere. Each war in history has its own events, actors, and context, but on the ground the job of every soldier is roughly the same: follow orders and kill people who are defined as the enemy. The broad sociological issue is why wars continue, despite shared recognition of the harms of war. Asserting that the cause and justification for war is economic is not a complete answer. It is critical to engage in an institutional analysis of the relationships, hierarchies, and cultural arguments that support war efforts.

A sociological analysis of the *institution* of war requires that we look at how just war theory is related to the practice of war in social relations. An institution is a large-scale pattern of actions and beliefs that sustains itself over time and is socially reproduced (Douglas

1986). An institutional analysis of the politics of war is an analysis that focuses on the norms of behavior held by states and soldiers who are located at various levels of the military apparatus. For instance, because of norms related to the chain of command, soldiers on the ground tend to avoid theorizing war in their conversations and actions. Instead, their beliefs and acts are shaped by their understanding of the appropriate role of the soldier as an occupation (Moskos 1977).

This understanding is derived, in part, from their training as soldiers. Research indicates that soldiers tend to see the role of a soldier as an occupation, not a political task. The occupation of soldier is characterized by cohesion within units and strict compliance with the chain of command (Kestnbaum 2009; Moskos 1977). Recent research in the field of military sociology looks at the quality of the social bonds, or social cohesion, within military units, in light of the increasing delegation of military tasks to private contractors, who are integrated into soldier's units (Kelty 2009). According to Kelty, the soldiers compared themselves with contractors, and those comparisons had a negative influence on perceptions of unit cohesion.

The work of soldiers is conducted by and between individuals in military units, but it accumulates into collective violence. The structure and norms of the military lead to reproducing war, sometimes in violation of moral theories of war. This is in part the case because war is not just ordinary politics using violence (Clausewitz [1832] 1976). War is also not simply the multiplication of street fighting—so many fights added together to make a war. Instead, war is a social process supported by institutional patterns and structured relationships. The structured relationships include the distinctions among state leaders, military leaders, and ordinary soldiers, who are organized into hierarchies. Institutional behaviors (or patterned behaviors) are driven by different occupational and professional norms operating at different levels of the military.

War as Ordinary Politics

According to a classical theorist of war, Carl von Clausewitz ([1832] 1976), *war* is defined as the continuation of politics by other means. What he meant is that war is a form of ordinary politics, using different tools. For instance, while politicians use legislative action, military officers and soldiers use violence. Different tools are used to reach the same political end. But is war really just ordinary politics, plus the use of guns and bombs? Interestingly, Clausewitz also defined war as *nothing more* than a duel or wrestling match between individuals, carried out on a larger scale (Bassford 2008; Clausewitz [1832] 1976). But is war simply the addition or multiplication of street fighting? Is it just interpersonal violence—so many separate fights combined into one? To understand classical theories of war, it is important to realize that the Clausewitz definitions are reductionist. Both conceptions *reduce* war to other types of human behavior (ordinary politics or street fighting). War is not just ordinary politics, nor is it merely small-scale fighting carried out at a larger scale. War is a qualitatively different phenomenon that combines elements of ordinary politics and violent conflict but is a different animal altogether. Because of the scale of war, it becomes something else entirely—not politics and not street fighting. It is a new social dynamic taking place at the collective level (Bassford 2008). War is an institutional pattern that reproduces itself because of key features of its social structure, including actions and beliefs. The actions taken at the higher levels of the state and military include making deci-sions to go to war and making public statements intended to explain or legitimate the war. But war is actually carried out at the lower levels of the military, in the execution of orders. At the level of the soldier carrying out orders, there are distinct beliefs about the appropri-ate role of the soldier and the meaning of the war. Thus, war is the result of different actions and norms operating at different levels of the military and political structure.

Even if we acknowledge that war is a unique animal, it still seems as though the work of soldiers is linked to the politics of war, as carried out by states, in a straightforward way. At the top level, influential actors in the state apparatus determine when and how collective violence is justified or can be legitimated. Their decisions filter down, through the chain of command, from officer to officer, and finally to the soldier or soldiers who actually enact violence. The relationship between the theories of war and policy debates over war, on the one hand, and wars as experienced by soldiers, on the other hand, is not straightforward. The question becomes: How are the politics of war, including theories of just war, and the structure of the military command, related to the individual experiences of soldiers on the ground? How does the institutional pattern of going to war get reproduced through these social relationships?

To explore this question, we will use two films about the 1991 Iraq invasion: *Jarhead* (Sam Mendes, 2005) and *Three Kings* (David O. Russell, 1999). While both include stories of soldiers being frustrated by government policies in the Gulf War, they offer different views on the politics of war. *Jarhead* offers a view of the alienated soldier trying to do his job—if only he can figure out what that job is. *Three Kings* offers an idealistic, if unrealistic, picture of soldiers taking matters into their own hands and changing the pursuit of war from what they see as an unjust mission to a humanitarian one. Sociological concepts addressed in this reading include *legitimation, collective violence, politics of war*, and *just war theory*, as well as basic sociological concepts of *structure, action, social roles*, and *norms*. The central argument of this reading is that the politics of war is an institutional process sus-tained and reproduced by the gap between theorizing what constitutes a just war within the mediated public sphere and actually pursuing a course of war in practice on the ground.

Cinematic Method and Institutional Analysis

The method of using film to examine the institutional patterns and legitimation of war might be questioned, because movies are not "real." Nevertheless, watching a movie can be a valid method for examining social life. This is because films accomplish some of the interpretative work necessary to understand history and social actions, including for example the politics of war, so long as we keep the facts of history in mind. Watching a movie can be a form of nonparticipant observation, especially when combined with his-torical or comparative analysis. For these reasons, the following discussion of *Jarhead* and *Three Kings* includes historical information about the Iraq invasion in 1991.

While distinctions must be maintained between historical documentation and cine-matic representation, it must also be acknowledged that the politics of war itself relies on competing representations. What one state or group understands to be terrorism, another interprets as a justified war. Competing representations are bolstered by historical informa-tion and arguments offered by both sides. What is a fact to one group, in a debate over the politics of war, is a biased interpretation to another group. History and representations of history are intertwined in the politics of war.

When considering the politics of war as sociologists, we might first ask about the patterns and constraints that shape policy decisions about war. What are the justifications for war? How are these justifications expressed in theories about just war? Who has a voice in the public debate over whether a particular war is legitimate or not? More specifically, we can ask about the social relationships that lead to particular outcomes or patterns of behavior. Instead of theorizing the just or unjust nature of war, we can examine the social structure of the military, the state, and the chain of command to determine how this structure leads to its own reproduction in the practice and politics of war. In this reading, we will examine just war theory and how theories are related or disconnected from the role of the soldier as her or she falls in the chain of command. It can be argued that the reproduction of war over time is supported by a disconnect between theories of just war and the actual conduct of war.

By examining the soldier's role as depicted in *Jarhead* and *Three Kings*, we are able to see that it is precisely the *disconnect* between the occupational role of the soldier and the politics of war pursued in institutional discourse that allows wars to be reproduced despite problems of legitimacy. There is a gap between just war theory and the practice of war. When legitimating war in public discourse, state actors and elites might discuss the elements of a just war in theoretical and logistical terms, but on the ground, every war is (arguably) the same in terms of the soldier's experience. Soldiers follow the chain of command and form small, cohesive units within which they strive to survive.

Because soldiers tend to focus on the job of shooting and exploding (even as they wait around for it to occur), the political and moral justifications for war are removed from their daily interactions. The occupation of killing takes place at a great social distance from the debates over legitimacy. In *Jarhead*, for example, there are questions about the legitimacy of the 1991 Iraq invasion, but there is no resolution of those concerns. We watch the soldiers suffer through their experience, at the bottom end of the chain of command, until finally they come home and it is over. In contrast, in *Three Kings* (somewhat more hopefully, but less realistically), the soldiers do find a resolution. From the beginning, they take matters into their own hands, at first seeking their own economic gain, only to then shift priorities and work on resolving one of the problems of the war: the mistreatment of civilians.

Legitimacy, the State, and the Politics of War

A central theme in *Jarhead* is the legitimation of political violence as seen through the eyes of an individual soldier and his military unit. *Legitimation* is the process of defining an event, an actor, or an action as appropriate or worthwhile. Legitimacy is attributed to a war via an institutional process that can be termed the *politics of war*. The sociological concern is the legitimation of war in the public sphere in contrast to the individual experience of war in the occupation of soldier. How does the occupation of another country by a state relate to the occupation (or job) of a soldier on the ground?

In *Jarhead*, we learn that Anthony Swofford (Jake Gyllenhaal) is a young man who "got lost on the way to college," and somehow ended up in the Marines during the U.S.-led invasion of Iraq in 1991. The film is based on the book *Jarhead*, a memoir of the real-life Swofford who served in the Persian Gulf War. In narrative early in the film, Swofford reflects on the meaning of *jarhead*:

Jarhead (noun): Slang for Marine.

Origin: From the resemblance to a jar . . . to the regulation high-and-tight haircut.

The Marine's head by implication, therefore . . . also a jar.

An empty vessel.

Toward the end of the film, Swofford says that "every war is different, every war is the same." After watching *Jarhead*, we might ask: is every war the same? Is every war different? How can it be true that every war is the same *and* every war is different? The answer to this simple paradox is found in the social distance, or structural gap, that exists between war as legitimated and war as conducted. Built into the structure of the military is a separation of theory and practice. The primary actor in the justifications for war is the state, while the primary actor in the conduct of war is the soldier. The state and soldier, however, use different logics of action, which, when combined, lead to the pursuit of wars that may not be justifiable. On the international stage, a national government or state, or alliance of states, engages in justifications for war but does not take concrete action. That is to say, the state itself is not violent. On a micro level, the soldier engages in concrete action, enacting violence, but does not theorize the justifications for war (which makes sense, given that he or she is "empty-headed"). To understand this structural gap, it is important to have at least a preliminary understanding of what a *state* is.

Photo 9.2   Waiting around for war in *Jarheads*. Boredom, heat, and minimal military action lead soldiers in the 1991 Gulf War to pass the time in a variety of ways.

In his essay "Politics as a Vocation," Max Weber defines a *state* as "a human community that (successfully) claims the monopoly of the legitimate use of physical force within a given territory" ([1918] 1946:78). Weber did not mean that *only* states engage in violence, but instead that only states engage in *legitimate* violence. Although definitions of the term *state* vary, for our purposes a state is a political community with authority over a territory. Violence is rendered legitimate, or acceptable, only if pursued by a recognized state, in accord with proper channels, such as a military chain of command—or if pursued via an appropriate delegation to private authorities, including military contractors. The state holds this monopoly so it can maintain its territory, but as we will see in the discussion of the Gulf War, the legitimacy of war has been extended beyond territorial boundaries. According to theories of war, the use of collective violence by groups or entities *other* than states, or their delegates, is never considered legitimate. The right to conduct war is a right monopolized by states. Collective violence by other actors is considered illegitimate (C. Carr 2002).

The *politics of war* is an active process of legitimating the use of military violence by states through justifications offered in public discussions, such as in congressional debates or in the mediated public sphere. Military organizations within the government actually study the reasons for war and the technologies of war, engaging in internal studies of the possible—or unthinkable—future that might include world destruction. These studies were previously known as "scenario planning" during the Cold War era (Kahn 1962; M. Carr 2010). Moving beyond internal planning, state actors and civil society actors also engage in public dialogue about the legitimacy of particular wars, at least in democratic settings (Strahm 2007). The politics of war is thus a process of debating the pros and cons of going to war in a particular historical context. Further, the politics of war can be understood to include the practice of war through the chain of command. As we will see in the analysis of these films, below, the institutional logics of war are sustained by (1) theories of just war, offered in public discourse by states and other actors, and (2) the disconnection of those theories and public debates from the actual conduct of war by soldiers.

Just War? In Theory and in Practice

While some people argue that wars can be justified, others argue that the idea of a *just war* is ambiguous. Still others argue, on moral or religious grounds, that no war can ever be justified (U.S. Institute for Peace 2002). Assuming, for the sake of argument, that wars can be justified, the moral reasons for war have to be in line with just war theory (JWT) if the war is to be considered legitimate in the international community (Orend 2008; Walzer 1977). The elements of JWT are organized chronologically, starting with the declaration of war, then moving to the practice of war and then, finally, to its consequences. The theory is divided into three parts: (1) *jus ad bellum*, regarding the reasons for resorting to war; (2) *jus in bello*, regarding the practice or conduct of war; and (3) *jus post bellum*, regarding peace agreements and the termination of war (Orend 2008). While the theory dates to ancient times—and is complex and evolving with modern technologies of war—the elements can summarized in three parts.

1. ***Last resort.*** According to JWT, war must be a last resort, pursued only after other alternatives have been exhausted (Orend 2008; U.S. Institute for Peace 2002). This means that the war must be, in some sense, unavoidable. This sounds good, in theory, but the problem is that while people generally agree that war must be a last resort to be justified, there is often disagreement over when the turning point has been reached and going to war is necessary as a last resort. The concern for many people, including members of civil society and state actors, is that there are limited—or perhaps no—circumstances in which war can lead to peace.

2. ***Humane treatment.*** A second element of JWT is that there has to be humane treatment of both civilians and captured or surrendering soldiers. This principle was codified in the Geneva Conventions in 1949 after the end of World War II. For example, under Geneva principles, civilians are not supposed to be the targets of fighting, and care must be used to avoid civilian casualties.

3. ***Positive outcome.*** A third element of JWT is that the world (sometimes defined as the community of nations or limited to the countries affected by the war) must be better off because of the war. The war should lead to a positive outcome. Whether an outcome is positive is measured by contrasting the world after the war with the world situation that existed before, or the world situation that might have come about if the war had not been pursued. The problem here is that alternative outcomes cannot always be controlled or known. War is an unstable condition within the territory where it is conducted. Conflict theorists might argue that war can create certain stabilities—for instance, in a state organized around warfare that benefits from a war economy—but outcomes are far from certain in war-torn areas.

Because decisions to go to war are made and justified at the institutional level in the dialogue between state actors and elites in the mediated public sphere, sociological research on the politics of war often focuses on the decisions of state actors and the media representations of war by elite newspapers and television reporters (Abdolali and Ward 1998; Strahm 2007). In democratic settings, governments are held accountable to citizens, however, and so the public discourse is expected to be transparent and provide reasonable justifications rendering one war legitimate and another illegitimate.

There are important, historical differences in the justifications given for the U.S. decisions to enter World War II in 1941, Vietnam in the early 1960s, and the Persian Gulf in 1990–91. There were still other reasons offered for the 2003 invasion of Iraq. Some of these arguments followed JWT, saying that these wars were last resorts that protected civilians, proceeded according to proper channels and procedures, and left the world in a better condition.

There are differences in how each war is legitimated, and questioned, in public discourse (Smith 2005; Strahm 2007). The specific events and actors considered relevant in the politics of war vary across wars. Yet a similar pattern of legitimation exists in the unfolding debates over war (Smith 2005). According to Smith, in the buildup to a war, there is an escalation of narratives in which the proposed war is presented as a last resort that is likely to achieve a positive outcome. Moreover, in these narratives, the genre of storytelling is often apocalyptic rather than an exercise in calculating the costs and benefits in rational terms. Smith argues that moral representations about the legitimacy or reasons for war have causal effects on following events in a social process. The arguments for and against war include competing interpretations of prior events and relevant actors. As Smith makes clear, the different interpretations themselves "become influential," meaning that beliefs about events and actors tend to support (or fail to support) the competing claims made about the legitimacy of collective violence (Smith 2005:35).

Complicating Factors

The politics of war is complicated by many factors, including variations in the capacity for violence, which tends to increase as we move from two people in a street fight to small collectivities of people—and then to the many thousands of people who make up a nation, state, or other large-scale collectivity. During the Cold War between the United States and the U.S.S.R., for example, international political relations were marked by decades of tension over competing visions for the world held by two large nation-states and their allies. The Cold War started shortly after the end of World War II and continued until the collapse of the Soviet Union in 1991. The Cuban Missile Crisis in 1962 marked a high point in the level of threat from nuclear war during those decades.

Technologies of war also change the politics of war and the balancing of factors in JWT. Does the experience of war change as we move from hand-to-hand combat and sniper shots to aerial strikes? In the terrorist attacks of September 11, 2001, a relatively small group of people were able to use commercial airplanes as weapons of mass destruction (WMD), killing thousands of civilians and affecting the lives of many more thousands. The decision in that case to go ahead with the "war on terror" followed the common pattern of legitimating a war; the character of the political actors also made a difference. The Al Qaeda network is not considered a legitimate state, and, according to JWT, wars waged between states are differentiated from wars waged by cells of terrorists. A state is considered a legitimate actor, while a terrorist cell is not (C. Carr 2002).

Regarding the topic of war technologies, scholars have argued that the Iran-Iraq war was the last conventional war—meaning it was the last war to include trench warfare. In post-conventional war, there is a diminished role for the individual soldier as worker, because technology (or faith in technology) has overcome the responsibilities of individual, human action. The threat of annihilation makes conventional war obsolete (Arendt 1963). Moreover, common understandings of who is—and who is not—a legitimate actor in warfare have changed. Social scientists have started to theorize the concept of the "new war," although that terminology is the subject of debate (Kestnbaum 2009).

Jarhead: The Sameness of War for Ordinary Soldiers

In *Jarhead*, there is a scene in which the Marines briefly discuss the politics of war. They soon dismiss the relevancy of politics, however, and focus on doing their job. The Marines are in a convoy of trucks heading into the desert.

Marine 1:   This defensive position stuff sucks, huh? We need to get out of this shithole soon. I need to shoot something.

Marine 2:   You're going to get all you want soon enough.

Marine 3:   First to fucking fight!

Marine 4:   Yeah, for what? I've been around these old, white motherfuckers all my life. They got their fat hands in Arab oil. Motherfuckers drink it like it's beer. That's why we're here. To protect their property.

This statement causes the others to object.

Troy: He's full of shit. He's full of shit.

Troy motions with his hand across his neck, as if to say "Cut it out" or "Stop it."

Marine 5:   Fuck politics. We're here. The rest is bullshit.

The chain of command is vital to every soldier or Marine portrayed in *Jarhead*. This occupational logic connects directly to the politics of war at the level of public debate, because it is not for the individual soldier or Marine to decide if a war is legitimate or just. Those decisions are left to the state, which holds the monopoly on legitimate violence. The state, together with the public, decides which wars are to be pursued and supported.

The status of the soldier as a worker leads to a commonality of experience among all ordinary soldiers. This sense of cohesion is illustrated in *Jarhead*. At the end of the movie, Swofford makes a remark about wars being the same and different during a bus ride home from the Gulf War. Local residents and family members stand in the streets, watching and cheering. At one stop, an aging Vietnam veteran climbs aboard and asks if he can join the ride. The young Marines stare at him, a bit surprised at his request. He congratulates each Marine, one by one, expressing thanks for the Marine's military service. The implication is that the Vietnam vet is offering to the Gulf War vets the acknowledgment and honors he may not have received when he came home from war. (Debate continues about the treatment of Vietnam veterans on their return home.)

By the time the Vietnam War ended with the Fall of Saigon in 1975, an increasing number of people in the United States saw the conflict as illegitimate. Questions included why the United States entered the Vietnam conflict and the policies pursued during the war. Some, including Martin Luther King, Jr. (1967), believed that the threat of Communist rule was used as a veil to mask an imperialist agenda. Debate also continues about these political and economic reasons for the Vietnam War versus the legitimation offered: protection of South Vietnam from Communist takeover.

Yet, as we see in movies about Vietnam and movies about the Gulf War, the ordinary soldier experiences his everyday life at a social location far removed from these political-economic debates. Quite obviously, soldiers are not engaged in policy analysis but instead in killing and exploding. The role of a soldier is to engage in combat. Conceptions of a soldier's work have not changed much, but what has changed, with the modern technology of war, is the amount of action seen by soldiers on the ground. In the film *Apocalypse Now*

(Francis Ford Coppola, 1979) about the Vietnam War, the soldiers see a lot of action. Flash forward to the 1990s, however, and in *Jarhead* the soldiers spend a great deal of time waiting around. They have time to watch movies, including *Apocalypse Now*. When they see the famous helicopter scene in which the roaring song "Ride of the Valkyries" is played, they sing along in unison. They have the cohesion of soldiers in Vietnam, but they only hope to see that much action. The Gulf War lasted only a few weeks in the beginning of 1991. It started with an Iraqi invasion of Kuwait in August 1990. This invasion was condemned in the international community, including by the United Nations Security Council. Next, the United States started a peaceful campaign known as Operation Desert Shield. The goal was to prevent Iraq from invading nearby Saudi Arabia, but the effort also served the purpose of a military buildup.

During this time, soldiers on the ground level waited around for months without seeing military action. In *Jarhead*, this time of heat and boredom leads to several ridiculous interactions with the embedded media. Working with and for the media is not understood as one of the roles of a soldier. Swofford and the others start to go a bit crazy. After Swofford is blamed for a fire started by a fellow soldier, Fergus (Brian Geraghty), Swofford breaks the soldier's code of cohesion and threatens Fergus with violence. He later gets demoted because of the fire and spends hours cleaning latrines and burning excrement. These metaphoric scenes in *Jarhead* are the depiction of a worker (soldier) who wants to do his job, but is not entirely sure whether his job is to shoot people or to waste time.

After the deadline passed for an Iraqi withdrawal from Kuwait, Operation Desert Shield gave way to Operation Desert Storm. This military effort primarily consisted of a massive air strike in January 1991. Then–U.S. president George H. W. Bush (Bush I) relied, in part, on the Carter Doctrine to justify the war effort, but this doctrine was overtly material and less morally oriented than JWT. Under the Carter Doctrine, the use of force by Iraq to seize control of the Persian Gulf region could rightfully be regarded as an assault on U.S. interests—that is, economic interests—even though the Gulf is outside U.S. territory. In legitimating the Gulf War in public debate, Bush I also justified the invasion on the basis of potential threats to Saudi oil fields.[1]

The massive air strike again confirmed that the occupation of the soldier was shifting in technological circumstances of new war. While the war itself was cast as a last resort in accord with JWT, because peaceful efforts to demand withdrawal did not succeed, the concrete action was a destructive air strike. In the film, the long hot wait for action does not give Swofford and the other soldiers in his unit the opportunity to do their job of fighting the enemy, as promoted by the apocalyptic narratives in the run-up to the war. They do not see enemies in combat. Instead, they march along a highway where civilians tried to escape the air strike. Civilians were not protected, despite the moral terms of JWT. The soldiers encounter burned vehicles and bodies, and, finally, the burning oil wells. The oil pours down from the sky onto the faces, symbolizing that the focal point of the war is the struggle over oil.

Finally, Swofford and Troy (Peter Sarsgaard) get an actual combat mission, one that takes them beyond the boredom, the waiting, and the photo opportunities with media. They are supposed to execute sniper shots of Iraqi officers in an airport; yet right before they can do their job, a commanding officer appears and orders them to stand down because the air strike is coming. They scream and yell and ask for the chance to take the shot. Swofford was trained as a military sniper and wants to do his job, but instead he is told to stop in favor of the air strike, a technological advance in warfare. The preferred method of waging war is now an aerial strike that takes out everyone and everything in its path, not the precision hit of a sniper.

The sniper scene serves as a commentary on the new war. In historical terms, the Gulf War was offered as a last resort, but the competing scenarios appear to be centered on lasting access to oil, not making a lasting improvement in world conditions. Untold numbers of other soldiers and civilians were targeted in the air strike, in violation of the other element of JWT.[2] After the soldiers of *Jarhead* return home, they go their separate ways, but on the way, Swofford makes his comment regarding the common experience of all soldiers. All wars are the same. This comment could be interpreted to suggest that the common experience is to do the job and not ask why, as the politics of war are beyond the role of the individual soldier. This interpretation makes sense because all soldiers follow the chain of command rather than make policy choices that cast a war as legitimate or illegitimate, just or unjust.

Three Kings: Can Ordinary Soldiers Make a Different War?

Jarhead is distinct from *Three Kings*, because in *Kings* there is an arc or transformation in the soldiers' actions. At first they do not want to get involved in the politics of the war—for instance, the plight of the civilians who are being abandoned when the United States withdraws. By the end of the film, after witnessing and experiencing violence and torture, they take action to do the right thing in accord with the second element of JWT: the just treatment of civilians. Ironically, this change of heart has the soldiers deciding that acts of mercy and justice in relation to the civilians are the last resort, *after* the pursuit of economic gain alone becomes unsatisfying or unjustifiable. Rather than portraying acts of war as the last resort, *Kings* depicts acts of justice as the last resort.

In *Kings,* the premise is that a small group of U.S. military men decide to heist millions in stolen Kuwaiti gold at the end of the Gulf War, but do so strictly in accord with their own creative chain of command: Major Archie Gates (George Clooney) is in charge, followed by Sergeant First Class Troy Barlow (Mark Wahlberg), Chief Elgin (Ice Cube), and, finally, Private First Class Conrad Vig (Spike Jonze). During their illicit adventure, the four maintain military rank and continue to follow rank.

That being said, the opening scene of *Kings* puts the idea of the chain of command directly into play. The film has a satiric tone that allows it to explore the meaning and purposes of the chain of command, in contrast to *Jarhead*, which has a sardonic tone and stands back from direct commentary on the themes of just war. When the camera lens opens in *Kings*, we hear Barlow asking again and again if the command is to shoot. He does not try to determine whether the Iraqi soldier he is targeting is armed or ready for combat, or is trying to surrender. Barlow only wants to know what the current orders are. He says, "Are we shooting? Are we shooting?" He wants to know if the command is to shoot, not whether shooting is the right thing to do. When he does shoot the man, who is a surrendering Iraqi, and then runs over to see what happened, he sees a man in the agony of death. At that point, Barlow looks away in shame and disgust. The chain of command theme comes up again when Barlow orders Vig to remove an object—turns out it is a treasure map—from the rectum of another surrendering Iraqi soldier. He says that Vig has to do it, pointing out, "That's how the chain of command works."

While they have gone on a misadventure that violates U.S. policy in heading off on their own, the soldiers of *Three Kings* do not try to change the course of the war. They do not ask what is the right action to make the world a better place as theorized in the first element of JWT. They are more concerned with whether the Iraqi military will try to interfere with their finding the gold. In a way, their self-assigned purpose or mission is parallel to a critical view of U.S. policy in the Gulf War, in which, under the Carter Doctrine, material interests were expressly at stake. Activists who questioned the U.S-led invasion of Iraq argued that the sole purpose was protecting and amassing wealth in the region, not freeing the Iraqi people from an evil leader, even though that storyline was the apocalyptic narrative (Smith 2005). In *Kings*, when the men wonder about facing opposition, they are assured by Gates that the Iraqi military will let them do what they like without interference.

It is not until Gates, as their leader, decides that circumstances have changed do the other men consider the possibility and value of helping the civilians who were left behind by the evacuating forces. After witnessing the shooting of an Iraqi by the Iraqi military, the soldiers of *Three Kings* decide to change course and no longer only pursue the gold, but instead pursue a just conclusion to the war. While not likely or realistic, the narrative turns toward having ordinary soldiers make a difference in the outcome of the war—by deciding for themselves what the purpose should be. Through most of the film, however, the gang pursues their own interests and assumes that the soldiers on the other side will do the same, each side guarding its own property. The soldiers tell each other that the problems of the Iraqi people, who were abandoned by U.S. forces at the end of the war, are "not our problem."

One of the concerns in *Three Kings* is whether war is a game of action or of justice. As the four men are on their way to get the gold, Gates allows them to shoot off a few rounds because they want to see action. That is their occupational or professional imperative. Vig, as the low man on the totem pole, is not well versed in what is right or wrong in the situation. He goes a bit too far and blows up a football, only to complain that so far in the war, he has not seen any action. Gates then shows him what action produces as they look at the burned bodies of people who were trying to escape the air strike. They see body parts sticking out of the sand.

While the soldiers in *Three Kings* do not openly discuss the Geneva Convention and treatment of civilians in war, the film presents the issue in visual detail. If these images are accurate portrayals of what happened along the highway as civilians tried to escape, then at least one of the promises of JWT was not kept. In a similar storyline, Barlow is captured and tortured in violation of Geneva principles.

Although the marines in *Jarhead* and *Three Kings* are apolitical, that does not mean the films are apolitical. To the contrary, both *Jarhead* and *Three Kings* use micro level analysis to address questions about why wars persist and the problems with legitimating war in public discourse. Both films also explore the issues of "new war" posed by media and technology. The films offer viewers a chance to see the points at which institutional legitimations for war—and collective representations about good and evil in the public sphere—break down and become less intelligible. In both films, the men want to fulfill their imperative, which is to "see action" or "shoot something"—that is, to kill.

In *Jarhead*, there is a scene in which a Marine separates from his group. Swofford calls out to him, telling him to come back and dig where he was told to dig. He does not comply, and so the Marines go over the hill, where their fellow Marine is sitting with a dead Iraqi. The Marine says, "The whole goddamn desert is shitting dead ragheads. Have we done anything? Have we done anything but walk around in the sand?" The ending scenes of *Three Kings* present a different picture. The soldiers in *Three Kings* have taken justice into their own hands, in violation of existing orders, to save the civilians that the U.S. military abandoned. Instead of stealing the gold and running, they decide to make the world a better place. In reality, soldiers are not likely to succeed or do well in making their own policy choices. Instead, the farce or comedy of the film suggests that if pursuing justice is possible for the ordinary soldier, it is possible for politicians as well.

Conclusion

Having explored issues of legitimacy, the structure of collective violence, just war theory, and the politics of war, as well as the occupational norms of soldiers, we can start to unravel the puzzle of why collective violence persists. We saw that micro level behaviors in war—that is, the ordinary behaviors of soldiers in maintaining small-group cohesion and seeking to do their job, or fulfill their occupational imperative (to kill)—are related to the institutional level goals of pursuing collective violence. Under JWT, there has to be a moral reason for declaring and pursing war, but these reasons are often coupled with material and territorial reasoning and *decoupled* from the reasoning used by individual soldiers as they follow the chain of command.

The separation of macro and micro levels in the conduct of a war means that soldiers aim for survival and proper behavior as workers at the bottom of a military structure while elite actors make decisions and legitimate their decisions about warfare in the public sphere. This hierarchical structure or relationship tends to separate the *justifications* for war from the *conduct* of war. The soldiers think there is one response to policy issues. It does not matter: the important thing is to do your job.

Are there other possible responses for Marines and soldiers at the individual level of behavior? Soldiers might report their concerns to higher-ups in the military, or in interviews with the media, but as we saw in *Jarhead*, most cultural representations to the outside world are controlled by media. In *Jarhead* and *Three Kings*, the officers demand that those below them in the chain of command only make certain representations to those outside the military. If the Marines and soldiers had reported their concerns that nothing was being accomplished in the desert, or that civilians were being killed, what would have happened to the Marines and soldiers? Would they have faced discipline?

Another set of questions for further consideration is the relationships between military personnel and media actors in these films. Because journalists were embedded in the units with ordinary soldiers, the more usual separation of military action from public discourse and investigation shifted in the Gulf War.

Following on these analyses, we also might ask about different types of military violence. When and how are terrorist acts of violence recast and then legitimated as acts of just war in accord with JWT? Is it true that only states engage in war? Is war, as pursued by states in modern conditions, the same as terrorism (C. Carr 2002)? In working through these questions, it is important to use specific, sociological concepts to theorize *who* engages in war, the processes by which war is legitimated, and the structures that tend to promote or defeat collective violence. As outlined in this reading, collective violence is not the simple aggregate of one-on-one violence but a distinct social phenomenon. It is reproduced, in part, because of a unique, institutional configuration: the structural relationship between states and soldiers.

References

Abdolali, N. and D. Ward. 1998. "The Senate Armed Services Committee and Defense Budget Making: The Role of Deference, Dollars, and Ideology." *Journal of Political and Military Sociology* 26(2):229–53.

Arendt, H. 1963. *On Revolution.* New York: Viking.

Bassford, C. 2008. *Clausewitz and His Works.* Retrieved July 2011 (http://www.clausewitz.com/readings/Bassford/Cworks/Works.htm).

Carr, C. 2002. *The Lessons of Terror: A History of Warfare against Civilians, Why It Has Failed and Why It Will Fail Again.* New York: Random House.

Carr, M. 2010. "Slouching toward Dystopia: The New Military Futurism." *Race & Class* 51(3):13–32.

Clausewitz, C. von. [1832] 1976. *On War.* Edited and translated by M. Howard and P. Paret. Princeton, NJ: Princeton University Press. Also available online at the Gutenberg Project in another translation (http://www.gutenberg.org/files/1946/1946-h/1946-h.htm).

Douglas, M. 1986. *How Institutions Think.* Syracuse, NY: Syracuse University Press.

Foer, F. 2005. "The Trouble with Sources." *New York Magazine,* May 21.

Hiatt, F. 2005. "Politics of War." *Washington Post,* November 14. Retrieved January 20, 2012 (http://www.washingtonpost.com/wp-dyn/content/article/2005/11/13/AR2005111301062.html).

Kahn, H. 1962. *Thinking about the Unthinkable.* New York: Horizon.

Kelty, R. 2009. "Citizen Soldiers and Civilian Contractors: Soldiers' Unit Cohesion and Retention Attitudes in the 'Total Force.'"*Journal of Political and Military Sociology* 37(2):133–59.

Kestnbaum, M. 2009. "The Sociology of War and the Military." *Annual Review Of Sociology* 35:235–54.

King, M. L., Jr. 1967. "Beyond Vietnam: A Time to Break Silence." Speech delivered April 4 at a meeting of Clergy and Laity Concerned, Riverside Church, New York City. Retrieved January 20, 2012 (http://www.hartford-hwp.com/archives/45a/058.html).

Moskos, C. C. 1977. "From Institution to Occupation: Trends in Military Organization." *Armed Forces and Society* 4(1): 41–50.

Orend, B. 2008. "War." *Stanford Encyclopedia of Philosophy.* Fall 2008 ed. Retrieved January 20, 2012 (http://plato.stanford.edu/entries/war/#2).

Smith, P. 2005. *Why War? The Cultural Logic of Iraq, the Gulf War, and Suez.* Chicago: University of Chicago Press.

Strahm, A. M. 2007. "Prestige Press Reporting of War and Occupation: Enemy Combatants or a Coalition of the Willing? (Iraq War)." Unpublished dissertation, University of Oregon.

U.S. Institute for Peace. 2002. *Teaching Guide on the Justification of War.* Washington, DC: United States Institute for Peace. Retrieved January 20, 2012 (http://www.usip.org/publications/justification-war).

Walzer, M. 1977. *Just and Unjust Wars: A Moral Argument with Historical Illustrations.* New York: Basic Books.

Weber, M. [1918] 1946. "Politics as Vocation." Pp. 77–128 in *From Max Weber: Essays in Sociology,* edited by H. H. Gerth and C. Wright Mills. Oxford, England: Oxford University Press.

Notes

1. The Second Gulf War, also known as Operation Iraqi Freedom but more commonly referred to as the Iraq War, started in March 2003 under the direction of U.S. president George W. Bush (Bush II). In the Iraq War, under the direction of Bush II, a coalition of U.S. and British troops invaded Iraq. This war was based on the justification that Iraq had weapons of mass destruction (WDM). The alleged WDM were never found (see Foer 2005; Hiatt 2005).

2. After the Gulf War ended, it was announced that the U.S.-led coalition had liberated the Kuwaiti people, but questions remained regarding why the war was cut short with Iraqi president Saddam Hussein still in power (Smith 2005).

Outtake

Zombie Apocalypse: Understanding the Perceptions of Health versus Nonhealth

Andrew Hund

The film *28 Days Later* (Danny Boyle, 2002) is a useful tool for analyzing the social construction of health as well as illness behavior. The zombies are portrayed as urban dwellers who operate in a pack or horde and engage in eating the flesh of the nonzombies. The origin of the disease has been attributed to captive primates reported to be suffering from "aggressiveness," later found to be a symptom of the disease. The zombies are illustrative of a highly contagious and infectious epidemic. Once infected, the zombies are no longer human but transform into the virus itself. The zombies are a highly mobile and aggressive disease vector. Being ill lasts approximately 20 to 30 seconds; then the virus overwhelms the person, transforming him or her into the virus itself, and the healthy or uninfected need to immediately kill the person to prevent further spread of the disease.

A major theme of this film and other zombie films is the preservation of human health. In this film, "good" versus "bad" health is characterized by noninfected humans' judgments of relative degrees of infection. Subtle and overt messages regarding how health and illness are thought about in society, especially prejudices and behavior toward the unhealthy, are exposed in the dialogue and behavior of noninfected characters. Getting "infected" or becoming unhealthy by being bitten, scratched, or exposed to a drop of infected zombie blood results in healthy humans killing off the newly infected with little or no remorse. During one scene, zombies are attacking Mark, Jim, and Selena at Jim's parent's home. Mark, during a zombie confrontation, acquires a scratch on his arm. When Selena realizes Mark has been scratched and he tries to plead for his life, Selena chops off his arm and violently proceeds to finish him off without a second thought. After killing Mark, Selena says to Jim (who appears to be in a state of shock), "I would expect you to do the same." Her words and violent actions in this scene demonstrate the extreme feeling of fear and prejudice associated with the perception of infection or an unhealthy state.

Another predominant theme of the film is "othering." The idea of othering is expressed in the extreme behaviors and communication of characters related to their perceptions of infection or an unhealthy state. A scene that exemplifies the healthy humans' strong aversion and fear of being infected involves Frank, a middle-aged taxi driver, and his teen daughter, Hannah. Upon reaching the safe zone, Frank gets a drop of diseased zombie blood in his eye. Realizing the ramifications, he immediately tells his daughter how much he loves her and to get away from him. Without delay, he also starts to physically and psychologically quarantine himself from his daughter and the other humans (Selena and Jim). When his daughter does not heed his warning to "stay away from me" and tries to approach him, he yells at her in a loud, angry, aggressive voice. He also tells Selena and Jim to "get her away from me." Frank's behavior illustrates the negative perception humans have about being infected, especially Frank's evident feelings of self-loathing when he realizes he has been infected and has become the Other.

Even though the film portrays the zombies as diseased members of a mindless horde, there are numerous subtle and nuanced messages in the films about society's perceptions, prejudices, and behaviors related to healthy versus nonhealthy humans. The film aids us in understanding the relative "influence and meaning" of health and illness at the individual, group, and society levels. For example, a parallel can be drawn to modern society, where people will take extreme measures to maintain a healthy image, such as cosmetic surgery, inordinate exercising, nutritional fads, or Botox treatments, in an effort to maintain health or not appear symbolically as a zombie. The need to appear healthy can take on a hypervigilant or obsessive nature, as shown by the characters in the film. Yet our ability to identify the infected in modern societies is less definite.

CHAPTER 10

Global Connections

Max Cohen: Restate my assumptions: One: Mathematics is the language of nature. Two: Everything around us can be represented and understood through numbers. Three: If you graph the numbers of any system, patterns emerge. Therefore, there are patterns everywhere in nature. Evidence: The cycling of disease epidemics; the wax and wane of caribou populations; sunspot cycles; the rise and fall of the Nile. So, what about the stock market? The universe of numbers that represents the global economy. Millions of hands at work, billions of minds. A vast network, screaming with life. An organism. A natural organism.

—*Pi* (1998)

Lauren Adrian: Since when did you start putting corporate responsibility above the truth?

George Morgan: The days of investigative reporting are over, Lauren. The news isn't news anymore. It's as dead as the typewriter I used to write it on. Corporate America is running the show now and their news agenda is free trade, globalization, and entertainment. That's our glorious future!

—*Bordertown* (2006)

Max Cohen's observation that the global economy is a "vast network . . . an organism" can be found in sociological theories of globalization. As sociologist Piotr Sztompka (1994) wrote, all people living on the globe constitute a social entity such that "one may speak of a global structure of political, economic, and cultural relations extending beyond any traditional boundaries and binding separate societies into one system" (p. 86). In this section, our focus is on the global context, with two readings addressing different dimensions of the "complex connectivity" that is globalization (Tomlinson 1999:2).

In the first reading, Roberto Gonzales focuses on the politics of international immigration in the film *Dirty Pretty Things*, providing a sociological analysis at the macro and micro levels. He notes that the dual (and often conflicting) structures of the labor market and systems of immigration push immigrants to the margins of society, where they are rendered invisible to the larger society. The contradictions of the situation are made clear as the immigrants are sought out to fill the unmet needs of a shifting economy, and then have to fight exploitation and violation of their humanity at every turn.

Gonzales encourages application of the sociological imagination to understand immigration in the global economy and uses the stories of desperation told in the film to highlight the human costs. We see the social networks that allow Okwe and Senay to survive the most challenging of circumstances, reminding us that human agency is also involved in the process of immigrant adaptation. At the same time, despite the bonds and loyalties established, Okwe and Senay cannot overcome the structured inequality they face.

In the second reading, Alison Moss and Jerome Hendricks use the popular film *Slumdog Millionaire* to explore the intersecting social processes of globalization and neoliberalism underlying the expansion of Western capitalism. The film revolves around the outcome of a game show, specifically whether or not Jamal (a "slumdog" in the globalizing city of Mumbai) will win (against all odds) and become a millionaire. The people of Mumbai watch with great anticipation, longing for his victory, as Moss and Hendricks point out, to "succeed in the face of unfairness."

The complex political economy of Mumbai is seen in the extremes of wealth and poverty written on the landscape in the form of mansions, bright lights, and modern highways juxtaposed with the garbage dump three children call home after fleeing the anti-Muslim riots in the slum where their families lived.[1] The unfolding of their stories reveals the ways that their life chances are shaped by poverty, ethnicity, religion, gender, and location on the globe (south). The myth of mobility promises freedom of choice, but as Moss and Hendricks point out, this choice "does not include options that would alter current institutional practices or promote new institutional means of social reform." In other words, systems of inequality remain intact whether Jamal wins the game show or not.

Together these two readings invite us to think about how our lives, opportunities, resources, and worldviews are shaped by our location in the world today. Through film, we have a close-up view of the networks of globalization and the various "flows of capital, commodities, people, knowledge, information, ideas, crime, pollution, diseases" across national and geographic boundaries (Tomlinson 1999:2). Watching this movement, we can think about the institutional domains across cultures (the economy, military, family, religion) and how individuals in different parts of the world both are shaped by these domains and give shape to them.

References

Sztompka, P. 1994. *The Sociology of Social Change.* Cambridge, MA: Blackwell.

Tomlinson, J. 1999. *Globalization and Culture.* Chicago: University of Chicago Press.

Note

1. Slum tourism to Mumbai has increased since the movie's release. According to Chris Way, co-owner of the company that gives tours of Dharavi, "the people have little material wealth, but are always smiling and happy" (retrieved January 25, 2012, from http://www.smh.com.au/travel/travel-news/slumdog-reality-20090304-8nyl.html).

Okwe: We are the people you don't see. We are the ones who drive your cabs; we clean
your rooms . . .

Dirty Pretty Things (2002)

International migration and immigrant adaptation have long been important subfields
of sociology. Among its many strands, the sociology of immigration provides sociological frameworks to understand the important questions of why people migrate; how
immigrants experience life, work, and the adaptation process in the host country; and how
they, in turn, shape society, influence labor markets, and affect government expenditures.
This important subfield also helps us to understand the ways in which social structures
facilitate the assimilation and acculturation processes for certain immigrant populations,
while serving to marginalize others.

The quickening pace of globalization and the fluid movement of capital, ideas, and culture have prompted social scientists to question the salience of the nation-state and argue
that national borders have weakened (Mann, 1990; Tambini, 2001). However, the complexities of contemporary international migration provide evidence to counter such claims.
Particularly, during the past three or four decades, there has been an intensification of labor
migration and recruitment from developing countries to developed countries. Within these
rapid changes, contradictions have become evident, as immigration law has failed to keep
pace with labor needs created by the new economies. As a result, immigrants find themselves caught in a complex web of interests. One important and unfortunate consequence
of this mismatch between immigration policies and the needs of capital is the growth of
large, vulnerable migrant populations in developed countries to serve the needs of local and
national economies. Without access to important benefits and protections, however, few of
them are given the means to successfully integrate into society and the economy.

Dirty Pretty Things and
the Immigrant Metropolis

Through a consideration of film and video, teachers and students alike have been able to
engage important topics, such as immigration, beyond the textbook, thereby providing an
additional dimension from which to flesh out important and sometimes abstract concepts.

Dirty Pretty Things (2002) offers a means of exploring the consequences of complex immigration processes through its depiction of contemporary immigrants in a global city. It provides both micro- and macrolevel perspectives of immigration, as well as a tightly woven story about immigrant survival in the face of a labor market and an immigration system that oftentimes leaves immigrants out on the margins of society and renders invisible these countless, faceless low-wage immigrant workers.

Dirty Pretty Things offers a critical lens through which we might examine and critique the various mechanisms that impact the lives of international migrants. While its setting is contemporary London, the film's narrative allows us to draw comparisons with U.S. cities such as New York, Chicago, or Los Angeles. On the macrolevel, it offers a glimpse into a city that has seen a dramatic transformation in its racial and ethnic landscape, largely due to demographic and economic shifts. As immigrants have been sought out to fill the needs of the economy, the film demonstrates the ways in which these arrangements produce vulnerability and exploitation.

As the immigrant characters in the film are looked on to provide needed cheap labor, they are often rendered marginal within society and subject to the punitive arm of the state's immigration raids and deportation processes.

On the microlevel, *Dirty Pretty Things* captures what some of the day-to-day struggles involved in immigrant life might look and feel like. Using the sociological imagination (Mills, 1959), we see the structure of the global economy, and the individual-level experiences of immigrants today. Through the film, we come to know the characters and relate to the processes of adaptation, which often involve sacrifice, loss of social status, and desperation. While some manage to hold on to their dreams and maintain their dignity and integrity, these limits are tested at every turn.

Globalization and Increasing Inequality

Dirty Pretty Things brings together macro- and microlevel analyses in a carefully crafted case study of contemporary immigration, and the not always fluid or easy incorporation processes immigrants face in what sociologist Saskia Sassen (2001) and others call global cities. According to the literature, cities such as Amsterdam, London, Frankfurt, Hong Kong, Los Angeles, New York, Paris, Sydney, Tokyo, and Zurich have emerged as command centers for the global economy and, as such, have undergone massive and parallel changes. Within these cities is a growing stratum of jobs employing high-income professionals and low-wage jobs held by immigrants. Inherent in this arrangement is increased inequality. While the connection immigrants and low-wage service work have to the global economy dominated by finance and specialized services may not be directly obvious, Sassen argues that immigrants fulfill a number of important functions that are essential to keeping the society and economy running smoothly.

In fact, these global cities incorporate large numbers of immigrants in activities that service strategic sectors of the economy. Sassen argues that these new economies require a flexible workforce to service the needs of the professional and managerial classes. These professionals require services that facilitate an intensive time commitment to work and have grown accustomed to certain amenities that are dependent on a low-wage service workforce. A corresponding and related growth in these cities' informal economies increases the level of flexibility in a broad range of activities and contributes to a growing presence of casual labor markets and a growing casualization of the employment relation. Immigrants are in a position that renders them a likely workforce, and they are absorbed into these low-wage jobs, meeting these various needs as an invisible "serving class."

Seemingly taking its cue from this literature, *Dirty Pretty Things* chooses to focus on this often underdiscussed and invisible side of the contemporary city. London, as seen through these lenses, is bifurcated between the haves and the have-nots and a city where many of its ethnic minorities and foreign-born struggle to make ends meet. Represented as a multiethnic city, where most of the immigrants toil in low-wage service and informal sectors, it is also a relentless city that many of these marginalized immigrants want to leave.

We see the city through the lives of its immigrant characters. Therefore, we see the world of low-wage and unauthorized immigrants. From this perspective, London is as much a city of low-wage workers and ethnic enclaves as it is a corporate world-class city. Dense ethnic communities, like Chinatown, serve the dual purposes of keeping poor immigrants out of public sight when they go home, while also allowing immigrants to hide some of their own secrets, as Okwe (Chiwetel Ejiofor) does when he attempts to hide Senay (Audrey Tautou) from immigration authorities. We also see cab stands, run by North African immigrants to serve the more affluent, and outdoor markets staffed by a collection of immigrants from across the globe.

The hotel, however, provides the most salient example and critique of the cleavages of inequality that are produced by globalization, as it is a site of both production and consumption, of service and leisure. While tourists and global professionals see the hotel as a place of leisure amid city touring or business, it is where many others make their living, servicing the needs of the guests. We see this through the film's main characters, as well as when scanning the faces of the hotel maids who line up for work every day. These two populations live in radically different worlds, yet come together under these arrangements. The hotel also brings together most of the film's central characters, and we see the ways in which their lives are impacted by the dual processes of migration and globalization. This dichotomy is expressed well by Sneaky (Sergi López) in his statement to Senay: "Come on. You've cleaned their shit for so long. Now you can be one of them."

Contexts of Reception

While the literature on global cities covers the ways in which globalization has manifested within cities and among immigrant populations, it still leaves many questions unanswered, namely why certain immigrants achieve some success in the integration process and others do not fare quite as well. Indeed, contemporary immigration challenges much of the conventional wisdom on immigrant assimilation, as today's immigrants are absorbed differently into the immigration system and in the labor market than were international migrants at the turn of the 20th century. Much of the contemporary scholarship on immigrant adaptation has focused on the interplay between individual level characteristics and structural considerations in examining how and why immigrant families fare differently. Sociologists Alejandro Portes and Rubén G. Rumbaut (2001) argue that modes of incorporation in the adaptation process of immigrants are shaped by various contexts of reception. Immigrants bring skills in the form of education, job experience, and language knowledge. The currency of these skills, however, is determined by the larger contexts that receive their respective groups. Portes and Rumbaut point out that among other contexts, the policies of the receiving government and the conditions of the host labor market are instrumental in structuring opportunities.

The Categorizations of the State

While global processes create the need for immigrant workers, the laws of the state shape the ways in which they are incorporated into the economy and society. As Aleinikoff (2001) contends, the state creates immigration laws that shape immigrant integration, and therefore plays a significant role in opportunities for work, rights, and social benefits. Moreover, it regulates who stands inside or outside the law and who qualifies to participate in society, as it dictates who has access to resources. Sociologist Cecilia Menjívar (2000, 2006) builds on this notion by adding that citizenship as legal status—by way of granting rights and responsibilities to the individual in the state—plays the dual role of determining immigrants' membership in society, while also conditioning their understanding of their place within that society.

The categories under which immigrants are designated within a country's particular immigration system determine the extent to which they are entitled by law to participate in society. Certain designations allow immigrants to work, vote, receive benefits, and travel outside of the country. However, not all immigrants have access to such privileges. Portes and Rumbaut (2001) outline three important government responses to immigrants—exclusion, passive acceptance, and active encouragement—and their benefits and limitations.

Immigrants who enter the country without the proper authorization encounter exclusion by the host country and end up in the underground economy. These unauthorized migrants are excluded from most forms of participation, as they cannot legally work, vote, drive in most states, receive benefits, nor travel outside of the country. These immigrants have little to no rights in the host country and, as such, are outside of the law. At any time, these immigrants can be jailed and deported. They often live and work in the shadows of society and are susceptible to employers and others who prey on their vulnerability.

On the other hand, immigrants who are granted legal status enjoy a range of entitlements in the host country. They can legally participate in the society and labor market and are eligible to receive state entitlements. Beyond these rights, however, the government does not endow special benefits to the vast majority of these immigrants. Portes and Rumbaut refer to this type of government response as a passive acceptance. However, some immigrants receive an active reception by the government. This group is made up of refugees and a small number of asylum seekers, who are provided with government assistance for resettlement. This type of government support is important because it offers these newcomers access to an array of resources that do not exist for other immigrants, including job-skill training programs, adaptation programs, access to special loans, and monetary assistance. For those who possess high human capital, governmental assistance can translate into an opportunity for rapid upward mobility.

Having an understanding of the ways in which the state shapes immigrant integration is helpful in understanding the different experiences of the immigrant characters in *Dirty*

Pretty Things. The particular legal designations of the state's system mark immigrants as either insiders or outsiders. Kitty Calavita (1998, 2005) argues that immigration laws, rather than regulating immigration, control and marginalize immigrants. That is, immigrants are conditioned to recognize and accept their place in society and to be fearful of the watchful eye of the state. They understand the ways in which the laws restrict them and behave accordingly (Chavez, 1991, 1998; Coutin, 2000, 2002; Hagan, 1994). Susan Coutin (1996, 1998) concurs, asserting that these laws in effect criminalize migrant behavior. However, Coutin (2002) points out that migrants do exercise agency as they create what she calls legitimate spaces for work, political, and social life.

Dirty Pretty Things provides a useful representation of immigrants living in contemporary London, through a detailed examination of its five central characters—Okwe, an unauthorized immigrant from Lagos who works clandestinely as a cab driver and hotel porter; Senay, a Turkish asylum seeker who, out of necessity, violates the conditions of her visa by working as a maid in the hotel and accepting rent money; Ivan (Zlatko Buric), the Russian immigrant doorman at the hotel; Mr. Juan, or Sneaky, the Spanish head porter at the hotel, who meddles in the underground economy by operating an illegal organ selling business; and Guo Yi (Benedict Wong), an ethnically Chinese refugee (presumably from Southeast Asia) who works as a mortician.

These characters fit into the range of Portes and Rumbaut's taxonomy of governmental reception of immigrants: exclusion, passive acceptance, and active encouragement. Through these lenses, we can see the ways in which their respective statuses shape their experiences and their available options.

Okwe, the film's central character, is an unauthorized immigrant. As such, he is excluded from access to any supports in London. He works without the authorization of the state, collecting fares as a cab driver and receiving his wages as a hotel porter in cash payments. Although he has plenty of human capital by virtue of his medical training, his immigrant status locks him out of the formal economy and opportunities to participate in regular society. He is constantly reminded of the limitations of his status throughout the film as he lives his day-to-day life in the shadows, hidden in dense ethnic communities, and constantly on the hideout from immigration officials. Even his good friend, Guo Yi, reinforces this reality when he cautions him: "You're an illegal, Okwe. You don't have a position here. You have nothing. You are nothing." We see that Okwe internalizes this position when he lectures Senay, "For you and I, there is only survival. It is time you woke up from your stupid dream."

Similarly excluded, Senay finds herself living in the shadows and working clandestinely. Her immigrant status differs from that of Okwe as she is actually legally in London, seeking asylum. However, the conditions of her petition are that she cannot receive money in the form of wages or rent payments. Unable to survive under the existing law, Senay works illegally at the hotel. Like Okwe, she finds that she cannot make ends meet with one low-wage job, so she offers her friend and coworker, Okwe, her couch for rent. Once she violates the conditions of her status, she finds herself outside the law and propelled into the punitive arm of the state. Senay dreams of a better life in New York, but she is continually forced to confront the limitations of her status. "Always we must hide," she tells Okwe in frustration.

The remaining characters are seemingly legal immigrants of one particular status or another. While we do not know as much about Ivan (his character is not central in the story line), we can assume that he is a legal immigrant, albeit without access to higher paying jobs.

He works as the doorman of the hotel. As such, he is subjected to the sometimes harsh cycles of London's weather and does what he can to earn extra money on the job. We see and hear of Ivan's schemes to hustle unknowing hotel guests and his accepting money to keep quiet about the goings on at the hotel.

Sneaky's situation is slightly more complicated. A Spanish immigrant (also presumably legal) employed as the head porter of the hotel, Sneaky supplements his income by moonlighting in the underground economy. Like many of the immigrants in the film, Sneaky has realized that he cannot make ends meet by merely working at the hotel. His position at the hotel and his legal status earn him a good position within the underground economy. Unlike Okwe who must hide, Sneaky is able to use legal status as a "middle-man minority" (Light & Bonacich, 1988) between well-established professionals such as doctors and underground counterfeiters to serve an endless supply of desperate immigrants in need of his services. Sneaky appears to also have more money and material possessions than the others. He drives a Mercedes, drinks champagne, and wears expensive clothes. When he says, "My whole business is based on happiness," he has put into simple terms the complexity of the underground economy and the different interests involved. Moreover, this admission also speaks to the ways in which Sneaky has internalized the ideals of capitalism and a desire to assimilate.

Positioned similarly as legal immigrants, Ivan and Sneaky face certain limitations, presumably due to their inability to get better jobs. As a result, both are entrepreneurial, doing what they can to hustle extra money. Sneaky, however, seems to have a better grasp of navigating both worlds in order to be successful in the informal economy.

Finally, Guo Yi, Okwe's closest friend, is a refugee of Chinese origin, perhaps from Southeast Asia. Of all the characters, Guo Yi has probably the best position within the formal economy, as a mortician. While we do not know what governmental benefits Guo Yi might receive, we know he has a good and stable job and a car. We do not see Guo Yi struggle like the other characters. He has a position within society and has a decent job to match his education and skill levels. As such, Guo Yi is also in a position to assist his friends, namely Okwe and Senay. He provides ongoing advice to Okwe and assists him in finding a place to hide Senay. He also provides Okwe and Senay a much needed ride to the airport.

The Conditions of Work

While the government context is important in determining where immigrants begin their lives in the host country and the resources available to them, their labor market experience is arguably as important in determining social and economic mobility. Unlike immigrants at the turn of the 20th century who were almost uniformly labor migrants being absorbed into expanding industrial economies, contemporary immigrants across the globe are received both as professionals with advanced degrees and as labor migrants with little formal education or skills. Portes and Rumbaut (2001) underscore the importance of such human level variables in determining where and how immigrants enter the labor market. This theorizing is consistent with the findings of segmented labor market scholars, who examine the structural and institutional constraints of work (Averitt, 1968; Massey et al., 1998; Piore, 1979).

Such scholars argue that the labor market stratifies firms and workers into primary and secondary sectors. Whereas the primary sector meets basic demands of the economy, the secondary sector meets fluctuating or seasonal demands and relies primarily on lower paid, flexible, labor intensive jobs primarily occupied by immigrants. Highly skilled immigrants in fields such as health care, engineering, and computer science begin their lives in the new country with professional jobs that pay well. However, certain groups of immigrants and racial minorities are systematically excluded from particular employment opportunities, while slotted into the lower levels of the labor force and therefore unable to gain access to better jobs that provide higher wages, job security, and opportunities to advance. These workers are said to earn lower wages than domestic workers, even when human capital is held constant.

The immigrants seen in *Dirty Pretty Things* are overly represented within the secondary sector of the labor market. With the exception of Guo Yi, they all occupy the bottom rungs of the labor force. Cab drivers, maids, and janitors are all nonwhite and speak English with accents. We do not fully know to what extent these barriers are due to low levels of education, English language fluency, country of origin, racial or ethnic group, or exclusion from the regular workforce because of immigrant status. However, these are indeed among the range of barriers that direct immigrants into secondary sector jobs. We know that Okwe is trained as a doctor and forced into the world of low-wage work because of his immigrant status. As such, he experiences a loss of status and is left to piece together low-wage jobs to make ends meet. His coworkers at the hotel and the taxi stand, and the immigrants captured by the camera's eye within the hospitals and on the streets, make up a less educated and skilled low-wage work force.

Scholarly research has demonstrated that most of these immigrant workers, without advanced levels of education, have a difficult time breaking into primary sector jobs. These immigrant characters are invisible to the vast majority of society, yet they comprise increasing numbers in secondary and informal labor markets. As such, they work for low wages and take the dirty jobs that most of the native-born shun. To survive in the city, they have to hustle, take more than one job, work illegally, and participate in the informal economy. Okwe works around the clock, with very little sleep. We do not know whether he is saving money for his family in Lagos, but we do know that his two jobs do not pay him well. This is corroborated by the evidence from other characters. Senay cannot survive in London without work, so she works illegally. She also cannot make ends meet, so she rents her couch to Okwe. Ivan does what he can to make extra money, taking advantage of every opportunity at the hotel to make an extra dollar.

Like Okwe, Guo Yi possesses a high degree of human capital. He speaks the Queen's English and has been educated in the medical field. We do not know whether he was a doctor in his home country, but we do know that he has enough formal education to qualify for a job as a mortician. Refugee status and the accompanying privileges allowed him to translate his previous education and job training into a professional job that pays enough money to afford a car and other amenities. Guo Yi's character allows us to see the effects of both government reception and labor market participation. His training and background match that of Okwe, but as a certified refugee, Guo Yi is able to reap the benefits of his education and training in the host country, whereas Okwe cannot. Similarly, Guo Yi is a legal immigrant in London and entitled to many of the benefits as other immigrants like Ivan and Sneaky. However, his education clearly allows him to bypass the lower strata of the labor market. While we do not know a lot of the specifics of the immigrants in the background of the film, Guo Yi's position in London's society and economy stands in direct contrast with those immigrants—the maids in the hotel, the janitors in the hospital, and the cab drivers—who possess low human capital, experience negative governmental reception, and experience discrimination in the labor market because of their racial or ethnic backgrounds.

Viewers do not get much insight into the domestic lives of the immigrant characters. Most of the film's activity takes place at the hotel or other places of work. However, we do see Senay's apartment, where Okwe rents the couch. This arrangement between Senay and Okwe tells us at least a couple of things. First, and especially for Okwe, home is only for sleeping (and even that is very limited). Between his two jobs, he works around the clock, with little time for a break (we even see him falling asleep at the hotel and taking herbs to help him stay awake). Second, the apartment is not big enough for both Okwe and Senay. They share one key, taking turns in the apartment. When Okwe is there, Senay is at work and vice versa. The apartment is small and quaint. While it is not run-down, it does not have many amenities and the plumbing is bad.

Human Agency and the Ethnic Community

This essay would be incomplete if I did not address the human agency that is involved in the process of immigrant adaptation, survival, and, for some, success. Despite extreme obstacles in the migration and incorporation processes, immigrants and their families manage to lead lives of dignity, to send children to college, and to improve their circumstances over time. A great many, however, are structurally locked into impoverished lives, poor and desperate communities, and jobs with very few opportunities for advancement. Even within these circumstances, opportunity is born out of struggle, as these same conditions have spawned labor movements, mass protest, and ongoing struggle for better lives. There is evidence of such agency throughout this film: Senay's pursuit of her dreams takes her over each barrier she faces; Okwe succeeds in guarding his immigrant status while preserving his morality; and Ivan finds ways to take advantage of the system and enjoy himself in the process.

The best articulation of agency in *Dirty Pretty Things* is in its depiction of the ethnic networks of immigrants and the advantage those bonds garner. In Portes and Rumbaut's modes of incorporation thesis, the ethnic community makes up the third category of importance in the adaptation process. Many scholars argue that immigrant coethnic networks cushion the impact of cultural change and provide immigrants with a wider set of resources from which to find jobs, housing, economic assistance, and support (Gibson, 1988; Waters, 1999; Zhou & Bankston, 1998). At the same time, some scholars argue that among networks of poor immigrants, there are insufficient resources to leverage advantage to individual members (Menjívar, 2000).

Dirty Pretty Things captures this tension. Certainly, the film depicts numerous examples of the ways in which low-wage and unauthorized immigrants exercise agency in assisting each other day to day: Okwe and Senay provide each other mutual support in their initial apartment sharing relationship; Okwe and Ivan help Senay when immigration officials show up at the hotel looking for her; Guo Yi offers Okwe a place to sleep when Okwe and Senay are forced to leave her apartment, as well as provides information on an apartment in Chinatown for Senay; Okwe assists the North African immigrants who sell their organs for passports; Senay teaches Okwe that it not useless to hold on to dreams; Okwe saves Senay from Sneaky; and they all band together in the end to outsmart Sneaky, beat the system, and get Okwe and Senay out of London.

Yet, the bonds between the film's characters are not enough to improve each other's working or living conditions. While Okwe and Senay manage to escape London (we might suspect that a similar fate awaits Senay in New York, and perhaps even for Okwe if he cannot practice medicine), the film does not offer an alternative to a life of low-wage work and fear for its immigrant characters who remain. Most of them do not have connections adequate enough to provide entrée into better paying jobs, for example. Okwe is powerless to help Senay find a good job when she is forced to leave the hotel, and Guo Yi does not have the ability to assist Okwe in his attempt to reestablish his status in the medical field. "All I bring you is bad luck," Okwe tells Senay, noting his limitations in helping her or himself move out of their structurally locked positions.

While it is clear that this is *the* point the film wants to make, by doing so it fails to provide any alternative for its immigrant characters. Human agency is reduced to the ability or inability to escape London or just to ease the day-to-day pain. This is reminiscent of the popular wave of urban films of the early 1990s—notably, *Boyz n the Hood* (1991) and *Menace II Society* (1993)—wherein the protagonists discover that the only path toward upward mobility is to leave the violence of the neighborhood. Just as these films did not offer the alternative of remaining in the community and working toward making it better, *Dirty Pretty Things* does not help viewers to envision a world where immigrants can organize collectively for civil, human, and worker rights.

Work, the State, and the Construction of Vulnerable Migrants

Shortcomings aside, *Dirty Pretty Things* gives viewers a no-holds-barred look at the implications of contemporary immigration policies and economic practices. Taken together, the harsh realities of the state and the limited opportunities of the labor market create lives of struggle and marginality for low-skilled immigrants. In fact, for many of these immigrants, the dual forces of the immigration system and the labor market work in tandem to create a low-wage labor force that is responsive to the needs of capital and vulnerable to a whole host of people—employers, immigration officials, and the dangerous world of the underground. It is perhaps here where *Dirty Pretty Things* launches its harshest critique and where it makes its most important contribution to the immigration debate. As such, it provides a means through which to make micro and macro connections, identify some of the key mechanisms that shape the fates of the immigrant characters, and gain insight into the consequences of the ways in which contemporary cities absorb and marginalize unskilled and unauthorized immigrants, producing vulnerability and industries of opportunists who take advantage of their limited and limiting circumstances.

Like the vulnerable immigrants in Leo Chavez's seminal work *Shadowed Lives* (1998), the characters in the film live *shadowed lives*. They must be careful not to draw attention to themselves, as it could lead them to jail, to deportation, or without the means to earn a living. They live in fear, often hidden in the shadows. They take bad jobs out of desperation and do their best not to interact with government agencies or officials because doing so could arouse suspicion and jeopardize their employment or result in deportation.

Okwe and Senay constantly look over their shoulders. As a woman, Senay may be even more vulnerable than Okwe. The conditions of her asylum request seem to be out of touch with the reality of contemporary urban life and survival. She has very little choice in London, other than to try to earn money. However, doing so puts her on the wrong side of the law and out of status. In other words, by violating the conditions of her asylum request, Senay loses the legal right to be in the country and thus becomes like Okwe, unauthorized. The seemingly tenable decision to work has dire consequences. When the immigration officials come for Senay, she is forced to go into hiding and change jobs and apartments. When the veil of security is lifted, Senay has to confront the totality of her vulnerability, as she has little choice other than to take an undesirable job at a sweatshop. When immigration officials show up at Senay's workplace, all of the workers run out. This is reminiscent of a similar scene in the film *El Norte* (1983) and suggests that all of the workers in the sweatshop are working without proper authorization and susceptible to immigration raids.

Senay's vulnerability becomes more extreme when immigration officials single her out to her employer. As a result, she is left even more vulnerable, as not only her labor is exploited but also her body. Her identification, not only as an unauthorized worker but as one who is being sought out by immigration authorities, gives the sweatshop owner a means to exploit her. This puts Senay in a dangerous situation, as her employer uses this information to blackmail her into performing sexual acts in exchange for his silence. As an immigrant out-of-status and as a woman, Senay's character illuminates the precariousness of life for unauthorized women. Without the protections of the state, many immigrant women are vulnerable to any number of employers, government officials, and men who hold power over them.

The film goes to great lengths to portray the manner in which immigrant vulnerability can manifest itself in extreme desperation. The central story line of the film underscores this point as its immigrant characters are revealed to be so desperate to gain legal status with the entitlements that come along with it, they are willing to sell their organs. This is reminiscent of the plot in *Sympathy for Mr. Vengeance* (2002), in which Ryu, the film's protagonist, turns to the black market to sell his own organs in order to pay for his sister's surgery. The horror of these desperate acts serves as a strong metaphor for these characters' utterly desperate living situations, as they willingly give up literal and physical parts of themselves in order to survive. This stark example is a chilling reminder of the dangers involved in the migration experience, as many international migrants risk their lives to cross into developed countries and have to continue to make life-preserving decisions once in the receiving country. This calls to mind images of bodies stacked up on makeshift rafts, humans locked in trunks and trailers, deaths from starvation and dehydration, and lives of indentured servitude that have come to be a part of the migration narrative.

Further, the theme of migrant vulnerability in the film speaks to the complicated relationships between sending and receiving countries. That is, the ways in which limited opportunities in sending countries and the enticement of available jobs at higher wages, prompt and push people toward migration. While we do not have the opportunity to view life in any of the characters' homelands (neither do the vast majority of citizens who come into contact with migrants), we are left to conclude that it must be dire enough that people would risk their lives and uproot themselves to travel across borders into strange lands.

Dirty Pretty Things compels us to ponder the link between the cumulative effects of migration and a subpopulation so desperate it is willing to trade their vital organs for money to live. Upon arrival, with very few options, many migrants find that while wages may be higher, the material conditions of immigrant life, coupled with the fear and anxiety produced by systems of surveillance and enforcement of the state, produce poor, desperate, and scared migrant workers. The characters live in the shadows of the receiving society, under poor working and living conditions, risking violence and imprisonment.

This vulnerability and extreme desperation make these immigrants susceptible to the unscrupulous acts of others. This reality illuminates the world in which contemporary immigrants live and work. Fearful of deportation and jail, immigrants become systematic prey to employers looking for cheap and pliant labor, they become less than their original selves, and they sacrifice their own values and even their own bodies to survive. Given these contexts, sacrifice is not only conceivable but a necessary requirement for survival.

Okwe and Senay, too, come to understand the contours of this world. Throughout the film we see Okwe doing his best to keep a low profile and stay out of the sight of authorities. But when he discovers a human heart in the hotel toilet, he finds himself caught in a dilemma between his need for survival and his sense of morality. In his confrontation with Sneaky, Okwe is quickly forced to make a decision. As Sneaky proceeds to call the police, so that Okwe can report what he has found, Okwe must assess his choices and his own vulnerability. He is left to hang up the phone, choosing to protect himself over doing what he believes is right. Sneaky's warning serves as an important reminder: "If you're so concerned, go to the police. Get yourself deported."

However, through his contact with desperate immigrant organ donors and the frustration of his own limitations, Okwe begins to come to terms with the complexities of such decisions. This growing awareness is brought to the fore when Okwe realizes that the one he loves, Senay, has given up her virginity and promised to sell an organ for a passport in order to escape. Okwe's dilemma between morality and survival comes together, as do the pieces of the film's complicated puzzle, as neither Okwe nor the viewer can overlook Senay's loss of innocence (and the right to control her own body) as a direct consequence of her quest for survival in a cruel, cruel city.

Conclusion

For sociologists and moviegoers alike, *Dirty Pretty Things* offers a glimpse into the world in which low-wage immigrants toil, struggle, and pursue their dreams. As a case study, it provides a snapshot of the contemporary global city. Behind large finance centers and corporations, beyond the glitz of the city, we find the foundational infrastructure, the women and men who keep the global economy running. Through this medium, the film-makers can delve deeply into the questions of how the macro is manifested in the micro;

that is, how do complex systems of global labor impact the lives of the most vulnerable, the low-wage and unprotected migrants.

Engaging with film alongside academic scholarship enhances our understanding of the theoretical while revealing to us the ways in which we might recognize sociology in mediums such as popular film. When used appropriately and creatively, film can animate important conceptual frameworks and provide a human face and engaging story line. In turn, our all-too-often causal viewing of films can be fortified by the development of critical lenses and, most important, a sociological imagination.

References

Aleinikoff, T. A. (2001). Policing boundaries: Migration, citizenship, and the state. In G. Gerstle & J. Mollenkopf (Eds.), *E pluribus unum? Contemporary and historical perspectives on immigrant political incorporation* (pp. 267–291). New York: Russell Sage Foundation.

Averitt, R. T. (1968). *The dual economy: The dynamics of American industry structure.* New York: Norton.

Calavita, K. (1998). Immigration, law, and marginalization in a global economy: Notes from Spain. *Law and Society Review, 32*(3), 529–566.

Calavita, K. (2005). *Immigrants at the margins: Law, race, and exclusion in southern Europe.* New York: Cambridge University Press.

Chavez, L. R. (1991). Outside the imagined community: Undocumented settlers and experiences of incorporation. *American Ethnologist, 18*(2), 257–278.

Chavez, L. R. (1998). *Shadowed lives: Undocumented immigrants in American society.* Fort Worth, TX: Harcourt Brace College Publishers.

Coutin, S. B. (1996). Differences within accounts of U.S. immigration law. *PoLAR: Political and Legal Anthropology Review, 19*(1), 11–19.

Coutin, S. B. (1998). From refugees to immigrants: The legalization strategies of Salvadoran immigrants and activists. *International Migration Review, 32*(4), 901–925.

Coutin, S. B. (2000). *Legalizing moves: Salvadoran immigrants' struggle for U.S. residency.* Ann Arbor: University of Michigan Press.

Coutin, S. B. (2002). Questionable transactions as grounds for legalization: Immigration, illegality, and law. *Crime Law and Social Change, 37*(1), 19–36.

Gibson, M. (1988). *Accommodation without assimilation: Punjabi Sikh immigrants in an American high school.* The Anthropology of Contemporary Issues Series. Ithaca, NY: Cornell University Press.

Hagan, J. M. (1994). *Deciding to be legal: A Maya community in Houston.* Philadelphia: Temple University Press.

Light, I., & Bonacich, E. (1988). *Immigrant entrepreneurs.* Berkeley: University of California Press.

Mann, M. (1990). *The rise and decline of the nation state.* Oxford, UK: Blackwell.

Massey, D. S., Arango, A., Hugo, G., Kouaouci, A., Pellegrino, A., & Taylor, J. E. (1998). *Worlds in motion: International migration at the end of the millennium.* Oxford: Oxford University Press.

Menjívar, C. (2000). *Fragmented ties: Salvadoran immigrant networks in America.* Berkeley: University of California Press.

Menjívar, C. (2006). Liminal legality: Salvadoran and Guatemalan immigrants' lives in the United States. *American Journal of Sociology, 111*(4), 999–1037.

Mills, C. W. (1959). *The sociological imagination.* London: Oxford University Press.

Piore, M. (1979). *Birds of passage: Migrant labor in industrial societies.* New York: Cambridge University Press.

Portes, A., & Rumbaut, R. G. (2001). *Legacies: The story of the immigrant second generation.* Berkeley and New York: University of California Press and Russell Sage Foundation.

Sassen, S. (2001). *The global city: New York, London, Tokyo* (updated 2nd ed.). Princeton, NJ: Princeton University Press.

Tambini, D. (2001). Post-national citizenship. *Ethnic and Racial Studies, 24*(2), 195–217.

Waters, M. C. (1999). *Black identities: West Indian immigrant dreams and American realities.* New York: Russell Sage Press.

Zhou, M., & Bankston, III, C. L. (1998). *Growing up American: How Vietnamese children adapt to life in the United States.* New York: Russell Sage Foundation.

SLUMDOG OR MILLIONAIRE—MAY I PHONE A FRIEND?

Neoliberalism and Globalizing the American Dream

Alison R. Moss and Jerome M. Hendricks

*S*lumdog Millionaire, opening scene, black background with white print:

Jamal Malik is one question away from winning 20 million rupees. How did he do it?

A: He cheated

B: He's lucky

C: He's a genius

D: It is written

Understanding Our Global Society

Neoliberalism, globalization, Americanization, McDonaldization: these terms and many others are often used to describe the social, economic, technological, and political changes that are connecting our contemporary world. In attempting to understand our complex global society, academic terms sometimes become bundled, conflated, or just plain confusing. In this case, confusion appears to result in socioeconomic, technological, and political stagnation: *when we don't understand what's happening, we can't understand what needs to be done.* Rather than arguing in favor of hegemonic, "Western" ideologies or a combination of spontaneous processes, we ask readers to consider a flexible yet purposeful modern capitalist project that relies on two individual, though concurrent, processes—*neoliberalism* and *globalization*—to survive.

Neoliberalism and globalization are distinct processes with unique features that benefit the expansion and elasticity of capitalism throughout the world. The intersection of these processes creates uneven, yet persistent, development that can be seen in the forms that capitalist states take, power dynamics between and within these states, and resulting global conflicts. Foundationally, these processes are rooted in U.S. capitalism, as the United States is the preeminent capitalist state; in the U.S., neoliberalism and globalization intersect, creating a characteristically "American" version of capitalism that we will call "Western" capitalism. In this sense, the means and practice of implementing neoliberal economic and social policy result in a global, generalized conception of how to attain the "American Dream." In the following analysis we will first define neoliberalism and globalization. With these terms intact, we will use the film adapted from Simon Beaufoy's novel *Slumdog*

Millionaire (Danny Boyle and Loveleen Tandan, 2008) to exemplify the ways in which neo-liberalism and globalization provide the material basis for a capitalist American Dream. As with all capitalist projects to date, the "dream" promised is only realized by a select few to the detriment of social "others."

Photo 10.1   The Indian version of the American Dream in *Slumdog Millionaire*. Jamal (Dev Patel), defies his social location as he continues to answer correctly on "Who Wants to be a Millionaire?"

Understanding Neoliberalism and Globalization

As stated above, we conceptualize neoliberalism and globalization as distinct processes within the ongoing history of capitalism. With this in mind, we offer the following definitions as tools for critical analysis and understanding of our global (social, economic, technological, and political) environment. Neoliberalism is best understood as a *blueprint* for capitalist development featuring an emphasis on less government regulation/involvement and increasing the role of the private sector. Globalization is the *transport* process where technology and practice facilitate the execution of the *blueprint*. These concepts are designed to assist the expansion of capitalism that generates fundamental disadvantages for those who do not control the means of production. Further, neoliberalism and globalization rely on a generalized consumer cultural ideology we refer to as the American Dream. Based on the rhetoric of individualism, freedom, and choice, the American Dream is prescribed as a solution for everyone and results in a consumer cultural ideology superimposed upon local norms (e.g., American consumer culture as an impetus for globalizing production jobs). While it is easy to see this cultural justification as the result of neoliberal policy through globalized means, the allure of consumer culture is also used to justify the implementation of neoliberalism. *Slumdog Millionaire* provides examples of the ways in which *all* individuals are implicated in and disenfranchised by the allure of consumer culture and the American Dream; however, the film shows that women and children bear the brunt of social inequalities produced by this modern capitalist project more often than anyone else.

It is important to understand that the mechanisms of capitalist expansion have similar features despite their evolution over time. Just as colonialism and the Industrial Revolution were made possible through economic and technological advances, modern capitalism has flourished because of neoliberalism and globalization. Despite the occasional economic depression or world war, capitalism has maintained relatively consistent growth over time (see Harvey 2010). These cycles of capitalist expansion have resulted in robust structures that encourage localized economies to perpetuate global inequalities via wealth discrepancies. For example, overlaying a modern capitalist structure in India, a Western project with Western cultural norms victimizes children of Mumbai/Bombay, who are bound by Indian cultural norms. Jamal (Ayush Mahesh Khedekar), Salim (Azharuddin Mohammed Ismail), and Latika (Rubina Ali) are ensconced in various moneymaking schemes as very young children. They are forced to the streets to steal, swindle, and beg their way through life as dictated by those in control. Children in this setting have few or no rights. Child welfare is nonexistent for Jamal, Salim, and Latika, and as such, the film highlights the ways in which these children endeavor to survive the harsh reality of impoverishment in the slums. In this sense, the tendency to reinvent the cycle is directly connected to the benefit it provides powerful individuals and organizations to the detriment of Indian children.

Sociology students may hear the terms *neoliberalism* and *globalization* but remain confused as to their importance in sociological analysis. Moreover, some may find they know very little about what distinguishes one from the other and use the terms in confusing or confounding ways. Our purpose is to distinguish between these terms so they may be used more clearly when assessing and understanding current global social and economic phenomena. Importantly, the constraints, barriers, privileges, and access that arise as a result of one's social location in the global political economy are influenced by the current capitalist expansion project. Thus, neoliberalism and globalization can be used to frame locations related to gender, class, race, sexuality, and nation.

Jamal, Salim, Latika, and Mumbai, India— Characters in a New Global Time and Space

The following analysis considers the lives of three Indian children from the slums of Mumbai, India, as viewed through the blockbuster feature film *Slumdog Millionaire.* Jamal and Salim are orphan brothers who experience life in the slums through various experiences of "work." As beggars, thieves, and hustlers, Jamal and Salim survive life in the slums working for crime bosses in the Mumbai street economy. Though Jamal and Salim are close companions as well as brothers, they are portrayed quite differently. Jamal is the main protagonist in the film. The viewers feel compelled to champion Jamal's cause as a lucky slumdog with the chance to become a megamillionaire. Salim, conversely, is the antagonist throughout the majority of the film. Salim is mostly complicit in various criminal activities, and though the viewer may sympathize with Salim, given his painful life experiences, Salim's character as the antagonist is villainous and unlikable. Latika is the third of the "Three Musketeers," according to young Jamal. Latika is also an orphan, but unlike Jamal and Salim, she has no one else to rely on for survival. Aside from early scenes including Jamal and Salim's mother before her murder, Latika is the only female character of note in the film. The three children attempt life as slumdogs together, surviving and failing in their own ways.

Secondary characters in the film are contextually important to our understanding of neoliberalism and globalization. They depict the sociopolitical and economic environment at given historical moments in the city of Mumbai (Bombay) through skin color, ethnic accent, moving between Hindi and English (where and when language shifts take place), and social class identifiers. Further, the city itself can be viewed as a "character" in this film. Different sections of Mumbai are shown to demonstrate social extremes: depressed economic conditions or booming capitalist industry, the wealth of crime bosses in mansions or the shacks of the slums, the bright lights and modern highway infrastructure or the dusty, grimy garbage dump with a makeshift tent where Jamal, Salim, and Latika sleep. All of these characters coalesce to create a film that captures the ways in which neoliberalism and globalization serve to expand Western capitalism globally.

Global Life through Film: Capitalism, Neoliberalism, and Globalization

In the context of contemporary capitalism, countries where the expansion of modern capitalism is particularly harmful due to absent or minimal socioeconomic resources (often referred to as "third-world countries") will be respectfully referred to as countries of the global "South." Previous literature (see Connell 2007) suggests moving away from conceptualizing regions/countries as "third world" due to negative connotations and use to further oppress and marginalize citizens of these Southern regions. In this reading, we show the ways in which modern Western capitalism is transported and implemented in the global South as depicted in *Slumdog Millionaire*. This film is an exemplar of life during contemporary social and economic shifts in our global community. Neoliberal social and economic shifts leave Southern slum dwellers of Mumbai located in the "center of the center" of global India, in dire straits as a result of historical, caste-based wealth and income inequalities.

The filmmaker presents the audience with two concurrent problems in attempting to globalize or transport Western theories of economic expansion: time (history) and space (geography). The film depicts Mumbai as distinctly different from American metropolitan areas. While the viewer may be temporarily blinded by the glossy advertisements, media influence, gridlock, and light pollution shown in the film, the consistent message is that Mumbai is distinctly Indian. This assertion of Indian nationalism is important in that we can discern the difficulties in mapping Americanized cultural assumptions onto Southern cultural contexts.

As nations in the global South attempt to implement neoliberal political and economic strategies, context-specific cultural norms, once taken for granted, are made unimportant by lived economic experiences. For example, in his youth, Jamal scratched out a living as a pretend tour guide at the Taj Mahal. He made money on Western tourists' ignorance of local culture and customs. The money Jamal made, however, was not always Indian rupees, the Indian national currency. Many times he made American dollars and coins. Having extensive experience with American money afforded Jamal the knowledge of whose face is on the American $100 bill. At the same time, he was not familiar with a basic Indian cultural symbol and therefore could not tell the crime boss that Ghandi is on the Indian 1000-rupee bill. The likelihood that Jamal would have come into contact with a 1000-rupee bill is small, given that he is from the slums and performed many jobs begging and working in the Mumbai street economy for little pay in rupees. Yet he is somehow able to fill this cultural void with lived globalized circumstances and experiences that he is able to take advantage of in the game show. Paying close attention to Jamal's "work history," through flashbacks to his youth, reveals not just how he comes up with the answers in the game show, but also the ways in which his life has been dictated by current social and economic shifts.

Using the framework of neoliberalism and globalization, we can better understand the way that Jamal, representing poor Indian youth (slumdogs), is negatively impacted by contemporary constraints while the promise of privilege is waiting behind the next (game show) question. The sharp distinction between rich and poor in the film leaves no room for the middle class who we assume are there somewhere, given the consumer culture that is ubiquitous in Mumbai (Bombay). Jamal's flashback to life in the slums as a restaurant employee, a few years after his "job" at the Taj Mahal, is an example of a slumdog in the shifting worlds between Bombay (as named by the colonizing British) and Mumbai (the politically reclaimed Indian name for the city).

Jamal's experience between the rich world of Bombay and the poor slums of Mumbai (though really the same city, just different sections) and Salim's experiences working for crime bosses resonate as examples of the constraints and privileges of adopting neoliberalism. Jobs are scarce, money is scarce, and resources are limited, which further separates and stratifies the rich and the poor. Though Salim and Jamal stood to make money at the Taj Mahal, more important to Jamal is Latika's safety in the slums of Mumbai, while Salim wanted the money.

Latika's position as a young girl growing up in the gendered social and economic environment of Mumbai proves to be extremely dangerous. Latika's occupational shifts from street beggar to exotic dancer to girlfriend of a crime boss reveal the very narrowly defined social position of what it means to be a girl/woman in political economies indifferent to the effects of "development" on women. As a young woman, Latika (Freida Pinto) is scarred, mentally and physically, by her experiences in the slums. When she is abducted by gangsters, her face is cut with a knife, marking her as the property of the crime boss and symbolically revealing her fettered status as a woman.

While gender constrains Latika's life as a woman, there are limited benefits for men in the changing world of Mumbai. On the one hand, they can continue to work in dead-end service jobs that do not pay a living wage. On the other hand, they can choose criminal activity, where they have a chance to make more money despite the constant threat of incarceration or death. Upward mobility is a dream, but as we see in the lives of the three main characters, the options available are crime (Salim), prostitution (Latika), and luck (Jamal). From the point of view of neoliberalism, individuals have the opportunity to utilize the circumstances presented to them, and they must bear the burden of the choices made. Fairness, or the lack of fairness, is an issue related to the uniqueness of individuals. To impose fairness on larger social groups is more unfair than harmful individual outcomes. In other words, the "choices" available to Jamal, Salim, and Latika may be unfair, but to impose policies that attempt to balance the opportunity structure would be *more* unfair.

This rationale suggests Jamal and Salim can stay the course in their service job or take a risk. For Salim, the risk is organized crime; by becoming a killer for hire, he gains financial opportunity, a sense of community, and power. For Jamal, a game show elevates him from a have-not to a national hero. The celebration of Jamal's "victory" reveals what Friedman (1980) pointed out about society's glorification of celebrity and games of chance—that society covets unfairness, or more specifically, society covets those that succeed in the face of unfairness. In this social atmosphere, then, risk that produces greater opportunity is better served at the disposal of those who are successful in the face of unfairness rather than rationed through government intervention.

The paths open to Jamal, Salim, and Latika directly contradict the value of hard work and the economic payoff implied in the American Dream. Could it be that their options are so limited because others are simply more or better equipped? Or could it be that their limitations are imposed by a history of inequality and a social arena articulated through differences as opposed to commonalities (Hardt and Negri 2001; Harvey 2005)? If one were to track any distribution of capital throughout history to determine how these resources came to be held, one would consistently uncover processes of violence and exploitation. Consider the development and outcomes of colonialism; robbery, piracy, slavery, rape, murder, and blackmail have served as a foundation for modern accumulation of capital (Marx [1867] 1978; Polanyi [1944] 1975). Today, the neoliberal state promotes a specific freedom of choice that does not include options that would alter current institutional practices or promote new institutional means of social reform.

A Marxist Understanding of Capitalism: The Foundation of Neoliberalism and Globalization

In capitalism, those who control the "means of production" pay others a wage for their labor. The means of production is a Marxian concept describing the nonhuman components necessary for producing commodities for a market. These means are almost exclusively held by the wealthy and privately owned organizations that operate with the single goal of creating and expanding profits. Through increased revenue and decreased costs, the ownership is compelled to exploit their workers in various ways. According to Marx ([1867] 1978),

> the capitalist process of production is a historically determined form of the social process of production in general. The latter is as much a production process of material conditions of human life as a process taking place under specific historical and economic production relations, producing and reproducing these production relations themselves, and thereby also the bearers of this process, their material conditions of existence and their mutual relations, i.e., their particular socio-economic form. (P. 439)

In *Slumdog Millionaire*, capitalism as the current mode of production is made obvious given the mise-en-scène, or the "look" of the film. Many scenes of the film show the capitalist expansion and evolution as it takes place in the city of Mumbai/Bombay, India. Flashbacks to Jamal's childhood as a beggar in the poverty-stricken slums, his participation in the local tourist economy at the Taj Mahal in the more contemporary "Bombay," and his work in a "legitimate" call center as a *chai wallah*, or assistant, give viewers a sense of capitalist development in an "exotic" place over time. Also, the specific linguistic and metaphorical uses of India's capital city suggest that India's history of colonization and current adoption of neoliberal policy have served to further stratify and disadvantage Indian social "others," or slumdogs.

Capitalism is as much a social arrangement between those with control and those without as it is an economic system. As reflected in Jamal's work history, the continued struggle between the haves and have-nots is continually reproduced. Jamal's position as a *chai wallah* at a Mumbai telephone call center is an example of an individual relationship to the social and economic means of production. Jamal's occupations shift and, in some respects, improve as he grows older, yet he is never freed from the constraints of domination. He is consistently controlled by those who have more power. Jamal is part of India's underclass, or working poor. Jamal's position as a beggar, a fake tour guide, and a *chai wallah* are examples of positions in which he is clearly exploited by those in power.

Definitions and connotations of occupational positions within Indian social structures do not seamlessly correlate with American understandings of the social class structure and the ways in which individuals are socially stratified. This is not an issue of lower class and upper class perceptions of a workplace; these positions are defined by an ascribed caste system. While the globalization of Western call centers to poverty -stricken "global" cities is neoliberal capitalism at its finest, the social meanings that surface within these new organizations are quite different. In this same sense, neoliberalism and globalization are distinct processes designed exclusively to assist the expansion of capitalism. The observed material outcomes of capitalist expansion such as intense poverty, wealth disparities, and violence inform our understanding of what capitalism does in the social sphere.

From the Slums to the Taj Mahal to the Call Center—Neoliberalism: The Blueprint of Global Inequality

As noted earlier, neoliberalism is the *blueprint* of capitalist expansion. Harvey has explained it as "a theory of political economic practices that proposes that human well-being can best be advanced by liberating individual entrepreneurial freedoms and skills within an institutional framework characterized by strong private property rights, free markets, and free trade" (2005:2). This doctrine originates from classical liberal economics and contains three components: individualism, open markets, and a noninterventionist state.

In classical liberalism, the advantage of individualism comes from the notion that each citizen is the best judge of her or his specific needs and wants. Society must, therefore, be structured to lower all barriers that would otherwise prohibit the realization of these pleasures, needs, and wants via entrepreneurial freedoms and skills (proffered by American doctrine as "life, liberty, and the pursuit of happiness"). The open market is lauded as the most efficient and effective avenue to support individual independence, allowing maximum access to free trade. Finally, the role of the government should be limited to the safety of the citizenry, the maintenance of individual rights, and the pursuit of competitive markets. In addition, neoliberalism contains a political rhetoric inspired by the work of conservative economic and political philosophers. This rhetoric is centered on a patriotic discourse of freedom, liberty, and equality that promotes a moral standard, is critical of undesirable laws, and believes in private property and the unrestricted expansion of the competitive market.

A very clear and interesting example of the *blueprint* of capitalist expansion as shown in *Slumdog Millionaire* is the role of the U.S.-based game show *Who Wants to Be a Millionaire*. The game is the same: questions worth increasing amounts of money, lifelines, audience participation via cheers and jeers, stage, lights, music, and suspense; however, the obvious differences are found in the assertions of Indian nationalism. For example, the game show questions refer to Indian popular culture, the increasing amounts of money are in Indian rupees rather than American dollars, and the game show host converses with Jamal and the audience in English and Hindi.

Close attention to the game show host reveals further examples of an Americanized *blueprint*; he (who has no name in the film, likely because he is meant to be a replication of "any other" American game show host) is very light skinned, appearing white next to Jamal. His English is only lightly accented with Hindi, except in each instance of pronouncing the word *millionaire*, when his accent sounds heavier and less Americanized.

The host's very character is an example of the American Dream. He is an Indian man, formerly from the slums of Mumbai, who "pulled himself up by his bootstraps" and "made it" out of the slums through the Mumbai street economy. As the host of Mumbai's most famous game show, he is now a millionaire, and one that has been corrupted by his fame and fortune. Given this context, the host covertly gives Jamal the wrong answer in an attempt to throw the game, thus relegating Jamal to his expected status of slumdog. However, Jamal outsmarts the host and chooses the alternative answer, "D," despite the host's coercion. Jamal knows what is best for him, decides to trust his instincts, and the strategy pays off as he continues on to the next question. By taking a risk, the new hero outwits the old: Jamal makes a choice, takes a risk, and wins within the rules of the game, thus allowing him more time on the game show in his attempt to rescue Latika from the crime boss who holds her captive in sexual servitude. It is clear that Jamal's desire to rescue Latika is limited by his access to resources. Thus, individualism and freedom take on specified, structured meanings within this particular context.

Transporting the Blueprint from the U.S. to Mumbai: Globalization and the Mechanisms of Neoliberal Transference

While *globalization* is often used as a blanket term in reference to "global forces" (Harvey 2003), a "new world order" (Marcos [1997] 2001), or a "borderless world" (Klein 2007), here we offer a new definition of globalization as the means and practices by which the *blueprint* of neoliberalism is *transported*. This blueprint discussed above (individualism, open markets, and a noninterventionist state resulting in "ultimate freedom") is transported and implemented in various, contextually specific ways.

We look to two extant features of current global social and economic change as the core of a responsible globalization definition. First, technological advances have decreased global time and space dimensions. Technology delivers information at lightening fast speeds; the continual advancement of the Internet and computer information systems makes our world seem smaller because quick, easy, and convenient modes of communication are now available. Just as advances in technology made colonialism possible, technological advances similarly facilitate and reinforce a unique, modern capitalist project. Drawing largely on Bourdieu (1977), the practice feature of globalization involves the system of dialectical (re)actions to information deemed relevant and objective. This aspect suggests that dominant world actors reorganize local and regional markets based on the momentum of past projects and interpretations of future goals. In other words, concepts or technologies that are understood as successful can appear to take on a life of their own, but their development is contingent on social understandings and goals. In sum, our definition of globalization works well with what Hardt and Negri (2001:32) describe as a monetary perspective where "we can see a horizon of values and a machine of distribution, a mechanism of accumulation and a means of circulation, a power and a language," or Marcos's ([1997] 2001:273) definition of globalization as simply "the totalitarian extension of the logic of the finance markets to all aspects of life."

Relevant Information

We are able to see the ways in which Jamal's life reflects the consequences of "totalitarian" market logic in his everyday life as a beggar and a kid from the streets of Mumbai. From early childhood, Indian popular culture supplanted formal education as a form of knowledge production in Jamal's life (as told through childhood flashbacks). Jamal's social location did not afford him a formal education, suggesting that he should be ignorant and therefore unable to succeed on a television game show based on getting the correct answers. Jamal's experiences produced a situated cultural knowledge that also happened to be the information needed to do well on *Who Wants to Be a Millionaire*. However, the stereotype of what it means to be a slumdog is pervasive in Indian culture and, as such, the stereotype leaves no room for a slumdog to be capable of winning 20 million rupees. By embracing the opportunities in front of him and "pulling himself up by his bootstraps," Jamal becomes a personified example of the American Dream in the face of rigid, traditional opposition.

Technological Advances

The arrival of new technologies, and the products that represent the transfer of these technologies to India, are seen as both enticing and problematic in the changing worlds of Mumbai/Bombay. From the moment that Maman (Ankur Vikal), a local crime boss, wakes young Jamal and Salim in their tent at a blistering hot landfill with an ice-cold "Coke and a smile," we know that their fate is sealed. As they accept the Coke, they become recruits in the underworld of crime in Mumbai/Bombay. We might consider these enticements or opportunities "with strings attached."

When new technologies are introduced, we see that they tend to produce much more harm despite their immediate functional effectiveness. We point specifically to the introduction of the revolver shown throughout the film. As a new and powerful technology, it aids Jamal and Salim in their quest to rescue Latika from Maman. Salim takes control of a life-or-death situation by killing Maman and facilitating the escape of the "Three Musketeers." However, the power the gun represents also contributes to Salim's downward spiral, ultimately producing a rift between brothers and further objectification of Latika. By the time the brothers reunite, some years later, Jamal (Dev Patel) is working as the lowly *chai wallah* while Salim (Madhur Mittal) is wearing shiny new clothes, driving fast expensive cars, and working for Khan, a rival crime boss in Mumbai. Latika is now the property of Khan. Introduction of the gun as technology might have served a limited purpose (rescue of Latika), but ultimately it was used to solidify Salim's criminal status and Latika's subservient status.

No discussion of globalization's dynamism is complete without discussion of the good and evil aspects of technological expansion. Just as our previous example suggests, we must question the long-term price of current practices. Keep in mind the cyclical nature of capitalism and how it consistently reinforces relations of inequality. Jamal's movement away from being a beggar to working in a "legitimate" job is an example of technological expansion. Without globalization of jobs and job markets, Jamal's job as a *chai wallah* would be nonexistent. Now he is able to work and be paid in a way that more closely mimics the job and pay structure in the Western world. However, Jamal is still unable to make enough money to change his poverty status, highlighting these inequalities. Perhaps as important as the good and evil aspects of technological expansion are the relationships behind globalization; for example, people make war and people can also utilize technology as a leveling force.

Too often, those with political power in countries of the global South welcome industrialization with little or no consideration for the workers. New economic and social policies are introduced to secure global financing where no alternatives are available for those dependent on past arrangements. Jamal, Salim, and Latika are pawns in this global game of chance. We see the ways in which each of their lives is affected by the changing socioeconomic conditions in Mumbai. There are no provisions in place, as the slum children, now adults, are no better off under the modern capitalist project than they were before its implementation. Latika, for example, is able to survive only by exchanging sex for a life of servitude (with some level of material comfort). In many ways she had more freedom as a child beggar despite the harsh conditions.

In terms of the definitions provided above, the ever-increasing speed in which neoliberal theory champions the modern capitalist project imposes this market logic upon every state, resulting in a historical decision-making exclusively driven by capitalist interests. Capitalist interests usurp social welfare and, as shown in the film, citizens of the underclass are those who most often pay the price through lack of sufficient employment, income, and resources, denying them the basic necessities of life.

Conclusion: Slumdog or Millionaire? Understanding Neoliberalism and Globalization as Concepts of Modern Capitalism

Slumdog Millionaire shows the ways in which globalizing the American Dream is not only an impractical endeavor due to cultural relativity, but also an intensely dangerous act, given the narrative of Jamal's life. Through the distinctions made throughout this chapter, it is our intent to provide a framework for analyzing the process and outcome of economic changes in the world today. By first identifying the continuous yet historically variable cycle of capitalist accumulation, we are better able to identify a starting point at which to further examine mechanisms like neoliberalism and globalization. Organizing the American Dream as the ideological basis and subsequent justification for neoliberal economic and political ideology allows dominant individuals and organizations to separate the hypothetical from the historical. In this case we see Jamal's appearance on the game show as the American Dream, or the hypothetical means of no longer being relegated to the slumdog underclass (Jamal's reality); however, Jamal is not in control of his destiny. Jamal's destiny, as shown throughout the film, is in the hands of others—the game show host, Salim, and crime bosses who, indeed, have more power and money than he. Thus, the implementation of the neoliberal *blueprint* through globalized means and practices is yet another advancement in a long history of economic systems designed to perpetuate stratifying inequalities.

The American Dream juxtaposed with realities of life in Mumbai for Jamal, Salim, and Latika illustrates the ways in which overlaying Western neoliberalism and capitalism onto regions of the global South is not only impractical but dangerous in the lives of the citizenry. Throughout *Slumdog Millionaire*, constant scene splicing and cutting from the slums of Mumbai to the wealth of the more "Americanized" Bombay places viewers in the shoes of young Jamal as he matures during the perpetually turbulent and violent implementation of modern capitalism in India. Additionally, if the viewer closes her or his eyes, the Indian game show host closely mimics Regis Philbin's "Millionaire" persona—that is, until he pronounces "mill-yo-naire." Jamal, Salim, and Latika experience the impact of consumer culture and globalized occupational structures in their work histories and limited life choices through the shifts of modern capitalism.

The dualism between what is clearly Americanized and what is native to Indian culture provides a specific cultural lens through which to understand the American Dream. Jamal's "destiny" hinges on the luck of the draw of questions in the game show. Without proper knowledge of Hindi and American popular culture, Jamal would have been rendered a loser, one who did not fulfill his destiny, one who had the American Dream at his fingertips and lost. As it is written, however, Jamal indeed fulfills his destiny—and with 20 million rupees in his pocket, he is a *chai wallah* no more. The divide between rich and poor, success and failure further signifies the contrast between Western and Indian culture as portrayed in the film. Painting broad strokes of the characters allows us to see the ways in which each is imperative to the plot of the film: Jamal, Salim, Latika, the game show host, and Mumbai/Bombay are all affected by modern capitalism.

This frame of analysis asks us to recognize underlying factors that assist and uphold global hierarchies and inequalities. The very systematic and market-driven nature of neoliberalism and globalization serve to uphold the capitalist project of exploitation. The American Dream is a consumer paradise where achievement is measured in material goods. As a measure, failure to attain the American Dream can serve as a call for neoliberal reform where governments have failed their citizenry. As a paradise, the American Dream can serve as an exemplar of what could be if we just keep working hard and avoid questions, analysis, and alternatives.

With this critical lens, scholars have an advantage over the general media consumer. In *Slumdog Millionaire*, average media consumers may see the industrial growth of Mumbai's urban core as industrialization, the movement of slum dwellers to the outskirts of the city as gentrification, and Jamal's position as a *chai wallah* as the transport of "American" jobs overseas. It is our intent to encourage sociologists to connect these localized explanations to modern capitalist projects achieved through globalizing neoliberalism.

References

Bourdieu, P. 1977. *Outline of a Theory of Practice (Esquisse d'une théorie de la pratique).* Translated by R. Nice. New York: Cambridge University Press.

Connell, R. 2007. *Southern Theory: The Global Dynamics of Knowledge in Social Science.* Crows Nest, Australia: Allen & Unwin.

Friedman, M. 1980. *Free to Choose: A Personal Statement.* 1st ed. New York: Harcourt Brace Jovanovich.

Hardt, M. and A. Negri. 2001. *Empire.* 1st ed. Cambridge, MA: Harvard University Press.

Harvey, D. 2003. *The New Imperialism.* Oxford: Oxford University Press.

Harvey, D. 2005. *A Brief History of Neoliberalism.* New York: Oxford University Press.

Harvey, D. 2010. *The Enigma of Capital: And the Crises of Capitalism.* New York: Oxford University Press.

Klein, N. 2007. *The Shock Doctrine: The Rise of Disaster Capitalism.* 1st ed. Toronto: Alfred A. Knopf Canada.

Marcos, S. [1997] 2001. "The Fourth World War Has Begun." Pp. 270–85 in *The Zapatista Reader,* edited by T. Hayden. New York: Thunder's Mountain Press/Nation Books.

Marx, K. [1867] 1978. "On the Realm of Necessity and the Realm of Freedom." Pp. 439–41 in *The Marx-Engels Reader.* 2nd ed., edited by R. C. Tucker. New York: W. W. Norton.

Polanyi, K. [1944] 1975. *The Great Transformation.* New York: Octagon Books.

Outtake

Arabs and Muslims in Hollywood's *Munich* and *Syriana*

Jack G. Shaheen

Finally, Hollywood is offering humane, equitable images of Arabs and Muslims. Stephen Gaghan's political drama *Syriana* and Steven Spielberg's *Munich* discard stale stereotypes. Instead, they forcefully and eloquently argue that unabated power and unconstrained violence serve to expedite terrorism and prevent peace.

Gaghan's lucid geopolitical thriller, *Syriana,* on which this writer did some minor consulting, stars George Clooney. The film probes contemporary questions, ruffling our senses and causing us to ponder seriously the consequences of what happens when corrupt, influential U.S. government and corporate executives mix together greed, oil and terrorism in order to maintain their monopoly on Arab oil. Power and money matter most.

Writer-director Gaghan projects *Syriana*'s Arabs, Pakistanis and Americans as multidimensional characters, complete with complex motives. In the clash of modernity and radicalism, Gaghan eschews stereotypes. For example, he presents unemployed Pakistani Muslim oil refinery workers not as hateful suicide bombers but as innocent victims, seduced by an Islamic fundamentalist.

Syriana does not vilify the Muslim world, its people, religion or culture. Instead, the film warns us to be wary of power moguls, men who consider the deaths of innocent people acceptable. In Gaghan's harsh, corrupt world, everyone is expendable: Educated Arabs seeking democracy, unemployed Pakistani immigrants desperate to find a meaningful purpose to their lives, covert CIA operatives pursuing justice, even Arab and American children.

As for *Munich*, I initially balked before seeing it because Hollywood has a history of demonizing all things Palestinian, and Spielberg, one of the world's most influential filmmakers, has not always been balanced in his portrayal of Arabs. In movies that Spielberg has been associated with, Egyptians are shown as Nazi sympathizers (*Raiders of the Lost Ark*), Arab terrorists try to machine-gun Michael J. Fox (*Back to the Future*), Dr. Moriarty's Egyptian cult kidnaps young girls and torches them alive (*Young Sherlock Holmes*), and fanatical Egyptian Christians are out to kill Indy (*Indiana Jones and the Last Crusade*).

In his skillful *Munich*, however, Spielberg portrays Palestinians and other Arabs not as demons but as thoughtful, ordinary human beings. He does not paint Palestinians in black and Israelis in white. Both have a conscience, both articulate thoughtful arguments about what it means to be a displaced people.

Munich is Hollywood's third film about the events surrounding the tragic deaths of 11 Israeli athletes. Previously, two TV movies, ABC's *21 Hours at Munich* (1976) and HBO's *Sword of Gideon* (1986) focused on the Israeli hit team tracking down Palestinian terrorists.

Spielberg's film, however, best captures the varied motives and emotions of Israeli assassins as they go about killing, one by one, Palestinians responsible for the deaths of the Israelis during the 1972 Summer Olympics.

Spielberg could have achieved more balance, however—not to mention accuracy—by showing the killings of innocent Arabs who had nothing to do with the Munich attack, such as the real-life assassination of an innocent Moroccan waiter in Norway who was shot dead by the Israeli hit team.

In the end, watching Israelis shoot Palestinians is as painful as watching assassins kill Israelis. In *Munich*, the lives of reel Palestinians are worth almost as much as the lives of reel Israelis.

Caring, intelligent Middle East thrillers like *Syriana* and *Munich* demand our attention because they pose incisive questions applicable to today's quest for Middle East peace: Are political objectives achieved by the acts of revenge, by an unending cycle of violence that continues to the present day? What has the use of force accomplished?

Thanks to the inventive vision of directors like Gaghan and Spielberg, we can better debate whether violence has brought us any closer to peace.

SOURCE: *Washington Report on Middle East Affairs.* March 2006 (Vol. 25, Issue 2), p. 73.

CHAPTER 11

Social Change

Donna: Have you ever read about the life of Mahatma Gandhi, Ronnie? Or Henry David Thoreau on civil disobedience? That essay changed my life—it taught me that people have a right to stand up and speak out when an injustice is being done— that it's their obligation, their duty as human beings. Gandhi believed that one person with the truth was a majority—could win. Even women are fighting for their rights, Ronnie!

—Born on the Fourth of July (1989)

Neville [talking to Ann about Bob Marley]:   He had this idea. It was kind of a virologist idea. He believed that you could cure racism and hate . . . literally cure it, by injecting music and love into people's lives. When he was scheduled to perform at a peace rally, a gunman came to his house and shot him down. Two days later he walked out on that stage and sang. When they asked him why, he said, "The people, who were trying to make this world worse . . . are not taking a day off. How can I? Light up the darkness."

—I Am Legend (2007)

In the film *I Am Legend* (2007), it is 2012 and scientists have genetically reengineered a virus that is the cure for cancer. Three years later the virus has mutated and seemingly killed most of humanity and turned the survivors into monsterlike creatures who can only survive in the dark. An earlier film version of the story, *The Omega Man* (1971), is set in 1977 two years after a virus caused by biological warfare between the People's Republic of China and the Soviet Union has killed the majority of earth's population, leaving a few mutant survivors. Both films project into the future, exploring how science run amok can destroy humankind and make the planet unsafe for living creatures. Robert Neville (Will Smith), explaining why he keeps searching against all odds for a cure, brings together key themes addressed in this chapter: war, violence, working for justice and peace, science and the environment, and the possibility of creating a better world in the future.

In the first reading, Christopher Podeschi uses science fiction films as "future myths," stories about the possible future direction of society. These myths are based on visions of society and its relationship with nature. Podeschi explores culture as a "site of struggle" where resistance to the exploitative relationship between society and nature is manifest in a call for the valuing of nature through sustainable economies and technology, as opposed to reproductive discourses where nature is a resource to be exploited for human need through technology.

Examining the most popular science fiction films of the second half of the twentieth century, Podeschi finds that most are based on reproductive discourses that present a "technologically saturated" future where environmental consequences are ignored. Exceptions to this approach are found in films that give warning about the dangers of nuclear warfare, such as *Planet of the Apes* and *Testament*, and technology that involves some sort of reproduction of humanity, as in *The Empire Strikes Back* and *The Matrix*. In keeping with the reproductive discourse, nature and animals are portrayed as dangerous, needing to be conquered or tamed, and valuable only insofar as they can be colonized to serve humankind.

In the second reading, Kathryn Feltey explores nonviolence in film as a strategy for challenging systems of domination, injustice, and inequality. Violence is endemic in film and society; its hegemony lies in the widespread public acceptance of violence as the only (or at least the most effective) method to gain and maintain power. Internationally, an orientation toward war is the organizing principle of relations, such that a significant amount of the world's resources are allocated to the production and distribution of arms and the training and maintenance of military personnel. Further, we are conditioned to invest our collective energy into expecting and preparing for the worst; what we imagine as possible in the future guides our decisions and actions in the present. Accordingly, "we can't work for what we can't imagine, so we cannot have a peaceful future if we cannot imagine it" (Boulding 1995:203).

Feltey asks us to use nonviolence as presented in film as a starting point for imagining a world in which *Satyagraha* and *ahimsa* are the organizing principles for nations and communities. Using *Gandhi* and *The Long Walk Home*, nonviolence as a model for social change is examined in the movement for home rule in India and the Montgomery bus boycott in the movement against racial apartheid in the United States. The methods used are designed to challenge and change the social order, and to shift the paradigm of power from might to right. As Donna (Kyra Sedgwick) tells Ron (Tom Cruise) in *Born on the Fourth of July*, Gandhi believed that "one person with the truth . . . could win."

The film *Witness* provides a contrast between a contemporary crime-ridden urban Philadelphia and the bucolic, peaceful setting of an Amish community not far away in miles, but a century away in lifestyle. Detective John Book (Harrison Ford), hiding out on an Amish farm, tells his partner, "Where I'm at is maybe 1890 . . . Make that 1790." Not only is the standard of living "primitive" by modern standards without the conveniences of technology, but the community is completely devoid of diversity across all dimensions. In sociological terms, this is a folk society, a gemeinschaft, where kinship ties, shared values, and a simple division of labor are central to the social order. To use Weber's language, mechanical solidarity creates social bonds that are reinforced by the Ordnung; nonviolence is central to this way of life.

In the third reading, Jeffrey Langstraat uses *The Long Walk Home, Norma Rae*, and *Milk* to explore the sociology of social movements. These three films focus on historical social movements in the United States that transformed social relations on the basis of race (the civil rights movement of the 1950s and 1960s), class/worker status (the labor and unionization movements of the twentieth century), and sexuality/gender (the LGBT movement of the late twentieth century). Introducing key concepts in social movement theories, Langstraat emphasizes that social change depends on individual and collective "cognitive liberation." In other words, people have to believe, within themselves and with one another, that change is possible and, as Langstraat states, "that their actions can help produce that change." As Donna tells Ronnie in *Born on the Fourth of July*, recognizing our "right to stand up and speak out when an injustice is being done" can be life altering for the individual as well as produce large-scale social change.

Together these three readings challenge us to think about social change and the future of society. What does society look like when people are asked to imagine a future they are not afraid to enter? Research with groups of people in countries around the globe reveals that their imagined futures share some common elements: communities are more rural than urban; lifelong education is valued; a spectator-leisure industry is absent; nation-states become less significant; peace-keeping brigades replace military armies; and living in harmony with the environment is a priority (Bakker 1993). In a similar vein, sociologists in future studies have identified a set of shared global values that promote the future health of all societies: individual responsibility; treating others as we wish them to treat us; respect for life; economic and social justice; nature-friendly ways of life; honesty; moderation; freedom (expressed in ways that do not harm others), and tolerance for diversity (Bell 2004). These values may be conceptualized as global, but they are highly contested within and across societies. As Langstraat demonstrates, change is possible, but it depends on factors such as state structure, policy context, mechanisms of social control, alliance and conflict systems, and movement leadership.

Ultimately, our survival on the planet may depend on the answer to a question posed by climatologist Jack Hall (Dennis Quaid) in *The Day after Tomorrow*: "Will be able to learn from our mistakes?"

References

Baaker, J. I. 1993. *Toward a Just Civilization: A Gandhian Perspective on Human Rights and Development*. Toronto: Canadian Scholars Press.

Bell, W. 2004. "Humanity's Common Values: Seeking a Positive Future." *The Futurist*, September–October, pp. 30–6.

Boulding, E. 1995. "The Dialectics of Peace." Pp. 196–203 in *The Future: Images and Processes*, edited by E. Boulding and K. Boulding. Thousand Oaks, CA: Sage.

READING 11.1

FROM EARTH TO COSMOS

Environmental Sociology and Images
of the Future in Science Fiction Film

Christopher W. Podeschi

W e need to take something for granted at the outset: the relationship between society and nature is problematic. While nature constrains societies (e.g., arid conditions make farming difficult), our concern here is with problems caused by humans, like deforestation and biodiversity loss, the impact of suburban sprawl on water quality, or what will continue to be a big focus for years: global warming.[1] These are serious problems not just for what they do to nature, but because human societies rely on the environment as a home, source of sustenance, and for various other "ecosystem services." Harm to the natural world can ultimately mean harm to people and society.

Responsibility for understanding these problems so that we can improve conditions in the future falls on the shoulders of citizens, politicians, and scholars alike. Among scholars, these problems need attention from disciplines other than the natural sciences like ecology, biology, or geology. Sociology must also play a central role. In this section, I introduce *environmental sociology* and present some of the scholarship in this area. Then, I examine images of the future in science fiction films as a way of looking at the "culture of nature," or how nature and society's relationship with nature are "social constructions." My aims are to demonstrate both the value of close examination of film content to environmental sociology and the contribution sociology can make to future sustainability through deepening understanding of important social and cultural processes.

Environmental Sociology

Talking about environmental problems as caused by humans is actually a good place to start introducing environmental sociology. With regard to climate change, the term *anthropogenic* is used to emphasize that it is caused by human activities (e.g., CO_2 emissions from fossil fuel use). But the term *human activity* is too vague for sociologists. Sociologists are interested in the social and cultural contexts that guide human behavior and history. For example, *humans* built and moved to the suburbs that now create water-quality problems when it rains,[2] but there's a *sociological* story to tell as well. At present, "growth machines" in many locales compete with other cities and towns to attract industries and people (see Logan & Molotch, 1987). During the Great Depression, the federal government contributed to urban sprawl by backing mortgages for new housing to stimulate the economy. Then, pushed by business interests, the government built the highways that made it easier to live outside of cities (Andrews, 1999). Further, many white Americans sought refuge from urban social conditions and the influx of racial and ethnic minorities to the city (see Szasz, 2007). In the end, it is clear that sprawl-induced water quality problems have a specific social history. Generic talk about "human activity" is inadequate because environmental problems are *social* problems.

Environmental sociologists also emphasize that society and nature are not really separate entities. Consider the consumption and disposal practices of human beings, for example. People in wealthy nations get their sustenance from grocery store shelves and send their waste from porcelain bowls through sewer pipes to treatment plants. Layers of social structure (the capitalist food production and distribution system), culture (dining and waste disposal habits), and technology (modern agriculture and waste treatment systems) have distanced people from nature, but the flow of material and energy that ties human bodies, and thus society, to continuous interchange with the earth *necessarily* remains intact. And this is just one illustration of the myriad ways in which society and nature are inextricably linked (see Carolan, 2005; Dunlap, 2002; Murphy, 2004).

Perhaps surprisingly, sociology long ignored the integration of society and the environment. In an early attempt to define environmental sociology, William Catton and Riley Dunlap (1978) asserted that by ignoring society-environment dynamics and ecological limits to economic growth, sociology was guilty of falling under a "human exceptionalist" or "exemptionalist" paradigm. They argued for a "New Ecological Paradigm" and for sociology to explicitly examine society-environment dynamics.

Recent scholarship by Dana Fisher (2006) provides an excellent example of this "integrationist" perspective.[3] Fisher is interested in why the United States has been reticent on the issue of climate change policy when compared to other nations. This stance is curious given the consensus among climate scientists that global warming is real, caused primarily by the burning of fossil fuels, and promises serious future consequences. Recent reports by the Intergovernmental Panel on Climate Change (the body that shared the 2007 Nobel Peace Prize with Al Gore) confirm this (see Intergovernmental Panel on Climate Change, 2007).[4] Fisher notes that while environmental sociologists have looked at *social* explanations for the U.S. position, they haven't yet looked at the role of "the material." Aiming to correct this, she relies on the notion of "conjoint constitution"—that is, the idea that social phenomena like policymaking can be understood as the result of the interaction of natural and social factors (Freudenburg, Frickel, & Gramling, 1995). Fisher looks at recent U.S. politics and finds the level of coal extraction in states to be an excellent predictor of both Senate votes on climate policy and state-level climate policies. Specifically, the presence of coal, a resource used to generate electricity and a huge contributor to climate change, predicts opposition to policies that might ameliorate climate change. She asserts that "including aspects of America's natural resource endowment helps to explain more fully climate change policy in the United States" (2006, p. 488).

While the integrationist approach is an important corrective, many environmental sociologists nonetheless feel it's important to not lose sight of the value of conventional sociology (i.e., sociology that remains focused on social and cultural factors rather than examining society-nature interaction directly). The "Treadmill of Production" model developed by Allan Schnaiberg serves as an excellent example of a conventional approach to environmental sociology (Schnaiberg, 1980; Schnaiberg & Gould, 1994).[5] For a nation like the United States, rather than becoming gradually more environmentally friendly, the Treadmill model envisions continued economic growth and ongoing pressure to prevent or weaken environmental regulations. Continued and increased environmental disorganization can thus be expected. The structure of modern capitalist societies is the cause, and so this path is seen as more or less inevitable absent mass political action to undermine capitalism.

Two phenomena are of central importance. One is what Schnaiberg (1980) calls the "growth coalition." Put simply, the major players in the economy, capitalists, government, and the working class, are unified in their commitment to continued economic growth. The working class has an interest in a higher standard of living and job security, both of which are seen as more likely if the economy is expanding. The government's role is to make sure the economy is profitable for capitalists *and* that the general population is content (see also O'Connor, 1973). These are known as the "accumulation" and "legitimation" functions, respectively. The former is accomplished through investments like highways on which goods can be transported, supporting university research of new technologies, and training future workers. Legitimation takes various forms, but examples include social programs like welfare to the poor or workplace safety regulations. The government becomes committed to growth because expansion provides the revenues via taxation that make it possible to "satisfy the demands of both constituencies" (Schnaiberg, 1980, p. 211).

The other key treadmill phenomenon is *competition* between capitalist firms. Competition compels capitalists to increase profits by limiting the cost of production. From this comes opposition to government regulation of business. But competition leads to growth because it compels capitalists to expand their enterprises through increased or innovative production (Schnaiberg, 1980). This allows a firm to undercut the competition's price and sell more product, increasing profits and possibly gaining investors. In the short run, the innovating firm wins out, but soon competition will invest in innovation and everyone is back to square one in terms of profitability. The difference, however, is that the capacity for production has expanded. And this goes on in every industry. Among other things, growth of output means more resources and energy are used and more pollution and trash are generated. Even with "green" technology, gains in efficiency are offset by growth (Schnaiberg & Gould, 1994).

While these production factors are central for understanding the push for continued growth, the problem of consumption arises as well. Companies making more products need more buyers. A number of strategies are available, such as selling in overseas markets, but marketing and the availability of credit (e.g., consumer credit cards) are most notable for the role they have played in creating demand and, in turn, the high and environmentally unsustainable levels of consumption present in the United States (Schnaiberg, 1980). Status concerns and the feeling of "relative deprivation" cultivated by marketing and by living in a stratified society like the United States are worth considering as well (see Schor, 1999).

Nature, the environment, society-environment relations, and environmental problems are both real phenomena *and* cultural objects (i.e., things imbued with meanings that impact perception and action). Environmental sociologists therefore turn attention to culture as well, and much of this work is "conventional" rather than "integrationist." Survey research looking at people's worldviews and attitudes with regard to the environment is one focus (for example, see Dietz, Kalof, & Stern, 2002; Dunlap, Van Liere, Mertig, & Jones, 2000; Jones & Carter, 1994). There is also a literature on the "social construction" of environmental problems—that is, the social process through which environmental issues get recognized and defined as problems.[6] Environmental problems like global warming are frequently not apparent or clearly problematic in people's everyday lives. As a result, recognition requires effort, called *claimsmaking,* on the part of activists and often scientists (for example, see Hannigan, 1995; Mazur & Lee, 1993; Ungar, 1998a). The success of claims depends on politics, media attention, and even on the "character" of the claims themselves, since some claims are made in ways that are more likely to draw people's attention and convince them the problem is serious (Snow & Benford, 1988; Snow, Rochford, Worden, & Benford, 1986).

At the same time, *counterclaims* are made by those who would undermine or prevent recognition of an issue. Usually, successful counterclaims *prevent* public recognition of a problem, but with global warming things have followed a different course. McCright and Dunlap (2003) point out that global warming had been successfully "constructed." Late 1990s poll results indicated that the majority of the American public was concerned and ready to support efforts to fix the problem. But since then, scientific consensus about the reality, human causes, and seriousness of the problem has continued to grow while public support in the United States has waned. Calling this the "delegitimation of global warming as a social problem" (p. 350), McCright and Dunlap show how organizations in the American conservative movement, an "elite-driven network of private foundations, policy-planning think tanks, and individual intellectuals" (p. 352), caused this by seizing on and promoting the views of just five scientists skeptical about climate change. With their financial clout and political influence, these organizations were able to get the climate skeptics' views heard by Congress and the media. Despite holding an exceedingly rare position, their views were presented alongside the view of the majority of climate scientists. These efforts effectively planted doubt in public opinion. Despite the overwhelming consensus among climate scientists, recent polls show that a remarkable number of Americans believe climate scientists disagree about climate change (Nisbet & Myers, 2007). According to McCright and Dunlap (2003), this public confusion "translates into political inaction and policy gridlock—disproportionately favoring powerful interests attempting to construct the nonproblematicity of environmental conditions" (p. 366).[7]

The Culture of Nature in Science Fiction Films

Environmental sociologists also look at the *social construction of nature.* Rather than looking at the social construction (or delegitimation) of environmental problems, the focus here is on meanings of nature itself and on the meaning of society's relationship with nature. Scholars have used survey research to explore these meanings, but they have also studied how nature is represented in cultural artifacts like prime time television shows, documentaries, advertisements, magazines, and children's textbooks (Lerner & Kalof, 1999; Papson, 1992; Shanahan & McComas, 1999; Ungar, 1998b). In my research, I have examined the meaning of nature and of society's relationship to nature in general audience magazines (Podeschi, 2007) and science fiction films (Podeschi, 2002). In both cases I used a historical approach to see if the modern environmental movement has impacted the presentation of nature in popular culture.

I use science fiction films as *future myths;* the opposite of origin myths, future myths are stories about where a society is headed or might be headed. Even though they can be outlandish, these visions are undoubtedly significant to society as hopeful projections, extrapolations, or warnings. In these future scenarios, whether intended or not, the producers provide a vision of the future value of nature and of society's relationship with nature.

So the question becomes: What is the *nature* of future myths? Theoretically, I see culture as serving the powerful through the distribution of ideas and information. However, power is tempered, imperfect, and incomplete. Plenty of ideas are circulating that counter the interests of powerful groups. Further, hegemony requires sustained effort and there are no guarantees that it will last. In short, culture should be seen as a place where power matters, but also as a site of struggle. Thus, we might expect science fiction films, in some ways and to some extent, to *transcode* (Ryan & Kellner, 1988) the thinking found in the environmental movement that challenges the existing and exploitative relationship between society and nature.

Using the most popular science fiction films from 1950 through 1999, I devised a scheme for interpreting the nature- and environmentally-relevant material in the films (the films are listed at the end of this reading). This scheme was grounded in efforts by sociologists to understand the key orienting discourses in environmentalism and the society at large (see Brulle, 1996; Olsen, Lodwick, & Dunlap, 1992). I called the environmentalist discourse *resistant* because it demanded changes in the existing society-nature relationship. As an ecological vision, environmentalist discourse calls for things like sustainable economics and technology and for seeing value in nature. Historically, the primary cultural stance toward nature in the United States has been called Manifest Destiny, the *dominant social paradigm* or the *technological social paradigm* (see Brulle, 1996; Brulle, 2000; Olsen et al., 1992), a discourse I call *reproductive* because the way society operates is left unchallenged. Sentiments here include an *anthropocentric* (human-centered) focus on nature as a resource to be used for human needs and wants *and* a trust in the potential of technology to provide great benefits and solve future problems with minimal attention to potential environmental consequences. In the resulting analysis, I explored two dimensions in science fiction film: the relationship of society with nature and the value of nature.

The Relationship of Society With Nature

Almost all of the futuristic films show society "colonizing the cosmos." The scale of the colonization varies. Futures like that in *Total Recall* (1990) only take us as far as the planets of our own solar system—humans have colonized Mars. In other films, like *Alien* (1979), *Aliens* (1986), *Forbidden Planet* (1956), *Planet of the Apes* (1968), and both the *Star Trek* (1979–2009) and *Star Wars* (1977–2005) series, the scale of colonization is grand. In *Alien* and *Aliens,* people have gone so far that there are "frontier" and "core" systems, and in the *Star Trek* films there are galactic political boundaries. Rather than small outposts on distant planets, the films show societal-level colonization and resource extraction. In *Star Wars,* the desert-planet Tatooine is significantly colonized in a manner reminiscent of earthly colonization of lands and peoples. Here humans appear to be intruding colonists, shown as "modern" and "western" relative to the desert people who tellingly fight them in guerilla-fashion. Extensive control is also depicted by the "taming" of a planet and a harvesting of its resources. The Genesis technology from *Star Trek II: The Wrath of Khan* (1982) and the terraformers in *Aliens* are both technologies that tame wild environments on the "frontier" of space and make them useful to humans. Similarly, the resources of other planets are mined in *Total Recall, Alien,* and *The Empire Strikes Back* (1980). Regardless of the details, this imagery is significant for resonating well with reproductive discourse. One can argue that these films envision a new manifest destiny, with space as the new wilderness frontier (rather than the North American West). Depictions of a planet-hopping future support reproductive discourse by implying that societies need not worry about resource scarcity or sustainability in the here and now.

Technology is important when considering society's relationship with nature as well. Technology involves both transforming and controlling nature to suit social interests and is a means through which societies interact with and impact nature.[8] And technology is of course a major presence in science fiction films. Historically, American culture has trusted and valued technology, viewing it as a source of progress and a benefit to humanity (see Olsen et al., 1992). This is the reproductive discourse. Some environmentally concerned thinkers continue in this tradition, confident future industrial society can develop new, environmentally sound technologies (see Hawken, Lovins, & Lovins, 2000; McDonough & Braungart, 2002). The more conventional resistant discourse, however, in both mainstream and radical environmentalism, questions the value of technology, technological developments, and heavily technological societies given the risks and hazards created by industrial capitalism, chemical-intensive agriculture, nuclear power, and the like (see Brulle, 2000). In this discourse, global warming is seen as resulting from societies' reliance on machines.

For the most part, visions of the future in science fiction films resonate with reproductive discourse by serving as uncritical celebrations of the potential of technology. Overall, future myths envision a technology-saturated future, but most telling is the fact that more than three-fourths of the films I analyzed present a future of extraordinarily powerful technologies. The list is considerable, but a few examples stand out, especially those that have significant power over nature. In many films, space travel is a regular event, but in the *Star Trek* films, spaceships use "warp" drives in which space itself is folded and then restored with "space matrix restoration coils." The film *Forbidden Planet* takes viewers to Altair IV where the technology of a long-extinct alien society is intact and materializes thoughts. Visitors to the planet who learn to use the technology have to be careful, however, because their subconscious desires can create monsters beyond their control. While this amazing device is clearly dangerous, and not a direct projection of future human technology, viewers are told in the end that it is the kind of thing "we" will eventually achieve. Also startlingly powerful, in *Star Trek II,* the Genesis device (mentioned above) can turn a lifeless environment into a lush paradise in a matter of moments. The devise is like a missile, and when it is detonated, "matter is reorganized" at the subatomic level "with life generating results." Rounding out the list is an example that seems tame relative to what we find in some films: in *Back to the Future Part II* (1980), the National Weather Service controls the Earth's weather with clock-like precision. Doc Brown (Christopher Lloyd), one of the main characters, at one point complains how the "post office isn't as efficient as the weather service."

Science fiction films promote reproductive discourse; risk and/or environmental consequences stemming from technologies are largely ignored. As a whole, the technologies depicted in the films rarely malfunction and risks are the exception rather than the rule. Telling in this regard is the fact that films from the 1970s and later depict nuclear technology as "naturalized" into the future social landscape. *Forbidden Planet, Star Wars, The Black Hole* (1980), *Back to the Future Part II, Star Trek II, Aliens, Star Trek IV: The Voyage Home* (1986), *Total Recall,* and *Demolition Man* (1993) all present nuclear power as an unproblematic aspect of the imagined future society. In *Back to the Future Part II*, there are even personal reactors that look like food processors. Such validation of this inherently risky technology is clearly controversial from a resistant environmentalist perspective. Further, in futuristic films when technological risk is acknowledged, the source of the trouble is never the technology itself. In *Aliens,* for example, a military force is sent to rescue an off-world colony from hostile alien creatures, but the aliens have built their den over "a big fusion reactor." The technology itself is not a threat, it's a naturalized part of the social landscape, but they do have to be careful not to shoot the reactor when fighting the aliens. Additionally, when risks are depicted, this depiction has to be read in context, and the broader context is frequently one of amazing technology that prevents the film from taking a truly critical or resistant stance. The *Star Trek* series, for example, includes devices that "beam" people from place to place by turning their matter into a signal and then reassembling them at their destination. In *Star Trek: The Motion Picture* (1979), the first film in the series, two people die from a malfunction of the beaming device, but this can't be read as the film taking a resistant stance toward technology in general because the broader context is one of technological splendor.

A remarkable number of films even use a "bait and switch" approach with regard to fears about technology: risk or serious concerns about a technology are acknowledged, but then ultimately contradicted by the plot. One has to wonder about the potential for this technique to cultivate faith in technology. In *Alien,* Ash (Ian Holm), the "artificial person," endangers his human crewmates by following programmed orders that have him work to ensure an extraordinarily violent alien makes it back to earth. This starts as sharp critique of technology: Ash is an important member of the crew, but in contrast to humans, he is valueless and unreflective and so not to be trusted. In *Aliens,* however, we meet and come to love Bishop (Lance Henriksen), the perfected artificial person reprogrammed to protect human life above all else. Three Cold War era films about nuclear technology use bait and switch as well: *Destination Moon* (1950), *The Beast From 20,000 Fathoms* (1953), and *Voyage to the Bottom of the Sea* (1961). *Destination Moon* focuses on a group of men who want to launch a nuclear-powered rocket to the moon despite fearful opposition from the public and the government. They launch anyway, and though they have some trouble getting home, the trip is a success. Concerns about technology are proven unfounded and viewers are given the message that they should trust technological innovations because their unfounded fears will delay the course of progress.

Star Trek II includes a particularly strong example of the bait and switch approach. The Genesis device, with the power to create life and transform environments, is initially strongly criticized. After learning about the technology, Bones (DeForest Kelley), the protagonist doctor, is outraged because of its power and potential for accident or aggressive misuse. Another key protagonist, Mr. Spock (Leonard Nimoy), concurs and points out that if detonated where life already exists, it would destroy that life by replacing its subatomic matrix. Bones is further angered: "We're talking about universal armageddon!" The rest of the film, however, operates to undermine this critique of nature-transforming technology. Genesis is touted for its potential to alleviate "cosmic food and population problems."

The technology is used twice with clear demonstration of its creative potential. The first experiment with the device takes place in a huge underground cavern. The result is a cavern filled with breathtaking natural beauty and fertile, bountiful nature. In the second use, the antagonist Khan (Ricardo Montalbn) attempts to destroy the protagonists and their space-ship, the *Enterprise*, by detonating a stolen Genesis device. The Enterprise escapes the attack and the detonation creates a beautiful and lush planet. Khan's evil is transformed into goodness and beauty. These positive depictions are backed up by the characters themselves. Mr. Spock dies at a critical moment, and in his eulogy Captain Kirk (William Shatner) diffuses sorrow for Spock's death by noting that it took place in the "shadow of new life" (the new planet). Near the end of the film, we are also provided shots of key characters gazing upon the beauty of the new creation. One can certainly read this as a film-length argument for trusting technology to fix environmental problems like resource scarcity. As with colonization of space, resistant discourse about creating sustainable societies is undermined.

On the whole, the films studied resonate with reproductive discourse for valorizing technology or raising and then countering fears about technological risks. There is, however, content more squarely critical of technology. Nuclear technology receives strong negative attention in the 1950s and 1960s. *On the Beach* (1960) and the *Planet of the Apes* films (1968–1972) are essentially psychological horror films about the effects or aftermath of nuclear war. *Them!* (1954) and *The Incredible Shrinking Man* (1957) articulate fears of fallout from nuclear weapons testing.

Another technology that is presented as negative or potentially harmful is technology that involves some sort of union with or simulation of humanity. Specifically, cyborgs, bionics, implants, and robots or artificial intelligence receive sustained critique as fundamentally flawed in futuristic films from 1969 forward. Implanted surveillance devices or other technological connections to the body are repulsed in *Total Recall, Demolition Man*, and *The Matrix* (1999). Cyborg slaves from *The Black Hole* and Darth Vader from the *Star Wars* series provide a critical vision of the union of technology and human bodies. The films *2001: A Space Odyssey* (1968) and *The Matrix* focus on artificial intelligence or simulated humanity gone awry. In these cases, computers become too much like human beings (i.e., the simulations are too good, and they gain consciousness and agency and threaten or enslave humanity).

The *Star Wars* films actually reverse the bait and switch approach described above and can be read as critical of technology as well, but in a more general manner. These films are set in a highly technological future where the protagonists (the rebels) and antagonists (the empire) rely on powerful and amazing technologies. On the surface, the films validate technology, but parallel to this is a latent opposition between good and evil serving as a critique of technology. First, the forces for good, the rebels, are grounded in nature. The rebel princess (Carrie Fisher) is from a lush blue planet resembling Earth and Yoda (voice of Frank Oz), the master of the good Jedi Knights, lives on a swamp planet teeming with life. By sharp contrast, the evil empire is grounded almost entirely in built technological environments like mind-bogglingly huge spaceships. Most telling, however, is the Death Star. This planet-sized sphere is the empire's "home" and so functions like an artificial planet. It is also a weapon powerful enough to destroy real planets, and it does destroy the Earthlike planet in the first film. So the films give us real nature destroyed by evil, simulated nature. In addition to this contrast, the lead antagonist, Darth Vader (voice of James Earl Jones), is a cyborg nightmare. Viewers are meant to infer that his body is damaged from a life of violence, and the damaged parts have been replaced with bionics. He is even forced to wear a mask and cannot breathe on his own. At one point, a key protagonist says of

Vader, "He's more machine now than man; twisted and evil," implying that the union with technology explains his brutality. In the end, even though both good and evil rely on technology in these films, this latent linkage of good with nature and evil with technology can be read as a warning for future societies.

On the Value of Nature

Turning to the status of nature relative to society in these projected futures, the question is whether the films project a cultural opposition between nature and society, with society more highly valued. On the one hand, futures containing continued domination of nature through colonization and technology can be seen as assigning nature a secondary status relative to society. But here we look at the direct "charge" given to animals and environments in these projected futures.

From a distance, environments are frequently positively charged as beautiful landscapes. But when environments and inanimate nature are more than background and salient in the narrative, they are usually hostile, harsh, or simply devalued. On its own, this clearly stands in contrast to "resistant" environmentalist discourses for devaluing nature and for failing to depict it in an ecological fashion, but it also reinforces that sense that future societies will colonize and control a new "wilderness."

In terms of devaluation of nature relative to society/humanity, *Star Trek II* defines an entire planet in terms of its potential usefulness to humanity. When the protagonists arrive at Regula I, Mr. Spock describes it as "a great rock in space" with "unremarkable ores." In other words, it is seen as good for nothing. *Forbidden Planet* uses a different approach. The inventor of a remarkably powerful robot demonstrates the safety of his creation by commanding it to destroy both a tree and the key protagonist. It vaporizes the tree, but refuses to harm the "rational being." Nonrational life beware!

The *Star Wars* series depicts natural settings as harsh and unpleasant. In the first film, we are introduced to a desert planet, Tatooine; in the second, an ice planet, Hoth; and finally a swamp planet, Degobah, in the third. All three are depicted as terribly unpleasant places for extreme heat and sterility, extreme cold, and muck, respectively. The swamp planet is perhaps most hostile for it is not only dark and covered with murky water, but filled with organisms that spark fear and disgust, like lizards and giant snakes. The protagonists from the future who find themselves in these places make their displeasure clear. For example, Luke Skywalker, the main protagonist, calls Degobah a "slimy mud hole." Tempering Degobah's negative depiction some is the fact that Yoda, one of the arch-protagonists and symbols of goodness in the films, lives on Degobah and appreciates the place, perhaps because its fecundity fuels his magic power (he's a Jedi Master of the Force). Otherwise, the only nonbuilt and friendly environment in the *Star Wars* trilogy is the forest moon Endor in *Return of the Jedi* (1983).

The films' depiction of animals parallels that of environments. Counter to resistant discourse, animals are not presented as inherently valuable in ecological terms, but tend to be hostile, disgusting, valued if domesticated, or merely lesser than the "civilized." The films project Arnold Arluke and Clinton Sanders's (1996) "sociozoologic scale" into the future. Good animals are docile pets and tools while bad animals refuse to stay in their proper place, entering society as freaks, vermin that contaminate or disgust, or as demons seeking to kill people.

In the *Star Wars* films the protagonists have to content with not only harsh environments, but a series of "demons" waiting there to consume them. In *Star Wars* and *The Empire Strikes Back*, tentacled creatures lurk in murky water. In *Return of the Jedi* and *The Empire Strikes Back* the protagonists barely escape from enormous worms, one of which could have swallowed their spaceship. The films *Alien* and *Aliens* focus on one type of creature, a part demon, part vermin "sea monster in space" that the planet-hopping humans have encountered (begging the question, who is the alien?). These "wild" animals are demons because they are unbelievably strong and fast, and can easily kill and devour humans. Amazing survivors, the creatures also can sustain themselves and blend physically into any type of environment. In *Alien*, the body of the creatures becomes metallic and imitates the "technology texture" of the ship, a curious and perhaps critical statement about evolution of life in future technological environments. The aliens are vermin because of their similarity with Earth pests. They can reproduce parasitically (in a human host in *Alien*) or by eggs (*Aliens* features a large and disgusting den). They are also reminiscent of snakes, spiders, and insects. The fact that they *infest* places is a particularly clear similarity to vermin. In *Alien*, one creature occupies and travels primarily via the internal structure of the spaceship in which the film takes place. In *Aliens* a whole host occupies the internal structure of a large building complex. In both cases, the films draw a clear parallel to rodent and insect infestation with which audiences are familiar. The infestations inspire dread because the protagonists never know where the aliens may be.

Two other trends counter resistant discourse. First of all, the films analyzed occasionally present us with valued domesticated animals in contrast to the wild and dangerous ones. For example, docile, gentle, and horselike "ton-tons" are opposed to an abominable snowman that captures the hero in *The Empire Strikes Back*. In *Alien*, Jonesy, the beloved spaceship cat, is set in stark opposition to the alien. As domesticated animals are *in the fold* of civilization, such contrasts reinforce a division between society and nature (see Arluke & Sanders, 1996). Secondly, apart from being portrayed as hostile, animals in these films are denigrated as simply of lesser value than humanity. Domesticated animals are no exception; they are valued in contrast to wild creatures, but they are still humans' pets or tools. For one of the best examples of this, we can turn again to the ton-tons from *The Empire Strikes Back*. In the beginning of this film, Han Solo (Harrison Ford) goes out into the hostile environment of the ice planet Hoth riding a ton-ton in search of the hero, Luke Skywalker (Mark Hamill). He does this knowing that his ton-ton is unlikely to survive plummeting temperatures as night falls. The ton-ton does indeed die, but Han saves Luke, notably by using the recently deceased animal's insides for warmth. Not only is the ton-ton domesticated in the service of humans, the ton-ton can be sacrificed in favor of human life.

To close, it must be noted that the devaluation of nature relative to society does not go wholly unchecked. In *Star Trek IV: The Voyage Home*, Mr. Spock tells Captain Kirk that "only human arrogance" would assume humans are the only intelligent form of life on Earth. In *Aliens*, appreciation for alien biology is expressed in scientific terms by one of the key protagonists. The films *Planet of the Apes* and *Beneath the Planet of the Apes* (1970) take a different approach, devaluing humanity by providing sharp critiques of human society as destructive. Such content cannot be ignored, but these are counterexamples against the primary thrust of the films. More common are dangerous or valueless environments and creatures.

In reality, of course, nature can be uncomfortable, scary, and dangerous. However, as the primary emphasis in the films, rather than a balanced or ecological view, this fits and reinforces reproductive discourse on the value of nature. Historically in the United States, nature has been seen as wild and dangerous or as something without value that needs to be controlled for human benefit (see Brulle, 2000; Nash, 1982). By contrast, resistant discourses in the history of both the radical and more mainstream arms of the environmental movement see nature, wilderness, and wildlife as inherently valuable and/or worth preserving, both for themselves and for humanity (see Brulle, 1996, 2000).

Conclusion

This reading introduced and examined basic concepts from environmental sociology. We then saw how environmental sociologists look at the potential for natural resources to impact social and political processes, how socioeconomic structures generate environmentally problematic economic growth, and how social actors politicize scientific perspectives on environmental problems and influence public opinion. Last, we saw how science fiction films can be used to study the culture of nature or the way that nature itself is socially constructed. This work is useful not just for what it reveals about the meaning of nature, but for what it reveals about imagery with regard to nature in the future.

I hesitate to paint my findings with too broad a brush. What's presented here already glosses over a fair amount of specificity worth examining and debating, but what stands out is the way that the films for the most part fail to resonate with resistant or environmentalist discourse. Instead, with some exceptions, they fit reproductive discourse by presenting future technological society in optimistic terms and reinforcing a sharp nature-society dualism by depicting nature as an obstacle or a thing of lesser value than humanity/society. This is the case despite the rise of the modern environmental movement in the early 1960s *and* despite survey results indicating that the culture has moved away from the technological or dominant social paradigm (see Olsen et al., 1992).

Films reflect the time periods in which they are made. For example, from the late 1960s forward, technologies that unite with or simulate humanity are strongly resisted (e.g., Darth Vader; Hal from *2001*), perhaps articulating some anxiety about the integration of computers into society. This generally fits resistant discourse concerns about technology, but is notably distant from *environmental* concerns. In contrast, nuclear technology's potential for environmental harm is debated in science fiction films made during the 1950s and 1960s when fears about nuclear weapons testing and the Cold War were significant. But after this, as the films focused on cyborg technologies, they also "naturalized" nuclear power in the depicted futures. This is particularly interesting given the visibility of the antinuclear and environmental movements and historical events such as Three Mile Island in 1979 and Chernobyl in 1986 (see Rothman, 2000).

Ultimately, the future presented in science fiction film is not one of technological caution, of sustainable living on earth, or of harmony with wild places and creatures, but is instead one of ubiquitous and powerful technology, of colonization of space and other planets, and of conflict and difficulty with hostile environments and creatures. Does this indicate a lack of responsiveness to the environmental movement in popular culture?

Maybe it is simply the case that commercial film producers are not interested in gritty science fiction films that question the future or the potential of technology, fearing fewer people will pay for tickets to pessimistic films.

References

Andrews, R. (1999). *Managing the environment, managing ourselves: A history of American environmental policy.* New Haven, CT: Yale University Press.

Arluke, A., & Sanders, C. R. (1996). *Regarding animals.* Philadelphia: Temple University Press.

Brulle, R. J. (1996). Environmental discourse and social movement organizations: A historical and rhetorical perspective on the development of U.S. environmental organizations. *Sociological Inquiry, 66,* 58–83.

Brulle, R. J. (2000). *Agency, democracy, and nature: The U.S. environmental movement from a critical theory perspective.* Cambridge: MIT Press.

Carolan, M. (2005). Realism without reductionism: Toward an ecologically embedded sociology. *Human Ecology Review, 12*(1), 1–20.

Catton, W. R., & Dunlap, R. E. (1978). Environmental sociology: A new paradigm. *The American Sociologist, 13*(February), 41–49.

Dietz, T., Kalof, L., & Stern, P. C. (2002). Gender, values and environmentalism. *Social Science Quarterly, 83*(1), 353–364.

Dunlap, R. E. (2002). Paradigms, theories and environmental sociology. In R. E. Dunlap, F. H. Buttel, P. Dickens, & A. Gijswijt (Eds.), *Sociological theory and the environment: Classical foundations, contemporary insights* (pp. 329–350). New York: Rowman & Littlefield.

Dunlap, R. E., Van Liere, K. D., Mertig, A., & Jones, R. E. (2000). Measuring endorsement of the new ecological paradigm: A revised NEP scale. *Journal of Social Issues, 56*(3), 425–442.

Fisher, D. (2006). Bringing the material back in: Understanding the U.S. position on climate change. *Sociological Forum, 21*(3), 467–494.

Foster, J. B. (1999). *The vulnerable planet: A short economic history of the environment.* New York: Monthly Review Press.

Freudenburg, W. R., Frickel, S., & Gramling, R. (1995). Beyond the nature/society divide: Learning to think about a mountain. *Sociological Forum, 10*(3), 361–392.

Freudenburg, W. R., & Gramling, R. (1993). Socioenvironmental factors and development policy: Understanding opposition and support for offshore oil. *Sociological Forum, 8*(3), 341–364.

Freudenburg, W. R., Gramling, R., & Davidson, D. (2008). Scientific certainty argumentation methods (SCAMS): Science and the politics of doubt. *Sociological Inquiry, 78*(1), 2–38.

Fuller, T., & Revkin, A. C. (2007, December 16). Climate plan looks beyond Bush's tenure. *The New York Times,* p. 1.

Hannigan, J. (1995). *Environmental sociology: A social constructionist perspective.* New York: Routledge.

Hawken, P., Lovins, A., & Lovins, H. (2000). *Natural capitalism: Creating the next industrial revolution.* New York: Little, Brown.

Intergovernmental Panel on Climate Change. (2007). *Climate change 2007: Synthesis report: Summary for policymakers.* New York: The United Nations. Retrieved December 20, 2007, from http://www.ipcc.ch/pdf/assessment-report/ar4/syr/ar4_syr_ spm.pdf

Jones, R. E., & Carter, L. F. (1994). Concern for the environment among black Americans: An assessment of common assumptions. *Social Science Quarterly, 75*(3), 560–579.

Lerner, J., & Kalof, L. (1999). The animal text: Message and meaning in television advertisements. *Sociological Quarterly, 40*(4), 565–586.

Libes, S. (2003). *Why we should all be "Waccamaw waterwatchers."* Distinguished Teacher-Scholar Lecture Series. Conway, SC: Coastal Carolina University.

Logan, J. R., & Molotch, H. (1987). *Urban fortunes: The political economy of place.* Berkeley: University of California Press.

Mazur, A., & Lee, J. (1993). Sounding the global alarm: Environmental issues in the US national news. *Social Studies of Science, 23*(4), 681–720.

McCright, A. M., & Dunlap, R. E. (2003). Defeating Kyoto: The conservative movement's impact on U.S. climate change policy. *Social Problems, 50*(3), 348–373.

McDonough, W., & Braungart, M. (2002). *Cradle to cradle: Remaking the way we make things.* New York: North Point Press.

Murphy, R. (2002). The internalization of autonomous nature into society. *The Sociological Review, 50*(3), 313–333.

Murphy, R. (2004, August). *Technological disasters, natural disasters, environmental disasters: Toward the integration of social constructionism and critical realism.* Paper presented at the Annual Meeting of the American Sociological Association, San Francisco, CA.

Nash, R. (1982). *Wilderness and the American mind.* New Haven, CT: Yale University Press.

Nisbet, M. C., & Myers, T. (2007). Twenty years of public opinion about global warming. *Public Opinion Quarterly, 71*(3), 444–470.

O'Connor, J. (1973). *The fiscal crisis of the state.* New York: St. Martin's Press.

Olsen, M., Lodwick, D., & Dunlap, R. (1992). *Viewing the world ecologically.* Boulder, CO: Westview.

Papson, S. (1992). "Cross the fin line of terror": Shark week on the Discovery Channel. *Journal of American Culture, 15,* 67–81.

Podeschi, C. (2002). The nature of future myths: Environmental discourse in science fiction films, 1950–1999. *Sociological Spectrum, 22*(3), 251–297.

Podeschi, C. (2007). The culture of nature and the rise of modern environmentalism: The view through general audience magazines, 1945–1980. *Sociological Spectrum, 27*(3), 299–331.

Rothman, H. (2000). *Saving the planet: The American response to the environment in the twentieth century.* Chicago: Ivan R. Dee.

Rudel, T. K. (2005). *Tropical forests: Regional paths of destruction and regeneration in the late 20th century.* New York: Columbia University Press.

Ryan, M., & Kellner, D. (1988). *Camera politica: The politics and ideology of contemporary Hollywood film.* Bloomington: Indiana University Press.

Schnaiberg, A. (1980). *The environment: From surplus to scarcity.* New York: Oxford.

Schnaiberg, A., & Gould, K. A. (1994). *Environment and society: The enduring conflict.* New York: St. Martin's Press.

Schor, J. B. (1999). *The overspent American: Why we want what we don't need.* New York: Harper Paperbacks.

Shanahan, J., & McComas, K. (1999). *Nature stories: Depictions of the environment and their effects.* Cresskill, NJ: Hampton Press.

Snow, D. A., & Benford, R. D. (1988). Ideology, frame resonance, and participant mobilization. *International Social Movement Research, 1,* 197–217.

Snow, D. A., Rochford, Jr., E. B., Worden, S. K., & Benford, R. D. (1986). Frame alignment processes, micromobilization, and movement participation. *American Sociological Review, 51,* 464–481.

Spector, M., & Kitsuse, J. I. (1987). *Constructing social problems.* Hawthorne, NY: Aldine de Gruyter.

Szasz, A. (2007). *Shopping our way to safety: How we changed from protecting the environment to protecting ourselves.* Minneapolis: University of Minnesota Press.

Ungar, S. (1998a). Bringing the issue back in: Comparing the marketability of the ozone hole and global warming. *Social Problems, 45*(4), 510–527.

Ungar, S. (1998b). Recycling and the dampening of concern: Comparing the roles of large and small actors in shaping the environmental discourse. *Canadian Review of Sociology and Anthropology, 35*(2), 253–276.

Warner, K., & Molotch, H. (2000). *Building rules: How local controls shape community environments and economies.* Boulder, CO: Westview.

York, R., Rosa, E., & Dietz, T. (2003). Footprints on the earth: The environmental consequences of modernity. *American Sociological Review, 68*(2), 279–300.

Appendix: Sample of Science Fiction Films

I selected two top box-office grossing films in each half-decade; then the next highest grossing film from any point in the decade was added. If more than one film from the same series was selected, these were only counted once toward the total of five for that decade.

1950s: *Destination Moon* (1950), *The Beast From 20,000 Fathoms* (1953), *Them!* (1954), *Forbidden Planet* (1956), *The Incredible Shrinking Man* (1957)

1960s: *On the Beach* (1960), *Voyage to the Bottom of the Sea* (1961), *Fantastic Voyage* (1966), *Planet of the Apes* (1968), *2001: A Space Odyssey* (1968)

1970s: *Beneath the Planet of the Apes* (1970), *A Clockwork Orange* (1972), *Star Wars* (1977), *Alien* (1979), *Star Trek: The Motion Picture* (1979)

1980s: *The Black Hole (1980), Star Wars: The Empire Strikes Back* (1980), *Star Trek II: The Wrath of Khan* (1982), *Star Wars: Return of the Jedi* (1983), *Aliens* (1986), *Star Trek IV: The Voyage Home* (1986), *Back to the Future Part II* (1989)

1990s: *Total Recall* (1990), *Demolition Man* (1993), *Jurassic Park* (1993), *Waterworld* (1995), *The Matrix* (1999)

Notes

1. It must be emphasized here that there is essentially no controversy among climate scientists the world over about whether global warming is occurring naturally or is caused by human activities: they believe it is caused by human activities. For background information, see *An Inconvenient Truth* (2006), directed by Davis Guggenheim, and "Climate Change 2007: Synthesis Report: Summary for Policymakers" by the Intergovernmental Panel on Climate Change (2007).

2. When it rains, some water soaks into the ground and some runs off into streams and rivers. The water runs off especially well from "impervious surfaces" like roads, parking lots, and buildings, and along the way it picks up pollutants, like oil from roads and bacteria from pet waste in yards (see Libes, 2003).

3. For other examples of integrationist environmental sociology, see Freudenburg, Frickel, and Gramling (1995), Freudenburg and Gramling (1993), and Murphy (2002, 2004).

4. Recent UN climate talks in Bali, Indonesia, confirm U.S. reticence, with American negotiators remaining "obstructionist until the final hour of the two-week convention and changing their

stance only after public rebukes that included boos and hisses from other delegates" (Fuller & Revkin, 2007). The talks ended with hope that more progress could be made during subsequent negotiations once a new U.S. president took office in 2009.

5. For other examples of environmental sociology that is both primarily conventional and structural, see Foster (1999), Rudel (2005), Warner and Molotch (2000), and York, Rosa, and Dietz (2003). Note that often this sort of work includes measured dependent variables that are non-social (e.g., deforestation rate), but these are placed in this category for looking primarily at conventional social factors and processes as driving forces rather than examining "feedback" from the environment.

6. This is a problem for all contentious issues, not just environmental problems. See Spector and Kitsuse (1987).

7. Research by Freudenburg, Gramling, and Davidson (2008) complements the work of McCright and Dunlap (2003) by highlighting how antienvironmental campaigns use "SCAMS" or "Scientific Certainty Argumentation Methods," preying on the reliance on statistical probabilism in scientific research.

8. Murphy (2004) in fact calls technology "recombinant nature."

THE ONLY POSSIBLE SOLUTION?

The Challenge of Nonviolence to the Hegemony of Violence in Film

Kathryn Feltey

Violence in film has received extensive attention from academics, journalists, political pundits, and the general population for some time now. As a viewing audience, we have grown accustomed to increasingly violent images in the media, with widespread acceptance of violence as the "normal" response and remedy to a wide range of threats, conditions, and problems. Not only do audiences accept the violence that is presented, but there has been an increase in popular demand for more graphic depictions of violence (Slocum, 2000). With the advantages of technology and big budgets, filmmakers have complied, giving audiences more "explicit, even exaggerated, portrayals of aggression and its grisly, splattering aftermath in shootings, slashings, explosions, and crashes" (Iadicola & Shupe, 2003, p. 55). The sensibility seems to be, as an Interpol agent exclaims in the film *Nighthawks* (1981), "To combat violence, you need greater violence. To defeat a violent people you need to be trained to react in a given situation, with ruthless, cold-blooded violence as well."

An interesting debate in the literature on violence in film focuses on the role of American cinema as either challenging or supporting dominant values and norms, while many argue that Hollywood serves as an agent of both social control and change (Slocum, 2000). Violence in this debate is interrogated in terms of how it is presented, who is using it, and to what end. Whether we see violence as legitimate and justified depends on the answers to these questions. One way that violence in film increases solidarity, and therefore contributes to the social order, is by identifying a common enemy for the viewing audience. The face of the enemy has changed throughout the history of cinema, influenced by the historical and cultural context. For example, films from the World War II era featured German and Japanese enemies, while Vietnam and post-Vietnam films such as the *Rambo* films focused on defeat of the Viet Cong and the communist threat. Violence in film has also served to highlight competing forces for social change, in films such as *Matewan* (1987), in which West Virginia coal miners, struggling to form a union, battle against the company and armed state agents.

A central concern about violence in film is whether the violence is contextualized for the viewing audience or presented gratuitously. Films that use violence in a ritualistic display of stereotypical masculinity (e.g., *Die Hard: With a Vengeance*, 1995) or for its shock value, as in hyperreal violent films (e.g., *Sin City*, 2005), ignore the causes and effects of violence on people and the communities in which they live. Symbolic violence, on the other hand, couples emotions and images of violence, requiring the viewing audience to grapple with the meaning of violence in the social contexts where it occurs. Films using symbolic violence include historical explorations, what Ed Guerrero (Chapter 4) calls "historical agonies," such as *Schindler's List* (1993), *Rosewood* (1997), and *Hotel Rwanda* (2004).

Despite the interrogation of film violence and concerns about decontextualized gratitutous violence, the use of violence or the portrayal of human struggles and conflict as requiring violent methods is, for the most part, left unchallenged. Even when the story is one in which social change is the goal, violence is not seen as (part of) the problem, only the misuse of violence by unhinged individuals or unjust rulers or regimes. In the right hands, violence in film becomes a celebration of righteous victory, the triumph of good over evil, and justice served. This is also true at the level of interpersonal conflict. For example, in films about domestic violence, the victimized wife is most victorious when she can use violence more effectively than her abusive husband, as in *Sleeping With the Enemy* (1991) and *Enough* (2002).

Widespread acceptance of violence as the only way to protect an individual or a nation from external threat is legitimized across social institutions, including the media (Iadicola & Shupe, 2003). The ubiquitous presence of violence in film promotes a worldview of violence as not only necessary, but as the only effective method for resolving conflict, settling differences, protecting interests and resources, and gaining and maintaining power. As Lieutenant Jean Rasczak explains in the film *Starship Troopers* (1997), "Naked force has settled more issues in history than any other factor. The contrary opinion 'violence never solves anything' is wishful thinking at its worst. People who forget that always pay. . . . They pay with their lives and their freedom."

What can the "wishful thinking" of nonviolence, as presented in film, teach us about alternative methods for challenging injustice and creating social change? Interestingly, the few films that fit this definition are documentaries and feature films based on historical events (true stories) involving the use of nonviolence. While countless fictional and fantasy films include aggression, violence, force, and warfare, very few use nonviolence as a central theme, either as a way of creating social change or as a way of life.

The paucity of alternatives to violence in film can be understood by thinking about film text as part of cultural hegemonic processes (Cooper, 1999). Hollywood's contribution to these processes can be seen in the ways that movies have promoted dominant American myths and values, such as individualism, power as dominance over, racial superiority, heteronormativity, and material success. Violence to protect and promote the American way of life is an integral part of these processes. Ultimately, hegemonic meanings and values are experienced as practices that define reality, and reinforce that definition so completely, that it becomes difficult for many to resist, much less challenge or change, what is defined as real (Williams, 2001).

In this reading, we will examine films that challenge the hegemony of violence by making nonviolence, as a method of resistance, a source of political power, and/or way of life, central to the story. For each film we will consider the following: (1) how nonviolence is presented—that is, what is the story of nonviolence in the context of the film; (2) whether the nonviolence story challenges or supports dominant values and norms in society; and (3) how alternatives to violence, as portrayed in film, might provide us with models for creating meaningful social change.

The Films

The first film we will consider is a biopic of the life of the one person who is most associated with nonviolence historically, Mohandas Karamchand Gandhi (Mahatma Gandhi). Making *Gandhi* (1982) was a 20-year dream of the film's director and producer, Richard Attenborough. Funding for the film was a problem; the project was rejected by every studio in the film industry. Finally, it was made with private money and only purchased for distribution after it was completed (Briley, 1996). Nonviolence changing the political and economic structure of a country across the ocean was apparently not seen as a potential moneymaker in the United States. Of course, the critical and popular acclaim of the film was tremendous. *Gandhi* was widely distributed and won a total of eight Academy Awards, including Best Picture, Actor, Director, Art Direction, Cinematography, Costume Design, Editing, and Original Screenplay. It was also nominated for Best Makeup, Original Score, and Sound.

The second film, *The Long Walk Home* (1990), is a fictional story set in Montgomery, Alabama, in 1955 during the 381-day bus boycott inspired by Martin Luther King, Jr., and his teachings on nonviolent protest. The film centers on two women, Odessa Cotter (Whoopi Goldberg) and Miriam Thompson (Sissy Spacek). Odessa has been working as a domestic in the Thompson household for nine years. Miriam is living the white, middle-class, mid-century life of a housewife and mother. The relationship between Miriam and Odessa, structured by class, race, and the regional politics of the U.S. South, provides insight into the political impact of the boycott within and between their respective communities.

The last film, *Witness* (1985), differs from the first two in that it is a work of fiction, without reference to particular historical events, although it takes place in the late 20th century in Pennsylvania. The film is a thriller/drama that explores two cultures, the Amish and English (non-Amish). Nonviolence as a value and way of life in the Amish community stands in stark contrast to the violent world of urban America. Sociologically, we gain insight into these cultures through the eyes of the outsider who visits. Rachel Lapp (Kelly McGillis) and her son Samuel (Lukas Haas) are immediately exposed to violent crime when they arrive in Philadelphia and Samuel witnesses a murder, while John Book (Harrison Ford) experiences deep culture shock when, after being shot and seriously wounded, he hides out with the Amish for a time to escape the men who are pursuing him.

In all three films, nonviolence is central to the story. However, it is important to note that it is not the absence of violence that qualifies these films as nonviolent. Rather it is the centrality of nonviolence not just as a method for changing the outcome of a particular situation, but as a complete, holistic way of life that structures the ways that people create and sustain their social worlds.

The Story of Nonviolence in Film

The story of nonviolence, as told through the selected films, is linked to and rooted in spiritual and religious beliefs. In *The Long Walk Home* and *Witness*, Christian beliefs are the foundation for choosing nonviolence and creating a nonviolent way of life. In *The Long Walk Home*, Odessa and her family find solace and comfort in their Christian beliefs and church community. Once the bus boycott has begun, Odessa joins in by refusing to take the bus to work, walking the nine miles to the Thompson home.[1] We see Odessa arrive home exhausted from long days at work and the long walk home, struggle to put her church shoes on swollen and bleeding feet, and attend services where Martin Luther King, Jr., gives stirring sermons of inspiration and hope to the weary boycotters. We never see King, but hear his stirring words of nonviolence, Christian faith, and fighting for justice at the Holt Street church:

> We are here, we are here this evening because we're tired now. And I want to say, that we are not here advocating violence. We have never done that. I want it to be known throughout Montgomery and throughout this nation that we are Christian people. . . . The only weapon that we have in our hands this evening is the weapon of protest. . . . And we are not wrong, we are not wrong in what we are doing. If we are wrong, the Supreme Court of this nation is wrong. If we are wrong, the Constitution of the United States is wrong. If we are wrong, God Almighty is wrong. If we are wrong, Jesus of Nazareth was merely a utopian dreamer that never came down to earth. If we are wrong, justice is a lie: love has no meaning. And we are determined here in Montgomery to work and fight until justice runs down like water and righteousness like a mighty stream.

In *Witness*, the Amish practice nonresistance, based on the belief that Christians should "turn the other cheek" when confronted by an enemy, and only return good to those who do them harm. At one point, Eli Lapp (Jan Rubes) tries to explain to his grandson, Samuel, why guns and violence are wrong, according to Amish beliefs: "This gun of the hand is for the taking of human life. We believe it is wrong to take a life. That is only for God. Many times wars have come and people have said to us: you must fight, you must kill, it is the only way to preserve the good. But Samuel, there's never only one way. Remember that." Confused by what he has seen in Philadelphia, Samuel tells his grandfather he would only kill the "bad men" who can be identified by what they do: "I can see what they do. I have seen it." Here is where we learn from Eli about the separateness of the Amish community from the larger society, as he tells his grandson that "having seen, you become one of them. . . . What you take into your hands, you take into your heart. Wherefore, come out from among them, and be ye separate, saith the Lord, and touch not the unclean thing."

Gandhi's approach to nonviolence is shaped by Hinduism, but he regards all religions as contributing to a message of unity and nonviolence. As he tells the group gathered with him during his fast to bring an end to the rioting between Hindus and Muslims, "Each night before I sleep, I read a few words from the Gita and the Koran and the Bible." He goes on to "share these thoughts of God" with his companions: "I will begin with the Bible where the words of the Lord are, "Love thy neighbor as thyself" . . . and then our beloved Gita, which says, "The world is a garment worn by God, thy neighbor is in truth thyself" . . . and finally the Holy Koran, "We shall remove all hatred from our hearts and recline on couches face to face, a band of brothers."

Based on these beliefs about the oneness of humanity, he developed the concept of *Satyagraha,* which he also called truth-force or soul-force, based in part on the principle of *ahimsa* (doing no harm in thought, word, or deed to any living being). While Gandhi recognized that the existence of a society necessitates *himsa* (the destruction of life) in small and subtle ways, he promoted the goal of minimizing harm at the individual and collective level (Lucien, 1984). This includes the way that people choose to live, their use of available resources, and the dependence of their lifestyle on the exploitation of others. We see in the film, for example, a stark contrast between the simple life that Gandhi lives in community with others and the Indians who are in government who live like the British, with all of the status symbols of material success. In one scene, when Gandhi first returns to India, a reception in his honor is held at the home of a successful Indian lawyer, during which we see:

> A splendid peacock, its tail fanned in brilliant display, lords it on a velvet lawn. A woman in a sumptuous silk sari is trying to feed it crumbs. Behind her, Gandhi's reception is in full spate—silver trays, tables covered in fine linen, Indian servants, a swimming pool, a small fountain, the grounds filled with Indian millionaires and dignitaries gathered with their wives to meet the new hero from South Africa. (Briley, 1982)

We soon discover that Gandhi's vision of India under home rule is the India of "seven hundred thousand 'villages', not a few hundred lawyers in Delhi and Bombay." He explains that the leadership of the home rule movement will never be successful without this understanding: "Until we stand in the fields with the millions who toil each day under the hot sun, we will not represent India—nor will we ever be able to challenge the British as one nation."

Unity is central to Gandhi's nonviolence—and this extends across national boundaries, as well as social divisions within a society by caste, religion, and gender. All of us, according to Gandhi, are human beings, no matter which side we are on, as he explains to photographer Margaret Bourke-White (Candice Bergen) when she visits him in prison, "Every enemy is a human being—even the worst of them. And he believes he is right and you are a beast. And if you beat him over the head you will only convince him. But you suffer, to show him that he is wrong, your sacrifice creates an atmosphere of understanding—if not with him, then in the hearts of the rest of the community on whom he depends."

The idea that passive nonresistance is a powerful response to violent conflict is a consistent message throughout the movie *Gandhi*. Early in his career, when Gandhi was a lawyer in South Africa, he was confronted with institutional and individual racism against Indians. Speaking with his Indian compatriots about the legal discrimination they experience, he urges them to join the nonviolent battle ahead, saying:

> I am asking you to fight! To fight against their anger, not to provoke it. We will not strike a blow, but we will receive them. And through our pain we will make them see their injustice, and it will hurt—as all fighting hurts. But we cannot lose. We cannot. They may torture my body, break my bones, even kill me. Then, they will have my dead body—not my obedience.

He stresses that fighting to expose injustice means being "willing to die a soldier's death" while never striking a blow.

The Challenge of Nonviolence in Film

Nonviolence in *Gandhi* and *The Long Walk Home* is the method and philosophy of the larger social movements occurring in India and the United States. In *Gandhi*, we see the struggle for Indian independence from British rule. Promoting the idea that the British can only rule if India allows herself to be ruled, Gandhi encourages Indians, Muslim and Hindu alike, to resist British rule through noncooperation. He stresses that reclaiming India does not require defining the British as an enemy to be conquered. Instead, Gandhi focuses on the humanity of all parties involved, saying, "I want to change their minds—not kill them for weaknesses we all possess."

Changing minds is not just a matter of debate, but is achieved through action. In the film, we see campaigns organized to communicate, symbolically, politically, and economically, that Indians will not participate in systems that oppress and exploit them. Gandhi's approach was systematic: first he gave careful consideration to the problem at hand, then he would begin communicating with the person(s) involved. Next he made the communication public, and last he informed the person(s) that he would resort to public campaigns to force the issue. According to Gandhi's grandson, he always did this with great politeness and with no intentions of inconveniencing the opposition (Meyer, 2005).

For example, in the film, Gandhi meets with British authorities after the Amritsar massacre of 1919, in which General Reginald Dyer (Edward Fox) ordered his troops to fire on a meeting of unarmed Indian civilians—men, women, and children—at Jallianwala Bagh, an enclosed courtyard, resulting in 400 deaths and 1,500 injured. In the shocked aftermath of this brutal attack, we see a meeting between the British (represented by the viceroy, two generals, a naval officer, two senior civil servants, and a senior police officer) and Indian leadership. The scene opens with the viceroy stating, "You must understand, gentlemen, that His Majesty's government—and the British people—repudiate both the massacre and the philosophy that prompted it."

Gandhi's response links the actions and philosophy that the British "repudiate" to the business-as-usual domination of one country by another: "We think it is time you recognized that you are masters in someone else's home. Despite the best intentions of the best of you, you must, in the nature of things, humiliate us to control us. General Dyer is but an extreme example of the principle. It is time you left." A flummoxed officer rhetorically asks, "You don't think we're just going to walk out of India?"

Gandhi, demonstrating the last course of action, announces that Indians will refuse to cooperate with British rule. He politely responds to the officer, "Yes. In the end, you will walk out, because 100,000 Englishmen simply cannot control 350 million Indians if those Indians refuse to cooperate. And that is what we intend to achieve: peaceful, nonviolent, noncooperation—'til you, yourselves, see the wisdom of leaving, Your Excellency."

Nonviolence as the organizing principle was a challenge to the British colonial authority; it was difficult to justify wholesale violence against a population that refused to use violence defensively, much less offensively. To try to contain the dissent and undermine the solidarity occurring among the Indian population, the British used military and police force, the legal system, and manipulation of Muslim-Hindu conflicts. In one scene, Gandhi is tried for sedition for advocating the overthrow of the British government. When asked by the Advocate

General at the trial whether he denies the charges, Gandhi responds, "Not at all." Turning to the judge, he continues, "And I will save the Court's time, m'Lord, by stating under oath that to this day I believe noncooperation with evil is a duty. And that British rule of India is evil. . . . And if you truly believe in the system of law you administer in my country, you must inflict on me the severest penalty possible." Gandhi's challenge is not limited to the judge in this one situation, but to the system of law established by the British to protect their (unjust) rule of India. By pushing the British to treat him as a criminal for his advocacy of home rule and sentence him to prison, the injustice of their domination and control over India is further revealed, to the British themselves and to the rest of the world.

The strategy of civil disobedience that Gandhi employed was central in the civil rights movement under the leadership of Dr. Martin Luther King, Jr. King was influenced by the teachings of Gandhi, as was Rosa Parks, whose arrest for refusing to give up her seat to a white bus rider sparked the Montgomery bus boycott. In the film *The Long Walk Home*, we only hear about Rosa Parks's, arrest through discussion in the black community about staying off the buses. Historically what we know is that Rosa Parks, an activist with the NAACP, had attended a workshop at the Highlander Folk School where she learned about Gandhi's nonviolent methods of protest just a few months before her arrest (Fisk, 2000).

In *The Long Walk Home*, we enter the Jim Crow South of the mid 20th century, where racial apartheid is reproduced through legally reinforced social customs and practices. In one scene, Miriam drops off Mary Catherine (Lexi Randall) and her friends at a park to play, under Odessa's supervision, while she goes to the beauty parlor. Odessa and the children are summarily escorted from the park by a young police officer, who yells at Odessa in front of the children that the park is for whites only. He is later forced to apologize to the children (and Odessa) when Miriam complains to the police chief about her daughter being thrown out of the park. Acknowledging that the children were with their maid, she defensively exclaims, "It's not like she was paradin' her own children around the park, for heaven's sake!"

In another example, we see black maids going to work on the bus, following the prescribed ritual of entering the front of the bus, dropping their coins in the fare box, exiting the bus and reentering through the rear door to find their seat at the back of the bus. Applying a sociological perspective, we understand that this ritual symbolically reinforces the legal system of racial apartheid, where blacks are defined and treated as different from and inferior to whites. It is a daily reminder of everyone's place in the racial/class hierarchy of the society. The disruption of this practice, enacted by several women prior to Rosa Parks's famous refusal to move,[2] reveals that systems of inequality are dependent on the acceptance and acquiescence of the oppressed. When the subordinated group refuses to obey unjust laws, the dominant group has no choice but to reinforce the law (throwing Odessa out of the park, arresting Rosa Parks on the bus) or change the law.

The bus boycott was a nonviolent challenge to the economic and political racial inequality on which the social order rested. For Miriam, it is an inconvenience since Odessa is frequently late to work, and exhausted as a result of her long walk. Miriam offers to drive her to and from work several days a week, but keeps this from her husband Norman (Dwight Schultz) who has joined the White Citizen's Council and is working to break the boycott and the burgeoning civil rights movement. When he finds out, he shouts angrily, "Here I am trying to hold my head up as a white man in this town, and you're carting a nigger maid." He forbids Miriam to drive, telling her that she needs to leave the decision

Photo 11.1   The Jim Crow south as depicted in *The Long Walk Home.*   Mary Katherine (Lexi Randall) with Odessa (Whoppie Goldberg) when the white men of Montgomery attempt to intimidate the African-American community.

making to him as the head of the household, the one who knows best. He goes on to explain that there can never be a real relationship between the races: "We don't know her, can't ever know her." On the other side of town, Odessa's husband is unhappy when she adds Miriam to their evening prayer, warning that "she don't know us, and she don't want to know us."

Yet, Miriam's beliefs about race and race relations are changing, and she is beginning to see Odessa not as a member of a racial group, or even as her maid, but as a woman who, like herself, is a wife and mother. At one point, she tells Odessa that she does "the real mothering," even to the extent of taking care of Mary Catherine when she had the chicken pox, "and you hadn't even had them yourself." She goes on to wonder, "Would I have done that for your daughter?" We, the viewing audience, know the answer; as a southern white woman, she never would have been in the position of caring for Odessa's children, who are growing up in a different Montgomery than the one Miriam's children know.

Odessa's children are directly affected by the bus boycott. Odessa has instructed them not to ride the bus under any circumstances, but her daughter, anxious to see her boyfriend, sneaks away from the house and onto one of the empty buses. She soon realizes she is in trouble when two white boys begin harassing her, and she runs from the bus only to realize they are in pursuit. Her brother, who has followed her, intervenes and ends up taking the beating intended for her. A follower of King's teachings, he refuses to strike back; as he repeatedly struggles to his feet, we see his hands at his sides gripped into fists, gradually releasing to an open palm. He has the strength of his convictions and is victorious in overcoming the desire to meet violence with violence. At church that night, he listens joyfully to the sermon, and joins in singing "Marching to Zion" with his worried, but proud, parents and remorseful sister.

The bus boycott continues, and King's house is firebombed; Miriam drives alone down his street to see the damage. We learn about the highly organized alternative transportation system established during the bus boycott when Miriam becomes a regular driver for the carpool. Odessa explains to her that the police have been ticketing and arresting drivers and passengers, and tells her that she could donate money if she wants to help, rather than putting herself at risk. Miriam is determined to do something, not just give money (which she notes is really Norman's anyway) to help bring the boycott to a successful end. Odessa explains to Miriam that the goal of the movement is much more far-reaching, and that the buses are just a beginning in the fight for justice and racial equality. She warns that "when it's all said and done, people are going to look at you, Miss Thompson. And they gonna say you were part of this."

The challenge of the boycott to the white supremacist system is made clear in the final scenes of the movie, which take place in the downtown parking lot that serves as the carpool center. Led by Norman's brother, members of the White Citizen's Council show up threatening the drivers and smashing out car windows. Intending to shut down the taxi service, they confront the work-weary domestics waiting for a ride home, shouting in one voice, "Walk, nigger, walk!" The women join hands, and begin singing, timidly at first and then in stronger voice, a gospel hymn. Miriam stands literally between two worlds, the black women who work as maids in the homes of white women like herself standing in solidarity, and the white men who rule in their homes and the community, by violence if necessary. One of the women reaches out her hand, and Miriam joins the line of women, with Mary Catherine by her side. The men, including Norman, are confused and frightened by the power of this nonviolent stand against their hatred and racism; in the end, they turn and walk away.

In *Witness*, there is no direct nonviolent challenge to dominant rulers or groups in society. The Amish live separately within the larger society, in communities based on shared values and beliefs, including rejection of modern technology and deep commitment to nonviolence. However, the Amish way of life provides an alternative to the dominant culture, demonstrating that violence is not necessary to create and sustain community. In the film, the centrality of violence and aggression in urban Philadelphia stands in stark contrast to the quiet, peaceful rhythm of life in the Amish community.

These two cultures clash early in the film when 8-year-old Samuel observes a homicide in the train station in Philadelphia. Questioned by detective John Book, he reveals that he saw the man who committed the murder—as it turns out a police officer, like the victim. As Samuel and his mother Rachel wait for what will happen next, they observe Book and the chief of homicide in an angry exchange. Samuel, frightened, asks, "Momma, are they angry with us?" She reassures him, "No, no. It's just the English way." Samuel has been introduced in ways large (murder) and small (an angry verbal exchange) to the world outside of the Amish community. However, Rachel makes clear that they want nothing to do with this crime or the community in which it occurred. When Book tells her that they are not free to go since Samuel is a material witness to a homicide, she tells him, "You do not understand, we have nothing to do with your laws!"

The tables are soon turned when Book is forced to hide at the Lapp farm in the Amish community after being shot by the police officer who committed the murder. He is immersed in a world without modern conveniences, where his way of life and his work are disdained. He defensively tells Rachel, "I am a cop. That's what I know and that's what I do." Rachel responds, "What you do is take vengeance, which is sin against heaven!" Reinforcing the divide between their worlds, Book observes, "That is your way, not mine." She corrects him, "It is God's way."

Book passes as a member of the Amish community, dressing like the other men, appearing "plain," which Rachel explains to him means not being vain or taking pride in one's appearance. The juxtaposition between his Amish appearance and who he is as a denizen of the modern world violates the expectations of the townspeople and tourists who visit to see the Amish and their way of life. In one encounter, a tourist asks to take his picture, and Book threatens, "Lady, you take my picture with that thing and I'm gonna rip your brassiere off and strangle you with it! You got that?"

In another scene, Book approaches several young men harassing an Amish man and his family. Rachel tells him that this happens from time to time, and that he should do nothing in response, urging him to "turn the other cheek." Book is furious and, confronting the young men, he explodes, knocking one unconscious and breaking the nose of another. A local man says to the gathering crowd, "Never seen anything like that in all my years!" The explanation given is that he is a cousin visiting from Ohio. The local man observes, "Well, them Ohio Amish sure must be different . . . around here the brethren don't have that kind of fight in them." He shouts after them, "This ain't good for the tourist trade, you know! You tell that to your Ohio cousin!"

The real challenge and power of nonviolence is revealed in the final scenes of the movie when Philadelphia police officers who are involved in the cover-up of the murder show up at the Lapp farm to kill John Book. In a gripping scene, Samuel is told to run to a neighboring farm to safety, but hearing gunshots he returns home, grabs the bell rope, and begins ringing to let the community know they need help. The community responds, making their way across the fields to the Lapp farm where they stand as witnesses to the violence occurring, bringing an end to the siege. In the end, we see Book leaving the farm, returning to his world, with Eli calling in farewell, "You be careful, John Book! Out among them English!"

Nonviolent Models for Social Change in Film

In this reading nonviolence as a method and goal of social change, as well as a way of life, is explored in film. In American society, violence has been naturalized in the sense that we see it as a normal and even necessary part of human life. However, the films analyzed here provide a different perspective on violence, challenging the dominant paradigm and perhaps suggesting alternative routes to creating social change and/or living nonviolently.

First, all three films direct our attention to the interconnectedness of personal experience and social structure, what in sociology we refer to as "the sociological imagination." In all of the films, the social structure and culture shape the lives of the individuals we meet, at the same time that they are social agents influencing, reinforcing, and/or changing the social worlds in which they live. In *Gandhi*, for example, we see Muslims and Hindus working together for Indian home rule, and British military and Indian police who brutalize those defying British rule in India. In *The Long Walk Home*, we see Miriam become an ally in the Montgomery bus boycott and the civil rights movement, while her husband joins a racist organization to break the boycott and undermine the movement. In *Witness*, Rachel and Book can see past their differences and even love one another, at the same time that their differences, rooted in cultural beliefs and practices, are irreconcilable.

Second, two of the films, *Gandhi* and *The Long Walk Home*, provide historical accounts of nonviolence as conceptualized and practiced in social movement activism at particular times and places in the 20th century. In both we see the power of the state, enacted by the police, military, government agencies, and citizen organizations, used to block nonviolent resistance and social change. The protagonists in both films engage in acts of great courage that cost them dearly. Gandhi and his followers are beaten, imprisoned, and killed. In Montgomery, those involved in the boycott are threatened, attacked, and arrested. We watch as Miriam, faced with the choice of complicity or acting outside of her race and class interests, loses her husband, her position and ties in the community, and her way of life. Odessa's son is beaten for protecting his sister from attack.

At the same time, we see individuals transformed by their activism and belief in the possibility of social change. We see groups of people brought together in common cause, breaking down barriers, undermining prejudices. For example, in the 240-mile march to the sea in the 1930 salt campaign in *Gandhi*, "we see an extraordinary variety of participants: old, young, students, peasants, ladies in saris and jewels, Muslims, Hindus, Sikhs, Christian nuns, Untouchables, merchants, some vigorous and determined, others disheveled, tired and determined" (Briley, 1982).

Third, in all three films, nonviolence works for those who choose it as a way of life and vehicle for social change. In *Gandhi* and *The Long Walk Home*, nonviolent social protest challenges and changes the society in which it occurs. The British leave India; Jim Crow laws are dismantled and racial inequality is (and continues to be) challenged in the United States. In contrast, in *Witness* nonviolence is part of the Ordnung, the unwritten social order that guides behavior in the community. In this *gemeinschaft*/folk society, homogeneity and conformity provide the context for shared values, including nonviolence. Eli warns Rachel that she will be shunned if she goes against the Ordnung: "Rachel, you bring this man to our house. With his gun of the hand. You bring fear to this house. Fear of English with guns coming after . . . Rachel, good Rachel, you must not go too far!" Living separately from the dominant culture allows the Amish to protect their way of life and to ensure that all live according to the Ordnung.

Last, these films provide a way of thinking about how we choose to live in society at this point in history. Do we accept injustice, inequality, and violence as the "American way" or do we seek to challenge and change structures that harm those who are not among the privileged in society? To choose nonviolence, do we need to separate from the dominant culture, rejecting values and beliefs rooted in and supportive of consumerism, individualism, accumulation, and violence? How do we go about envisioning the type of world we want to live in and working to create that world? Perhaps movies such as *Gandhi*, *The Long Walk Home*, and *Witness* provide a beginning for this exploration, as nonviolent alternatives to hegemony in film.

References

Briley, J. (1982). *Gandhi: The screenplay.* Retrieved February 21, 2012 (http://www.gandhiserve.org/video/gandhi_screenplay.html)

Briley, J. (1996). On "Gandhi" and "Cry Freedom": Two pivotal scripts in my life. *Creative Screenwriting, 3,* 3–12.

Burks, M. F. (1990). Trailblazers: Women in the Montgomery bus boycott. In V. L. Crawford, J. A. Rouse, & B. Woods (Eds.), *Women in the civil rights movement: Trailblazers and torchbearers, 1941–1965* (pp. 71–84). Bloomington: Indiana University Press.

Cooper, B. (1999). Hegemony and Hollywood: A critique of cinematic distortions of women of color and their stories. *American Communication Journal, 2*(2). Retrieved February 21, 2012 (http://digitalcommons.usu.edu/journalism_facpub/32/)

Fisk, L. J. (2000). Shaping visionaries: Nurturing peace through education. In L. J. Fisk & J. L. Schellenberg (Eds.), *Patterns of conflict, paths to peace* (pp. 159–193). Peterborough, ON: Broadview Press.

Iadicola, P., & Shupe, A. (2003). *Violence, inequality, and human freedom.* Lanham, MD: Rowman & Littlefield.

Jones, J. (1995). The Long Walk Home. In M. C. Carnes (Ed.), *Past imperfect: History according to the movies* (pp. 262–265). New York: Henry Holt.

Lucien, B. (1984). Nonviolence and Satyagraha in Attenborough's *Gandhi. Journal of Humanistic Psychology, 24*(3), 130–141.

Meyer, T. (2005). Creating a culture of nonviolence: A conversation with Arun Gandhi. *Nonviolent Communication.* Retrieved February 21, 2012 (http://www.nonviolentcommunication.com/freeresources/article_archive/arun_gandhi_tmeyer.htm)

Slocum, D. J. (2000). Film violence and the institutionalization of the cinema. *Social Research, 67,* 649–681.

Williams, R. (2001). Base and superstructure in Marxist cultural theory. In J. Higgins (Ed.), *The Raymond Williams reader* (pp. 158–178). Malden, MA: Blackwell.

Notes

1. While much of the historical focus on the boycott has been on the leadership, the success of the movement has been attributed to "the nameless cooks and maids who walked endless miles for a year to bring about the breach in the walls of segregation" (Burks, 1990, p. 82).

2. Early in 1955, 15-year-old Claudette Colvin refused to get up when the white section filled and the bus driver told the black riders to move back. The police were called; upon their arrival Claudette said, "I done paid my dime, I ain't got no reason to move." E. D. Nixon, former president of both the state and local NAACP chapters, prepared to take on Colvin's case until he learned she was pregnant and thought she would be discredited by the white press. He turned down the cases of two more women before he learned that Rosa Parks had been arrested. Rosa agreed to let her friend from the NAACP turn her case into a cause for the movement (Jones, 1995, p. 262).

Reading 11.3

"We Will No Longer Sit Quietly"

Social Movements Through Film

Jeffrey A. Langstraat

S ocial movements, like sociology itself, are a product of modernity (Buechler 2000). The historical roots of social movements may lie in more elemental forms of collective behavior, both empirically and theoretically (Buechler 2000, 2011; Tarrow 1996; Tilly 1995), but they have evolved into a distinct form of social activity with a specialized field of inquiry. Additionally, and more important for the lives of everyday people, they have shaped the course of history in areas like the extension of citizenship to the working classes and to women, the inclusion of gay men and lesbians in society, and the dismantling of Jim Crow segregation.

Within sociology, social movements are often linked with other forms of collective behavior. Indeed, the American Sociological Association section dedicated to studying social movements carries the title "Collective Behavior and Social Movements." However, social movements are distinct from other forms of collective behavior such as fads, riots, and crowds. Movement scholars William Gamson and David Meyer (1996:283) define the social movement as "a sustained and self-conscious challenge to authorities or cultural codes by a field of actors (organizations and advocacy networks), some of whom employ extrainstitutional means of influence." Often thought of as politics by other means, movements involve people engaging in purposive collective action to produce, or resist, social change. In this reading, several of the major theoretical concepts involved in the study of social movements are explored using the films *The Long Walk Home*, *Norma Rae*, and *Milk*.

Set during the Montgomery bus boycott, *The Long Walk Home* (Richard Pearce, 1990) tells the story of a relationship between two women divided by the South's color line. Miriam Thompson (Sissy Spacek) is the wife of a prominent white real estate developer and Odessa Cotter (Whoopi Goldberg) is her maid. Over the course of the film, their relationship undergoes a radical transformation as the racial barrier between them is breached and the former comes to understand the latter not just as a maid, but as a fellow human being. That personal transformation alters Miriam's understanding of the segregated society in which she lives and leads to her participation in the bus boycott as a driver in the carpools organized to transport black workers to and from their jobs.

Norma Rae (Martin Ritt, 1979) is about a union organizing campaign in a North Carolina textile mill and is based on the real-life story of Crystal Lee Sutton, who is portrayed in the character Norma Rae Webster (Sally Field). Norma is a single mother who, along with her parents and much of the community, works under oppressive conditions in a local textile mill that Reuben Warshowsky (Ron Leibman), an organizer for the Textile Workers Union of America, has come to unionize. He initially finds resistance among the workers and struggles to get them involved. The campaign picks up steam, though, when

Norma Rae joins his efforts by introducing him to community members and taking a lead recruitment role within the mill. While she is eventually fired and arrested for her activity, their efforts are successful, and workers at the mill vote to unionize.

The biopic *Milk* (Gus Van Sant, 2008) shows the last decade of pioneering gay activist Harvey Milk's (Sean Penn) life. "The story of Harvey Milk is, to a large extent, the story of the gay movement in San Francisco" (Shilts 1982:xiii). After losing three campaigns, he is elected to the San Francisco Board of Supervisors, making him the second "out" gay man elected to public office in the United States.[1] As a supervisor, he cosponsors and helps pass an antidiscrimination ordinance, one of the first gay rights laws in the nation. He also leads the fight against a California ballot initiative that would have barred gay men and lesbians from being public school teachers. At the end of the film, he and the mayor are assassinated by fellow supervisor Dan White (Josh Brolin).

These three films each involve personal and social transformation that takes place through collective action. They also provide illustrations of many of the major concepts that sociologists use to describe, explain, and analyze social movement activity. In this reading, examples from these films are used to explore those key ideas. In addition, since these movies are based on real people and/or events, they are also used as jumping-off points to discuss the social movements on which each is based. Whether the illustrations are drawn from the films themselves or from the actual social movements, the goal is to help readers come to a sociological understanding of social movements.

Grievances, Framing, and Identity

The Long Walk Home opens at a Montgomery, Alabama, bus stop where three black domestic workers are waiting for the bus. As the bus pulls up to the stop, each woman enters the front door of the bus, pays her fare, and exits to reenter through the back door, which was standard practice in the city's segregated buses (Morris 1984). In this scene, and throughout the film, viewers are confronted with practices associated with the South's Jim Crow segregation, which Aldon Morris (1984) described as a "tripartite system of domination" (p. 1). Based on economic deprivation, political exclusion, and interpersonal degradation, it produced objective hardships in the lives of black Americans.

Norma Rae and *Milk* also demonstrate how the organization of social life produces hardships that become the basis for social movement grievances. In a *Norma Rae* scene, set in the title character's kitchen, Reuben asks the assembled workers about conditions in the mill. They describe experiences such as being forced to stand for too long, management's refusal to accommodate medical problems, and a dehumanizing lack of respect. One of them compares working in the mill to a prison sentence. Such hardships, particularly the refusal to accommodate medical conditions, are illustrated throughout the film. In the first scene of the film, Norma Rae's mother is temporarily deafened by the noise in the mill, a condition that is ignored by the on-site doctor. Later, Norma Rae's father's left arm goes numb as he is working. The supervisor tells him to keep working until his scheduled break. He attempts to do so but falls into a bin of spindles, dead of a heart attack. The film illustrates how the workers' health, safety, and humanity are expendable in the pursuit of corporate profit.

In *Milk*, different systems of oppression are evidenced. The opening credits run over footage showing a common form of antigay repression for much of the twentieth century: police raiding gay bars and arresting their patrons. Later in the film, a similar bar raid takes place, but instead of simply arresting patrons, the police also physically assault them. In a subsequent scene, Harvey berates a police officer for his indifference to a gay man who was beaten to death on the street, and to the police department's general hostility toward San Francisco's gay population. Antigay violence and active state repression were regular features of gay life, even in "liberal" San Francisco.

In presenting the different hardships faced by their characters, each of these films demonstrates how systems of social organization produce the oppressive conditions the main characters are working to change. These are the grievances around which movement organizers attempt to mobilize people. Oppression and the grievances associated with it are not sufficient to produce movement activity, though. As Doug McAdam (1982) has noted, "segments of society may very well submit to oppressive conditions unless that oppression is collectively defined as both unjust and *subject to change*" (p. 34, emphasis in original). A scene in *Norma Rae* illustrates this, albeit on an individual level. Norma Rae is at a bar drinking with her future husband, Sonny (Beau Bridges), and Reuben. They are discussing Reuben's attempt to unionize the mill's workforce. Sonny notes that the odds are against the union, saying, "The big companies always get what they want. Everything goes to the rich man," to which Rueben responds, "Are you tired of it yet?" Sonny, having internalized the oppression produced by corporate hegemony, says that he drowns those tired feelings with beer. He may recognize that he is, as Reuben told Norma Rae's father, "underpaid, overworked and shafted up to his tonsils," but he has resigned himself to this state of affairs. Such acceptance must change in order for people to engage in collective action.

Photo 11.2 Charismatic leadership in *Milk*. Harvey Milk (Sean Penn) leads the gay and lesbian community of San Francisco in their pursuit of civil rights.

McAdam (1982) referred to the process of transforming how unjust conditions are understood as "cognitive liberation" (p. 34). For hardships to be turned into grievances, and then into social movement claims, people must understand that the conditions under which they are living are not necessarily the way they have to be. Not only must people believe change is possible, they must also believe that their actions can help produce that change. This process of "cognitive liberation" is simultaneously individual and collective. McAdam was referring to groups undergoing a change in their collective definition of the situation. However, that collective transformation also requires changes in individual consciousness. People like Sonny must come to believe that another world is possible.

The process of cognitive liberation is illustrated in *The Long Walk Home*. Montgomery's black citizens, already challenging Jim Crow through the bus boycott, have seemingly undergone this process. Odessa demonstrates this in a conversation with Miriam, who thinks "this whole mess" is solely about the buses.

And what about when it isn't just about the buses, when it's the parks and the restaurants, when it's colored teachers in white schools? What about when we start voting, Miss Thompson? 'Cause we are. And when we do, we're gonna put Negroes in office. What about when the first colored family moves into your neighborhood?

Odessa makes it clear that the current upheaval is about more than the buses, and that she and the city's other black citizens believe they can successfully challenge segregation's tripartite system of domination. This conversation takes place as Miriam is taking a role in the bus boycott movement by becoming a driver for the carpool.

Prior to that conversation, Miriam had already been driving Odessa to work a few days a week. But, after a confrontation with her husband over those rides and a heart-to-heart conversation with Odessa, she comes to see her maid as more than a domestic worker and recognizes the injustices that black Montgomery citizens face. She understands Jim Crow segregation, at least on the buses, as unjust and wrong and believes that she can play a part in dismantling it by shuttling boycotters in her car. In the sequence of interactions that lead to her participation, the processes of consciousness raising and cognitive liberation are taking place. Within the field of social movement studies, the interactive process through which this cognitive transformation takes place is referred to as "frame alignment" (Snow et al. 1986).

"Frames" are central to the study of both social movement claims-making activity and the social psychological processes involved in micromobilization (Benford and Snow 2000). These sociocognitive structures establish conceptual relationships between social actors, and between actors and the conditions in which they find themselves. They are "schemata of interpretation" (Goffman 1974:21) that help people define situations and determine appropriate courses of action. "Collective action frames," the type of frame at the heart of movement scholarship, "serve as accenting devices that either underscore and embellish the seriousness and injustice of a social condition or redefine as unjust and immoral what was previously seen as unfortunate but perhaps tolerable" (Snow and Benford 1992:137). Framing is the symbolic labor of constructing and communicating messages about unjust social conditions and attempting to motivate people to take action to change those conditions.

William Gamson (1992) has identified three primary components of collective action frames: identity, injustice, and agency. I have already discussed the issue of injustice. The social structural conditions demonstrated in these three films produce oppressive hardships for African Americans, mill workers, and gay men and lesbians. The key for movement activists is to frame those conditions in such a way that they are no longer accepted as "the way things are," but are instead understood as unjust and oppressive.

I have also noted how this framing activity must convince people that they can, indeed should, take action. As Klandermans and Oegema (1987) have demonstrated, the majority of people who agree with a social movement's goals and activities do not participate in collective action. I return to the organizational and structural issues surrounding mobilization below, but a scene from *Norma Rae* demonstrates the framing aspect of this phenomenon. In his first meeting with mill workers, Reuben describes how a union can transform their lives. Talking to a mixed-race group of workers assembled in a black church, he draws on the scriptures familiar to them, saying, "Yes, it comes from the Bible: 'According to the tribes of your fathers, ye shall inherit.' But it comes from Reuben Warshowsky: 'Not unless you make it happen.'" He uses religious language familiar to his audience to produce a message that "resonates" (Snow and Benford 1988) with the worldview they already have and motivates them to take action.

The final aspect of collective action frames involves identity and the construction of a collective "we." In *Norma Rae*, for example, people see themselves not so much as individual employees, but collectively as workers and union members. The recruitment scene I mentioned above illustrates this point. Rueben describes his grandfather's funeral. After noting the main family members present at the funeral, he continues:

> Also present were 862 members of the Amalgamated Clothing Workers and the Cloth Hat and Cap Makers Union of America, also members of his family. In death, as in life, they stood at his side. They had fought battles with him, had bound the wounds of battle with him, had earned bread together, and had broken it together. When they spoke, they spoke in one voice, and they were heard. And they were black, and they were white. They were Irish, and they were Polish. And they were Catholic, and they were Jews. And they were one. That's what a union is. One.

In this scene, Reuben is speaking of social solidarity, a sense of "we-ness" based on a shared status that is broadly referred to as "collective identity" (Taylor and Whittier 1992; Polletta and Jasper 2001). Reuben is framing union membership as an identity. It is that shared status of union member that transcends differences surrounding race, ethnicity, and religion that he is trying to foster among the gathered mill workers.

Reuben's construction of the "we" of union membership is linked to a construction of "they." In this case, it is the textile manufacturing industry, the owners of the plants that employ these workers. This industry, he tells them, is exploiting them. Identity framing involves more than just framing the movement itself. It also involves framing of opponents and authorities (Hunt, Benford, and Snow 1994). This we/them construction is also present in *Milk's* illustration of the rise of an antigay countermovement led by Anita Bryant and California senator John Briggs. These antigay proponents frame homosexuals as predators who recruit children. Harvey, in turns, frames the antigay movement as a threat to gay and lesbian lives. He also tries to undercut their framing, turning it on its head by ironically proclaiming, "I am here to recruit you" at the beginning of his speeches. "Framing contests" like this involve competing constructions of social conditions and attempts to undercut each other's messages (Dugan 2008; Fisher 2009).

Social movement actors frame messages for multiple audiences. They try to convince authorities to take a particular action, to undercut the messages of their opponents, and to mobilize constituents. In doing so, they construct hardships such as those imposed by the structures of segregation, class exploitation, and heterosexual supremacy as problems to be corrected. Such grievances are necessary for mobilization but are not by themselves suffi-cient. For people to engage in collective action, they must undergo a process of cognitive liberation and see conditions as amenable to change through movement participation. It is to the issue of mobilization itself that we now turn.

Mobilizing Structures and Movement Organization

During the first half of *Norma Rae*, Reuben experiences difficulty in enlisting mill workers to take part in, or even show interest in, the unionizing effort. An outsider in the close-knit community, he is unable to connect with its members. Additionally, as a nonemployee, he is excluded from the plant itself and is relegated to handing flyers to workers as they enter. After the above-noted recruitment meeting, he complains to Norma Rae that only 17 of the 800 people working in the mill attended. She explains to him that his outsider status is working against him and begins taking him around town, introducing him to people who work in the mill and helping him integrate into the community. This creates a network of personal relationships that he can draw on to mobilize participation in the campaign. Research has demonstrated that people who are embedded in social networks with social movement participants are more likely to participate themselves, particularly if there are strong communal ties involved (Oberschall 1973).

Such social networks, as well as the links between community and movement organiza-tions, are what movement scholars call "mobilizing structures" (McAdam, McCarthy, and Zald 1996). These are the formal and informal social networks, community and movement organizations, and other social groups that connect movement actors to the constituencies they claim to represent and try to mobilize.

The importance of social networks is also illustrated in the Montgomery bus boycott on which *The Long Walk Home* is based. Communal ties were fostered and reinforced in black churches. These institutions were significant for mobilization, providing an organizational infrastructure that linked community members with each other and that linked movement organizers with a mobilizable base (McAdam 1982; Morris 1984). Local organizations like the Women's Political Council and NAACP were looking for opportunities to challenge bus segregation but had a more limited membership base than the churches did. In joining with the city's black ministers to form the Montgomery Improvement Association, these organizations gained access to a new base of people. The communal networks existing within Montgomery's black churches facilitated mobilization because they provided activ-ists with an already organized constituency (McAdam 1982). While movement organizers in Montgomery were able to draw on the existing organizational structures of the churches, Reuben is attempting to build such an organizational infrastructure for workers in the mill. Communal networks exist there, but he is excluded from them until Norma Rae provides access, which facilitates mobilization.

Just as mobilization requires more than grievances, these networks and organizations are necessary but insufficient to produce it. Barriers must be overcome for people to get involved. For many blacks in Montgomery, like Odessa Cotter, not owning a car constituted an obstacle to participation in the boycott. Staying off the buses meant losing the transportation that took her to work. That loss could lead to unemployment and the loss of income. Similarly, workers in *Norma Rae* faced retribution for taking part in the unionization campaign, and Norma Rae is fired and arrested for her actions. In *Milk*, Harvey receives death threats while running for political office and as he is preparing to give a speech at the Gay Freedom Day Parade.

Such threats to life and economic security present very real barriers to movement participation. If activists are going to mobilize people, they need to overcome those barriers. *The Long Walk Home* demonstrates how some economic barriers were overcome during the Montgomery bus boycott. Organizers created a carpool system to shuttle boycotters around the city. They established specific sites for dropping off and picking up people who needed rides, and drivers used routes that mirrored those of the bus system. In doing so, they allowed the city's black citizens to act in nearly routine ways while still participating in the boycott.

Above I noted the role of black churches in providing a mobilizable base. They were also significant in maintaining the boycott. One of several church scenes in *The Long Walk Home* shows Odessa's family entering as the minister is soliciting help for the carpool. "If you own a car," he says, "but must be at work during the day, we have fine young men who can drive your cars, allowing you to still contribute to the boycott." People who were willing and able to make such a contribution were invited to come to the front of the church during the singing of a hymn. This work to recruit drivers and obtain funds to support the boycott is illustrative of what has become one of the dominant paradigms within social movement studies: "resource mobilization" (McCarthy and Zald 1977).

McCarthy and Zald posited that a new form of social movement has arisen in contemporary societies, one comprising professionally staffed organizations working to elicit resources to support their political activity. In this form of movement, mass mobilization and demonstration are often less important than funding the work of professional activists. McCarthy and Zald's position was rooted in the rational choice theory that came to dominate social movement studies after the publication of Swedish economist Mancur Olson's book, *The Logic of Collective Action* (1965). The economistic approach they drew on was particularly prominent in their description of the organizational aspects of movement activity. Again, they focused on formal, bureaucratic social movement organizations (SMOs). In the Montgomery mobilization, this would include organizations like the above-noted Montgomery Improvement Association, Women's Political Council, and NAACP. The collection of organizations within a movement composes the social movement industry (SMI). This would include the three groups just noted as well as others, such as the Southern Christian Leadership Conference. The accumulated industries from different movements make up the social movement sector (SMS) of a society.

The organizational model McCarthy and Zald developed doesn't work quite as well when analyzing resource-poor movements that rely on the mass mobilization of people and lack access to resource sources that McCarthy and Zald's model conceptualized. Indeed, Piven and Cloward (1979) argued that the formal bureaucratic organizations McCarthy and Zald emphasized could actually inhibit mass insurrections of the poor by diverting valuable resources away from mobilization efforts and toward organizational maintenance. While Piven and Cloward make an important point about how the mobilizing population influences the shape movements take, it is also true that organization and resources matter. The carpool illustrates this point; people with cars were recruited to drive others, and funds were solicited for things like fuel. The mobilization of resources was absolutely necessary to maintain the mobilization of people.

The just-noted scene from *The Long Walk Home*, in which the minister solicited resources for the carpool, also illustrates one of the ways that movement solidarity can be reinforced and mobilization maintained. The Cotters were late to that church service because their oldest son, Theodore (Richard Habersham), had been beaten up by white teens in a park. The family sits down in the church, and Theodore is shown with his lip bloodied and swollen from the assault. Initially, he appears angry and distant, but as he joins the congregation singing "Coming on to Zion," his expression changes to one of resolve. The ritual act of singing establishes a connection with the broader community of black citizens resisting Jim Crow. Indeed, as Doug McAdam (1982:129) has noted:

> In the case of most church-based campaigns [during the civil rights movement], it was not so much that movement participants were recruited from among the ranks of active churchgoers as it was a case of church membership being redefined to include movement participation as a primary requisite of the role.

Churches became movement organizations, and the ritual practices within them reinforced movement solidarity and collective identity while helping to maintain motivation.

Steven Buechler's (2011) discussion of Émile Durkheim's contribution to social movement theory is useful here. Although Durkheim ([1915] 1965) did not specifically focus on social movement activity, his work on religious ritual and social solidarity (Durkheim [1915] 1965) provides insights into issues that are important in sustaining movement activity. The practice of singing, as Eyerman and Jameson (1998) noted, can play such a ritualistic role in social movements. Coming together in ritual practice, such as singing songs of "getting over," reinforces membership in the group and the righteousness of the cause. In the Durkheimian sense, these practices strengthen collective identity and the sense of belonging to something larger. Theodore's feelings of membership in and obligation to the movement were renewed and reinforced. This experience is vital for the maintenance of the motivation necessary to sustain mobilization.

Above, I noted that the Women's Political Council and NAACP had been looking for opportunities to challenge bus segregation. They almost did so a few months prior to Rosa Parks's arrest, but decided against it because Claudette Colvin, the teenager who was arrested, was unmarried and pregnant (Morris 1984). While the selection of "appropriate" victims raises important concerns about the construction of a public image, the issue of greater concern here is that there are certain people within movements who make decisions about which goals to pursue, how to frame issues, and how to mobilize people. Movements have leaders. However, while many people point to the almost mythological images of charismatic leaders like Martin Luther King, Jr., and Harvey Milk, issues of leadership are more complex.

Leadership

Weber's (1946) work on authority and legitimacy is instructive for understanding the roles of leaders in movement activity. Weber detailed three particular forms of authority: rational-legal, charismatic, and traditional. The former two are particularly significant for social movement activity. The formal bureaucratic organizations described in McCarthy and Zald's resource mobilization approach are likely to draw on the rational-legal form of leadership. Harvey Milk is a classic example of charismatic leadership.

In *Milk*, Sean Penn portrays the personal characteristics that made Harvey Milk such an effective leader. Milk was an inspirational orator with a flair for the dramatic and an effervescent personality that drew people to him. He was skilled at pinpointing the issues people cared about and turning them into political campaigns. This combination of traits is illustrated on the night that Miami-Dade voters repealed a gay rights ordinance. The gay and lesbian community of San Francisco's Castro district is outraged and takes to the streets. Harvey climbs a stage in front of them and expresses the crowd's feeling, stating, "I know you're angry! I'm angry! Let's march the streets of San Francisco and share our anger!" His leadership is effective not only because his personality draws people to him. He is also able to channel the energy of those around him into a productive movement demonstration instead of an unfocused riot. These skills and personality traits allowed him to become a leader of the increasingly powerful San Francisco gay movement.

At the end of *Milk*, Harvey is assassinated by fellow supervisor Dan White. This tragedy illustrates a potential problem with charismatic leadership: if a charismatic leader is the driving force behind movement mobilization, the loss of that leader could lead to the movement's collapse. The maintenance of formal organizations, like the Textile Workers Union of America in *Norma Rae*, can be important, then, because it allows movements to outlive their leaders. Although Piven and Cloward's (1979) argument that organizations divert resources away from mobilization and toward organizational maintenance is a valid one, in situations like the murder of Harvey Milk—or someone like Malcolm X or Martin Luther King, Jr.—the existence of such organizations can facilitate movement continuity despite the loss of a charismatic leader.

Additionally, movement continuity requires the recruitment not merely of members, but also of people who can step into positions of leadership. The relationship between Harvey and Cleve Jones in *Milk* illustrates this point. On the night Wichita repeals its gay rights ordinance, Harvey gives Cleve his bullhorn and has him lead a march to City Hall, where Supervisor Milk will be waiting to "calm" the crowd. In the following scene, as Milk and Jones are reading an account of Harvey's "peacemaking," Harvey provides feedback and critiques Cleve's actions at the demonstration. Harvey is grooming the young Jones to take on a leadership position. As the film's epilogue notes, Jones did indeed continue in a leadership position after Milk's death, including his founding of the Names Project AIDS Quilt.

Leaders like Harvey Milk and Cleve Jones are important in movement activity. They can inspire people to give their time, energy, and money for movement activity. They make decisions about what course of action to take, and when to take it. However, these leaders need people willing to march on City Hall or boycott buses or sign union cards. They may be able to inspire or convince people to take action, but broader social networks and systems of social organization are also necessary for the mobilization of both people and resources. Such mobilization can entail risks because movement activity is contentious. It is to issues of conflict we now turn.

Context, Conflict, and Opposition

In the iconic scene from *Norma Rae*, the lead character, having just been fired, writes the word *Union* on a piece of cardboard and displays it to her coworkers as she stands on a work table. All of the workers on the floor turn off their machines in solidarity. Norma Rae is arrested and jailed for refusing to leave and instead continuing her union agitation— illustrating that, as noted above, movement participation may involve substantial risks. These risks flow from the fact that movement activity is contentious. It involves conflict with authorities and opponents.

When social movement scholars discuss the conflictual contexts in which movements act, they often use the concept of "political opportunity structures" (Kitschelt 1986). Kitschelt was referring to the institutional relations of power, authority, and social control that movements confront. There are a number of ways that state structure influences movement activity and outcomes. One involves how much and what kind of access citizens and movements have to political processes. A "closed" government, like segregationist states were to black citizens, presents few institutional channels for people to pursue change. Thus, organizers might be more likely to use disruptive protest like the bus boycott shown in *The Long Walk Home*. The refusal to ride city buses was an attempt to exert economic pressure by depriving municipal bus systems of the income generated by riders' fares. As Richard Flacks (2005:16) has noted, "the power of the powerless is rooted in their capacity to stop the smooth flow of social life." Southern blacks, lacking political and economic power, collectively refused to ride the buses. This was one of the few areas in which they could exert economic pressure and disrupt the everyday operation of Jim Crow segregation.

The people occupying positions within the state also matter. In *Milk*, Harvey runs for elective office several times, finally winning a position on the San Francisco Board of Supervisors on his fourth attempt. In that position, he pursues policies of importance to the city's gay and lesbian communities by acts such as sponsoring a nondiscrimination ordinance. While it can be important for movements to capture state institutions by electing members, the broader conflict and alliance systems are also significant. Harvey was able to draw on the support of Mayor Moscone and Supervisor Silver to help pass the gay rights ordinance. While unanimous elite support can help movements realize their goals, and unanimous opposition may inhibit such realization, splits among elites may also be exploited, depending on which elites line up in support and opposition of the movement.

Mechanisms of social control are another important part of the system of opportunities and threats activists confront. As noted, Norma Rae was arrested for her union activism.

Elites may use law enforcement tactics like selective enforcement or the use of violence against protesters and activists to resist changes sought by social movements. *The Long Walk Home* also shows the use of the police as a force of control and repression. In a scene in which Miriam is driving Odessa to work, a police motorcycle follows them as they drive past the carpool depot. Odessa explains, "Oh, they trying to break the boycott. They just follow behind people and try to give 'em tickets." State authorities may use intimidation and repression to confront and control movements, or they may use more mundane means, such as requiring permits or portable toilets in order to hold demonstrations.

Thus far, I have discussed opposition from institutional elites. Movements also often face opposition from "countermovements" or "opposing movements" (Meyer and Staggenborg 1996). In *Milk*, the rise of a specifically antigay countermovement is demonstrated in Anita Bryan's "Save Our Children" campaign. It emerged in Miami-Dade County and spread to Wichita, Eugene, and Saint Paul before arriving in California. Her movement arose in reaction to the gains made by the gay and lesbian rights movement and was successful in repealing antidiscrimination ordinances in those jurisdictions. In California, this effort was led by state senator John Briggs, who proposed legislation that would have barred gay men and lesbians from being public school teachers. Briggs' initiative was defeated, but the cultural and political conflicts between the gay and lesbian rights movement and the antigay religious right have continued for the last 35 years.

The relationships among movements, countermovements, and the state can take a variety of forms. *Milk* reveals two movements in conflict, each trying to influence state policy in its preferred direction with neither movement in control of the state. *The Long Walk Home* illustrates a different conflict system. The White Citizens' Council, of which Miriam's husband and brother-in-law are members, arose in response to black resistance to Jim Crow. It was also part of a longer-term semi-institutional white supremacist movement that included groups like the Ku Klux Klan. Members of these organizations were also business elites and state actors, leading to a situation in which there are not two movements fighting over the state, but one movement challenging a countermovement that is aligned with a repressive state and economic elite. The difference between the two films highlights an important aspect of the alliance and conflict systems composing political opportunity structures. There are multiple possible alignments of the relationships among movements, countermovements, and institutional elites, and these influence movement activities and outcomes.

State structure, policy context, control mechanisms, and alliance/conflict systems shape how movements act and influence their likelihood of success. However, movement activists' efforts are shaped by their understanding of those structures. Activists' analyses of the system of risks and opportunities, and of their chances of success, influence the choices they make. For example, the bus boycott in *The Long Walk Home* was based on an analysis concerning potential vulnerabilities in the Jim Crow laws.

While the Montgomery bus boycott is understood as a seminal mobilization in the history of the civil rights movement, it was not the first carried out by southern blacks. In 1953, a one-week boycott in Baton Rouge produced changes in that city's bus segregation policies, providing "evidence that the system of racial segregation could be challenged by mass action" (Morris 1984:25). The decision to challenge bus segregation in Montgomery was based not only on the grievances that black citizens of Montgomery had, but also on an understanding that the system might be vulnerable. That understanding was, at least partially, due to the successful Baton Rouge mobilization.

A similar boycott takes place in *Milk*. Harvey, working with union leaders, convinces the city's gay bars to boycott Coors beer. Boycotts, be they of beer companies or municipal buses, illustrate what Sidney Tarrow (1996) has called the "modular" character of social movement protest, or how a general form of collective action can be transported from one social setting or movement to another. Strikes, marches, sit-ins, and demonstrations are other examples of the actions composing movements' "repertoires of contention" (Tilly 1995), and activists choose from this repertoire based on their analysis of existing conditions.

Five months after the Montgomery boycott began, another bus boycott was initiated in Tallahassee, Florida, and subsequent boycotts were launched in Atlanta, Georgia; New Orleans, Louisiana; Birmingham, Alabama; Chattanooga, Tennessee and; and Rock Hill, South Carolina (McAdam 1982). The decision to boycott was made by movement actors seeking to influence state and business elites. These choices were based on their understanding of complex systems of opportunities and risks that confronted them in their attempts to overturn Jim Crow segregation. Such political opportunity structures are something all movement activists confront.

Conclusion

The Long Walk Home, Norma Rae, Milk, and the movements that inspired them provide insight into the sociology of social movements. Broadly, I divided the discussion into three theoretical sections. The first involved social movement grievances and how activists frame them. The next section concerned mobilizing structures and the organizational aspects of movement activity. Finally, there was the political context of risk and opportunity and the alliance and conflict systems that shape movement activity. These sections roughly represent widely accepted conceptual divisions within movement studies (Buechler 2011; McAdam, McCarthy, and Zald 1996).

While these three analytical areas focus on different aspects of movement activity, each interpenetrates the others. In the first section, for example, I discussed collective identity and its relationship to framing. However, as I discussed in the second section, collective identity is also rooted in the relationships people share in organizational contexts and the experience of social solidarity. Related to this, the alliance and conflict systems in which movements are embedded shape identity conflicts. Social identities are relational and contextual, and the issues addressed in each section are necessarily linked to those discussed in the other two. Thus, when considering how these concepts should be understood, it is vital to keep in mind that these distinctions are merely analytical. Rather than read them as distinct concepts, they must be understood in conjunction with each other.

The films *The Long Walk Home, Norma Rae*, and *Milk* illustrate social movements that have transformed life in the United States. The civil rights movement of the 1950s and 1960s dismantled the Jim Crow system of American apartheid. Working men and women enjoy workplace protections because of labor movement struggles. Workers (especially blue collar and low- and middle-income earners) see an increase in wages and benefits with unionization (Mishel and Walters 2003). Gay men and lesbians continue to experience greater levels of inclusion thanks to the LGBT rights movement. Other movements have likewise produced significant social change. As evidenced here, there is a vibrant field of research working to understand how social movements operate. Whatever direction this research moves in the future, it is undeniable that the object of study, social movements, will continue to be a driving force of social change.

References

Benford, R. D. and D. A. Snow. 2000. "Framing and Social Movements: An Overview and Assessment." *Annual Review of Sociology* 26:611–39.

Buechler, S. M. 2000. *Social Movements in Advanced Capitalism: The Political Economy and Cultural Construction of Social Activism.* New York: Oxford University Press.

Buechler, S. M. 2011. *Understanding Social Movements: Theories from the Classical Era to the Present.* Boulder, CO: Paradigm.

Dugan, K. B. 2008. "Just Like You: The Dimensions of Identity Presentation in an Antigay Contested Context." Pp. 21–46 in *Identity Work in Social Movements,* edited by J. Reger, D. J. Myers, and R. L. Einwohner. Minneapolis: University of Minnesota Press.

Dunbar, E. 2008. "Longtime State Sen. Allan Spear Dies." Retrieved July 3, 2011 (http://minnesota.publicradio.org/display/web/2008/10/12/spear_obit/).

Durkheim, É. [1915] 1965. *The Elementary Forms of Religious Life.* New York: Free Press.

Eyerman, R. and A. Jamison. 1998. *Music and Social Movements: Mobilizing Traditions in the Twentieth Century.* New York: Cambridge University Press.

Fisher, S. 2009. "It Takes (at Least) Two to Tango: Fighting with Words in the Conflicts over Same-Sex Marriage." Pp. 207–30 in *Queer Mobilizations: LGBT Activists Confront the Law,* edited by S. Barclay, M. Bernstein, and A.-M. Marshall. New York: New York University Press.

Flacks, R. 2005. "The Question of Relevance in Social Movement Studies." Pp. 3–19 in *Rhyming Hope and History: Activists, Academics and Social Movement Scholarship,* edited by D. Croteau, W. Hoynes, and C. Ryan. Minneapolis: University of Minnesota Press.

Gamson, W. A. 1992. *Talking Politics.* New York: Cambridge University Press.

Gamson, W. A. and D. S. Meyer. 1996. "Framing Political Opportunity." Pp. 275–90 in *Comparative Perspectives on Social Movements: Political Opportunities, Mobilizing Structures, and Cultural Framings,* edited by D. McAdam, J. D. McCarthy, and M. N. Zald. New York: Cambridge University Press.

Goffman, E. 1974. *Frame Analysis: An Essay on the Organization of Experience.* New York: Harper & Row.

Hunt, S. A., R. D. Benford, and D. A. Snow. 1994. "Identity Fields, Framing Processes, and the Social Construction of Movement Identities." Pp. 185–208 in *New Social Movements: From Ideology to Identity,* edited by E. Laraña, H. Johnston, and J. R. Gusfield. Philadelphia: Temple University Press.

Kitschelt, H. P. 1986. "Political Opportunity Structures and Political Protest: Anti-nuclear Movements in Four Democracies." *British Journal of Political Science* 16:57–85.

Klandermans, B. and D. Oegema. 1987. "Potential, Networks, Motivations, and Barriers: Steps Towards Participation in Social Movements." *American Sociological Review* 52(4):519–31.

McAdam, D. 1982. *Political Process and the Development of Black Insurgency, 1930–1970.* Chicago: University of Chicago Press.

McAdam, D., J. D. McCarthy, and M. N. Zald. 1996. "Introduction: Opportunities, Mobilizing Structures, and Framing Processes—Toward a Synthetic, Comparative Perspective on Social Movements." Pp. 1–20 in *Comparative Perspectives on Social Movements: Political Opportunities, Mobilizing Structures, and Cultural Framings*, edited by D. McAdam, J. D. McCarthy, and M. N. Zald. New York: Cambridge University Press.

McCarthy, J. D. and M. N. Zald. 1977. "Resource Mobilization and Social Movements: A Partial Theory." *American Journal of Sociology* 82(6):1212–41.

Meyer, D. S. and S. Staggenborg. 1996. "Movements, Countermovements, and the Structure of Political Opportunity." *American Journal of Sociology* 101(6):1628–60.

Mishel, L. and M. Walters. 2003. "How Unions Help All Workers." *Economic Policy Institute*. Retrieved July 22, 2011 (http://www.epi.org/publications/entry/briefingpapers_bp143/).

Morris, A. D. 1984. *The Origins of the Civil Rights Movement: Black Communities Organizing for Change*. New York: Free Press.

Oberschall, A. 1973. *Social Conflicts and Social Movements*. Englewood Cliffs, NJ: Prentice Hall.

Olson, M. 1965. *The Logic of Collective Action*. Cambridge, MA: Harvard University Press.

Piven, F. F. and R. A. Cloward. 1979. *Poor People's Movements*. New York: Vintage.

Polletta, F. and J. M. Jasper. 2001. "Collective Identity and Social Movements." *Annual Review of Sociology* 27:283–305.

Shilts, R. 1982. *The Mayor of Castro Street: The Life and Times of Harvey Milk*. New York: St. Martin's Press.

Snow, D. A. and R. Benford. 1988. "Ideology, Frame Resonance, and Participant Mobilization." Pp. 197–217 in *International Social Movement Research*. Vol. 1., edited by B. Klandermans, H. Kriesi, and S. Tarrow. Greenwich, CT: JAI Press.

Snow, D. A. and R. Benford. 1992. "Master Frames and Cycles of Protest." Pp. 133–55 in *Frontiers in Social Movement Theory*, edited by A. D. Morris and C. M. Mueller. New Haven, CT: Yale University Press.

Snow, D., A. E. B. Rochford, Jr., S. K. Worden, and R. D. Benford. 1986. "Frame Alignment Processes, Micromobilization, and Movement Participation." *American Sociological Review* 51(4):464–81.

Tarrow, S. 1996. *Power in Movement: Social Movements and Contentious Politics*. 2nd ed. New York: Cambridge University Press.

Taylor, V. and N. Whittier. 1992. "Collective Identity in Social Movement Communities." Pp. 104–29 in *Frontiers in Social Movement Theory*, edited by A. Morris and C. M. Mueller. New Haven, CT: Yale University Press.

Tilly, C. 1995. *Popular Contention in Great Britain, 1758–1834*. Cambridge, MA: Harvard University Press.

Weber, M. 1946. "The Sociology of Charismatic Authority." Pp. 245–64 in *From Max Weber: Essays in Sociology*, edited by H. H. Gerth and C. W. Mills. New York: Oxford University Press.

Notes

1. The film erroneously says that Milk was the first openly gay man to be elected to public office. However, at the time of Harvey's election, an openly gay man, Allan Spear, was serving in the Minnesota Senate (Dunbar 2008).

Outtake

Excerpt from "Thoughts . . . on the Spirit of Activism in Film"

John Farr

Great activist movies portray the ongoing struggle between the welfare of working people and larger societal forces, seemingly beyond their control, that threaten their integrity, livelihood, and often, their very survival. These quintessentially American films make inspiring David and Goliath stories, where average citizens take on powerful and entrenched "special interests" via the media, the courts, or the labor unions.

A perfect case in point is the landmark *Salt of the Earth* (1954). Filmed independently on a shoestring by blacklisted director Herbert Biberman, it too was blacklisted on release, the only movie in our country's history to earn that distinction. Using mainly nonactors, (this film) portrays the indigent lives of workers at a zinc mine in New Mexico, focusing on Ramon and Esperanza Quintero (Juan Chacon and Rosaura Revueltas). When Ramon, backed by the Union of Mine, Mill and Smelter Workers, leads a walk-out against the Empire Zinc Company, reprisals follow. The company eventually produces an injunction forcing the men off the picket line, so their wives step in and take over for them. Shot with a documentary-style immediacy, this historic effort still makes for stark, powerful cinema. (Note: Blacklisted actor Will Geer, later Grandpa in *The Waltons*, plays the sheriff).

Fast forward twenty-five years to Sally Field's Oscar-winning turn in *Norma Rae*. After hearing New York–based union organizer Reuben (Ron Leibman) deliver a speech at the Southern textile mill where she works, Norma Rae (Field) joins the effort to organize workers. Butting heads with management, and alienating husband Sonny (Beau Bridges) with her new activism, Norma Rae evolves from pliant employee to impassioned agitator for workers' rights. The interplay between Norma Rae and unlikely ally Reuben is interesting to watch, but ultimately it's the emergence of Norma Rae's righteous fire that's most memorable.

Director Mike Nichols would bring a chilling true story to life with *Silkwood* (1983), starring Meryl Streep as Karen Silkwood, an employee at a plutonium plant outraged at her management's blatant disregard for proper safety procedures, and the resulting risk of radioactive contamination. On her way to meet a journalist in November, 1974, Karen disappeared, never to be seen again.

One of the best films of the 1980s, John Sayles's brilliant *Matewan* (1987) takes us back to the 1920s and the primitive, perilous lives of coal miners in West Virginia. United Mine Workers union rep Joe Kenehan (Chris Cooper) has his hands full organizing this group, as it comprises white, black and Italian factions unaccustomed to interacting outside the pit. Joe's simple message: There is strength in numbers.

In *Separate but Equal* (1991), a recounting of events leading to the Supreme Court's 1954 landmark ruling on school desegregation, Sidney Poitier stars as Thurgood Marshall, the future Supreme Court justice who, on behalf of a small black community in South Carolina, squares off on the long-standing injustice of segregation against John W. Davis (Burt Lancaster) in the courtroom of Chief Justice Earl Warren (Richard Kiley).

(Continued)

(Continued)

And finally, don't miss Ken Loach's *Bread and Roses* (2000). Los Angeles organizer Sam Shapiro (Adrien Brody) wants to unionize a local janitorial service, largely composed of illegal immigrants. Without rights, these workers are regularly abused and mistreated for substandard wages. Worker Maya (Pilar Padilla) becomes a key supporter, risking her own position, much to the consternation of sister and fellow employee Rosa (Elpidia Carrillo), who must support a disabled husband and can't afford to lose her job. The conflict between principle and practical reality is deftly explored by Loach, and we learn again that within such sticky, complex issues lie no easy answers. This intense, authentic depiction of our most vulnerable workers' struggle for a decent life only underscores the importance of taking a stand, however daunting.

As most authentic activists will tell you, accepting the status quo is simply not an option.

SOURCE: John Farr, Best Movies by Farr (http://www.bestmoviesbyfarr.com/).

Film Index for Teaching Sociology

Age and Aging

About Schmidt (2002)

American Beauty (1999)

Away from Her (2006)

The Big Chill (1983)

Bubbeh Lee and Me (1996)

The Bucket List (2007)

Cocoon (1985)

Driving Miss Daisy (1989)

The Evening Star (1996)

For Better or Worse (1995)

A Gathering of Old Men (1987)

Grumpier Old Men (1995)

Grumpy Old Men (1993)

Harold and Maude (1971)

The Hours (2002)

How to Make an American Quilt (1995)

I Never Sang for My Father (1970)

Iris (2001)

Jack (1996)

Mrs Dalloway (1997)

Mrs Palfrey at The Claremont (2005)

Nobody's Fool (1994)

On Golden Pond (1981)

A Rumor of Angels (2000)

Salut Victor (1989)

Shirley Valentine (1989)

Strangers in Good Company (1990)

The Sunshine Boys (1975)

Terms of Endearment (1983)

Trip to Bountiful (1985)

Tuesdays with Morrie (1999)

Unforgiven (1992)

Water for Elephants (2011)

The Whales of August (1987)

Documentaries

Aging in America: The Years Ahead (2003)

Beauty before Age (1997)

Complaints of a Dutiful Daughter (1994)

Edie & Thea: A Very Long Engagement (2009)

Eager for Your Kisses: Love and Sex at 95 (2006)

Facing Death (2002)

42 Up (1999)

Number Our Days (1976)

Shameless: The Art of Disability (2006)

Still Doing It: The Intimate Lives of Women over 65 (2004)

Still Kicking: Six Artistic Women of Project Arts &

Longevity (2006)

Whisper: The Women (1989)

Young@Heart (2007)

Assimilation, Immigration, Pluralism, Colonialism

America, America (1963)

A Better Life (2011)

Bhaji on the Beach (1993)

Cabeza de Vaca (1991)

Chocolat (1989)

Coming to America (1988)

Como Era Gostoso o Meu Francês (How Tasty Was My Little Frenchman) (1971)

Crossing Over (2009)

Dirty Pretty Things (2002)

Double Happiness (1995)

El Norte (1983)

The Emerald Forest (1985)

Hotel Rwanda (2004)

In America (2002)

The Man Who Cried (2000)

The Mission (1986)

Mister Johnson (1991)

Moscow on the Hudson (1984)

My Big Fat Greek Wedding (2002)

My Family (1995)

The Namesake (2006)

Outsourced (2006)

Quilombo (1984)

Rabbit-Proof Fence (2002)

Rockford (1999)

Sunshine (1999)

Documentaries

Farmingville (2004)

Los Trabajadores (The Workers) (2003)

The Other Side of Immigration (2009)

Which Way Home (2009)

Work in the Naked City (2009)

The Body

Born on the Fourth of July (1989)

Coming Home (1978)

Death Becomes Her (1992)

G.I. Jane (1997)

Girl, Interrupted (1999)

Mask (1985)

My Left Foot (1989)

The Other Side of the Mountain (1975)

Road to Victory (2007)

Shallow Hal (2001)

Soul Surfer (2011)

Documentaries

Body Image: The Quest for Perfection (2000)

Body Politics (1995)

Fat, Sick and Nearly Dead (2010)

Nappy (2007)

Passion & Power: The

Technology of Orgasm (2007)

Pumping Iron (1977)

Thin (2006)

College Life

American Pie (1999)

American Pie 2 (2001)

Animal House (1978)

Back to School (1986)

Boys and Girls (2000)

Blue Chips (1994)

Breaking Away (1979)

Bring It on Again (2004)

Campus Man (1987)

College (2008)

College Confidential (1960)

DOA: Dead or Alive (2006)

Educating Rita (1983)

Fast Break (1979)

Good Will Hunting (1997)

The Graduate (1967)

Higher Learning (1995)

Horsefeathers (1928)

The House Bunny (2008)

The Human Stain (2003)

Love Story (1970)

Mona Lisa Smile (2003)

The Nutty Professor (1963; 1996)

The Program (1993)

Old School (2003)

Oleanna (1994)

Real Genius (1985)

Revenge of the Nerds (1984)

Revenge of the Nerds II (1987)

Rudy (1993)

School Daze (1988)

The Skulls (2000)

Spring Break (1983)

The Sure Thing (1985)

Van Wilder (2002)

Where the Boys Are (1960)

Where the Boys Are '84 (1984)

With Honors (1994)

Wonder Boys (2000)

Corporate and Organizational Deviance

Boiler Room (2000)

Casino Jack (2010)

Catch Me If You Can (2002)

The China Syndrome (1979)

A Civil Action (1998)

Class Action (1991)

A Constant Gardener (2005)

The Corporation (2003)

Duplicity (2009)

Erin Brockovich (2000)

The Firm (1993)

Fun with Dick and Jane (2005)

Glengarry Glen Ross (1992)

The Hudsucker Proxy (1994)

The Informant! (2009)

The Insider (1999)

Limitless (2011)

Lord of War (2005)

Margin Call (2011)

Michael Clayton (2007)

Owning Mahowny (2003)

The Rainmaker (1997)

Runaway Jury (2003)

She Hate Me (2004)

Syriana (2005)

Thank You for Smoking (2005)

Wall Street (1987)

Wall Street: Money Never Sleeps (2010)

Wall-E (2008)

Documentaries

The Corporation (2003)

Enron: The Smartest Guys in the Room (2005)

Iraq for Sale: The War Profiteers (2006)

Mickey Mouse Monopoly (2001)

Roger & Me (1989)

Crime, Criminology, Criminal Justice

Absence of Malice (1981)

The Accused (1988)

American Gangster (2007)

American Psycho (2000)

American Violet (2008)

...And Justice for All (1979)

Animal Kingdom (2010)

Badlands (1973)

Beautiful Boy (2010)

Bottle Rocket (1996)

Bowling for Columbine (2002)

Boyz n the Hood (1991)

Brooklyn's Finest (2010)

Brubaker (1980)

Casino (1995)

Catch Me If You Can (2002)

Cell 211 (2010)

Chinatown (1974)

A Clockwork Orange (1971)

Clockers (1995)

Crash (2004)

Criminal Justice (1990)

Dead Man Walking (1995)

Deadline (2012)

The Departed (2006)

Double Indemnity (1944)

Eye for an Eye (1996)

Fargo (1996)

Gangs of New York (2002)

Gangster's Paradise: Jerusalema (2010)

The Girl with the Dragon Tattoo (2011)

The Godfather (1972)

Goodfellas (1990)

The Green Mile (1999)

A History of Violence (2005)

Holy Rollers (2010)

In Cold Blood (1967)

J. Edgar (2011)

The Killing Jar (2010)

Man on a Ledge (2012)

Monster (2003)

Monster's Ball (2001)

Natural Born Killers (1994)

No Country for Old Men (2007)

The Outsiders (1983)

The Oxford Murders (2008)

Pathology (2008)

Pulp Fiction (1994)

Reservoir Dogs (1992)

Scarface (1983)

Serpico (1973)

The Shawshank Redemption (1994)

Slumdog Millionaire (2008)

Taken (2008)

Takers (2010)

To Kill a Mockingbird (1962)

The Town (2010)

Training Day (2001)

True Grit (2010)

12 Angry Men (1957; 1997)

Unforgiven (1992)

The Usual Suspects (1995)

We Need to Talk about Kevin (2011)

Winter's Bone (2010)

Zodiac (2007)

Zoot Suit (1981)

Documentaries

America's Brutal Prisons (2006)

Blind Spot: Murder by Women (2000)

Brother's Keeper (1992)

Crips and Bloods: Made in America (2009)

The Execution of Wanda Jean (2002)

Eyes in the Back of Your Head (2003)

The Farm: Angola, USA (1998)

Girlhood (2003)

Girls on the Wall (2010)

A Hard Straight (2004)

Lockdown: Inside America's Prisons (2006)

Mothers of Bedford (2011)

Murder on a Sunday Morning (2001)

No Tomorrow (2011)

Paradise Lost: The Child Murders at Robin Hood Hills (1996)

Paradise Lost 2: Revelations (2000)

Rape in a Small Town: The Florence Holway Story (2004)

The Trials of Darryl Hunt (2005)

Tulia, Texas (2008)

Un Coupable Idéal (Murder on a Sunday Morning) (2001)

What I Want My Words to Do to You: Voices From Inside a Women's Maximum Security Prison (2003)

Who Killed Vincent Chin? (1987)

Culture

After Hours (1985)

American History X (1998)

Apocalypto (2006)

The Body (2001)

Borat: Cultural Learnings of America for Make Benefit Glorious Nation of Kazakhstan (2006)

Crazy Like a Fox (2004)

Daughters of the Dust (1991)

The End of Violence (1997)

Eve's Bayou (1997)

The Gods Must Be Crazy (1980)

I Am Love (2009)

La Misma Luna (Under the Same Moon) (2007)

Local Hero (1983)

Lost in Translation (2003)

Meek's Cutoff (2011)

The Motorcycle Diaries (2004)

My Big Fat Greek Wedding (2002)

Namesake (2006)

The New World (2005)

Not Without My Daughter (1991)

Out of the Holes of the Rocks (2008)

Party Monster (2003)

Rabbit-Proof Fence (2002)

Saving Face (2004)

Scott Pilgrim vs. The World (2010)

A Separation (2011)

Slumdog Millionaire (2008)

The Social Network (2010)

Smoke Signals (1998)

Songcatcher (2000)

The Stoning of Saroya M (2008)

Take Me Home Tonight (2011)

This Is England (2006)

Witness (1985)

Documentaries

Baraka (1992)

Bowling for Columbine (2002)

Consuming Kids: The Commercialization of Kids (2008)

Guns in America (2008)

Do You Speak American? (2004)

The Empty Chair (2003)

Exit through the Gift shop (2010)

Good Hair (2009)

Made in China (2007)

NO! The Rape Documentary (2006)

Paris Is Burning (1990)

Party (2007)

Queer Icon: The Cult of Bette Davis (2009)

Split: A Divided America (2008)

A Tale of Two Hippies (2006)

Voices in Exile (2005)

A Walk to Beautiful (2007)

When We Were Kings (1996)

Deviance

Acts of Worship (2001)

Angus (1995)

Bonnie and Clyde (1967)

Borat: Cultural Learnings of America for Make Benefit Glorious Nation of Kazakhstan (2006)

The Boys in the Band (1970)

Cidade de Deus (City of God) (2002)

Crimes and Misdemeanors (1989)

The Dark Knight Rises (2012)

Edward Scissorhands (1990)

The Elephant Man (1980)

Enter the Void (2009)

The Girl with the Dragon Tattoo (2011)

A Home at the End of the World (2004)

I Love You Phillip Morris (2009)

Kids (1995)

Mask (1985)

Notes on a Scandal (2006)

One Flew over the Cuckoo's Nest (1975)

Party Monster (2003)

Rampart (2012)

Requiem for a Dream (2000)

Shame (2011)

Taxi Driver (1976)

Terri (2011)

Wanderlust (2012)

Documentaries

Cocaine Cowboys (2006)

Garbage Warrior (2007)

Girl Trouble (2004)

Girls on the Wall (2010)

Grass (1999)

The Life of Kevin Carter (2004)

Street Life: Inside America's Gangs (1999)

Very Young Girls (2007)

Ethnic Stratification

Angels and Insects (1996)

Braveheart (1995)

Cry, the Beloved Country (1995)

Gandhi (1982)

High Hopes (1989)

Losing Isaiah (1995)

Los Santos Inocentes (Holy Innocents) (1984)

The Man Who Cried (2000)

Metropolitan (1990)

My Beautiful Laundrette (1985)

Nothing but a Man (1964)

A Passage to India (1984)

Racing with the Moon (1984)

Raining Stones (1993)

Salaam Bombay! (1988)

Sammy and Rosie Get Laid (1987)

Sense and Sensibility (1995)

Six Degrees of Separation (1993)

Trading Places (1983)

White Man's Burden (1995)

Who's Who (1978)

Documentaries

The Color of Fear (1994)

Farmingville (2004)

I Have Never Forgotten You: The Life & Legacy of Simon Wiesenthal (2007)

9 Star Hotel (2007)

Screamers (2006)

Family

Addams Family Values (1993)

Alice Doesn't Live Here Anymore (1974)

American Beauty (1999)

Antwone Fisher (2002)

Baby Mama (2008)

A Better Life (2011)

Big Miracle (2012)

Cheaper by the Dozen (1950; 2003)

A Cool, Dry Place (1998)

Dan in Real Life (2007)

Daughters of Dust (1991)

A Day Without a Mexican (2004)

Dim Sum: A Little Bit of Heart (1985)

Erin Brockovich (2000)

Eulogy (2004)

Europa, Europa (1990)

Extremely Loud and Incredibly Close (2012)

Familia Rodante (Family Rodante) (2004)

The Family Stone (2005)

Far from Heaven (2002)

Father of My Children (2009)

Home for the Holidays (1995)

Germinal (1993)

Guess Who (2005)

Guess Who's Coming to Dinner (1967)

Home for the Holidays (1995)

The Incredibles (2004)

Jerry Maguire (1996)

The Joy Luck Club (1993)

The Kids Are All Right (2010)

Knocked Up (2007)

Kramer vs. Kramer (1979)

Let's Get Married (1960)

Life, Above All (2011)

Life with Father (1947)

Little Miss Sunshine (2006)

Losing Isaiah (1995)

Madea's Big Happy Family (2011)

Magnolia (1999)

Marvin's Room (1996)

Meet the Browns (2008)

Monsoon Wedding (2001)

Monster's Ball (2001)

Moolaadé (2004)

Mrs. Doubtfire (1993)

My Family (1995)

The Namesake (2006)

Ordinary People (1980)

Our Family Wedding (2010)

Real Women Have Curves (2002)

The Royal Tenenbaums (2001)

Rudy (1993)

Running with Scissors (2006)

A Simple Twist of Fate (1994)

Sling Blade (1996)

Soul Food (1997)

The Squid and the Whale (2005)

The Stone Boy (1984)

Used People (1992)

The Virgin Suicides (2000)

Warrior (2011)

The Wedding Banquet (1993)

What's Cooking? (2000)

White Man's Burden (1995)

White Oleander (2002)

Why Did I Get Married? (2007)

Win Win (2011)

Documentaries

Capturing the Friedmans (2003)

Chicks in White Satin (1994)

The Farmer's Wife (1998)

For the Bible Tells Me So (2007)

Love and Diane (2002)

The Motherhood Manifesto (2007)

Treeless Mountain (2008)

Out in Suburbia (1989)

Family Violence

Baby Boy (2001)

Bastard out of Carolina (1996)

Beauty and the Beast (1991)

Black and Blue (1999)

Boys on the Side (1995)

The Burning Bed (1984)

Carousel (1956)

The Color Purple (1985)

A Cry for Help: The Tracey Thurman Story (1989)

Deadly Matrimony (1992)

Double Parked (2000)

Enough (2002)

Fried Green Tomatoes (1991)

Precious (2009)

Radio Flyer (1992)

Sleeping with the Devil (1997)

Sleeping with the Enemy (1991)

This Boy's Life (1993)

Vegas (2009)

Waitress (2007)

What's Love Got to Do with It? (1993)

Documentaries

Abused Women Who Fight Back: The Framingham Eight (1994)

Defending Our Lives (1994)

Hostages at Home (1994)

Safe: Inside a Battered Women's Shelter (2001)

Shifting the Paradigm: From Control to Respect (1999)

Gender/Doing Gender

Albert Nobbs (2011)

The Associate (1996)

Battle of Little Jo (1993)

Birdcage (1996)

Blonde Venus (1932)

The Break Up (2006)

Bus Stop (1956)

College (2008)

Fast & Furious (2009)

Flawless (1999)

Funny Girl (1968)

Hooking Up (2009)

The House Bunny (2008)

The Iron Lady (2012)

Little Sister (1992)

Miss Congeniality (2000)

Mrs. Doubtfire (1993)

Mulan (1998)

Pirates of the Caribbean: At World's End (2007)

Pirates of the Caribbean: The Curse of the Black Pearl (2003)

Pirates of the Caribbean:

Dead Man's Chest (2006)

Pulp Fiction (1994)

Semi-Pro (2008)

Sex and the City (2008)

She's the Man (2006)

Some Like It Hot (1959)

No Strings Attached (2011)

This Means War (2012)

Tootsie (1982)

The Twilight Saga (2008–2011)

Victor/Victoria (1982)

White Chicks (2004)

Yentl (1983)

See also: all the James Bond films

Globalization

Babel (2006)

Blood Diamond (2006)

Children of Men (2006)

The Constant Gardener (2005)

A Day Without a Mexican (2004)

The Descendants (2011)

Dirty Pretty Things (2002)

El Norte (1983)

Green Zone (2010)

The Kite Runner (2007)

La Misma Luna (Under the Same Moon) (2007)

Life, Above All (2010)

Lord of War (2007)

White Material (2009)

Documentaries

Control Room (2004)

The Corporation (2003)

Darfur Now (2007)

Darwin's Nightmare (2004)

Fast Food Nation (2006)

Inside Job (2010)

Iraq for Sale: The War Profiteers (2006)

King Corn (2007)

Life and Debt (2001)

Mardi Gras: Made in China (2005)

Zoned for Slavery (1995)

Health and Health Care

As Good as It Gets (1997)

At First Sight (1999)

The Doctor (1991)

Gattaca (1997)

John Q (2002)

Miss Evers' Boys (1997)

Outbreak (1995)

Passion Fish (1992)

Philadelphia (1993)

Documentaries

The American Experience: The Pill (2003)

Big Bucks, Big Pharma: Marketing Disease & Pushing Drugs (2006)

Deadly Deception: The Mark Hacking Story (2004)

A Healthy Baby Girl (1997)

La Operación (1982)

Trade Secrets: A Moyers Report (2001)

Health Care: Experiencing Illness and/or Disabilities

Boys on the Side (1995)

The Bucket List (2007)

I Am Sam (2001)

Living & Dying (2007)

My Left Foot: The Story of Christy Brown (1989)

One True Thing (1998)

On Golden Pond (1981)

The Other Sister (1999)

My Life Without Me (2003)

Philadelphia (1993)

Regarding Henry (1991)

Terms of Endearment (1983)

What's Eating Gilbert Grape (1993)

Documentaries

Live and Let Go: An American Death (2002)

On Our Own Terms: Moyers on Dying in America

The Suicide Tourist (2007)

Health Care: Mental Health and Substance Abuse

American Gangster (2007)

American Psycho (2000)

As Good as It Gets (1997)

The Basketball Diaries (1995)

A Beautiful Mind (2001)

Benny & Joon (1993)

Black Swan (2010)

Blow (2001)

Charlie Bartlett (2007)

Clean, Shaven (1993)

Clean and Sober (1988)

50 First Dates (2004)

Frances (1982)

Girl, Interrupted (1999)

Harvey (1950)

The Hours (2002)

Iron Weed (1987)

I Am Sam (2001)

Lady Sings the Blues (1972)

Leaving Las Vegas (1995)

Little Miss Sunshine (2006)

One Flew over the Cuckoo's Nest (1975)

Postcards from the Edge (1990)

Proof (2005)

Rachel Getting Married (2008)

Requiem for a Dream (2000)

Running with Scissors (2006)

Shine (1996)

Shock Corridor (1963)

The Snake Pit (1948)

Shutter Island (2010)

The Soloist (2009)

28 Days (2000)

When a Man Loves a
Woman (1994)

Documentaries

Addiction: Why Can't
They Just Stop (2007)

Asylum—A History of the
Mental Institution in
America (1999)

Back from Madness: The
Struggle for Sanity (1990)

Depression out of the
Shadows (2008)

Homeless in Paradise
(2005)

Making a Killing: Philip
Morris, Kraft, and Global
Tobacco (2000)

The Meth Epidemic (2006)

The New Asylums (2005)

A Revolving Door (2007)

The Secret Passage: A
Journey of Black Women
and Depression (2001)

Health Care: Professionals and Institutions

Awakenings (1990)

Critical Care (1997)

Extraordinary Measures
(2010)

Gross Anatomy
(1989)

The Hospital (1971)

House Calls (1978)

One Flew over the
Cuckoo's Nest (1975)

Patch Adams (1998)

Vital Signs (1990)

Documentaries

Selling Sickness (2004)

Sicko (2007)

A Walk to Beautiful (2007)

Health Care: Reproductive Health

Cider House Rules (1999)

Citizen Ruth (1996)

4 Luni, 3 Saptamâni si 2
Zile (4 Months, 3 Weeks,
and 2 Days) (2007)

A Handmaid's Tale (1990)

If These Walls Could Talk
(1996)

Juno (2007)

Knocked Up (2007)

Rambling Rose (1991)

Vera Drake (2004)

Waitress (2007)

Documentaries

The Abortion Diaries (2005)

Lake of Fire (2006)

La Operación (1982)

High School

American Graffiti (1973)

Angus (1995)

The Blackboard Jungle (1955)

Breakfast Club (1985)

Bring It On (2000)

Can't Buy Me Love (1987)

Can't Hardly Wait (1998)

College (2008)

Cooley High (1975)

Dazed and Confused (1993)

Easy A (2010)

Election (1999)

Fame (1980)

Fast Times at Ridgemont High (1982)

Flirting (1992)

Friday Night Lights (2004)

Get Real (1999)

Heathers (1989)

High School Musical (2006)

Just One of the Guys (1985)

Mean Girls (2004)

Mr. Holland's Opus (1995)

My Bodyguard (1980)

Napoleon Dynamite (2004)

Pretty in Pink (1986)

Risky Business (1983)

Rushmore (1999)

She's All That (1999)

Sixteen Candles (1984)

Stand and Deliver (1988)

Terri (2011)

To Sir with Love (1967)

The Virgin Suicides (2000)

Documentary

Hoop Dreams (1994)

Life Course

Another Year (2010)

Barney's Version (2010)

The Curious Case of Benjamin Button (2008)

Fried Green Tomatoes (1991)

Going in Style (1979)

Gran Torino (2008)

Greenberg (2010)

The Human Stain (2003)

The Illusionist (2010)

Please Give (2010)

The Straight Story (1997)

Tea with Mussolini (1999)

Tell Me a Riddle (1980)

The Tree of Life (2011)

Waking Ned Devine (1999)

Men and Masculinity

Affliction (1997)

American Beauty (1999)

American Gangster (2007)

American History X (1998)

American Pie (1999)

The Benchwarmers (2006)

Breakin' All the Rules (2004)

City Slickers (1991)

College (2008)

The Cowboys (1972)

Death of a Salesman (1985)

The Dilemma (2011)

Fight Club (1999)

40 Days and 40 Nights (2002)

40-Year-Old Virgin (2005)

Full Monty (1997)

Ghost Rider: Spirit of Vengeance (2012)

The Godfather (1972)

The Godfather: Part II (1974)

The Godfather: Part III (1990)

Gran Torino (2008)

The Grey (2012)

The Hangover (2009)

The Hangover Part II (2011)

He Got Game (1998)

I Love You, Man (2009)

Inside Man (2006)

Knocked Up (2007)

Lars and the Real Girl (2007)

Monster's Ball (2001)

Rio Bravo (1959)

Road to Victory (2007)

Robin Hood (2010)

The Searchers (1956)

Superbad (2007)

Take Shelter (2011)

Take the Lead (2006)

3:10 to Yuma (2007)

Wall Street (1987)

White Chicks (2004)

The Wrestler (2008)

Documentaries

Boys Will Be Men (2002)

Hip-Hop: Beyond Beats and Rhymes (2006)

Hoop Dreams (1994)

Men's Lives (1974)

Michael Kimmel on Gender (2008)

Paris Is Burning (1990)

Tough Guise: Violence, Media & the Crisis in Masculinity (1999)

White Scripts and Black Supermen (2011)

Wrestling with Manhood (2002)

Mothers and Mothering

Almost Famous (2000)

Baby Boom (1987)

Chocolat (2000)

The Good Mother (1988)

The Grifters (1990)

In America (2002)

The Joy Luck Club (1993)

Little Man Tate (1991)

Mommie Dearest (1981)

Mother (1996)

Mother and Child (2009)

Not Without My Daughter (1991)

Ordinary People (1980)

The Positively True Adventures of the Alleged Texas Cheerleader-Murdering Mom (1993)

Serial Mom (1994)

Steel Magnolias (1989)

Stepmom (1998)

Surviving My Mother (2007)

Terms of Endearment (1983)

Todo Sobre Mi Madre (All About My Mother) (1999)

What's Eating Gilbert Grape (1993)

Documentaries

Ima Hozeret Habayta
(A Working Mom)
(2008)

The Motherhood
Manifesto
(2007)

The Mother's House (2005)

Refrigerator Mothers (2003)

Politics and Political Economy

Advise & Consent (1962)

All the King's Men
(1949)

All the President's Men
(1976)

The American President
(1995)

The Best Man (1964)

Bob Roberts (1992)

Bobby (2006)

Bulworth (1998)

The Candidate (1972)

Che: Part One (2008)

Che: Part Two (2008)

Citizen Cane (1941)

Dave (1993)

Dr. Strangelove, or
How I Learned to Stop
Worrying and Love the
Bomb (1964)

Fail Safe (1964)

Frost/Nixon (2008)

The Ghost Writer (2010)

Good Night, and Good
Luck (2005)

La Muerte de un
Burócrata (Death of a
Bureaucrat) (1966)

The Manchurian
Candidate (1962; 2004)

Man of the Year (2006)

Meet John Doe (1941)

Mr. Smith Goes to
Washington (1939)

Nixon (1995)

Primary Colors (1998)

Reds (1981)

Seduction of Joe Tynan
(1979)

Seven Days in May (1964)

State of the Union (1948)

Three Days of the Condor
(1975)

Viva Zapata! (1952)

W (2008)

Wag the Dog (1997)

Documentaries

American Blackout
(2006)

The Big One (1997)

Casino Jack and the
United States of Money
(2010)

Inside Job (2010)

Farenheit 911

14 Women (2007)

No End in Sight (2007)

Please Vote for Me (2008)

"Surviving the Good Times:
A Moyers Report" (2000)

The Tilman Story (2010)

The Yes Men Fix the
World (2009)

The War Room (1993)

Poverty and Homelessness

Cidade de Deus (City of
God) (2002)

Dark Days (2000)

The Fisher King (1991)

God Bless the Child (1988)

Joyeux Calvaire (1996)

Kicking It (2008)

Metal (1999)

The Pursuit of Happyness
(2006)

The Soloist (2009)

With Honors (1994)

Documentaries

America's War on Poverty (1995)

Life below the Line: The World Poverty Crisis (2007)

1 More Hit (2007)

Poverty Outlaw (1997)

Stairway from Hell (2010)

Strong Bodies Fight (2010)

Prejudice and Discrimination

American Violet (2008)

Bad Day at Black Rock (1954)

Black Like Me (1964)

Boys Don't Cry (1999)

The Defiant Ones (1958)

The Diary of Anne Frank (1959)

Do the Right Thing (1989)

Far from Heaven (2002)

The Help (2011)

Home of the Brave (1949)

Il Giardino dei Finzi-Contini (The Garden of the Finzi-Continis) (1970)

Intruder in the Dust (1949)

Jungle Fever (1991)

Map of the Human Heart (1993)

No Way Out (1950)

Nothing but a Man (1964)

A Passage to India (1984)

Rabbit-Proof Fence (2002)

Schindler's List (1993)

This Is England (2006)

To Kill a Mockingbird (1962)

White Man's Burden (1995)

Documentaries

Bowling for Columbine (2002)

"Frontline: A Class Divided" (1985)

Prom Night in Mississippi (2009)

Race and Ethnicity

American History X (1998)

Babel (2006)

Bamboozled (2000)

Boyz n the Hood (1991)

Bread & Roses (2000)

A Bronx Tale (1993)

Come See the Paradise (1991)

The Constant Gardener (2005)

Corina, Corina (1994)

Crash (2004)

Cry, the Beloved Country (1995)

Dangerous Minds (1995)

A Day Without a Mexican (2004)

Dim Sum: A Little Bit of Heart (1985)

Dirty Pretty Things (2002)

Do the Right Thing (1989)

A Dry White Season (1989)

Europa, Europa (1990)

Finding Forrester (2000)

Get on the Bus (1996)

Glory (1989)

Guess Who's Coming to Dinner (1967)

The Help (2011)

Hotel Rwanda (2004)

In My Country (2004)

La Misma Luna (Under the Same Moon) (2007)

Land of Plenty (2004)

Maid in America (1982)

Maid in Manhattan (2002)

Maria Full of Grace (2004)

Malcolm X

Mi Vida Loca (1993)

Miss Evers' Boys (1997)

Mississippi Burning (1988)

Mississippi Masala (1991)

My Family (1995)

The Namesake (2006)

Our Family Wedding (2010)

Once We Were Warriors (1994)

187 (1997)

Panther (1995)

Rabbit-Proof Fence (2002)

School Daze (1988)

Secrets & Lies (1996)

Stand and Deliver (1988)

Strictly Ballroom (1992)

Taxi Driver (1976)

The Wedding (1998)

The Wedding Banquet (1993)

West Side Story (1961)

What's Cooking (2000)

A World Apart (1988)

Zebrahead (1992)

Zoot Suit (1981)

Documentaries

Black Is . . . Black Ain't (1994)

Crips and Bloods: Made in America (2008)

Crossing Arizona (2006)

Ethnic Notions (1986)

Farmingville (2004)

Free Indeed (1995)

Incident at Oglala (1992)

Journeys in Black: Jamie Foxx (2005)

Los Trabajadores (The Workers) (2003)

Mexico: A Death in the Desert (2004)

Surviving the Good Times: A Moyers Report (2000)

Troubled Harvest (1990)

Understanding Race (1999)

Walking the Line (2005)

What's Race Got to Do with It? (2006)

Who Killed Vincent Chin? (1987)

Race/Class/Gender Intersectionality

Bend It Like Beckham (2002)

Casa de los Babys (2003)

The Color Purple (1985)

Daughters of the Dust (1991)

Heaven & Earth (1993)

Higher Learning (1995)

Jungle Fever (1991)

Just Another Girl on the I.R.T. (1992)

The Long Walk Home (1990)

Maria Full of Grace (2004)

Menace II Society (1993)

Mississippi Masala (1991)

Monster's Ball (2001)

187 (1997)

Set It Off (1996)

Skin Deep (1989)

Whale Rider (2002)

White Man's Burden (1995)

Documentaries

The Letter: An American Town and "The Somali Invasion" (2003)

Mickey Mouse Monopoly (2001)

U People (2009)

What's Race Got to Do with It? (2006)

Religion

Agnes of God (1985)

The Apostle (1997)

Avatar (2009)

The Body (2001)

Brother Sun, Sister Moon (1972)

Bruce Almighty (2003)

The Chosen (1981)

The Da Vinci Code (2006)

Der Himmel Über Berlin (Wings of Desire) (1987)

Dogma (1999)

Doubt (2008)

Elmer Gantry (1960)

The Exorcist (1973)

Harry Potter and the Goblet of Fire (2005)

The Last Temptation of Christ (1988)

The Mission (1986)

Not Without My Daughter (1991)

Of Gods and Men (2011)

The Prince of Egypt (1998)

Sister Act (1992)

Sister Act 2: Back in the Habit (1993)

Stigmata (1999)

Documentaries

Baraka (1992)

Jesus Camp (2006)

A Jihad for Love (2007)

New Muslim Cool (2009)

Religulous (2008)

Sister Rose's Passion (2006)

Trembling before G-d (2001)

With God on Our Side (2004)

Science Fiction

The Adjustment Bureau (2011)

Alien (1979)

Aliens (1986)

Back to the Future Part II (1989)

Battle: Los Angeles (2011)

The Beast from 20,000 Fathoms (1953)

Beneath the Planet of the Apes (1970)

Black Hole (1980)

Blade Runner (1982)

Born in Flames (1983)

A Clockwork Orange (1972)

Demolition Man (1993)

Destination Moon (1950)

Fantastic Voyage (1966)

Forbidden Planet (1956)

The Hunger Games (2012)

Inception (2010)

The Incredible Shrinking Man (1957)

Jurassic Park (1993)

The Matrix (1999)

Monsters (2010)

On the Beach (1960)

Planet of the Apes (1968)

RoboCop (1987)

Soylent Green (1973)

Star Trek: The Motion Picture (1979)

Star Trek II: The Wrath of Khan (1982)

Star Trek IV: The Voyage Home (1986)

Star Wars (1977)

Star Wars: The Empire Strikes Back (1980)

Star Wars: Return of the Jedi (1983)

Them! (1954)

Total Recall (1990)

2001: A Space Odyssey (1968)

Voyage to the Bottom of the Sea (1961)

Waterworld (1995)

Sexuality and Gender

The Adventures of Priscilla, Queen of the Desert (1994)

Before Night Falls (2000)

Bliss (1997)

Boys Don't Cry (1999)

Breakfast on Pluto (2005)

Brokeback Mountain (2005)

The Crying Game (1992)

If These Walls Could Talk 2 (2000)

In & Out (1997)

The Incredibly True Adventure of Two Girls in Love (1995)

Kinsey (2004)

M. Butterfly (1993)

Ma Vie en Rose (1997)

Milk (2008)

Normal (2003)

Shame (2011)

Stonewall (1995)

Transamerica (2005)

Torchsong Trilogy (1988)

The Watermelon Woman (1996)

Documentaries

The Celluloid Closet (1995)

I Was a Teenage Feminist (2005)

Juggling Gender/Still Juggling (1992/2008)

Last Call at Maud's (1993)

Out of the Past: The Struggle for Gay and Lesbian Rights in America (1997)

Paris Is Burning (1990)

Small Town Gay Bar (2006)

The Times of Harvey Milk (1984)

Transgeneration (2005)

Tongues Untied (1989)

Trembling before G-d (2001)

Sex Work(ers)

American Gigolo (1980)

Breakfast at Tiffany's (1961)

Claire Dolan (1998)

Dangerous Beauty (1998)

Irma la Douce (1963)

The Man from Elysian Fields (2001)

Mighty Aphrodite (1995)

My Own Private Idaho (1991)

Pretty Baby (1978)

Pretty Woman (1990)

Midnight Cowboy (1969)

Priceless (2006)

Soap Girl (2002)

Sweet Charity (1969)

Working Girls (1986)

Documentaries

Born into Brothels: Calcutta's Red Light Kids (2004)

The Good Woman of Bangkok (1991)

Live Nude Girls Unite! (2000)

Not a Love Story: A Film about Pornography (1981)

Sacrifice (2000)

Shinjuku Boys (1995)

Sisters and Daughters Betrayed (2002)

Trading Women (2003)

Social Class and Inequality

Amar te duele (2002)

American Psycho (2000)

Attica (1980)

Born Yesterday (1950)

Bread & Roses (2000)

The Color Purple (1985)

Dirty Dancing (1987)

Educating Rita (1983)

8 Mile (2002)

Gosford Park (2001)

Grapes of Wrath (1940)

The Greatest Game Ever Played (2005)

The Great Gatsby (1974)

Hey Hey It's Esther Blueburger (2008)

Jane Eyre (2011)

The Ice Storm (1997)

Inventing the Abbotts (1997)

La Règle du Jeu (The Rules of the Game) (1939)

Le Charme Discret de la Bourgeoisie (The Discreet Charm of the Bourgeoisie) (1973)

Matewan (1987)

Miss Pettigrew Lives for a Day (2008)

My Fair Lady (1964)

The Nanny Diaries (2007)

Native Son (1986)

Norma Rae (1979)

Please Give (2010)

Pride & Prejudice (2005)

The Pursuit of Happyness (2006)

Pygmalion (1938)

Reds (1981)

The Remains of the Day (1993)

Room at the Top (1959)

Save the Last Dance (2001)

Six Degrees of Separation (1993)

The Soloist (2009)

Step Up (2006)

The Swimmer (1968)

Trading Places (1983)

The War (1994)

Documentaries

Morristown: In the Air and Sun (2007)

The Overspent American (2004)

People Like Us: Social Class in America (2001)

Unnatural Causes: Is Inequality Making Us Sick? (2008)

Social Class: Private Schools

The Bells of St. Mary's (1945)

Chasing Holden (2001)

Dead Poets Society (1989)

The Emperor's Club (2002)

Finding Forrester (2000)

Goodbye, Mr. Chips (1969)

The History Boys (2006)

The Lords of Discipline (1983)

Outside Providence (1999)

School Ties (1992)

Taps (1981)

Social Interaction

Annie Hall (1977)

The Big Chill (1983)

The Break-Up (2006)

Clerks (1994)

The Graduate (1967)

Harold and Maude (1971)

The King's Speech (2010)

Lars and the Real Girl (2007)

Midnight in Paris (2011)

Open Water (2003)

Pretty Woman (1990)

Sisterhood of the Traveling Pants (2005)

Six Degrees of Separation (1993)

12 Angry Men (1957)

35 Shots of Rum (2010)

When Harry Met Sally . . . (1989)

Who's Afraid of Virginia Woolf? (1966)

Social Movements and Social Change

Bloody Sunday (2002)

Butterfly (1982)

Deadly Deception (1987)

Gandhi (1982)

In the Name of the People (2000)

Iron-Jawed Angels (2004)

Kilomètre Zéro (Kilometer Zero) (2003)

Love and Anarchy (1974)

Lumumba (2000)

Made in Dagenham (2010)

Making a Killing (2002)

Malcolm X (1992)

Matewan (1987)

Medium Cool (1969)

Romero (1989)

Salt of the Earth (1954)

The Take (2007)

Documentaries

Amandla! A Revolution in Four Part Harmony (2002)

At the River I Stand (1993)

Before Stonewall (1984)

Berkeley in the Sixties (1990)

Daisy Bates: First Lady of Little Rock (2010)

Eyes on the Prize: America's Civil Rights Movement 1954–1985 (1987)

The FBI's War on Black America (1990)

The Fight in the Fields: Cesar Chavez and the Farmworkers' Struggle (1997)

War and Gender

War and Violence

In Darkness (2012)

The Killing Fields (1984)

Lacombe Lucien (1974)

The Last of the Mohicans (1992)

La Vita è Bella (Life Is Beautiful) (1997)

The Longest Day (1962)

MASH (1974)

Master and Commander:

The Far Side of the World (2003)

No Man's Land (2001)

Oh! What a Lovely War (1969)

Paths of Glory (1957)

Patton (1970)

The Pianist (2002)

Platoon (1986)

Red Tails (2012)

Regeneration (1997)

Ride with the Devil (1999)

Salvador (1986)

Saving Private Ryan (1998)

Schindler's List (1993)

The Thin Red Line (1998)

Three Kings (1999)

Welcome to Sarajevo (1997)

Documentaries

Darfur Now (2007)

Inheritance (2008)

Pray the Devil Back to Hell (2009)

Standard Operating

Procedure (2008)

Taxi to the Dark Side (2007)

Restrepo (2010)

Women and Gender

Anchorman: The Legend of Ron Burgundy (2004)

Antonia's Line (1995)

Bagdad Cafe (1990)

Because I Said So (2007)

Bend It Like Beckham (2002)

Bhaji on the Beach (1993)

The Birdcage (1996)

The Break-Up (2006)

Calendar Girls (2003)

Chocolat (1989; 2000)

The Circle (2004)

Girlfight (2000)

The Girl with the Dragon Tattoo (2011)

The Handmaid's Tale (1990)

Haywire (2012)

Ice Princess (2005)

The Incredibly True Adventure of Two Girls in Love (1995)

In Her Shoes (2005)

I've Heard the Mermaids Singing (1987)

Just Like a Woman (1992)

Made in Dagenham (2010)

The Magdalene Sisters (2002)

Material Girls (2006)

Mean Girls (2004)

Mrs. Doubtfire (1993)

Mujeres al Borde de un Ataque de Nervios (Women on the Verge of a Nervous Breakdown) (1988)

Mulan (1998)

Muriel's Wedding (1994)

North Country (2005)

Personal Velocity: Three Portraits (2002)

Real Women Have Curves (2002)

Shirley Valentine (1989)

Snow Flower and the Secret Fan (2011)

The Stepford Wives (1975; 2004)

Strangers in Good
Company (1990)

Thelma & Louise (1991)

Whale Rider (2002)

What Women Want
(2000)

White Chicks (2004)

Documentary

Michael Kimmel on Gender (2008)

Women and Work

Bread & Roses (2000)

Cheaper by the Dozen (2003)

The Devil Wears Prada
(2006)

Fast Food Fast Women
(2000)

Nine to Five (1980)

Norma Rae (1979)

North Country (2005)

Silkwood (1983)

Sunshine Cleaning
(2008)

Women Buddy Films

Alice Doesn't Live Here
Anymore (1974)

Bagdad Cafe (1990)

Beaches (1988)

Bridesmaids (2011)

Coup de Foudre (Entre
Nous) (1983)

Crimes of the Heart
(1986)

Desert Hearts (1985)

Divine Secrets of the Ya-Ya
Sisterhood (2002)

Dreamgirls (2006)

The First Wives Club
(1996)

Julia (1977)

A League of Their Own
(1992)

Leaving Normal (1992)

Mystic Pizza (1988)

Nine to Five (1980)

Passion Fish (1992)

Personal Best (1982)

The Prize Winner of
Defiance, Ohio (2005)

Shirley Valentine (1989)

Sisterhood of the Traveling
Pants (2005)

The Turning Point (1977)

The Women (2008)

Women's Sexuality

About Schmidt (2002)

Ad Ogni Costo (Grand
Slam) (1968)

American Gigolo (1980)

Antonia's Line (1995)

As Good as It Gets (1997)

The Banger Sisters (2002)

Being Julia (2004)

The Bliss of Mrs. Blossom
(1968)

Boomerang (1992)

Bull Durham (1988)

Calendar Girls
(2003)

A Change of Seasons
(1980)

Cocoon (1985)

Daughters of the Dust
(1991)

Desert Hearts (1985)

A Dirty Shame (2004)

The Evening Star (1996)

The Graduate (1967)

The Girl with a Dragoon Tattoo (2011)

Grandma's Boy (2006)

Grumpy Old Men (1993)

Harold and Maude (1971)

How Stella Got Her Groove Back (1998)

Innocence (2004)

Ladies in Lavender (2004)

La Pianiste (The Piano Player) (2001)

La Vie Devant Soi (Madame Rosa) (1977)

The Madness of King George (1994)

Meet the Fockers (2004)

Moonstruck (1987)

Must Love Dogs (2005)

The Opposite of Sex (1998)

The Piano (1993)

Roman Spring of Mrs. Stone (2003)

Sammy and Rosie Get Laid (1987)

Saving Face (2004)

Shirley Valentine (1989)

Something's Gotta Give (2003)

Songcatcher (2000)

The Squid and the Whale (2005)

Steel Magnolias (1989)

A Streetcar Named Desire (1951)

A Summer Place (1959)

Sunset Blvd. (1950)

Terms of Endearment (1983)

Thomas Crown Affair (1999)

A Touch of Class (1973)

Under the Tuscan Sun (2003)

Unfaithful (2002)

An Unmarried Woman (1978)

Wedding Crashers (2005)

Witches of Eastwick (1987)

Documentaries

Edie & Thea: A Very Long Engagement (2009)

Our Bodies, Our Minds (2001)

The Right to Femininity (2004)

Still Doing It: The Intimate Lives of Women over 65 (2004)

Work and the Workplace

Blue Collar (1978)

Bread & Roses (2000)

Coyote Ugly (2000)

Daddy Day Care (2003)

The Devil Wears Prada (2006)

Employee of the Month (2006)

The Firm (1993)

Freedom Writers (2007)

Gigante (2009)

Glengarry Glen Ross (1992)

Horrible Bosses (2011)

Michael Clayton (2007)

Modern Times (1936)

Nine to Five (1980)

Norma Rae (1979)

On the Waterfront (1954)

The Pursuit of Happyness (2006)

10,000 Black Men Named George (2002)

Social Work (2010)

Documentaries

American Dream
(1990)

Life and Times of Rosie
the Riveter (1980)

Roger & Me
(1989)

Work in Restaurants

Alice Doesn't Live Here
Anymore (1974)

As Good as It Gets (1997)

Cocktail (1988)

Five Easy Pieces (1970)

Frankie and Johnny
(1991)

Heavy (1995)

Home Fries (1998)

It Could Happen to You
(1994)

Little Man Tate (1991)

Mystic Pizza (1988)

Nurse Betty (2000)

Office Space (2000)

Pay It Forward (2000)

Pleasantville (1998)

Return to Me (2000)

Thelma & Louise (1991)

Untamed Heart (1993)

Waiting (2005)

Waitress (2007)

The Wedding Singer
(1998)

Thanks to the following for contributing to this list of films:

For the constant flow of film recommendations from our colleagues on the Sociologist
for Women in Society (SWS) listserv.

American Society of Criminology

Introduction to Criminology Syllabi Collection

Denise Paquette Boots (University of Texas at Dallas) and William Reese (Augusta State
University), editors: Recommended Media List

Editor: Rick J. Scheidt, Ph.D.

http://apadiv20.phhp.ufl.edu/cinema.htm

Criminal Justice film site:

http://www.mastersincriminaljustice.com/blog/2008/top-100-crime-movies-of-all
-time/

War films:

http://www.channel4.com/film/newsfeatures/microsites/W/greatest_warfilms/
results/5-1.html

Guide to documentary and independent films:

http://www.bullfrogfilms.com/index.html

And to the following individuals for their contribution of film titles: Michelle Bemiller, Kim Cook, Mark Cox, Kristen DeVall, Erin Farley, Katie Gay, Wendy Grove, Michael Kimmel, Christina Lanier, Jess MacDonald, Mike Maume, Diane Moran, Abigail Reiter, Miranda Reiter, John Rice, Rachel Schneider, Angela Wadsworth.

Photo Credits

Photo 2.1a, page 35: DANCES WITH WOLVES, Kevin Costner, Graham Greene, 1990. ©Orion Pictures/ Courtesy: Everett Collection.

Photo 2.1b, page 35: AVATAR, Zoe Saldana (right), 2009. TM & Copyright ©20th Century Fox. All rights reserved/Courtesy Everett Collection.

Photo 2.2, page 45: THE MATRIX, Laurence Fishburne, 1999. ©Warner Bros./ Courtesy: Everett Collection.

Photo 3.1, page 78: DANGEROUS MINDS, Michelle Pfeiffer, 1995. ©Buena Vista Pictures/courtesy Everett Collection.

Photo 4.1, page 110: CRASH, Thandie Newton, Matt Dillon, 2005, ©Lions Gate/ courtesy Everett Collection.

Photo 5.1, page 137: TERMINATOR 2: JUDGEMENT DAY, Arnold Schwarzenegger, 1991, ©TriStar/courtesy Everett Collection, TR2 162, Photo by: Everett Collection (81269).

Photo 5.2, page 170: TRANSAMERICA, Felicity Huffman, 2005, ©IFC Films/ Courtesy Everett Collection.

Photo 6.1, page 198: MR. MOM, Michael Keaton (center), 1983, ©MGM/courtesy Everett Collection, MRMM 003, Photo by: Everett Collection (34212).

Photo 7.1, page 220: THE DARK KNIGHT, Heath Ledger, Christian Bale, 2008. ©Warner Bros./Courtesy Everett Collection.

Photo 8.1, page 264: ROAD TO EL DORADO, The Chief, Miguel, 2000. ©DreamWorks/courtesy Everett Collection.

Photo 8.2, page 290: GRAN TORINO, from left: Clint Eastwood, Bee Vang, Brooke Chia Thao, Chee Thao, Ahney Her, 2008. ©Warner Bros./Courtesy Everett Collection.

Photo 9.1, page 307: DOUBT, from left: Meryl Streep, Philip Seymour Hoffman, 2008. ©Miramax/courtesy Everett Collection.

Photo 9.2, page 351: JARHEAD, 2005, ©Universal/courtesy Everett Collection.

Photo 10.1, page 381: SLUMDOG MILLIONAIRE, from left: Dev Patel, Anil Kapoor, 2008. ©Fox Searchlight/courtesy Everett Collection.

Photo 11.1, page 419: THE LONG WALK HOME, Whoopi Goldberg, Lexi Faith Randall, 1990, ©Miramax/courtesy Everett Collection.

Photo 11.2, page 426: MILK, Sean Penn, 2008. ©Focus Features/Courtesy Everett Collection.

About the Editors

Jean-Anne Sutherland is an assistant professor of sociology at the University of North Carolina Wilmington, where she teaches courses in Introduction to Sociology, Gender and Society, Sociological Theory, Public Sociology, Social Psychology, and Sociology through Film. Her research spans two areas: the sociology of mothering and sociology through film. She has published work on mothering in *Sociology Compass*, *The Encyclopedia of Motherhood*, and *Mama Ph.D.: Women Write about Motherhood and Academic Life* (Rutgers University Press, 2008). She is currently working on a project analyzing the representations of feminism in film (1970–present). Jean-Anne also authors a quarterly article on film and culture in *TILT* (*Therapeutic Innovations in Light of Technology*) magazine (http://www.online therapymagazine.com/).

Kathryn Feltey is an associate professor at the University of Akron in the Department of Sociology, where she teaches Qualitative Methods, Sociology of Gender, College Teaching of Sociology, and Sociology through Film. Her areas of research include homeless women and children, violence against women, and the experiences of settler and colonized women in nineteenth-century North America. She is the editor of the Gender Section of the online journal *Sociology Compass*.

About the Contributors

Carleen R. Basler is an assistant professor of sociology and American studies at Amherst College. She completed her BA at the University of California, Los Angeles, and her PhD at Yale University. Her teaching and research are primarily concerned with race and ethnicity, political identity, social stratification, and social movements. Dr. Basler is a Mexican American who splits her time between residences in Amherst, Massachusetts, and Los Angeles, California.

Mary K. Bloodsworth-Lugo is a professor of critical culture, gender, and race studies at Washington State University. She has published in the areas of race, gender, and sexuality; post-9/11 discourse and cultural production; film and U.S. popular culture; and contemporary continental social and political philosophy. In addition to journal articles, Bloodsworth-Lugo is author of *In-Between Bodies: Sexual Difference, Race, and Sexuality* (2007); coeditor of *A New Kind of Containment: "The War on Terror," Race, and Sexuality,* with Carmen R. Lugo-Lugo (2009); coauthor of *Animating Difference: Race, Gender, and Sexuality in Contemporary Films for Children,* with C. Richard King and Carmen R. Lugo-Lugo (2010); and coauthor of *Containing (Un)American Bodies: Race, Sexuality, and Post-9/11 Constructions of Citizenship,* with Carmen R. Lugo-Lugo (2010).

David Boyns is an associate professor of sociology at California State University at Northridge. He studies general social theory, cultural sociology, media studies, the sociology of deviance, and the sociology of emotions. He has published on such topics as sociological theory, the emotional dynamics of the self, social construction processes in virtual worlds, the sociology of deviance, and the sociology of education. His current research investigates the human-technology interface, media experience and everyday life, and the sociology of wellness and creativity.

Robert C. Bulman is a professor of sociology at Saint Mary's College of California. He received his BA in sociology from the University of California at Santa Cruz in 1989 and his PhD in sociology from the University of California at Berkeley in 1999. His areas of expertise include the sociology of education, the sociology of adolescence, the sociology of culture, and the sociology of film. He has published a book on the depiction of high schools and adolescents in Hollywood films—*Hollywood Goes to High School: Cinema, Schools, and American Culture* (Worth Publishers, 2005).

Valerie J. Callanan, PhD, is an assistant professor in the Department of Sociology at the University of Akron. She specializes in corrections, suicide, and media and public opinion of crime. She is the author of *Feeding the Fear of Crime: Crime-Related Media and Support for Three-Strikes* (New York: LFB Scholarly Press, 2005). Her research has been published in *Crime and Delinquency, Feminist Criminology, Journal of Criminal Justice, Policing & Society, Sex Roles, Gender Issues*, and *Suicide & Life-threatening Behavior*.

Janet Cosbey is a Professor Emerita of Sociology at Eastern Illinois University, Charleston, Illinois, where she still teaches part time. She is also an adjunct professor at the University of Indianapolis, where she teaches for the Center for Aging and Community in the School for Adult Learning and in the Social Sciences Department. She teaches courses on aging, gerontology, family, and gender. She has published articles in *Teaching Sociology* and several gerontology journals.

Harry F. Dahms (PhD, New School for Social Research, 1993) is an associate professor of sociology and an associate director of the Center for the Study of Social Justice at the University of Tennessee, Knoxville; an affiliated faculty member at the University of Innsbruck, Austria; and the editor of *Current Perspectives in Sociology*. Previously, he taught at Florida State University and at the University of Göttingen, Germany. He has published articles in *Sociological Theory, Current Perspectives in Social Theory, Soziale Welt, International Journal of Politics*, and *Culture and Society*, in addition to numerous book chapters and encyclopedia entries. Book publications: *The Vitality of Critical Theory* (2011); as editor: *Transformations of Capitalism: Economy, Society, and the State in Modern Times* (2000); in the Current Perspectives in Social Theory series: *Globalization between the Cold War and Neo-imperialism* (2006); *No Social Science without Critical Theory* (2008); *Nature, Knowledge, and Negation* (2009); *Theorizing the Dynamics of Social Processes* (with Lawrence Hazelrigg, 2010); *The Diversity of Social Theories* (2011). Among other projects, he is currently working on a book manuscript to be published in 2012, entitled *Modern Society as Artifice: Theorizing the Dynamics of Alienation, Anomie, and the Protestant Ethic* (Ashgate).

James J. Dowd holds the rank of Professor of Sociology at the University of Georgia. He studied sociology at St. Peter's College (BS), the University of Maryland (MA), and the University of Southern California (PhD). He regularly teaches Introduction to Sociology, as well as courses on culture, social theory, and the military. He has taught Sociology in Film for over 15 years, and has published a number of papers having to do with films and the film industry in journals such as *Teaching Sociology, Current Perspectives in Social Theory*, and *Sociological Perspectives*.

Karla A. Erickson is an associate professor of sociology at Grinnell College. She is currently finishing her next book, entitled *How We Die Now: Intimacy, Labor and the Social Organization of Dying* (Temple University Press, 2013), which examines the interactions among staff, residents, their families, and administrators in long-term care facilities. In 2009, Erickson's study of gender, sociability, and connection in a Tex-Mex restaurant, entitled *The Hungry Cowboy: Selling Service and Smiles, and Community in a Neighborhood Restaurant*, was published by the University Press of Mississippi. She coedited *Feminist Waves, Feminist Generations: Life Histories of a Movement* with Hokulani Aikau and Jennifer Pierce (University of Minnesota, 2007). Erickson received her PhD in American studies and feminist studies from the University of Minnesota in 2004, her MA in liberal studies from Hamline University in 1998, and her BA in English and women's studies from Illinois Wesleyan University in 1995.

Rebecca J. Erickson is a professor in the Department of Sociology at the University of Akron. Dr. Erickson's social psychological research on the experience and management of emotion now spans 22 years. During this time, she has examined how emotion processes affect the mental and physical health of individuals both at home and at work. Her most recent investigation is supported by a grant from the National Science Foundation and focuses on the occupational experiences of registered nurses and how the emotional demands of the nursing profession impact nurses' health.

John Farr started his career as an ad executive, rising at Ogilvy & Mather to senior partner. After nearly 20 years on Madison Avenue, Farr departed to pursue his first love: identifying and promoting the best of film—old and new, domestic and foreign. What started as a popular local movie club and newspaper column is now a multimedia enterprise called Best Movies by Farr. Farr's mission is to demystify great films, applying engrained selling techniques to promote the best movies available, particularly those prone to being over-looked or forgotten. His website, bestmoviesbyfarr.com, lists close to 1,500 timeless film titles on DVD, searchable by genre, mood, decade, actor, director, and even country.

Henry A. Giroux holds the Global TV Network Chair in English and cultural studies at McMaster University in Canada. His most recent books include *America on the Edge* (2006); *Beyond the Spectacle of Terrorism* (2006), *Stormy Weather: Katrina and the Politics of Disposability* (2006), *The University in Chains: Confronting the Military-Industrial-Academic Complex* (2007), and *Against the Terror of Neoliberalism: Politics beyond the Age of Greed* (2008). His newest book is *Youth in a Suspect Society: Democracy and the Politics of Disposability* (2009).

Susan Searls Giroux is an associate dean of humanities and an associate professor of English and cultural studies at McMaster University in Hamilton, Ontario. Her most recent book, *Between Race and Reason: Violence, Intellectual Responsibility, and the University to Come* (Stanford University Press), won the prestigious Gary A. Olson Award for Best Book Published in Rhetoric and Cultural Studies in 2010. She is also the author, with Henry A. Giroux, of *Take Back Higher Education: Race, Youth and the Crisis of Democracy in the Post–Civil Rights Era* (Palgrave, 2004) and, with Jeffrey T. Nealon, *The Theory Toolbox: Critical Concepts for the Humanities, Arts and Social Sciences* (Rowman and Littlefield, 2003). A revised, expanded edition of *The Toolbox* appeared in August 2011. Additionally, she has published over 30 articles and book chapters on U.S. racial politics, the persistence of racism in the post–civil rights era, the history and politics of the university, and antiracist pedagogy, which have appeared in *Third Text, Social Identities, Patterns of Prejudice, Cultural Studies ↔ Critical Methodologies, The CLR James Journal, JAC, Works and Days, Cultural Critique, College Literature*, and *Tikkun*. She has been managing editor of the interdisciplinary *Review of Education, Pedagogy, and Cultural Studies* for over a decade.

Roberto G. Gonzales is an assistant professor at the University of Chicago School of Social Service Administration. Professor Gonzales's research focuses on the ways in which legal and educational institutions shape the everyday experiences and the transitions to adulthood of poor, minority, and immigrant youth.

Ed Guerrero is a professor of cinema studies and Africana studies at New York University. Professor Guerrero's influential books, *Framing Blackness* (Temple U. Press) and *Do the Right Thing* in the Modern Classics series (British Film Institute), explore black cinema, its critical discourse and political economy. Professor Ed Guerrero has also written extensively on black cinema, its movies, culture and politics for such journals as *Sight & Sound, CINEASTE, Film Quarterly, Discourse, Journal of Popular Film and Television, Callaloo,* and *Ethnic and Racial Studies.* Ed Guerrero has served on numerous editorial and professional boards including those of *Cinema Journal, Quarterly Review of Film and Video,* and *Race/ Ethnicity* and the National Film Preservation Board of the Library of Congress.

Jerome M. Hendricks is a graduate student at the University of Illinois at Chicago. His research interests include the relationships among capitalism, economic sociology, organizations and organizing, and difference and inequality. His dissertation work explores the effect of technology on consumer markets and the social construction of value during periods of field change.

Jeanne Holcomb is a lecturer at the University of Dayton in the Department of Sociology, Anthropology, and Social Work. She studied sociology and psychology as an undergraduate at the University of Florida and continued her studies at UF, receiving her MA and PhD in sociology. Her teaching and research interests focus primarily on family experiences, especially those related to the transition to parenthood. Her past research includes a qualitative study of women's experiences breastfeeding. She has taught classes on marriages and families, sociology of childhood, and sociology of motherhood.

Andrew Hund is a recent PhD graduate (2010) from Case Western Reserve University in medical sociology and gerontology. Andrew has taught sociology for six years at four campuses. He is presently an independent academic and working on a book investigating epidemic outbreaks in the circumpolar North. His research interests are social epidemiology, the social history of illness, the political economy of health, biotechnology in aging populations, disaster research, science and technology studies, and sociology of education.

Michael Kimmel is a Distinguished Professor of Sociology at SUNY at Stony Brook. His books include *Men Confront Pornography* (1990); *Against the Tide: Profeminist Men in the United States, 1776–1990* (1992); *The Politics of Manhood* (1996); *Manhood: A Cultural History* (1996; 10th-anniversary second edition, 2006); and *The Gendered Society* (2nd edition, 2003). He coedited *The Encyclopedia on Men and Masculinities* (2004) and *Handbook of Studies on Men and Masculinities* (2004). He is the founder and editor of *Men and Masculinities,* the field's premier scholarly journal; editor of a book series on Gender and Sexuality at New York University Press; and editor of the Sage Series on Men and Masculinities. He is the spokesperson for the National Organization for Men Against Sexism (NOMAS) and lectures extensively in corporations and on campuses in the United States and abroad. His new book, *Guyland: The Perilous World Where Boys Become Men* (HarperCollins, 2008), has been optioned by DreamWorks for a feature film.

Neal King is an associate professor of sociology at Virginia Tech. He is author of *Heroes in Hard Times* and *The Passion of the Christ* (Palgrave Controversies series) and coeditor of *Reel Knockouts.* He has published articles on gender, class, age, and culture in such journals as *Gender & Society, The Journal of Film and Video, Postmodern Culture,* and the *International Journal of Sociology and Social Policy.*

Jeffrey A. Langstraat is an assistant professor of sociology at the University of North Dakota. His research focuses on the intersection of social movements and mass media, with a particular focus on how sexual minority movements challenge underrepresentation and stereotypical images while working to gain coverage of the issues and communities for which they advocate.

Betsy Lucal is an associate professor of sociology at Indiana University South Bend, where she also teaches in the women's studies program. She teaches courses on gender and sexuality, sociological theory, social movements, and sociology of food. She is a member of Indiana University's Faculty Colloquium on Excellence in Teaching and winner of the IU South Bend Distinguished Teaching Award and the all-IU Sylvia Bowman Award for Excellence in Teaching. She currently serves as chair of the American Sociological Association's Section on Teaching and Learning in Sociology. She also is a deputy editor of *Gender & Society,* journal of Sociologists for Women in Society.

Carmen R. Lugo-Lugo is an associate professor of critical culture, gender, and race studies at Washington State University. She engages in research on empire, "the War on Terror," and popular culture. In addition to numerous journal articles (with Mary K. Bloodsworth-Lugo) on the United States–led "War on Terror," she has published essays on the representation of Latinos and other minoritized groups within U.S. popular culture. Her books include *A New Kind of Containment: "The War on Terror," Race, and Sexuality* (2009, edited with Bloodsworth-Lugo); *Animating Difference: Race, Gender, and Sexuality in Contemporary Films for Children* (2010, with Bloodsworth-Lugo and C. Richard King), and *Containing (Un)American Bodies: Race, Sexuality, and Post-9/11 Constructions of Citizenship* (2010, with Bloodsworth-Lugo).

Elizabeth E. Martinez is an assistant professor of sociology at Fresno Pacific University and an attorney licensed to practice in California. She works in the law and society tradition, using a variety of data and methods to address issues of legal change, contentious politics, civil liberties, crime, deviance, and the mediated public sphere.

Theresa Martinez is an associate professor of sociology and assistant vice president for academic outreach at the University of Utah. Her teaching and research deal with issues of race, class and gender, deviant behavior, juvenile delinquency, and popular culture. Professor Martinez has published articles in *Sociological Perspectives, Sociological Spectrum,* the *Utah Law Review,* and *Race, Gender & Class: An Interdisciplinary Journal.* In addition, she and Professor Marcia Texler Segal coedited an anthology titled *Intersections of Gender, Race, and Class: Readings for a Changing Landscape* (2007), published by Oxford University Press.

Michael O. Maume is an associate professor in sociology and criminology at the University of North Carolina Wilmington. His areas of research interest are macrosocial correlates of lethal violence, communities and crime, and intimate partner violence. His work has been published in *Criminology, Violence Against Women,* and *Journal of Quantitative Criminology.* He teaches courses in criminology, methods and statistics, and white collar crime.

Michael A. Messner is a professor of sociology and gender studies at the University of Southern California, where he teaches courses on sex and gender. His most recent books are *It's All for the Kids: Gender, Families and Youth Sports* (University of California Press, 2009), and *King of the Wild Suburb: A Memoir of Fathers, Sons and Guns* (Plain View Press, 2011).

Andrea D. Miller is a fellow of the Institute for Human Rights and Humanitarian Study at Webster University. She is the coordinator of the Year of International Human Rights for the College of Arts and Sciences at Webster University. Miller also led Webster University's inaugural Human Rights Summer Institute for high school students in the St. Louis area. She is a faculty member in the Behavioral and Social Sciences Department and the Human Rights Program, where she teaches courses on gender, sexuality, and bisexuality. Miller holds an MA and a doctoral degree in sociology from American University. Miller's work focuses on gender and sexuality at the local and global levels. Her current research project focuses on "hacker culture" and the gendered and sexualized component of this subculture.

Susanne C. Monahan is an associate dean for program and curricular development and past chair of the Department of Sociology & Anthropology at Montana State University. She is coauthor of *Religion Matters: What Sociology Teaches Us About Religion in Our World* (with Michael Emerson and William Mirola) and coeditor of *Sociology of Religion: A Reader* (with Michael Emerson and William Mirola). She has published articles and reviews in *Journal for the Scientific Study of Religion*, *Review of Religious Research*, *Sociology of Religion*, *Journal of the American Academy of Religion*, *Theoretical Criminology*, *Justice Quarterly*, *Child Development*, *Addiction*, *Journal of Studies on Alcohol*, *Addictive Behaviors*, and *Contemporary Sociology*. She received her BA from Swarthmore College and her MA and PhD from Stanford University.

Jeffrey Montez de Oca is an assistant professor of sociology at the University of Colorado, Colorado Springs, with broad research interests in sociological theory, sport, media, identity, and inequality. He specializes in theoretically oriented research on sport during the cultural cold war and American Indian boarding schools as technologies of citizenship. His research has been published as peer-reviewed articles in *Signs*, *American Studies*, and the *Journal of Historical Sociology*. He also has chapters in *East Plays West: Essays on Sport and the Cold War* (Routledge, 2006) and *The Blackwell Companion to Sport* (in press).

Alison R. Moss is a doctoral student at the University of Illinois, Chicago. Through her feminist studies, teaching, research, and scholarship, she applies a critical lens to global systems of oppression. Her master's project research (forthcoming publication in the *Journal of GLBT Family Studies*, 2012) focuses on "doing family" for bisexual women who are married to men while simultaneously long-term partnered with women (i.e., married, bisexual, polyamorous women). Her current research focuses on the institution of marriage as a social control mechanism that secures the persistence of heteropatriarchy through intersecting individual and social ideologies.

Kathleen C. Oberlin is a PhD candidate and associate instructor in the Department of Sociology at Indiana University. She recently completed the Preparing Future Faculty Program. At present she is preparing for publication an activity she uses in the classroom, which involves students' responding to a series of statements regarding U.S. health statistics and trends by taking steps forward or backward as appropriate. This physical movement requires them to consciously draw on their own experiences and compare themselves to their peers to complete the activity.

Erica Orange is the vice president of Weiner, Edrich, Brown, Inc., a leading futurist consulting group. Orange has authored several articles on various social, technological, economic, and political trends, and has written extensive white papers on such topics as *The Human/*

Machine Interface, The Future of Family and Household Formation, and *Climate Change and the Travel & Tourism Industry*. Orange received her B.A. in political science and psychology from the University of Rochester in Rochester, New York.

Bernice A. Pescosolido is a Distinguished Professor of Sociology at Indiana University. She is founder and director of the ConCEPT I Health & Illness Program (Contemporary Concepts for Emerging Policy & Theory Issues in Health & Illness) at IU, which includes both dedicated undergraduate/graduate minors and a graduate program. Along with Brian Powell, she is cofounder and codirector of Sociology's Preparing Future Faculty Program. The recipient of numerous teaching and research awards, Pescosolido has served in leadership roles for the Medical Sociology and Mental Health Sections of the American Sociological Association and as vice president of the ASA.

Christopher W. Podeschi is a member of the sociology faculty at Bloomsburg University of Pennsylvania. His research focuses primarily on culture and the environment. Forthcoming work looks at images of nature in children's books over time, and recently published work examines the role of place attachment in fostering environmental concern. A project under way examines how parents and the character of household culture predict young people's environmental worldview. In the past he has taught environmental sociology, but recent teaching includes sociological theory, introductory sociology, race and ethnic relations, and qualitative methods.

Nicole Rafter, who teaches at Northeastern University, has authored five monographs: *Partial Justice: Women, State Prisons, and Social Control; Creating Born Criminals; Shots in the Mirror: Crime Films and Society; The Criminal Brain*; and (with M. Brown) *Criminology Goes to the Movies*. In addition, she has translated (with M. Gibson) the major criminological works of Cesare Lombroso and published over 50 journal articles and chapters. In 2009 she received the American Society of Criminology's Sutherland Award; other honors include a Fulbright Fellowship and several fellowships at Oxford University. Currently she is studying genocide, focusing on its criminological implications. Rafter teaches courses in crime films, biological theories of crime, and crimes against humanity.

Mark Rubinfeld is a professor and the department chair of sociology at Westminster College. Specializing in the sociology of popular culture, Mark's articles and reviews have appeared in the *American Journal of Sociology, International Journal of the History of Sport, Popular Music and Society*, and *Teaching Sociology*. He is the author of *Bound to Bond: Gender, Genre, and the Hollywood Romantic Comedy* (Praeger, 2001). His newest book, *American Pop: Exploring the Sociology of Popular Culture*, will be published by Pine Forge Press, a SAGE subsidiary.

Jack G. Shaheen is the author of *Reel Bad Arabs: How Hollywood Vilifies a People* (2001), *Arab and Muslim Stereotypes in American Popular Culture* (1997), and *The TV Arab* (1984).

Robert Wonser is an associate lecturer of sociology at College of the Canyons. His interests are popular culture, social inequality, and sociological theory. His research interests include the sociology of social media and subcultural studies. He has a broad range of teaching specializations, including the sociology of deviance, popular culture, and social inequality.

⑤SAGE research**methods**
The Essential Online Tool for Researchers

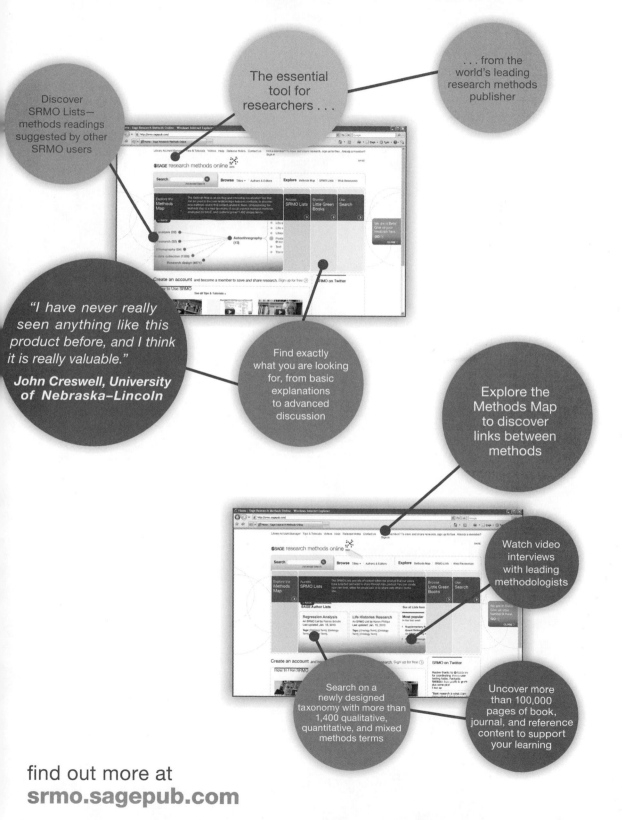

Discover SRMO Lists—methods readings suggested by other SRMO users

The essential tool for researchers . . .

. . . from the world's leading research methods publisher

"*I have never really seen anything like this product before, and I think it is really valuable.*"

John Creswell, University of Nebraska–Lincoln

Find exactly what you are looking for, from basic explanations to advanced discussion

Explore the Methods Map to discover links between methods

Watch video interviews with leading methodologists

Search on a newly designed taxonomy with more than 1,400 qualitative, quantitative, and mixed methods terms

Uncover more than 100,000 pages of book, journal, and reference content to support your learning

find out more at
srmo.sagepub.com